# Sweden

## THE ROUGH GUIDE

D0057774

There are more than one hundred Rough Guide titles
covering destinations from Amsterdam to Zimbabwe

### Forthcoming titles include
Jamaica • New Zealand • South Africa
Southwest USA

### Rough Guide Reference Series
Classical Music • The Internet • Jazz • Opera • Rock Music • World Music

### Rough Guide Phrasebooks
Czech • French • German • Greek • Hindi and Urdu • Indonesian • Italian •
Mandarin Chinese • Mexican Spanish • Polish • Portuguese • Russian •
Spanish • Thai • Turkish • Vietnamese

### Rough Guides on the Internet
http://www.roughguides.com/
http://www.hotwired.com/rough

# ROUGH GUIDE CREDITS

**Text editor:** Catherine McHale
**Series editor:** Mark Ellingham
**Editorial:** Martin Dunford, Jonathan Buckley, Samantha Cook, Jo Mead, Amanda Tomlin, Ann-Marie Shaw, Vivienne Heller, Paul Gray, Sarah Dallas, Chris Schüler, Helena Smith, Kirk Marlow (UK); Andrew Rosenberg (US)
**Production:** Susanne Hillen, Andy Hilliard, Judy Pang, Link Hall, Nicola Williamson, Helen Ostick

**Cartography:** David Callier and Melissa Flack
**Online Editors:** Alan Spicer (UK); Andrew Rosenberg (US)
**Finance:** John Fisher, Celia Crowley, Catherine Gillespie
**Marketing & Publicity:** Richard Trillo, Simon Carloss, Niki Smith (UK); Jean-Marie Kelly (US)
**Administration:** Tania Hummel, Alexander Mark Rogers

# ACKNOWLEDGEMENTS

On this first edition of the Rough Guide to Sweden, **thanks** are due to the Swedish Youth Hostel Association; Anne-Charlotte Carlsson from the Swedish Travel & Tourism Council in London, the world's leading authority on Swedish bus timetables; Jane Wilde for providing yet more timetables; Juliet Shaffer for words of wisdom; Per Henriksson in Stockholm, whose summer cottage and good humour provided needed relief; and to all those tourist offices that supplied free coffee along the way. Big thanks also go out to Adam Claus for his friendship and great support, both practical and emotional; Claus Feldthusen of Malmö for his tireless pursuit of offbeat information; Tomas Larson of Gothenburg for his social insight and hospitality; Eric Lindfeldt of Jönköping for his opinions; and Jonas Ludvigsson of Lidköping for fantastic advice about discovering Sweden's underside. Also to all those other people who opened their homes and gave of their time, particularly Brita Anhoff, Christer Jacobsson, Charlotta Lindell and Per Nilsen. And finally to Catherine McHale, who kept her cool when the going got tough, and who never realized that reindeer could be so interesting.

### The authors

**Jules Brown** first visited Sweden in 1986. Apart from this book, he has also written and researched four more *Rough Guides*, as well as various titles for other travel publishers and numerous newspaper and magazine articles.

**James Proctor** first travelled to Sweden as a student. Attracted by the open nature of Swedish society, he taught himself Swedish and finally fulfilled a long-standing desire to live in Stockholm while working as the BBC's Sweden correpondent. He now works for BBC Radio Five Live, where he presents a daily European news programme.

**Neil Roland** is a law graduate living in Didsbury, Manchester, who has worked as a freelance features-writer since escaping the clutches of the legal profession. He has been editor of Greater Manchester Theatre magazine and of the Jewish Gazette newspaper, and has written on travel, sex, the law and entertainment in a variety of publications. He has also broadcast several short stories for radio and is now concentrating on writing fiction.

# PUBLISHING INFORMATION

This first edition published April 1997 by Rough Guides Ltd, 1 Mercer St, London WC2H 9QJ.
Distributed by the Penguin Group:
Penguin Books Ltd, 27 Wrights Lane, London W8 5TZ
Penguin Books USA Inc., 375 Hudson Street, New York 10014, USA
Penguin Books Australia Ltd, 487 Maroondah Highway, PO Box 257, Ringwood, Victoria 3134, Australia
Penguin Books Canada Ltd, 10 Alcorn Avenue, Toronto, Ontario, Canada M4V 1E4
Penguin Books (NZ) Ltd, 182–190 Wairau Road, Auckland 10, New Zealand
Typeset in Linotron Univers and Century Old Style to an original design by Andrew Oliver.
Printed in the UK by Bath Press, Bath.
Illustrations in Part One & Part Three by Edward Briant; illustrations on p.1 and p.409 by Henry Iles.

# Sweden

## THE ROUGH GUIDE

written and researched by

## Jules Brown, James Proctor
## and Neil Roland

THE ROUGH GUIDES

TRAVEL GUIDES • PHRASEBOOKS • MUSIC AND REFERENCE GUIDES

 We set out to do something different when the first Rough Guide was published in 1982. Mark Ellingham, just out of university, was travelling in Greece. He brought along the popular guides of the day, but found they were all lacking in some way. They were either strong on ruins and museums but went on for pages without mentioning a beach or taverna. Or they were so conscious of the need to save money that they lost sight of Greece's cultural and historical significance. Also, none of the books told him anything about Greece's contemporary life – its politics, its culture, its people, and how they lived.

So with no job in prospect, Mark decided to write his own guidebook, one which aimed to provide practical information that was second to none, detailing the best beaches and the hottest clubs and restaurants, while also giving hard-hitting accounts of every sight, both famous and obscure, and providing up-to-the-minute information on contemporary culture. It was a guide that encouraged independent travellers to find the best of Greece, and was a great success, getting shortlisted for the Thomas Cook travel guide award,

and encouraging Mark, along with three friends, to expand the series.

The Rough Guide list grew rapidly and the letters flooded in, indicating a much broader readership than had been anticipated, but one which uniformly appreciated the Rough Guide mix of practical detail and humour, irreverence and enthusiasm. Things haven't changed. The same four friends who began the series are still the caretakers of the Rough Guide mission today: to provide the most reliable, up-to-date and entertaining information to independent-minded travellers of all ages, on all budgets.

We now publish 100 titles and have offices in London and New York. The travel guides are written and researched by a dedicated team of more than 100 authors, based in Britain, Europe, the USA and Australia. We have also created a unique series of phrasebooks to accompany the travel series, along with an acclaimed series of music guides, and a best-selling pocket guide to the Internet and World Wide Web. We also publish comprehensive travel information on our two web sites:

http://www.hotwired.com/rough
and http://www.roughguides.com/

## HELP US UPDATE

We've gone to a lot of effort to ensure that this first edition of **The Rough Guide to Sweden** is as up-to-date and accurate as possible. However, if you feel there are places we've under-rated or over-praised, or find we've missed something good or covered something which has now gone, then please write; suggestions, comments or corrections are much appreciated.

We'll credit all contributions, and send a copy of the next edition (or any other Rough Guide if you prefer) for the

best letters. Please mark letters: "Rough Guide Sweden Update" and send to:
Rough Guides, 1 Mercer St, London WC2H 9QJ, or
Rough Guides, 375 Hudson St, 9th floor,
New York NY 10014.
Or send e-mail to: sweden@roughtravl.co.uk
Online updates about this book can be found on Rough Guides' website (see above for details)

# CONTENTS

Introduction ix

## ● CHAPTER 3: THE SOUTHWEST 159–234

## ● CHAPTER 4: THE SOUTHEAST 235–301

## ● CHAPTER 5: THE BOTHNIAN COAST: GÄVLE TO HAPARANDA 302–349

# • CHAPTER 6: CENTRAL AND NORTHERN SWEDEN 350—407

## PART THREE  CONTEXTS  409

# LIST OF MAPS

## MAP SYMBOLS

| | | | |
|---|---|---|---|
| ═══ | Motorway | ∴ | Ruin |
| ══ | Major road | ♦ | General point of interest |
| ── | Minor road | ▲ | Mountain peak |
| - - - - | Path | ⓘ | Tourist office |
| ──■── | Railway | ⊠ | Post office |
| ▪▪▪ | Wall | ⓒ | Telephone |
| — — | Ferry route | P | Parking |
| ～～ | Waterway | ⬯ | Swimming pool |
| ┴┴┴┴ | Canal | ✡ | Synagogue |
| ─ ─ ─ | Chapter division boundary | ★ | Bus stop |
| ■─■─■ | International boundary | ▮ | Building |
| ▬ ▬ ▬ | County boundary | ⊞ | Church (town map) |
| ✕ | Airport | ✝✝✝ | Cemetery |
| ◉ | Hotel | | Park |
| ♕ | Castle | | National park |
| 🏛 | Stately home | | Forest |
| ⛪ | Church | | Sand/beach |
| ♟ | Museum | | |

# INTRODUCTION

**S**weden conjures resonant images: snow-capped peaks, reindeer wandering in deep green forests and the twenty-four hour daylight of the Midnight Sun – not to mention a standard of living that is one of the highest in the world. But beyond the household names of Abba, Ikea and Volvo, much of Sweden is relatively unknown. Indeed, the largest of the Scandinavian countries, with a land mass twice the size of Britain (and roughly the same size as California), but with a population of barely nine million, it could be said to be one of Europe's best-kept secrets – not least, perhaps, because of its legendarily high prices. However, if this is the reason you've given the country a wide berth in recent years, you may be in for a surprise. Sweden can still be expensive, it's true, but what you get for your kronor is always of the highest quality; and, if you know where to look, it's not that difficult to travel on a budget.

## The Swedes

The other Nordic nations love to make fun of the **Swedes**. Witness the joke about the ten Nordic men stranded on a desert island. On day one the two Finns have felled half the trees on the island for firewood. On day two the two Norwegians have constructed a fishing boat from some of the wood to catch fish for supper. On day three the Danes have set up a cooperative to organize all the work. On day four the Icelanders decide to lift everyone's spirits with tales of the brave men of the ancient sagas. And on day five the two Swedes are still waiting to be introduced to each other!

It is certainly true that the Swedes are not the easiest of people to get to know, and are often thought of by foreigners as distant and reserved. On the whole they're straight-talking, saying what they mean with a minimum of words and fuss. For many people used to the expressiveness of the southern Europeans this can often be interpreted as lack of interest or even downright rudeness, but that's unlikely to be the case, and it's worth reassuring yourself with the fact that the Finns think the Swedes are too talkative. In short, overt expressions of emotion, wild gesticulations and raucous conversations are not the name of the game in Sweden – at least until the weekend, when in many parts of the country beer and aquavit help people throw off their inhibitions.

Many tourists come to Sweden looking forward to **wild sex** and easy pick-ups. Most return home disappointed. Somehow over the years the open Swedish attitude to nudity and sexuality has become confused with sex. Contrary to popular belief, Sweden isn't populated solely with people waiting for any opportunity to tear their clothes off and make passionate love under the midnight sun. People may talk about sex openly, but when it comes down to it the Swedes can be rather puritanical. Sex and nakedness are two totally different things; go to a beach in Sweden on a hot summer's day and you'll often be stretched to find anyone with clothes on, but it's certainly not an invitation for a love-in. Nudity is often seen – but not really looked at.

## Where to go

Sweden is principally a land of forests and lakes. Its towns and cities are small by European standards and mostly to be found in the southern third of the country, where most Swedes live. The **south** is also the most cosmopolitan part of the country, owing something to the proximity of Denmark and the rest of the European continent. The country's second city, **Gothenburg**, on the west coast, is one of the country's most appealing destinations; Gothenburgers have a reputation for being among the most friendly people in the whole of Sweden, and its network of canals and spacious thoroughfares is reminiscent of Amsterdam. Other historic southern ports include

**Helsingborg** and the third city, **Malmö**, both opposite the Danish island of Zeeland. The southern province of **Skåne** consists of flat farming land and is the breadbasket of Sweden – the first view of Sweden for many travellers and a far cry from the high mountains of the far north. Southern towns are neat and tidy, virtually pollution free, and, thanks to a seemingly endless string of welfare benefits, free of homeless people and beggars. **Bästad**, on the border of Skåne and Halland, is a popular summer holiday destination for city Swedes, and home to Swedish tennis. Off the southeast coast, the Baltic islands of **Öland** and **Gotland** are the country's most hyped resorts, and with good reason, offering a lazy beach life to match that of the best southern European spots, but without the hotel blocks, crowds and tat.

**Central and northern Sweden** is the country of the tourist brochures. The further north you travel the more isolated the towns become – you'll often be covering vast distances in these regions just to get to the next village, and you shouldn't be surprised if you're the only one on the road. This is the land of reindeer and elk, of swiftly flowing rivers and of coniferous forest, all traversed by endless hiking routes that give you a chance to experience the pioneering edge of the country. You don't come here for the cities and towns, but the modern and likeable cities of **Sundsvall**, **Umeå** and **Luleå** on the **Bothnian Coast** are certainly worth visiting and very handy for ferry routes across the Gulf of Bothnia to Finland.

**Two rail routes** link the north of Sweden with districts further south. The eastern run, close to the Bothnian coast, stretches up close to the Finnish border; the trains of the private Inlandsbanan strike through some of the country's most beautiful scenery clearing reindeer, and occasionally bears, off the track as they go. This route begins in **Dalarna** – literally "The Dales", an area of rolling hills, villages of red and white wooden houses that is for Swedes the most "Swedish" part of Sweden; it's also home to **Lake Siljan**, one of the country's most beautiful lakes. Both rail routes eventually meet in the far north of Sweden, across the **Arctic Circle**, in the home of the Lapps or **Same** – Sweden (and Scandinavia's) oldest indigenous people. This is where you will experience the **Midnight Sun**: in high summer the sun never sets, allowing you to read the newspaper or play golf at twelve midnight. In midwinter the opposite is true, and months of complete darkness (not to mention the extreme weather conditions) make this one of the most difficult parts of the country to travel through.

Of the cities, **Stockholm** is supreme. Sitting elegantly on fourteen different islands, where the waters of Lake Mälaren meet the Baltic Sea, the city boasts some fantastic architecture, fine museums and by far the best culture and nightlife in the country. Its wide tree-lined boulevards, the narrow medieval streets of the Old Town and some modern, state-of-the-art buildings make Stockholm one of the most beautiful cities in Europe. And it needn't be expensive. Competition between restaurants and bars has led to prices plummeting over recent years, and it's possible to turn up some real bargains.

## When to go

**Summer** in Sweden is short. Most Swedes take their summer holiday between mid-June and mid-August, which is when the weather is at its best and events are thick on the ground. In the south of the country the winter snow has generally gone by the end of March or beginning of April and temperatures are slowly starting to rise. Bear in mind, though, that if you're heading north in late spring you're likely to encounter snow until well into May. In general, May to September is a good time to visit Sweden – north or south. Summer is generally hotter than in Britain, and recent summers in Stockholm have seen temperatures pushing 30°C.

Roughly speaking, if southern Sweden is having a hot summer, it'll be miserably cold and rainy in the north – and vice versa. By the end of August in northern Sweden leaves are starting to turn colour and night frost is not uncommon. The first snows fall in the north in September. In Stockholm snow starts to fall in October but doesn't generally

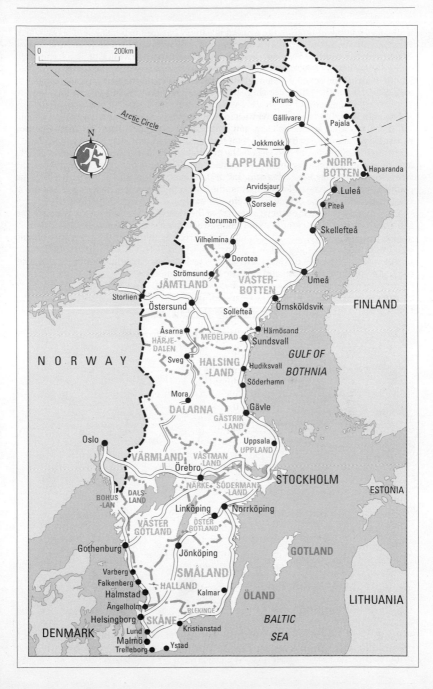

settle. By November, though, the ground is usually covered in a blanket of snow, which will last until the following March or even April when there can still be snow showers. **Winters** in the south of Sweden are mild, and the southern province of Skåne can often escape snow completely. Swedes go to great lengths, however, to point out that a cold snowy winter is far better than a milder, greyer one: a cover of snow on the ground acts as a reflector for the little light there is in the winter months and goes a long way to brightening things up.

**Daylight** is in short supply in **winter**. In **Stockholm** in December it doesn't get light in the mornings until around 9.30am and will normally be dark again by 3pm. **Further north**, things are more extreme. North of the Arctic Circle, in Kiruna, for example, there's twenty-four darkness from mid-December to mid-January, and the merest twinkle of light at noon during the months immediately either side. This is also the time of year when the **Northern Lights**, or *Aurora Borealis*, are at their most spectacular in the far north of the country. An eerie shifting glow of light in the sky, generally green, blue or pale orange in colour, and in the shape of long wisps, they're thought to be electric in origin.

In the height of **summer** there's no part of Sweden which is dark for very long. Even the **south** of the country only experiences a few hours of darkness; in Stockholm in June it doesn't get properly dark at all. From 11pm or midnight there's a sort of half-light, with the sun only just below the horizon, which lasts just a few hours. At 3am it's bright daylight again. In the far **north** there's twenty-four daylight from the end of May to the end of June, and April and July are very light months.

## CLIMATE CHART

Average daily temperatures (°C, max and min) and precipitation (mm)

|  | Jan | Mar | May | June | July | Aug | Oct | Dec |
|---|---|---|---|---|---|---|---|---|
| **Jokkmokk** | | | | | | | | |
| °C | -17 | -8 | 6 | 12 | 14 | 12 | 1 | -14 |
| mm | 30 | 24 | 35 | 48 | 78 | 74 | 41 | 32 |
| **Umeå** | | | | | | | | |
| °C | -9 | -4 | 7 | 13 | 15 | 14 | 4 | -7 |
| mm | 49 | 41 | 41 | 44 | 53 | 78 | 65 | 56 |
| **Östersund** | | | | | | | | |
| °C | -7 | -4 | 7 | 12 | 13 | 12 | 4 | -6 |
| mm | 27 | 23 | 35 | 57 | 76 | 60 | 37 | 31 |
| **Stockholm** | | | | | | | | |
| °C | -3 | 0 | 11 | 16 | 17 | 16 | 8 | -1 |
| mm | 39 | 26 | 30 | 45 | 72 | 66 | 50 | 46 |
| **Gothenburg** | | | | | | | | |
| °C | -2 | 1 | 11 | 15 | 16 | 16 | 9 | 0 |
| mm | 62 | 50 | 51 | 61 | 68 | 77 | 84 | 75 |
| **Visby** | | | | | | | | |
| °C | -1 | 0 | 10 | 14 | 16 | 16 | 8 | 1 |
| mm | 48 | 32 | 29 | 31 | 50 | 50 | 50 | 51 |
| **Lund** | | | | | | | | |
| °C | -1 | 2 | 11 | 15 | 17 | 17 | 9 | 1 |
| mm | 54 | 44 | 43 | 54 | 66 | 63 | 60 | 65 |

# PART ONE

# THE

# BASICS

# GETTING THERE FROM BRITAIN

Given the long distances involved in reaching Sweden, especially the northern stretches of the country, flying is by far the best option. The train from London to Stockholm takes about 30 hours – the plane takes two. But if you're planning to travel around Sweden by train, it may be worth considering an InterRail or ScanRail ticket to help cut the initial travel costs of getting there. If you want to take your car, there are direct sailings from Harwich and Newcastle to Gothenburg, and driving on Sweden's straight and quiet roads is a joy – but bear in mind the high cost of petrol once you're there. Travel by long-distance bus is the stuff horror movies are made of and only to be recommended to the extremely hardy.

## FLIGHTS

Over recent years, there's been a great expansion in the number of airlines linking Sweden and Britain, which in turn has led to an increase in destinations. The airlines have latched on to the fact that London is the Swedes' favourite European location for short breaks, and competition on routes has seen prices fall. Having said that, flying to Sweden still isn't particularly cheap. Low-cost charter flights from Britain to Sweden don't really exist, but the first stop for the **best deals** (and cheap scheduled flights to Stockholm) should be *Strata Travel* (see "Discount flight agents"), whose summer charters from

Stansted to Stockholm via Malmö go for around £160 return. Another good way to find cheap flights is to look in the classified sections in the Sunday newspapers or on ITV's teletext service. If you live in London, *Time Out* magazine or the *Evening Standard* can sometimes throw up good offers. Failing that, go straight to a discount flight agent like *STA Travel* or *Campus Travel*; they specialize in youth and student flights as well as discounted fares for the over 26s.

It's also worth trying the **airlines** directly – the most useful ones are *Scandinavian Airlines (SAS)*, *British Airways, Finnair, British Midland* and *Air UK*. Fares are standard all year round but special offers such as *British Airways'* World Offers (generally in the spring) can bring the price of a return flight down by up £20 or £30, which is then matched by the other airlines. The cheapest deals are known under various names at the different airlines – "Jackpot" with *SAS*, **Apex** with *British Airways* and "Save Fare" with *Finnair*. They all include a minimum stay of one Saturday night and generally have to be booked at least seven days in advance. Flights in June, July and August are often sold out months before at the lower fares. If you're under 25 ask about the availability of youth fares, although generally they're nothing to write home about. All the prices quoted below are the cheapest scheduled fares.

Of all the scheduled airlines, *SAS* has more direct flights from more British cities, with five flights a day from **Heathrow to Stockholm** (£205; 2hr 25min) and two a day to Gothenburg (£190; 1hr 55min) – *British Airways* and *Finnair* also operate direct flights for around the same prices (see "Airlines and agents" for a full run-through of all the possibilities). There's a handy new route from London City Airport to Stockholm's equivalent, Bromma (£240), via Malmö (£225), with *Malmö Aviation*.

*SAS* also flies direct once daily (except Sat) from **Manchester to Stockholm** (£210; 2hr 20min); as does *Finnair* for around £10 less. From Birmingham, Newcastle, Edinburgh and Glasgow you have to fly to Copenhagen first. *SAS* flies from Newcastle; *British Midland* serves Glasgow and Edinburgh; while *Maersk Air* is the only airline to operate out of Birmingham. To get to Copenhagen costs round £170–180 with all the airlines, and connections on to Stockholm bring

## AIRLINES AND AGENTS

**Air UK** (☎0345/666777). *Stansted to Copenhagen (2 daily).*

**British Airways** (☎0345/222111). *Heathrow to Stockholm (4 daily); Gatwick to Stockholm (2 daily); Heathrow to Gothenburg (2 daily); Gatwick to Gothenburg (1 daily); Heathrow to Copenhagen (4 daily); Gatwick to Copenhagen (2 daily).*

**British Midland** (☎0345/554554). *Edinburgh to Copenhagen (1 daily); Glasgow to Copenhagen (2 daily; afternoon flight via Edinburgh). Connections with SAS to Gothenburg and Stockholm.*

**Finnair** (☎0171/408 1222, ☎0161/436 2400). *Gatwick to Stockholm (2 daily); Manchester to Stockholm (1 daily). No advance booking needed.*

**Maersk Air** (*British Airways partner carrier*; ☎0345/222111). *Gatwick to Copenhagen (2 daily), Birmingham to Copenhagen (2 daily).*

**Malmö Aviation** (☎01293/530839). *London City Airport to Malmö and then onto Stockholm's city airport, Bromma (Mon–Fri 1 daily; Sun from Sweden only).*

**Scandinavian Airlines** (☎0345/010789; ☎0345/090900). *Heathrow to Stockholm (1 daily); Heathrow to Gothenburg (2 daily); Heathrow to Copenhagen (5 daily); Manchester to Stockholm (1 daily); Manchester to Copenhagen (3 daily); Newcastle to Copenhagen (2 daily); Aberdeen to Stavanger (2 daily) with connections to Gothenburg and Stockholm via Oslo. Connections available through Copenhagen to Stockholm, Borlänge, Gothenburg, Jönköping, Kalmar, Karlstad, Malmö (hovercraft), Norrköping, Örebro, Västerås and Växjö.*

**Varig Brazilian Airlines** (☎0171/287 3131). *London to Copenhagen (1 on Wed, Fri & Sun).*

## DISCOUNT FLIGHT AGENTS

**Benz Travel**, Regent St, London W1 (☎0171/439 4181).

**Campus Travel**, 52 Grosvenor Gdns, London SW1W 0AG (Europe ☎0171/730 3402); 541 Bristol Rd, Selly Oak, Birmingham B29 6AU (☎0121/414 1848); 61 Ditchling Rd, Brighton BN1 4SD (☎01273/570226); 39 Queen's Rd, Clifton, Bristol BS8 1QE (☎0117/929 2494); 5 Emmanuel St, Cambridge CB1 1NE (☎01223/324283); 53 Forest Rd, Edinburgh EH1 2QP (☎0131/668 3303); 166 Deansgate, Manchester M3 3FE (☎0161/833 2046); 105–106 St Aldates, Oxford OX1 1DD (☎01865/242067). *Student/youth travel specialists, with branches also in YHA shops and on university campuses all over Britain.*

**Council Travel**, 28a Poland St, London W1V 3DB (☎0171/437 7767). *Flights and student discounts.*

**STA Travel**, 86 Old Brompton Rd, London SW7 3LH, 117 Euston Rd, London NW1 2SX, 38 Store St London WC1 (☎0171/361 6161); 25 Queens Rd, Bristol BS8 1QE (☎0117/929 4399); 38 Sidney St, Cambridge CB2 3HX (☎01223/366966); 75 Deansgate, Manchester M3 2BW (☎0161/834 0668); 88 Vicar Lane, Leeds LS1 7JH (☎0113/244 9212); 36 George St, Oxford OX1 2OJ (☎01865/792800); and branches in Birmingham, Canterbury, Cardiff, Coventry, Durham, Glasgow, Loughborough, Nottingham, Warwick and Sheffield. *Worldwide specialists in low cost flights and tours for students and under-26s.*

**Strata Travel**, 9 Central Parade, Green St, Enfield EN3 7HG (☎0181/805 1555).

**Trailfinders**, 42–50 Earls Court Rd, London W8 6FT (☎937 5400); 194 Kensington High St, London, W8 7RG (☎0171/938 3939); 58 Deansgate, Manchester M3 2FF (☎0161/839 6969); 254–284 Sauchiehall St, Glasgow G2 3EH (☎0141/353 2224); 22–24 The Priory, Queensway, Birmingham B4 6BS (☎0121/236 1234); 48 Corn St, Bristol BS1 1HQ (☎0117/929 9000). *One of the best-informed and most efficient agents.*

**Travel Bug**, 597 Cheetham Hill Rd, Manchester M8 5EJ (☎0161/721 4000). *Large range of discounted tickets.*

**Travel Cuts**, 295 Regent St, London W1 (☎0171/255 1944).

the price up to £230 and to Gothenburg to £210 (an example of flight journey times via Copenhagen: from Manchester 1hr 45min, plus one hour's wait, then a 30min flight to Stockholm). From Aberdeen, *SAS* offers flights to Stavanger, with connections on to both Stockholm and Gothenburg for the same prices. Flights to Copenhagen can also be useful for southern Sweden, particularly Malmö, which is just a thirty-minute ride away across the Öresund Strait by inexpensive jetfoil (for bus services from the airport see p.55).

**SAS Airpasses** are sold in connection with Jackpot tickets and can be useful for exploring Sweden by air (see "Getting around").

## TRAINS

Taking the **train** doesn't work out a lot cheaper than flying, and is in fact more expensive if you're over 26. But a number of discounted tickets and passes make it possible to cut costs (see below).

Trains to Sweden **from London** go via Brussels, Cologne, Hamburg and Copenhagen. There are no direct trains from London, and a typical journey will involve changing trains two or three times. The best connection with the minimum of hassle is to take the *Eurostar* leaving Waterloo at 12.27pm to Brussels Midi, where you change onto the Nord Express leaving at 18.47pm, which has through coaches, including couchettes and sleeping cars, to Copenhagen. You then have to change again for an onward connection to Stockholm or Gothenburg. The standard fare from London to Stockholm is £470 return.

If you're travelling **from the north of England or Scotland** you may well prefer to take the overnight service with *North Sea Ferries* from Hull to Rotterdam and then the train from Rotterdam at 12.37pm for Amersfoort, changing there for Copenhagen (arrives 22.59pm). There's a night train from here (23.15pm) that arrives in Stockholm the next morning (7.53am). There is no through ticket for this journey; the cheapest way to do it is with an *InterRail* pass (see below), with the ferry cost of about £55 on top. Alternatively, to cut the long slog south through England, take the new *Eurostar* night sleepers that are set to begin operations from Scotland, Wales and the West of England to the Continent during 1997.

### DISCOUNT TICKETS AND PASSES

If you are under 26, a **BIJ** ticket gives up to 50-percent discount on ordinary fares. Available through *Eurotrain* or *Wasteels (see* "Travel information" for details) and from youth and student travel agents (see opposite), these allow as many stopovers as you like and are valid for two

months. You can follow a choice of routes to Sweden and buy a ticket to more or less anywhere.

Better value by far, especially if you are taking in a number of other countries on the way, is an **InterRail pass**, available to anyone who is under 26 and resident in the 26 participating European countries for six months. A zoning system applies for all of the countries valid under the pass, and the price is determined by the number of zones you want to travel in and for how long. Supplements, seat reservations, couchettes and/or sleeping cars are extra, but you do get discounts on British trains and on *Eurostar*, and some hefty discounts on ferries round Scandinavia, including Sweden. To reach Sweden you'll need a pass covering zone E (France, Belgium, Netherlands, Luxembourg), zone C (Germany, Switzerland, Austria and Denmark), and one for zone B for Sweden itself if you intend to see the country by train (also covers Norway and Finland). A pass for three zones for one month currently costs £245. Anyone over 26 could get an **InterRail "26-Plus" pass**; this, however, excludes Belgium and France so you would have to travel to the Hook of Holland first and make your way from there. At the moment a 15-day pass costs £215, a one-month pass £275. The passes are available from *British Rail* and youth/student travel agencies.

A serious rival to *InterRail*, and invaluable if you're planning to visit Norway, Finland and Denmark as well as Sweden, is the **ScanRail pass**. Valid on the rail networks of all four countries, the pass comes in two forms, *ScanRail Flexi* and *ScanRail*. A full 21-day *ScanRail* pass in standard class costs £194, for one month £254; 12- 25-year-olds get around 25-percent discount. *ScanRail Flexi* is available for travel on any five days in a 15-day period (adult £130; youth £98) or any ten days in a month (adult £176; youth £132). The passes are also available in first class at higher fares. *ScanRail* gives 50-percent discount on a number of ferry routes, including Stockholm–Helsinki, Stockholm–Turku, Umeå–Vaasa, Gothenburg–Fredrikshavn, Nynäshamn/Oskarshamn–Visby, as well as 50-percent discount on the privately run *Inlandsbanan* in central and northern Sweden. The pass can be bought before you leave from *Deutsche Bann*.

Another alternative for travelling in Sweden (and through Scandinavia) is *British Rail's*

## TRAIN INFORMATION

**British Rail**, International Rail Centre, Victoria Station, London SW1 1JY (☎0171/834 2345).

**Deutsche Bann**, Suite 4, 23 Oakhill Grove, Surbiton, Surrey KT6 6DU (☎0181/390 8833).

**Eurostar**, EPS House, Waterloo Station, London SE1 8SE (☎0345/881881).

**Eurotrain**, 52 Grosvenor Gdns, London SW1W 0AG (☎0171/730 3402).

**Le Shuttle**, PO Box 300, Cheriton Parc, Folkstone, Kent CT19 4QD (☎0990/353535).

**Wasteels**, Victoria Station (by platform 2), London SW1V 1JY (☎0171/834 7066).

## BUS INFORMATION

**Eurolines**, *National Express*, 164 Buckingham Palace Rd, London SW1 (☎0990/808080).

**Freedom pass**, which offers unlimited train travel (including supplements on high-speed trains) within any one of 25 European countries including Sweden, Denmark, Finland and Norway. For each country you have to buy a separate pass, which is good for a certain number of travel days within a one-month period and comes in under-26 and standard-class versions. The prices for Sweden are: three days for £69 and £99; five days for £99 and £129; and ten days for £129 and £179. Exactly the same deal can also be purchased from *Eurotrain*, which calls its pass a **EuroDomino**.

Finally, if you're 60 or over, the **Rail Europe Senior Card** gives 30-percent discounts on train travel in 25 European countries including *Eurostar* and train-connected sea crossings. More details from *British Rail*.

Information on Swedish rail passes is given in "Getting around" on p.27.

## BUSES

**Bus services** to Sweden can be an endurance test but are the best option for anyone on a really tight budget and over 26. *Eurolines* operate a service three times a week **from London**'s Victoria Bus Station to Stockholm (34hr; from £147 return) and Norrköping (32hr; same price). The service to Helsingborg (22hr; £124), Gothenburg (25hr; £124 return) and Kristinehamn (30hr; £162 return) runs twice a week. **From the**

**north of England and Scotland** *National Express* run direct daily bus services to the ferry terminal in Hull for the sailing to Rotterdam. Principal pick-up points are Bradford, Edinburgh, Glasgow, Leeds, Manchester, Middlesborough, Newcastle, Oldham, Sunderland and York; details from *National Express*.

Travellers flying to Denmark and making their own way over **from Copenhagen** can take advantage of a very useful bus service that connects Kastrup airport with the south of Sweden. *Kustlinjen* buses (buy tickets on the bus with Danish or Swedish currency) depart from right outside the arrivals terminal building and run eight times a day linking Kastrup with Helsingborg (110kr), Ängelholm (120kr), Båstad (130kr) and Halmstad (150kr). At Helsingborg you can connect up with the Swedish rail network and take a direct train to Stockholm; Halmstad is on the main line between Malmö and Gothenburg, with frequent services to Gothenburg. There are also fourteen daily buses from Copenhagen to Malmö (100kr), which use the ferry over to Limhamn, just south of Malmö city centre.

## FERRIES

There is only one ferry company that provides a direct link between Britain and Sweden, **Scandinavian Seaways** (see opposite for a full run-through of all the routes and ferry company details). Although crossings are long, if you are taking your car they do save a lot in petrol and frayed tempers – don't underestimate the length of the drive up from France or Belgium through the Netherlands, Germany and Denmark before southern Sweden finally comes into sight. The drive from Copenhagen to Stockholm will take around eight to ten hours depending on the weather, much longer in winter. This long haul north makes taking your car on *Le Shuttle* services across to France not worth the bother, unless you are doing a really extensive tour (see the "Train Information" above for *Le Shuttle* details). The only other ferry routes that make any sense are those to the Netherlands, giving you a head start on the driving to Sweden.

**Fares** with *Scandinavian Seaways* are expensive; the cheapest ticket with couchette accommodation for a car and four passengers from

## USEFUL FERRY ROUTES

| Route | Company | Frequency | Duration |
|---|---|---|---|
| Harwich–Gothenburg | Scandinavian Seaways | 2 weekly | 24hr |
| Newcastle–Gothenburg | Scandinavian Seaways | June to mid-Aug only 1 weekly | 24hr |
| Newcastle–Hamburg | Scandinavian Seaways | April–Oct only 1–2 weekly | 24hr |
| Harwich–Esbjerg | Scandinavian Seaways | 3–4 weekly | 20hr |
| Hull–Rotterdam | North Sea Ferries | 1 daily | 14hr |
| Harwich–Hook of Holland | Stena Sealink | 2 daily | 7hr |

### FERRY OPERATORS

**Scandinavian Seaways**, Parkeston Quay, Harwich, CO12 4QG (☎0990/333000).
**North Sea Ferries**, King George Dock, Hedon Rd, Hull HU9 5QA (☎01482/377177).
**Stena Sealink Line**, Charter House, Park St, Ashford, TN24 (☎01223/647047).

Harwich or Newcastle to Gothenburg (both take 24hr) in July or August costs £619. For foot passengers, the cheapest ticket is the Seapex (these have to be booked 21 days in advance and don't allow you to travel on Fri or Sat); a return in July or August from Harwich or Newcastle to Gothenburg is £200. Students get a 50-percent discount on standard returns and Seapex fares. Conditions on board are extremely good with saunas, cinemas and discos helping to while away the long hours. Bear in mind, though, that especially in winter a 24-hour crossing of the North Sea can be a stomach wrenching experience.

### PACKAGE TOURS

Don't be put off by the idea of an inclusive **package**. Sweden can be expensive, and a package can sometimes work out the cheapest way of doing things, and may be a much easier way of reaching remote areas of northern Sweden in winter. **City breaks** invariably work out less costly than arranging the same trip independently. Prices include return travel, usually by plane, and accommodation (with breakfast), with most operators offering a range from hostel to luxury-class hotels. As a broad guide, four-night stays in Stockholm and Gothenburg go for around £250–300 a head. Go for a week and rates per night fall considerably.

There are also an increasing number of operators offering **special interest holidays** to Sweden, from camping tours to Arctic expeditions. Prices for the latter are costly and some may not be worth it – Norvista (see box overleaf for details) run a four-day Arctic safari based in Abisko in northern Lapland for £948! Many also offer **skiing** and **winter sports holidays**, with skiing packages offering some of the best deals: one week in one of the major resorts, Storlien, costs around £300 in January with Ski Scandinavia. For general information on skiing holidays in Sweden you can ring the Swedish Travel and Tourism Council's **Ski Sweden Information Line** on ☎0171/724 5868. For more on skiing and winter sports in Sweden see also "Sports and outdoor pursuits", p.46.

## SPECIALIST TOUR OPERATORS

**Anglers World Holidays**, 46 Knifesmith Gate, Chesterfield, S40 1QR (☎01246/221717). *Angling holidays; cottage and hotel stays.*

**Arctic Experience**, 29 Nork Way, Banstead, SM7 1PB (☎01737/362321). *Specialize in trips to Lapland.*

**Crystal Holidays**, Crystal House, The Courtyard, Arlington Rd, Surbiton, Surrey KT6 6BW (☎0181/399 5144). *The biggest ski operator on the market, with packages to Åre and Storlien for reasonable prices.*

**Holiday Scandinavia Ltd**, 28 Hillcrest Rd, Orpington, BR6 9AW (☎01689/824958). *Swedish cabin holidays.*

**Mountain & Wildlife Ventures**, Compston Road, Ambleside, Cumbria LA22 9DJ (☎015394/33285). *Vastly experienced company dealing in Nordic ski touring, mountain skiing, ski courses and expeditions.*

**Norvista**, 227 Regents St, London W1R 8PD (☎0171/409 7334). *Hiking holidays around Arvidsjaur; and a four-day Arctic safari – but neither is worth the exhorbitant prices.*

**Scandinavian Seaways**, Scandinavia House, Parkeston Quay, Harwich, CO12 4QG (☎01255/240234, ☎0171/493 6696). *Extensive range of motoring and cabin holidays as well as city breaks – good deals out of season.*

**Scantours**, 21–24 Cockspur St, London, SW1Y 5BN (☎0171/839 2927). *City breaks, cruises on the Göta canal, budget scheduled flights.*

**Ski Scandinavia**, Whetstone Lodge, The Dicken, Whetstone, Leicester LE8 6LE (☎0116/275 2750). *The cheapest ski operator to Sweden with packages to Åre and Storlien.*

**Sovereign Scanscape**, First Choice House, Gatwick Approach, London Rd, Crawley RH10 2EX (☎0161/742 2288). *City breaks, charter holidays and fly-drive holidays.*

**Tracks**, Evegate Park Barn, Smeeth, Ashford, Kent TN25 6SX (☎01303/814949). *Group camping tours for 18- 38-year-olds.*

**Travellers**, Waterside, Kendal, Cumbria LA9 4HE (☎015396/20196). *Dog sledging holidays in Arctic Sweden, with accommodation in mountain cabins in the national parks.*

**Winge of Scandinavia**, Broadmead House, 21 Panton St, London SW1 (☎0171/839 5341). *Bus tours, city breaks and good deals on flights.*

# GETTING THERE FROM IRELAND

**With no ferry services from Ireland to any Scandinavian port, the best and only direct** way to travel to Sweden is to fly. If you are planning a wider European tour that includes Britain, travelling by train on an InterRail pass is another option worth considering. Alternatively, you might find it more economical to make your way to London and pick a flight, bus or package deal from there – all of which are detailed above.

The cheapest airline ticket from Ireland is an **Apex**; these require you to stay for a minimum of one Saturday night and to book at least seven days in advance (all the prices quoted below are Apex fares). In general, there isn't much in the way of seasonal special deals, although airline fare structures change regularly, so it's always a good idea to check with the airlines or with your local travel agent.

It's possible to cut costs further by approaching an **agent**. Several of the discount agents (addresses below), and in particular *USIT*, are good for discount deals; if you're under 26 or a student, you can generally secure fares from Dublin to Stockholm for around IR£238.

From the **Republic of Ireland**, *SAS* are the only airline offering direct flights to Sweden, with daily services from **Dublin to Stockholm** (IR£280; 3hr 50min); flights to Gothenburg are routed via Copenhagen (IR£260; 4hr). *Aer Lingus* also operates daily flights to Stockholm via

Copenhagen and Amsterdam, with the best prices on the latter route (IR£286). Alternatively, travellers heading for southern Sweden can take a flight to Copenhagen with either airline (IR£169; 2hr) and travel on from there by bus or by jetfoil (see "Getting there from Britain" for more details).

From **Belfast**, *British Airways* flies to London Heathrow, where connections can be made to

## AIRLINES

**Aer Lingus**, 46 Castle St, Belfast, BT1 1HB (☎01232/314844); 2 Academy St, Cork (☎021/327155); 40 O'Connell St, Dublin 1 (☎01/844 5440); 136 O'Connell St, Limerick (☎061/474239). *Daily flights to Stockholm via Copenhagen and Amsterdam.*

**British Airways**, 9 Fountain Centre, College St, Belfast, BT1 6ET (☎0345/222111); Dublin reservations (☎01/676 8080; ☎1800/768080). *Belfast to Heathrow with connections to Stockholm (4 daily).*

**British Midland**, Belfast reservations (☎0345/554554); Nutley, Merrion Rd, Dublin 4 (☎01/283 8833). *Belfast to Heathrow, then onward flights on SAS to Stockholm and Gothenburg.*

**Scandinavian Airlines**, reservations (☎01/844 5440). *Daily direct flights from Dublin to Stockholm; and daily to Gothenburg via Copenhagen.*

## FERRY OPERATORS

**Irish Ferries** (same company as *B&I*), 16 Westmoreland St, Dublin 2 (☎01/661 0511); 2–4 Merrion Row, Dublin 2 (☎01/661 0511); 24hr information service (☎01/661 0715); St Patrick's Bldgs, Cork (☎021/504333). *Dublin–Holyhead; Rosslare to Pembroke; also hooks up with* Scandinavian Seaways *to Sweden and* P&O *to France.*

**P&O European Ferries**, Rosslare, Co. Wexford (☎053/33115); c/o Tourist Office, Grand Parade, Cork (☎021/272 965); c/o Tourist Office, Arthurs Quay, Limerick (☎061-316 259); Terminal building, Larne Harbour, Co. Antrim, N. Ireland (☎01574/274321; ☎1800/409049). *Larne–Cairnryan (onward tickets at an inclusive fare for Hull to Zeebrugge or Rotterdam, and Newcastle to Esbjerg, Hamburg or Gothenburg).*

## DISCOUNT TRAVEL AGENTS

**Discount Travel**, 4 South Great Georges St, Dublin 2 (☎01-679 5888).

**Flight Finders International**, 13 Baggot St Lower, Dublin 2 (☎01/676 8326).

**Joe Walsh Tours**, 8–11 Baggot St, Dublin (☎01/676 3053). *General budget fares agent.*

**Liffey Travel**, Abbey Mall, 13 Lower Liffey St, Dublin 1 (☎01/873 4900). *Package tour specialists.*

**Neenan Travel**, 12 South Leinster St, Dublin 2 (☎01/676 5181). *European city breaks.*

**Student & Group Travel**, 71 Dame St, Dublin 2 (☎01/677 7834). *Student specialists.*

**Thomas Cook**, 11 Donegall Place, Belfast (☎01232/240833); 118 Grafton St, Dublin

(☎01/677 1721). *Package holiday and flight agent, with occasional discount offers.*

**Travel Shop**, 35 Belmont Rd, Belfast 4 (☎01232/471717).

**USIT**, Fountain Centre, Belfast BT1 6ET (☎01232/324073); 10–11 Market Parade, Patrick St, Cork (☎021-270900); 33 Ferryquay St, Derry (☎01504/371888); Aston Quay, Dublin 2 (☎01/679 8833); Victoria Place, Eyre Square, Galway (☎091/565177); Central Buildings, O'Connell St, Limerick (☎061/415064); 36-37 Georges St, Waterford (☎051/72601). *Student and youth specialists for flights, trains and European city breaks.*

Stockholm (£260 and upwards; 6–8hr) four times a day. *British Midland* also flies from Belfast to Heathrow and offers connections and through fares with their partner airline, *SAS*, to Stockholm and Gothenburg (£369 & £325; both take around 5hr). It's often cheaper to buy two separate tickets instead of one through fare, for example: Belfast–Heathrow return (around £60) plus Heathrow–Stockholm return (around £205).

If you want to travel to Sweden **by train**, then buying an **InterRail pass** (available from *USIT* – see box on p.9 for details) makes a lot of sense, especially if you are taking in a number of other countries on the way. From both the North and the Republic, you need the same pass as a traveller from Britain. Another useful train pass is the **ScanRail pass**, which allows free travel within Sweden, Denmark, Norway and Finland. For full details of both passes see "Getting there from Britain".

Attempting to take the **bus** all the way to Sweden would involve connecting up with ser-vices from Britain and would take up to three days; for the money it saves it really isn't worth the hassle. Similarly, anyone wanting to take their car to Sweden is facing a long and tiring journey. *Irish Ferries* "Landbridge" tickets allow you to travel via Britain and link up with *Scandinavian Seaways* **ferries** to Sweden (see "Getting there from Britain" for a full run-through of their routes), while *P&O* services to France are only worth it if you are touring the other countries on the way. On the Larne-to-Cairnryan route from Northern Ireland, *P&O* offer an inclusive onward fare for their services from Newcastle to Gothenburg (see the box on p.9 for ferry company details).

As yet there are very few **packages** available from Ireland to Sweden, and the agents listed on p.9 only have a limited range of city breaks and skiing holidays on offer. Probably your best bet is to connect up with one of the packages offered by the British-based tour operators (see p.4).

## GETTING THERE FROM THE US AND CANADA

**With only two airlines operating direct flights from the USA to Sweden and no direct flights from Canada, you will more than likely have to transit via another European city. To reduce costs you might consider flying to London first and then tak-ing a flight, train or ferry (see "Getting there** from Britain"). If Sweden is part of a wider European tour, buying a Eurail pass before you go can be one of the most cost-effective ways to travel (see the box on European passes on p.14).**

### SHOPPING FOR TICKETS

Barring special offers, the cheapest of the air-lines' published fares is usually an **Apex** ticket, although this will carry certain restrictions: you have to book – and pay – at least 21 days before departure, spend at least seven days abroad (maximum stay three months), and you tend to get penalized if you change your schedule. On transatlantic routes, there are also winter **Super Apex** tickets, sometimes known as "Eurosavers" – slightly cheaper than an ordinary Apex, but limiting your stay to between 7 and 21 days. Some airlines also issue Special Apex tick-ets to people younger than 24, often extending the maximum stay to a year. Many airlines offer youth or student fares to **under-26s**; a passport or driving licence are sufficient proof of age, though these tickets are subject to availability and can have eccentric booking conditions. It's worth remembering that most cheap return fares involve spending at least one Saturday night away and that many will only give a percentage refund if you need to cancel or alter your journey, so make sure you check the restrictions carefully before buying a ticket.

## DISCOUNT AGENTS, CONSOLIDATORS AND TRAVEL CLUBS

**Air Brokers International**, 323 Geary St, Suite 411, San Francisco, CA 94102 (☎1-800/883-3273 or 415/397-1383; fax 415/397-4767; email: air-broker@aiment.com). *Consolidator.*

**Air Courier Association**, 191 University Blvd, Suite 300, Denver, CO 80206 (☎303/278-8810). *Courier flight broker.*

**Airhitch**, 2641 Broadway, New York, NY 10025 (☎1-800/326-2009 or 212/864-2000). *Standby-seat broker: for a set price, they guarantee to get you on a flight as close to your preferred destination as possible, within a week.*

**Airtech**, 584 Broadway, Suite 1007, New York, NY 10012 (☎1-800/575-TECH or 212/219-7000). *Standby-seat broker; also deals in consolidator fares and courier flights.*

**Cheap Tickets, Inc**, offices nationwide (☎1-800/377-1000 or 212/570-1179). *Consolidator.*

**Council Travel**, 205 E 42nd St, New York, NY 10017 (☎1-800/226-8624), and branches in many other US cities. *Student/budget travel agency. A sister company, Council Charter (☎1-800/800-8222), specializes in charter flights.*

**Educational Travel Center**, 438 N Frances St, Madison, WI 53703 (☎1-800/747-5551 or 608/256-5551). *Student/youth and consolidator fares.*

**High Adventure Travel**, 353 Sacramento St, Suite 600, San Francisco, CA 94111 (☎1-800/428-8735 or 415/912-5600; fax 415/912-5606; Website: http://www.highadv.com; email: airtracks@highadv.com).

**International Student Exchange Flights**, 5010 E Shea Blvd, Suite 104A, Scottsdale, AZ 85254 (☎602/951-1177). *Student/youth fares, student IDs.*

**Interworld Travel**, 800 Douglass Rd, Miami, FL 33134 (☎1-800/468-3796). *Consolidator. Specializes in Scandinavia.*

**Last Minute Travel Services**, Offices nationwide (☎1-800/LAST-MIN). *Specializes in standby flights.*

**Nouvelles Frontieres/New Frontiers**, 12 E 33rd St, New York, NY 10016 and other branches in LA and San Francisco (☎1-800/366-6387); in Canada: 1001 Sherbrook East, Suite 720, Montreal, H2L 1L3 (☎514/526-8444). *French discount travel firm.*

**Now Voyager**, 74 Varick St, Suite 307, New York, NY 10013 (☎212/431-1616). *Courier flight broker and consolidator.*

**Skylink**, 265 Madison Ave, 5th Fl, New York, NY 10016 (☎1-800/AIR-ONLY or 212/573-8980) with branches in Chicago, Los Angeles, Montreal, Toronto, and Washington DC. *Consolidator.*

**STA Travel**, 10 Downing St, New York, NY 10014 (☎1-800/777-0112 or 212/627-3111), and other branches in Los Angeles, San Francisco and Boston. *Worldwide discount travel firm specializing in student/youth fares.*

**TFI Tours International**, 34 W 32nd St, New York, NY 10001 (☎1-800/745-8000 or 212/736-1140), and other offices in Las Vegas and Miami. *Consolidator.*

**Travac Tours**, 989 6th Ave, New York NY 10018 (☎1-800/872-8800 or 212/563-3303). *Consolidator and charter broker. If you have a fax machine you can have a list of fares faxed to you by calling toll-free 888/872-8327.*

**Travel Avenue**, 10 S Riverside, Suite 1404, Chicago, IL 60606 (☎1-800/333-3335 or 312/876-6866). *Full-service travel agent that offers discounts in the form of rebates.*

**Travel CUTS**, 187 College St, Toronto, ON M5T 1P7 (☎416/979-2406), and other branches all over Canada. *Canadian student travel organization specializing in student fares, IDs and other travel services.*

**Travelers Advantage**, 311 W Superior St, Chicago, IL 60610 (☎1-800/255-0200). *Travel club; annual membership required.*

**UniTravel**, 1177 N Warson Rd, St Louis, MO 63132 (☎1-800/325-2222 or 314/569-2501). *Consolidator.*

**Worldtek Travel**, 111 Water St, New Haven, CT 06511 (☎1-800/243-1723 or 203/772-0470). *Discount travel agency.*

**Worldwide Discount Travel Club**, 1674 Meridian Ave, Miami Beach, FL 33139 (☎305/534-2082). *Travel club; annual membership required. Call for membership kit.*

You can normally cut costs further by going through a **specialist flight agent** – either a **consolidator**, who buys up blocks of tickets from the airlines and sells them at a discount, or a **discount agent**, who in addition to dealing with discounted flights may also offer special student and youth fares and a range of other travel-related services such as travel insurance, rail passes, car rentals, tours and the like. Bear in mind, though, that penalties for changing your plans can be stiff. Remember, too, that these companies make their money by dealing in bulk – don't expect them to answer lots of questions. Some agents specialize in **charter flights**, which may be cheaper than anything available on a scheduled flight, but again departure dates are fixed and withdrawal penalties are high (check the refund policy). If you travel a lot, **discount travel clubs** are another option – the

annual membership fee may be worth it for benefits such as cut-price air tickets and car rental.

Don't automatically assume, however, that tickets purchased through a travel specialist will be the cheapest – once you get a quote, check with the airlines and you may turn up an even better deal. Be advised also that the pool of travel companies is swimming with sharks – exercise caution and never deal with a company that demands cash up front or refuses to accept payment by credit card.

**Students** might be able to find cheaper flights through the major student travel agencies *STA Travel*, *Nouvelles Frontieres* and, for Canadian students, *Travel Cuts* (see the box on p.11 for details).

Regardless of where you buy your ticket the **fare** will depend on the time of year you travel: fares are highest between June and August,

## AIRLINES IN THE US AND CANADA

**Air Canada** (BC ☎1-800/663-3721; Alberta, Saskatchewan & Manitoba ☎1-800/542-8940; eastern Canada ☎1-800/268-7240; US ☎1-800/776-3000). *Toronto to Frankfurt and Zurich daily, and five weekly flights to Paris, with connections to Stockholm on SAS and Air France.*

**Air France** (US ☎1-800/237-2747; in Canada ☎1-800/667-2747). *Flies daily from many major US and Canadian cities to Paris with connections to Stockholm.*

**American Airlines** (☎1-800/433-7300). *Direct flights to Stockholm from Chicago and Miami.*

**British Airways** (US ☎1-800/247-9297; Canada ☎1-800/668-1059). *Flies daily from 26 different US and Canadian cities to London, with connecting flights to Stockholm.*

**Continental Airlines** (☎1-800/231-0856). *Connects most major North American cities with direct SAS flights from New York to Stockholm and offers daily flights from New York to many major European cities with connections to Stockholm.*

**Delta Airlines** (☎1-800/241-4141). *Flies daily from major North American cities via Atlanta and New York to Brussels, with Stockholm connections on Sabena.*

**Finnair** (☎1-800/950-5000). *Flights from New York to Stockholm via Helsinki (year round; 6–7 weekly); also from San Francisco (summer only; 3*

*weekly), Miami (winter only on Sun), and Toronto (summer only; 2 weekly).*

**Icelandair** (☎1-800/223-5500). *Flies to Stockholm via Reykjavik from New York (daily), Baltimore (6 weekly), Boston (4 weekly), Orlando (3 weekly) and Halifax (2 weekly) – frequencies given here are for high season; they vary throughout the year. Option to break your flight with 1–3 nights' stay in Reykjavik.*

**Scandinavian Airlines** (**SAS**; ☎1-800/221-2350). *Direct daily flights from New York to Stockholm; also operates indirect daily flights from Seattle and Chicago via Copenhagen. You can connect up with all their flights from other North American cities on American and United.*

**TWA** (☎1-800/892-4141). *Services from all major cities in North America to Frankfurt and Paris; connects with Lufthansa or SAS to Stockholm.*

**United Airlines** (☎1-800/538-2929). *Connects most major North American cities with SAS direct flights from New York to Stockholm.*

**US Air** (☎1-800/622-1015). *Flies from Philadelphia and Boston to many major European cities, with connecting flights to Stockholm on other carriers.*

**Virgin Atlantic Airways** (☎1-800/862-8621). *Daily flights from the major US and Canadian cities to London with connections to Stockholm.*

when the weather is best; they drop during the "shoulder" **seasons** of mid-March to May and September to October, and are cheapest during the low season, November to mid-March (excluding Christmas and New Year when prices are hiked up and seats are at a premium). Double-check with each airline for specific season dates. Flying **on weekends** (including Friday) adds about US$50–60 to the round-trip fare.

## FLIGHTS

**Direct flights** from the US to Sweden are with *Scandinavian Airlines (SAS)*, which flies from New York to Stockholm daily, and *American Airlines*, with daily flights from Chicago and Miami. There are also **indirect flights** offered by *Icelandair, Finnair* and *SAS* from numerous US cities to Stockholm, with one stop in their respective hubs of Reykjavik, Helsinki and Copenhagen – see the box opposite for full details of airlines and routings. Otherwise, you can choose from a number of other carriers offering flights from across the States to major European cities, from where you can pick up a second flight to Stockholm with another airline.

Although direct flights are usually cheaper than indirect or connecting flights, there is really very little difference, and it is always worth shopping around to get the cheapest fares for the dates you want to travel. The price ranges quoted below are all based on the airlines' Apex tickets and exclude taxes and airport fees.

From **New York**, a round-trip midweek fare to Stockholm (an 8hr journey on a direct flight; overwise around 10hr) will cost US$900–1000 in high season; US$750–850 during the shoulder seasons; and anywhere between US$450 and 650 in the low season. *Icelandair* are currently offering some of the best deals. From **Chicago** (9hr on a direct flight; at least 11hr otherwise), prices are much the same, although some airlines charge US$100 more than the top fares from New York. *American Airlines'* direct flight is the cheapest midwest option. Travelling from the **West Coast** (at least 12hr), you'll pay around US$1250 in high season; US$1050 in the shoulder seasons; and US$650–900 in low season. Some of the cheapest fares are with *SAS* from Seattle and *Finnair's* summer-only flight from San Francisco.

## SPECIALIST TOUR OPERATORS

**American Express Vacations** ☎1-800/446-6234. *Flight-plus-hotel packages to Stockholm.*

**Bennett Tours** (☎1-800-221-2420; Website: http://www.bennett-tours.com). *Scandinavia specialists. Offers cheap weekend breaks or fully escorted bus tours throughout Scandinavia.*

**Bergen Line** (☎1-800-323-7436). *For cruises around the Swedish archipelago and the Baltic Sea. In Canada call Finncharter (☎1-800/461-8651 or 416/222-0740).*

**Borton Overseas** (☎1-800/843-0602). *Company specializing in adventure vacations (hiking, rafting, cross-country skiing etc).*

**Contiki Tours** (☎1-800/CONTIKI). *Tours of Scandinavia and Russia for 18- to 35-year-olds.*

**Euro-Bike** (☎1-800/321-6060). *Offers a summer bicycling tour of Sweden and Denmark.*

**EuroCruises** (☎1-800/688-3876). *For cruises of the Baltic Sea and the canals of Sweden.*

**Euroseven** (☎1-800/890-3876). *Independent hotel-plus-flight packages from New York, Baltimore or Boston to Scandinavia.*

**Passage Tours** (☎1-800-548-5960). *Specializes in Scandinavia. Offers escorted and unescorted tours and cheap weekend breaks.*

**Pedersen World Tours** (in Canada 1-800/973-3377; in the US ☎1-800/933-6627). *A Canadian tour operator specializing in Swedish tours.*

**Scanam World Tours** (☎1-800/545-2204 or 201/835-7070). *Specializes in Scandinavian tours and cruises for groups and individuals. Also cheap weekend breaks.*

**Scandinavian Airlines (SAS**; ☎1-800/221-2350 ext. 4). *Also offers tours and fly-drive deals.*

**Scandinavian Special Interest Network** (☎201/729-8961; Website: http://www.sitravel.com). *Offers hundreds of different special interest tours in Scandinavia.*

**Scantours** (☎1-800/223-7226). *Major Scandinavian holiday specialists offering vacation packages and customized itineraries, including cruises and city sightseeing tours.*

**Vantage Deluxe World Travel** (☎1-800/322-6677). *Deluxe group tours and cruises in Scandinavia.*

With no direct flights from **Canada**, travellers can take **indirect flights** to Stockholm with *Finnair*, who operate a summer service from Toronto via Helsinki, or with *Icelandair* from Halifax via Reykjavik. Several other airlines also operate flights from Toronto and Vancouver to European cities, with connections on to Stockholm – see the box on p.12 for full details of airlines and routings.

**Fares** from Toronto (journey time 9–13hr depending on connections) are CAN$1000–1250 in high season, CAN$800–950 in shoulder season, and CAN$750–960 in low season. From Vancouver (journey time 13–18hr) you can expect to pay around CAN$400 more in all seasons. The cheapest fares are with *Finnair* and *Icelandair*. It might well also be worth investigating cheap flights to New York, Chicago or Seattle and linking up with one of *SAS's* or *American Airlines'* direct flights from there (see box on p.12).

If Sweden is only one stop on a longer journey, you might want to consider buying a **Round-the-World (RTW) ticket**. As Stockholm and the other Scandinavian capitals are not among the most popular destinations, you would need a custom-designed RTW ticket. This will have you touching down in about half a dozen cities aside from your Scandinavia stopoff, but is apt to be more expensive than a standard RTW ticket; depending on your route it could cost up to US$3000.

## PACKAGES AND ORGANIZED TOURS

There are a large number of companies operating **package holidays** and **tours** of Sweden, ranging from deluxe cruises to bicycling holidays. Group tours can be very expensive, and occasionally do not include airfare, so check what you are getting for the price. If your visit is

## EUROPEAN RAIL PASSES FOR NORTH AMERICAN AND AUSTRALASIAN TRAVELLERS

There are a number of European rail passes that can only be purchased before leaving home, though consider carefully how much travelling you are going to be doing: these all-encompassing passes only really begin to pay for themselves if you intend to see a fair bit of Sweden and the rest of Europe.

The best-known and most flexible is the **Eurail Youthpass** (for under-26s), which costs US$419/A$575 for 15 days, and there are also one-month and two-month versions; if you're 26 or over you'll have to buy a first-class **Eurail** pass, which costs US$522/A$720 for the 15-day option. You stand a better chance of getting your money's worth out of a **Eurail Flexipass**, which is good for a certain number of travel days in a two-month

period. This, too, comes in under-26/first-class versions: 10 days for under-26s costs US$438/A$635, for over-26s US$616/A$895; and 15 days costs US$588/A$855 and US$812/A$1175.

North Americans and Australasians are also eligible to purchase a pass specifically for travel in Scandinavia only (Sweden, Denmark, Finland and Norway) called the **ScanRail pass**. These also come in under-26/first-class versions and are valid for five days of travel within 15 days (under-26s US$132/A$177; over-26s US$278/A$236) and 10 days within one month (US$209/A$294; US$278/A$392); there are also one month passes. For information on passes for travel in Sweden only that you can also buy before you go see "Getting around", p.27.

### RAIL CONTACTS IN NORTH AMERICA

**CIT Tours** (☎1-800/223-7987). *Eurail passes only.*

**DER Tours/GermanRail**, 9501 W Divon Ave, Suite 400, Rosemont, IL 60018 (☎1-800/421-2929). Eurail *and* ScanRail *passes*.

**Rail Europe**, 226 Westchester Ave, White Plains, NY 10604 (☎1-800/438-7245). *Official* Eurail *agent in North America; also sells* ScanRail *passes*.

**ScanTours**, 1535 6th St, Suite 205, Santa Monica, CA 90401 (☎1-800/223-7226). Eurail *and* ScanRail *passes*.

### RAIL CONTACTS IN AUSTRALIA

**CIT**, 123 Clarence St, Sydney (☎02/9299 4574); offices in Melbourne, Adelaide, Brisbane and Perth (☎09/322 1090). No NZ office – enquiries and reservations via Australian offices. *Comprehensive range of rail passes.*

centred on Stockholm you could simply book a hotel-plus-flight package, which can work out cheaper than booking the two separately. *Bennett Tours, Scanam* and *Passage Tours* offer very reasonable weekend deals in the low season. You can get a round-trip flight on *SAS* from New York (Newark) and two nights in a Stockholm hotel for as little as US$438 per person (based on double occupancy). For general information on package tours, the *Swedish Travel and Tourism Council* (☎212/949-2333) can provide tour brochures and useful advice.

## GETTING THERE FROM AUSTRALIA & NEW ZEALAND

There are no direct flights from Australia or New Zealand to Sweden; instead you have to fly to either a European or Asian gateway city where you can get a connecting flight or alternative transport. Fares are pretty steep, so if you're on a tight budget it's worth flying to London (see "Getting there from Britain"), Amsterdam or Frankfurt first and picking up a cheap flight. If you intend to take in a number of other European countries on your trip,

### AIRLINES AND ROUTINGS

**Air New Zealand** (Auckland ☎09/366 2803; Sydney ☎02/9223 4666). *Several flights weekly to London via Auckland and LA and daily flights to Bangkok from major Australian and New Zealand cities (connects with SAS in Bangkok).*

**Britannia Airways** (Sydney ☎02/9251 1299; no NZ office). *Several charter flights to London and Amsterdam per month during their charter season (Nov–March) from major Australian cities and Auckland via Singapore and Abu Dhabi.*

**British Airways** (Sydney ☎02/9258 3300; Auckland ☎09/356 8690). *Daily flights to London from major Australian cities via Asia and from New Zealand cities via Los Angeles.*

**Canadian Airlines** (Sydney ☎02/9299 7843; Auckland ☎09/309 0735). *Flies twice weekly to Vancouver and Toronto from Sydney, Melbourne and Auckland (connects with SAS to Copenhagen then on to Stockholm and Gothenburg).*

**Finnair** (Double Bay, NSW ☎02/9326 2999; no NZ office). *Code-share with Qantas/Thai four flights weekly from Sydney via Bangkok/Tokyo to Helsinki and with Singapore Airlines twice weekly from Auckland via Singapore to Helsinki and then on to Stockholm and Gothenburg.*

**Garuda** (Sydney ☎02/9334 9944; Auckland ☎09/366 1855). *Fly several times weekly via Jakarta or Denpasar to Gatwick and Amsterdam from major Australian cities and from Auckland twice weekly.*

**Lufthansa/Lauda-Air** (Sydney ☎02/9367 3888; Auckland ☎09/303 1529). *Three flights weekly to Frankfurt and Vienna from major Australian cities*

*and Auckland via Sydney and Singapore (code-share with Ansett and Air New Zealand).*

**Malaysia Airlines** (Sydney (local-call rate) ☎13 2627; Auckland ☎09/373 2741). *Several flights weekly to London, Amsterdam, Paris and Zurich from major Australian and New Zealand cities via Kuala Lumpur.*

**Philippine Airlines** (Sydney ☎02/9262 3333; no NZ office). *Twice weekly to London and Frankfurt from Brisbane, Sydney and Melbourne via Manila.*

**Qantas** (Sydney ☎02/9957 0111; Auckland (☎09/357 8900). *Daily flights to London, Singapore and Bangkok from major cities in Australia and New Zealand; connects with SAS and Finnair to Stockholm and Gothenburg.*

**Scandinavian Airlines** (**SAS**; Sydney ☎02/9299 6688; Auckland ☎09/309 7750). *SAS-Qantas/Air new Zealand have several flights weekly to Stockholm and other destinations in Scandinavia from major cities in Australia and New Zealand via Copenhagen.*

**Singapore Airlines** (Sydney (local-call rate) ☎13 1011; Auckland ☎09/379 3209). *Several flights weekly to London via Singapore from major Australian cities and twice weekly from Auckland (connects with Finnair to Helsinki).*

**Thai Airlines** (Sydney ☎02/9844 0999 or toll-free 1800/422 020; Auckland ☎09/377 3886). *Several times weekly to Stockholm and Copenhagen via Paris and Bangkok from major Australian cities and Auckland (connects with Finnair).*

**Accent on Travel**, 545 Queen St, Brisbane (☎07/3832 1777).

**Anywhere Travel**, 345 Anzac Parade, Kingsford, Sydney (☎02/9663 0411).

**Brisbane Discount Travel**, 260 Queen St, Brisbane (☎07/3229 9211).

**Budget Travel**, 16 Fort St, Auckland; other branches around the city (☎09/366 0061; toll-free 0800/808 040).

**Destinations Unlimited**, 3 Milford Rd, Milford, Auckland (☎09/373 4033).

**Flight Centres**, Australia: Circular Quay, Sydney (☎02/9241 2422); Bourke St, Melbourne (☎03/9650 2899); plus other branches nationwide. New Zealand: National Bank Towers, 205–225 Queen St, Auckland (☎09/209 6171); Shop 1M, National Mutual Arcade, 152 Hereford St, Christchurch (☎03/379 7145); 50–52 Willis St, Wellington (☎04/472 8101); other branches countrywide.

**Harvey World Travel**, 631 Princes Highway, Kogarah, Sydney (☎02/9567 6099); branches nationwide.

**Northern Gateway**, 22 Cavenagh St, Darwin (☎08/8941 1394).

**Passport Travel**, Kings Cross Plaza, Suite 11a, 4010 St Kilda Rd, Melbourne (☎03/9824 7183).

**STA Travel**, Australia: 855 George St, Ultimo, Sydney (☎02/9212 1255; toll-free 1800/637 444); 256 Flinders St, Melbourne (☎03/9654 7266); other offices in Townsville, state capitals and major universities. New Zealand: Travellers' Centre, 10 High St, Auckland (☎09/309 0458); 233 Cuba St, Wellington (☎04/385 0561); 90 Cashel St, Christchurch (☎03/379 9098); other offices in Dunedin, Palmerston North, Hamilton and major universities.

**Thomas Cook**, Australia: 321 Kent St, Sydney (☎02/9248 6100); 330 Collins St, Melbourne (☎03/9602 3811); branches in other state capitals. New Zealand: Shop 250a St Luke's Square, Auckland (☎09/849 2071).

**Topdeck Travel**, 65 Glenfell St, Adelaide (☎08/8232 7222).

**Tymtro Travel**, 428 George St, Sydney (☎02/9223 2211).

**UTAG Travel**, 122 Walker St, North Sydney (☎02/9956 8399); branches throughout Australia.

it might well be worth buying a Eurail pass before you go (see the preceding box on European passes).

From Eastern Australian cities **fares** are **common rated**; from Perth and Darwin you can expect to pay A$100–200 less via Asia or A$200–400 more via Canada and the US. In New Zealand, fares from Christchurch and Wellington are NZ$150–300 more than from Auckland. Prices also vary significantly with the **season**. For most major airlines low season is mid-January to the end of February and October to November 30; high season is from mid-May to August 31 and December to mid-January; shoulder seasons cover the rest of the year. There's no variation in price during the week. Tickets purchased direct from the **airlines** tend to be expensive, with common-rated **published fares** listed at: low A$2399/NZ$2699; shoulder A$2599–2799/ NZ$2899–3150; and high A$2999/NZ$3399. **Travel agents** offer better deals on fares and have the latest information on limited special deals such as free stopovers en route and fly-drive/accommodation packages. *Flight Centres*

and *STA* (fare reductions for *ISIC* card holders and under 26) generally offer the best discounts – see the box above for agents' details. All the prices quoted below are for discounted fares.

**To Sweden** *Scandinavian Airlines* (*SAS*) and *Finnair* (in conjunction with airlines out of Australia and New Zealand) offer the best connecting services with daily flights to Stockholm and Gothenburg via Copenhagen and Helsinki respectively for around A$2100/2400/2700 and NZ$2250/2600/2900.

Of fares to **other European cities**, the lowest are on *Britannia* to London – during their limited charter season from November to March A$1200/1450/1800 and NZ$1420/1840/2130. Generally you can expect to pay A$1499/ NZ$1999–A$1899/NZ$2450 on *Philippine Airlines* and *Garuda*; A$1800/NZ$2300–$2100/ NZ$2700 on *Malaysia Airlines*, *Thai Airways* and *Lufthansa/Lauda-Air* and A$2399/NZ$2999– A$2699/NZ$3399 on *British Airways*, *Qantas*, *Singapore Airlines*, *Air New Zealand* and *Canadian Airways*. For details of all the airlines and full run-down of routes see the box on p.15.

## SPECIALIST TOUR OPERATORS

**Bentours**, Level 11, 2 Bridge St, Sydney (☎02/9241 1353). *Ferry, rail, bus and hotel passes and a host of scenic tours throughout Scandinavia, including a four-day ferry journey down the Gota Canal between Stockholm and Gothenburg from A$1190/NZ$1300, including meals.*

**European Travel Office**, 122 Rosslyn St, West Melbourne (☎03/9329 8844); Level 20, 133 Castlereagh St, Sydney (☎02/9267 7727); 407 Great South Rd, Penrose, Auckland (☎09/525 3074). *Stockholm hotel accommodation from A$79 twin share and sightseeing tours by bus or boat.*

**Explore Holidays**, 1st Floor, Oasis Centre cnr Pennent Hills & Marsden Rds, Carlingford, Sydney (☎02/9872 6222). *Stockholm mini-stays from A$490/NZ$517 twin share and 21-day adventure tour through central and northern Sweden and coastal Norway (including Oslo) from A$1660/NZ$1700.*

**Wiltrans/Maupintour**, Level 10, 189 Kent St, Sydney (☎02/255 0899). *14–21 day luxury all-inclusive tours of Scandinavia travelling by boat and train and overnighting in spendid hotels and quaint lodges from US$2869.*

**Airpasses** that allow for discounted flights within Europe, including Sweden, such as the Visit Scandinavia Pass from *SAS* and the *BA-Qantas* Airpass, are only available if you fly with the issuing airline and must be purchased before you depart. Expect to pay between A/NZ$120 and A/NZ$180 per coupon.

For extended trips, **Round The World (RTW)** tickets, valid for up to a year, make good sense. Tickets that take in Sweden include the combined *SAS-Thai-United* fare (A$2999/NZ$3299) with six stopovers, open-jaw travel and backtracking permitted, and the *Qantas-BA* Global Explorer (A$2499–3099/NZ$2699–3299) with no backtracking allowed.

Travellers who want to take a **package holiday** to Sweden will find there are very few to choose from with only a small number of tour operators offering holidays specifically to Sweden, or even Scandinavia as a whole. Your best bet is *Bentours* (see box above for details), who will put together a package for you and are about the only agents willing to deal with skiing holidays. Alternatively you could wait until you get to Europe, where there's a greater choice of holidays and prices (see "Getting there from Britain") – none of the prices given in the box above include the plane fare.

# RED TAPE AND VISAS

European Union, American, Canadian, Australian and New Zealand citizens need only a valid passport to enter the country and can stay for up to three months. If you want to stay longer, you can often get a short extension (there's no fixed period and you may have to leave the country first to get one) via the local police, although after this has expired you won't be allowed back into Sweden, or any of the other Nordic countries, for a further six months. All other nationals should consult the relevant embassies about visa requirements.

In spite of the lack of restrictions, **checks** are sometimes made on travellers at the ports in

### SWEDISH EMBASSIES ABROAD

**AUSTRALIA:** Turrana St, Yarralumla, ACT (☎06/273 3033).

**CANADA**: 377 Dalhousie St, Ottawa, Ontario K1N 9N8 (☎613/241-8553).

**NEW ZEALAND**: Consulate General at 13th Floor, Aitken St,Thordon, Wellington (☎04/499 9895).

**REPUBLIC OF IRELAND**: Sun Alliance House, 13–17 Dawson St, Dublin 2 (☎01/715 822).

**UK**: 11 Montagu Place, London W1H 2AL (☎0171/724 2101).

**US**: 1501 M Street NW, Washington, DC 20005 (☎202/467-2600).

Note: visa information is also available on the Internet; address email to Info@zvs.com.

Malmö, Helsingborg and Gothenburg. If you are young and have a rucksack, be prepared to prove that you have enough money to support yourself during your stay. You may also be asked how long you intend to stay and what you are there for. Be polite and you will have no trouble. There are few border formalities between the Nordic countries so once you're in Sweden, in effect, you've made it into the rest of Scandinavia.

### CUSTOMS ALLOWANCES

The following list details the amount of tobacco and alcohol UK and Republic of Ireland citizens can take into Sweden when tax has already been paid (restrictions on duty-free items are much tighter): 300 cigarettes, or 150 cigarillos, or 75 cigars, or 400g of pipe tobacco; one litre of spirits (more than 22° of alcohol by volume), 5 litres of wine and 15 litres of strong beer (more than 3.5 percent of alcohol by volume). North Americans and Australasians are allowed even less so check before you leave.

You can take meat, fish and fruit into Sweden for your own use, but potatoes cannot be imported. An import permit is required for pets: for an application contact the economic section of your Swedish embassy.

# INSURANCE

Most people will find it essential to take out some kind of comprehensive travel insurance. Bank and credit cards (particularly American Express) often have certain levels of medical or other insurance included, especially if you use them to pay for your trip. This can be quite comprehensive, anticipating anything from lost or stolen luggage to missed connections. Similarly if you have a good "all risks" home insurance policy it may well cover your possessions against loss or theft even when overseas, and many private medical schemes also cover you when abroad – make sure you know the procedure and the helpline number.

If you plan to participate in **water sports,** or do some **hiking**, you'll probably have to pay an extra premium; check carefully that any insurance policy you are considering will cover you in case of an accident. Note also that very few insurers will arrange on-the-spot payments in the event of a major expense or loss; you will usually be reimbursed only after going home. In all cases of loss or **theft** of goods, you will have to contact the local **police** to have a **report** made out so that your insurer can process the claim; for medical claims, you'll need to provide supporting bills. Keep photocopies of everything you send to the insurer and note any time period within which you must lodge any claims.

## BRITISH AND IRISH COVER

**In Britain** and **Ireland**, travel insurance schemes (from around £23 a month) are sold by many **travel agents**, **banks** and by **specialist insurance companies**. Policies issued by *Campus Travel* or *STA*, *Endsleigh Insurance*, *Frizzell Insurance*, *USIT* or *Columbus Travel Insurance* are all good value. *Columbus* also does an annual multi-trip policy which offers twelve months' cover for £125.

## US AND CANADIAN COVER

Before buying an insurance policy, check that you're not already covered. **Private health plans** typically provide some overseas medical coverage, although they are unlikely to pick up the full tab in the event of a mishap. Holders of official **student/teacher/youth cards** (see p.23) are entitled to accident coverage and hospital in-patient benefits – the annual membership is far less than the cost of comparable insurance. **Students** may also find that their student health coverage extends during the vacations and for one term beyond the date of last enrollment. Homeowners' or renters' insurance often covers theft or loss of documents, money and valuables while overseas. After exhausting the possibilities above, you might want to contact a specialist

travel insurance company; your travel agent can usually recommend one, or see the box below.

The best **premiums** are usually to be had through student/youth travel agencies – *ISIS* policies, for example, cost US$48–69 for fifteen days (depending on level of coverage), US$80–105 for a month, US$149–207 for two months, US$510–700 for a year. If you're planning to do any "dangerous sports" (skiing, mountaineering etc.), be sure to ask whether these activities are covered: some companies levy a surcharge.

Most North American travel policies apply only to items lost, stolen or damaged while in the custody of an identifiable, responsible third party – hotel porter, airline, luggage consignment, etc. Even in these cases you will have to contact the local police within a certain time limit to have a complete report made out so that your insurer can process the claim.

## AUSTRALIAN AND NEW ZEALAND COVER

Travel insurance is available from travel agents or direct from insurance companies (see box below). Policies are broadly comparable in premium and coverage: a typical one will cost A$190/NZ$220 for one month, A$270/NZ$320 for two months and A$330/NZ$400 for three months.

---

## TRAVEL INSURANCE SUPPLIERS

### AUSTRALIA AND NEW ZEALAND

**AFTA**, 181 Miller St, North Sydney (☎02/9956 4800).

**Cover More**, Level 9, 32 Walker St, North Sydney (☎02/9968 1333; toll-free 1800/251 881).

**Ready Plan**, 141–147 Walker St, Dandenong, Victoria (toll-free ☎1800/337 462); 10th Floor, 63 Albert St, Auckland (☎09/379 3399).

**UTAG**, 347 Kent St, Sydney (☎02/9819 6855; toll-free 1800/809 462).

### BRITAIN AND IRELAND

**Access America** (☎1-800/284-8300).
**Campus Travel**, ☎0171/730 8111.
**Columbus Travel Insurance**, ☎0171/375 0011.
**Endsleigh Insurance**, ☎0171/436 4451.

**Frizzell Insurance**, ☎01202/292333.
**STA**, ☎0171/361 6262.
**USIT**, Belfast ☎01232/324073; Dublin ☎01/679 8833.

### US AND CANADA

**Carefree Travel Insurance** (☎1-800/323-3149).
**Desjardins Travel Insurance** – Canada only (☎1-800/463-7830).
**International Student Insurance Service** (**ISIS**) – sold by *STA Travel* (☎1-800/777-0112).

**Travel Assistance International** (☎1-800/821-2828).
**Travel Guard** (☎1-800/826-1300).
**Travel Insurance Services** (☎1-800/937-1387).

# HEALTH

EU nationals can take advantage of Sweden's health services under the same terms as residents of the country. For this you'll need form E111, available in the UK through post offices and DSS offices. You'll have to show your E111 if you need medical treatment. Citizens of non-EU countries will be charged for all medical services, but North American visitors in particular will find that medical treatment is far less expensive than they are accustomed to in the US – even so it is advisable to take out travel insurance (see "Insurance"). For emergency assistance from the police, fire brigade or ambulance services dial ☎112; emergency calls from pay phones are free of charge.

There's no local doctor system in Sweden: go to the nearest hospital with your passport and for around 140kr they'll treat you. There's a charge of 80kr per 24 hours if you need to stay in hospital overnight. The casualty department is called *Akutmottagning*. **Prescriptions** can be taken to the nearest pharmacy (*Apotek*). Pharmacies will fill prescriptions written by Scandinavian doctors with no problem; if you are coming from other EU countries you'll need to show your E111 form with your prescription.

For **dental treatment** EU citizens are liable to pay for all work costing up to 700kr, for bills from 701kr to 1350kr you pay 65 percent and from 1351kr upwards you pay 30 percent. For **dental surgeries** look for the sign "*Tandläkare*" or "*Folktandvården*". An emergency dental service is available in most major towns and cities out of hours.

**Medicines** may be taken into Sweden if intended for your own use. Narcotics used as medication can also be taken into the country if intended for personal use for a maximum of five days. You must have a medical certificate proving that you need them.

## SURVIVING THE SUMMER – MOSQUITOES

The **mosquito** goes by the rather fetching name of *mygg* in Swedish – it's a word you'll become painfully familiar with during your stay. If you're planning to spend any time at all outside the confines of towns and cities (and even here the little critters are merciless), it's imperative that you protect yourself. Swedish mosquitoes don't carry hideous diseases, but they can torment your every waking moment from the end of June onwards, when the warmer weather causes them to hatch. They are found in their densest concentrations in the north of the country, where the sky has been known to turn black as swarms of the things appear from nowhere.

Mosquitoes are most active early in the morning and in the late afternoon/early evening; the best way to protect yourself is to wear thick, preferably bright clothing, avoid large stretches of water, especially lakes and pools, make a smoky fire of, for example, damp peat (mosquitoes don't like smoke), rub mosquito **repellent** like crazy on all exposed flesh. And, easier said than done, don't scratch mosquito bites (*myggbett*); treat them instead with *Salubrin* or *Alsolsprit*, or something similar – both available from local chemists.

## SURVIVING THE WINTER

There's no two ways about it, seven to eight months of snow can make **winter in Sweden** pretty grim. But visiting in the depths of winter can be quite fun if you protect yourself against the extreme cold – often below -30°C in the north of the country. Swedes cope by wearing several **layers of clothes**, preferably cotton, which is good at keeping out the cold. A warm winter coat alone won't suffice. You'll need a good woolly hat, snug-fitting gloves or mittens and thick socks as well – between 30 to 50 percent of body heat is lost from the feet and head. Be prepared, though, to shed layers when you go into shops and other buildings, which are often heated to oven temperature.

Bring **boots** or stout shoes with good grips that will hold onto the finely polished compacted snow that covers streets and pavements in winter. Before venturing onto the ice ask the advice of local people to make sure it'll hold your weight. Although even Swedes get it wrong, and reports of people going under the ice are commonplace in newspapers during the winter months. **Drivers** often take shortcuts in their cars across frozen lakes in winter – if you're going to do it, too, make sure you stick to the route that has either been laid out or the existing well-worn tracks in the ice. In towns and cities, it can even be dangerous just walking along the pavement – keep your eyes peeled for dagger-shaped **icicles** hanging from

roofs and gutters; sooner or later they'll come crashing to the ground and you don't want to be underneath when that happens. Death by icicle appears on more death certificates than you'd imagine.

## TRAVELLERS WITH DISABILITIES

Sweden is in many ways a model of awareness for the traveller with disabilities, and help, if needed, is forthcoming from virtually all Swedes. Both public buildings and public

transport throughout the country are geared up for people with disabilities. According to Swedish law, all public buildings must be accessible to people with disabilities and

### CONTACTS FOR TRAVELLERS WITH DISABILITIES

#### AUSTRALIA AND NEW ZEALAND

**ACROD (Australian Council for Rehabilitation of the Disabled)**, PO Box 60, Curtin ACT 2605 (☎06/682 4333); 55 Charles St, Rydo (☎02/0809 4400).

**Disabled Persons Assembly**, PO Box 10, 138 The Terrace, Wellington (☎04/472 2626).

#### BRITAIN AND IRELAND

**Disability Action Group**, 2 Annadale Ave, Belfast BT7 3JH (☎01232/91011).

**Holiday Care Service**, 2nd floor, Imperial Building, Victoria Rd, Horley RH6 9HW (☎001293/774535).

**Holiday Scandinavia Ltd**, 28 Hillcrest Rd, Orpington BR6 9AW (☎01689/824958).

**Irish Wheelchair Association**, Blackheath Drive, Clontarf, Dublin 3 (☎01/833 8241). *A nation-*

*al voluntary organization working with people with disabilities with related services for holidaymakers.*

**RADAR**, 12 City Forum, 250 City Rd, London EC1V 8AS (☎0171/250 3222; Minicom ☎0171/250 4119). *A good source of advice on holidays and travel abroad.*

**Tripscope**, The Courtyard, Evelyn Rd, London W4 5JL (☎0181/994 9294).

#### SWEDEN

**Svenska Handikappidrottsförbundet**, Idrottenshus, S-123 87, Farsta, Sweden (☎08/605 60 00; fax 724 85 40). *Information on sports facilities for people with disabilities.*

**Swedish Federation of Disabled Persons (De Handikappades Riksförbund; DHR)**, Katrinebergsvägen 6, S-117 43, Stockholm (☎08/18 91 00; fax 645 65 41).

#### US AND CANADA

**Directions Unlimited**, 720 N Bedford Rd, Bedford Hills, NY 10507 (☎1-800/533-5343). *Tour operator specializing in custom tours for people with disabilities.*

**Mobility International USA**, PO Box 10767, Eugene, OR 97440 (Voice and TDD: ☎503/343-1284). *Information and referral services, access guides, tours and exchange programmes. Annual membership $20 (includes quarterly newsletter).*

**Society for the Advancement of Travel for the Handicapped (SATH)**, 347 5th Ave, New

York, NY 10016 (☎212/447-7284). *Non-profit travel-industry referral service that passes queries on to its members as appropriate; allow plenty of time for a response.*

**Twin Peaks Press**, Box 129, Vancouver, WA 98666; ☎206/694-2462 or 1-800/637-2256). *Publisher of the Directory of Travel Agencies for the Disabled (US$19.95), listing more than 370 agencies worldwide; Travel for the Disabled (US$19.95); the Directory of Accessible Van Rentals (US$9.95) and Wheelchair Vagabond (US$14.95), loaded with personal tips.*

have automatic doors. **Any building with three or more stories must legally have a lift installed**, and around towns and cities wherever there are lots of steps there's often a lift nearby. **Wheelchair access is usually available on trains (intercity trains often have special carriages with hydraulic lifts and wide aisles and large toilets for easy access), and there are lifts down to the platforms at almost every metro station in Stockholm. Also specially converted minivans are used as taxis across the country.**

**Hotels** are also geared up to cater for their disabled guests with specially adapted rooms (as are some chalet villages which have cabins with wheelchair access). Generally hotels, hostels, museums and other public places are very willing to help and will often have other facilities aside from those mentioned above. **Getting there**, too, is getting easier: *Scandinavian Seaways* ferries have specially adapted cabins, and *Silja Line* offers discounts for travellers with disabilities on its routes between Sweden and Finland. A useful holiday guide is available from Swedish tourist offices (see "Information and maps" for their addresses abroad).

### PLANNING A HOLIDAY

There are **organized tours and holidays** specifically for people with disabilities – the contacts in the box on p.21 will be able to put you in touch with any specialists for trips to Sweden. If you

want to be more independent, it's important to become an authority on where you must be self-reliant and where you may expect help, especially regarding transportation and accommodation. It's also vital to be honest with travel agencies, insurance companies and travel companions. It's worth thinking about your limitations and making sure others know them, too. If you don't use a wheelchair all the time but your walking capabilities are limited, remember that you are likely to need to cover greater distances while travelling (sometimes over rougher terrain and in hotter/colder temperatures than you are used to). If you use a wheelchair, it is always wise to have it serviced before you go and carry a repair kit.

People with a pre-existing medical condition are sometimes excluded from travel **insurance policies**, so read the small print carefully. To make your journey simpler, ask your travel agent to notify airlines or bus companies, who can cope better if they are expecting you, with, for example, a wheelchair provided at airports and staff primed to help. A **medical certificate** of your fitness to travel, provided by your doctor, is also extremely useful; some airlines or insurance companies may insist on it. Make sure that you have extra supplies of drugs – carried with you if you fly – and a prescription including the generic name in case of emergency. Carry spares of any clothing or equipment that might be hard to find; if there's an association representing people with your disability, contact them early in the planning process.

# COSTS, MONEY AND BANKS

**It's a widely held belief that Sweden is the most expensive country in Europe. However, this is not true any more. There's no doubt that it can be expensive, but on average Sweden is cheaper than the other Scandinavian countries and no more expensive than, say, France or Germany. If you like drinking coffee and eating cakes all day long, travelling by taxi and tripping off to the theatre of an evening you'll leave Sweden a pauper. If, however, you don't mind eating the main meal of the day at lunchtime, like the Swedes, or having picnics in the midnight sun with goodies bought from the supermar-**

ket, travelling by the efficient public transport system and going easy on the nightlife, you'll find Sweden isn't the financial investment you thought it was going to be.

## CURRENCY

The Swedish **currency** is the *krona* (kr; plural *kronor*), made up of 100 *öre*. It comes in coins of 50öre, 1kr, 5kr and 10kr; and notes of 20kr, a new 50kr note as of 1996, 100kr, 500kr, 1000kr and 10,000kr. There's no limit on the amount of Swedish and foreign currency you can take into Sweden. Currently there are 10kr to £1; that's 7.5kr to US$1. The different Scandinavian currencies are not interchangeable, but on inter-Nordic ferries all the currencies can generally be used.

## COSTS

**Accommodation** in Sweden is good value: youth hostels are of a very high standard and charge only 70–125kr a night for members (£7–12.50/US$10–16); in summer, hotels offer special low prices to tourists; and campsites are plentiful and cheap. **Admission prices** to museums and galleries are also low or indeed don't exist at all; and if you flash an *ISIC* card (see opposite), it's likely to bring a reduction. There are also reductions of around 30 to 50 percent at most places for children and senior citizens, and often younger children get in for free.

When buying **food** look for produce marked "*extrapris*", which denotes a special offer, or "*fynd*", which is supposed to be literally that, a bit of a find. Avoid anything in tins or frozen, coffee, sweeties and breakfast cereals. Fresh fish, seafood, sausages and beef are all quite reasonable.

**Restaurant eating** can work out a good deal if you stick to the *Dagens Rätt* (dish of the day), served at lunchtime in most restaurants and cafés and consisting of salad, a main meal (often a choice between two or three dishes), bread, a drink and a coffee – all-in for 40–60kr (£4–6/US$6–9). What will cost you money in Sweden is **alcohol**; a strong beer served in a bar costs a dizzy 35–55kr (£3.50–5.50/US$5–8). A bottle of wine in a restaurant will set you back around 200kr (£20/US$30); and the cost of a whisky or cognac is likey to bring on early heart trouble.

Put all this together and you'll find you can exist – camping, self-catering, hitching, no drink-

ing – on a fairly low budget (around £15/$22 a day), though it will be a pretty miserable experience and only sustainable for a limited period of time. Stay in hostels, eat the *Dagens Rätt* at lunchtime, get out and see the sights and drink the odd beer or two and you'll be looking at doubling your expenditure. Better meals in restaurants with wine, a few taxis, coffees and cakes and hotel accommodation and you'll be getting through considerably more (£60–75/US$90–115).

Remember that although some Swedish prices will amaze you (especially the cost of books), the quality is always high and that goods are clean, new, bright – and, most of all, they work.

## YOUTH AND STUDENT DISCOUNTS

Full-time students are eligible for the **International Students ID Card (ISIC)**, which entitles the bearer to special fares on local transport and discounts at museums, theatres and other attractions. For Americans there's also a health benefit, providing up to US$3000 in emergency medical coverage and US$100 a day for sixty days in hospital, plus a 24-hour hotline to call in the event of medical, legal or financial emergency. The card, which costs £5 in the UK, £7 in Ireland, US$16 in the US and CAN$15 in Canada, is available from branches of *USIT* in Ireland, and *Council Travel*, *STA* and *Travel CUTS* around the world.

If you're 25 or younger you qualify for the **Go-25 Card**, which costs the same as the *ISIC* card and carries the same benefits. It can be purchased through *Council Travel* in the US and *Hostelling International* in Canada (see "Accommodation"), and *STA* in Australia and New Zealand.

*STA* also sells its own ID card that's good for some discounts, as do various other travel organizations. A university photo ID might open some doors, too.

## TRAVELLERS' CHEQUES, CASH AND CARDS

Although you're unlikely to be mugged in Sweden, it's safest to carry your money as **travellers' cheques**, available for a small commission (usually one percent of the amount ordered) from most banks and building societies, and from branches of *Thomas Cook* and *American Express*. You must always keep the purchase agreement and a record of cheque serial numbers separate from the cheques themselves. In the UK banks also issue current account holders with a **Eurocheque card** and chequebook, with which you get cash in Sweden direct from your own bank account; you'll pay something in service charge and a fee for the card itself but the card, in particular, can be very useful in getting money out of the wall virtually everywhere without the interest charged by credit cards for cash advances.

The major **credit and charge cards** (*Visa, Access/Mastercard, American Express* and *Diners Card*) are accepted almost everywhere in return for goods or cash. *Visa* and *Access/Mastercard* with pin numbers are good for taking money out of cash machines, although machines which accept *Visa* are slightly more common. British and Irish chequebooks don't work in Sweden; bank cards only work if they have a *Visa* or *Access* facility on them.

## BANKS AND EXCHANGE

**Exchanging money** is easy but quite expensive. Banks have standard exchange rates but commissions can vary enormously, and it's always worth shopping around. Some places charge per cheque, others per transaction, so it's common sense to take large denominations with you, or to try to change as much as you feel you can handle at once.

You can change money in **banks** all over Sweden; opening hours are Mon–Fri 9.30am–3pm, with extended hours on Thurs until 5.30pm. In some cities banks may stay open to 5.30pm. All banks are closed at weekends and on public holidays. Banks at airports, ports and main train stations generally have longer opening hours – but often worse rates of exchange.

The **best place to change money** is at the yellow **Forex** offices which pay 3–18 percent more for your currency than the banks. You'll find them in city centres in Stockholm (also at the Central Station), Gothenburg, Malmö, Lund, Uppsala and Trelleborg. There are also branches at Arlanda airport in Stockholm, Landvetter airport in Gothenburg, Sturup airport in Malmö and at the ferry terminals in Helsingborg and Ystad.

It's also possible to change money in **post offices**: look out for the "*Växel*" (exchange) sign. In the more remote areas, you'll often find that hostels, hotels and campsites will also change money; in general forget hotels, because their exchange rates are abysmal.

## EMERGENCY CASH

If, as a foreign visitor, you run out of money or there is some kind of emergency, the quickest way to get **money sent out** is to contact your bank at home and have them wire the cash to the nearest bank. You can do the same thing through *Thomas Cook* or *American Express*, if there is a branch nearby. Americans and Canadians can also have cash sent out through *Western Union* to a nearby bank or post office. Make sure you know when it's likely to arrive, since you won't be notified by the receiving office. Remember, too, that you'll need some form of identification when you pick up the money.

# INFORMATION AND MAPS

## SWEDISH TRAVEL AND TOURISM COUNCIL

**Australia:** No office but the Swedish Embassy handles tourist information (see p.18).

**Britain:** 11 Montagu Place, London, W1H 2AL (☎0171/724 5868; fax ☎0171/724 5872).

**Canada:** Contact the Swedish Embassy for tourist information (see p.18).

**Ireland:** No office but the Swedish Embassy handles tourist information (see p.18).

**New Zealand:** The Swedish Consulate supplies tourist information (see p.18).

**US:** PO Box 4649, Grand Central Station, New York, NY 10163–4649 (☎212/949-2333; fax ☎212/697-0835).

**Before you leave it's worth contacting the Swedish Travel and Tourism Council (the national tourist board) in your own country for free maps and brochures – though don't go overboard as much of it can easily be obtained later in Sweden. Any timetables for trains, planes and buses are worth taking along with you, as are the booklets listing accommodation. Addresses of the Swedish Travel and Tourism Council are given opposite.**

## TOURIST OFFICES

Once in Sweden every town and some villages have a **tourist office** from where you can pick up free town plans and information, brochures and other bumph. Many book private rooms (sometimes youth hostel beds), rent bikes, sell local discount cards and change money. During the summer they're open until late evening; out of season shop hours are more usual, and in the winter they're normally closed at weekends. You'll find full details of individual offices throughout the text.

## MAPS

The **maps and plans** printed in this guide are fine for general reference, but drivers, cyclists and hikers will probably require something more detailed. Tourist offices give out reason-

able road maps and town plans but anything better you'll have to buy – see the map shops listed overleaf.

The most useful **map of Stockholm** can only be bought when you arrive in the city: the *Stockholmskartan* is available from the local transport authority, *Storstockholms Lokaltrafik*, at their offices underneath the central train station and also at the entrance to Sergels Torg metro station and at Slussen metro. This has the added advantage of showing all bus and metro routes in the capital and a street index. For maps of the whole country, go for the *Terrac* (1:1,000,000) or *Hallwag* maps. There are also regional maps produced by *Kartförlaget* (1:400,000).

If you're staying in one area for a long time or are **hiking** or **walking** you'll need something more detailed still – a minimum scale of 1:400,000, though preferably much larger if you're doing any serious trekking. The 1:300,000 *Esselte Kartor* are excellent, but the one to beat them all if you're in the northwestern mountains is the *Fjällkartan* series at a scale of 1:100,000 produced by *Lantmäteriet* – though this is unfortunately rather expensive both in Sweden and abroad. You'll find that the larger tourist offices sometimes have decent hiking maps or leaflets giving descriptions of local hiking routes. *Svenska Turistföreningen* (Swedish Touring Club, Box 25, S-101 20 Stockholm; ☎08/463 21 00) also has a good stock of maps and guides.

## MAP OUTLETS

### AUSTRALIA AND NEW ZEALAND

**The Map Shop**, 16a Peel St, Melbourne, VIC 3000 (☎08/8231 2033).

**Bowyangs**, 372 Little Burke St, Adelaide, SA 5000 (☎03/9670 4383).

**Perth Map Centre**, 891 Hay St, Perth, WA 6000 (☎08/9322 5733).

**Specialty Maps**, 58 Albert St, Auckland (☎09/307 2217).

**Travel Bookshop**, 20 Bridge St, Sydney, NSW 2000 (☎02/9241 3554).

### BRITAIN

**Daunt Books**, 83 Marylebone High St, London W1 (☎0171/224 2295).

**John Smith and Sons**, 57–61 St Vincent St, Glasgow G2 5TB (☎0141/221 7472).

**National Map Centre**, 22–24 Caxton St, London SW1 (☎0171/222 4945).

**Stanfords\***, 12–14 Long Acre, London WC2 (☎0171/836 1321); 52 Grosvenor Gdns, London SW1W 0AG; 156 Regent St, London W1R 5TA.

**The Travel Bookshop**, 13–15 Blenheim Crescent, London W11 2EE (☎0171/229 5260).

*Note: Maps by **mail or phone order** are available from *Stanfords*; ☎0171/836 1321.

### CANADA

**Open Air Books and Maps**, 25 Toronto St, Toronto, ON M5R 2C1 (☎416/363-0719).

**Ulysses Travel Bookshop**, 4176 St-Denis, Montréal (☎514/289-0993).

**World Wide Books and Maps**, 1247 Granville St, Vancouver, BC V6Z 1E4 (☎604/687-3320).

### IRELAND

**Easons Bookshop**, 40 O'Connell St, Dublin 1 (☎01/873 3811).

**Fred Hanna's Bookshop**, 27–29 Nassau St, Dublin 2 (☎01/677 1255).

**Hodges Figgis Bookshop**, 56–58 Dawson St, Dublin 2 (☎01/677 4754).

**Waterstone's**, Queens Bldg, 8 Royal Ave, Belfast BT1 1DA (☎01232/247355).

### US

**The Complete Traveler Bookstore**, 199 Madison Ave, New York, NY 10016 (☎212/685-9007); 3207 Fillmore St, San Francisco, CA 92123 (☎415/923-1511).

**Forsyth Travel Library**, 9154 W 57th St, Shawnee Mission, KS 66201 (☎1-800/367-7984).

**Map Link Inc**, 25 E Mason St, Santa Barbara, CA 93101 (☎805/965-4402).

**Phileas Fogg's Books & Maps**, #87 Stanford Shopping Center, Palo Alto, CA 94304 (☎1-800/233-FOGG in California; ☎1-800/533-FOGG elsewhere in US).

**Rand McNally\***, 444 N Michigan Ave, Chicago, IL 60611 (☎312/321-1751); 150 E 52nd St, New York, NY 10022 (☎212/758-7488); 595 Market St,

San Francisco, CA 94105 (☎415/777-3131); 1201 Connecticut Ave NW, Washington, DC 20003 (☎202/223-6751).

**Sierra Club Bookstore**, 730 Polk St, San Francisco, CA 94109 (☎415/923-5500).

**Travel Books & Language Center**, 4931 Cordell Ave, Bethesda, MD 20814 (☎1-800/220-2665).

**Traveler's Bookstore**, 22 W 52nd St, New York, NY 10019 (☎212/664-0995).

*Note: *Rand McNally* now has 24 stores across the US; call ☎1-800/333-0136 (ext 2111) for the location of your nearest store or for maps by mail order.

# GETTING AROUND

The public transport system in Sweden is possibly the most efficient in the whole of Europe; it operates in all weathers on time. There's a comprehensive train network in the south of the country; in the north travelling by train isn't quite so easy – many branch lines have been closed as Swedish State Railways tries to save money. However, it's still possible to reach the main towns and cities in the north by train. Where trains no longer exist, buses generally cover the same routes (in some cases rail passes are valid on these routes).

## TIMETABLES

All train, bus and ferry schedules are contained in the giant **Rikstidtabellen** (National Timetable), which currently costs 80kr and is available from train stations. It's not really worth buying and carrying with you, given its size; instead ask for photocopies of the relevant pages from tourist offices or travel agents. Alternatively for train times pick up a copy of the handy and free **Tur & Retur booklets** available from stations, which give listings to major destinations in Sweden. But the most useful booklets if you're doing a lot of travelling by train are the **Tågtider** (Train Times) and **Tåg Till Utlandet** (Trains Abroad), again available from train stations for 10kr. The former lists most train departures on most routes in Sweden, the latter connections to destinations in the rest of Europe – both are in

Swedish but are easy to figure out. Each train route also has its own timetable leaflet available free from the local station.

Remember that in winter train and bus services, in particular, are reduced (especially in the north where they may even dry up alltogether). At holiday times (see "Opening hours and festivals", p.45) and between mid-June and mid-August services are often heavily booked; it's worth making reservations as far in advance as you can (in Britain *Deutsche Bann* – see p.6 – can help).

Watch out for city and **regional discount cards**, which often give free use of local travel (bus, ferry, tram, sometimes train), free museum entry and other discounts. Often these cards are only on sale during the summer (notable exceptions are those in Stockholm, Gothenburg and Malmö); the most useful ones have been detailed in the text. Elsewhere it's worth asking at local tourist offices as schemes change frequently.

If you're planning on jetting round the country **by plane** using one of the two airpass systems in operation, you'll find it handy to have a copy of the **Inrikestidtabellen** (Domestic Timetable), which lists every route within Sweden – not just *SAS* – and is available from airports, tourist offices, travel agents and airline offices.

## TRAINS

**Swedish State Railways** (*SJ – Statens Järnvägar*, ☎08/696 75 40 from abroad, or on local call rate ☎020/75 75 75) has an **extensive network** stretching from the far south of the country up through northern Sweden, over the Arctic Circle and across the border to Narvik in Norway – the northernmost line in Europe. Other than flying, it's the quickest and easiest way of covering Sweden's vast expanses. The service is excellent, especially on the main routes, and prices are not too expensive. The standard-class return journey from Stockholm to Gothenburg, for example, will cost you 505kr, and from Stockholm to Kiruna 780kr, with a couchette; one-way fares are half the return price.

Sweden is currently introducing a new **high-speed train**, the X2000, on main intercity routes (see table overleaf for routes and approximate journey times), which can save you a couple of hours

## X2000 ROUTES AND JOURNEY TIMES

| | |
|---|---|
| Stockholm–Malmö | 4hr 30min |
| Stockholm–Gothenburg | 3hr 15min |
| Stockholm–Karlstad | 2hr 30min |
| Stockholm–Jönköping | 3hr |
| Stockholm–Falun (Dalarna) | 2hr 25min |
| Stockholm–Mora (Dalarna) | 3hr 30min |
| Stockholm–Sundsvall | 4hr |
| Stockholm–Härnösand | 5hr |
| Stockholm–Växjö | 3hr 30min |
| Gothenburg–Malmö | 3hr |

on most routes. They have sockets for listening to the radio (bring your own headphones), onboard telephone, fax and photocoping services in first class and a bistro car. Fares are, not surprisingly, more expensive: for example, the Stockholm-to-Gothenburg fare on X2000 standard class costs 710kr. Seat reservations are included in the ticket price. If you buy a ticket abroad or have a rail pass, you pay a 100kr supplement. Bear in mind, you always have a choice as ordinary intercity trains also operate on all the routes in the box above.

If you're travelling overnight in Sweden, it's worth paying for a **couchette** (women-only compartments are available) or a **sleeping car** – Swedish train seats don't pull out to form a bed, unlike their equivalents in many other European trains. Prices are low, though; a couchette within Sweden (you'll be sharing with five others) costs 85kr, roughly the same as a night in a youth hostel, and slightly more on international services. A two-berth standard-class sleeping car is a lot more; prices vary according to destination but start at 220kr. Sleepers run between Stockholm and the following final destinations: Gothenburg, Malmö, Helsingborg, Kalmar, Sundsvall, Östersund, Storlien, Umeå, Luleå and Kiruna; also abroad to Oslo and Copenhagen (prices slightly more). There's a hot shower and hair dryer in the end of every sleeping car as well as a socket for the radio (bring your own headphones).

The night train from Stockholm to Kiruna and Luleå and from Gothenburg to Luleå is an experience in itself. The **Nordpilen** (Northern Arrow) has a cinema onboard where you can catch up with the latest releases before heading off for the bistro for a bite to eat or for a quick jive to your favourite tunes from the jukebox – all as you slip painlessly through the Swedish night.

### TICKETS AND DISCOUNTS

Individual **train tickets** are rarely cost-effective, despite the comprehensive (and downright confusing) system of discounts, which seem to change as soon as they've been brought in. Visitors doing a lot of touring by train are much better off buying a train pass (see below). If you do need to buy an individual ticket it's worth checking the latest on any special deals that may be available. In Sweden one-way tickets cost half of the return price, but note also that reservations (20kr) are compulsory on all ordinary intercity trains.

The main **discounts** are known as the **röd avgång** (red departure) because they're marked by a red blob in the timetables (note these don't appear every day) and give a range of discounts depending on the distance you are travelling. However, you need what's known as a **reslustkort** (literally a "wanderlust card"!; 150kr; valid for one calendar year) in order to be able to use the red departure times. The *reslustkort* also includes a number of other discounts, and one card entitles two people travelling together to the same discount.

The system becomes even more confusing on public holidays; for full details ask at any train station in Sweden or from agents abroad (see the relevant "Getting there" section). It's worth pointing out that nearly all train staff in Sweden speak good English, which means that you've got a sporting chance of buying the right ticket every time; conversely it's difficult to be convincing if you're caught by the conductor in possession of an invalid or wrong ticket.

In the end most people are best off avoiding the headache and getting a **pass** instead, such as *InterRail*, *Eurail* or *ScanRail* (see the relevant "Getting there" section for details) or, if you are only touring Sweden, a **Sweden Rail Pass**. This gives unlimited travel throughout the country on all *SJ* trains. A standard class seven-day pass costs £130 and first class £171; 14 days costs £174 and £226. Supplements are payable on intercity and express services. You have to buy the pass before you leave home – it is not available in Sweden – at present there is no agent in Australia or New Zealand.

### THE INLANDSBANAN

The fate of the **Inlandsbanan** (Inland Railway; ☎063/12 76 95, fax 10 15 90), which runs through northern Sweden, became a hot topic of debate in

Sweden when *SJ* announced that they were planning to close it down on grounds of cost. After the last *SJ* trains ran on the line – which stretches over 1300km from Mora to Gällivare – in 1992, it was sold off to a private company, *Inlandståget AB*, which now runs services during the summer months only. *ScanRail* and *InterRail* and *Eurail* holders are entitled to discounts of 50 percent; reduced-fare tickets can be bought onboard the trains but advance reservations aren't possible. If you're in Sweden for any length of time, travelling at least a section of the route is a must. Timetables change from year to year but in general the *Vildmarkståget* (Wilderness Express), with its vintage 1930s carriages and restaurant, runs several times a week making numerous stops along the route. It also has guides who point out items of interest along the way and is by far the best way to cross the Arctic Circle – an opportunity for much whistle blowing and snapping of piccies. A normal stopping service without the frills also operates up and down the line. For more on the *Inlandsbanan*, see p.354.

## PÅGATÅGEN

In Sweden's southernmost province, Skåne, a local private company, *Pågatågen*, operates trains between Helsingborg, Lund and Malmö, and between Malmö and Ystad. These are fully automated and you buy your tickets from a machine on the platform, which accepts coins and notes. Prices on the short hops are low; *InterRail* and *ScanRail* cards are valid.

## BUSES

Although **buses** are cheaper than the train, they are never a good alternative for long distances – except, of course, where there are no trains. Services are a lot slower (for example, Stockholm to Malmö takes 4hr 30min on the X2000; by bus it's 9hr 20min) and in general less frequent. However, travelling by bus does cost around half the price of the train.

Most **long-distance buses** are operated by two companies, *Swebus* (from abroad call ☎08/655 00 90; in Sweden call on local rate ☎020/64 06 40) and *Svenska Buss* (☎020/67 67 67). **Swebus** offer the most extensive network in Sweden, with departures to over four hundred destinations from Malmö in the south up as far as Luleå and Haparanda on the far northern coast. **Svenska Buss** operate in the south of the country, going no further north than Falun and Borlänge. There are two types of buses run by both companies: *Expressbussar* run daily, usually complementing rather than competing with the train network, while the cheaper *Veckoslutsbussar* only run at weekends (Fri & Sun). With *Swebus*, **fares** range from 20kr to 350kr depending on the length of the journey, with under-17s going for half price and children under 6 for free. Students and young people between the ages of 17 and 21 get a 30-percent discount; while senior citizens can travel at a 50-percent discount from Monday to Thursday and on Saturday.

There are also a number of **smaller companies** running only one or two routes, including *Y-Bussen* (☎08/23 14 40), the only company operating services from Stockholm to the High Coast, Sollefteå and Östersund, and *Stockholms-expressen* (☎010/256 99 69), which operates buses between Stockholm and Umeå.

**Regional bus services** also exist throughout the country, particularly in the north where they carry mail to isolated areas. Several companies operate daily services, and fares are broadly similar (usually 100–150kr for a 1–2hr journey). Major routes are listed in the "Travel Details" at the end of each chapter, and you can pick up a comprehensive timetable at any bus terminal. Local buses also exist in towns and cities. Count on using them, as many hotels and particularly hostels and campsites can be a fair distance from town centres. Flat fares cost 12–20kr, the ticket usually valid for an hour. Most large towns operate some sort of discount system where you can buy cheaper books or tickets – details are in the text or can be obtained from the local tourist offices.

## PLANES

The **domestic plane** network is operated by a number of companies, the key players being *SAS* and *Transwede*. Various deals can make flying a real steal, especially considering the time saved. Individual so-called Jackpot tickets (much the same as an Apex), which can be booked right up to departure, aren't particularly cheap (around 1000–1500kr return depending on destination); for information on domestic flights and fares in Sweden call ☎020/72 70 00.

Both companies offer airpasses, which can make flying a serious alternative to *InterRail* or

*ScanRail*. **SAS Airpasses** have to be bought in conjunction with a Jackpot ticket to Sweden (you can buy up to six with each Jackpot) and cost £50 per pass (child £38). *SAS* passes are also valid on flights within and between Denmark, Norway and Sweden and between Sweden and Finland. One airpass permits travel on one flight only.

The **Nordic Airpass**, offered by *Transwede* in cooperation with *Finnair/Braathens* and *Maersk Air*, is less useful for Sweden, because the airline only operates to a handful of destinations in the country. It does, however, offer greater possibilities if your visit to Sweden is part of a larger Scandinavian trip, because it takes in countless routes in Finland with *Finnair*, in Norway with *Braathens* and in Denmark with *Maersk*. The pass is incredibly user-unfriendly, its impenetrable rules best explained by the airlines themselves. In Sweden you can contact *Transwede* on ☎020/22 52 25 or try *Finnair*, *Braathens* or *Maersk* in your home country before you leave.

Alternatively, young people under the age of 25 can make a killing by flying **standby**. Buy tickets at Stockholm's Arlanda airport when you arrive and put yourself in the queue – a standby ticket currently costs 280kr. A telephone service in Swedish only gives information on availability of flights; if you don't speak Swedish call *SAS* on the above number and ask them if you're likely to get a seat.

### FERRIES AND BOATS

**Domestic ferry** services in Sweden are few. The main domestic ferry route is between Visby on the Baltic island of Gotland and the mainland (Nynäshamn near Stockholm and Oskarshamn). High-speed **catamarans** also operate on the Nynäshamn-to-Visby route. These routes are very popular in summer and you should try to book ahead. The *ScanRail* pass gives a 50-percent discount on the Gotland crossings (for more detail see p.5).

The various archipelagos off the coast, particularly the **Stockholm archipelago** with its 24,000 islands, have ferry services which link up the main islands. If you're in Stockholm make sure you venture out into the archipelago – the peace and quiet and vistas of water, rocks and skerries is something special. An island-hopping boat pass is available in Stockholm; see p.98 for more details.

With your own boat, it's possible to cross between Stockholm and Gothenburg on the **Göta Canal**, or alternatively you can take an expensive cruise along the same route onboard an atmospheric old steam boat; ticket and journey details are given on p.148. Cheaper day cruises are possible along stretches of the Göta Canal and the Trollhätan Canal; more details are given in the text.

### CAR, TAXIS AND HITCHING

As far as road conditions go, **driving in Sweden** is a dream. Traffic jams are rare (in fact in the north of the country you'll often be the only car on the road), roads are well maintained and motorways, where they exist, are tollfree. The only real dangers are **reindeer** (in the north) and **elk** (everywhere), which wander onto the road without warning. It's particularly difficult to see them at dusk, and when it's properly dark all you'll see is two red eyes, as the animal leaps out in front of your car. The Swedes have now taken to spraying pungent-smelling artificial wolf urine on the edge of roads where accidents involving elk are common; elk and wolves don't get on together at all well. If you hit an elk or deer, not only will you know about it (they're as big as a horse), you're bound by law to report it to the police.

To drive in Sweden you'll need a **full licence**; an international driving licence isn't required, though a green card or other insurance documents are essential. **Speed limits** are 110kph on motorways, 90kph on dual carriageways and many other roads, 70kph where unsigned, and 50kph in built-up areas. For cars and caravans (with brakes) the limit is 70kph. You must drive with your headlights on 24hr a day (don't forget to turn them off when you leave the car!), and it's useful to fit a headlamp adaptor if you're bringing over a right-hand drive car to avoid dazzling oncoming traffic with your lights. Warning triangles are compulsory, as is the wearing of seatbelts both in the back and in the front; children can use any seat but must use a seat belt or a special child safety seat. Studded tyres for driving on snow and ice are allowed between November 1 and the first Monday after the Easter holiday; when in use they must be fitted to all wheels. If you're motoring in northern Sweden, it's worth fitting mudflaps to your wheels and stoneguards to the front of caravans.

Swedish **drink-driving laws** are among the strictest in Europe and random breath tests are commonplace. Basically, you can't even have one

## CAR RENTAL FIRMS

**AUSTRALIA**
**Avis** ☎1800/225 53.
**Budget** ☎13 2848.
**Hertz** ☎13 1918.

**BRITAIN**
**Avis** ☎0181/848 8733.
**Europcar/InterRent** ☎01345/222 525.
**Eurodollar** 01895/233300.
**Budget** ☎0800/181181.
**Hertz** ☎0990/996699.
**Holiday Autos** ☎0990/300400.

**IRELAND**
**Avis** ☎01232/240404.
**Budget** ☎01232/230700.
**Europcar** ☎01232/450904 or 01232/423444.
**Hertz** ☎01/660 2255.
**Holiday Autos** ☎01/454 9090.

**NEW ZEALAND**
**Avis** ☎09/525 1982.
**Budget** ☎09/275 2222.
**Hertz** ☎09/309 0989.

**NORTH AMERICA**
**Auto Europe** ☎1-800/223-5555.
**Avis International** ☎1-800/331-1084.
**Budget** ☎1-800/527-0700.
**Dollar** ☎1-800/421-6868.
**Europe by Car** ☎1-800/223-1516.
**Hertz International** ☎1-800/654-3001; in Canada ☎1-800/263-0600.
**Holiday Autos** ☎1-800/422-7737.

For the main car rental firms **in Sweden** see the "Listings" sections of Stockholm and Gothenburg chapters.

beer and still be under the limit; the blood alcohol level is 0.2 percent. If you're found to be over the limit you'll lose your licence (always), face a fine (often) and a prison sentence (not infrequently). For **speeding** and the like **fines** are levied on the spot.

If you **break down** call either the police or the *Larmtjänst* (☎020/91 00 40 for towing; ☎020/22 00 00 for other accidents), a 24-hour rescue organization run by Swedish insurance companies. You should only use the emergency telephone number (☎112) in the event of an accident and injuries. It's not mandatory to call the police in the case of an accident, but drivers must give their name and address to the other parties involved and shouldn't leave the scene until that's done. Drivers who don't stop after an accident may be liable to a fine or even imprisonment.

### CAR RENTAL AND PETROL

If driving in Sweden is a dream – forking out for car rental and petrol is more the stuff of nightmares. **Car rental** is uniformly expensive; the only way to bring down the ludicrous prices is to hunt for special weekend rates (tourist offices are a good source for these) or try the national chain

of filling stations, *Statoil*, which often rents out vehicles at near bargain prices over weekends, generally Friday afternoon to Monday morning. If you fail to find a special deal, reckon on paying 3000kr a week and upwards for a VW Golf or similar-sized car with unlimited mileage in the summer months. Be warned, though, that deals in the remoter parts can be even more expensive than this. The major international companies are represented in all the main towns and cities (in out-of-the-way places, airports are often the only source of car rental). To rent a car in Sweden you must be over 21 and have held a driving licence for at least one year.

You may well find it cheaper, especially if you are travelling from North America, to arrange things before you go; airlines sometimes have special deals with car rental companies if you book your flight and car through them. Alternatively, if you don't want to be tied down, try an agency such as *Holiday Autos*, who will arrange advance booking through a local agent and can usually undercut the big companies considerably (see the box above for details of car rental companies).

The cost of **petrol** (*bensin*) is also very high. Normal types of petrol available are 98 octane (equivalent to 4-star), unleaded and diesel. A litre of petrol is currently around 8kr. Most filling stations are self-service (*Tanka själv*), where you either pay a machine at the pump that accepts 20kr or 100kr notes, or head for the pumps marked "*Kassa*", which allow you to pay inside at the till. The Swedish for unleaded is *blyfri*.

### TAXIS

**Taxi** fares are quite simply horrific. Before you get in the taxi the clock will be showing at least 35kr; it will continue to tick over as you stand at traffic lights. A three-kilometre ride can easily set you back around 100kr. Given the phenomenal fares they charge, taxi drivers don't expect a tip. In some areas there are also surcharges for ordering a taxi by phone. Save your money and take the excellent public transport instead.

### HITCHING

Despite the amount of holiday traffic and the number of young Swedes with cars, **hitching** is rarely worth the effort, as long-distance lifts are few and far between. Shorter hops are easier to find, especially when travelling along the coasts and in the north, but don't rely on hitching as your main means of transport. If you do try it, always use a sign and be prepared for long, long waits and to be scoffed at by passing drivers.

## CYCLING

The best way to get round independently is to **cycle**, and some parts of the country were made for it: Stockholm, the southern provinces and Gotland, in particular, are ideal for a leisurely pedal. Many towns are best explored by bike, and tourist offices, campsites and youth hostels often rent them out from around 80kr a day, 400kr a week. Taking a bike on the train involves a bit of forward planning, however; you have to hand it in three days in advance for registration and it will cost you 125kr.

Sweden has a large number of signposted cycle trails; one of the most popular is the **Sweden Trail** (*Sverigeleden*), which links all the larger ferry ports and takes in many of the country's main sights. *Svenska Cyckelsällskapet* (Swedish Cycling Association, Box 6006, S-164 06 Kista; ☎08/751 62 04; fax 751 19 35) has more information; also try *Cyckelfrämjandet*, Box 6027, S-102 31 Stockholm (☎08/32 16 80). The *STF* (the Swedish youth hostels association) has details of cycling holidays in Sweden that include youth hostel accommodation, meals and cycle rental.

# ACCOMMODATION

Finding somewhere cheap to stay in Sweden isn't difficult. There's an extensive network of youth hostels (of an exceptionally high standard) and campsites, while private rooms and bed and breakfast places are common in the towns and cities. Discounts make hotels affordable at weekends and during the summer months, and special deals available as part of the discount card schemes available in many of the larger places also help to bring down the cost.

## YOUTH HOSTELS

**Youth hostels** in Sweden (*vandrarhem*: literally "wanderers' home") turn up in the unlikeliest of places: converted lighthouses, old castles and prisons, historic country manors, schoolrooms and even on boats. Nearly all have well-equipped self-catering kitchens and serve a buffet breakfast. Quite simply they offer some of the best accommodation in the country. Forget any preconceptions about youth hostelling: in Sweden dormitories are few, rooms are family oriented, modern, clean and hotel-like. There are over three

## YOUTH HOSTEL ASSOCIATIONS

**AUSTRALIA**

**Australian Youth Hostel Association**, Level 3, 10 Mallet St, Camperdown, Sydney (☎02/9565 1325). *Annual membership costs A$42.*

**CANADA**

**Hostelling International/Canadian Hostelling Association**, Room 400, 205 Catherine St, Ottawa, ON K2P 1C3 (☎613/237-7884 or ☎1-800/663-5777). *Annual membership: adults CAN$26.75, children under 18 free when accompanied by parents; two-year memberships cost CAN$35.*

**ENGLAND AND WALES**

**Youth Hostel Association (YHA)**, Trevelyan House, 8 St Stephen's Hill, St Alban's, Herts AL1 2DY (☎01727/855215). London information office: 14 Southampton St, London WC2 7HY (☎0171/836 1036). *Annual membership costs £9.30 .*

**IRELAND**

**Youth Hostel Association of Northern Ireland**, 22 Donegall Rd, Belfast BT12 5JN

(☎01232/324 733); **An Oige**, 61 Mountjoy St, Dublin 7 (☎01/830 4555). *The price in Northern Ireland is the same as in England and Wales; in the Republic annual membership costs £7.50.*

**NEW ZEALAND**

**Youth Hostel Association of New Zealand**, PO Box 436, Christchurch (☎03/379 9970). *Annual membership costs NZ$45.*

**SCOTLAND**

**Scottish Youth Hostel Association**, 7 Glebe Crescent, Stirling, FK8 2JA (☎01786/451181). *Annual membership costs £6.*

**US**

**Hostelling International-American Youth Hostels (HI-AYH)**, 733 15th St NW, Suite 840, PO Box 37613, Washington, DC 20005 (☎202/783-6161). *Annual membership: adults US$25, youths (under 18) US$10, seniors (55 or over) US$15, families US$35.*

---

hundred youth hostels and around sixty fell stations out in the mountains (also see p.396). Youth hostels cost between 70kr and 125kr; fell stations are slightly more expensive at 135–365kr. In the youth hostels themselves **children** pay up to 75kr per night if their parents are association members, otherwise 85kr.

The hostels are run by *Svenska Turistföreningen* (*STF*, Vandrarhem-savdelningen, Box 25, S-101 20 Stockholm; ☎08/463 21 00; fax 678 19 58). To get membership rates at Swedish hostels you can either join the youth hostel association in your home country (see box above for details) or get a **Hostelling International (HI)** card at any Swedish hostel for 225kr. You can also take advantage of the discounts on entry to some museums, ferry crossings and sightseeing trips that membership cards provide. Non-members can use the hostels but will pay slightly more – a sizeable sum over a couple of weeks given the low cost of annual membership.

To sleep at an *STF* hostel you'll need a **sheet sleeping bag**, the only kind allowed in *HI* hostels (although some Swedish hostels allow the use of

sleeping bags in winter). They can be rented at the hostels and are on sale at camping shops; alternatively you can stitch a couple of old sheets together and take a pillowcase. If you're planning to cook for yourself using youth hostel kitchens, bear in mind that a few don't provide pots and pans and utensils – take at least the basic equipment with you.

It would be impossible to list all three hundred or so youth hostels in this guide – instead consult *Hostelling International: Europe and the Mediterranean*, which lists every hostel in Sweden.

**Some tips**: Hostels are used by Swedish families as cheap hotel-standard accommodation and can fill quickly, so always ring ahead in the summer. Hostels are usually closed between 10am and 5pm, curfews around 11pm/midnight. Some hostels (particularly those in the north) close out of season.

Apart from the *STF* hostels there are a number of **independently run hostels**, usually charging similar prices. Many are listed in the booklet of non-affiliated hostels (*SVIF*), and local tourist offices will have more details.

---

The pensions and hotels listed in the guide have been price-graded according to the scale outlined below; the number indicates the price for the least expensive double room. Many hotels offer considerable reductions at weekends (year round) and during the summer holiday period (mid-June to mid-Aug); in these cases the reduction is either noted in the text or, where it falls into another price band, given after the number for the full price. Single rooms, where available, usually cost between 60 and 80 percent of a double.

① under 500kr    ② 500–700kr    ③ 700–900kr    ④ 900–1200kr    ⑤ over 1200kr

---

In conjunction with the *InterRail* programme, the **YMCA/YWCA** has a string of hostels, known as **InterRail Points**, in Sweden, open in summer to anyone with a membership card. These have kitchens and laundry facilities; although usually less luxurious, they are often cheaper than the *STF* hostels. Membership cards and information are available from the main *YMCA* and *YWCA* in your home country. You can also join on your first night's stay at any *InterRail Point* hostel.

### HOTELS AND PENSIONS

**Hotels** and **pensions** needn't be expensive, and although there's little chance of any kind of room under 250kr a night, you can be lucky in summer, especially in July, when business people who fill the hotels during the week are on holiday. Also many Swedes head south out of the country during the summer. Out-of-season rooms are much cheaper at weekends (when the business people are at home) than midweek. On average for a room with TV and bathroom you can expect to pay from 350kr for a single, 500kr for a double. Nearly all hotels include a huge self-service buffet breakfast in the price, which will keep you going for much of the day. It's perhaps worth noting that in summer some of the larger hotels drop their prices even lower than their usual discount rate if you turn up after 6pm without a booking. This is obviously a risky strategy (and breakfast often isn't included in these late deals), but it can mean some very cheap rooms.

The **best package deals** are those operated in Malmö, Stockholm and Gothenburg, where 300–365kr minimum gets you a hotel bed for one night, breakfast and the relevant city discount card thrown in. These schemes are often valid from mid-June to mid-August and at weekends throughout the year, but see the accommodation details under the city accounts for more exact information.

The other option is to buy into a **hotel pass** scheme, where you pay in advance for a series of vouchers that allow discounts or free accommodation in various chains throughout the country. The vouchers can be bought before you leave for Sweden; for the latest details, it's best to consult your travel agent or the *Swedish Tourism and Travel Council* (see "Information and maps"), which also publishes *Hotels in Sweden*. This contains a comprehensive listing of Swedish hotels with information on special discount schemes.

### PRIVATE ROOMS, B&B AND SELF-CATERING

A further option is the **private rooms** in people's houses that most tourist offices can book for you in any reasonably sized town. From around 90–140kr a head (plus a 30–50kr booking fee), they're an affordable and pleasant option. Out in the countryside look for roadside signs saying "*Rum*" or "*Logi*". All have access to showers and/or baths and sometimes a kitchen; hosts are rarely intrusive.

**Farms** throughout Sweden offer **bed and breakfast** accommodation and self-catering facilities. For more information contact local tourist offices or *Bo på Lantgård* (Living on a farm), Skåne Tourist Board, Skiffervägen 38, S-223 78 Lund, Sweden (☎046/12 43 50; fax 12 23 72). It costs roughly 250–300kr a night per person, with discounts for children. The *Swedish Travel and Tourism Council* have the latest details on farm B&Bs and farm holidays, and should be able to help you book your accommodation before you leave.

If you fancy renting a **self-catering** private apartment or a couple of rooms for a week or so, contact local tourist offices (details given in the text), where staff will book them for you, or one of the companies listed in the box overleaf. Apartments cost between 2000kr and 3000kr a week.

## SELF-CATERING APARTMENTS

**STOCKHOLM**
**Allrum** ☎08/21 37 89; fax 21 01 76.
**Hotelltjänst/Caretaker** ☎08/10 44 37;
fax 21 37 16.

**GOTHENBURG**
**Foretagsbostäder** ☎031/17 00 25;
fax 711 2460.
**SGS** ☎031/81 33 71; fax 81 24 97.
**Svenska Turistlägenheter** ☎031/30 06 00;
fax 81 24 97.

**MALMÖ**
**Takvåningen Triangeln** ☎040/795 94;
fax 97 67 70.
**SEM** ☎040/12 61 70; fax 12 71 35.

## CAMPSITES

Practically every town or village has at least one **campsite**, and these are generally of a high standard. To pitch a tent at any site you'll need the **Swedish Camping Card**, which costs 49kr and includes accident insurance while staying at the site. Cards can be issued at the first site you visit or before you leave. The International Camping Card is no longer available in Sweden.

It costs around 100kr for two people to pitch a tent in July and August (50kr the rest of the year). Most sites are open from June to September, some – around two hundred in winter sport areas – throughout the year. A camping brochure with details of all sites plus a detailed motoring and camping map is available from offices of the *Swedish Travel and Tourism Council* (see p.25 for details). A comprehensive listings book, *Camping Sverige*, is also available from bookshops in Sweden or from the bigger map shops worldwide (see p.26). Note also that only **propane gas** – for example, *Primus* – is normally available in Sweden. It's illegal and also highly dangerous to burn propane in equipment designed for butane.

Propane and the associated cooking, heating or lighting equipment are inexpensive and widely available at more than two thousand *Primus* dealers.

Thanks to a tradition known as *Allemansrätten* (Everyman's Right; see p.47), it's perfectly possible to **camp rough** throughout the country. This gives you the right to camp anywhere for one night without asking permission provided you stay a reasonable distance (100m) away from other dwellings. In practice (and especially if you're in the north), there'll be nobody around to mind if you camp in one spot for longer, although it's as well – and polite – to ask first should you come across someone. The wide-open spaces within most town and city borders make free camping a distinct possibility in built-up areas too.

## CABINS, CHALETS, AND MOUNTAIN HUTS

Mant campsites also boast **cabins**, usually decked out with bunk beds, kitchen and equipment, but not sheets. It's an excellent alternative to camping for a group or a couple; cabins go for around 250–350kr for a four-bed number. Again it's wise to ring ahead to secure one.

Sweden also has a whole series of cabins for rent that are often in beautiful locations in the middle of the forest or by a lake shore or on the coast. On the whole they offer high-standard accommodation at prices to match. Contact the local tourist office (addresses and telephone numbers in the text) or the *Swedish Travel and Tourism Council* or book through a travel agent at home (see the relevant "Getting there" section).

In the more out-of-the-way places, *STF* operate a system of isolated **mountain cabins** strung out along hiking trails and in the national parks. This really is a chance to get away from it all; usually staffed by a warden and with cooking facilities, the huts cost between 120–200kr for members (slightly more in winter). More details and information from *STF* (see p.34 for details).

# EATING AND DRINKING

There's no escaping the fact that eating and drinking is going to take up a large slice of your budget in Sweden – though perhaps no more so than in any other northern European country. At its best Swedish food is delicious, largely fish-meat-and-potato based but very varied and always tasty and well presented. Unusual specialities generally stem from the north of the country and include reindeer, elk meat and wild berries; while herring and salmon come in so many different guises that fish fiends will always be content. Vegetarians, too, should have no problems, with plenty of non-meat options available especially in the bigger towns. Drinking is more uniform, the lager-type beer and imported wine providing no surprises; the local spirit akvavit, however, is worth trying at least once – it comes in dozens of weird and wonderful flavours.

## FOOD

**Sauces** feature prominently in Swedish cooking and are often worked around dill or parsley – making a wonderful complement to fish dishes – or numerous delicious cream concoctions. Generally, though, it's hard to beat the various **salmon** dishes: divine and delectable either warm or cold and a main feature of any Swedish *Smörgåsbord* (lunchtime menu, see p.39) worth its salt. **Herring** is mostly served raw, but don't let that put you off; it tastes surprisingly good.

Of the food from the north, **reindeer** is the most obvious one to try; it has a delicious flavour when smoked and is something akin to beef but with virtually no fat; **elk meat** is decidedly less appetizing, but it is good for burning up calories – you'll expend as many chewing the stuff as you'll get from it. Wild berries appear in many dishes, especially the **lingonberry**, which is something like cranberry, making a good accompaniment to Swedish meatballs, which are praised by many a Swede as a delicacy of the country. You'll also be able to taste orange-coloured sweet **cloudberries**, which grow in the marshes of Lapland and are delicious with ice cream to follow any main dish.

**Eating** well and cheaply in Sweden needn't be mutually exclusive aims. The best strategy is to fuel up on breakfast and lunch, both of which offer good-value options. Breakfast is often included in the cost of a night's accommodation, and most restaurants have lunchtime specials that time and again are the best-value meals you'll find. There are a large number of foreign restaurants – Chinese and Italian mostly, Indian less often – but don't expect them to serve up cheap evening meals. In Sweden Chinese food, in particular, can be really quite expensive and tasteless.

## BREAKFAST

**Breakfast** (*frukost*) is almost invariably a help-yourself buffet in the best Swedish tradition; you go up to the serving table as many times as you like and eat until you're fit to explode. There's generally an endless supply of breakfast cereals, muesli, cheeses, ham, salad, caviar and paté, boiled eggs, Danish pastries, coffee, tea and juice. Swankier venues will usually offer warm food as well, usually bacon, scrambled egg and sausages, as well as porridge, herring, yoghurt and fruit. Youth hostels charge around 50kr for breakfast; it's about the same in restaurants. If you stay in a hotel, it'll be included in the price of your accommodation. Something to watch out for is the jug of *filmjölk* (sometimes just called *fil*) or **soured milk** that you'll find next to the ordinary milk on the breakfast table. Swedes rave about the stuff and pour lashings of it on their cereals. It's thicker than normal milk, and you might find it tastes better if you mix it with some of the regular stuff. It's also eaten by itself, sometimes with a dollop or two of jam and a pinch of cinnamon.

**Coffee** is something the Swedes excel at: always freshly brewed, strong and delicious. Coffee breaks are a national institution, encapsulated in the word *fika*, which English renders rather longwindedly as "to put your feet up and enjoy a good cup of coffee". A coffee costs 10–15kr, but the price usually buys you more than one cup; the word *påtår* indicates that all cups after the first are either free or cost just a few kronor. **Tea** isn't up to scratch – weak *Liptons* as a rule – and costs just one or two kronor less than coffee. There are, however, some excellent speciality teas in Sweden – look around when you're in a café, and if they have *Södermalmsblandning* (named after the southern island in Stockholm), give it a try.

## SNACKS AND LIGHT MEALS

For **snacks** and **light meals** you're really looking at the delights dished up by the **Gatukök** (street kitchen) or **Korvstånd** (sausage stall). A *Gatukök* is often no more than a hole in the wall – generally noticeable by the snaking queue and gaggle of teenagers it attracts – serving sausages, burgers, pizza slices (sometimes), chicken bits (sometimes), chips, soft drinks and ketchup. A sausage or burger and chips is generally around 45kr. The *Korvstånd* usually limits itself to sausages, though may have chips and burgers as well. These outlets are to be found on every street in every town and village, and until ten years ago were often the only source of nourishment open after 5pm in smaller places. Thankfully things have changed now. If you feel like really pushing the boat out you could hit one of the country's **burger bars**: *Clockburger* is Sweden's own chain and usually a couple of kronor cheaper than the usual outlets of *McDonalds* and *Burger King*. At the very best these places offer the cheapest source of coffee – if you can stomach the surroundings.

It's often nicer to hit the **konditori**, a coffee and cake shop of the first order. You should try a konditori at least once while you're in Sweden, but unfortunately this is where your money will simply vanish. An open sandwich (*smörgås*), a pastry (*wienerbröd*) and a coffee (*kaffe*) will set you back 80–90kr. Remember, though, that coffee is generally free after your first cup. This is as

good a place as any to try a Swedish **open sandwich**, piled high with an elaborate variety of toppings. Favourites include prawns in mayo with or without caviar, smoked salmon, egg slices and anchovy, cheese (often with green peppers or cucumber), paté, meatballs, and in the north sometimes reindeer. They go for 40–50kr.

## SELF-CATERING

For the cheapest eating it's hard to beat the **supermarkets** and **market stalls**. Of the supermarkets, the cheapest is *Vivo*, followed by *ICA* and *Konsum*. Swedes don't really go in for huge out-of-town supermarkets; most of them are small local affairs selling just the basics and a few other bits and pieces. If it's choice you're after, and you're in one of the bigger towns and cities, you should try the food halls in the department stores, *Åhléns* and *Domus*, which have a much wider selection. Alternatively head for the indoor or outdoor markets, which often have fresher produce than the supermarkets and at lower prices.

Fish is always excellent value, especially salmon. Pork and beef aren't too bad either; chicken is slightly more expensive. If you buy **fresh meat** and it smells slightly funny when you peel back the wrapping don't be alarmed; it's because Sweden uses few preservatives in fresh produce, and dead meat in Sweden smells like just that. Swedish chicken tastes like the chicken you had when you were little – succulent and tender.

As for **bread**, it's best to avoid the fluffy white loaves that you'll hardly notice you've eaten; go instead for the darker, more filling stuff. Sweden is a country rich in **cheeses**, all of which are reasonably good value and make great sandwich fillers; the range runs from stronger ripened cheeses such as *Västerbotten* and *Lagrad Svecia* to milder types like *Grevé* and *Herrgårdsost*; *Prästost* (priest's cheese) is also a particular favourite. Also handy for sandwiches are the packs of sliced ham that are available in all supermarkets, though not especially cheap, and **Kalles Kaviar**, found in blue tubes with a silly smiling little boy on – he's Kalle (Charlie) and something of a folk hero. It's not real caviar but made from cod roe and is especially good on **crispbread** (*knäckebröd*), which is another area where the Swedes excel. It's easy to be overwhelmed by the different varieties available, but you can try a good few as prices are low.

There's also loads of different **yoghurts** and varieties of *filmjölk* (see p.37) to choose from – all very healthy and inexpensive – as is **milk**, which comes in three varieties: *lättmjölk* (skimmed), *mellanmjölk* (semi-skimmed) and *mjölk* (full-fat). **Fruit** and **salad** are expensive but not exorbitantly so; generally bananas and mushrooms are the most expensive items. A pack or jar of **coffee** constitutes a serious financial investment; tea less so, but it is still not especially cheap. Pasta, rice, potatoes, eggs, onions and bacon are all low priced.

The only goods to steer well clear of are those in tins (except mussels, mackerel and tomatoes), because they are invariably extremely expensive.

### RESTAURANTS

Don't treat **restaurants** (*restaurang*) as no-go areas: they can be perfectly affordable and offer some delicious high-quality food. Swedes eat their main meal of the day at lunchtime; do the same and you'll save lots of cash. But you don't have to restrict yourself to eating at **lunchtime**; many restaurants also offer special deals in the evening, and even if they don't you're bound to find something on their menu that will fit your pocket. The dish to go for at lunchtime in any restaurant is the **Dagens Rätt** or dish of the day, which costs between 40–60kr and is one example of Swedish *Husmanskost* or home cooking. Served from 11am to 2pm, *Dagens Rätt* offers the choice of a main meal (usually at least two choices), along with salad and bread/crispbread, soft drink/light beer and coffee. Some Swedish dishes like *pytt i panna* (a fry-up of potatoes and meat with beetroot and a fried egg) and *köttbullar* (meatballs) are standards. You'll also find various pizza and pasta dishes on offer in Italian restaurants, basic meals in Chinese restaurants (sometimes on a help-yourself basis) and meat and fish dishes in other places. Most cafés also offer some sort of *Dagens Rätt* but may not be as good as restaurants; train stations and department stores, however, are worth trying. If you're travelling with children look out for the word for childrens' menu, **Barnmatsedel**.

Whilst you're in Sweden you should try a **Smörgåsbord** – expensive but good for a blowout, available in the larger restaurants and in hotels for around 150kr. A good table will be groaning under the weight of dishes: salmon (both boiled and smoked), *gravad lax* (see "Swedish specialities" in the box on pp.40–41), shrimps, herring, eel, *Janssons frestelse*, scrambled eggs, oven-baked omelettes, fried sausages, smoked reindeer, liver paté, beef, hot and cold meats, eggs, fried and boiled potatoes, vegetables, salad, pastries, desserts, fruit, cheese – the list is endless. It's important to pace yourself: don't fill up your plate the first time you go to the table; you can return as many times as you like. If you're a traditionalist you should start with *akvavit*, drink beer throughout and finish with coffee. Coffee will be included in the price – alcohol won't, except on Sundays when fancier and dearer spreads generally include it in the price.

A variation on the theme is the **Sillbricka** or herring table made up of a dozen or so dishes based on Sweden's favourite food, cured and marinated herring. Once again this is excellent (if you like raw fish) and runs to about the same price as the *Smörgåsbord*.

A not-too-upmarket **evening meal** in a restaurant will cost you 70–100kr without alcohol. A three-course meal will naturally cost more; expect to pay something in the region of 150–200kr. Add around 40kr for a strong beer, 200kr for an average bottle of wine. Dishes usually have some sort of salad accompaniment and come with bread. In the box on pp.40–41 are listed many of the traditional Swedish dishes that are on offer in most restaurants. Bear in mind that Swedes eat early; lunch will be served from 11am, dinner from 6pm.

### ETHNIC RESTAURANTS

For years the only **ethnic** choice in Sweden was between the pizzeria and the odd Chinese restaurant; in provincial towns this is often still the case, but even here the number of ethnic restaurants has increased dramatically. **Pizzerias** offer the best value; you'll get a large, if not strictly authentic pizza, for 50–60kr, usually with free coleslaw and bread. As well as the local restaurants, *Pizza Hut* can be found in Sweden, though the chain is a lot more expensive than in the US or Britain. **Chinese** restaurants nearly always offer a set lunch, but in the evenings prices shoot up. They aren't particularly good value for money and the food is often bland and inauthentic. If there's a group of you, however, putting dishes together can work out reasonably in price terms. **Middle Eastern** kebab takeaways and cafés

## GLOSSARY OF SWEDISH FOOD AND DRINK TERMS

### Basics and snacks

| | | | | | | | |
|---|---|---|---|---|---|---|---|
| *Bröd* | Bread | *Knäcke* | Crispbread | *Ris* | Rice | *Tårta* | Cake |
| *Bulle* | Bun | *-bröd* | | *Salt* | Salt | *Vinäger* | Vinegar |
| *Glass* | Ice cream | *Olja* | Oil | *Senap* | Mustard | *Våffla* | Waffle |
| *Grädde* | Cream | *Omelett* | Omelette | *Småkakor* | Biscuits | *Ägg* | Egg |
| *Gräddfil* | Sour cream | *Ost* | Cheese | *Smör* | Butter | *Ättika* | Vinegar for |
| *Gröt* | Porridge | *Pastej* | Paté | *Smörgås* | Sandwich | | pickling |
| *Kaka* | Cake | *Peppar* | Pepper | *Socker* | Sugar | | |
| *Keks* | Biscuits | *Pommes* | Fries | *Sylt* | Jam | | |

### Meat (*Kött*)

| | | | | | |
|---|---|---|---|---|---|
| *Biff* | Beef | *Köttbullar* | Meatballs | *Renstek* | Roast reindeer |
| *Fläsk* | Pork | *Kyckling* | Chicken | *Rådjursstek* | Roast venison |
| *Kalvkött* | Veal | *Lammkött* | Lamb | *Skinka* | Ham |
| *Korv* | Sausage | *Lever* | Liver | *Älg* | Elk |
| *Kotlett* | Cutlet/chop | *Oxstek* | Roast beef | | |

### Fish (*Fisk*)

| | | | | | |
|---|---|---|---|---|---|
| *Ansjovis* | Anchovies | *Kräftor* | Freshwater | *Sardiner* | Sardines |
| *Blåmusslor* | Mussels | | crayfish | *Sik* | Whitefish |
| *Fiskbullar* | Fishballs | *Lax* | Salmon | *Sill* | Herring |
| *Forell* | Trout | *Makrill* | Mackerel | *Sjötunga* | Sole |
| *Hummer* | Lobster | *Räkor* | Shrimps/ | *Strömming* | Baltic herring |
| *Kaviar* | Caviar | | prawns | *Torsk* | Cod |
| *Krabba* | Crab | *Rödspätta* | Plaice | *Ål* | Eel |

### Vegetables (*Grönsaker*)

| | | | | | |
|---|---|---|---|---|---|
| *Blomkål* | Cauliflower | *Morötter* | Carrots | *Svamp* | Mushrooms |
| *Brysselkål* | Brussel sprouts | *Potatis* | Potatoes | *Tomater* | Tomatoes |
| *Bönor* | Beans | *Rödkål* | Red cabbage | *Vitkål* | White cabbage |
| *Gurka* | Cucumber | *Sallad* | Lettuce; salad | *Vitlök* | Garlic |
| *Lök* | Onion | *Spenat* | Spinach | *Ärtor* | Peas |

### Fruit (*Frukt*)

| | | | | | |
|---|---|---|---|---|---|
| *Ananas* | Pineapple | *Hallon* | Raspberry | *Persika* | Peach |
| *Apelsin* | Orange | *Hjortron* | Cloudberry | *Päron* | Pear |
| *Aprikos* | Apricot | *Jordgubbar* | Strawberries | *Vindruvor* | Grapes |
| *Banan* | Banana | *Lingon* | Lingonberry; | *Äpple* | Apple |
| *Citron* | Lemon | | red whortleberry | | |

### Culinary terms

| | | | | | |
|---|---|---|---|---|---|
| *Blodig* | Rare | *Kall* | Cold | *Ungstekt* | Roasted/ |
| *Filé* | Fillet | *Kokt* | Boiled | | baked |
| *Friterad* | Deep fried | *Lagom* | Medium | *Varm* | Hot |
| *Genomstekt* | Well done | *Pocherad* | Poached | *Ångkokt* | Steamed |
| *Gravad* | Cured | *Rökt* | Smoked | | |
| *Grillat/halstrat* | Grilled | *Stekt* | Fried | | |

## Drinks

| | | | | | |
|---|---|---|---|---|---|
| *Apelsinjuice* | Orange juice | *Mineral-* | Mineral | *Te* | Tea |
| *Chocklad* | Hot chocolate | *vatten* | water | *Vatten* | Water |
| *Citron* | Lemon | *Mjölk* | Milk | *Vin* | Wine |
| *Fruktjuice* | Fruit juice | *Rödvin* | Red wine | *Vitt vin* | White wine |
| *Grädde* | Cream | *Saft* | Juice | *Öl* | Beer |
| *Kaffe* | Coffee | *Starköl* | Strong beer | *Skål* | Cheers! |
| *Lättöl* | Light beer | *Storstark* | Large strong | | |
| *Mellanöl* | Medium-strong | | beer | | |
| | beer | | | | |

## Swedish specialities

| | | | |
|---|---|---|---|
| *Bruna bönor* | Baked, vinegared brown beans, usually served with fried pork | *Mesost* | Brown, sweet whey cheese; a breakfast favourite |
| *Filmjölk* | Soured milk | *Ostkaka* | Curd cake made from fresh curds and eggs baked in the |
| *Fisksoppa* | Fish soup usually including several sorts of fish, prawns and dill | | oven served with jam or berries |
| *Getost* | Goat's cheese | *Pepparkakor* | Spiced thin gingerbread bis- cuits popular at Christmas |
| *Glögg* | Mulled wine usually fortified with spirits to keep out the cold, and drunk at Christmas | *Plättar* | Thin pancakes often served with pea soup |
| | | *Potatissallad* | Potato salad often flavoured with dill or chives |
| *Gravad lax* | Salmon marinated in dill, sugar and seasoning; served with mustard sauce and lemon | *Pytt i panna* | Cubes of meat and fried pota- toes with a fried egg and beetroot |
| *Hjortron* | A wild orange-coloured berry served with fresh cream and/or ice cream. Also made into jam | *Semla* | Sweet bun with almond paste and whipped cream; associated with Lent |
| *Janssons frestelse* | A potato and anchovy bake with cream | *Sillbricka* | Various cured and marinated herring dishes; often appears as a first course in restaurants at lunchtime |
| *Kryddost* | Hard cheese spiced with seeds, sometimes caraway seeds or cloves | *Sjömansbiff* | Sailor's beef casserole, thin slices of beef baked in the oven with potatoes and |
| *Köttbullar* | Meatballs served with a brown creamy sauce and lingonberries | | onion topped with parsley |
| | | *Smultron* | Wild strawberries, known for their concentrated taste |
| *Kräftor* | Crayfish often served with *kryddost* and eaten in August | *Strömming* | Baltic herring |
| | | *Surströmming* | Baltic herring fermented for months until it's rotten |
| *Lingon* | Lingonberry (sometimes known as red whortleber- ries), a red berry made into a kind of jam and served with meat dishes as well as on pancakes and in pud- dings eaten at Christmas | | and the tin it's in buckles – very smelly and eaten in very, very small quantities. Not for the faint hearted! |
| | | *Ärtsoppa* | Yellow pea soup with pork spiced with thyme and marjoram; a winter dish traditionally eaten on Thursdays |
| *Långfil* | A special type of soured milk from northern Sweden | | |
| *Lövbiff* | Sliced, fried beef with onions | *Ål* | Eel, smoked and served with |
| *Matjessill* | Sweet-pickled herring | | creamed potatoes or scrambled eggs (*Äggröra*) |

have also sprung up over recent years; here you can find something substantial in pitta bread for around 30–40kr. **Japanese** is popular and not too pricey, but other ethnic options are not such good deals: **Indian** food is hard to find and quite expensive; anything **French** is expense-account stuff and not worth the money.

## VEGETARIAN FOOD

It's not too tough being **vegetarian** in Sweden given the preponderance of buffet-type meals; most of these are heavy with salads, cheeses, eggs and soups. For those who eat fish, there'll be no problem at all. The cities, too, have salad bars and sandwich shops, where you'll have no trouble feeding yourself; and if all else fails the local pizzeria will always deliver the non-meaty goods. At lunchtime you'll find that the *Dagens Rätt* in many places has a vegetarian option; it's always worth asking.

## DRINK

Drinking in Sweden is notoriously expensive, but there are ways of softening the blow. Either you forgo bars and buy your booze in the state-run liquor shops, the *Systembolaget* (see opposite), or you hunt out the **happy hours** (same term in Swedish) offered at many pubs and bars. The timing of happy hours has no rhyme or reason so keep your eyes peeled for signs either in the window or on the pavement outside. They can bring down the price of a strong beer to under 25kr – and that's a real bargain. If you miss happy hour, content yourself with the fact that Swedes, too, think booze is overpriced, and you won't be expected to participate in expensive rounds. It's also perfectly acceptable to nurse one drink through the entire evening, if that's all you can afford.

## WHAT TO DRINK

**Beer** is the most common alcoholic drink in Sweden, and even though it's expensive it is very good. Competition in Stockholm, Gothenburg and Malmö has brought down the price considerably; be prepared to pay a third more in the provinces for the same thing. Whether you buy beer in a café, restaurant or a bar, it'll cost roughly the same: on average 30–40kr for half a litre of lager-type brew (in nightclubs, it'll be more like 50–60kr).

Unless you specify it will be *starköl*, the strongest Class III beer with an alcohol content of five percent or slightly over; if this is what you want ask for a *storstark*. *Mellanöl*, another Class III brew, costs slightly less than a *starköl* because it contains less alcohol. Class II or *folköl* is the stuff that's sold in supermarkets and contains slightly less alcohol than a normal lager in Britain and is very similar in strength to *mellanöl*. Cheapest of all is *lättöl*, which is the beer served with *Dagens Rätt* at lunchtime; even though it contains virtually no alcohol at all, it is palatable with food. *Lättöl* is also available in supermarkets; Class III, however, is only available in the *Systembolaget*, where it's around a third of the price you'll pay in a bar. *Pripps* and *Spendrups* are the two main brands; a good *mellanöl* is *Three Towns* (green labelled bottle). Watch out also for a brew called *50/50*, which is half *Pripps* and half *British Samuel Smiths*.

**Wine** in restaurants is pricey; a bottle will set you back something like 200kr: a glass will be around 40kr. You can buy a good bottle of red or white in the *Systembolaget* for 40–50kr.

It's also worth trying the **akvavit** or schnapps, which is made from potatoes. Served ice-cold in tiny shots, it's washed down with beer – check the small print of your insurance policy first, though. There are numerous different flavours of *akvavit* – spices, herbs, citrus fruits – added to the finished concoction to produce some memorable headaches. Or if you're in Sweden at Christmas don't go home without having sampled **glögg**: mulled red wine with cloves, cinnamon, sugar and more than a shot of *akvavit*.

## WHERE TO DRINK

You'll find **bars** in all towns and villages. In Stockholm and the larger cities the move is towards brasserie-type places – smart and flash. The British pub – and, more recently, the Irish pub – is also popular in Sweden, although the atmosphere inside never quite lives up to the original. Elsewhere – and particularly in the north of the country – you'll come across more down-to-earth drinking dens, occasionally sponsored by the local trades union. Drink is no cheaper here, and the clientele is heavily male and usually drunk: for outsiders, especially in small provincial villages, they can be intimidating places – drinking seems

## THE SYSTEMBOLAGET: A USER'S GUIDE

The **Systembolaget** is the only shop in any Swedish town or city that sells wine, strong beer and spirits. It's run by the state, is only open office hours from Monday to Friday, and keeps all its alcohol in locked glass cabinets. Walking into any *Systembolaget* is a trip into the twilight zone, if you can find one at all: stores are often tucked away in obscure places, and they're forbidden by law to advertise.

Buying alcohol (minimum age 20; you may need to show ID) is made as unattractive as possible: first you take a queue number from the machine by the door. This will give you your place in the queue and may even tell you how long you'll have to wait: a quarter of an hour is about average, though on Friday afternoons it can be up to an hour and over. You select your bottle of the hard stuff by number

(each bottle in the cabinets has its number displayed alongside); when your turn comes you then quote your number to the cashier who scuttles off to retrieve your booty. Hand over your cash (paying on credit is not allowed) and the dirty business is over. Should you wish to choose your tipple from the comfort of your own armchair, the *Systembolaget* produces a handy catalogue, which you can take home to peruse at your leisure.

The system is designed to make Swedes think about how much they drink, and prices are accordingly very high — 70cl of whisky costs 250kr. But it's estimated that for every four bottles of booze consumed in Sweden only two are bought from the *Systembolaget*; one is smuggled into the country whilst the other is moonshine, distilled illegally at home.

to be the main way of coping with eight months of winter. Generally, though, with the fall in the price of alcohol over recent years, more and more people are now going out to bars of an evening. On Friday and Saturday nights in particular, they're the place to be seen.

In the summer, café-bars spill out onto the pavement, which is better for children and handy

for just a coffee. In out-of-the-way places when you want a drink and can't find a bar, head for the local hotel — but be prepared to pay for it. Bar opening hours are elastic and drinking-up time is generally some time after midnight; in the big three — Stockholm, Gothenburg and Malmö — you can go on drinking all night, if your wallet can take the pace.

# MAIL, TELECOMMUNICATIONS AND THE MEDIA

Communications within Sweden and abroad are good; in general it is easy to phone or fax anywhere in the world, even from smaller towns.

Most Swedes speak some English, and the operators are usually extremely accomplished (although you may have to use German with older employees). International mail services also work very efficiently and post offices are easy to use if you don't know Swedish, though in remoter places collections and deliveries can take a bit longer.

## MAIL SERVICES

**Post offices** are open Monday to Friday (9am–6pm) and Saturday (10am–1pm) but closed Sunday. You can buy **stamps** (*frimärken*) at post offices, most newspaper kiosks, tobacconists, hotels, bookshops and stationers' shops. International letters (*internationella brev*) and postcards (*vykort*) within Europe cost 6kr for up to 20g; within Sweden 3.70kr for "A-post" (first class) or 3.35kr for "Ekonomipost"

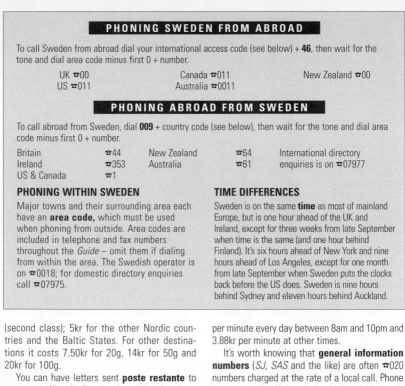

### PHONING SWEDEN FROM ABROAD

To call Sweden from abroad dial your international access code (see below) + **46**, then wait for the tone and dial area code minus first 0 + number.

| | | |
|---|---|---|
| UK ☎00 | Canada ☎011 | New Zealand ☎00 |
| US ☎011 | Australia ☎0011 | |

### PHONING ABROAD FROM SWEDEN

To call abroad from Sweden, dial **009** + country code (see below), then wait for the tone and dial area code minus first 0 + number.

| | | | | |
|---|---|---|---|---|
| Britain | ☎44 | New Zealand | ☎64 | International directory |
| Ireland | ☎353 | Australia | ☎61 | enquiries is on ☎07977 |
| US & Canada | ☎1 | | | |

#### PHONING WITHIN SWEDEN

Major towns and their surrounding area each have an **area code,** which must be used when phoning from outside. Area codes are included in telephone and fax numbers throughout the *Guide* – omit them if dialing from within the area. The Swedish operator is on ☎0018; for domestic directory enquiries call ☎07975.

#### TIME DIFFERENCES

Sweden is on the same **time** as most of mainland Europe, but is one hour ahead of the UK and Ireland, except for three weeks from late September when time is the same (and one hour behind Finland). It's six hours ahead of New York and nine hours ahead of Los Angeles, except for one month from late September when Sweden puts the clocks back before the US does. Sweden is nine hours behind Sydney and eleven hours behind Auckland.

(second class); 5kr for the other Nordic countries and the Baltic States. For other destinations it costs 7.50kr for 20g, 14kr for 50g and 20kr for 100g.

You can have letters sent **poste restante** to any post office in Sweden by addressing them "Poste Restante" followed by the name of the town and country. When picking up mail you'll need to take your passport, and make sure they check under middle names and initials as letters can get misfiled.

### PHONES

Occasionally you'll find telephone offices marked *Tele* or *Telebutik* from where you can call abroad. But for **international telephone calls** you can also dial direct from **public payphones**. This is very easy: the phones take 1kr and 5kr coins (note minimum charge 2kr), and the operators all speak good English if you have trouble. Or you can call from a public cardphone using a **phonecard**, which can be bought from newsagents. Alternatively whip out your **credit card** and dial from a credit card phone marked "CCC"; these are widely available. Calls within Europe cost 4.62kr

per minute every day between 8am and 10pm and 3.88kr per minute at other times.

It's worth knowing that **general information numbers** (*SJ, SAS* and the like) are often ☎020 numbers charged at the rate of a local call. Phone boxes are plentiful and almost invariably work; English instructions are normally posted up inside. To reverse the charges call the operator and ask to make a **collect call**. Paying for international calls from **hotels** will give you nightmares for months after and is only worth it in an emergency.

International and domestic **fax** service is widely available at most hotels across the country and is free to use if you are a resident. Post offices in Sweden do not have fax machines for public use.

### THE MEDIA: NEWSPAPERS, TV AND RADIO

Assuming you don't read Swedish, you can keep in touch with world events by buying **English-language newspapers** in the major towns and cities, sometimes on the day of issue, more usually the day after. In recent years, there's also been an English-language paper in the summer, **N & D**, giving essential listings and hip information about where to be seen and what to do in Stockholm; it's available in bars and pubs. The main **Swedish papers** are *Dagens Nyheter* and *Svenska Dagbladet* – their Friday supplements may be useful for Stockholm listings – and the tabloids, *Expressen* or *Aftonbladet*. If you're in Stockholm you can pick up a copy of *Metro*, a free newspaper available at tube stations, which has lots of information about what's on in the capital.

## TELEVISION AND RADIO

Swedish TV won't take up much space on your postcards home. There are **two state channels**, Kanal 1 and TV2, operated by *SVT* (*Sveriges Television*), worth watching if only for the wooden cross-eyed in-vision continuity announcers. TV3 is a **cable station** shared with Norway and Denmark and is pretty dire, although there's a good chance you'll manage to catch up with an old episode of *Kojak*, if you like that sort of thing. Sweden's only **commerical station** is TV4 whose evening news programme, *Nyheterna*, is an attempt to portray news as public entertainment; unfortunately, though, the end result is pretty naff. On all the channels imported pro-grammes are in their original language, which makes for easy viewing; Kanal 1 and TV2 show a lot of excellent BBC documentaries and comedy programmes; even Julian Clarey has been known to hit Swedish TV screens.

On the **radio** you'll find pop/rock music on P3; commercial music is on P2, and Swedish speech is on P1 (frequencies differ throughout the country) – all operated by **Swedish Radio**, the state broadcaster. **Commercial stations** have now sprung up in towns and cities across Sweden, and in Stockholm the ones worthy of your interest are Radio City 105.9 FM, Megapol 104.3 FM and Classic FM 107.5 FM. You'll find **news in English** on 89.6 FM in Stockholm and on 1179 kHz medium wave throughout the rest of the country courtesy of **Radio Sweden** (Swedish Radio's international arm). Their English news broadcasts can be heard in Stockholm at 1.30pm, 2.30pm, 3.30pm, 7.30pm, 9.30pm, 10.30pm, 11.30pm and throughout the night. The evening broadcasts should be audible on kHz medium wave throughout Sweden. You can also hear BBC World Service on 89.6 FM in Stockholm from 6am to 7am or at other times by tuning to either 6195, 9410, 12095 or 15070 kHz short wave.

## OPENING HOURS AND FESTIVALS

**Opening hours are generally from 9am to 6pm on weekdays and 10am to 4pm on Saturdays. In larger towns department stores remain open until 8pm or 10pm on weekdays, and some are also open on Sundays between 12 noon and 4pm. In country areas shops and petrol stations general-ly close between 5pm and 6pm. Museums and galleries operate various opening hours but are generally closed on Mondays. (For banks see p.24 and post offices see p.43.) Banks, offices and shops are closed on pub-lic holidays (see box overleaf). They may also be closed or have earlier closing hours on the eve of the holiday.**

Swedish **festivals** are for the most part orga-nized around the seasons. Most celebrations are lively events as Swedes are, perhaps surprisingly, great party people – especially when the beer begins to flow. The highlight of the year is the **Midsummer** festival when the whole country gets involved, and wild parties last well into the early hours.

## PUBLIC HOLIDAYS IN SWEDEN

New Year's Day (Jan 1)
Epiphany (Jan 6)
Good Friday
Easter Sunday
Easter Monday
Labour Day (May 1)
Ascension Day (May 1)
Whit Sunday (the seventh Sunday after Easter)

Whit Monday (the Monday after Whit Sunday)
Midsummer's Eve (June 21)
Midsummer's Day (June 22)
All Saints' Day (Nov 2)
Christmas Eve (Dec 24)
Christmas Day (Dec 25)
Boxing Day (Dec 26)
New Year's Eve (Dec 31)

## MAJOR ANNUAL FESTIVALS AND EVENTS

**Valborgsmässoafton** (April 30): Walpurgis Night; bonfires and songs welcome the arrival of spring nationwide.

**Labour Day** (May 1): a marching day for the workers' parties.

**Stockholm Marathon** (June 1): one of the biggest events of its kind.

**Swedish National Day** (June 6): in existence since 1983, a bit of a damp squib and not a public holiday; worthy speeches are held in the evening.

**Midsummer** (June 21–23): the celebration to beat them all; the Swedish Maypole, an old fertility symbol, is erected at popular gatherings across Sweden. The Maypole is raised in June because it's often still snowing in northern Sweden in May.

**Crayfish parties** (Aug): held in the August moonlight across the country to mark a wistful farewell to the short Swedish summer.

**Stockholm Water Festival** (Aug): special events and entertainment mark the capital's close links with the water – also see p.89.

**Surströmming** (late Aug): parties in northern Sweden; foul-smelling fermented Baltic herring prepared in tins that turn spherical under the pressure of the gas from the fermentation process.

**Eel parties** (Sept): parties held in the southern province of Skåne.

**St Martin's Eve** (Nov 10): people from Skåne get together to eat goose – the traditional symbol of the province.

**Nobel Prize Day** (Dec 10): held in Stockholm.

**St Lucia's Day** (Dec 13): a procession of Swedish children led by a girl with candles in her hair sing songs to mark one of the darkest periods of the year.

# SPORTS AND OUTDOOR PURSUITS

**Sweden is a wonderful place if you love the great outdoors, with great hiking, fishing and, of course, skiing opportunities. Best of all you won't find the countryside overcrowded – there's plenty of space to get away from it all, especially in the north. You'll also find Swedish beaches refreshingly relaxed and always clean. For information on cycling see "Getting around".**

## SKIING AND WINTER PURSUITS

The sport of **skiing** began in Scandinavia. During the winter months skiing is incredibly popular and in the north of the country people even ski to work. In northern Sweden you can ski from the end of

October well into April, and at Låktatjåkko in Lapland, Sweden's highest tourist facility, you can ski year round. Kiruna is a good place to base yourself for other winter sports, whether you fancy dog sledging, snowmobile riding, snowboarding, a night in the world's biggest igloo, the *Ice Hotel* at Jukkasjärvi, ice fishing or even a helicopter tour out into the snowy wilderness. Bear in mind, though, that the area around Kiruna is one of the coldest in the country and at Nikkaluokta and Naimakka the mercury can sink to -50°C during a really cold snap (also see "Surviving the winter" on p.20). If the mere thought of such temperatures chills you to the bone, it's worth noting that Stockholm also has a ski slope within the city boundary (contact any of the Stockholm tourist offices for more information).

## THE COUNTRYSIDE – SOME GROUND RULES

In Sweden you're entitled by law to walk, jog, cycle, ride or ski across other people's land, provided you don't cause damage to crops, forest plantations or fences; this is the centuries' old **Allemansrätten** or **Everyman's Right.** It also allows you to pick wild berries, mushrooms and wild flowers (except protected species), fish with a rod or other hand tackle, swim in lakes, and moor your boat and go ashore where there are no nearby houses. But this right brings with it certain obligations: don't get too close to houses or walk over gardens or on land under seed or crops; don't pitch a tent on land used for farming; don't camp close to houses without asking permission; don't cut down trees or bushes and don't break branches or strip the bark off trees. Nor are you allowed to: drive off-road (look out for signs "*Ej motorfor-*

*don*", no motor vehicles, or "*Enskild väg*", private road); light a fire if there's a risk of it spreading; or disturb wildlife.

### Other rules and advice

It's also common sense to be wary of frightening **reindeer herds** in the north of Sweden, since if they scatter it can mean several extra days hard work for the herders; also avoid tramping over moss-covered stretches of moorland, which is the reindeer's staple diet. If you do pick flowers, berries or mushrooms it's worth checking the latest advice from the authorities – post Chernobyl. As you might expect, any kind of hunting is forbidden without a permit. National parks have special regulations which are posted on huts and at entrances and are worth reading and remembering.

Some of the most popular **ski resorts** include Åre, Sälen, Storlien, Jukkasjärvi and Riksgränsen. These resorts and many others are packed out during the snow season when prices hit the roof. If you do intend to come to ski, it is essential to book accommodation well in advance thorugh the tourist office or take a package holiday – see the relevant "Getting there" sections. For more on skiing and winter sports possibilities also see the above destinations in the *Guide*.

### HIKING

Sweden's **Right of Public Access** means you can walk freely right across the entire country. A network of more than forty long-distance footpaths covers the whole of Sweden, with overnight accommodation available in mountain stations and huts. The most popular route is the *Kungsleden*, the King's Route, which unfortunately at times is a little too busy but still enjoyable. The path stretches for 460km through some spectacular landscape in the wild and isolated northwest of the country between Abisko (on the train line between Kiruna and Narvik in Norway) and Hemavan; the trail takes in Sweden's highest mountain, Kebnekaise (2078m). If you want to find out more about walking in Sweden contact the very helpful *Svenska Turistföreningen* (Swedish Touring Club) at Drottninggatan 31–33 in Stockholm and at Drottningtorget 6 in Gothenburg. For a guide to the dos and don'ts of

hiking in Sweden see "Hiking in the national parks", p.395.

### GOLF AND FISHING

**Golf** has become incredibly popular in Sweden over recent years. There are now over three hundred courses in the country; most are concentrated in the south and are available year-round, but it's also possible to play above the Arctic Circle in the light of the Midnight Sun. For more information contact the *Swedish Golf Federation*, PO Box 84, S-182 11, Danderyd, Stockholm; ☎08/622 15 00; fax 755 84 39.

Sweden is an ideal country for **anglers**; in fact salmon are regularly caught from opposite the Parliament building right in the centre of Stockholm, because the water there is so clean and fishing there is free. Fishing is also free along the coastline and in the larger lakes including Vänern, Vättern and Mälaren. In most areas you need a permit for freshwater fishing – ask at local tourist offices. For more information contact *Top 10 Fishing*, S–566 93 Brandstorp, Sweden; ☎0502/502 00, fax 502 02.

### CANOEING AND WHITEWATER RAFTING

There are almost 100,000 lakes and thousands of miles of rivers and canals in Sweden and needless to say on summer afternoons taking to a **canoe** is a popular pastime. Good centres for canoeing holidays include the Voxnadalen Valley in Hälsingland to the north of Stockholm, Älshult canoe base in Småland in the southeast and the Nordmarken canoe centre in western Värmland on the southern border with Norway.

For more fast-flowing action, the northern rivers are ideal for **whitewater rafting**, as are areas in Värmland and just to the north in Dalarna. Particularly good spots include: the Kukkola rapids

in the Torne Valley north of Haparanda; the Torneälv river in Norrbotten in the far northeast, where there are various lengths and grades of difficulty; and the Indalälven river, in Jämtland on the border with Norway, which offers moderately difficult to difficult rafting. The Strängforsen rapids in Värmland are somewhat tamer, with easy whitewater trips in paddle boats.

# POLICE, CRIME AND CULTURAL ATTITUDES

**Sweden is in general a pretty safe country to visit, including for women travelling alone; however, it would be foolish to assume that the naive trouble-free country of just a few years ago still exists. It doesn't. But although people no longer leave their doors unlocked when they go out shopping, Sweden is still a far cry from crime-ridden London or New York and as long as you take care, especially at night in the bigger towns and cities, you should have no problems. If you do meet trouble you can dial ☎112 for emergency assistance from the police, fire brigade or ambulance; emergency calls from pay phones are free of charge.**

## PETTY CRIME AND MINOR OFFENCES

Stockholm and the bigger cities have their fair share of **petty crime**, fuelled as elsewhere by a growing number of drug addicts and alcoholics after easy money. But keep tabs on your cash and passport (and don't leave anything valuable in your car when you leave it) and you should have little reason to visit the **police**. If you do, you'll

find them courteous, concerned and most importantly usually able to speak English. If you have something stolen make sure you get a **police report** – essential if you want to make a claim against your insurance.

As for **offences** *you* might commit, **topless sunbathing** is universally accepted in all the major resorts (elsewhere there'll be no one around to care). **Nude bathing** is best kept for quieter spots but is very common and perfectly accepted – you'll have no problems finding a beach (even an island for that matter) that you can call your own; should anyone stumble on you they'll either ignore you or apologize for cramping your style. **Camping rough** creates no problem and is enshrined in law (see p.47). The big no-no is **drinking alcohol in public places,** and being drunk on the streets can get you arrested – **drink-driving** is treated especially rigorously (see p.31). **Drugs** offences, too, meet with the same harsh attitude that prevails throughout the rest of Europe.

### RACISM

The biggest problem you may encounter in Sweden is the ugly and fast-spreading **racism** that stems from a small but vocal neo-Nazi movement, called White Arian Resistance or VAM. Slogans like *"Behålla Sverige Svenskt"* (Keep Sweden Swedish) can sometimes be seen daubed on walls of towns and cities and in the Stockholm metro. Over recent years unemployment has shot up from the steady one or two percent it used to be during the heyday of Social Democracy; Sweden's skinheads blame the country's one million immigrants for stealing jobs from Swedes. There have been several racist murders and countless attacks on dark-skinned foreigners over the last couple of years, and it pays to be vigilant: keep your eyes and ears open and avoid trouble, especially on Friday and Saturday nights when drink fuels these prejudices.

## SEXUAL HARASSMENT AND THE WOMEN'S MOVEMENT

Sexual harassment in Sweden is rare. In general the social and economic position of women is one of the most advanced in Europe – something that becomes obvious after just a short time here. Sweden has one of the highest percentages in the world of women in the workplace, and international surveys continually put Sweden at the top of the list when it comes to equality: 50 percent of Sweden's government ministers are women. Many women are in traditionally male occupations, which means that Swedish men have been forced to become more aware of the rights of women. You can walk around almost everywhere in comparative comfort and safety, although in Stockholm and Gothenburg you can occasionally expect to receive unwelcome attention. If you do have any problems the fact that almost everyone understands English makes it easy to get across an unambiguous response.

The **women's movement** is strongly developed, riding on the back of welfare reforms introduced by the Social Democratic governments since World War II. You'll find women's centres in most major towns.

## GAY AND LESBIAN SWEDEN

**Swedish attitudes** to gay men and lesbians are at first sight remarkably liberal when compared to most other western countries, with both the government and the legal system proudly geared towards equality and the promotion of gay rights. The official age of sexual consent is 15 whether you are gay or straight, and gay couples can now register their relationships legally as "registered partnerships", giving them the same rights as their married straight counterparts.

However, among the wider population, and certainly outside the bigger towns and cities, there is still embarrassment and unease whenever the subject is mentioned. And even in Stockholm and Gothenburg, you are unlikely to see gay or lesbian couples holding hands or kissing in public. Paradoxically the "gay scene" in Sweden is much less visible than in countries with more regressive official policies towards minority sexuality; and outside Stockholm and Gothenburg, there is no independent commercial scene.

Instead, gay community life, like everything else in Sweden, is run on highly organized and rigid lines, with the state-sponsored **national gay and lesbian association**, *RFSL* (*Riksförbundet för Sexuellt Likaberättigande*; Sveavägen 57–59, PO Box 350, 10126 Stockholm; ☎08/736 02 13, fax 30 47 30), running almost everything to do with gay issues. *RFSL* operates a switchboard and/or helpline in most of the larger towns, though it's unlikely that callers will get further than an answering machine in Swedish. It runs discos and pub nights in the official local venues either once a week or, more likely, once a month. *RFSL* also organizes a Midsummer party to which foreign visitors are very welcome. Unless you are Swedish speaking, it's worth contacting the main *RFSL* offices in Stockholm or Gothenburg; tourist offices invariably have no information about gay venues or events. The international gay guide, *Spartacus*, has lots of useful information about gay and lesbian happenings in Sweden; however, you may be disappointed if you try out the bars, discos, cafés and restaurants listed in the guide as "mixed gay"; compared to those at home, many are not particularly gay-orientated at all.

## DIRECTORY

**ADDRESSES** In Sweden addresses are always written with the number after the street name. In multi-floored buildings the ground floor is always counted as the first floor, the first the second, etc.

**ALPHABET** The letters å, ä and ö come at the end of the alphabet after z. Remember this also applies inside words; for example, a listing for *frigång* comes after *frigjord*.

**ARCTIC CIRCLE** An imaginary line drawn at approximately 66° 33′ latitude that stretches across northern Sweden and denotes the limit beyond which there is at least one day in the year when the sun never sets *completely* and one on which it never rises *completely*.

**BOOKS** You'll find English-language books in almost every bookshop and in the bigger department stores, though at roughly twice the price you're used to paying. Libraries, too, stock foreign-language books.

**DEPARTURE TAX** This is currently a nominal 12kr.

**LUGGAGE** In most train stations, ferry terminals and long-distance bus stations there are lockers where you can leave your bags for a small fee. At train stations there is sometimes also hand-in type storage. Tourist offices may also watch your stuff but generally make a charge.

**MUSEUMS AND GALLERIES** As often as not there's a charge to get in, though other than for the really major collections, it's rarely very much; flash an *ISIC* card and it's likely to bring a reduction. Opening hours vary widely though more often than not Monday is closing day.

**NORTHERN LIGHTS** (*Aurora Borealis*) A shifting coloured glow visible during winter in northern Sweden, thought to be of electrical origin – though you'll need to be in luck to see a really good display. The sky often turns peculiar colours most dark winter nights in the far north.

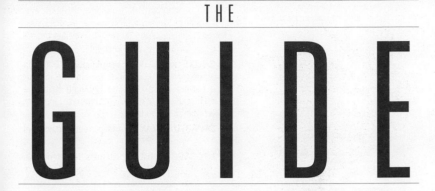

# PART TWO

## THE

# GUIDE

# CHAPTER ONE

# STOCKHOLM AND AROUND

**S**tockholm is without a shadow of a doubt one of the most beautiful cities in Europe. Built on no fewer than fourteen islands, where the fresh water of Lake Mälaren meets the brackish Baltic Sea, the city certainly lives up to the tourist office hype of "Beauty on Water". Fresh air and open space.

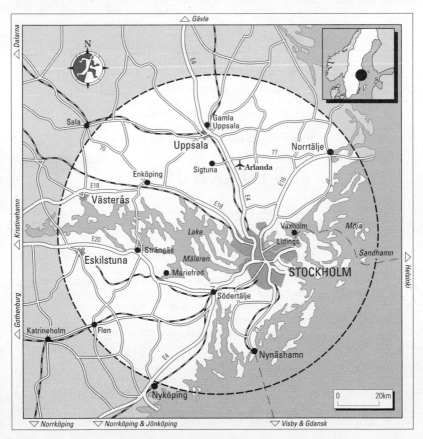

are in plentiful supply here – one-third of the city's total area is made up of water, another third comprises parks and woodlands, including the world's first urban national park, where you can swim and fish just minutes from the city centre. Quality of life is important to Stockholmers – a seat on the metro and elbow room on even the most crowded shopping street are regarded as virtual birth rights. As a result the capital is one of Europe's saner cities and a delightful place in which to spend time. Broad boulevards lined with elegant buildings are reflected in the deep blue water, and alongside the cobbled waterfront, rows of painted wooden houseboats bob gently in the tide. Yet Stockholm is also a hi-tech metropolis, with futuristic skyscrapers and a bustling commercial hub. The modern centre is a consumer's heaven, full of stylish and expensive shops and home to the city's cinemas and many of its bars and restaurants, of which Stockholm has more per capita than most other European capitals.

Move away from Stockholm and it's not difficult to appreciate its unique geographical location. Water surrounds the city and, although you can travel by train and bus, it's worth making the effort to ply the serene waters of Lake Mälaren or the archipelago by boat. The Stockholm **archipelago** is made up of a staggering 24,000 islands, rocks and skerries, the Swedish mainland slowly splintering into the Baltic Sea. The islands are a summer paradise for holidaying city dwellers and are easily accessible from the centre. Another must is a boat trip inland along Lake Mälaren to **Drottningholm**, the seventeenth-century royal residence right on the lakeside; on the way you'll glide slowly past purple reedbeds and rocky outcrops topped with bronzed naked bodies drinking up the long hours of summer sunshine. Another easy trip on Lake Mälaren leads to the equally important castle of **Gripsholm** at Mariefred; and still within day-trip reach are the ancient Swedish capital and medieval university town of **Uppsala** and Sweden's oldest village, **Sigtuna**, complete with its rune stones and ruined churches, accessible by boat or by frequent train services from Central Station.

# STOCKHOLM

*"It is not a city at all", he said with intensity. "It is ridiculous to think of itself as a city. It is simply a rather large village, set in the middle of some forest and some lakes. You wonder what it thinks it is doing there, looking so important."*

Ingmar Bergman interviewed by James Baldwin

Self-important perhaps, but **STOCKHOLM** is without doubt a disparate capital; its status as Sweden's most contemporary, forward-looking city is at odds with the almost pastoral feel of its wide open spaces and ageing monumental buildings. First impressions of the city can be of a distant and unwelcoming place. It's no surprise then that provincial Swedes drawn to Stockholm for work sometimes dub the city "the Ice Queen". But don't be put off; on a Friday or Saturday night you'll see its second side – when Stockholmers let their hair down, and the night air buzzes with conversation.

**Gamla Stan** (pronounced "Gam-la Starn" and Swedish for Old Town) was the site of the original settlement of Stockholm. Today it's an atmospheric mixture of pomp and historical authenticity: ceremonial buildings surrounded on all sides by a latticework of medieval lanes and alleyways. The tiny island of

> The telephone code for Stockholm is ☎08.

**Skeppsholmen** (pronounced "Shepps-holm-en"), site of the two most central youth hostels, with fantastic views of the curving waterfront, is close by and can be reached by ferry. To the north of the Old Town, **Norrmalm** takes over, trading tradition for a thoroughly contemporary feel – shopping malls, huge department stores and a conspicuous, showy wealth; the lively central park, Kungsträdgården, and Central Station are here, too. Most of Stockholm's eighty or so **museums and galleries** are spread across this district and those to the east: the more residential **Östermalm**, with its mix of grand avenues and smart houses, and to the southeast the green park island of **Djurgården**. Here the extraordinary seventeenth-century warship, **Vasa**, rescued and preserved after sinking in Stockholm harbour, and **Skansen**, oldest and best of Europe's open-air museums, both receive loud and deserved acclaim. The island of **Södermalm**, to the south of the Old Town, is known rather precociously in English as "the Southside" or as plain "Söder" to its right-on inhabitants. This was traditionally the working-class area of Stockholm, but today is known for its cool bars and restaurants and lively streetlife. To the west of the centre is the island of **Kungsholmen**, which is fast becoming a rival to its southern neighbour for trendy restaurants and drinking establishments.

# Arrival and information

Most planes – international and domestic – arrive at **Arlanda airport** (☎797 60 00), an annoying 45km north of Stockholm. Terminal 2 is used by *Austrian Airlines, Finnair, Maersk, Sabena, Swissair* and *Transwede*, and Terminal 5 by all other international airlines. *SAS* domestic flights leave from Terminal 4; other domestic airlines use Terminal 3. Airport buses, *Flygbussarna* (6.30am–11.30pm; 60kr; ☎600 10 00), call at all terminals and run every ten minutes (every 5min at peak times) from Arlanda to **Cityterminalen** (Stockholm's long-distance bus station; see overleaf) in about forty minutes; you buy your ticket on the bus. **Buses to the airport** leave Cityterminalen (4.25am–10pm; 30min); tickets are sold at the booth in the departure area, *not* on the bus. These buses will be replaced in 1999 by a high-speed rail link from Central Station. **Taxis** from the airport into town should cost around 350kr – an affordable alternative for a group; choose the ones that have prices displayed in their back windows, rather than the cowboy operators who prey on unsuspecting tourists, charging them upwards of 800kr.

Flights from London operated by *Malmö Aviation* arrive at the more central **Bromma airport**, which is also connected to Cityterminalen by *Flygbussarna* – buses run in connection with flight arrivals and departures. Buses to the airport leave from Gate 23 (40kr; 20min). There are also services between both airports (7.15am–11.10pm; 60kr; 45min).

By **train**, you'll arrive at **Central Station**, a cavernous (but heated) structure on Vasagatan in the central Norrmalm district of town. Inside there's a **Forex** money exchange office and a very useful **room-booking service**, *Hotellcentralen* (see "Accommodation" for full details). All branches of the **Tunnelbana**, Stockholm's efficient metro system, meet at T-Centralen, the metro station directly below the main station. The regional trains that run throughout Greater

Stockholm, **Pendeltågen**, leave from the main train platforms on the ground level – not from underground platforms.

By **bus**, your arrival point will be at the huge glass structure known as **Cityterminalen**, a hi-tech bus terminal adjacent to Central Station and reached by a series of escalators and walkways from the northern end of the main hall. It handles all bus services: airport, ferry shuttle (see below), domestic and international. There's also a money exchange office.

### Arriving by boat

There are two main **ferry** companies that connect Stockholm with Helsinki and Turku in **Finland** and with Mariehamn in the Finnish Åland Islands. For *Viking Line* arrivals at Vikingterminalen on the island of Södermalm, it's a thirty-minute walk along the water's edge and through Gamla Stan to the modern centre; or take a bus from outside the terminal to Slussen, from where the *Tunnelbana* leaves every couple of minutes to T-Centralen. Ferries on the *Silja Line* arrive on the northeastern edge of the city at Siljaterminalen; it's a short walk to either Gärdet or Ropsten metro station on the red line, from where trains run into town. When leaving Stockholm by ferry, note the Swedish names for your Finnish destinations: Helsinki is *Helsingfors* and Turku confusingly is *Åbo*.

The other main operator is *Estline*, with sailings from Tallinn in **Estonia** arriving at Frihamnen at the end of the #41 bus route, which will take you all the way into town; if you're heading for Central Station get off at the junction of Kungsgatan and Vasagatan and walk the short distance – the bus also goes directly past the Cityterminalen.

The boats that ply the **Göta Canal** from Gothenburg dock at the quay on the island of Riddarholmen, just a couple of minutes' walk from Gamla Stan and the rest of the centre.

# Information

You should be able to pick up a map of the city at most points of arrival, but you are best off visiting one of the city **tourist offices**. Each hands out fistfuls of free information, with a functional (if tiny) **map** in most of the brochures and booklets – though it's probably worth paying 15kr for the better, larger plan of Stockholm and the surrounding area. You'll also be able to buy the valuable Stockholm Card (see "Getting around") from any of the tourist offices.

The **main office** is on Hamngatan in Norrmalm, on the ground floor of **Sverigehuset** (Sweden House; June–Aug Mon–Fri 8am–6pm, Sat & Sun 9am–5pm; rest of the year Mon–Fri 9am–6pm, Sat & Sun 9am–3pm; ☎789 24 90, excursion information on ☎789 24 15; information by email on @stoinfo.se or from their website at http://www.stoinfo.se). Pick up *Stockholm This Week*, a free listings and entertainments guide, as well as any number of brochures and timetables. Upstairs, the **Swedish Institute** has a good stock of English-language books on Sweden as well as calendars, videos and the like; detailed factsheets on all aspects of Sweden (economy, geography, society, etc) cost 1kr each. There's also information to be had on working and studying in the country.

**Other tourist offices** are in Stadshuset at Hantverkargatan 1 on Kungsholmen (May–Oct daily 9am–3pm; no telephone enquiries) and at the Kaknäs TV tower on Djurgården (daily 9am–10pm; ☎789 24 35). Lastly

**Kulturhuset,** the monster cultural centre at Sergels Torg 3 in Norrmalm, has a desk on the ground floor with limited city information (Tues–Fri 11am–6pm; Sat & Sun noon–5pm; ☎700 01 00).

# City transport

Stockholm winds and twists its way across islands, over water and through parkland, a thoroughly confusing place. To find your way around, the best bet is to equip yourself with one of the tourist **maps** and walk: it takes about half an hour to cross central Stockholm on foot, east-west or north-south. Sooner or later, though, you'll have to use some form of **transport** and, while routes are easy enough to master, there's a bewildering array of **passes** and **discount cards** available; the brief rundown below should help. One thing to try to avoid is paying as you go on the city's transport system – a very expensive business. The city is zoned, a trip within one zone costing 13kr, with single tickets valid within that zone for one hour; cross a zone and it's another 6.50kr. Most journeys you want to make will generally cost 19.50kr.

## Public transport

*Storstockholms Lokaltrafik (SL)* operates a comprehensive system of buses and trains (metro and regional) that extends well out of the city centre. The main *SL* information office, the **SL-Center** (Mon–Fri 8am–6pm, Sat 8am–1pm), is at Sergels Torg just by the entrance to T-Centralen and has timetables for the city's buses and metro system, regional trains and archipelago boats, as well as a useful **transport map** showing all bus routes and street names for 42kr (for other *SL* offices see "Listings"). The map should also be available from *Pressbyrå* newsagents.

The quickest and most useful form of transport is the **Tunnelbana** (T-bana), Stockholm's metro system, based on three main lines (red, green and blue), with a smattering of branches. Entrances are marked with a blue letter "T" on a white background. It's the swiftest way to travel between Norrmalm and Södermalm, via Gamla Stan, and it's also handy for trips out into the suburbs – to ferry docks and to distant youth hostels and museums. Signs above each platform give the final destination, making it easy to use. Trains runs from early morning until around midnight, but on Fridays and Saturdays there are services all through the night. The *Tunnelbana* is something of an artistic venture, too, many of the stations looking like Functionalist scupltures: T-Centralen is one huge papier-maché cave and Kungsträdgården is littered with statues, spotlights and fountains. Others to look out for are Akalla (ceramic pictures of daily life), Rissne (wall paintings with historical scenes) and Midsommarkransen (wooden sculptures of a massive wreath of flowers).

**Buses** can be less direct due to the nature of Stockholm's islands and central pedestrianization — for help consult the bus-route map on the back of the *Stockholms Innerstad* bus timetable. You should board buses at the front, get off

---

For **public transport information**, call ☎600 10 00.

at the back or in the middle and buy tickets from the driver. **Night buses** replace the metro after midnight, except on Friday and Saturday when trains are still running. In an effort to cut pollution, many city buses now run on ethanol – some of it produced from Spanish red wine – instead of diesel, which is supposed to be better for the environment; you'll notice a strange smell when one of these buses goes by. Stockholm's buses are also pushchair and pram-friendly; a special area halfway down the bus has been set aside for various baby-pushing contraptions. If you're travelling with a dog, sit as far back as you can, as the seats at the front of the buses are intended for people with allergies.

**Ferries** provide access to the sprawling archipelago from outside the *Grand Hotel* on Strömkajen (see "Around Stockholm" for more details); they also link some of the central islands: Djurgården is connected with Nybroplan in Norrmalm via Skeppsholmen (July & Aug only), and with Skeppsbron in Gamla Stan (year round). **Cruises** on Lake Mälaren leave from outside Stadshuset on Kungsholmen, and **city boat tours** leave from outside the *Grand Hotel*, as well as from round the corner on Nybroplan.

## Travel passes and tickets

The best pass to have, certainly if you're planning to do any sightseeing at all, is the *Stockholmskortet* or the **Stockholm Card**, which gives unlimited travel on city buses, ferries, metro and regional trains, free museum entry, discounts on boat trips and tours, plus free parking and many other discounts. Cards are sold undated and stamped on first use, then valid for 24 hours (175kr); one card will cover one adult and two children under eighteen. From mid-May to the end of August the card includes an hour's free sightseeing by boat. It isn't valid, though, on ferries to Djurgården and the direct airport buses to Arlanda. Buy the card from any tourist office in the city, including *Hotellcentralen* in Central Station.

Of the other options, all issued by *SL*, the *Turistkort* or **Tourist Card** is valid for 24 hours (56kr) or 72 hours (107kr) and gives unlimited travel from the time the card is stamped on buses, metro and regional trains, and on the ferries and trams (the city's only line from Norrmalmstorg) to Djurgården. In addition, the 72-hour card gives you free admission to Skansen, the Kaknäs TV tower, Gröna Lund amusement park and the tram museum at Tegelviksgatan 22. As with all *SL* tickets, young people travel at reduced rates up to and including the month in which their eighteenth birthday falls, senior citizens as from the month in which their sixty-fifth birthday falls (24hr card 33kr; 72hr card 70kr). The cards are oddly not available at the barriers to the metro stations — buy them instead from any *Pressbyrå* or city tourist offices.

Otherwise you can buy a strip of twenty reduced-price *SL* **ticket coupons**, known as *rabattkuponger* (85kr) – you'll have to stamp at least two for each journey. Buy them at the ticket barriers to any metro station. If you're staying in Stockholm for a week or a fortnight, it's worth considering a *Månadskort* or **Monthly Card**, which brings fares tumbling down: it offers unlimited travel on virtually everything that moves throughout the whole of Greater Stockholm for a mere 355kr. If you're spending several months in the city, there are some great-value **season cards** (*Säsongskort*) available. All the above cards require a photograph and can be bought from any *SL-Center*. Once again reduced fares are available on all cards for under eighteens and senior citizens.

One-way **tickets** for ferries linking the central islands cost 15kr and for longer trips out into the archipelago up to 65kr, depending on how far you are going.

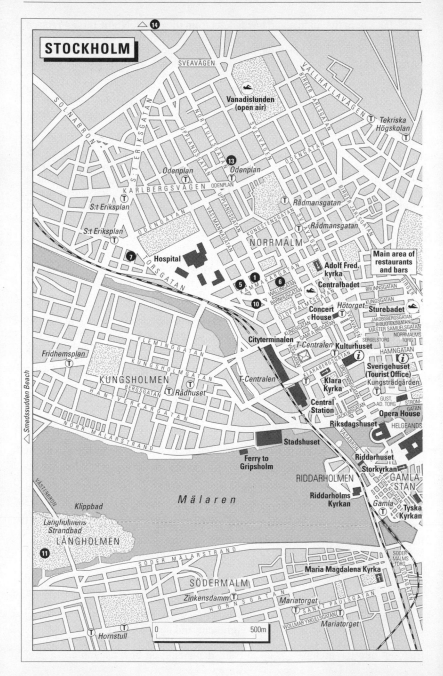

STOCKHOLM

SVEAVÄGEN

Vanadislunden
(open air)

Tekriska
Högskolan

Odenplan

Odenplan

Rådmansgatan

S:t Eriksplan

Rådmansgatan

S:t Eriksplan

NORRMALM

Hospital

Adolf Fred.
kyrka

Main area of
restaurants
and bars

Centralbadet

Concert
House

Hötorget

Sturebadet

Cityterminalen

T-Centralen

Kulturhuset

Sverigehuset
(Tourist Office)

Fridhemsplan

T-Centralen

Klara
Kyrka

Kungsträdgården

KUNGSHOLMEN

Rådhuset

Central
Station

Opera House

Riksdagshuset

HELGEANDS

Stadshuset

Ferry to
Gripsholm

Riddarhuset

Storkyrkan

GAMLA
STAN

RIDDARHOLMEN

*Mälaren*

Riddarholms
Kyrkan

Gamla

Tyska
Kyrkan

Klippbad

Langholmens
Strandbad

LÅNGHOLMEN

SÖDER MÄLARSTRAND

Maria Magdalena Kyrka

SÖDERMALM

Zinkensdamm

Mariatorget

Hornstull

Mariatorget

0          500m

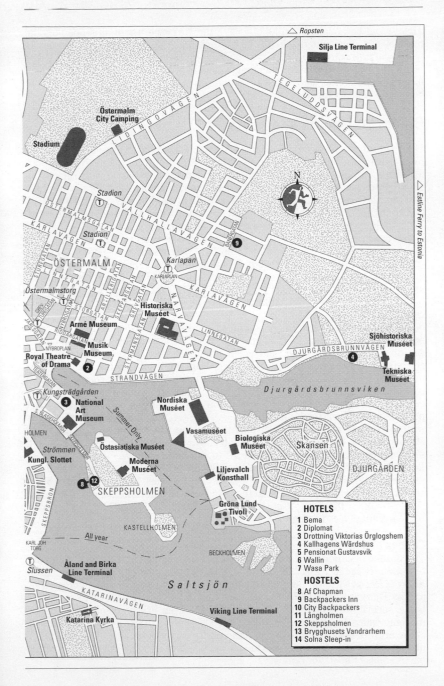

△ Ropsten

**Silja Line Terminal**

△ Estline Ferry to Estonia

Östermalm
City Camping

Stadium

*Stadion*

*Stadion*

ÖSTERMALM

*Karlapan*

*Östermalmstorg*

**Historiska
Muséet**

**Armé Museum**

**Musik
Museum**

**Royal Theatre
of Drama**

STRANDVÄGEN

DJURGÅRDSBRUNNVÄGEN

**Sjöhistoriska
Muséet**

**Tekniska
Muséet**

*Djurgårdsbrunnsviken*

*Kungsträdgården*

**National
Art
Museum**

**Nordiska
Muséet**

HOLMEN

*Summer Only*

*Strömmen*

**Östasiatiska Muséet**

**Vasamuséet**

**Biologiska
Muséet**

**Skansen**

**Kungl. Slottet**

**Moderna
Muséet**

**Liljevalch
Konsthall**

DJURGÅRDEN

SKEPPSHOLMEN

**Gröna Lund
Tivoli**

KASTELLHOLMEN

*All year*

BECKHOLMEN

KARL JOH
TORG

*Slussen*

**Åland and Birka
Line Terminal**

*Saltsjön*

KATARINAVÄGEN

**Katarina Kyrka**

**Viking Line Terminal**

**HOTELS**

1 Bema
2 Diplomat
3 Drottning Viktorias Örglogshem
4 Kallhagens Wärdshus
5 Pensionat Gustavsvik
6 Wallin
7 Wasa Park

**HOSTELS**

8 Af Chapman
9 Backpackers Inn
10 City Backpackers
11 Långholmen
12 Skeppsholmen
13 Brygghusets Vandrarhem
14 Solna Sleep-in

Tickets can be bought from the offices of the **ferry company** that operates the majority of sailings into the archipelago, *Waxholms Ångfartygs AB* (more commonly known as *Waxholmsbolaget*) on Strömkajen outside the *Grand Hotel*, or on the boats themselves. If you are intending to spend a week or so exploring different islands in the archipelago, there are a couple of cards available that will help cut costs; see "The archipelago" on p.98.

## Bikes, taxis, cars and boats

**Bike rental** is centrally available from *Skepp O'Hoj* at Galärvarvsvägen 10 (☎660 57 57), just over the bridge that leads to Djurgården or from the nearby *Cykel-och Mopeduthyrningen* at Kajplats 24 along Strandvägen (☎660 79 59); reckon on 180kr per day or 800kr per week for the latest mountain bike, less for a bone shaker. Other less central places include *Cykelstallet* at Sankt Eriksgatan 34 (☎650 08 04), to the northwest of Norrmalm, and *Servicedepån* at Kungsholmsgatan 34 on Kungsholmen (☎651 00 66), which also has tandems for rent.

You can either hail a **taxi** in the street (low-success rate) or ring one of the four main operators: *Taxi Stockholm* (☎15 00 00), *Taxi Kurir* (☎30 00 00), *Top Cab* (☎33 33 33) or *Taxi 020* (☎85 04 00). If you do phone the metre will show around 25kr before you even get in and will then race onwards and upwards at an alarming speed: 93kr or thereabouts for every 10km during the day, 103kr per 10km between 7pm and 6am and 110kr per 10km at weekends. A trip across the city centre will cost 100 – 120kr.

**Drivers** should be extremely careful where they park. You are not allowed to park within ten metres of a road junction, whether it be a tiny residential cul-de-sac or a major intersection, and you'll often see people goose-stepping in an attempt to measure out the exact distance. **Parking** is also prohibited within ten metres of a pedestrian crossing, and in bus lanes and loading zones. Disabled parking spaces are solely for the use of disabled drivers, a rule which is rigorously enforced – it can cost you over 800kr if you disobey. In the centre, parking isn't permitted on one particular night a week (see the rectangular yellow street signs with days and times in Swedish only, below the "no stopping" sign on every street) to allow for cleaning and, in winter, snow clearance. If your car is towed away (a regular occurrence), it will go to the compound at Gasverksvägen in Ropsten (Mon–Fri 8am–7pm, Sat 11am–2.30pm; ☎651 00 00) – a short walk from the metro station, where surly staff will demand at least 1500kr to hand it back, and more for every day it spends in the compound. In short, if in doubt, don't park there – look for the signs "*Gatukontoret*" or "*Parkeringsbolaget*" for valid spaces. For **car rental** see "Listings".

### Canoes and kayaks

The dozens of **canoes** and **kayaks** you see being paddled around Stockholm are testament to the fact that one of the best ways to see the city is from the water. *Skepp O'Hoj*, at Galärvarvsvägen 10 (☎660 57 57), and *Tvillingarnas Båtuthyrning*, just by Djurgårdsbron (☎663 37 39), are two of the best places in town to rent boats; special weekend deals are often available from Friday evening to Monday morning with a canoe going for 400kr; otherwise about 100kr per day. For canoes in the **archipelago** try *Skärgårdens kanotcenter* on Vaxholm, one of the most popular islands (☎54 13 77 90), or ask locally on the other islands – corner shops often have canoes or boats for rent.

# Accommodation

Stockholm has plenty of **accommodation** to suit every tourist's taste and pocket, from elegant upmarket hotels with waterfront views to youth hostels in unusual places – two on boats and another in a former prison. If you are looking for one of the cheaper hotel rooms or a hostel bed in the centre of town, don't turn up late in summer. In fact it is always a good idea to book your first night's accommodation in advance (especially during the Water Festival; see p.89), either through the **Sverigehuset** tourist office, on Hamngatan in Norrmalm, or the hotel or hostel direct.

Alternatively use the services of the excellent **Hotellcentralen**, the room-booking service in the main hall of Central Station (June–Aug daily 7am–9pm; Sept & May daily 8am–7pm; Oct–April daily 9am–6pm; ☎789 24 25), which holds comprehensive listings of **hotels and hostels**. Where they score over ringing yourself is having the latest special offers direct from the hotels; if you call into the office for a room right away, there's a booking fee of 40kr per room, 15kr for a hostel room, but if you ring ahead the fee is waived. *Hotellcentralen* also features the **Stockholm Package** (see "Hotels and pensions").

## Youth hostels and private rooms

Stockholm has wide range of good, well-run **hostels**, costing from 70kr to 150kr a night per person. There are no fewer than six official *STF* youth hostels in the city, two of which – *Af Chapman* and *Långholmen* – are among the best hostels in Sweden. There are also a number of independent places, which tend to be slightly more expensive. Nearly all Stockholm's hostels are in the centre of the city or within easy access of it.

Another good low-cost option is a **private room**; to book one contact *Hotelltjänst*, Vasagatan 15–17 (☎10 44 67), just a few minutes' walk from Central Station. Tell them how much you want to pay, and where in the city you want to stay (most rooms are out of the centre), and you should land somewhere with fridge and cooking facilities for around 250kr per person per night; you can usually arrange better deals for longer stays.

### STF hostels

**Af Chapman**, Västra Brobänken, Skeppsholmen (☎679 50 15, fax 611 98 75); T-bana Kungsträdgården or bus #65 direct from Central Station. This square-rigged 1888 ship – a landmark in its own right – has unsurpassed views over Gamla Stan, at least for the price. Without an advance written reservation (try a fortnight before you arrive), the chances of a space in summer are slim: the drawbacks to nautical accommodation are no kitchen and a lockout (11am–3pm). Open all year; reception 7am–noon & 3–10pm, closes every night at 2am. 100kr per bed.

**Backpackers Inn**, Banérgatan 56, Östermalm (☎66 07 51, fax 665 40 39); T-bana Karlaplan exit Valhallavägen or bus #41. Quite central old school residence with washing machines available. Open late June to mid-July; 85kr.

**Hökarängen**, Munstycksvägen 18 (☎94 17 65). Out of the city on the green metro line in the direction of Farsta Strand, get off at Hökarängen and walk 10min from the station. Nice old place with 46 beds. Open late June to mid-Aug; 85kr.

**Långholmen**, Kronohäktet, Långholmen (☎668 05 10, fax 720 85 75); T-bana Hornstull and follow the signs. Stockholm's grandest *STF* hostel is inside the old prison building (built in 1724) on the island of Långholmen; the cells converted into smart hotel and hostel rooms, still with extremely small windows. The hostel is open all year, but between mid-Sept and mid-April there are only 26 beds available (at other times 254). A great location, with beaches nearby, and buses to Kungsholmen and the whole of Södermalm on the doorstep. Fantastic views of Stockholm and of Lake Mälaren. Open all day; 125kr.

**Skeppsholmen**, Västra Brobänken, Skeppsholmen (☎679 50 17, fax 611 71 55); T-bana Kungsträdgården or bus #65 direct. A dead-central hostel, at the foot of the gangplank to *Af Chapman*. Immensely popular, this former craftsman's workshop is little better for speculative arrivals than the ship, though. Again there's no kitchen or washing/drying facilities. Open all year; lockout between noon and 3pm. Beds go for either 70kr or 100kr.

**Zinkensdamm**, Zinkens Väg 20, Södermalm (☎616 81 00, fax 616 81 20); T-bana Hornstull or Zinkensdamm. Huge hostel with 466 beds available in summer (202 at other times). Kitchen and washing facilities (also see "Hotels and pensions"). Open all year and all day; beds go for 100kr or 125kr.

### Independent hostels

**Brygghusets Vandrarhem**, Norrtullsgatan 12N, Norrmalm (☎31 24 24, fax 31 02 06); T-bana Odenplan. Close to the top end of Sveavägen around the lively area of Odenplan; has 57 beds. June–Aug; 110kr.

**City BackPackers Vandrarhem**, Barnhusgatan 16 (☎20 69 20, fax 31 02 06); T-bana T-Centralen. Very central all-year hostel with 40 beds; 110kr.

**Columbus Hotell & Vandrarhem**, Tjärhovsgatan 11, Södermalm (☎644 17 17, fax 702 07 64); T-bana Medborgarplatsen. This friendly hostel/hotel (also see "Hotels and pensions") is open all year; beds at around 120kr, doubles from 300kr.

**Gustav af Klint**, Stadsgårdskajen 153, Södermalm (☎640 40 77, fax 640 64 16); T-bana Slussen. Floating hostel/hotel has fine hostel rooms, but if full don't be tempted to take a hotel room – they're not worth it. Good central location, just a few minutes' walk from the Old Town. Open all year; cabin beds for around 120kr.

**Solna Sleep-In**, Haga Södra, Annerövägen, Norrmalm (☎34 46 80, fax 30 98 57); bus #69 or a good 20min walk from Odenplan. Housed in a former *SAS* terminal, it's open all year but groups only Oct–April; around 150kr.

## Hotels and pensions

In summer, it's a buyer's market in Stockholm as the business trade declines, with double rooms as low as 450kr. The cheapest choices on the whole are found to the north of Cityterminalen in the streets to the west of Adolf Fredriks kyrka. But don't rule out the more expensive places either: there are some attractive weekend and summer prices that make a spot of luxury nearer the waterfront a little more affordable. Also most of the hotels and pensions offer the **Stockholm Package** (mid-June to mid-Aug and at weekends year round), an arrangement whereby accommodation booked at certain establishments is charged at a much reduced room rate and a Stockholm Card (normally costing 175kr) is thrown in free for each night's stay. At the bottom end of the scale it can work out cheaply: 300kr per person in a twin room with breakfast, going up to around 500kr per person for a room in something quite posh. This package can only be booked through *Hotellcentralen*; you can specify which hotel you'd like by ringing ahead (and if you do this, they also waive the 40kr fee – see p.63), whereas on the day you'll be given what's available. At the time of writing, all the hotels and pensions given below were part of the scheme, but the list of participants changes every year; all the following also include breakfast in the price, unless otherwise stated.

**Alexandra**, Magnus Ladulåsgatan 42 (☎84 03 20, fax 720 53 53); T-bana Medborgarplatsen. Small modern Södermalm hotel in peaceful location whose summer and weekend reductions make it a pleasant and affordable option. ③/②

**Anno 1647**, Mariagränd 3 (☎644 04 80, fax 643 37 00), near Slussen, Södermalm; T-bana Slussen. A seventeenth-century building handy for the Old Town, with pine floors and period furniture; not recommended for people with disabilities. ③/②

**Bema**, Upplandsgatan 13 (☎23 26 75, fax 20 53 58); bus #47 & #69 from Central Station. Small pension-style hotel with en-suite rooms, 10min walk from the station. Modern Swedish decor, with beechwood furniture. Summer and weekend deal brings the cost down to the bottom of the price-code range. ②

**Castle**, Riddargatan 14 (☎679 57 00, fax 611 20 22); T-bana Östermalmstorg. Fine central hotel popular with jazz and blues musicians (jazz on summer evenings). All rooms have baths; good breakfast buffet. ③/②

**Central**, Vasagatan 38 (☎22 08 40, fax 24 75 73); T-bana T-Centralen. Modern hotel and the cheapest of all the hotels around the station. ④/③

**Columbus Hotell & Vandrarhem**, Tjärhovsgatan 11, Södermalm (☎644 17 17, fax 702 07 64); T-bana Medborgarplatsen. Simple rooms in a building that looks like a school. Rooms not en-suite. Summer and weekend deals. ②

**Diplomat**, Strandvägen 7C (☎663 58 00, fax 783 66 34); T-bana Östermalmstorg or buses #47 & #69. Rooms with a view out over Stockholm's grandest boulevard and inner harbour. This turn-of-the-century town house has suites at top end of range which represent much better value than the cheaper rooms at the *Grand*. Summer and weekend deals. ⑤

**Drottning Viktorias Örlogshem**, Teatergatan 3, Norrmalm (☎611 01 13, fax 611 31 50); T-bana Kungsträdgården. Old pension owned by the Swedish Navy, excellent value for such a central location – some en-suite rooms. Summer and weekend deals. ③

**First Hotel Reisen**, Skeppsbron 12–14 (☎22 32 60, fax 20 15 59); T-bana Gamla Stan or Slussen. Traditional hotel with heavy wooden panelled interior. All rooms with bathtubs; excellent view over the Stockholm waterfront. ⑤/④

**Gamla Stan**, Lilla Nygatan 25; T-bana Gamla Stan. Really the only halfway affordable Old Town hotel. Wonderfully situated, elegant building with rooms to match; all 51 are individually decorated. ④/③

**Grand**, Södra Blasieholmshamn 8, Norrmalm (☎679 35 00, fax 611 86 86); T-bana Kungsträdgården. A late nineteenth-century harbourside building overlooking Gamla Stan, Stockholm's most refined hotel provides the last word in luxury at world-class prices (even with reductions). Only worth it if you're staying in the best rooms – otherwise, the *Diplomat* has suites with a view for the same price. Summer and weekend reductions. ⑤

**Källhagens Wärdshus**, Djurgårdsbrunnsvägen 10 (☎665 03 00, fax 665 03 99); bus #69 from Central Station & town centre. Highly recommended. Twenty rooms painted in different colours in a fantastic spot overlooking the serene water of Lake Djurgårdsbrunnsviken. ⑤/③

**King's Lodge**, Kungsgatan 37, Norrmalm (☎20 88 02, fax 733 50 18); T-bana Hötorget. Four former offices now converted into an excellent central hotel, ideal for exploring Sveavägen and cinemaland. Advance booking necessary. No en-suite rooms. ②/①

**Lady Hamilton**, Storkyrkobrinken 5 (☎23 46 80, fax 411 11 48); T-bana Gamla Stan. Traditional hotel with rooms done out in old-fashioned Swedish/British style – lots of antique furniture. ⑤/④

**Lord Nelson**, Västerlånggatan 22 (☎23 23 90, fax 10 10 89); T-bana Gamla Stan. The narrowest hotel in Sweden – only five metres wide. Small rooms with a maritime feel – teak floors and lots of mahogany and brass. ⑤/④

**Mälardrottningen**, Riddarholmen (☎24 36 00, fax 24 36 76); T-bana Gamla Stan. An elegant white ship moored by the side of the island of Riddarholmen; cabin-style rooms in need of a lick of paint and bit of a polish, but still good value for such a central location. ③/②

**Pensionat Gustavsvik**, Västmannagatan 15 (☎21 44 50); buses #47, #53 & #69 from Central Station. Small and cheap pension, within 10min walk of the station. Summer and weekend deals. ①

**Queen's**, Drottninggatan 71A, Norrmalm (☎24 94 60, fax 21 76 20); T-bana Hötorget. Good mid-range pension-style hotel, with en-suite rooms and breakfast buffet. Summer and weekend deals. ②

**Scandic Crown**, Guldgränd 8, Södermalm (☎22 96 20; fax 21 62 68); T-bana Slussen. Lots of wooden floors throughout this expensive chain hotel, but worth it if you can get one of the rooms at the front with fantastic views out over Gamla Stan. ⑤/④

**Stockholm**, Norrmalmstorg 1 (☎678 13 20, fax 611 21 03); T-bana Östermalmstorg or Kungsträdgården. Penthouse hotel on the top floor of a central office building; good views out over Strandvägen and the harbour. Squeaky wooden floors and faded bathrooms – recommended. ⑤/②

**Tre Små Rum**, Högbergsgatan 81, Södermalm (☎641 23 71, fax 642 88 08); T-bana Mariatorget. Clean modern rooms with a Japanese flavour in the heart of Södermalm. Very popular and often full. Summer and weekend deals. ①

**Wallin**, Wallingatan 15, Norrmalm (☎20 15 20, fax 791 50 50); buses #47 & #69 from Central Station. Decent central hotel with en-suite rooms; 10min walk from the station. ④/②

**Wasa Park**, St Eriksplan 1, Norrmalm (☎34 02 85, fax 30 94 22); T-bana Sankt Eriksplan. A clean, simple hotel; a bit out of the centre but cheap. No en-suite rooms. Summer and weekend deals. ①

**Zinkensdamm**, Zinkens Väg 20, Södermalm (☎616 81 10, fax 616 81 20); T-bana Hornstull or Zinkensdamm. Hotel rooms in a separate wing of the youth hostel (see p.64). A good choice for the price. ③/②

## Camping

With the nearest year-round campsites well out of the city centre, **camping** in Stockholm can prove a bit of a burden. However, a summer-only city campsite does exist in Östermalm. The tourist offices have free camping booklets available detailing facilities at all Stockholm's campsites. It costs around 100kr for two people to pitch a tent in July and August (50kr the rest of the year).

**Bredäng** (☎97 70 71, fax 708 72 62); T-bana Bredäng on the red line towards Norsborg. Southwest of the city with views over Lake Mälaren. Open all year.

**Östermalms Citycamping**, behind the Stockholm stadium at Fiskartorpsvägen 2 (☎10 29 03); T-bana Stadion. The most central campsite in town; late June to mid-Aug.

**Solvalla Citycamping**, Sundbybergkopplet, behind the Solvalla horse trotting track (☎627 03 80, fax 627 03 70); T-bana Rissne on the blue line towards Hjulsta, then walk 1km. Open all year.

**Ängby** (☎37 04 20, fax 37 82 26); T-bana Ängbyplan on the green line towards Välingby. West of the city on the lakeshore. Open all year.

# The City

Seeing the sights is a straightforward business in Stockholm: everything is easy to get to, opening hours are long, and the city is spacious and relaxed. And, though, the sights and museums have changed, visitors have noted Stockholm's aesthetic qualities for 150 years. Once, in the centre, there were country lanes, great orchards, grazing cows, even windmills. The downside then was no pavements (until the 1840s) and no water system (until 1858), open sewers, squalid streets and crowded slums. Later, in the twentieth century, a huge modernization programme was undertaken as part of the Social Democratic out-with-the-old-and-in-with-the-new policy; Sweden was to become a place fit for working people to live in: old areas were torn down as "a thousand homes for a thousand Swedes", as the project was known, were constructed. The result, unfortunately, can be seen only too clearly around Sergels Torg: five high-rise carbuncles and an ugly rash of soulless concrete buildings that blot the city-centre landscape. There was even a plan to tear down the whole of the Old Town and build a modern city in its stead; thankfully the scheme was quickly dismissed. Today Stockholm, for the most part, is a bright and elegant place, and, with its great expanses of open water right in the centre, it offers a city panorama unparalleled anywhere in Europe.

The capital also boasts an amazing range and number of **museums**; the most interesting are described in detail in the following account of the city – for a brief run-through of the best and worst of the rest, see "Stockholm's other museums" on p.82.

# Old Stockholm: Gamla Stan and Riddarholmen

Three islands make up the **oldest part of Stockholm** – Riddarholmen, Staden and Helgeandsholmen – the whole history-riddled mass a cluster of seventeenth- and eighteenth-century Renaissance buildings backed by hairline medieval alleys. Here, on three adjoining polyps of land, Birger Jarl erected the first fortification in 1255, and for centuries this was the first city of Stockholm. Rumours abound about the derivation of the name Stockholm; it's thought that some sort of wooden drying frames, known as "stocks", were erected on the island that is now home to Gamla Stan, thus making it the island, *holm*, of *stocks*. Incidentally, today the word *stock* means log.

Although strictly speaking only the largest island, Staden, contains **Gamla Stan** (the Old Town), it's a name that is usually attached to the buildings and streets of all three islands. Once Stockholm's working centre, nowadays Gamla Stan is primarily a tourist city, an eminently strollable concentration of royal palace, parliament and cathedral, and one that represents an extraordinary tableau of cultural history. The central spider's web, especially if you approach it over Norrbron or Riksbron, invokes potent images of the past: sprawling monumental buildings and high airy churches form a protective girdle around the narrow streets. The tall dark houses in the centre were mostly those of wealthy merchants, still picked out today by intricate doorways and portals bearing coats of arms. Some of the alleys in between are the skinniest thoroughfares possible, steeply stepped between battered walls; others are covered passageways linking leaning buildings. It's easy to spend hours wandering around here, although the atmosphere these days is not so much medieval as mercenary: there's a dense concentration of antique shops, art showrooms and chi-chi cellar restaurants, though, to be fair, the frontages don't really intrude upon the otherwise light-starved streets. Not surprisingly, this is the most exclusive part of Stockholm in which to live.

## Riksdagshuset and the Medeltidsmuseum

Almost every time you enter or leave the Old Town, you'll walk past the **Riksdagshuset** (late June to late Aug; daily guided tours in English at 12.30pm

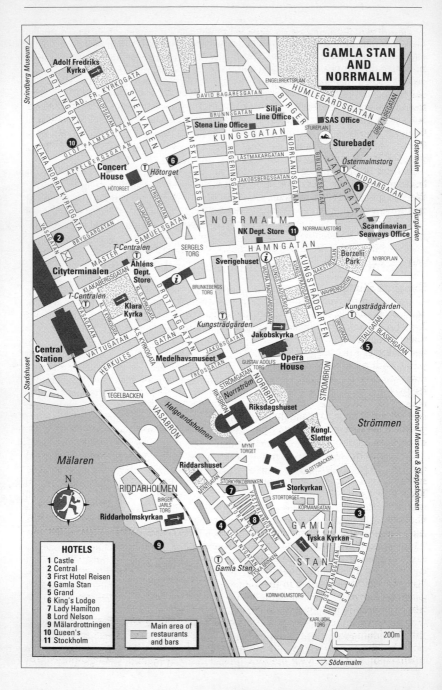

# GAMLA STAN AND NORRMALM

Strindberg Museum

Adolf Fredriks Kyrka

ENGELBREKTSPLAN

HUMLEGÅRDSGATAN

DAVID BAGARESGATAN

DROTTNINGGATAN
UPPLANDSGATAN
ADOLF FR. KYRKOGATA
SVEAVÄGEN
OLOF PALMESGATAN
APPELBERGSGATAN
KLARA NORRA KYRKOGATA

BRUNNSGATAN

Silja Line Office

Stena Line Office

BIRGER JARLSGATAN

SAS Office

STUREPLAN

Sturebadet

KUNGSGATAN

LÄSTMAKARGATAN

REGERINGSGATAN
MALMSKILLNADSGATAN

10 Queen's

6 Hötorget

Concert House

HÖTORGET

JAKOBSBERGSGATAN

BIBLIOTEKSGATAN
NORRLANDSGATAN

Östermalmstorg

RIDDARGATAN

1

△ Östermalm

GREV TUREGATAN

△ Djurgården

N O R R M A L M

NK Dept. Store  11

NORRMALMSTORG

Scandinavian Seaways Office

2

VASAGATAN
MÄSTER SAMUELSGATAN

T-Centralen

T

Åhléns Dept. Store

SERGELS TORG

HAMNGATAN

Sverigehuset

i

Berzelii Park

NYBROPLAN

Cityterminalen

KLARABERGSGATAN

T-Centralen

T

Klara Kyrka

BRUNKEBERGS TORG

i

DROTTNINGGATAN

KUNGSTRÄDGÅRDSGATAN
VÄSTRA TRÄDGÅRDSGATAN

HAMNGATAN
NÄSTRÅGATAN
WAHRENDORFFSGATAN

KUNGSTRÄDGÅRDEN

Kungsträdgården

STALLGATAN

BLASIEHOLMSGATAN

5

△ National Museum & Skeppsholmen

Central Station

△ Stadshuset

VATTUGATAN

HERKULESGATAN

KLARA S. KYRKOGATA

Medelhavsmuséet

JAKOBSGATAN

T

Kungsträdgården

Jakobskyrka

Opera House

STRÖMBRON

FREDSGATAN
GUSTAV ADOLFS TORG

VASAGATAN

TEGELBACKEN

STRÖMGATAN

RIKSBRON

Norrström

NORRBRO

Strömmen

Mälaren

VASABRON

Helgeandsholmen

Riksdagshuset

Kungl. Slottet

N

RIDDARHOLMEN

Riddarshuset

MYNT TORGET

SLOTTSBACKEN

Riddarholmskyrkan

BIRGER JARLS TORG

MYNTGATAN

STORKYRKOBRINKEN

7

STORKYRKAN
STORTORGET

Storkyrkan

KÖPMANGATAN

3

4

8

G A M L A

9

Tyska Kyrkan

S T A N

Gamla Stan

KORNHOLMSTORG

KARL JOH. TORG

SKEPPSBRON
ÖSTERLÅNGGATAN
VÄSTERLÅNGGATAN

## HOTELS

1 Castle
2 Central
3 First Hotel Reisen
4 Gamla Stan
5 Grand
6 King's Lodge
7 Lady Hamilton
8 Lord Nelson
9 Mälardrottningen
10 Queen's
11 Stockholm

Main area of restaurants and bars

0        200m

△ Södermalm

& 2pm; free), the Swedish parliament building. You'll often see Swedish politicians nipping in and out or lunching in one of the nearby restaurants. There's even a creche inside for MPs' children – it's been known for offspring to be breastfed in the chamber during particularly dull parliamentary debates. The building itself was completely restored in the 1970s (though only seventy years old then), and is today a deceptive place, as the columned, stately and original front (viewed to best effect from Norrbron) is hardly ever used. The business end is the new glassy bulge at the back (which you see when coming into Stockholm from the south by train), and it's around here that **guided tours** perambulate. Being Sweden, the seating for members is in healthy, non-adversarial rows, grouped by constituency and not by party.

In front of the Riksdag (pronounced "Reeks-da"), accessible by a set of steps leading down from Norrbron, the **Medeltidsmuseum** (Tues–Sun 11am–4pm, Wed till 6pm; 30kr) is a museum of medieval Stockholm. Medieval ruins, tunnels and walls were discovered during excavations under the parliament building and have been incorporated into a walk-through underground exhibition. There are reconstructed houses to poke around, models and pictures, boats, skeletons and street scenes. With the detailed English labelling that goes with it, it's a splendid display, and great fun for children, too.

## Kungliga Slottet

Cross over a second section of bridges and up rears the most distinctive monumental building in Stockholm, **Kungliga Slottet** (the Royal Palace) – a low, yellowy-brown square building, whose two front arms stretch down towards the water. Stockholm's old Tre Kronor castle (Three Crowns) burned down at the beginning of King Karl XII's reign, leaving his architect, Tessin the Younger (see p.97), with a free hand to design a simple and beautiful Renaissance structure. Finished in 1754, the palace is a striking achievement: uniform, sombre outside, its magnificent Baroque and Rococo interior is a swirl of state rooms and museums. The sheer size and limited opening hours conspire against you seeing everything at once. Outside the hours detailed below, the different sections of the palace have varying and often restricted opening times (the Armoury is the only exception), and some may close entirely for state visits and ceremonies.

The **Apartments** (June to Aug daily 10am–4pm; 45kr) form a relentlessly linear collection of furniture and tapestries. It's all basically Rent-a-Palace stuff, too sumptuous to take in and inspirational only in terms of colossal size. The **Treasury** (June–Aug daily 10am–4pm; 30kr), on the other hand, is certainly worthy of the name. Its ranks of jewel-studded crowns grab the eye, the oldest that of Karl X (1650), the most charming belonging to princesses Eugéne (1860) and Sofia (1771). Also worth catching is the **Armoury** (daily year round 11am–4pm; 45kr), less to do with weapons and more to do with ceremony – suits of armour, costumes and horse-drawn carriages from the sixteenth century onwards. It certainly couldn't be accused of skipping over historical detail. King Gustav II Adolf died in the Battle of Lützen in 1632, and the museum displays his horse (stuffed) and the blood- and mud-spattered garments retrieved after the enemy had stripped him down to his boxer shorts on the battlefield. For those with the energy, the **Palace Museum** (June–Aug daily 11am–4pm; 10kr) contains part of the older Tre Kronor castle, its ruins underneath the present building. Also there's the **Museum of Antiquities** (June–Aug daily 10am–4pm; rest of the year opening times subject to change; 40kr) and the **Hall** of State (same opening times and hours; 10kr) for real palace junkies. Reopening in 1997, the **Royal Coin Cabinet**, at Slottsbacken 6, is home to a stash of coins, banknotes and medals as well as a number of silver hoardes from Viking days.

## Into Gamla Stan: Stortorget and around

Beyond the Royal Palace you're into Gamla Stan proper, the streets suddenly narrower and darker. The highest point of the old part of Stockholm is crowned by **Storkyrkan**, almost the first building you stumble upon: the Great Church, consecrated in 1306. Pedantically speaking, Stockholm has no cathedral, but this rectangular brick church is now accepted as such, and the monarchs of Sweden married and were crowned here. Storkyrkan gained its present shape at the end of the fifteenth century, with a Baroque remodelling in the 1730s. The interior is marvellous: twentieth-century restoration has removed the white plaster from the red-brick columns, and although there's no evidence that this was intended in the original church it gives warm colouring to the rest of the building. Much is made of the fifteenth-century Gothic sculpture of *St George and the Dragon*, certainly an animated piece but easily overshadowed by the royal pews – more like golden billowing thrones – and the monumental black and silver altarpiece. Organ recitals take place every Saturday at 1pm.

**Stortorget**, Gamla Stan's main square, is still handsome and elegantly proportioned. Crowded by eighteenth-century buildings, whose walls bear wrought-iron lamps, it's well placed for access to the surrounding narrow shopping streets. In 1520, Christian II used the square as an execution site during the "Stockholm Blood Bath" (also see p.414), dispatching his opposition en masse with bloody finality. Now, as then, the streets **Västerlånggatan** and **Österlånggatan**, **Stora Nygatan** and **Lilla Nygatan** run the length of the Old Town, although today their time-worn buildings harbour a succession of art and craft shops and restaurants. Happily the consumerism here is largely unobtrusive and in summer buskers and evening strollers clog the narrow ways, making it an entertaining area to wander – and to eat and drink. There are few real targets, though at some stage you'll probably pass the copy of the George-and-Dragon statue in **Köpmantorget** (off Österlånggatan). Take every opportunity, too, to scuttle up side streets, where you'll find fading coats of arms, covered alleyways and worn cobbles at every turn.

Just off Västerlånggatan, on Tyska Brinken, **Tyska kyrkan**, or German Church (Sat & Sun noon–4pm), once belonged to Stockholm's medieval German merchants, serving as the meeting place of the Guild of St Gertrude. A copper-topped red-brick church atop a rise, it abandoned its secular role in the seventeenth century, which was when Baroque decorators got hold of it: the result, a richly fashioned interior with the pulpit dominating the nave, is outstanding. Sporting a curious royal gallery in one corner, designed by Tessin the Elder, it came complete with mini palace roof, angels and the three crowns of Swedish kingship.

## Riddarhuset and Riddarholmen

If Stockholm's history has gripped you, it's better to keep right on as far as the handsome Baroque **Riddarhuset** (Mon–Fri 11.30am–12.30pm; 20kr), the seventeenth-century "House of Nobles". It was in its Great Hall that the Swedish aristocracy met during the Parliament of the Four Estates (1668–1865), and their coats of arms – around two and a half thousand of them – are splattered across the walls. Some six hundred of the noble families survive, the last ennoblement having taken place in 1974. Take a look downstairs, too, at the Chancery, which stores heraldic bone china by the shelf load and racks full of fancy signet rings – essential accessories for the eighteenth-century noble-about-town.

Riddarhuset shouldn't really be seen in isolation. It's only a matter of seconds to cross the bridge onto **Riddarholmen** (Island of the Knights) proper, to **Riddarholmskyrkan** (daily noon–4pm; 20kr). Originally a Franciscan monastery, for over six centuries the church has been established as the burial place of Swedish royalty. Since Magnus Ladulås was sealed up here in 1290, his successors have rallied round to create a Swedish pantheon and, amongst others, you'll find the tombs of Gustav II Adolf (in the green marble sarcophagus), Karl XII, Gustav III and Karl Johan XIV, plus other innumerable and unmemorable descendants. Walk around the back of the church for stunning views of Stadshuset, the City Hall, and Lake Mälaren. The island to the left of Västerbron – the bridge in the distance – is Långholmen; in winter people skate here and take their dogs for walks on the ice as the water freezes solid right up to the bridge and beyond.

# Skeppsholmen and Kastellholmen

Off Gamla Stan's eastern reaches lies the island of **Skeppsholmen** (a 10min walk from Stortorget: cross Strömbron, turn right and cross Skeppsholmbron; you can also take a ferry from Nybroplan, see p.59), home to most younger travellers in Stockholm, who end up at one of the island's two youth hostels. Other than this convenience, the reason for being here is an eclectic clutch of **museums**; the first of which, the National Art Museum, is actually just before the bridge.

## The National Art Museum

On the way to Skeppsholmen as you approach Skeppsholmsbron, you'll pass the striking waterfront **National Art Museum** (Tues 11am–8pm, Wed–Sun 11am–5pm; 40kr), looking right out over the Royal Palace. This impressive collection of European fine and applied arts from the late medieval period to the nineteenth century is contained on three floors. The **ground floor** is taken up by changing exhibitions of prints and drawings, and this is where you'll have to leave your bags (in the refundable lockers provided). There's a museum shop and café here, too.

The **first floor** is devoted to applied art and, if it's curios you're after, this museum has the lot – beds slept in by kings, cabinets leaned on by queens, plates eaten off by nobles – mainly from the centuries when Sweden was a great power. There's modern work alongside the ageing tapestries and furniture, including Art Nouveau coffee pots and vases, and the intelligent simplicity of Swedish wooden chair design.

It's the **second floor**, though, that's of most engaging interest. There's a plethora of European and Mediterranean sculpture and some mesmerizing sixteenth- and seventeenth-century Russian icons. The paintings are equally wide ranging and of a similarly high quality, including works by El Greco, Canaletto, Gainsborough, Gauguin and Renoir. Something of a coup for the museum is Rembrandt's *Conspiracy of Claudius Civilis*, one of his largest monumental paintings, in room 33. Picturing a scene from Tacitus's *History*, the bold work shows a gathering of well-armed chieftains. There are also some fine works by **Swedish artists** from the sixteenth to early twentieth centuries – most notably paintings by Sweden's nineteenth-century masters Anders Zorn and Carl Larsson, and one, by Carl Gustav Pilo, a late eighteenth-century painter, depicting the coronation of Gustav III in Storkyrkan in Gamla Stan. The detail here is interesting, since it shows the church with white plaster columns and not the red-brick of today.

So much is packed into this museum that it can quickly become confusing and overwhelming. To wade through it all, splash out on the **guidebook** – money well spent.

### The museums of modern art, eastern antiquities and architecture
On Skeppsholmen itself, Stockholm's Museum of Modern Art, the **Moderna Museet**, is one of the better modern art collections in Europe, with a comprehensive selection of work by some of the twentieth-century's leading artists. At the time of writing, however, it was closed for renovation – with a projected reopening date of February 1998 – and in the meantime, the exhibits have been cramped into premises in the north of the city at Birger Jarlsgatan 57, near Eriksbergsplan in Norrmalm (Tues–Thurs noon–7pm, Fri–Sun noon–5pm; 50kr). Although the surroundings aren't perfect, you can still view Dali's monumental *Enigma of William Tell* showing the artist at his most conventionally unconventional, and Matisse's striking *Apollo*. Look out for Picasso's *Guitar Player* and a whole host of Warhol, Lichtenstein, Kandinsky, Miró and Magritte. To get to the temporary premises take bus #46 from Slussen or Skeppsbron in Gamla Stan; once the museum has reopened take #65 from Central Station.

A steep climb up the northern tip of the island brings you to **Östasiatiska Museet**, the Museum of Far Eastern Antiquities (Tues noon–8pm, Wed–Sun noon–5pm; 40kr). The reward is an array of objects displaying incredible craftsmanship. Many of the exhibits are from China – Swedish archeologists' favourite hunting ground – and you can wander past fifth-century Chinese tomb figures, intricate ceramics from the seventh century onwards and fine Chinese paintings on paper and silk. Alongside these, take a look at the astounding assembly of sixth-century Buddhas, Indian watercolours and gleaming bronze Krishna figures, and from Japan a magnificent set of Samurai armour, a gift from the Crown Prince of Japan in the 1920s. In short, a visit here is half a day well spent.

Other than this there's little to detain you on Skeppsholmen or on adjacent microscopic **Kastellholmen**, connected by a bridge to the south. Both islands are in the Baltic and proved attractive enough to induce the Swedish Navy to settle there in the nineteenth century, and some of the old barracks are still visible. If you're taking a stroll around the islands, though, be aware of Skeppsholmen's other diversion — **Arkitektur Museet**, on Västra Brobänken next to *Af Chapman* youth hostel (Tues 11am–8pm, Wed–Sun 11am–5pm; 20kr), which stages temporary exhibtions on various aspects of architecture and urban planning within Sweden. Perhaps one for a rainy day.

# Norrmalm and Kungsholmen

Modern Stockholm lies immediately to the north and east of Gamla Stan and is split into two distinct sections. **Norrmalm**, to the north, is the commercial heart of the city, a compact area full of shops and offices, restaurants, bars and cinemas that is always bustling with people and streetlife – it also, unfortunately, has a high count of ugly modern buildings. To the east, **Kungsholmen** has a very different feel, with wider, residential streets, larger parks, select shops and Stockholm's town hall. Norrmalm is easy to get round on foot, and it's only a short walk across Stadshusbron to Kungsholmen.

## Around Gustav Adolfs Torg

Down on the waterfront, at the foot of Norrbron, is **Gustav Adolfs Torg**, more a traffic island than a square these days, with the nineteenth-century **Operan** (Opera House) its proudest, most notable – and ugliest – building. It was here in an earlier opera house on the same site, at a masked ball in 1792, that King Gustav III was shot by one Captain Ankarström, an admirer of Rousseau and member of the aristocratic opposition. The story is recorded in Verdi's opera *Un ballo in maschera*, and you'll find Gustav's ball costume, as well as the assassin's pistols and mask, displayed in the Palace Armoury in Gamla Stan (see p.69). The opera's famous restaurant, *Operakällaren*, which faces the water, is hellishly expensive, the trendy café less so.

A statue of King Gustav II Adolf marks the centre of the square, between the Opera and the Foreign Office opposite. Look out, too, for fishermen pulling salmon out of **Strömmen**, the fast-flowing water that winds its way through the centre of the city. Stockholmers have had the right to fish this outlet from Lake Mälaren to the Baltic since the seventeenth century; it's not as difficult as it sounds, and there's usually a group of hopefuls on one of the bridges around the square.

Just off the square, at Fredsgatan 2, in the heart of Swedish government land (several ministries are located in the surrounding streets), is **Medelhavsmuseet**, a sparkling museum devoted to Mediterranean and Near Eastern Antiquities (Tues 11am–9pm, Wed–Sun 11am–4pm; 40kr). Its enormous Egyptian display covers just about every aspect of Egyptian life up to the Christian era. As well as several whopping great mummies, the most attractive pieces are the bronze weapons, tools and domestic objects from the time before the Pharaohs. The Cyprus collections are also huge, the largest such gathering outside Cyprus itself, depicting life through a period spanning six thousand years. Additionally the museum contains strong Greek displays and comprehensive collections of Etruscan and Roman art. A couple of rooms examine Islamic culture through pottery, glass and metal work, as well as decorative elements from architecture, Arabian calligraphy and Persian miniature painting.

Walking back towards the Opera House and continuing across the main junction onto Arsenalsgatan, you'll soon come to **Jakobs kyrka** (daily 11am–5pm). The church is one of the many hidden away in Stockholm, and can easily be missed. It's the pulpit that draws the attention, a great, golden affair, while the date of the church – 1642 – is stamped high up on the ceiling in gold figures. There are weekly concerts here as well: organ and choir recitals on Saturday at 3pm.

## Kungsträdgården

Just beyond the Jacobs kyrka and the Opera House, Norrmalm's eastern boundary is marked by **Kungsträdgården**, reaching from the water northwards as far as Hamngatan, the most fashionable and central of the city's numerous parks. The mouthful of a name literally means "the king's gardens", though if you're expecting perfectly designed flower beds and rose gardens you'll be sadly disappointed – it's a great expanse of concrete with a couple of lines of trees. The area may once have been a royal kitchen garden, but those days are long gone. Today the area is Stockholm's main meeting place, especially in summer, when there's almost always something going on: free evening gigs, live theatre and other performances take place on the central open-air stage. Look out, too, for the park's cafés – if you are here in spring you'll see winter-weary Stockholmers sitting in the open-air café, lapping up the much-missed sunshine. One of the cafés is a very good place to meet the capital's gay men and lesbians (also see "Gay Stockholm"). In winter the park is equally as busy; the **Isbanan**, an open-air ice rink at the **Hamngatan** end of the park, rents out skates (Oct–April daily 9am–6pm; skate rental 30kr). The main tourist office is here, too, at the corner of Hamngatan in Sverigehuset (see p.56 for details).

Hamngatan runs east to **Birger Jarlsgatan**, the main thoroughfare that divides Norrmalm from Östermalm and now a mecca for eating and drinking, but until 1855 the site of two pillories and largely rural. Look out too for the stone pillars near the water with their snaking lines of multicoloured illuminated lights – they're an indication of how clean the city's air and water are at the moment. Carry on along this street and you'll reach no. 57, near Eriksbergplan, where the paintings from the Moderna Museet are currently being exhibited (see p.72).

## Sergels Torg to Hötorget

At the western end of Hamngatan, past the enormous *NK* department store, lies **Sergels Torg**, the ugliest part of modern Stockholm. It's an unending free show centred around the five seething floors of **Kulturhuset** (Tues–Fri 11am–6pm, Sat & Sun noon–5pm), whose windows look down upon the milling concrete square. Inside this building, devoted to contemporary Swedish culture, are temporary art and craft exhibitions together with workshops open to anyone willing to get their hands dirty. The reading room (*Läsesalongen*) on the ground level is stuffed with foreign newspapers, books, records and magazines – handy if it's wet and windy outside. Check with the information desk as you come in for details of poetry readings, concerts and theatre performances; admission to Kulturhuset is free, but admission fees are charged for exhibitions and performances. At the café on the top floor, you can indulge in delicious apple pie and custard and take in the best views of central Stockholm – although the service here often leaves something to be desired.

From the café you have a bird's eye view of the singularly ugly, tall, wire-like column that dominates the massive square outside and the surrounding spewing fountain (often obscured by soap suds – the local youth think it's a real wheeze to pour packets of washing powder into it). Down the steps, below Sergels Torg, is **Sergels Arkaden**, a set of grotty underground walkways, home to buskers, brass bands and the demented lottery ticket vendors. Look out for the odd demonstration, too, or oddball game: you may see lots of young Stockholmers running around shivering in their underwear, having tied the rest of their clothes together in a line to see whose line is longest – somehow a very Swedish pastime. There's also an entrance into **T-Centralen**, the central T-bana station, as well as an entrance in Stockholm's other main department store, *Åhléns*, not quite as posh as *NK* and easier to find your way around.

A short walk along Klarabergsgatan, west of Kulturhuset, brings you to **Central Station** and **Cityterminalen**, hub of virtually all Stockholm's transport. The area around here is given over to unabashed consumerism, but as you explore the streets around the main drag, **Drottninggatan** (Queen Street), there's little to get excited about – the run-of-the-mill clothing shops, twee gift shops punctuated by *McDonalds* and the odd sausage stand. In summer the occasional busker or jewellery stall livens up what is essentially a souless grid of pedestrianized shopping streets. One highlight is **Klara kyrka** (Mon–Fri 10am–6pm; Sat 10am–7pm, Sun 8.30am–6pm), just to the right off Klarabergsgatan, another of Stockholm's overlooked churches, with only the spires visible from the streets around. Hemmed in on all sides, the church is particularly delicate, with a light and flowery eighteenth-century painted interior and an impressive golden pulpit. Out in the churchyard, a memorial stone commemorates the eighteenth-century Swedish poet Carl Michael Bellman, whose popular, lengthy ballads are said to have been composed extempore; his unmarked grave is somewhere in the churchyard.

Three blocks further up Drottninggatan in the cobbled-square **Hötorget** you'll find an open-air fruit and veg market as well as the wonderful indoor **Hötorgshallen**, a tantalizing array of Middle Eastern sights and smells and a good place to pick up ethnic snacks. Why not grab a bite to eat from the market and sit yourself on the steps of the **Konserthuset**, one of the venues for the presentation of the Nobel Prizes; if you're lucky, you may well catch one of the classical music recitals that are held here in summer (usually Sunday afternoons). From the steps look out across the square to the tall building opposite; this former department store is where Greta Garbo began life as a sales assistant in the hat section. And if you want to see a movie, you only have to walk across the square to Stockholm's biggest cinema complex, *Filmstaden*, while to the east, **Kungsgatan**, running down to Stureplan and Birger Jarlsgatan, has most of the rest of the city's cinemas (also see "Drinking, nightlife and culture"), interspersed with agreeable little cafés.

## North to Adolf Fredriks kyrka

From Hötorget, the city's two main streets, Drottninggatan and **Sveavägen**, with its excellent restaurants and bars and Stockholm's gay centre at *Hus1* (see p.93), run parallel uphill and north as far as Odengatan and the **Stadsbiblioteket**, the City Library, in its little park. In secluded gardens, not far north of Hötorget on Sveavägen, sits **Adolf Fredriks kyrka**. Although the church has a noteworthy past – the French philosopher Descartes was buried in the church's cemetery in 1650; his body was taken back to France in 1661 – it would have remained an almost unnoticed eighteenth-century church, its yard full of lunching office workers, were it not for one of the most tragic – and unexplained – events in modern Swedish history: the murder of the former prime minister **Olof Palme** (see box overleaf).

Continuing north along Drottninggatan, you'll soon come to the excellent **Strindbergsmuseet** at no. 85 (Tues–Sun 11am–4pm; 25kr), housed in the "Blue Tower", the last building in which the author August Strindberg lived in Stockholm. The house, which was the writer's home between 1908 and 1912, has been preserved to the extent that you must put plastic bags on your feet to protect the floors and furnishings. The study is as he left it on his death, a dark and gloomy place – he wrote with venetian blinds and heavy curtains closed against the sunlight. Upstairs is his library, a musty room with all the books firmly behind glass, which is a shame because Strindberg wasn't a passive reader: he underlined heavily and criticized in the margins as he read, though rather less eruditely than you'd expect. "Lies!", "Crap!", "Idiot!" and "Bloody hell!" tended to be his favourite comments. Good English notes are supplied free, and the nearest T-bana stop is Rådmansgatan, on the green line (direction Fridhemsplan and Hässelby Strand).

## THE ASSASSINATION OF OLOF PALME

Adolf Fredriks kyrka is of immense significance to modern Swedes as the final resting place of **Olof Palme**; a simple headstone and flowers mark his grave. He was shot on the way home from the cinema on Sveavägen, and his death sent shockwaves through a society unused to political extremism of any kind. Like most Nordic leaders his fame was his security, and he died unprotected, gunned down in front of his wife in February 1986. A politically instructive end, it has sadly led to a radical rethink of Sweden's open government policy, pursued for decades.

Sweden's biggest ever murder **inquiry** was launched and as the years went by so the allegations of police cover-ups and bungling grew. When Christer Pettersson was jailed for the murder (see the history section of *Contexts*, p.419), most Swedes thought that was the end of the story, but his eventual release only served to reopen the bitter debate, with consequent recriminations and resignations within a much-derided police force. Although in the past the most popular suspects were immigrant Kurdish extremists, right-wing terror groups or even a hitman from within the police itself, new allegations suggest that the corrupt regime in South Africa was behind the killing. These claims are being treated very seriously in Sweden – Palme was an outspoken critic of apartheid and led calls in the 1980s for an economic blockade against Pretoria.

A simple plaque now marks the spot on Sveavägen, near the junction with Olof Palmes Gatan, where the prime minister was gunned down; the assassin escaped up the nearby flight of steps.

Heading further north, the city gradually peters out into a number of rather diverse parks and gardens (for more on which see p.78). The closest to town – officially in the area north of the centre called **Vasastaden** – and only a twenty-minute walk along Sveavägen from Adolf Fredriks kyrka, is **Vanadislunden**. Inside the park is a watersports and activities centre called **Vanadisbadet** (mid-May to mid-Sept daily 10am–6pm; 50kr), where you can while away some hours splashing about in the water if it's raining outside. To get there from the centre, you can either walk from the T-bana at Odenplan, or take bus #52 from Central Station or Sergels Torg towards Karolinska Sjukhuset.

## Kungsholmen: Stadshuset

Take the T-bana back to the centre, get off at T-Centralen and it's only a matter of minutes from there, across Stadshusbron, to the island of **Kungsholmen** and Stockholm's City Hall. Finished in 1923, **Stadshuset** (June–Aug daily guided tours at 10am, 11am, noon & 2pm; at other times subject to change; 30kr) is one of the landmarks of modern Stockholm and one of the first buildings you'll see when approaching the city from the south by train. Its simple, if somewhat drab, exterior brickwork is no preparation for the intriguing detail inside. If you're a visiting Head of State you'll be escorted from your boat up the elegant waterside steps; for lesser mortals, the only way to view the innards is on one of the guided tours, which reveal the kitschy Viking-style legislative chamber and impressively echoing Golden Hall. The City Hall is also the departure point for **boats** to Drottningholm, Mariefred, Sigtuna, Skokloster and Uppsala (see "Around Stockhom") .

But don't just stop at Stadshuset; venture further into Kungsholmen and you'll discover a rash of great new bars and restaurants (see also the sections on eating, drinking and nightlife that began on p.85), and an excellent **beach** at

Smedsudden (buses #54 and #62 to Västerbroplan, then a five-minute walk). There's also the popular park, **Rålambshovsparken**, where swimming offers fantastic views of the City Hall and the Old Town.

# Östermalm

East of Birger Jarlsgatan the streets become noticeably broader and grander, a uniform grid as far as Karlaplan. **Östermalm** was one of the last areas of central Stockholm to be developed and, with the greenery of Djurgården (see overleaf) beginning to make itself felt, the impressive residences are as likely to be consulates and embassies as fashionable houses. The first place to head for is the water's-edge square, **Nybroplan**, just east along Hamngatan from Sergels Torg (from Gamla Stan it's a fifteen-minute stroll across Strombron or take the T-bana to Östermalmstorg or bus #55) and marked with the white-stone relief-studded **Kungliga Dramatiska Teatern**, Stockholm's showpiece theatre. The curved harbour in front is the departure point for all kinds of archipelago **ferries** and tours (see p.98) and for a ferry that makes the short journey via Skeppsholmen across to the Nordiska and Vasa museums over on Djurgården (daily July & Aug only every 15min; 20kr).

At the back of the theatre, at Sibyllegatan 2, is the innovative **Musikmuseet** (Tues–Sun 11am–4pm; 30kr), containing a range of instruments that visitors can play ("carefully", pleads the notice). The museum charts the history of music in Sweden using photographs, instruments and sound recordings. Best are the sections that deal with the late nineteenth century, a time when *folkmusik* had been given fresh impetus by the growing labour movement. The concluding parts on "progressive" and "disco" music are very brief and uninteresting, with the merest mention of punk and, astonishingly, nothing on Abba.

The chief feature of this end of the city was once the barracks: it's a link continued today by the presence of **Armémuseet**, opposite the Musikmuseet at Riddargatan 13. Hardly anyone comes to visit its displays of precision killing machines, uniforms, swords and medals. Indeed you'll probably be outnumbered by museum attendants, who seem to consider an interest in the exhibits as proof of social deviancy, and who stay keenly alert and omnipresent. At the time of writing, the museum was undergoing repairs and alterations; check at a tourist office for the new opening date.

Just back from the museums, up the hill of Sibyllegatan, **Östermalmstorg** is an absolute find: the square is home to the rather ritzy **Östermalmshallen**, an indoor market hall. Although it looks very similar to Norrmalm's Hötorgshallen, this place offers more delicatessen items – reindeer hearts and the like – and attracts a chic clientele to match. Wander round at lunchtime and you'll spot fur-coated ladies and gents sipping Chardonnay and munching on shrimp sandwiches.

## Historiska Museet

As you wend your way around Östermalm's rich streets, you're bound to end up at the circular **Karlaplan** sooner or later: a handy T-bana and bus interchange, full of media types coming off shift from the Swedish Radio and Television buildings at the eastern end of Karlavägen. From here, it's a short walk down Narvavägen – or you can jump on a #44 bus – as far as the **Historiska Museet** at no. 13–17 (Tues–Sun 11am–5pm; 55kr); from Norrmalm, hop on bus #56, which runs via Stureplan and Linnégatan. The most wide-ranging historical display in Stockholm, it's really two large collections, a Museum of National Antiquity and the new Gold Room, with its magnificent fifth-century gold collars and other fine pieces of jewellery, housed in an underground vault. On the ground floor, the pre-history section has labelling in English, and highlights include the ideal Stone Age household – flaxen-haired youth, stripped-pine benches and rows of neatly labelled herbs – and a mass of Viking weapons, coins and boats. Upstairs there's a worthy collection of medieval church art and architecture, with odds and ends gathered up from all over the country, evocatively housed in massive vaulted rooms. If you're moving from Stockholm to Gotland, be sure to take in the reassembled bits of stave churches uncovered on the Baltic island – some of the few examples that survive in Sweden.

# Djurgården

When you tire of the streets, it's time to utilize part of Stockholm's National City Park, just to the east of the centre. Originally royal hunting grounds throughout the sixteenth to eighteenth centuries, **Djurgården** (pronounced "Yoor-gorn") is actually two distinct park areas separated by the water of **Djurgårdsbrunnsviken** – a popular area for **swimming** in summer and **skating** in winter, when the channel freezes over. Aside from taking time out from the city, you can also visit some of Stockholm's finest **museums**. Top of the list are the massive open-air Skansen, an amazing conglomeration of architecture and folk culture from around the country, and Vasamuseet, which houses a wonderfully preserved seventeenth-century warship. You can walk to Djurgården through the centre out along Strandvägen, but it's quite a hike: take bus #44 from Karlaplan, or from the Norrmalm buses #47 and #69 (only as far as the bridge, Djurgårdsbron, over onto the island); or the ferries from Skeppsbron in Gamla Stan (all year) or Nybroplan (July & Aug only).

## Nordiska Museet, Skansen and Gröna Lunds Tivoli

A full day is just about enough to see everything on Djurgården. Starting with the palatial **Nordiska Museet** (Tues–Sun 11am–5pm; 50kr), just over Djurgårdsbron from Strandvägen, is the best idea, if only because the same cultural themes pop up repeatedly throughout the rest of the exhibits on the island. The displays are a recent attempt to represent Swedish cultural history (from over the past five hundred years) in an accessible fashion, and the *Sami* section is particularly good. On the ground floor of the cathedral-like interior is Carl Milles's phenomenal statue of Gustav Vasa, the sixteenth-century king who drove out the Danes, and an inspirational figure who wrought the best from the sculptor (for more of whom, see p.96).

It's for **Skansen** (daily 9am–10pm; July & Aug 55kr, rest of the year 45kr), though, that most people come: a vast open-air museum, with 150 reconstructed buildings, from a whole town to windmills and farms laid out on a region-by-region basis, with each section boasting its own daily activities – traditional handicrafts, games and displays – that anyone can join in. Best of the buildings are the small *Sami* dwellings, warm and functional, and the craftsmen's workshops in the old town quarter. You can also potter around a small **zoo** and a bizarre **aquarium**, fish cheek by jowl with crocodiles, monkeys and snakes. Partly because of the attention paid to accuracy, partly due to the admirable lack of commercialization (something a lack in Sweden as a whole), Skansen manages to avoid the tackiness associated with similar ventures in other countries. Even the snack bars dole out traditional foods and in winter serve up great bowls of warming soup.

Immediately opposite Skansen's main gates and at the end of the #44 bus route (bus #47 also goes by), **Gröna Lunds Tivoli** (May to mid-Sept daily noon to midnight; rest of the year restricted hours; 40kr) is not a patch on its more famous namesake in Copenhagen, though its decidedly cleaner and less seedy. It's definitely more of a place to stroll through rather than indulge in the rides (none included in the entrance fee), which are tame. At night the emphasis shifts as the park becomes the stomping ground for Stockholm's youth, with raucous music, cafés and some enterprising chat-up lines.

## Vasamuseet

In a brand-new building, close to Nordiska Museet, **Vasamuseet** (mid-June to mid-Aug daily 9.30am–7pm; rest of the year daily 10am–5pm, Wed until 8pm; 45kr) is without question head and shoulders above anything else that Stockholm has to offer in the way of museums. Built on the orders of King Gustav II Adolf, the *Vasa* warship sank in Stockholm harbour on its maiden voyage in 1628. Preserved in mud for over three hundred years, the ship was raised along with twelve thousand objcts in 1961, and now forms the centrepiece of a startling, purpose-built hall on the water's edge. The museum itself is built over part of the old naval dockyard and was designed to give the impression of a large, soft copper tent, the materials used supposed to relate to navy colours and designs: stone and ochre, tarred and black beams mixed with whites, reds and the green of Djurgården.

Impressive though the building is, nothing prepares you for the sheer size of the **ship**: 62m long, the main mast originally 50m over the keel, it sits virtually complete in a cradle of supporting mechanical tackle. Surrounding walkways bring you nose to nose with canon hatches and restored decorative relief, the gilded wooden sculptures on the soaring prow designed to intimidate the enemy and proclaim Swedish might. With the humid atmosphere (the ship will take decades to dry out) and the immediacy of its frightening bulk, it's not difficult to understand the terror that such ships must have generated. Adjacent **exhibition halls** and presentations on several levels take care of all the retrieved bits and bobs. There are reconstructions of life on board, detailed models of the *Vasa*, displays relating to contemporary social and political life, films and videos of the rescue operation, excellent English notes and regular English-language **guided tours** – in short, a must.

## Thielska Galleriet

At the far eastern end of Djurgården (bus #69 from Norrmalm), **Thielska Galleriet** (Mon–Sat noon–4pm, Sun 1–4pm; 40kr) is one of Stockholm's major treasures, a fine example of both Swedish architecture and art. The house was built by Ferdinand Boberg at the turn of this century for banker Ernet Thiel, who then sold it to the state in 1924, when it was turned into an art gallery. Thiel, who knew many contemporary Nordic artists, gathered an impressive collection of paintings over the years, many of which are on display today – there are works by Carl Larsson, Anders Zorn, Edvard Munch, Bruno Liljefors and even August Strindberg. The views, too, are attractive enough to warrant a trip out here.

## The TV tower: Kaknästornet

Bus #69 from Norrmalm will also take you directly to Stockholm's famous TV tower, in the northern stretch of parkland known as **Ladugårdsgärdet** (or more commonly as plain Gärdet), but it's also possible to walk here from Djurgården proper – head northwards across the island on Manillavägen over Djurgårdsbrunnsviken. At 160m, **Kaknästornet** (daily 9am–10pm; 20kr) is the highest building in Scandinavia, providing excellent views over the city and archipelago, and there's a restaurant about 120m up for an airborne cup of coffee. If you choose to take the bus here, you'll pass a gaggle of sundry museums – Maritime, Technical and Ethnographical – listed on pp.83–84; and beyond Ladusgårdsgärdet, north of the tower, where windmills used to pierce the skyline, lies first Frihamnen, where the Estonia ferry docks, and just beyond that, Värtahamnen and the *Silja Line* ferry terminal for Finland.

# Södermalm

Whatever you do in Stockholm, don't miss the delights of the city's southern island, **Södermalm**, more often known simply as "Söder", whose craggy cliffs, turrets and towers rise high above the clogged traffic interchange at Slussen. The perched buildings are vaguely forbidding, but venture beyond the main roads skirting the island and a lively and surprisingly green area unfolds, one that is at heart emphatically working class but Swedish style – there were never any slums here. To get to the island you can either take bus #46 or #48 from Norrmalm and get off at Bondegatan, or jump on the #53 to Folkungagatan; alternatively ride on the T-bana to either Slussen or, to save an uphill trek, Medborgarplatsen or Mariatorget.

Walking, you reach the island over a double bridge from Gamla Stan onto Södermalmstorg, the square around the entrance to the T-bana at Slussen. Just to the south is the rewarding **Stadsmuseet** (Tues–Sun 11am–5pm; 30kr), hidden in a basement courtyard. The Baroque building, designed by Tessin the Elder and finished by his son in 1685, was once the town hall for this part of Stockholm; now it houses a set of collections relating to the city's history as a seaport and industrial centre. Nearby the Renaissance-style **Katarina kyrka**, on Högbergsgatan, stands on the site where the victims of the so-called "Stockholm Blood Bath" were buried in 1520, the betrayed nobility of Sweden who had opposed King Christian II's Danish invasion. Their bodies were burned as heretics outside the city walls, and it proved a vicious and effective coup, Christian disposing of the opposition in one fell swoop.

That's about as far as specific sights go on Södermalm, but it is worth wandering westwards to **Mariatorget**, a spacious square where the influence of Art Nouveau on the buildings is still evident. This is one of the most desirable places for Stockholmers to live – and be close to the action: a glut of stylish bars and restaurants that are the favourite haunts of Stockholm's young and terminally hip. If you're having a bad-hair day and not looking your best, you can escape the latest fashions and regress to your childhood at the Museum of Toys, **Hobby-och Leksaksmuseum** at Mariatorget 1C (Tues–Fri 10am–4pm, Sat & Sun noon–4pm; 30kr, children 15kr), which contains everything from tin soliders to space guns, although there's more to interest big kids than little ones, with few toys you can actually play with.

The island is also home to one of Stockholm's most popular parks, **Tantolunden**, located close to the Hornstull T-bana at the end of Lignagatan,

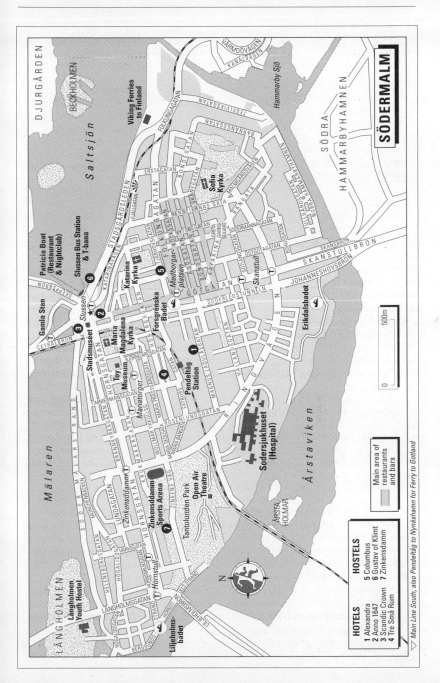

complete with open-air theatre in summer. It's also the place to come for **swimming pools**; there are three of them in fairly close proximity: *Forsgrénskabadet* (Medborgarplatsen T-bana), *Erikdalsbadet* (Skanstull T-bana) and the wonderful little *Liljeholmsbadet* (Hornstull T-bana), a pool in a boat-like pontoon contraption that floats in Lake Mälaren. There's single-sex nude swimming here on certain days of the week (see p.95). The water is never less than 30°C and there's an excellent sauna.

Although you'll probably end up in one of Söder's bars or restaurants when night falls, it's best to get your bearings during the day, as the streets in the dark become terribly confusing. The main streets to aim for are **Götgatan**, **Folkungagatan**, **Bondegatan** and **Skånegatan** (also see the sections on eating, drinking and nightlife that begin on p.85).

### Långholmen

The name **Långholmen** means "long island" and it's just that, a skinny finger of land that lies off the northwestern tip of Södermalm, crossed by the mighty Västerbron bridge linking Södermalm with Kungsholmen. There's a couple of popular **beaches** here: **Långholmens Strandbad** to the west of the bridge, rocky **Klippbad** to the east, and opposite the beach at **Smeddsudden** on Kungsholmen. Leafy and peaceful, Långholmen is a delightful place to take a walk; on the way you'll also get some stunning views of the city towards Stadhuset and Gamla Stan.

One of the better places to stay in the city is the youth hostel/hotel (see "Accommodation"), sited in what used to be Långholmen's large prison building. There's a café here in the summer, where you can sit outside in the former exercise yard – narrow, bricked-up runs with iron gates at one end. Alternatively you could nip back over onto Södermalm and sample the excellent *Lasse i Parken* café (see p.88).

Get to Långholmen by taking the T-bana to Hornstull and following the signs to the youth hostel and the island Bus #54 is also handy; it crosses Västerbron on its way between Södermalm, Kungsholmen, Vasastaden (to the northeast of Norrmalm) and Östermalm – incidentally, the bus ride is an excellent way of seeing a lot of the city for very little cost.

## Stockholm's other museums

Stockholm has eighty-odd **museums** scattered within its limits, and although you'd have to be very keen to want to see the lot, some of the minor collections are worth seeking out: what follows is a brief (and biased) rundown of the best – and worst. Full details are in the booklet *Stockholm's Museums*, available from all good tourist offices: note that the Stockholm Card gets free entry into most of them and that most are also closed on Mondays.

### Aquaria

Djurgården, Falkenbergsgatan 2; bus #44 or #47. Tues–Sun 10am–4.30pm; 45kr.

Stockholm's water museum covers every conceivable aspect of the water cycle; and a portion of the admission charge proceeds is donated to rainforest projects.

## Biologiska Museet

Djurgården; bus #44 or #47. Daily 10am–4pm, closed Mon out of season; 20kr.

A tired panorama of stuffed animals and birds from the Scandinavian countries; this is ever so pointless, but is housed in a rather pleasing copy of a Norwegian stave church.

## Cosmonova, Naturhistoriska Riksmuseet

Frescativägen 40; T-bana Universitetet. Daily 10am–6pm, Thurs till 8pm; 45kr.

Films in the country's only Omnimax theatre show the world of natural history in vivid technicolour; also planetarium shows.

## Dansmuseet

Dansens Hus, Barnhusgatan 12–14; T-bana T-Centralen. Tues–Sun noon–4pm; 30kr.

A push-button film archive of world dance, with costume displays – supposedly the only dance museum in the world.

## Ethnografiska Museet

Djurgårdsbrunnsvägen 34; bus #69. Tues, Thurs & Fri 11am–4pm, Wed 11am–8pm, Sat & Sun noon–5pm; 30kr.

More plundered Asian ethnographical stuff that wouldn't fit into any other museum.

## Hallwylska Museet

Hamngatan 4, Norrmalm. Tues–Sun noon–4pm, Wed till 7pm; 50kr.

Guided tours only (in English at 1pm on Sunday; ring for details of possible English tours at other times) around this private collection of the Countess von Hallwyl, whose middle name was not discrimination. Eceletic is hardly the word – paintings, silver, porcelain, weapons, furniture, tapestries and the kitchen sink.

## Hologram Grottan

Rörstrandsgatan 27; regional *pendeltåg* to Karlberg. Mon–Fri noon–6pm, Sat 10am–2pm; free.

Set in a cave, disembodied limbs and faces loom out of the wall as you walk round: only the first hologram is unsettling; the twentieth is totally unimpressive.

## Junibacken

Galärparken, Djurgården; bus #44 or #47. Tues & Sun 10am–8pm, Wed–Sat 10am–6pm; 75kr, children 55kr.

A family museum based on the stories of the writer Astrid Lindgren.

## Liljevachs Konsthall

Djurgårdsvägen 60; bus #44 or #47 or ferry from Skeppsbron (year round) or Nybroplan (summer only). Tues & Thurs 11am–8pm, Wed, Fri, Sat & Sun 11am–5pm; 40kr.

A difficult one to pigeonhole. Constantly changing exhibitions revolve around modern art, everything from photographs of naked men to sculpture displays, Swedish and international. One of the best times to visit is in February and March when the Spring Salon selects and displays the winners of the annual art competition. Consistently good; you may have to queue to get in. The excellent café next door makes this one a must for a Sunday afternoon.

## Marionettmuseet

Brunnsgatan 6, Norrmalm; T-bana Hötorget or Östermalmstorg. Tues–Sun 1–4pm; 15kr.

A dull collection of four thousand puppets, marionettes and associated mind-numbing paraphernalia, mainly from Asia. To be avoided.

## Postmuseum

Lilla Nygatan 6, Gamla Stan; T-bana Gamla Stan. Tues–Sun 11am–4pm; free.

Fans of Swedish stamp design will be in their element. Lesser beings will be bored rigid.

## Riksidrottsmuseet

Arenaslingan 5, Södermalm; T-bana Globen. Tues–Sun 11am–4pm; 20kr.

Famous Swedish sportsmen and sportswomen go through their paces on newsreel and in exhibition displays.

## Sjöhistoriska Museet

Djurgårdsbrunnsvägen 24; bus #69. Daily 10am–5pm; 30kr.

A glance into the Swedish fascination with the sea at this excellent Maritime Museum. Much is revealed of early boat building; there's a selection of scale models, some from the seventeenth century, and a perfunctory look at the modern Swedish navy, who are evidently proud of their torpedoes.

## Spårvägsmuseet

Tegelviksvägen 22; bus #46 from Slussen. Mon–Fri 10am–5pm; Sat & Sun 11am–4pm; 20kr.

SL's transport museum and a good one for children. Trams, buses and metro trains to poke at.

## Tekniska Museet

Museivägen 7, off Djurgårdsbrunnsvägen; bus #69. Mon–Fri 10am–4pm, Sat & Sun noon–4pm; 30kr.

Contains everything you'd expect of a museum of science and technology. If you drool at the prospect of bulky displays on iron production, the history of electricity and Swedish building technology, you'll be in seventh heaven (though nothing is marked in English). The museum also contains the **Teknorama** science centre and the **Telemuseum** (both same times), which deals with telecommunications, radio and television; in each there's a veritable haven of things to touch and buttons to press.

## Vin & Sprithistoriska Museet

Dalagatan 100; T-bana Odenplan. Tues 10am–7pm, Wed–Fri 10am–4pm, Sat & Sun noon–4pm; 30kr.

An unexpectedly fascinating place covering all aspects of wine-making and distilling processes. Worth visiting just for the mechanical sniffing cabinet, whereby you sniff one of the 55 spices used to flavour *akvavit*, guess what it is and press the button for confirmation. Needless to say in alcohol-obsessed Sweden, no free samples.

# Eating

**Eating out** in Stockholm needn't be expensive – observe a few rules and accept a few facts and you'll manage quite well. If money is tight, switch your main meal of the day to lunchtime, when almost every café and restaurant offers an excellent-value set menu, *Dagens Rätt*, for 50–60kr, though this is only Monday to Friday. In the evening look around for the best deals, but don't necessarily assume that Italian and Chinese places will be the least expensive; more often than not they're overpriced and the food is tasteless. Having said that, alongside the usual range of Mediterranean- and American-style food on offer, there are plenty of other good foreign food restaurants – particularly Japanese and Thai – among the many traditional Swedish places. In fact the latest culinary craze in Stockholm is for "crossover" dishes, a blend of Swedish cooking with other world cuisines that can lead to some surprising and delicious combinations.

## Breakfast, snacks, markets and supermarkets

Stockholmers don't really go out for **breakfast**, and there are very few early-morning eating places. If your hotel or hostel doesn't do breakfast, *Köket och en bar* in Norrmalm is a good option (see overleaf), or if you want to really fill up, try the restaurant at the Central Station, which lays out a large buffet between 6.30am and 10am daily; it's 50kr per person and good value at that. If you just want a cheap light meal or **snack**, you are best off avoiding burgers: at *McDonalds* you'll pay around 40kr for a large burger and fries – only 10kr less than the *Dagens Rätt* at lunchtime elsewhere. However, *McDonalds* and the Swedish equivalent, *Clock Burger*, are good for coffee, which is less costly than at most cafés. When the nibbles strike, it's much cheaper to pick up a *korv*, a grilled or fried sausage in bread for 10–15kr, from one of the many street vendors. In general, Stockholm hasn't got that many daytime cafés, where you can sit over coffee and cake and just watch the world go by. To save lots of tramping round it's worth noting the best ones before you set out for the day: *Wayne's* in the city centre; *Saturnas* in Östermalm; and in Södermalm *Indigo*, the studenty *String* and *Lasse i Parken* (for addresses see the listings on pp.86–89).

### Markets and supermarkets

Of the indoor **markets** (both closed Sun), Hötorgshallen in Hötorget (see p.75) is cheaper and more varied than Östermalmshallen in Östermalmstorg (see p.77). The former is awash with small cafés and ethnic snacks, but be sure to buy your fruit and veg outside, where it's less expensive. The latter is posher and downright expensive, with all kinds of unusual eats. It's pleasant for a wander, but you'll find most things at lower prices in the city's biggest **supermarket** in the basement of *Åhléns* department store at Sergels Torg. There are also several other central supermarkets: try *Konsum* in Järntorget and *Metro* in the underground arcade at Sergels Torg – although neither will be particularly cheap. If you're out in the suburbs look out for *Vivo* supermarkets – the cheapest chain in Sweden.

Other good places for **fruit and veg** are the summer stalls outside most T-bana stations, especially in the suburbs; two more central and year-round options are outside Slussen and Brommaplan T-bana.

# Cafés and restaurants

The main areas for decent eating, day or night, are the city-centre triangle marked out by Norrmalmstorg, Birger Jarlsgatan and Stureplan, Grev Turegatan in Öster-malm, and around Folkungagatan, Skånegatan and Bondegatan in Södermalm. In Kungsholmen, restaurants are more spread out so you need to know your destination before you set off. Several restaurants in Gamla Stan are also worth checking out, though they tend to be expensive. For the best choice of price and eating place head south for Södermalm, here you'll find more trendy and chic **cafés** and **restaurants** and a broader range of cuisines. In the listings below, we have given the following guide to cost: **inexpensive** means you can get a main dish for under 80kr, **moderate** means that main dishes cost between 80kr and 120kr, and **expensive** that they are over 120kr.

Some of the places below also appear in the "Drinking, nightlife and culture" section, as there's a fairly fine line between cafés, restaurants and bars in the whole of Sweden, not just in Stockholm, many offering music and entertainment in the evening as well as food throughout the day.

## Norrmalm

**Biblos**, Biblioteksgatan 9. A wonderfully trendy spot right in the centre of town – a good place to observe. Smoked salmon from 85kr.

**Birger Bar**, Birger Jarlsgatan 5. If you're a pasta freak this is the place – excellent, cheap pasta until it comes out of your ears. Always busy.

**East**, Stureplan 13. One of the city's finest restaurants. Trendy to a T and excellent food – lots of fish and Asian-style dishes – but expensive: lunch 74–106kr; dinner around 150kr.

**Enzo & Matilde**, Birger Jarlsgatan 9. A wonderful little Italian place tucked away in Birger Jarlspassagen; run by a lively Italian woman, who serves up delicious home-made spinach and salmon lasagne and other pasta treats. Moderate.

**Fredsgatan 12**, Fredsgatan 12. A delicious mix of Swedish and international cuisine, though on the expensive side. Check out the summer outside bar – it's 5m long.

**Hus1**, Sveavägen 57. If you want to eat among other gay people, this is the place to come; unfortunately the food is rarely up to much and too pricey for what it is (for more on gay Stockholm see p.93).

**KB**, Smålandsgatan 7. Excellent Swedish food in posh surroundings and a favourite haunt of authors and artists. Very expensive.

**Köket och en bar**, Sturegallerian 30. Very popular place for eats when the nightclubs have turned out – open from 8pm till 6.30am – but quite pricey.

**Lao Wai**, Luntmakargtan 74. This was Sweden's first East Asian restaurant and is decidedly good, though not especially cheap.

**Leonardo**, Sveavägen 55. Some of the tastiest pizzas (with the only wood-burning oven in town) and pasta in Stockholm – always fresh and delicious. Moderate.

**Operakällaren**, Operahuset, Gustav Adolfs Torg. A bill at the famous Opera House restaurant will seriously damage your wallet (starters from 150kr) but the daily *Smörgåsbord* (Mon–Sat 11.30am–3pm, Sun noon–6pm) is fabulous and just about affordable – around 250kr per person for a spread beyond compare. Otherwise the daily lunch in *Café Opera* around the back is about 100kr.

**Peppar**, Torsgatan 34. Attractive Cajun restaurant with decent-sized portions. Expensive.

**Prinsen**, Mäster Samuelsgatan 4. Old and traditional place frequented by artists and musicians and the like.Very expensive.

**Rolfs Kök**, Tegnérgatan 41. Popular central restaurant close to Hötorget with a special line in Asian and Cajun stir-fried food; fairly expensive prices.

**Sawadee**, Olofsgatan 6. Next to Hötorget T-bana. Attractive Thai restaurant with a wonderful 150kr special dinner and reasonably priced drinks.

**Svea Bar & Matsal**, Sveavägen 53, just by Rådmansgatan T-bana. Excellent place for a cheap and filling lunch around 60kr. Set menus in the evenings with dishes for around 100kr; cheap beer.

**Wayne's**, Kungsgatan 14. A popular café for smart city types, who pretend to be reading foreign newspapers whilst sipping cappuccinos.

## Östermalm

**Aubergine**, Linnégatan 38. An upmarket and expensive place on one of Östermalm's busiest streets. Lots of wood and glass. The separate bar menu brings things within reach – chicken on a skewer for 85kr is good.

**Berns**, Berzelii Park, Nybroplan. One of the chicest places to eat in town. Made famous by writer August Strindberg, who picked up character ideas here for his novel, *The Red Room*. Moderately priced international food under a huge chandelier.

**Grevens Bakficka**, Grev Turegatan 7. Affordable and cosy place for lunch with pork for 82kr, plaice 95kr and around 100kr for a string of other dishes.

**Grodan**, Grev Turegatan 16. Swedish for "the frog", hence the name *La Grenouille* on the outside, and a favourite haunt for many Stockholmers. French cuisine at moderate prices.

**Gröna Linjen**, Mäster Samuelsgatan 10, 2nd floor. A nineteenth-century building housing Scandinavia's oldest vegetarian restaurant. There's a good buffet here, too. Moderate.

**IKKI**, Grev Turegatan 7. A very popular Japanese restaurant, especially at lunchtime. Lots of fish and things grilled on skewers. Moderate.

**Il Conte**, Grev Turegatan 16. Rumoured to be the best Italian in town. The pasta is excellent and very good value.

**Mikael Mat & Dryck**, Karlavägen 73. Good tasty Swedish home cooking at excellent prices.

**PA & Co**, Riddargatan 8. Trendsetting fashionable restaurant with international dishes, some good old Swedish favourites and a few inventive "crossovers". Moderate.

**Samuraj**, Kommendörsgatan 40. A good Japanese place known for its fine food and friendly staff. Expensive.

**Saturnus**, Erikbergsgatan 6. Good, moderately priced pasta, huge cakes and massive sandwiches – a café that becomes a restaurant in the evening.

**Stolen**, Sibyllegatan, close to T-bana exit at Östermalmstorg. The name means "chair" after the dozens of different chairs in the restaurant. Good Italian-style food at reasonable prices – the chicken dishes are especially delicious.

**Vassilis Taverna**, Valhallavägen 131. Stockholmers say this is the best Greek restaurant in town – try the moussaka, which slips down a treat. Moderate.

**Wedholms Fisk**, Nybrokajen 17. Expensive but classy fish restaurant.

**Örtagården**, Nybrogatan 31. Top-notch vegetarian restaurant, with veggies dished up under a huge chandelier and in turn-of-the-century surroundings. Dozens of different salads, warm dishes and soups. Expensive.

## Gamla Stan

**Bistro Ruby**, Österlånggatan 14. French bistro in the heart of the Old Town, tastefully done out in Parisian style, but pricey. Main dishes go for around 150kr; there's a wide selection of beers.

**Eriks**, Österlånggatan 17. One of the best places in the Old Town – good food at moderate prices – and very popular as a result.

**De Fyras Krog**, Järntorgsgatan 5. As good a place as any to eat traditional Swedish food – choose between the posh, more expensive restaurant or the simple farmhouse-style bit.

**Den Gyldene Freden**, Österlånggatan 51. Stockholm's oldest restaurant, "The Golden Peace" was opened in 1772; expect to pay around 350kr for just two courses, without drinks, but the atmosphere, food and style are unparalleled in Stockholm.

**Hermans Hermitage**, Stora Nygatan 11. Vegetarian restaurant well worth checking out for hearty dishes. Open Mon–Sat till 8pm, Sun to 7pm. Moderate.

**Krokodil**, Österlånggatan 7. A good lunch place with a wide and varied menu – reasonable prices.

**Lilla Karachi**, Lilla Nygatan 12. Pakistani restaurant with vegetarian options and moderate prices; an interesting change for Stockholm, housed in some of Gamla Stan's old cellar vaults.

**Mårten Trotzig**, Västerlånggatan 79. A classic known throughout Sweden for its excellent and stylish food – lovely setting attracting luvvies and business types from across Stockholm. Very expensive.

**Skitiga Duken**, Stora Nygatan 35. The name means "dirty tablecloth" – a great little Italian place. Moderate.

## Södermalm

**Blå Dörren**, Södermalmstorg 6. Beer hall and restaurant with excellent, but expensive, Swedish food.

**Bonden Mat & Bar**, Bondegatan 1C. Small and cosy restaurant with rough brick walls; try the delicious fillet of chicken with oyster mushrooms in red wine sauce and potato gratin – a winner every time. Moderate.

**Bröderna Olssons**, Folkungagatan 84. If you like garlic this is the place for you, with every conceivable dish laced with the white stuff. Expensive.

**Creperie Fyra Knop**, Svartensgatan 4. A rare treat in Stockholm – excellent crepes and affordable prices: all around 50kr.

**Dilan**, Nytorget 6. Kurdish restaurant on the south side of the island where the food comes as spicy as you like it – the *kofteg* and lamb cutlets are particularly good. Inexpensive.

**Dionysos**, Bondegatan 56. Over-the-top Greek decor gives this place a friendly feel, and the food is excellent: moussaka for 85kr, chicken souvlaki for 70kr.

**Ett Rum och Kök II**, Blekingegatan 63A. Nothing more than one tiny room and a kitchen serving up French food. Try the salmon with spinach in lime sauce or the fillet of goose. Closed Sun. Expensive.

**Hannas Krog**, Skånegatan 80. A firm favourite and popular haunt of Söder trendies with a mooing cow's head to greet you just inside the entrance. It's crowded and noisy with lunch deals for 58kr, evening dishes for around 100–150kr. Also a popular drinking haunt; see p.91.

**Hosteria Tre Santi**, Blekingegatan 32. One of Södermalm's better Italian restaurants and excellent value for money – always busy.

**Indigo**, Götgatan near exit from Slussen T-bana. The ideal place to stop off for an afternoon cappuccino. Good pastries, too – the carrot cake is a house speciality. Small evening menu. Moderate.

**Indira**, Bondegatan 3B. The area's biggest Indian restaurant, with a good tandoori-based menu. Takeaway food also. Inexpensive.

**Kvarnen**, Tjärhovsgatan 4. Small beer hall with simple Swedish food – lunch for only 40kr. Evening dishes, fish and meat, for 80–90kr.

**Lasse i Parken**, Högalidsgatan 56. Café housed in an eighteenth-century house with a pleasant garden that's very popular in summer; also handy for the beaches at Långholmen. Moderate.

**Mellis**, Skånegatan 83–85. Another popular restaurant on this busy restaurant street. Greek, French and Swedish dishes – reasonable prices. A nice place for coffee and cakes, too.

**Mosebacke**, Mosebacke Torg 3. The place to come of a sunny lunchtime: sit outside and enjoy views over the harbour and the old town. The salmon is particularly good. Expensive.

**Pelikan**, Blekingegatan 40. Atmospheric, working-class Swedish beer hall with excellent traditional food, *pytt i panna* for 58kr.

**Sjögräs**, Timmermansgatan 24. A modern approach to Swedish cuisine, influenced by world cuisines; always packed. Moderate.

**Snaps/Rangus Tangus**, Medborgarplatsen. Good old-fashioned Swedish food in a three-hundred-year-old building. Very popular. Expensive.

**Soldaten Svejk**, Östgötagatan 15. Lively Czech-run joint that draws in a lot of students. Simple menu around the 100kr mark. Large selection of Czech beers; Pilsner Urquell for 39kr.

**Spisen**, Renstiernas Gata 30. Another trendy hang-out in the heart of Söder's restaurant land with emphasis on nouvelle cuisine; lunch 58kr; try the delicious pecan smoked breast of chicken with lemon. Moderate.

**String**, Nytorgsgatan 38. If you fancy yourself as a brilliant new writer, or if you just fancy yourself, you'll fit in well in this studenty café. Adopt a ponderous air. Good for moderately priced cakes and snacks.

**Tre Indier**, Möregatan 2. Slightly tucked away in a tiny street off Åsögatan (take bus #55 in the direction of Södra Hammarbyhamnen), but well worth hunting out. A lively Indian restaurant with adjoining bar. Also a very popular bar here; see *7:e himlen*, p.91. Moderate.

**Österns Pärla**, Götgatan 62. Reasonable Chinese food, around 80kr a dish.

## Kungsholmen

**Helmers**, Scheelegatan 12. Without a doubt the best restaurant on Kungsholmen. Southern American food with lots of Cajun spices. Very trendy and very busy. Expensive.

**Hong Kong**, Kungbrostrand 23. A popular good-value Chinese restaurant.

**La Famiglia**, Alströmergatan 45. One of Kungsholmen's better Italian places and a good one for that first date. Expensive.

**Mamas & Tapas**, Scheelegatan 3. Delicious reasonably priced Spanish food that deservedly attracts people from across Stockholm.

**Salt**, Hantverkaregatan 34. On the island's main road, it serves stodgy traditional Swedish fare. Salt is no bad name either – drink a lot of water if you're eating the slabs of pork they serve up. Inexpensive.

**Vildsvin M Fl**, corner of Flemingatan & Agnegatan. The name means "wild boar and more" – a Basque-run restaurant with a delicious and original menu from that region. Expensive.

# Drinking, nightlife and culture

There's plenty to keep you occupied in Stockholm, from pubs, gigs and clubs to the cinema and theatre. In the bars and pubs, there's a good **live music** scene, but you'll generally have to pay a cover charge of around 60–80kr. Also, if you don't want to feel scruffy, wear something other than jeans and training shoes – many places won't let you in dressed like that anyway. Be prepared too to cough up around 10kr to leave your coat at the cloakroom, a requirement at many bars as well as at discos and pubs, and particularly so in winter. Apart from the weekend, Wednesday night is an active time in Stockholm, with usually lots going on and queues to get into the more popular places. Swedes, and especially Stockholmers, are fairly reserved, so don't expect to immediately get chatting to people – in fact it is positively fashionable to be cool and aloof. However, after a few drinks, it's usually easy enough to strike up conversation.

For **information** on what's on and if your Swedish is up to it, there's a free monthly paper, *Nöjesguiden*, that details all manner of entertainment – from the latest films to a club guide. You'll see it in bars and restaurants; pick up a copy and get someone to translate. In summer, look out for a similar guide in English, *N&D*. Other useful sources of information are the special Saturday supplement of the *Dagens Nyheter* newspaper, *På Stan*. Also, the latest issue of *Stockholm This Week*, free from the tourist office, is particularly good for arts listings. It contains day-by-day information about a whole range of events – gigs, theatre, festivals, dance – sponsored by the city, many of which are free and based around Stockholm's many parks. Popular venues in summer are Kungsträdgården and Skansen, where there's always something going on.

One of Stockholm's most popular events is the **Stockholm Water Festival**, a ten-day annual jamboree held in August and featuring open-air gigs, street parties, fishing contests, exhibitions, sailing displays and children's activities; it closes with a stunning firework display. The tourist office has more specific details about each year's events. If you're planning your stay to coincide with the festival, book accommodation in advance. You'll also have to sharpen your elbows and prepare to forge your way through the crowds that briefly transform Stockholm into a bustling city. Luckily the change is but brief.

# Bars, brasseries and pubs

The scourge of Swedish nightlife – high alcohol prices – is gradually being neutralized due to increased competition. Over recent years, there's been a veritable explosion in the number of bars and pubs in Stockholm, in particular Irish theme pubs. **Beer prices** have dropped considerably and, on Södermalm especially, there are some very good deals. Look on the bright side, though: you no longer need a bank loan to see you through a night out in Stockholm, and Swedish beer is stronger than the stuff you're likely to be used to drinking. **Happy hours** at various places also throw up some bargains – watch out for signs outside bars and pubs advertising their particular times.

Although there are a lot more places to drink than there used to be, it's still the case that the majority of Stockholmers do their drinking and eating together, and several of the places listed below are first and foremost cafés and restaurants. Nonetheless, if you do want to do some serious drinking the capital certainly has enough establishments to choose from, and nearly all are open seven days a week.

### Norrmalm and Östermalm

**Bryggeriet Landbyska Verket**, Birger Jarlsgatan 24. Cheap beer that attracts Stockholm's lads; very busy.

**Café Opera**, Opera House, Gustav Adolfs Torg. If your Katherine Hamnett gear isn't too crushed and you can stand just one more Martini, join the queue outside. Daily till 3am.

**Dubliners**, Smålandsgatan 8. One of the busiest Irish pubs in town with live music most evenings.

**East Bar**, Stureplan. Loud music, loud dress and loud mouths. Great fun.

**Lydmar**, Sturegatan 10. Definitely one of the most popular bars in Stockholm – and very elegant. Dress up a little to get in past the beefcake bouncers.

**Mushrooms**, Nybroplan 6. An ugly low-level building hidden away at Nybroplan, but full to bursting with loud happy drinkers.

**Sturecompagniet**, Sturegatan 4. Three floors of bars; something for everybody and worth a look. Expensive beer.

**Svea Bar & Matsal**, Sveavägen by exit to Rådmansgatan T-bana. Cheap beer and a upbeat atmosphere from early evening onwards.

**Tranan**, Karlbergsvägen 14. Pricy French restaurant upstairs, but downstairs there's an atmospheric old workers' beer hall.

**Trap Bar**, Engelbrektsgatan 3. A tiny place that soon gets packed and very claustrophobic.

### Gamla Stan

**Gråmunken**, Västerlånggatan 18. Cosy café-pub, usually busy and sometimes with live music to jolly things along.

**Magnus Ladulås**, Österlånggatan 26. Rough brick walls and low ceilings make this bar-cum-restaurant an appealing place for a drink or two.

**Mårten Trotzig**, Västerlånggatan 79. Smart surroundings for an early evening drink before dinner – wear your finest garb.

## Södermalm

**Fenix**, Götgatan 40. A cheap and nasty American-style bar that's always busy and noisy.

**Gröne Jägaren**, Medborgarplatsen. Some of the cheapest beer in Stockholm; *storstark* 24kr until 9pm – perhaps inevitably the clientele tend to get raucously drunk.

**Hannas Krog**, Skånegatan 80. A good place for a drink before eating in the same excellent restaurant.

**Kvarnen**, Tjärhovsgatan 4. Another busy beer hall – a favourite haunt of southside football fans.

**O'Learys**, Götgatan 11–13. Södermalm's most popular Irish pub – great fun and good for stumbling back to the nearby T-bana at Slussen.

**Pelikan**, Blekingegatan 40. A fantastic old beer hall full of character – and characters.

**7:e himlen**, on the corner of Åsögatan & Möregatan. In the same building as the *Tre Indier* Indian restaurant and very popular with southside trendies. The name means "seventh heaven".

**Sjögräs**, Timmermansgatan 24. A wonderful local little bar that is always busy and lively.

**WC**, Skånegatan 51. Very busy at weekends with people from across town – handy for the restaurants around Skånegatan and Blekingegatan.

# Live music: rock and jazz

Apart from the cafés and bars already listed, there's no shortage of specific venues that put on **live music**. Most of these will be local bands, for which you'll pay around 60–70kr entrance, but nearly all the big names make it to Stockholm, playing at a variety of seated halls and stadiums – tickets for these are, of course, much more expensive. The **main large venues** are the *Stockholm Globe Arena* (supposedly the largest spherical building in the world); *Johanneshov* (T-bana Gullmarsplan; ☎600 34 00); *Konserthuset* in Hötorget (☎10 21 10); and the *Isstadion*, to the north of Östermalm (☎600 34 00) – ring for programme details or ask at the tourist offices.

**African Centre**, inside Rådhuset T-bana station, Norrmalm. Regular African and reggae gigs in this cavernous Algerian-run club; discos until 3am and beyond when there's no band.

**Cirkus**, Djurgården. Occasional rock and R&B performances.

**Cityhallen**, Drottninggatan 28, Norrmalm. A big bright bar-restaurant with live Nordic rock and R&B nightly; cheapish food and drink, too.

**Engelen**, Kornhamnstorg 59, Gamla Stan. Live jazz, rock or blues nightly until 3am, but arrive early to get in; the music starts at 8.30pm (Sun 9pm).

**Gino**, Birger Jarlsgatan 27, Norrmalm. Catch Swedish and international bands perform at one of the city's top music venues.

**Fasching**, Kungsgatan 63, Norrmalm. Local and foreign contemporary jazz; also a place to go dancing; see overleaf. Open Mon–Sat.

**Hard Rock Café**, Sveavägen 75. R&B bands (often American) several times per week.

**Kaos**, Stora Nygatan 21, Gamla Stan. Live music from 9pm nightly; rock bands on Fri and Sat in the cellar; and reasonable late-night food.

**Melody**, Kungsträdgården, Norrmalm. Part of the *Dagens Nyheter* complex, this central rock venue hosts the most consistent range of live contemporary music in town – everything from grunge to techno-influenced outfits.

**Mosebacke Etablissement**, Mosebacke Torg 3, Södermalm. Music and cabaret venue, putting on anything from jazz and swing to folk gigs and stand-up comedy.

**Stampen**, Stora Nygatan 5, Gamla Stan. Long-established and rowdy jazz club, both trad and mainstream; occasional foreign names, too.

**Tre Backar**, Tegnérgatan 12–14, Norrmalm; T-bana Rådmansgatan. Good, cheap pub with a live cellar venue. Music every night Mon–Sat; open until midnight.

# Clubs

The **club scene** in Stockholm is limited, and several places are also restaurants – where you have to eat – and bars. Cover charges aren't too high at around 40–50kr, but beer gets more expensive as the night goes on, reaching as much as 50kr. In Stockholm, as in the rest of Sweden, there is very little real crossover with the gay scene and none of the following clubs have mixed nights – for more on gay Stockholm see opposite.

**Abstrakt**, Gamla Brogatan 46, Norrmalm. A hang-out for trendy transvestites and other chic people about town. Atmosphere varies from risque to downright suggestive.

**Aladdin**, Barnhusgatan 12–14, Norrmalm. One of the city's most popular dance restaurants close to the Central Station – live bands often performing. An expensive night out.

**Fasching**, Kungsgatan 63, Norrmalm. Dancing to live jazz music from midnight onwards.

**G-klubben**, Skeppsbrokajen, Tullhus 2. Fri night is trendy people night – don't dance too much or your sweat stains will make you unattractive to the other beautiful people.

**King Creole**, Kungsgatan 18, Norrmalm. Mainstream disco worth checking out for nostalgia value – regular blasts from anything from Big Band to 1960s sounds.

**Patricia**, Stadsgårdskajen, Slussen, Södermalm. A former royal yacht for Britain's Queen Mother, today a restaurant-disco-bar with fantastic views of the city out across the harbour and Swedish stand-up comedy nights. The food is quite simply fantastic. Wed–Sun; gay on Sun (see opposite).

**Sturecompagniet**, Sturegatan 4, Norrmalm. Strut to house and techno and a fantastic light show – also three floors of bars. Very popular.

# Classical music, theatre and cinema

**Classical music** is always easy to find in Stockholm. Many museums – particularly Historiska Museet and Musikmuseet – have regular programmes; there's generally something on at *Konserthuset* in Hötorget, Norrmalm (☎10 21 10); *Berwaldhallen*, Strandvägen 69, Östermalm (☎784 18 00); *Gamla Musikaliska Akademien*, Blasieholmstorg 8, near the National Art Museum (☎20 68 18) and *Myntet*, Hantverkargatan 5 (☎652 03 10).

If you're after **church music**, you'll find it in Norrmalm at Adolf Fredriks kyrka (lunchtime), St Jakobs kyrka (Sat at 3pm) and Johannes kyrka; and in Gamla Stan at Storkyrkan. For more details consult *Stockholm This Week*.

The main **Opera House**, *Operan* (☎24 82 40), is Sweden's most famous operatic venue, though for less rarefied presentations of the classics, check the programme at *Folkoperan*, Hornsgatan 72, Södermalm (☎658 53 00).

## Theatre and cinema

There are dozens of **theatres** in Stockholm, but only one has regular performances of **English-language productions**: the *Regina*, Drottninggatan 71 (☎20 70 00), which features touring plays – tickets and more information from the theatre. If you want tickets for anything else theatrical, it's often worth waiting for reduced-price standby tickets, available from the kiosk in Norrmalmstorg.

**Cinemas** are incredibly popular, with screenings of new releases nearly always full. The largest venue in the city centre is *Filmstaden* in Hötorget, but there's also a good number of cinemas along the entire length of Kungsgatan between

Sveavägen and Birger Jarlsgatan, a very lively street on Saturday night. Tickets cost around 70kr and films are thankfully *never* dubbed into Swedish.

Finally **Kulturhuset** in Sergels Torg has a full range of artistic and cultural events – mostly free – and the information desk on the ground floor has programmes to give away.

# Gay Stockholm

Given that Stockholm is a capital city, the **gay scene** is disappointingly small and closeted. Attitudes in general are tolerant but you won't see gay couples walking hand in hand or kissing in the street – just one of the false perceptions of Sweden. Until just a few years ago, when the country freed itself from tax rules imposed on bars and restaurants, there was only one gay place in the whole of the city. Thankfully, today things have changed, and bars are springing up all over the place. Unfortunately, though, a kneejerk reaction by the government with the advent of AIDS has forced all gay saunas to close. The four main **bars** and **clubs** to be seen at – and to definitely do the seeing – are listed below. However, they are all mostly male hang-outs; lesbians in Stockholm have an even lower profile, and even the beaches listed below are male only.

You can find the latest information from *Hus1* on Sveavägen 57. *Hus 1* is the city's main gay centre; the offices above house Sweden's **gay rights group**, *Riksförbundet för sexuellt likaberättigande (RFSL)* – the National Association for Sexual Equality – which is a great source of knowledge (☎736 02 12). They also offer HIV advice (☎736 02 11); run a free newspaper, *Kom Ut;* a bookshop, *Rosa Rummet*; a restaurant, bar and club (see below and p.86) and a radio station. **Gay Pride Week** is the second week of August and centres on special events run by *Hus1*.

## Bars and clubs

**Gossip**, Sveavägen 36; T-bana Hötorget. A huge club on two floors with lots of dark little corners – great fun. Also an outdoor café in summer. Be there on Thurs, Fri and Sat.

**Hus1**, Sveavägen 57; T-bana Rådmansgatan (pronounced "hoos-et" meaning "the house"; ☎30 83 38 & 31 34 80). Stockholm's main gay mens' venue – a club, restaurant and bar all rolled into one – and very popular, especially on Fri and Sat nights. Open daily.

**Klubb Häktet**, Hornsgatan 82; T-bana Zinkensdamm. A wonderful place with two bars, front and back as well as a quiet sitting room and a beautiful outdoor courtyard – a real haven in summer. Very popular on Wed nights, especially with women. Also open Mon, Tues and Fri to Sun.

**Patricia**, Stadsgårdskajen; T-bana Slussen. The Queen Mother's former royal yacht attracts queens and more from across Stockholm for fun on Sun evenings (no entrance fee). Eat before you groove – a great place for romantic evenings staring out across the harbour. Often hosts drag acts or stand-up comedy.

## Gay beaches

**Freskati**, T-bana Universitetet. Turn left out of the underground station, past *Pressbyrån*, walk under the bridge and towards the trees. A popular sunbathing spot.

**Kärsön**, T-bana Brommapla, then buses #301–323 towards Drottningholm palace. Get off at the stop over the bridge and take the path to the right along the water's edge. If you want to sunbathe nude and swim in Lake Mälaren, this island is the place to come; woodpeckers in the trees, deer in the forest and people dozing in the sunshine; a truly wonderful place.

# Listings

**Airlines** *Aer Lingus*, Dalagatan 3 (☎24 93 26); *Aeroflot*, Sveavägen 20 (☎21 70 07); *Air France*, Norrmalmstorg 16 (☎679 88 55); *Air New Zealand*, Kungsbron 1G (☎21 91 80); *American Airlines* at Arlanda airport (☎24 61 45); *British Airways*, Hamngatan 11 (☎679 78 00); *Cathay Pacific* at Arlanda airport (☎797 85 80); *Delta Airlines*, Kungsgatan 18 (☎796 96 00); *Finnair*, Norrmalmstorg 1 (☎679 93 30); *Icelandair*, Kungstensgatan 38 (☎31 02 40); *KLM* and *Northwest* at Arlanda airport (☎59 36 24 30); *Lufthansa*, Norrmalmstorg 1 (☎611 22 88); *Malmö Aviation* (☎020/55 00 10); *SAS* Stureplan 8 (international ☎020/72 75 55; domestic ☎020/72 70 00); *Singapore Airlines*, Grev Turegatan 10 (☎611 71 31); *Transwede*, Vasagatan 36 (☎020/22 52 25); *Qantas*, Kungsgatan 64 (☎24 25 02); *United Airlines*, Kungsgatan 3 (☎678 15 70).

**Airports** Arlanda airport (☎797 60 00); *SAS* flight enquiries at Arlanda (☎797 30 30, other airlines ☎797 61 00); Bromma airport (☎797 68 00).

**American Express** Birger Jarlsgatan 1 (☎679 52 00); Mon–Fri 9am–5pm.

**Banks and exchange** Banks are generally open later in central Stockholm than in the rest of the country – Mon–Fri 9.30am–3pm, though some stay open until 5.30pm; the bank at Arlanda is open longer hours, and there's also a cashpoint machine in the departures hall. *Forex* exchange offices offer better value than the banks and are in: the main hall at Central Station (☎411 67 34) and downstairs in the T-bana area (☎24 46 02); Cityterminalen (☎21 42 80); Vasagatan 14 (☎10 49 90); in Sverigehuset (☎20 03 89); and at Arlanda airport Terminal 2 (☎59 36 22 71). Also try *Valutaspecialisten* at Kungsgatan 30 (☎10 30 00) and at Arlanda Terminal 5 (☎797 85 57).

**Beaches** City beaches are Långholmens Strandbad and Klippbad on Långholmen – T-bana Hornstull; Smedsudden on Kungsholmen – bus #62 from Central Station towards Fredhäll, get off at Västerbroplan; Hellasgården lake in Nacka – bus #401 from Slussen; Saltsjöbaden – take the Saltsjöbanan train from Slussen; good sandy beaches in the archipelago on the island of Grinda (see p.101) – boats from Strömkajen.

**Bookshops** *Akademibokhandeln*, corner of Regeringsgatan & Mäster Samuelsgatan; *Rönnells* secondhand bookshop, Klarabergsgatan 50; *Aspingtons* secondhand bookshop, Västerlånggatan 54; *Hedengrens Bokhandel*, Sturegallerian, Stureplan 4; *Sweden Bookshop*, Sverigehuset, Hamngatan 27.

**Buses** For *SL* bus information see "*SL* travel information" below; for long-distance bus information call *Swebus* (☎020/64 06 40) or *Swenska Buss* (☎020/67 67 67).

**Car rental** *Avis*, Sveavägen 61 (☎34 99 10), Vasagatan 16 (☎20 20 60), Arlanda airport (☎59 51 15 00), general enquiries (☎020/78 82 00); *Budget*, Sveavägen 115 (☎33 43 83), Arlanda airport (☎797 84 70); *Europcar*, Vretenvägen 8, Solna (☎627 48 00), Arlanda airport (☎59 36 09 40), general enquiries (☎020/78 11 80); *Eurodollar*, Klarabergsgatan 33 (☎24 26 55); *Hertz*, Vasagatan 26 (☎24 07 20), Arlanda airport (☎797 99 00), general enquiries (☎020/21 12 11); *Holiday Autos* at *Eurodollar* offices (see above); also a desk at Arlanda airport.

**Car trouble** If you need towing call *Larmtjänst* (☎020/22 00 00).

**Dental problems** Emergency dental care at St Eriks Hospital, Fleminggatan 22; daily 8am–7pm. After 9pm ring the duty dentist (☎644 92 00).

**Doctor** Tourists can get emergency outpatient care at the hospital for the district they are staying in; check with the *Medical Care Information* (☎644 92 00).

**Embassies and consulates** *Australia*, Sergels Torg 12 (☎613 29 00); *Canada*, Tegelbacken 4 (☎453 30 00); *Ireland*, Östermalmsgatan 97 (☎661 80 05); *New Zealand* – use the Australian Embassy; *UK*, Skarpögatan 6–8 (☎671 90 00); *US*, Strandvägen 101 (☎783 53 00).

**Emergencies** Ring ☎112 for police, ambulance or fire services.

**Ferries** Tickets for Finland from *Silja Line*, Stureplan or Värtahamnen (☎22 21 40), and *Viking Line*, Stadsgårdsterminalen (☎452 42 55); tickets for Estonia from *Estline*, Frihamnen (☎667 00 01); for Britain from *Scandinavian Seaways*, Birger Jarlsgatan (☎450 46 00); for Denmark and other lines in Europe from *Stena Line*, Kungsgatan 12–14 (☎14 14 75); for cruises from *Birka Cruises*, Södermalmstorg 2 (☎714 55 20); for the archipelago from *Waxholms Ångfartygs AB*, Strömkajen (☎679 58 30).

**Laundry** Self-service launderettes at Sturegatan 4 and St Eriksgatan 97; or try the youth hostels.

**Left luggage** Lockers at Central Station (from 20kr per day), the Cityterminalen bus station and the *Silja* and *Viking* ferry terminals. Central Station also has a left-luggage office (☎762 25 49).

**Lost property** Offices at Central Station (☎762 20 00); Police, Bergsgatan 39 (☎769 30 00); *SL*, Rådmansgatan T-bana station, Mon–Fri 10am–5pm (☎736 07 80).

**News in English** *Newsday* and *Europe Today* from BBC World Service can be heard on 89.6FM in Greater Stockholm at 6–7am. Radio Sweden also provides news in English, about Sweden only, on the same frequency at several times during the day (information on ☎784 74 00).

**Newspapers** Buy them at kiosks in Central Station, Cityterminalen or at the *Press Center*, with branches in the *Gallerian* shopping centre on Hamngatan and also at Sveavägen 52. Read them for free at Stadsbiblioteket (City Library), Sveavägen 73, or at Kulturhuset, Sergels Torg.

**Pharmacy** 24-hour service at *C W Scheele*, Klarabergsgatan 64 (☎24 82 80).

**Police** Headquarters at Agnegatan 33–37, Kungsholmen (☎401 00 00), but local city-centre police stations at Bryggargatan 19, Tulegatan 4 and Södermangatan 5 in the city centre.

**Post office** Main office at Vasagatan 28–34, Mon–Fri 8am–6.30pm, Sat 10am–2pm; for Poste Restante take your passport.

**Skiing** There are thirty downhill ski slopes in the county, most reached easily by public transport. More information from the tourist offices.

**SL travel information** Bus, T-bana and regional train (*pendeltåg*) information on ☎600 10 00. *SL Centers* at Sergels Torg, Mon–Fri 7am–6.30pm, Sat & Sun 10am–5pm; Slussen Mon–Fri 8am–6pm, Sat 8am–1pm; Gullmarsplan (Södermalm) Mon–Thurs 7.30am–6.30pm, Fri 7.30am–5.30pm; Tekniska Högskolan, Mon–Fri 7am–6.30pm, Sat 10am–3pm; Fridhemsplan (Kungsholmen) Mon–Fri 7am–6.30pm.

**STF** (*Svenska Turistföreningen*), Drottninggatan 31–33 (☎463 21 00). Information about Sweden's youth hostels, mountain huts, hiking trails, maps and youth hostel membership.

**Swimming pools** Outdoors at *Vandisbadet*, in Vanadislunden park, Sveavägen, and at *Eriksdalbadet*, Eriksdalslunden, Södermalm. Indoors at *Forsgrénskabadet*, Medborgarplatsen 2–4; *Centralbadet*, Drottninggatan 88; *Sturebadet* inside Sturegallerian shopping centre, Stureplan (also has masseurs); and at *Liljeholmsbadet*, Bergsunds Strand, Liljeholmen, where there's nude male-only swimming sessions on Fri, women-only Thurs; non-nude mixed sessions Tues, Wed and Sat.

**Systembolaget** Norrmalm: Klarabergsgatan 62; Regeringsgatan 55; Sveavägen 66; Vasgatan 25; Odengagan 58 & 92. Gamla Stan: Lilla Nygatan 18. Södermalm: Folkungagatan 56 & 101; Götagatan 132; inside Söderhallarna shopping centre in Medborgarplatsen.

**Toilets** Central public toilets in *Gallerian* shopping centre, *Åhléns* and *NK* department stores, T-Centralen and Cityterminalen.

**Train information** Tickets and information for domestic and international routes with *SJ* (Swedish State Railways) on ☎020/75 75 75; from abroad ring ☎08/696 75 40.

**Travel agents** *KILROY travels*, Kungsgatan 4 (☎23 45 15), and out at the University in Freskati at Universitetsvägen 9 (☎16 05 15), for discounted rail and air tickets and *ISIC* cards; *Ticket* Kungsgatan 60 (☎24 00 90); Sturegatan 8 (☎611 50 20); Sveavägen 42 (☎24 92 20); *Transalpinó Wasteels resor*, Birger Jarlsgatan 13 (☎679 98 70); for cheap flights also check the travel section of the main *Dagens Nyheter* newspaper.

# AROUND STOCKHOLM

Such are Stockholm's attractions, it's best to overlook the city's surroundings; yet after only a few kilometres the countryside becomes noticeably leafier, the islands less congested, the water brighter. As further temptation, some of the country's most fascinating sights are within easy reach, like the spectacular **Millesgården** sculpture museum and **Drottningholm**, Sweden's greatest royal palace. Further out is the little village of **Mariefred**, containing Sweden's other great castle, **Gripsholm** – and like Drottningholm, it's accessible by a fine boat ride on the waters of Lake Mälaren. Other trips in the stunning **archipelago** or to the university town of **Uppsala** really merit a longer stay, though it is possible to get there and back within a day.

To help cut travel costs, a Stockholm Card or *Turistkort* are valid on the bus, T-bana and regional train services within Greater Stockholm, but not on the more enjoyable boat services to Drottningholm or in the archipelago. The quickest way to get to Uppsala is by regional train from Central Station – both cards are valid as far as Märsta, from where you'll have to buy a supplementary ticket for the final part of the journey – though it only costs 50kr. There's also a summer boat service to Uppsala, stopping at medieval Sigtuna and the Baroque castle at Skokloster on the way; it leaves Stadshusbron, outside the City Hall on Kungsholmen, daily from mid-June to mid-August at 10am, arriving Sigtuna at 12.15pm, Skokloster at 1.10pm and finally turning into Uppsala at 5.30pm. Boats to Mariefred and Drottningholm also leave from Stadshusbron.

# Lidingö and Millesgården

**Lidingö**, where Stockholm's well-to-do live, is a residential, commuter island just northeast of the city centre, which you'll already have glimpsed if you arrived from Finland or Estonia by ferry, as they dock immediately opposite. It's worth a second look though: eagle eyes may have spotted, across the water, the tallest of the statues from the startling **Millesgården** at Carl Milles Väg 2 (daily 10am–5pm; 50kr), the outdoor sculpture collection of **Carl Milles** (1875–1955), one of Sweden's greatest sculptors and collectors. To get there, take the T-bana to Ropsten, then the rickety *Lidingöbanan* over the bridge to Torsvikstorg, then walk down Herserudsvägen.

The statues are seated on terraces carved from the island's steep cliffs, many of Milles's animated, classical figures perching precariously on soaring pillars, overlooking the distant harbour: ranked terraces of gods, angels and beasts. A huge *Poseidon* rears over the army of sculptures, the most remarkable of which, *God's Hand*, has a small boy delicately balanced on the outstretched finger of a monumental hand. If you've been elsewhere in Sweden much of the work may seem familiar, copies and casts of the originals adorning countless provincial towns. If this collection inspires, it's worth tracking down three other pieces by Milles in the capital – his statue of *Gustav Vasa* in the Nordic Museum on Djurgården and the *Orpheus Fountain* in Norrmalm's Hötorget. Also out at Nacka Strand (bus #404 from Slussen or *Waxholm* boat from Strömkajen), there's the magnificent *Gud på Himmelsbågen*, a claw-shaped vertical piece of steel topped with the figure of a boy, a stunning entrance marker to Stockholm harbour.

## Lidingöloppet

The island is also the venue for the world's biggest cross-country running race, the **Lidingöloppet**, held on the first Sunday in October. It's been going since 1965, the 30km course attracting an international field of around thirty thousand runners – quite a sight as they skip or crawl up and down the island's hills. For more information, or if you want to take part, ask the tourist office in Stockholm.

# Drottningholm and Birka

Even if your time in Stockholm is limited, try not to miss the harmonious royal palace of **Drottningholm** (May–Aug daily 11am–4.30pm; Sept Mon–Fri 1–3.30pm, Sat & Sun noon–3.30pm; 40kr), beautifully located on the shores of leafy Lovön island, 11km west of the centre. To get here take the lovely fifty-minute boat trip (see below).

Drottningholm is perhaps the greatest achievement of the architects **Tessin**, father and son. Work began in 1662 on the orders of King Karl X's widow, Eleonora, with Tessin the Elder modelling the new palace in a thoroughly French style – leading to the usual tedious descriptions of a Swedish Versailles. Apart from anything else, it's considerably smaller than its French contemporary, utilizing false perspective and *trompe l'oeil* to bolster the elegant, though rather narrow interior. On Tessin the Elder's death in 1681, the palace was completed by his son, already at work on Stockholm's Royal Palace. Inside good English notes are available to help you sort out each room's detail, a riot of Rococo decoration largely dating from the time when Drottningholm was bestowed as a wedding gift on Princess Louisa Ulrika (a sister of Frederick the Great of Prussia). No hints, however, are needed to spot the influence in the Baroque "French", and later "English", **gardens** that back onto the palace.

Since 1981 the Swedish royal family has slummed it out at Drottningholm, using the palace as a permanent home, a move that has accelerated efforts to restore parts of the palace to their original appearance – so that the monumental **Grand Staircase** is now exactly as envisaged by Tessin the Elder.

Another sight worth visiting is the **Court Theatre** (Slottsteater), which is nearby in the palace grounds (May–Aug daily noon–4.30pm; Sept 1–3.30pm; 40kr). It dates from 1766, but its heyday was a decade later when Gustav III imported French plays and acting troupes, making Drottningholm the centre of Swedish artistic life. Take a guided tour and you'll get a flowery but accurate account of the theatre's decoration: money to complete the building ran out in the eighteenth century, meaning that things are not what they seem – painted papier-maché frontages are krona-pinching substitutes for the real thing. The original backdrops and stage machinery are still in place, though, and the tour comes complete with a display of eighteenth-century special effects: wind and thunder machines, trapdoors and simulated lighting. If you're in luck you might catch a **performance** of drama, ballet or opera here (usually June–Aug). The cheapest **tickets** cost 95kr, though decent seats are more in the region of 260kr – check the schedule at Drottningholm or ask at the tourist offices in the city. You can book tickets by phone using *BiljettDirekt* (☎077/170 70 70) or call Drottningholm direct (☎08/660 82 25 or ☎660 82 81). You can also book from abroad by writing to *Drottningholms teatermuseum*, Föreställningar, Box 270 50, S-102 51, Stockholm, or by fax (☎08/665 14 73). With time to spare, the extensive palace grounds also yield the **Chinese Pavilion** (same hours as above), a sort of eighteenth-century royal summer house.

### Getting there

The finest way to reach Drottningholm is by **ferry**, which takes just under an hour each way (50kr one-way; 70kr return) and leaves daily every hour, on the hour, from Stadshusbron on Kungsholmen, to coincide with the opening times. Or take the T-bana to Brommaplan and then buses #301–323 from there – a less thrilling ride, but covered on the Stockholm Card or the *Turistkort*.

## Further into Lake Mälaren: Birka

**BIRKA**, on the island of **Björkö** (island of birches), is Sweden's oldest town and on the UNESCO World Heritage List. Founded in around 750AD, it was a Viking trading centre at its height during the tenth century. A few obvious remains lie scattered about, including the remnants of houses and a vast cemetery. Major excavations were carried out here from 1990 to 1995 and a museum, **Birka the Viking Town** (May to mid-Sept daily 10am–5pm; 185kr including boat trip to the island from Stockholm) now displays rare artefacts as well as scale models of the harbour and craftsmen's quarters.

Björkö is a green island in Lake Mälaren that is known for its rich flora, good beaches and ample swimming opportunities. To get there take the *Strömma Kanalbolaget* boat from Stadshusbron on Kungsholmen (May to mid-Sept daily 10am, return trip at 3.30pm from Birka; information on ☎08/23 33 75); you buy your ticket on board.

# The Archipelago

If you arrived in Stockholm by ferry from Finland or Estonia, you'll already have had a tantalizing glimpse of the **Stockholm archipelago**. In Swedish the word for archipelago is *skärgården* (pronounced "share-gord-en") – literally "garden of skerries" and a pretty accurate description. The array of hundreds upon hundreds of pine-clad islands and islets is the only one of its kind in the world.

The archipelago can be split into three distinct sections – inner, centre and outer. In the inner archipelago, there's more land than sea; in the centre, it's pretty much fifty-fifty; and in the outer archipelago, distances between islands are much greater. Here sea and sky merge to form one, and the nearest island is often no more than a dot on the horizon. From November to April, life in the archipelago can be tough, with the winter ice stretching far out into the Baltic and throwing the boat timetables into confusion. But in summer the archipelago is at its best: the air is heavy with the scent of fresh pine, and seemingly endless forests are reflected in the deep blue of the sea. It's worth bearing in mind that when it's cloudy in Stockholm, chances are the sun is shining somewhere out in the islands. Even if your stay in the capital is short, it is well worth making time to day-trip out here.

## Practicalities

**Getting out to the islands** is easy and cheap, with *Waxholmsbolaget* operating the majority of sailings into the archipelago. Most boats leave from Strömkajen in front of the *Grand Hotel* and the National Museum; others from just round the corner at Nybroplan, next to the *Kungliga Dramatiska Teatern* (see p.77). You can either buy tickets on the boat or from the *Waxholmsbolaget* office on Strömkajen, where you can pick up free timetables to help you plan your route. Timetables are also posted up on every jetty (Swedish: *brygga*). Ticket prices are very reasonable, ranging from 15kr to 65kr depending on the length of the journey. Most boats have a cafeteria or restaurant onboard. If you're planning to visit several islands, it might be worth buying the **Interskerries Card** (*Båtluffarkort*; 250kr), which gives sixteen days unlimited travel on all *Waxholmbolaget* lines. Or alternatively, if you've already got an *SL* monthly travel card (see p.59), buy a **supple-**

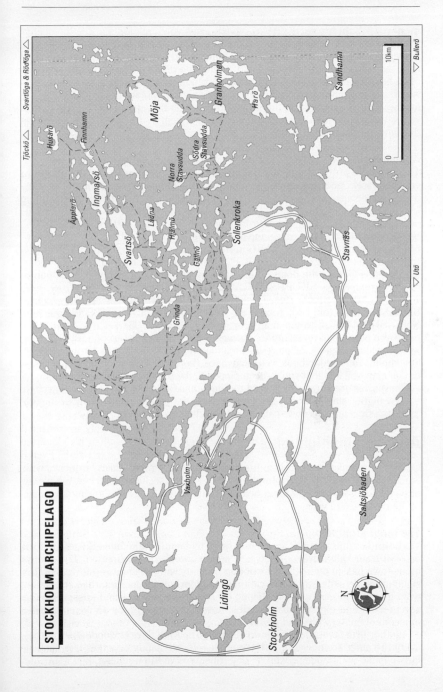

**STOCKHOLM ARCHIPELAGO**

Svartlöga & Rödlöga ◁

Tjôckö ◁

Husarö

Finnhamn

Äpplarö

Möja

Ingmarsö

Norra Stavsudda

Södra Stavsudda

Granholmen

Harö

Sandhamn

▷ Bullerö

10km

0

Svartsö

Ladna

Hjälmö

Gällnö

Sollenkroka

Stavräs

▷ Utö

Grinda

Vaxholm

Saltsjöbaden

Lidingö

Stockholm

N

mentary **Waxholm card** (215kr), which gives you one month's free travel anywhere in the archipelago.

**Departures** to the closest islands (often around four a day) are more frequent than those to the outer archipelago; if there's no direct service, connections can often be made on the island of Vaxholm. When boarding the boat, you'll be asked which island you're heading for. When you're out in the archipelago and waiting for the boat, you must raise the semaphore flag on the jetty to alert the boat that you're there and intending to travel; torches are kept in the huts on the jetties for the same purpose at night.

## Accommodation

Though there are few hotels in the archipelago, well-equipped and comfortable **youth hostel accommodation** is plentiful, and all hostels are open in the summer. The details for hostels on Finnhamn, Gällnö and Utö are given under "Archipelago highlights"; the rest are as follows: **ARHOLMA** in the outer archipelago and one of the northernmost islands (open all year; ☎0176/560 18; 100kr); **STORA KALHOLMEN** (mid-June to mid-Aug; ☎08/54 24 60 23; 95kr) in the central archipelago; and **FJÄRDLÅNG** in the south of the outer archipelago near Utö (mid-June to mid-Aug; ☎08/50 15 60 92; 95kr). There are also a number of mainland hostels (where the boats stop) that may prove useful as hopping-off points into the archipelago: **SKEPPSMYRA** for Arholma (open all year; ☎0176/940 27; 100kr); **KAPPELSKÄR** for Tjockö (open all year; ☎0176/441 69; 100kr); **SMÅDALARÖ** for Utö (open all year; ☎08/50 15 30 73; 100kr) and **NYNÄSHAMN** for Utö (open all year; ☎08/52 02 08 34; 95kr).

It's also possible to rent summer **cottages** on the islands for around 900–1200kr a week for four people – for more information on prices contact the tourist office in Stockholm. You need to book well in advance, though – at least six months before – or you may well find that you've been pipped to the post by holidaying Swedes.

**Campsites** are surprisingly hard to find; you'll be much better camping rough – a few nights' stay at most places won't cause any problems. Remember though that open fires are prohibited all over the archipelago.

# Archipelago highlights

Of the vast number of islands in the archipelago, several are firm favourites with Stockholmers, notably **Vaxholm**; others offer more secluded beaches and plenty of opportunity for walking amid beautiful surroundings. The following are some of the best ones to visit.

## The inner archipelago

**Vaxholm** lies only an hour from Stockholm by boat (or take bus #670, #671, #672 or #673 from Valhallavägen) and is a popular weekend destination. The eponymous town has an atmospheric wooden harbour with an imposing fortress. This structure superseded the fortifications at Riddarholmen and guarded the waterways into the city, successfully staving off attacks from Danes and Russians in the seventeenth and eighteenth centuries; nowadays, though, it's an unremarkable museum of military bits and pieces.

Another firm favourite is **Grinda** (2.5hr by boat), a thickly wooded island typical of the inner archipelago, with some magnificent sandy beaches. It is particularly popular with families, who do day-trips here on the weekend.

## The central archipelago

**Gällnö** is a low-lying island in the central archipelago. Covered with thick pine forest, it's been designated a nature reserve: spot deer in the forest or watch the eider ducks diving for fish. It takes around two hours to get here from the city. The **youth hostel** (May–Sept; ☎08/57 16 61 17; 100kr) is easy enough to find; the track leading to it is well signposted.

**Svartsö** lies in what's considered to be the most stunning part of the whole archipelago, not too far from the island of Möja (see overleaf). Known for its fields of grazing sheep, virgin forest and crystal clear lakes, Svartsö has good roads, making the island ideal for cycling or walking. The journey time is about two hours.

## Norrtälje, Grisslehamn and the outer archipelago

If you're heading into the southern **outer archipelago** and are short of time you can cut the journey time by up to two hours by taking bus #434 from Slussen to either **Sollenkroka** or **Stavsnäs** – the furthest point on the mainland – and picking up the boat from there. If you're heading for the northern islands, there's a fair chance you'll end up changing buses in the mainland town of **NORRTÄLJE**, where there's a tourist office at Lilla Torget (June to mid-Aug Mon–Fri 9.30am–7pm, Sat 9.30am–5pm, Sun 11am–5pm, rest of the year Mon–Fri 9am–5pm; ☎0176/719 90). It's worth a quick look round between buses – its an old spa town and capital of the Roslagen region, with a quirky cartoon museum and regional Roslagen museum (July & Aug daily noon–4pm; 10kr), housed in an old gun factory in the centre of town. Norrtälje is also a handy jumping-off point for trips to **GRISSLEHAMN** in the north, a small fishing village where you'll find the pretty home of early twentieth-century writer and artist Albert Engström, with paintings and knick-knacks displayed inside. Note that there are **ferry connections** (2–3 daily; 2hr; 60kr) from Grisslehamn to Eckerö on the Finnish Åland islands.

Starting off in the north of the outer archipelago, the first main island of interest is **Tjockö**. Life here is much as it was decades ago. A wonderful little place with forests, meadows and open fields, Tjackö also has a good sandy beach, as well as smooth rocks ideal for soaking up the sun. To get here take bus #640 or #644 from Tekniska Högskolan to Norrtälje, then bus #631 to Rafsnäs, from where it's a ten-minute boat trip.

To the south and much further out towards Finland are **Svartlöga** and **Rödlöga**. Svartlöga is the only island to consist totally of deciduous forest and was one of the few to escape Russian incursions in 1719. There are several good rocky beaches on which to rest up after a truly wonderful journey through the entire archipelago. Neighbouring Rödlöga is a much tinier red-granite affair, with no roads, just leafy paths, overgrown hedgerows thick with wild roses and wonderful secluded beaches. Journey time is four hours from Stockholm or one-and-a-half hours from Furusund, which is reached by bus #635 from Tekniska Högskolan.

Three hours by boat from Stockholm, the tiny island of **Finnhamn** is good for walking through forests, meadows and along cliff tops. The **youth hostel** is open all year (☎08/54 24 62 12; 100kr).

**Möja** (roughly pronounced "Murr-ya") is one of the most popular islands and is home to around three hundred people, who make their living from fishing and farming. There's a small craft museum in the main town, **Berg**, and even a cinema; but the island isn't good for bathing. The journey time is three and a half hours.

In the southern stretch of the archipelago, **Bullerö** (three hours from Stockholm) is about as far out as you can go in the archipelago before falling into the sea. This beautiful island is home to a nature reserve, with trails and an exhibition of the archipelago's plentiful flora and fauna. Take the train from Slussen to Saltsjöbaden, from where boats leave for the island of Nämdö; change at Idöborgs jetty for a shuttle service to Bullerö.

**Sandhamn** has been a destination for seafarers since the 1700s and remains so today; its tiny harbour is packed full of sailing yachts of all shapes and sizes. The main village is a haven of narrow alleyways, winding streets and overgrown verandahs. The journey time is three-and-a-half hours from Stockholm, one hour from Stavsnäs.

Lying far out in the southern reaches of the archipelago, **Utö** is ideal for cycling, and the sandy beaches at Ålö Storsand are perfect for a picnic. Alternatively, you can walk over the bathing cliffs at Rävstavik. There are also excellent views from the island's windmill. It takes three hours to get here by boat from Stockholm, one hour from Årsta Havsbad near Västerhaninge, which is accessible by *pendeltåg*. The **youth hostel** (May–Sept; ☎08/57 16 61 17; 100kr) is near where the ferry docks.

# Mariefred and Gripsholm

If you've only got time for one boat trip outside Stockholm, make it to **MARIEFRED**, a tiny village about an hour west of the city, whose own peaceful attractions are bolstered by one of Sweden's most enjoyable castles. To get there take the *S/S Mariefred* **steamboat**, which leaves from Klara Mälarstrand near Stadshuset on Kungsholmen (mid-May to mid-June Sat & Sun 10am; mid-June to mid-Aug Tues–Sun 10am; mid-Aug to mid-Sept Sat & Sun 10am; 100kr one way, 160kr return); buy your ticket on board for the three-and-a-half-hour journey. Outside summer, you'll have to travel by **train** to **Läggesta** (trains for Eskilstuna), from where connecting buses shuttle passengers into Mariefred. There's also an irregular bus (#40 to Strängnäs) from outside Liljeholmen T-bana station; you can get details from the operator, *Länstrafiken*, in the neighbouring county of Sörmland (☎020/22 40 00), but don't expect it to be going when you want to go.

Mariefred itself – the Swedish name is derived from an old monastery, Pax Mariae, or Mary's Peace – is as quiet, and quintessentially Swedish, as such villages come. It's surrounded by clear water; a couple of minutes up from the quayside and you're strolling through narrow streets, whose well-kept wooden houses and little squares haven't changed much in decades. The water and enveloping greenery make for a leisurely stroll around: if you call in at the central **Rådhus**, a fine eighteenth-century timber building, you can pick up a map from the **tourist office** inside (June & Aug Mon–Fri 10am–7pm, Sat & Sun 10am–6pm; July daily 10am–6pm; late Aug to mid-Sept Wed–Sun 10am–3pm; ☎0159/297 90). You could also ask here about **bike rental** (85kr per day; 400kr per week).

Steam train freaks will love the **Railway Museum** in the village – you'll probably have noticed the narrow-gauge tracks running all the way to the quayside. There's an exhibition of old rolling stock and workshops, given added interest by the fact that the steam trains still run to and from Mariefred; details below, under "Practicalities".

## Gripsholm Castle

Lovely though the village is, touring around it is really only a preface to seeing **Gripsholm** (May, June & Aug daily 10am–4pm; July 9am–5pm; April & Sept

Tues–Sun 10am–3pm; Oct–March Sat & Sun noon–3pm; 40kr), the imposing red-brick castle built on a round island just to the south. If you walk up the quayside, you'll be able to see the path to the castle running across the grass by the water's edge.

In the late fourteenth century, Bo Johnsson Grip, the Swedish High Chancellor, began to build a fortified castle at Mariefred, although the present building owes more to two Gustavs – Gustav Vasa, who started rebuilding in the sixteenth century, and Gustav III, who was responsible for major restructuring a couple of centuries later. Rather than the hybrid that might be expected, the result is rather pleasing – a textbook castle, whose turrets, great halls, corridors and battlements provide an engaging tour. The guide will point out most of the important bits and pieces as you go: there's a vast portrait collection, which includes recently commissioned works of political and cultural figures as well as assorted royalty and nobility; some fine decorative and architectural work; and like Drottningholm, a private theatre, built for Gustav III. It's too delicate to use for performances these days, but in summer plays and events take place out in the castle grounds; more information from the tourist office in Mariefred.

### Practicalities

Mariefred warrants a night's stay, if not for the sights – which you can exhaust in half a day – then for the pretty, peaceful surroundings. There's only one **hotel**, *Gripsholms Värdhus*, Kyrkogatan 1 (☎0159/130 20, fax 109 74; ⑨), that's a beautifully restored inn (the oldest in Sweden) a wonderfully luxurious option overlooking the castle and the water. Otherwise ask in the tourist office about **rooms** in the village, which range from 150kr per person per night to 420kr. There are also six-person **cabins** for rent for 500kr. The nearest **youth hostel** is 15km to the northwest in **STRÄNGNÄS** (open all year but advance booking necessary Sept–May; ☎0152/168 61; 100kr) and is connected by regular bus.

As for eating, treat yourself to **lunch** in *Gripsholms Värdhus*. The food is excellent and around 200kr will get you a turn at the herring table, a main course, drink and coffee – all enhanced by the terrific views over to Gripsholm. Alternatively try *Skänken* at the back of the *Värdhus*, where lunch goes for around 70kr. Another good midday spot is the classy *Strandrestaurangen* on the lakeside near the church, which serves up delicious fish dishes for 60kr. Or there's the friendly but basic *Jakobs Bistro* opposite the castle. For coffee and cakes head for *Konditori Fredman* in the main square, opposite the town hall.

When it comes to **leaving Mariefred**, consider taking the **narrow-gauge steam train** that leaves roughly hourly (mid-June to mid-Aug daily; May & Sept Sat & Sun ☎0159/210 06; 36kr return; half-price for children and rail-pass holders) between 11am and 5pm for **LÄGGESTA**, a twenty-minute ride away. From here it's possible to pick up the regular *SJ* train back to Stockholm; check for connections on the timetable at the tourist office before you leave. Of course, you could always come to Mariefred from Stockholm this way, too.

# Eskilstuna

Around an hour west of Mariefred, **ESKILSTUNA** (on the main train line from Stockholm) is mostly known for the precision tools and instruments manufactured here, but also for its unusually high incidence of violence and murders. Much is made of Eskilstuna's impressive industrial heritage in a series of fine museums based in and around the town's oldest houses, which date from the seventeenth century. Here in the **Radermacher Forges** (*Radermachersmedjorna*) museum, smiths and wrights work by traditional methods (June–Aug Mon–Fri 10am–6pm, Sat & Sun 10am–4pm; Sept–Nov Tues–Sun 10am–4pm; Dec–March Tues–Sat 10am–4pm; April & May daily 10am–4pm; free). Nearby, on an island reached by crossing the main Hamngatan and taking a narrow path over the river to Faktoriholmarna, is **Faktorimuseet** (Factory Museum; Tues–Sun 11am–4pm; free), which has three floors of displays, including several steam engines coaxed into life every Sunday between 1pm and 3pm. Next door is **Vapentekniska Museet** (Weapons Museum; June–Aug Tues–Sun 11am–4pm; rest of the year Tues, Sat & Sun 11am–4pm; free). To reach these museums from the **train station**, walk fifteen minutes down Drottninggatan and turn left. The tourist office is also out here (see "Practicalities" below for details).

More museums can be found in the town centre. **Konstmuseet** (Art Museum) is at Kyrkogatan 9 (Tues–Sun noon–4pm; Thurs also 7–9pm; free) and is worth a glance for its temporary exhibitions on the ground floor. On the first floor, there's a permanent collection of works of art from the seventeenth century onwards – look out for the thirty-odd paintings by local boy **Gustave Albert**. Born in Eskilstuna in 1866, he moved to France in 1891 and, heavily influenced by the Impressionist movement, become a respected and well-known artist by his death in 1905. In Sweden today he is still virtually unknown, but the museum is aiming to change all that by creating a new special exhibition on the artist's life. With time on your hands you may also want to poke around **Teatermuseet** at Gillbergavägen 2 (July–Sept Tues, Wed, Fri noon–4pm, Thurs noon–8pm; Aug & Sept also Sat & Sun noon–4pm; 30kr), an odd collection of old photos and newspaper cuttings of old theatre productions and a library with a good collection of literature on Swedish regional theatre – in Swedish and only for the dedicated.

## Practicalities

Hourly **trains** leave from Stockholm's central station for Eskilstuna. The **tourist office** is in Munktellstorget near the museums (June to late Aug Mon–Fri 9am–6pm, Sat & Sun 10am–4pm, rest of the year Mon–Thurs 9am–5pm, Fri 10am–5pm; ☎016/10 70 00). When it comes to **accommodation**, the cheapest option is the **youth hostel**, right by a nature reserve at *Vilsta Camping* (open all year; ☎016/51 30 80; 100kr), a couple of kilometres south of the centre. To get there, you turn right out of the station, head along Västermarksgatan to a roundabout, then turn right onto Kyrkogatan and follow the river until you come to the second bridge; the youth hostel is the other side of the river next to an open-air swimming pool. Of the central **hotels**, the cheapest is *Hotell City* (☎016/13 74 25, fax 12 42 24; ③/①) at Drottninggatan 15. For greater luxury try *Hotell Smeden* (☎016/13 76 90, fax 12 75 27; ④/②) or *Stadshotellet Best Western* (☎016/13 72 25, fax 12 75 88; ④/②) at Hamngatan 9–11.

For **eating and drinking** the best places are concentrated in the central pedestrianized area. The best of the bunch is *Brasserie Oscar* at Nybrogatan 5, which has special student prices and is popular with all ages. Another brasserie-style restaurant-cum-bar is *Perrongen* nearby at Nybrogatan 1 – also with student discounts on food. For finer surroundings check out *Restaurang Tingsgården* at Rådhustorget 2 – the fish is particularly good, but all meals are expensive. Greek food can be had at *Restaurang Akropolis* in Fristadstorget. For a good night's drinking try *Oliver Twist*, a popular pub at Careliigatan 2; *McEwans* at Nybrogatan 5 and *Hamlet Pub Restaurang* at Teatergatan 1. Avoid *Le Club & Games* at Alva Myrdals gata 4, which is where Eskilstuna's likely lads hang out looking for trouble and new boys in town.

## The Sigurd Carving

Twelve kilometres from town in a shady glade near **SUNDBYHOLM**, the **Sigurd carving** is a thousand-year-old runic inscription running for four metres along a slab of stone. The runes are an epitaph for Sigrid, who built a bridge at the site, and are illustrated by scenes from the Icelandic epic poem of Sigrid and the dragon slayer. To get here from Eskilstuna, take the #25 bus (5 daily; 15kr) from the bus station near the church – it passes very close to the stone. There's also excellent **swimming** to be had here in Lake Mälaren.

# Uppsala

First impressions as the train pulls into **UPPSALA**, only an hour from Stockholm, are encouraging. The red-washed castle looms up behind the railway sidings, the cathedral dominant in the foreground. A sort of Swedish Oxford, Uppsala clings to the past through a succession of striking buildings connected with and scattered about its cathedral and university. Primarily the city is regarded as the historical and religious centre of the country, and it's as a tranquil daytime alternative to Stockholm (and for an active student-geared nightlife) that Uppsala draws the traveller.

## Arrival, information and accommodation

Uppsala's **train** (several services an hour from Stockholm; 45min) and **bus stations** are adjacent to each other, and it's not far to walk down to the **tourist office** at Fyris Torg 8 (end June to mid-Aug Mon–Fri 10am–6pm, Sat 10am–3pm, Sun noon–4pm; rest of the year Mon–Fri 10am–6pm, Sat 10am–3pm; ☎27 48 00), where you can pick up a handy English guide to the town. This is also the place to rent **bikes** from 60kr per day. The **boats** for Skokloster, Sigtuna and Stockholm arrive and depart from the pier south of the centre, at the end of Bävernsgränd. Bus #801 runs between Uppsala bus station and **Arlanda airport**, so if you wish you can bypass Stockholm on your way in or out of Sweden (daily every 15–30min from 4.40am to 11.40pm calling at Terminals 2, 4 and 5; journey time 30min).

### Accommodation

Though it's so close to Stockholm, staying over in Uppsala can be an attractive idea. There are two **youth hostels**: an official one at Sunnerstavägen 24 (May–Aug; ☎32 42 20; 100kr), 6km south of the centre at *STF*'s beautifully sited *Sunnersta Herrgård* (bus #20 from Nybron by Stora Torget), and a non-*STF* affiliated one in the centre of town at Dragarbrunnsgatan 18 (open all year; ☎10 43 00; 150kr). Uppsala has a fair range of central **hotels** (see below), but the cheapest, *Hotell Årsta Gård*, is a bus ride away in suburbia. For a night's unofficial **camp-**

The telephone code for Uppsala is ☎018.

**ing**, head the few kilometres north to the open spaces of Gamla Uppsala (see p.109). Or there's a regular site with two-person cabins available (☎27 60 84) at *Sunnersta Camping* by Lake Mälaren at **GRANEBERG**, 7km out (bus #20 from Nybron) near the youth hostel.

**Grand Hotell Hörnan**, Bangårdsgatan 1 (☎13 93 80, fax 12 03 11). A wonderfully elegant place with large old-fashioned rooms and restaurant. ④/③

**Gillet**, Dragarbrunnsgatan 23 (☎15 53 60, fax 15 33 80). A stone's throw from the cathedral but with average, overpriced, shag-piled rooms. Kitsch fans should head for the restaurant. ⑤/③

**Linné**, Skolgatan 45 (☎10 20 00, fax 13 75 97). Completely overpriced tiny rooms – a last resort when everything else is full. ⑤/③

**Plantan**, Dragarbrunnsgatan 18 (☎ & fax 10 43 00). Simple, bright and clean rooms with en-suite bathroom and a tiny kitchen. Same price all year. ①

**Svava**, Bangårdsgatan 24 (☎13 00 30, fax 13 22 30). A newly built hotel with all mod-cons, including specially designed rooms for people with disabilities and those with allergies. ④/③

**Provorbis Hotell Uplandia**, Dragarbrunnsgatan 32 (☎10 21 60, fax 69 61 32). A modern hotel that's gone in for a lot of wood – and small rooms. ⑤/③

**Årsta Gård**, Jordgubbsgatan 14 (☎ & fax 25 35 00). This large cottage-style building in the outskirts is the cheapest hotel in town; take bus #7 or #56 to Södra Årsta (15min). Same price all year. ①

# The City

Centre of the medieval town and a ten-minute walk from the train station is the great **Domkyrkan** (daily 8am–6pm; free), Scandinavia's largest cathedral. Built as a Gothic brag to the people of Trondheim in Norway that even their mighty church could be overshadowed, it loses out to its competitor by reason of the building material – local brick rather than imported stone. Only the echoing interior remains impressive, particularly the French Gothic ambulatory, sided by tiny chapels and bathed in a golden, decorative glow. One chapel contains a lively set of restored fourteenth-century wall paintings that recount the legend of Saint Erik, Sweden's patron saint: his coronation, crusade to Finland, eventual defeat and execution at the hands of the Danes. The Relics of Erik are zealously guarded in a chapel off the nave: poke around and you'll also find the tombs of Reformation rebel Gustav Vasa and his son Johan III, and that of Linnaeus, the botanist, who lived in Uppsala. Time and fire have led the rest of the cathedral to be rebuilt, scrubbed and painted to the extent that it resembles a historical museum more than a thirteenth-century spiritual centre; even the characteristic twin spires are late nineteenth-century additions.

The other buildings grouped around the Domkyrkan can all claim a cleaner historical pedigree. Opposite the towers, the onion-domed **Gustavianum** (daily July & Aug 11am–3pm; Sept–June noon–3pm; 15kr) was built in 1625 as part of the university and is much touted by the tourist office for its tidily preserved anatomical theatre. The same building houses a couple of small collections of Egyptian, Classical and Nordic antiquities with a small charge for each section (July & Aug daily 11am–3pm).

The current **University** building (Mon–Fri 8am–4pm) is the imposing nineteenth-century Renaissance edifice over the way. Originally a seminary, today it's used for lectures and seminars and hosts the graduation ceremonies each May. The more famous of its alumni include Carl von Linné (Linnaeus) and Anders Celsius, inventor of the temperature scale. No one will mind you strolling in for a quick look, but to see the locked rooms (including the glorious Augsberg Art Cabinet, an ebony treasure chest presented to Gustav II Adolf), you need to ask in the office inside, to the right of the main entrance (*Vaktmästeriet*); or catch a **guided tour** (May–Aug daily 12.30pm & 2pm; 15kr).

A little way beyond the university is the **Carolina Rediviva** (Mon–Fri 9am–5pm, Sat 10am–4pm), the university library. On April 30 each year the students meet here to celebrate the first day of spring (usually in the snow), all wearing the traditional student cap that gives them the appearance of disaffected sailors. It's one of Scandinavia's largest libraries, with around four million books. Adopt a student pose and you can slip in for a wander round and a coffee in the common room. More officially, take a look in the **manuscript room**, where there's a collection of rare letters and other paraphernalia. The beautiful sixth-century Silver Bible is on permanent display, as is, oddly, Mozart's original manuscript for *The Magic Flute*.

After this, the **castle** (no admission) up on the hill is a disappointment. In 1702 a fire that destroyed three-quarters of the city did away with much of the castle, and only one side and two towers remain of what was once an opulent rectangular palace. But the facade still gives a weighty impression of what's missing, like a backless Hollywood set.

Seeing Uppsala, at least the compact older parts, will take up a good half a day; afterwards why not take a stroll along the river that runs right through the centre of town. In summer, there are several resting places that are good for an hour or two's sunbathing and enough greenery to make this stretch a pleasant place to wander. One beautiful spot is **Linnaeus Gardens** (daily May–Aug 9am–9pm; Sept 9am–7pm; 10kr), over the river on Linnégatan. The university's first botanical gardens, they were relaid by Linnaeus in 1741; some of the species he introduced and classified still survive.

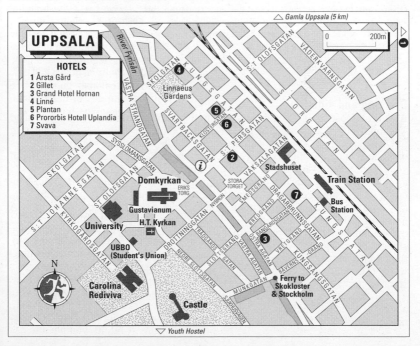

# Eating, drinking and nightlife

**Eating and entertainment** are straightforward in this university town, easier still if you have some form of student ID. For light daytime eating there are plenty of cafés, particularly in summer, when a glut of open-air places re-emerge, the most popular on the river. *Café Linné*, just down the street from the Linnaeus Gardens, and *Åkanten*, below St Eriks Torg, are among the best. Many stay open until the early hours, an unusual bonus (also see "Drinking and nightlife" below). For **snacks** and cheap coffee you can also try the *Alma* café in the basement of the university building. The following all offer more substantial eating options:

**Alexander**, Östra Ågatan 59. Completely OTT Greek place with busts of famous Ancient Greeks at every turn. Lunch deal for 50kr.

**Café Katalin**, Svartbäcksgatan 19. Does reasonably priced veggie food in a similar set-up to *Sten Sture & Co* (see below), and equally as popular.

**Caroline's**, Övre Slottsgatan 12. A cheap pizzeria up by the university. Lunch for 45kr.

**Domtrappkälaren**, St Eriks Gränd. One of the most chi chi places in town – old vaulted roof and great atmosphere. Nothing under 200kr; excellent lunch upstairs for 60kr, though.

**Elaka Måns**, Smedsgränd. A modern bistro-style restaurant with the usual run of fish and meat dishes. Very popular, not too expensive and definitely worth a look.

**Fågelsången**, Munkgatan 3. Café and lunch place that's full of posey students.

**Güntherska hovkonditori**, Östra Ågatan 31. Old-fashioned style café with simple lunch dishes.

**Hallen**, St Eriks Torg. A very popular if somewhat expensive restaurant. Try the duck in lime sauce or the flounder.

**Landings**, Kungsängsgatan 5. Busy café in the main pedestrian area.

**Ofvandahls**, Sysslomangatan 3–5. Near the old part of town, this lively café has old wooden tables and sofas – don't leave town without trying the homemade apple, rhubarb or blueberry pie.

**Sten Sture & Co**, Nedre Slottsgatan 3. For vegetarian food, it's difficult to beat lunch at this large ramshackle wooden house immediately below the castle: jazz while you eat and plenty of young trendies around. Outdoor tables in summer. A must.

**Svenssons krog/bakficka**, Sysslomangatan 15. A wonderful restaurant decked out in wood and glass next to the *bakficka* section that serves pasta dishes.

## Drinking and nightlife

**At night** most of the action is generated by the **students** in houses called "Nations", contained within the grid of streets behind the university, backing onto St Olofsgatan. Each a sort of college fraternity, they run dances, gigs and parties of all hues and most importantly boast very cheap bars. The official line is that if you're not a Swedish student you won't get into most of the things advertised around the town; in practice being foreign and nice to the people on the door generally yields entrance, and with an *ISIC* card it's even easier. As many students stay around during the summer, functions are not strictly limited to term time. A good choice to begin with is *Uplands Nation*, off St Olofsgatan and Sysslomangatan near the river, with a summer outdoor café open until 3am. Non-student bars include: *Svenssons Taverna*, Sysslomangatan 14, diagonally opposite the other *Svenssons* (see opposite), which is a great place for a beer and nibbles; while *O'Connors* is a first-floor Irish pub with food, tucked away in the main square Stora Torget (open after 4pm).

*Sten Sture & Co* puts on **live bands** in the evenings, while *Café Katalin* (see above) is open late and has jazz nights. *Club Dacke* is a student-frequented summer-only **disco** on St Olofsgatan, near the Domkyrkan, while one of the liveliest joints is *Rackis*, a music bar out near the student residences on St Johannesgatan (bus #1 to Studentstaden) – there's live music here nearly every night.

# Gamla Uppsala

Five kilometres to the north of the present city three huge **barrows**, royal burial mounds dating back to the sixth century, mark the original site of Uppsala, **Gamla Uppsala**. This was a pagan settlement – and a place of ancient sacrificial rites. Every ninth year the festival of *Fröblot* demanded the death of nine people, hanged from a nearby tree until their corpses rotted. The pagan temple, where this bloody sacrifice took place, is now marked by the Christian **Gamla Uppsala kyrka** (Mon–Fri 8.30am to dusk, Sat & Sun 10am to dusk), built over pagan remains when the Swedish kings first took baptism in the new faith. What survives is only a remnant of what was, originally, a cathedral – look inside for the faded wall paintings and the tomb of Celsius, of thermometer fame. Set in the wall outside, there's an eleventh-century rune stone.

There's little else to Gamla Uppsala, and perhaps that's why the site remains mysterious and atmospheric. There's an **inn** nearby, *Odinsborg*, where – especially if you've got children – you might want to sample the "Viking lunch": a spread of soup, hunks of meat served on a board, and mead, which comes complete with the horned helmet, an essential item if you're considering pillaging and plundering the afternoon away. And there's an opportunity, too, if you're discreet, to **camp** beyond the inn, amid the ghosts.

To get to Gamla Uppsala, take **bus** #2 (three hourly Mon–Fri) or #54 (half-hourly Sat afternoon after 3pm and Sun from 6pm to midnight) from Dragarbrunnsgatan.

# Listings

**Banks** *Handelsbanken*, Vaksalagatan 8; *Nordbanken*, Stora Torget; *SE-Banken*, Kungsängsgatan 7–9.

**Bus enquiries** *Uppsalabuss* (☎27 37 01); city buses leave from Stora Torget; long-distance buses from the bus station adjacent to the train station (see Stockholm "Listings" for phone numbers).

**Car rental** *Avis*, Spikgatan (☎12 55 01); *Budget*, Kungsgatan 80 (☎12 42 80); *Europcar*, Kungsgatan 103 (☎17 17 30); *Hertz*, Kungsgatan 97 (☎12 20 20); *Statoil*, Gamla Uppsalagatan 48 (☎20 91 00); *Q8* Vaksalagatan 95 (☎25 26 60).

**Cinemas** *Filmstaden/Spegeln*, Västra Ågatan 12; *Fyrisbiografen* St Olofsgatan 10B; *Sandrew* Smedsgränd 14–20.

**Exchange** *Forex*, Fyris Torg 8 (☎10 30 00), adjacent to tourist office.

**Pharmacy** at Akademiska Sjukhuset (out of town; ask at the tourist office for directions), entrance 70, Mon–Fri 8.30am–9pm, Sat & Sun 9am–9pm (☎66 34 55).

**Police** ☎ 16 85 00.

**Post office** Dragarbrunnsgatan (☎17 96 31).

**Systembolaget** The off-licence at Svavagallerian is open Mon–Thurs 9.30am–6pm, Fri 8am–6pm; at Skolgatan 6 Mon–Wed & Fri 9.30am–6pm, Thurs 9.30am–7pm.

**Taxis** *Taxi Direkt* (☎12 53 60); *Taxi Uppsala* (☎23 90 90).

**Telephone** *Telia Butik* on Svartbäcksgatan & Bredgränd.

**Train station** Information on ☎65 22 10.

**Travel agent** *Kilroy*, Bredgränd; *Ticket* Östra Ågatan 33 & Bangårdsgatan 13.

## travel details

### Trains

**From Stockholm** to Boden (2 daily; 14hr); Gothenburg (17 daily; 3hr 15min by X2000, 4hr 30min by intercity); Gällivare (2 daily; 16hr); Gävle (hourly; 2hr); Helsingborg (8 daily; 5hr by X2000, 6hr 30min by intercity); Kiruna (2 daily; 17hr); Luleå (2 daily; 14hr); Läggesta (for Mariefred; 32 daily; 45min by X2000); Malmö (11 daily; 4hr 45min by X2000, 6hr by intercity); Mora (7 daily; 4hr by X2000, 5hr by intercity); Nynäshamn *pendeltåg* for ferries to Gotland (hourly; 1hr); Sundsvall (6 daily; 4hr by X2000, 5hr by intercity); Umeå (1 daily; 11hr); Uppsala (50 daily; 45min); Östersund (4 daily; 6hr).

**From Eskilstuna** to Laggesta (for Mariefred; 32 daily; 15min by X2000); Stockholm (32 daily; 1hr by X2000).

**From Läggesta** to Stockholm (32 daily; 45min).

**From Uppsala** to Gällivare (2 daily; 15hr); Gävle (hourly; 1hr); Kiruna (2 daily; 16hr); Luleå (2 daily; 13hr); Mora (7 daily; 3hr 15min by X2000, 4hr 15min by intercity); Stockholm (50 daily; 45min); Sundsvall (6 daily; 3hr by X2000, 4hr by intercity); Umeå (1 daily; 10hr); Östersund (4 daily; 5hr).

### Buses

**From Stockholm** to Borlänge (2 Fri & Sun; 3hr); Falun (2 Fri & Sun; 3hr 30min); Gothenburg (2 daily Mon–Wed, 3 Thurs, 5 Fri & Sun, 1 Sat; 4hr 30min, or 7hr 20min via Kristinehamn or Jönköping); Gävle (3 Fri, 5 Sun; 2hr 20min); Halmstad (1 Fri & Sun only; 7hr 30min); Haparanda (1 Fri & Sun; 12hr 45min); Helsingborg (1 daily Mon–Thurs, 2 Fri & Sun; 8hr); Jönköping (1 daily Mon–Thurs, 2 Fri & Sun; 4hr 50min); Kalmar (5 daily; 6hr 30min); Kristianstad (1 Mon, Thurs, Fri & Sun; 9hr 30min); Kristinehamn (2 Mon–Thurs & Sat, 3 Fri & Sun; 3hr); Luleå (1 Fri & Sun; 12hr); Malmö (1 Fri, 2 Sun; 10hr 20min); Mora (2 Fri & Sun; 4hr 40min); Norrköping (2 daily Mon–Wed, 3 Thurs, 4 Fri & Sun, 1 Sat; 2hr); Rättvik (2 Fri & Sun; 4hr 10min); Skellefteå (1 Fri & Sun; 11hr); Sollefteå (1 Fri & Sun; 8hr 15min); Umeå (1 Fri & Sun; 9hr 20min); Östersund (1 Fri & Sun; 8hr 30min).

### International trains

**From Stockholm** to Copenhagen (9 daily; 8hr 30min); Narvik (2 daily; 20hr); Oslo (2 daily; 6hr 30min); Trondheim (3 daily; 12hr).

### Ferries

For details of city ferries see p.59 and for the services to the archipelago see p.98.

### International ferries

**From Stockholm** to Helsinki (1 *Viking Line* & 1 *Silja Line* daily; 15hr); Turku (2 *Viking Line* & 2 *Silja Line* daily; 1 daily on each route via the Åland islands); Tallinn (1 every second day); Eckerö on the Åland islands (2–3 daily; 3hr; a bus leaves Tekniska Högskolan T-bana 2hr before the ferry's departure from Grisslehamn).

**From Nynäshamn** to Gdansk (3 weekly; 19hr).

# CHAPTER TWO

# GOTHENBURG AND AROUND

O f all the cities in southern Sweden, the grandest is the western port of **Gothenburg**. Designed by the Dutch in 1621, the city boasts splendid Classical architecture, masses of parkland and a welcoming and relaxed spirit.

Gothenburg is Sweden's second largest city and Scandinavia's largest seaport; these facts, allied with its industrial heritage as a ship-building centre, have been enough to persuade many travellers arriving in the country by ferry to move quickly on to the surrounding countryside. But beyond the gargantuan shipyards, the cityscape of broad avenues, elegant squares, trams and canals is one of the prettiest in Sweden. Moreover, Gothenburg is a surprisingly cultured place, with a new and burgeoning café society, and is worth a lot more time than most

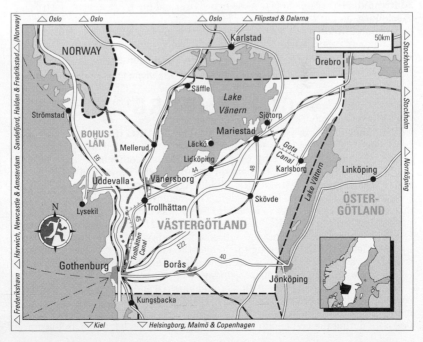

ferry arrivals give it. The city's image has also suffered from the inevitable comparisons with the capital, and while there is a certain resentment on the west coast that Stockholm wins out in the national glory stakes, many Swedes far prefer Gothenburg's easier-going atmosphere – and its closer proximity to western Europe. Talk to any Gothenburger and he or she will soon tell you about the more frenetic lives of the "08-ers" – 08 being the telephone code for Stockholm.

The counties to the north and east of the city are prime targets for domestic tourists. To the north, the craggy **Bohuslän coastline**, with its uninhabited islands, tiny fishing villages and clean beaches, attracts thousands of holidaymakers all the way to the Norwegian border. The coast is popular with the sailing set, and there are many guest harbours along the way, but the highlight is the glorious fortress island of **Marstrand**, an easy and enjoyable day-trip from Gothenburg.

To the northeast of city, the vast and beautiful lakes of **Vänern** and **Vättern** provide the setting for a number of historic towns, fairy-tale castles and some splendid inland scenery, all of which are within an hour's train journey from Gothenburg. The lakes are connected to each other (and to the east and west coasts) by the cross-country **Göta Canal**, and if you're inspired by the possibilities of water transport you could always make the complete four-day trip by boat from Gothenburg to Stockholm. First leg of the journey is up the Trollhättan Canal to **Trollhättan**, a wonderful little town built around the canal and a good place to aim for if you only have time for a short trip out from the city. Beyond here, though, other agreeable lakeside towns vie for your attention, with attractions including the elk safaris on the ancient hills of Halleberg and Hunneberg, near **Vänersborg** on the tip of Lake Vänern, the picturesque medieval kernel of **Mariestad**, further up the lake's eastern shore, and the huge military fortress at **Karlsborg**, on the western shore of Lake Vättern.

**Trains** and **buses** run through most of the region with a regular, efficient service; the only area you may find difficult to explore without a car is the Boshulän coast. **Accommodation** is never a problem, with plenty of hotels, hostels and camping sites in each town.

# GOTHENBURG

With its long history as a trading centre, **GOTHENBURG** (Göteborg in Swedish; pronounced "Yur-te-boy") is a truly cosmopolitan city. Founded on its present site in the seventeenth century by Gustavus Adolphus, Gothenburg was the fifth attempt to create a centre not reliant on Denmark – the Danes had enjoyed control of Sweden's west coast since the Middle Ages and had extracted extortionate tolls from all water traffic into Sweden. The medieval centre of trade had been 40km up the Göta river, but to avoid the tolls it was moved to a site north of the present city. It wasn't until Karl XI chose the island of Hisingen as the location for Sweden's trading nucleus that the settlement was first called Gothenburg. This, however, fell to the Danes during the battle of Kalmar, and it was left to Adolphus to find the vast ransom. Six years later, when it had finally been paid off, he founded the city where the main square is today.

Although Gothenburg's reputation as an industrial and trading centre has been severely eroded in recent years – clearly evidenced by the stillness of the cranes in the shipyards by the harbour – the British, Dutch and German traders who settled here during the eighteenth and nineteenth centuries left a rich architectural

The telephone code for Gothenburg is ☎031.

and cultural inheritance. The city is graced with terraces of grand merchant hous-es, all carved stone, stucco and painted tiles. The influence of the Orient was also strong, reflecting the all-important trade links between Sweden and the Far East, and is still visible in the chinoiserie detail on many buildings. This trading route was monopolized for over eighty years by the hugely successful East India Company, whose auction house, selling exotic spices, tea and fine cloth, attracted merchants from all over the world.

Today the city remains a sort of transit camp for business people, though their presence in the flashy hotels in the centre says much less about Gothenburg than the restrained opulence of the older buildings, which not only echoes its bygone prosperity but also the understatement of its citizens. Gothenburgers may tell you that they think their surroundings are nothing special, but don't believe them; this is simply the result of Swedish reserve and Gothenburg modesty – in reality, they are immensely proud, and rightly so, of their elegant and friendly city.

# Arrival and information

**Car ferry** connections from England are with *Scandinavian Seaways*, which oper-ates twice-weekly sailings from **Harwich** (mid-June to mid-Aug Sun & Tues; rest of year Fri & Sun; journey time 24hr), and a once-weekly summer service from **Newcastle** (mid-June to mid-Aug Fri; 24hr). Both arrive at **Skandiahamn** on Hisingen, north of the river, but there are special **buses** that will shuttle you to Nils Ericsonsplatsen, behind the central train station (30kr). When leaving, the same bus returns from platform V, ninety minutes before the ship leaves. The Gothenburg Card (see overleaf) is *not* valid on this bus.

*Stena Line* operates ferries between Gothenburg and Frederikshavn in **Denmark** (3–6 daily; 3hr 15min) and dock just twenty minutes' walk from the city centre. The trip costs 70kr, but with a Gothenburg Card you can do a free day-trip if travelling after 2pm. Alternatively, you can cut down the journey time by taking *SeaCat*'s catamaran service (1hr 45 mins; 70kr, the Gothenburg Card allows two for the price of one). *Stena Line* also operates one daily sailing between Gothenburg and Kiel in **Germany** (7pm from both countries; 14hr). The ferry drop-off is 3km away from the city, but the #86 bus or #3 tram will bring you into the centre. When leaving for Kiel, *Stena Line* runs a bus from Nils Ericsonsplatsen at 5.50pm in time for the 7pm crossing. For more on ferry com-panies see "Listings".

## Trains and buses
All trains arrive at **Central Station**, which forms one side of Drottningtorget (see p.121 for more on its impressive interior). Also here is a **Swebus** office (Mon–Fri 7am–6pm, Sun 10.30am–6pm), where you can buy bus tickets for services between Gothenburg and Oslo; buses leave from just outside. Otherwise, buses to and from destinations north of Gothenburg use **Nils Ericsonsplatsen** (ticket office Mon–Fri 7.30am–5.45pm, Sat 8am–2pm), just behind train station. From destinations south of Gothenburg, you arrive at **Heden** terminal at the junction of Parkgatan and Södra Vägen, with easy tram connections to all areas of the city.

## The airport

From **Landvetter** airport, 25km east of the city, buses run every fifteen minutes into the centre, stopping at Korsvagan, a junction just outside Liseberg Amusement Park to the south of the city centre, and in Drottningtorget outside Central Station (*Flygbuss* daily 5am–11.15pm; 50kr, Gothenburg Card not valid; 35min). For airline addresses and airport information, see "Listings".

## Information

Gothenburg has two **tourist offices**. Handiest for recent arrivals is at the **kiosk** in *Nordstan*, the indoor shopping centre near Central Station (Mon–Fri 9.30am–6pm, Sat 9.30am–3pm). The **main office** is on the canal front at Kungsportsplatsen 2 (May Mon–Fri 9am–6pm, Sat & Sun 10am–2pm; June–July daily 9am–6pm; Aug daily 9am–8pm; Sept–April Mon–Fri 9am–5pm, Sat 10am–2pm; ☎10 07 40). From the train station, it's just five minutes' walk across Drottningtorget and down Stora Nygatan; the tourist office is on the right opposite the statue of the so-called "Copper Mare" (see p.126). Both offices provide information, free city and tram maps, a room-booking service, restaurant and museum listings, as well as selling the Gothenburg Card. You can also get a copy of the fortnightly *Göteborgam*, which has information about what's on, including an English section at the back.

### The Gothenburg Card

Buying a **Gothenburg Card** (*Göteborgskortet*) is a real bonus if you want to pack in a good bit of sightseeing. It is available from either of the tourist offices, *Pressbyrån* kiosks and hotels, and it gives: unlimited bus and tram travel within the city; free entry into all the city museums and the Liseberg Amusement Park (but not the rides themselves); free car-parking (see below); boat excursions, including a day-trip to Fredrikshavn in Denmark; and a two-for-one reduction at several other sights. You can buy a card for 24 hours (125kr; children 75kr), 48 hours (225kr; 125kr) or 72 hours (275kr; 150kr). An accompanying Gothenburg Card booklet explains in detail how it can save you money.

# City transport

Apart from excursions north of the river or to the islands, it is **easy to walk** to almost anywhere of interest in Gothenburg. The wide streets are all pedestrian-friendly, and the canals and the grid system of avenues make orientation simple. If staying further out, however, or approaching from the central transport terminals, some sort of transport may be necessary. A free **transport map** (*Linje Kartan*) is available at both tourist offices.

## Public transport

The most convenient form of public transport is the **tram** system (see the map overleaf). Trams clunk around the city and its outskirts on a colour-coded, eight-line system, passing all central areas every few minutes – you can tell at a glance which line a tram is on as the route colour appears on the front. The main pick-up

## VINTAGE TRAMS

An atmospheric way of seeing the city is to take a ride on one of the **vintage trams** that spend the summer trundling noisily from the old town to both Liseberg, south-east of the centre, and Slottskogen in the southwest. Since the beginning of the century, trams have played a important role in Gothenburg life, from those decked with ribbons as mothers jolted home with their newborns, to black-hearse trams pushing coffins with mourners in the front carriage. Today white-gloved enthusiasts steer exquisitely preserved models – ranging from 1902 to the 1940s – complete with all their original leather, polished wood, etched glass and candles. The pre-1933 models have swastikas on the hub caps, painted on before the ancient religious symbol was appropriated by the Nazis, and many still have doors on the left – a last reminder that Sweden drove on the left from the late eighteenth century, when the British industrialists held sway, until 1967. Vintage trams run daily between July and August and on weekends in April and September; tickets cost the same as on ordinary trams. You can also go on special **guided tours** around city from Kungsportsplatsen – book through the tourist office.

points are outside Central Station and in Kungsportsplatsen. During summer, vintage trams ply the Liseberg and Slottskogen routes (see above). Gothenburg also has a fairly extensive **bus** network, using much the same routes, but central pedestrianization can lead to some odd and lengthy detours. You shouldn't need to use them in the city centre; routes are detailed in the text where necessary.

All public transport is free within the city with a Gothenburg Card, but otherwise, tickets are available from tram and bus drivers. There are no zones, and fares cost a standard 16kr for adults, while seven- to sixteen-year-olds go for half price and under sevens for free. If you are staying for a couple of days, it's cheaper to buy ticket cards from *Tidpunkten* offices (travel information centres) at Brunnsparken, Drottningtorget and Nils Ericsonsplatsen, *Pressbyrån* or *Ja* kiosks. A ten-trip ticket card costs 100kr. Stick these in the machines on a tram or bus, press twice for an adult, once for a child. The trams run from 5am to midnight, after which there is a night service at double the price.

**Fare-dodgers** tend to avoid the front carriage and the driver, but ticket inspectors in yellow jackets are on the increase and the instant fine is 600kr – since all the ticket information is in English on boards posted at bus and tram stops, ignorance is no defence.

A popular way to first get acquainted with the city is to take a **paddan boat ride** (late April to mid-June 10am–5pm; mid-June to early Aug 10am–9pm; Aug to mid-Sept 10am–5pm; mid-Sept to early Oct noon–3pm; 65kr; free with Gothenburg Card after 2pm). This classic canal and harbour tour offers a well-spent 55-minute trip past the city's historical sites. There are regular departures from their moorings on the canal by Kungsportsplatsen.

# Cars, taxis and bikes

There is no shortage of **car parks** in the city, with a basic charge of 15kr per hour in the centre. The Gothenburg Card comes with a free parking card, but this is invalid for privately run or multistorey car parks or any car parks with attendants, so always check first. The most useful car parks are the new *Ullevigarage* at

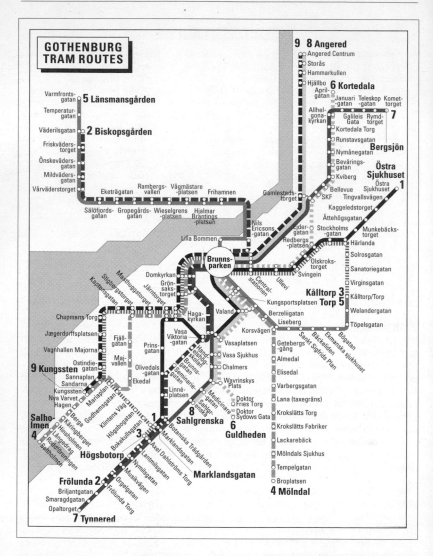

Heden, near the bus terminal, the *Lorensbergs* car park near Avenyn, *Gamla Ullevi* on Allen, south of Kungsportsplatsen, and two multistorey car parks at *Nordstan* near Central Station and *Garda-Focus* close to Liseberg. Without a Gothenburg Card, roadside parking areas marked with blue signs are cheaper than parking meters. Some of the larger hotels provide a discount at the multistorey car parks.

**Taxis** are summoned by calling ☎65 00 00. There is a twenty-percent reduction for women travelling at night – check with driver first. For information on **car rental** see "Listings".

It's easy and popular to **cycle** in the city, with a comprehensive series of cycle lanes and bike racks. The most central place to **rent a bike** is from *Sportkalleren* at Bohusgatan 2 (☎16 23 46), five minutes from Kungsportsplatsen on the far side of Heden. Alternatively try *Cyckelogen* at Bjorcksgatan 45c (☎21 11 11) – to get there take tram #1 or #3 to Härlanda – or *Cykelspecialisten* at Delsjovagen 5B (☎40 23 24) – take tram #5 to St Sigfridsplan, east of the city centre. To rent a bike for two days will cost you 250–300kr, for a week 325–500kr.

# Accommodation

Gothenburg has plenty of good accommodation to choose from, with no shortage of comfortable **youth hostels** – though many are out of the centre – **private rooms** and a number of big, central **hotels**. Most of these are clustered together around the train station and offer a high standard of service, if with fairly uniform and uninspiring decor. Summer-time reductions mean that even the better hotels can prove surprisingly affordable, and most places also take part in the Gothenburg Package, which can cut costs further (see "Hotels and pensions"). Whenever you turn up, you should have no trouble finding accommodation, though in summer it's a good idea to book ahead if you are limited to the cheaper hotels, or if you want to stay in the most popular youth hostels (see the listings below).

## Youth hostels and private rooms

The cheapest options for accommodation are booking a **private room** (costing 150kr per person in a double room, 200kr for a single) through the tourist office (which charges a booking fee of 60kr; ☎10 07 40 for details), or staying in one of the **youth hostels**. All the hostels listed below are *STF*, except for *Nordengarden,* and are open all year unless otherwise stated. For stays of a week or more, it is worth contacting *SGS Bostader*, Utlandgatan 24 (Mon–Fri 11am–3pm), who rent out **furnished rooms** with kitchens for around 1200kr a week. Sheets are included, but not kitchen utensils.

**Karralunds Vandrarhem**, Olbergsgatan (☎84 02 00). This hostel is 4km from the centre, close to Liseberg Amusement Park (take tram #5 to Welandergatan; direction Torp) and has non-smoking rooms available. Breakfast can only be ordered by groups. Also offers cabins and a campsite (see p.120). A bed costs 100kr per night. Fills up quickly in summer, so book ahead.

**Kviberg Vandrarhem**, Kvibergsvägen 5 (☎43 50 55, fax 43 26 50). Ten minutes by tram #6 or #7 from Central Station. In Gamlestad (the Old Town before present Gothenburg was founded), the hostel has four-bed rooms, with beds costing 110kr; 25kr extra for sheet rental.

**Masthuggsterrassen**, Masthuggsterassen 8 (☎ & fax 42 48 20). Within a couple of minutes' walk of the *Stena Line* ferry terminal from Denmark. A bed in four-bed rooms costs 125k.

**M/S Seaside**, Packhuskajen (☎10 10 35, fax 711 60 35). A moored ship at the harbour next to Maritima Centrum, this unusual option has twenty one-to-four bed cabins. A bed in a shared dormitory costs 100kr a night, while a cabin to yourself costs 175kr; breakfast and sheets extra. Open April–Sept.

**Nordengarden**, Stockholmsgatan 16 (☎19 66 31). Take tram #1 or #3 to Stockholmsgatan or tram #6 to Redbergplatsen. This is a private hostel with a kitchen and free showers. Advisable to book ahead; 80kr a night in dormitory rooms only.

---

**ACCOMMODATION PRICES**

The pensions and hotels listed in the guide have been price-graded according to the scale outlined below; the number indicates the price for the least expensive double room. Many hotels offer considerable reductions at weekends (year round) and during the summer holiday period (mid-June to mid-Aug); in these cases the reduction is either noted in the text or, where it falls into another price band, given after the full price. Single rooms, where available, usually cost between 60 and 80 percent of a double.

① under 500kr    ② 500–700kr    ③ 700–900kr    ④ 900–1200kr    ⑤ over 1200kr

---

**Ostkupan**, Mejerigatan 2 (☎40 10 50, fax 40 10 51). Bus #64 from Brunnsparken to Graddgatan or tram #5 to St Sigfridsplan then bus #62 to Graddgatan (Kalleback direction). A busy hostel that's only open June–Aug; if booking outside the season, call *Karralunds Vandrarhem* (above). 100kr a night.

**Partille**, Landvettervagen, Partille (☎ & fax 44 61 63). Fifteen kilometres east of the city (take bus #503 or #513 from Heden bus terminal; 30min), this hostel has a solarium and day-room with TV. 100kr a night.

**Slottskogen**, Vegagatan 21 (☎42 65 20, fax 14 21 02). Superbly appointed, family-run hostel that's the best in town. Just two minutes' walk from Linnegatan and not far from Slottskogen Park, the stylish apartment complex has a great living area/TV lounge, fine kitchen and well-designed rooms. Take tram #1 or #2 to Olivedahlsgatan. It costs 100kr a night and the breakfast at 40kr is excellent.

**Torrekulla**, Kallered (☎795 14 95, fax 795 51 40). Fifteen kilometres south of the city, this is a pleasantly situated hostel with lots of room, a free sauna and a nearby bathing lake. Best to take bus #705 from Heden or a 10-minute journey on a local train from Central Station followed by a 15-minute walk. 100kr a night for members.

# Hotels and pensions

The **Gothenburg Package**, coordinated by the tourist office (do not approach the hotels direct), is a real bargain as it brings together accommodation, breakfast and a Gothenburg Card for 360–650kr per person in a twin bedroom. With around thirty good central hotels taking part, the scheme is valid every Friday to Monday from early June to the end of August, all major holidays, winter sports holidays and over Christmas. Some of the hotels operate it on Thursdays and others all year round. There is a fifty-percent discount for **children** sharing with one parent at some hotels, while others allow extra beds in single rooms – the tourist office will advise. At the time of writing all the hotels listed below were involved in the Gothenburg Package, and all include breakfast in the price unless otherwise stated.

**Alleyn**, Parkgatan 10 (☎10 14 50, fax 11 91 60). Very central, sensibly priced hotel close to Avenyn and the old town. Prices include room service and parking. ③/②

**City**, Lorensbergsgatan 6 (☎18 00 25, fax 18 81 90). Not to be confused with *City Hotel Ritz* (see below), this is a cheapish and popular place, excellently positioned close to Avenyn on a street named after the *Lorensberg Theatre*, the city's first "democratic" theatre (see p.128). For en-suite rooms you'll pay 300kr more. ①

**City Hotel Ritz**, Burggrevegatan 25 (☎80 00 80, fax 15 77 76). Close to Central Station and airport buses, this comfortable hotel has en-suite WC, shower/bath and cable TV in all rooms. There is a free sauna for residents and solarium (30kr). ③

**Eggers**, Drottningtorget (☎80 60 70, fax 15 42 43). The original station hotel, this very characterful establishment has individually furnished bedrooms and a wealth of grand original features. One of the best-value central hotels, with a really low Gothenburg Package price. ⑤/③

**Ekoxen-Kung Karl**, Norra Hamngatan 38 (☎80 50 80, fax 80 58 17). A merge of the stylish, family-run *Kung Karl* and the new *Ekoxen* has resulted in this big, central hotel close to the train station providing sauna, bubble pool/spa and cable TV. Rather tired decor. ③/②

**Europa**, Köpmansgatan 38 (☎80 12 80, fax 15 47 55). With an amorphous facade attached to the *Nordstan* shopping centre, this is reputedly the largest hotel in Sweden. Inside is very plush with lots of marble, breakfast is a huge, international-style buffet and every en-suite room has a bath tub (unusual for Sweden). ⑤/③

**Excelsior**, Karl Gustavsgatan 9 (☎17 54 35, fax 17 54 39). Shabbily stylish 1880 building in a road of classic Gothenburg houses between Avenyn and Haga. It's been a hotel since 1930; Greta Garbo and Ingrid Bergman both stayed here as, more recently, did The Animals and Sheryl Crow. Classic suites with splendid nineteenth-century features, cost no more than plain rooms – Garbo's room is no. 535. ④/②

**Hotel 11**, Maskingatan 11 (☎779 11 11, fax 779 11 10). At the harbour, with views across to Hisingen and dramatic summer reductions, this is one of the city's most interesting and stylish places to stay. Built on the site of an old ship-building yard and using lots of the original structure, it organizes bungy jumping at 300kr a go. Take tram #1, #3, #4 or #9 from Järntorget, then the boat, *Älv Snabben* (Mon–Fri every 30min 6am–11.30pm, shorter hours on weekends; 16kr, free with Gothenburg Card), in the direction of Klippan from in front of the *Opera House* at Lilla Bommen – get off at Eriksberg. ⑤/③

**Lilton**, Föreningsgatan 9 (☎82 88 08, fax 82 21 84). One of Gothenburg's least-known pensions, close to the Haga district, this small, old, ivy-covered nine-bedroom place is set among trees. Splendid National Romantic and Art Nouveau buildings directly opposite. ③/②

**Maria Erikssons Pensionat**, Chalmersgatan 27A (☎20 70 30, fax 16 64 63). Just ten rooms, but well positioned on a road running parallel with Avenyn. Breakfast not included. ①

**Robinson**, Södra Hamngatan 2 (☎80 25 21, fax 15 92 91). Facing Brunnspark, this mediocre hotel still boasts its original facade – the building was part of the old Furstenburg Palace (see p.126). A few features have survived decades of architectural messing like the original etched windows depicting Skansen Leijonet (the fortress tower) on the lift. All rooms have cable TV, but en-suite rooms cost 160kr more; there are some family rooms. ②/①

**Sheraton**, Södra Hamngatan 59–65 (☎80 60 00, fax 15 98 88). Opposite the train station and exuding all the usual glitz of a costly hotel (double rooms at the standard price go for 1880kr). The atrium foyer is like a shopping mall with glass lifts and fountains; bedrooms are all pastel shades and birch wood. The *Frascati Restaurant* here serves up truffles, duck and salmon (fish dishes alone cost over 200kr); while set lunches offer two courses at 215kr. ⑤/④

# Cabins and campsites

Several campsites provide **cabins**, which are a worthwhile idea if you are sharing with more than one other. Facilities are invariably squeaky clean and in good working order – there is usually a well-equipped kitchen – but you'll have to pay extra for bedding. Prices for cabins are given below; if you want to **camp**, you'll pay around 100kr for two people in July and August (50kr the rest of the year).

**Askims** (☎28 62 61, fax 68 13 35). Twelve kilometres from the centre; take tram #1 or #2 to Linneplatsen, then bus #83, or better still the *Blo Express* (Blue Express) direction Saro from Drottningtorget outside Central Station. Beside sandy beaches, *Askims* is open May–Aug (office 9am–noon & 3pm–6pm, slightly later Thurs–Sat) and has four-bed cabins costing 615kr high season, otherwise 495kr.

**Karralunds** (see "Youth hostels and private rooms" on p.117 for details). Set among forest and lakes, it's open from June 24 to the end of August; four-bed cabins cost 615kr, or 695kr with your own toilet (50kr cheaper during the rest of the year).

**Lilleby Havsbad** (☎56 08 67, fax 56 16 05). Take bus #21 from Nils Ericsonsplatsen and change to the #23 at Kongshallavagen. It takes an hour to reach, but has a splendid seaside location.

# The City

Nearly everything of interest in **Gothenburg** is south of the Göta river, and with one exception, the **Volvo factory** on the northern island of **Hisingen**, there's no need to cross the water.

At the heart of the city is the historic **old town**, and although Gothenburg's attractions are by no means restricted to this area, its picturesque elegance makes it about the best place to start. Tucked between the Göta river to the north and the zigzagging canal to the south, old Gothenburg's tightly gridded streets are lined with impressive facades, interesting food markets and a couple of worthwhile museums – the **Stadmuseum** and, up by the harbour, the museum of **maritime history**. Just across the canal that skirts the southern edges of the old town is **Trädgårdsforeningen** park, which in summer is full of floral colour and picnicking city dwellers.

Heading further south into the modern centre, **Avenyn** is Gothenburg's showcase boulevard, alive with showy restaurants and bars. However, it's the roads off Avenyn that hold the area's real interest, with more alternative 24-hour café-bars and some of Gothenburg's best museums: in a small district called **Vasaplan** to the southwest, you'll find the **Röhsska Museum** of applied arts and, further south in **Götaplatsen**, the city **Art Museum**. For family entertainment day or night, the classic **Liseberg Amusement Park**, just to the southeast of the Avenyn, has been a focal point for Gothenburgers since the 1920s.

Vasaplan stretches west to **Haga**, the old working-class district now a haven for the trendy and monied. Haga Nygatan, the main thoroughfare, leads on to Linnegatan, the arterial road through **Linne**. Fast establishing itself as the most vibrant part of the city, it's home to the most interesting evening haunts, with new cafés, bars and restaurants opening up alongside long-established antique emporiums and sex shops. Further out the rolling **Slottskogen** park holds the **Natural History Museum**, but is more alluring as a pretty place to sunbathe.

Gothenburg is a fairly compact and easy city to get around, so if you only have a day or two here you can cover most of the sights, but to get the most from your stay give the city at least four days and slow your pace down to a stroll – which will put you in step with the locals.

## The old town and the harbour

The **old town** is divided in two by the **Stora Hamn Canal**, to the north of which are most of the main sights and the harbour, where the decaying, but still impressive, shipyards make for a dramatic backdrop. The streets south of the Stora Hamn stretching down to the southern canal are just right for an afternoon's leisurely stroll, with some quirky cafés, food markets and antique/junk shops to dip into, as well as Sweden's oldest synagogue. Straddling the Stora Hamn is the stately main square, **Gustav Adolfs Torg**, and starting your day here gives easy access to the whole area.

## Gustav Adolfs Torg

At the centre of **Gustav Adolfs Torg**, a copper statue of Gustavus Adolphus points ostentatiously at the ground where he reputedly declared: "Here I will build my city." This, however, isn't the original German-made statue of the city founder; that one was kidnapped on its way to Sweden, and rather than pay the ransom Gothenburgers commissioned a new one.

Although there is little attempt to encourage visitors to enter the buildings surrounding the square, it is worth persisting to discover some exceptional interiors. To the east of the square, with the canal behind you, stands the **Rådhus** – not a town hall as the name suggests, but the criminal law courts since 1672. Beyond its rather dull Classical facade, the interior of its extension is of international acclaim. Designed by the ground-breaking Functionalist architect E G Asplund in l936, it features the original glass lifts, mussel-shaped drinking fountains and huge areas of laminated aspen – the latter creating the impression of standing inside a giant 1930s cocktail cabinet.

There are also some rather fine rooms, with grand chandeliers and trompe l'oeil ceilings, tucked away in the old building, but to see them you'll have to attract the attention of a court assistant and wait for the rooms to be opened. Your time is better spent trying to convince attendants at the white, double-columned 1842 **Borhuset** to let you in. Facing the canal, this former Exchange has banqueting and concert halls of magnificent opulence, while smaller rooms are a riot of red and blue stucco, inspired by the eighteenth-century excavations at Pompeii. Visitors are not encouraged in any numbers as the fabric of the building is under strain, but once inside staff will usually give an enthusiastic and informed commentary.

## North to the harbour

Heading north from the square along the erstwhile canal, Östra Hamngatan, you'll pass Sweden's biggest shopping centre, **Nordstan**. A dark and dreary complex, its few saving graces are a 24-hour pharmacy and a second tourist office. If you have time to spare and haven't yet seen the city's impressive **Central Station**, take a short detour along Burggrevegatan to Drottningtorget. The oldest train station in the country (dating from 1856), behind its original facade is a grand and marvellously preserved interior – take a look at the wood beam-ends in the ticket hall, every one carved in the likeness of the city-council members of the day. Although it's usually behind closed doors, you might be able to persuade a guard to let you see the staffroom. This was once the royal waiting room, and is still resplendent, with hand-painted ceilings and gilt-topped pillars.

Otherwise walk up to the end of Östra Hamngatan and onto **Lilla Bommen**, where Gothenburg's industrial decline is juxtaposed with its artistic regeneration to dramatic visual effect: to the west beyond the harbour, redundant shipyard cranes loom across the sky, making a sombre background to the bronze and pink-granite sculptures dotted along the waterfront – most of which share an industrial theme. The new **Opera House** (daily noon–6pm; for guided tours ☎10 80 50, for opera details ☎701 80 70) to the left was designed with deliberate industrial

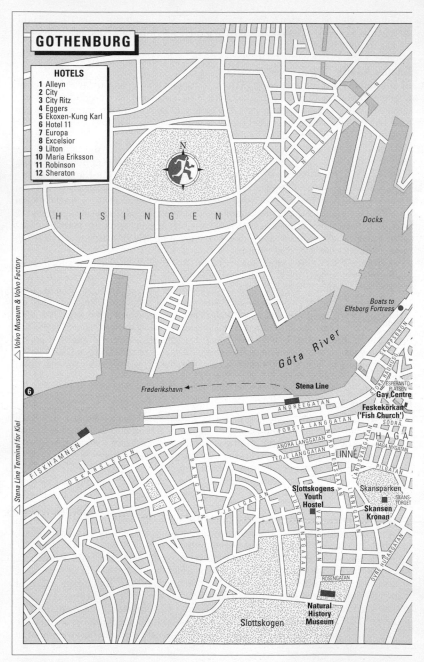

# GOTHENBURG

**HOTELS**
1 Alleyn
2 City
3 City Ritz
4 Eggers
5 Ekoxen-Kung Karl
6 Hotel 11
7 Europa
8 Excelsior
9 Lilton
10 Maria Eriksson
11 Robinson
12 Sheraton

N

HISINGEN

Docks

△ Volvo Museum & Volvo Factory

△ Stena Line Terminal for Kiel

Boats to
Elfsborg Fortress

Göta River

❻

Frederikshavn ◀───

Stena Line

ANDREEGATAN

ESPERANTO-
PLATSEN

Gay Centre

Feskekörkan
('Fish Church')

SÖDRA

FORSTA LANGGATAN

HAGA

HAGA NYGATAN

ANDRA LANGGATAN

TEDJE LANGGATAN

LINNE

PILGATAN

FISKHAMNEN

OSKARSLEDEN

SKARSLEDEN

BANGATAN

FJÄLLGATAN

JUNGMANSGATAN

KESJÖGATAN

Slottskogens
Youth
Hostel

Skansparken

SKANS-
TORGET

Skansen
Kronan

ROSENGATAN

ÖVRE HUSARGATAN

Natural
History
Museum

Slottskogen

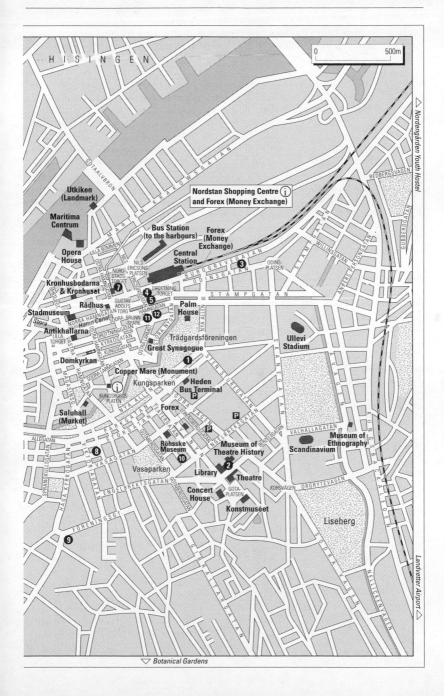

HISINGEN

Nordengården Youth Hostel ▷

0    500m

Utkiken
(Landmark)

Nordstan Shopping Centre ⓘ
and Forex (Money Exchange)

REDBERGSVÄGEN

Maritima
Centrum

Opera
House

Bus Station
(to the harbours)

Forex
(Money
Exchange)

Central
Station

❸

ODINS-
PLATSEN

Kronhusbodarna
& Kronhuset

❼

NORD-
STADS-
TORGET

NILS
ERICSONS-
PLATSEN

DROTTNING-
TORGET

❹
❺

STAMPGATAN

Råthus

Stadmuseum

GUSTAV
ADOLFS
TORG

Hamn Canal

SÖDRA BRUNN-
SPARK

Palm
House

❶❶ ❶❷

Antikhallarna

Domkyrkan

LILLA
TORGET

Trädgårdsföreningen

Ullevi
Stadium

Great Synagogue

❶

Copper Mare (Monument)

Kungsparken

Heden
Bus Terminal
Ⓟ

Forex

Ⓟ

Röhsske
Museum
❶⓪

Museum of
Theatre History

VALHALLAGATAN

Museum of
Ethnography
Scandinavium

Saluhall
(Market)

❽

Vasaparken

Library

❷

Theatre

Concert
House

GÖTA-
PLATSEN

KORSVÄGEN    ORGRYTEVÄGEN

Liseberg

Konstmuséet

❾

Landvetter Airport ▷

▽ Botanical Gardens

styling, the idea being that stage sets should be created within the building as part of a production flow. It's worth wandering inside whether you're an opera buff or not. To the right, the **Utkiken** or "Look Out" (Jan to mid-May & early Sept to mid-Dec Sat & Sun 11am–4pm; May to early Sept daily 11am–7pm; 25kr), which was designed by the Scottish architect Ralph Erskine in the late 1980s, is an 86m-high office building shaped and coloured like a half-used red lipstick. Its top storey offers panoramic views of the city and harbour.

Walking west along the quay, it is just a couple of minutes to **Maritima Centrum** (May–June & Aug daily 10am–6pm; July daily 10am–9pm; March–April & Sept–Nov daily 10am–4pm; 45kr, free with a Gothenburg Card), which describes itself as "the largest ship museum in the world". Not a dull experience, even for non-enthusiasts of things maritime, the museum comprises a dozen boats, including a 1915 lightship, a submarine and a firefloat, each giving a glimpse of how seamen lived and worked on board. The most impressive ship is a monstrous naval destroyer, complete with a medical office, where the amputa-tion of a leg and hand is more amusing than informative – far-fetched clothes-shop dummies do the honours. A special blue-arrow route has been designed for any-one wanting to avoid the ship's steep steps. The toilets and washrooms on board are an experience in themselves, being original and open for public use. There is a rather good café and restaurant here, too.

## The Kronhuset and the Stadsmuseum

From the maritime museum, it's a short walk southwest to Gothenburg's oldest sec-ular building, **Kronhuset** on Kronhusgatan (Tues–Fri 11am–4pm, Sat & Sun 11am–5pm). It was built by the Dutch in 1642 as an artillery depot for the city's gar-rison, and five-year-old Karl XI was proclaimed king here in 1660. Set picturesque-ly in the eighteenth-century wings that surround the original building is **Kronhusbodarna** (Mon–Fri 11am–4pm, Sat 11am–2pm), a cluster of small, pricey shops specializing in making gold, silver and glass. The silversmith will sell you a copy of the city's oldest key, but the money would be better spent at the vaulted, atmospheric café, which serves dunes of meringues as well as sandwich lunches.

A couple of blocks further south, the **Stadsmuseum** or City Museum (April–Sept Mon–Fri noon–6pm, Sat–Sun 11am–4pm; rest of the year closed Mon; 40kr) has emerged, after an extensive reshuffling of the city's museums, as the mother of them all, incorporating several into one building. It is housed at no. 12 Ostindiska Huset, the 1750-built offices, store and auction house of the enormously influential East India Company. Envious of the major maritime nations, two Gothenburg-based industrialists, Colin Campbell and Niklas Sahlgren, set up the Swedish **East India Company** in the early eighteenth cen-tury. Granted the sole right to trade with China in 1731, the company monopo-lized all Swedish trade with the Far East for over eighty years, the only condition being that the bounty – tea, silk, porcelain and spices and arrack, an East Indian snaps used to make Swedish punch – had to be sold and auctioned in Gothenburg. The Chinese influence of these great sea trips pervaded Gothenburg society, and wealthy financiers styled their homes and gardens with Chinese motifs. By 1813, the unrest of the French Revolution and competition from British and Dutch tea traders meant profits slid, and it was decreed that "East India trade could be pursued by anyone so inclined". The headquarters, however, remain an imposing reminder of the power and prestige the company, and Gothenburg, once held.

The museum itself is well worth a browse, not least for its rich interior, a mix of squat, carved-stone pillars, stained glass and frescoes. Your first port of call should be the third floor, where there are exhibitions on the East India Company. There is very little English labelling, but the numerous display cabinets full of the Chinese goods and treasures are a wonderful insight into the company's history. The renovated auction hall, where the city's grandest auctions took place, however, is surprisingly modest. From here you move on to the rather incongruously placed exhibition of **1950s' life**, based around fashions and film stars; you'll see showcases of pointy bras and Vespa motorbikes.

The museum's most impressive section is the **industrial history** exhibition. Using sound effects, clever design and plenty of English commentary, the exhibition focuses on twentieth-century history, starting with the textile and timber trade, which were central to Gothenburg's wealth. At the beginning of the century, working conditions in the city's factories were extremely poor, and a third of the workforce at some textile factories was children. The main working-class neighbourhood was Haga, and the exhibition highlights the importance of Järntorget (The Iron Square), just northwest of Haga Nygatan, which was a hotbed of unrest during the Great Strike of 1909. The exhibition moves on to the middle decades of the century, when massive industrial growth saw the building of the shipyards, and the ball bearings and car industries, and onto the 1950s and 1960s when the first foreign labour had to be recruited to deal with demand. The present-day situation is summed up by a plaque at the end: "Once, the city had one engineer and one hundred workers to make a ship engine. Now, a large group of engineers design an engine part to be built by factories abroad."

Most of the city's other smaller and none too thrilling museums have been incorporated within this building, with the exception of one, the **Banking Museum** on the opposite side of Stora Hamn canal at Södra Hamngatan 11 (Sun noon–3pm, guided tours in English 2pm). Inside you can visit the vaults, but really the building's facade is the best bit.

## South of Stora Hamn – Lilla Torget to Brunnsparken

Across Stora Hamn just to the west of the Stadsmuseum lies **Lilla Torget**, which in itself is nothing to get excited about, but having nodded at the statue of Jonas Alstromer, who introduced the potato to Sweden in the eighteenth century, walk on to the quayside at **Stenpiren** (stone pier). In 1638, this is where hundreds of emigrants said their last goodbyes before sailing off to create New Sweden in the United States. The original granite **Delaware Monument** was carted off to America in the early part of this century, and it wasn't until 1938 that celebrated sculptor Carl Mille cast a replacement in bronze, which still stands here looking out to sea.

Today boats leave from Stenpiren for the popular excursion to the island fortress of **Nya Elfsborg** (early May to Aug hourly 9.30am–3pm; 20min; 65kr, free with a Gothenburg Card). Built in the seventeenth century to defend the harbour and the city, the surviving buildings have been turned into a **museum** and café. There are guided tours in English (included in the price of the boat trip) around the square tower, chapel and prison cells, which detail violent confrontations with the Danes and some of the methods used to keep prisoners from swimming away – check out the set of iron shackles weighing over 36kg.

Back in Lilla Torget, it's worth taking the tiny opening on the western side of the square and making the steep but short climb to **Drottning Kristinas Jaktslott** (Queen Kristina's Hunting Lodge) at Otterhallegatan 16. Never a hunting lodge, and absolutely nothing to do with Queen Kristina, who died the century before it was built, it is instead a quaint café (daily 11am–4pm) that serves particularly good waffles.

Walking down Västra Hamngatan, which leads off the southern side of the square, it is only a short walk to the city's cathedral; on the way you'll pass **Antik Hallarna** (Mon–Fri 10am–6pm, Sat 10am–2pm), a clutch of pricey antique shops. It is the building, however, that warrants your attention, with its fantastic gilded ceiling and regal marble stairs, leading up to the second floor and a café. A few blocks south of Antik Hallarna and left off Västra Hamngatan is the classically styled cathedral **Domkyrkan** (Mon–Fri 8am–5pm, Sat 8am–3pm, Sun 10am–3pm), built in 1827 (the two previous cathedrals were destroyed by fires at a rate of one a century). Four giant sandstone columns stand at the portico, and inside there's an alterpiece full of gilded opulence. The plain white walls concentrate the eye on the unusual post-resurrection cross – devoid of a Jesus, but his gilded grave clothes are strewn over ground below. Another quirky feature is the twin glassed-in verandas that run down either side; looking like glamorous trams with net curtains, they were actually designed for the bishop's "private conversations".

Continuing east past the cathedral and north towards Stora Hamn, the leafy square known as **Brunnspark** soon comes into view, with Gustav Adolfs Torg just across the the canal. The sedate house facing the square is now a snazzy restaurant and nightclub called *The Palace* (see p.135), but the house was once home to Pontus and Gothilda **Furstenburg**, the city's leading arts patrons in the late nineteenth century. They opened up the top floor as Gothenburg's first art gallery to be lit with electric as well as natural light, and later donated their entire collection – the biggest batch of Nordic paintings in the country – to the city Art Museum. As a tribute to the Furstenburgs, the museum made over the top floor into an exact replica of the original gallery (see p.129). Staff at *The Palace* know little of its history, but you can still wander upstairs and see the richly ornate plasterwork and gilding much as it was.

## Along the southern canal

Following the zigzagging canal that marks the southern perimeter of old Gothenburg – a moat during the days when the city was fortified – makes for a fine twenty-minute stroll, past pretty waterside views and a number of interesting diversions.

Just east of Brunnspark, **Stora Nygatan** wends its way south along the canal's most scenic stretch; to one side are Classical buildings all stuccoed in cinnamon and cream, and to the other is the green expanse of Trädgårdsföreningen park (see "Avenyn and around"). Among all the architectural finery sits Sweden's oldest synagogue, **Great Synagogue** (for tour times call ☎17 72 45), which was inaugurated in 1855. Its simple domed exterior belies one of the most exquisite interiors of any European synagogue. The ceiling and walls are all covered in rich blues, reds and gold, and Moorish patterns are interwoven with Viking leaf designs – a combination that works to stunning effect. It also has some unusual features: the lofty interior contains two levels of upper women's galleries and at the back – extremely rare in synagogues – a splendid organ first played at the inauguration ceremony. The original congregation were Orthodox German Jews, though it now serves as a Conservative synagogue for all the community.

South from the synagogue, you'll pass **Kungsportsplatsen**, in the centre of which stands a useful landmark, a sculpture known as the "Copper Mare" –

though it's fairly obvious if you look from beneath that this is no mare (the main tourist office is also on the square). A few minutes further on, and one block in from the canal at Kungstorget, is **Saluhallen** (Mon–Fri 9am–6pm, Sat 9am–2pm), a pretty barrel-roofed indoor market built in the 1880s. Busy and full of atmosphere, it's a great place to wander through (for more on food markets in Gothenburg see "Eating"); outside there's a flower market.

Five minutes from here is another food market, whose strong aromas may well hit you long before you reach its door, the neo-Gothic **Feskekorka**, or "Fish-church" (Tues–Thurs 9am–5pm, Fri 9am–6pm, Sat 9am–1.30pm). Despite its undeniably ecclesiastical appearance, the nearest the 1874-built *Feskekorka* comes to religion is the devotion shown by the fish lovers who come to buy and sell here. Inside, every kind of fish from smoked to shellfish lie in gleaming pungent mounds of silver, pink and black flesh; while in a gallery upstairs, there's a very small, very good restaurant (see "Eating" for more details). Just behind the *Feskekorka* is Gothenburg's **gay centre** at Esperantoplatsen 7. Unfortunately, though, the café inside, *Café Hellmans*, is rarely open (Mon 7–11pm, Thurs & Sun 7–10pm), the bookshop has hardly any books in it (Thurs & Sun 7–10pm), and the library even fewer (Thurs & Sun 7–9pm) – for more information on Gothenburg's low-key gay scene, see "Drinking, nightlife and culture".

# Avenyn and around

Across the canal from Kungsportsplatsen and running all the way southeast to Götaplatsen is the wide, cobbled length of Kungsportsavenyn. Known more simply as **Avenyn** or "the Avenue", this is Gothenburg's showiest thoroughfare. It's teeming with life; the ground floor of almost every grand old nineteenth-century home has been converted into a café, bar or restaurant. The young and beautiful strut up and down and sip overpriced drinks at tables that spill onto the street from mid-spring to September. It's enjoyable enough to sit and watch people go by, but for all its glamour, the tourist-orientated shops and brasseries are mostly bright and samey, and the grandeur of the city's industrial past is easier to imagine in the less spoiled mansions along Parkgatan – running at right angles to Avenyn and parallel to the canal – and other roads off the main drag to the southwest. Here, in the area known as **Vasaplan**, you'll find Gothenburg's **museum of applied arts**, and further south on **Götaplatsen**, the extensive **fine art museum**.

## The Trädgårdsföreningen

Before you reach the crowds of Avenyn, you might want to take time out and relax in the well-groomed **Trädgårdsföreningen** or "Garden Society Park" (May–Aug 7am–9pm; Sept–April 7am–6pm; May–Aug 10kr, rest of year free), which really does live up to its blurb: "a green oasis in the heart of the city". The main entrance to the park is just over the canal bridge to your left. Once inside there are a number of attractions to visit. The most impressive is the 1878-built **Palm House** (June–Aug daily 10am–6pm; Sept–May daily 10am–4pm; 20kr, which also gives entry to the Botanical Gardens; see p.131); looking like a huge English conservatory, it contains a wealth of very un-Swedish plant life, with tropical, Mediterranean and Asian flowers. Close by is the **Butterfly House** (April, May & Sept daily except Mon 10am–4pm; June–Aug daily 10am–5pm; Oct–March Tues–Fri 10am–3pm, Sat–Sun 11am–3pm: 35kr), where you can walk among vast, free-flying butterflies from Asia and the Americas. The eighty-percent humidity keeps the creatures alive for double their natural lifespan. Further on is the **Rosarium**, a rose garden with nearly three thousand varieties of rose, arranged in a vivid rainbow of colours. During summer the place goes into overdrive with lunchtime concerts and a special children's theatre.

## Vasaplan and the Rohsska Museum

Once you've had your fill of Avenyn, take one of the roads off to the west and wander into **Vasaplan**, where the streets are lined with fine nineteenth-century and National Romantic architecture, and the cafés are cheaper and more laid-back. On Vasagatan, the main street through the district, is the excellent **Rohsska Museum**, Sweden's only museum of applied arts (May–Aug Mon–Fri noon–4pm, Sat & Sun noon–5pm; Sept–April Tues noon–9pm, Wed–Fri noon–4pm, Sat–Sun noon–5pm; 35kr). The 1916-built museum is an aesthetic Aladdin's cave, with each floor concentrating on different areas of decorative and functional art, from early dynasty Chinese ceramics to European arts and crafts of the sixteenth and seventeenth centuries. Far more arresting, however, is the first floor, which is devoted to twentieth-century decor and features all manner of recognizable designs from the 1910s to 1990s – enough to send anyone over the age of ten on a giddy nostalgia trip.

Heading away from Avenyn down **Vasagatan**, or its parallel street **Engelbrektsgatan**, you'll come across solid, stately and rangy buildings that epitomize Gothenburg's nineteenth-century commercial wealth and social pride. White-stuccoed or red-and-cream brick facades are decorated with elaborate ceramic tiles, intricate stone and brick animal carvings, shiny metal cupolas and Classical window porticoes. With the detail spread gracefully across these six-storey terraces, the overall effect is of restrained grandeur. Many of the houses also have Continental-style wrought-iron balconies; it's easy to imagine high-society gatherings spilling out into the night on warm summer evenings. In contrast, interspersed among all this nineteenth-century swagger are some perfect examples of early twentieth-century National Romantic architecture, with rough-hewn stone and Art Nouveau swirls in plaster and brickwork; look particularly at the early numbers along Engelbrektsgatan, furthest from Avenyn.

## Götaplatsen and the Kontsmuseum

At the top of Avenyn, **Götaplatsen** is modern Gothenburg's main square. and in the centre stands Carl Milles's **Poseidon** – a giant bronze body-builder, nude with a staggeringly ugly face. The size of the figure's penis caused moral outrage when the sculpture first appeared in 1930, and was subsequently dramatically reduced. Today, although from the front Poseidon appears to be squeezing the living daylights out of a large-fanged fish – symbolic of local trade – if you climb the steps of the **Concert Hall** to the right, it's clear that Milles won the battle over Poseidon's manhood to stupendous effect. To the left of the statue and standing back from the City Library is the columned **Lorensberg Theatre**, one of Gothenburg's few private theatres run entirely on a commercial basis. It was designed as the first "democratic" theatre, having no boxes, just standard price stalls. Few tourists are likely to take in a show here, though, as the *Lorensberg* (like many other theatres in Sweden) is closed during the summer and only puts on shows in Swedish (for more on theatre in Gothenburg see "Drinking, nightlife and culture").

Behind *Poseidon* stands the square's most impressive attraction, the much-respected **Konstmuseum** or Art Museum (May–Aug Mon–Fri 11am–4pm;

Sept–April Tues 11am–4pm, Wed 11am–9pm, Thurs–Fri 11am–4pm, Sat–Sun 11am–5pm; 35kr). Its massive, symmetrical facade is reminiscent of the Fascist architecture of 1930s' Germany. This is one of the city's finest museums, and it's easy to spend half a day absorbing the diverse and extensive collections. The following is only a brief guide to some of the highlights.

First off on the ground floor, the **Hasselblad Centre** shows excellent changing photographic exhibitions; while on the floor above, a display of post-1945 Nordic art gives space to contemporary Scandinavian painters and sculptors. Another room has some works by the celebrated masters of French Impressionism; others hold a range of minor works by Van Gogh, Gauguin and Pissarro, a powerful and surprisingly colourful Munch and a couple of Rodin sculptures. Moving on to floor five, you'll find Italian and Spanish paintings from 1500 to 1750, including works by Canaletto and Francesco Guardi, Rembrandt's *Knight with Falcon* and Rubens's *Adoration of the Magi.*

Best of all, however, and the reason to spend time at the museum, are the **Furstenburg Galleries** on the sixth floor. These celebrate the work of some of Scandinavia's most prolific and revered turn-of-the-century artists. Well-known paintings by Carl Larsson, Anders Zorn and Carl Wilhelmson reflect the seasons and landscapes of the Nordic countries and evoke a vivid picture of Scandinavian life in the early years of the century. Paintings to look out for include Larsson's *Lilla Suzanne,* which touchingly depicts the elated face of a baby and is one of his most realistic works; Anders Zorn's *Bathers,* flushed with a pale pink summer glow and exemplifying the painter's feeling for light and the human form; and the sensitive portraits of Ernst Josephson, most notably his full-length portrait of Carl Skånberg – easily mistakable for the young Winston Churchill. The Danish artist Peter Kroyer's marvellous *Hip Hip Horay* again plays with light, and a couple of works by Hugo Birger deserve attention, too. One depicts the interior of the original Furstenburg Gallery, complete with electric lights, while his massive *Scandinavian Artists' Breakfast in Paris,* dominating an entire wall, will help put some faces to the artists' names. Also worth a look is an entire room of Larsson's fantastical and bright wall-size paintings.

A delightful little park, **Nackros Dammen** (which means "Waterlily Park"), lies just behind Götaplatsen and, with its big pond full of ducks and late-spring rhododendrons, it's just the place to relax after a morning of intensive art appreciation.

## Liseberg Amusement Park and Museum of Ethnography

Just a few minutes' walk southeast from Götaplatsen – or take tram #5 from the old centre – is **Liseberg Amusement Park** (late April–June & late Aug daily 3–11pm; July to mid-Aug daily noon–11pm; Sept Sat 1–11pm, Sun noon–8pm; 40kr, under 7s free; all-day ride pass 195kr, or limited ride tickets for 90kr or 150kr). Opened in 1923, Sweden's largest amusement park is great fun for adults as well as children. A league away from the hyped neon and plastic mini-cities that make up so many theme parks around the world, with its flowers, trees, fountains and clusters of lights, Liseberg is much more Hansel and Gretel than Disneyland. Old and young dance to live bands, and although more youth dominated and louder at night (especially Saturdays), it is safe to stroll. The newest attraction is an ambitious roller coaster called "Hangover".

If you visit Liseberg during the day, it's worth teaming it up with the surprisingly interesting **Museum of Ethnography** at Avagen 24, a ten-minute walk north of the park (Tues–Fri 11am–4pm, Mon 11am–9pm, Sat & Sun 11am–5pm), just over the highway. The best exhibits are those on American Indian culture, with brilliantly lit textiles that are up to two-thousand years old and some other more grisly finds, including skulls deliberately trephined (squashed) to ward off bad spirits.

# Haga

On the other side of Avenyn, and a ten-minute stroll up Vasagatan (alternatively take tram #1, #3, #4 or #9 towards Linnegatan), is the city's oldest working-class suburb, **Haga**, which today is one of Gothenburg's most picturesque quarters. The transformation took place in the early 1980s when the area was so run-down that demolition was on the cards. The tables were turned, however, when someone saw potential in the web of artisans' homes known as "governor's houses". These distinctive buildings, made up of a stone ground floor and two upper wooden storeys, were built to prevent the devastation caused by city fires. After one particularly bad blaze, the city governor decreed that no building should have more than two floors of wood. At the time solid stone was too expensive and heavy for the clay ground – hence the combination.

Haga is now Gothenburg's mini version of Greenwich Village, the domain of the well-off and socially aware twenty- and thirty-somethings. The thick smattering of cafés and shops along its cobbled streets are style conscious and not at all cheap. Although there are a couple of good restaurants (see "Eating") along the main thoroughfare, **Haga Nygatan**, this is really somewhere to come during the day, when tables are put out on the street and the atmosphere is friendly and villagey – if a little self-consciously fashionable. Apart from the boutiques, which tend towards the likes of Art Deco light fittings, calmative crystals and nineteenth-century Swedish kitchenware, it's worth noting the apartment buildings between. These red-brick edifices were originally almshouses donated by the Dickson family, the city's British industrialist forefathers who played a big part in the success of the East India Company – the name of Robert Dickson is still emblazoned on their facades.

Adjoining Haga to the south, **Skansparken** is hardly a park at all, being little more than the raised mound of land on which stands the **Military Museum** (Tues, Wed noon–2pm, Sat & Sun noon–3pm; 20kr), housed in one of Gothenburg's two surviving seventeenth-century fortress towers. The steep climb is worth it for the views north across the city to the harbour rather than for the incredibly feeble museum, whose entire collection consists of wax models in military uniforms throughout the ages.

# Linne

To the west of Haga is the cosmopolitan district of **Linne**, named after the botanist Carl Von Linné, who originated the system for classifying plants that's used the world over. In recent years, so many stylish cafés and restaurants have sprung up along the main thoroughfare, Linnegatan (this leads on from Haga Nygatan), that Linne is now considered Gothenburg's "second Avenyn" – but without the attitude. The street is lined by Dutch-inspired nineteenth-century architecture, tall and elegant buildings cut through with steep little side roads.

However, it's the main roads leading off Linnegatan that give the area its real character. Prosaically named Long Street (Långgatan) First, Second, Third and

Fourth, the not-very-long second and third streets contain a mix of dark antique stores, glittering with massive chandeliers, basement cafés and upfront sex shops. Antiques go for high prices here, so if you're interested, it is well worth checking out the sale times at the popular Auction House on Third Street (Tradje Långgatan 7–9; ☎12 44 30), where a large amount of silver, porcelain and jewellery is mixed in with total tat.

**Slottskogen**, a five-minute walk south from Linnegatan (tram #1 or #2 stopping at Linneplatsen), is a huge, tranquil mass of parkland, with farm animals and birdlife, including pink flamingos in summer. The rather dreary **Natural History Museum** (Tues–Fri 11am–3pm, Sat & Sun 11am–5pm), within the grounds of the park, prides itself on being the city's oldest, dating from 1833. Its endless displays of stuffed birds appear particularly depressing after seeing the living ones outside, and although the museum supposedly contains ten million animals, most of these are minute insects, which sit unnoticed in drawers that fill several rooms. The only items that really capture the attention are a bottle containing the macabre nineteenth-century pickled foetuses of conjoined twins, and the world's only stuffed blue whale. Harpooned in 1865, the whale now contains a Victorian café complete with original red velvet sofas – the top half of the animal neatly secured to its underside by hinges. Unfortunately, these days the whale is only opened in election years, as the Swedish for 'election' is the same as for 'whale'. On the south side of Slottskogen are the large **Botanical Gardens** (daily 9am–dusk; glasshouses May–Aug daily till 6pm, rest of the year Mon–Fri 10am–3pm, Sat & Sun noon–4pm; free entrance with ticket to the Palm House; see p.127).

# North of the river

There is little need to venture north across the Göta river onto Hisingen, Sweden's fourth largest island, though car enthusiasts might be tempted by a visit to the **Volvo Museum** (Tues–Fri 10am–5pm, Sat 11am–4pm; 30kr); take tram #2 or #5 to Eketrägatan, then bus #28 to Götaverken Arendal. There is little effort made at the museum to create a special ambience for the many pristine exhibits, but if you enjoy classic cars, there are rare examples of most models, including "Phillip", an unusual American-style Volvo with fins, of which only one was ever produced, and plenty of gleaming classics, such as Volvo Amazons and the sporty P1800s, along with some not very interesting Volvo commercial vehicles.

The quite separate, and free, **Volvo Factory** has more general appeal (ask for times at the tourist office). The company was founded in 1927 by two engineers from a Gothenburg ball-bearings factory. Today Volvo's "factory" is a vast, city-like complex, with buses wending their way across leafy hills and stopping at places called Volvo Hall and Volvo Park. Geared towards people who are speculating about buying a car, the tour includes film shows and talks in English that are just like one long advertisement. More interesting, if you want to see just how advanced technology is used at each stage in the car's creation, is the **Blue Train tour** (free), a tram-like link of carriages that takes visitors through the vast site and through the 2km-long factory building, where you can watch robots (and even a few humans) create the cars from start to finish. There's a full commentary in English, which thankfully steers clear of technical jargon. From the centre of town, bus #29 runs in summer from Drottningtorget platform M, outside the main post office, right up to the Volvo Factory (40min). To reach the museum from the factory, take bus #29 to Eketrägatan and then change onto bus #28.

# Eating

Gothenburg has a multitude of **eating** places, catering for every budget and for most international tastes. The city's status as a trading port has led to a huge number of ethnic restaurants, everything from Lebanese to Thai (though these places tend to come and go very quickly); the only thing you won't see much of, at least at the lower end of the market, is Swedish food. The city is also a great centre for fish restaurants, and these are among the most exclusive around. For less costly eating, there is a growing trend towards low-price pasta places to complement the staple of pizza parlours and burger bars.

During the past few years, **café life** has really come into its own in Gothenburg, the profusion of new places throughout the city adding to the traditional **konditori** (bakery with tea-room attached). Nowadays, it's easy to stroll from one café to another at any time of day or night, and tuck into humongous sandwiches and gorgeous cakes. Cafés also offer a wide range of light meals and are fast becoming about the best places to go for good food at reasonable prices. The most interesting cafés are concentrated in the fashionable Haga and Linne districts.

### Markets and snacks

The bustling, historic **Saluhallen** at Kungstorget is a delightful sensory experience, with a great choice of meats, fish, fruits, vegetables and a huge range of delectable breads; there are also a couple of cheap coffee/snack bars here. A new arrival on the market scene is **Saluhall Briggen** on the corner of Tredje Långgatan and Nordhamsgatan in the Linne area. More Continental and much smaller than *Saluhallen*, this one specializes in good-quality meats, fish and cheese and mouthwatering deli delights. For excellent fresh fish, **Feskekorka** (see p.127) is an absolute must; while for the serious fish fetishist, there's the auction at **Fiskhamnen** (Fish Harbour; Tues–Fri 7am) a couple of kilometres west of the centre – take tram #3 or #4 to Stigbergstorget. The **Konsum** supermarket on Avenyn (daily till 11pm) sells a wide range of fruits, fish, meats and the usual superstore foods, and has a good deli counter.

## Cafés and restaurants

If you want to avoid paying over the odds, then with just a few exceptions, it's a good idea to steer clear of Avenyn, where prices are almost double what you'll pay in Haga or Linne, and to eat your main meal at **lunchtime**, when *Dagens Rätt* deals fill you up for not very much (40–60kr). For a useful guide to night-time eating for under 100kr, consult the Friday edition of Gothenburg's daily paper, *Göteborgs Posten*. In the following selection, we have given a guide to price: **inexpensive** means you get a main dish for under 80kr, **moderate** means that main dishes cost between 80kr and 120kr, and **expensive** that they are over 120kr.

### The old town

**Ahlstroms Konditori**, Korsgatan 2. A classic café/bakery of the old school. The original features have been watered down with modernization, but it's still worth a visit for its good selection of cakes and *Dagens Rätt* for 52kr.

**Broderna Dahlbom**, Kungsgatan 12 (☎701 77 84). Two celebrated brothers run this fine restaurant, serving Swedish and international *haute cuisine*. Mon–Sat till 11pm. Expensive.

**Feskekorka,** in the eponymous fish market (☎13 90 51). Excellent fish restaurant but prices seem particularly high when you can see the real cost of the ingredients below. Tues–Thurs 9am–5pm, Fri 9am–6pm, Sat 9am–1.30pm.

**Froken Olssons Kafe,** Östra Larmgatan 14. Dunes of sandwiches, salads and sumptuous desserts in a country-style (but not twee) atmosphere. Look out for their mountains of giant meringues on tiered, silver cake trays. Sandwiches 25–50kr.

**Mat & Dryck,** adjoining *Saluhallen* market. A pleasant, if basic, place for salad with dressings and fresh, country breads. Daily lunch at 52kr and a choice of twenty beers.

**Matilda's,** by the side of *Saluhallen* market. This central, friendly café is good for a soupbowl of *café au lait* and a cake.

## Avenyn and around

**GG12,** Avenyn 12 (☎10 58 26). A well-respected fish restaurant, but extremely expensive.

**Gothia Hotel,** Massansgatan 24 (☎40 93 00). Glossy, glitzy hotel, the main attraction being the panoramic views afforded at the piano-bar restaurant on the glass-walled top floor – Gothenburg's highest. They serve, among other fabulously expensive meals, superb king-prawn sandwiches at a whopping 110kr.

**Java Café,** Vasagatan 23, Vasaplan. Parisian feel to this studenty coffee house serving a wide range of coffees and breakfasts at 28kr. Decor includes a collection of thermos flasks dotted among shelves of books. A good Sunday-morning hang-out.

**Junggrens Café,** Avenyn 37. The only reasonably priced Avenyn café, with excellent snacks and sandwiches. Run for decades by a charismatic old Polish woman and her sulky staff. Drop by just for its quirky, convivial atmosphere, its wall paintings and chandeliers. Coffee at only 10kr, sandwiches from 12–20kr.

**Lai Wa,** Storgatan 11, Vasaplan. One of the better Chinese restaurants with a wide variety of dishes at reasonable prices. Good lunches. Try the excellent Peking soup.

**Le Chablis,** Aschebergsgatan 22 (☎20 35 45). A somber and elegant fish restaurant set in the candle-lit grandeur of an unusual early twentieth-century stuccoed building with Art Nouveau turrets. It's all fanned napkins and crisp linen. Extremely expensive.

**Restaurant Frågetecken,** Södra Vägen 20. Just a minute's walk from Götaplatsen, with a name that translates as "restaurant question mark", this is a very popular spot. Eat in the conservatory, or inside and watch the chefs at work, carefully preparing Balkan-influenced food. They boast of being "famous for breasts": duck at 219kr is the most expensive thing on the menu. Pasta for under 100kr. Mon–Fri 11am–11pm, Sat 2pm–midnight, Sun 2–10pm.

**Skåne Café,** Södra Vägen 59. Big, freshly made sandwiches, like smoked salmon for just 20kr, in a very small, basic café, well worth the five-minute walk from Avenyn or Liseberg.

**Smaka,** Vasaplatsen 3, Vasaplan (☎13 22 47). Very traditional Swedish dishes are eaten by a lively, young crowd in a striking, modern interior. Moderate.

**Tai Pak,** Arkivsgatan, just off Avenyn near Götaplatsen. A goodish, traditional-style Chinese restaurant serving a two-course special for 69kr. Individual courses around 65–75kr. Open seven days a week; till 11.30pm on Sat & Sun. Inexpensive.

**28+,** Götabergsgatan parallel with Avenyn. Very fine French-style gourmet restaurant. The name refers to the fat percentage of its renowned cheese; there's a fine cheese shop (9am–11pm) near the entrance. Specialities include goose liver terrine. Service is excellent and not snobbish. Lunch Mon–Fri 11.30am–2pm, dinner Mon–Sat 6–11pm. Expensive.

**Wasa Kallare,** Vasaplatsen 4, Vasaplan (☎13 36 33). Excellent restaurant serving such delights as pickled raw salmon with stewed potatoes. Snacks like smoked eel sandwich at 55kr. Inexpensive.

## Haga

**Café Engelen,** Engelbrektsgatan. Home-baked, excellent-value food at this friendly studenty café. Baked potatoes, lasagne and big sandwiches for 38kr. There's always a vegetarian selection and a good 27kr breakfast. Glorious home-made ice cream and massive range of fruit teas, too. Open 24 hours seven days a week.

**Hemma Hos**, Haga Nygatan 12 (☎13 40 90). Popular restaurant full of quaint old furniture and serving upmarket Swedish food – reindeer and fish dishes. Expensive.

**Jacob's Café**, Haga Nygatan 10. *The* place to sit outside and people watch; pretty decor with some of the finest *Jugend* (Swedish Art Nouveau) lamps.

**Sjöbaren**, Haga Nygatan 27. A small new fish and shellfish restaurant on the ground floor of a traditional governor's house building (see p.130). Open Tues–Sat till 11pm, Sun till 9pm. Moderate (see p.130).

**Solrosen**, Kaponjargatan 4A (☎711 66 97). The oldest vegetarian restaurant in Gothenburg with a wide range of dishes. Moderate.

**Tintin Café**, Engelbrektsgatan 22 (☎16 68 12). Very busy, 24-hour café with mounds of food and coffee at low prices (big plate of chicken salad for 40kr) in a laid-back, studenty atmosphere.

## Linne

**Cedars House**, Andra Långgatan 21. Serves traditional Lebanese food with fifteen-dish mezzes for 225kr (minimum 4 people). Try the wonderful couscous and lamb dishes. Big variety and portions. Belly dancing on Fri and Sat nights. Mon–Thurs 11.30am–11pm, Fri 11.30am–midnight, Sat 2pm–midnight, Sun 1–9pm. Inexpensive to moderate.

**Hos Pelle**, Djupedalsgatan 2 (☎12 10 31). Lovely and sophisticated wine bar off Linnegatan. Snacky options as well as full meals, and wonderful abstract artwork. Moderate.

**Johansson's Café & Curiosity Shop**, Andre Långgatan 6. Pleasant café, where you can buy the antique ornaments and furniture around you. Sandwiches from 22kr.

**Krakow**, Karl Gustavsgatan 28 (☎20 33 74). Burly staff serving big, basic and very filling Polish food in this large, dark restaurant. Moderate.

**Le Village**, Tredje Långgatan 13 (☎24 20 03). Lovely, candle-lit restaurant serving very well-presented but smallish dishes and connected to a big antique shop. Everything you sit on and at is for sale, though much of it is British and at inflated prices. While it's expensive in the main dining area, the trick is to pick a table at the cheaper bar area where meals are from 65kr. Mon–Thurs & Sun till midnight, Fri & Sat till 1am.

**Linnes Trädgård,** Linnegatan 38. This bar and restaurant is a popular, stylish meeting place, with huge windows taking full advantage of its corner position. Beautifully presented, if limited number of, fish, meat and pasta dishes. Try the blueberry mousse or the deliciously indulgent honey and pecan parfait. This is also a perfect place for a relaxed drink. Daily in summer 11am–2am. Expensive.

**Louice Restaurant**, Värmlandsgatan 18, off Andra Långgatan. Justifiably popular and unpretentious neighbourhood restaurant, with occasional live music. Standard mains are expensive, but look out for the excellent-value specials at 79kr. There's a full children's menu in English at 35kr.

**Solsidan Café**, Linnegatan. Lovely café, with delicious cakes and outside seating.

**Thai Garden**, Andra Långgatan 18 (☎12 76 60). Nothing special to look at, but big portions and excellent service with good prices. Moderate.

# Drinking, nightlife and culture

There's an excellent choice of places to **drink** in Gothenburg, but aside from a small number of British- and Irish-style pubs, even the hippest bars also serve food and have a restaurant atmosphere. The following listings are some of the most populars pubs and bar/restaurants in the city; however, many of the cafés and restaurants given above are also good places to have a beer, especially in the busier night-time areas of Avenyn and Linne. Just west of Avenyn in Vasaplan and further on in Haga, the 24-hour studenty cafés listed above are great places to drink into the early hours, and on Avenyn itself, it's less a matter of choosing the best than spotting a table. Although there are a number of long-established bars in the old town, the atmosphere is generally a bit low key at night.

There's plenty of other things to do in Gothenburg at night besides drink. The city has a brisk **live music scene** – jazz, rock and classical – as well as the usual cinema and theatre oportunities. The details below should give you some ideas, but it is worth picking up the Friday edition of the *Göteborgs Posten*, which has a weekly supplement called "Aveny" full listings for bars, concerts, clubs and almost anything else you might want to know about – it's in Swedish but not very difficult to decipher. The notice boards in the main hall at the entrance to *Studs*, the student bar in Haga, are also good for gigs, parties and other information on what's going on in the city.

Gothenburg's **gay scene** surprises even Gothenburgers with its half hearted-ness, largely put down to the high levels of tolerance towards lesbian and gay sexuality in the wider community. Most gay activity is run on ultra-organized, rigid lines by the state sponsored national gay association *RFSL* at Esperantoplatsen 7 (see p.127 for details). The city's few gay clubs are given overleaf.

# Drinking

Although it is not uncommon for Gothenburgers to drink themselves to oblivion, the atmosphere around the bars is generally non-aggressive. Avenyn, late on a Saturday night, is really the only place where you might feel even slightly unsafe.

### The old town

**Beefeater Inn**, Plantagegatan 1. One of a bevy of British-orientated neighbourhood pubs, very in vogue with Gothenburgers. This one really goes overboard, with a stylistic mish-mash of red-telephone-box doors and staff in kilts to match the tartan walls.

**Dubliners**, Östra Hamngatan 50B. Swedes have for a while been swept with a nostalgia for all things old and Irish – or at least what they imagine is old and Irish. This is the most popular Irish-style pub with a Swedish interpretation of Dublin *bonhomie*.

**Gamle Port**, Östra Larmgatan 18. The city's oldest watering hole with British beer in the downstairs pub and an awful disco upstairs (see "Clubs and live music").

**Norrlands Nation**, Västra Hamngatan 20. Formerly a university venue, the place is now licensed and is open late. Occasional comedy gigs and music.

**The Palace**, Brunnsparken. The rather splendid former home of the Furstenburgs and their art galleries (see p.126), this upmarket bar and restaurant is very popular – but costs.

### Avenyn

**Brasserie Lipp**, Avenyn 8. No longer the hippest place on Avenyn, *Lipp* is expensive and so attracts a slightly older crowd – but a crowd it is, especially during summer. Connected to the brasserie is *Bubbles Nightclub* (see "Clubs and live music").

**Harley's**, Avenyn 10. Very loud young crowd. Not a place for a drink and a chat, unless you spill out onto the street.

**Niva**, Avenyn 9. Bar and restaurant on different levels. Modern, mosaic interior – a stylish bar that's becoming more and more popular.

**Scandic Rubinen**, Avenyn 24. Glitzy hotel-foyer style bar. Always packed with tourists and right at the heart of Avenyn.

## Haga

**Dog & Duck**, Viktoriagatan 5. An all-British pub/restaurant, with a valiant attempt at a cosy, nineteenth-century atmosphere. Serves light meals, nachos, burgers and chicken shish-kebabs all at around 65kr. Mon–Thurs & Sun till 1am, Fri & Sat till 3am.

**Indian Palace Pub**, Järntorget 4. Just northwest of Haga Nygatan, this place is rather unappealing from outside, with neon arrows coaxing you in. There is a restaurant on the ground floor with a basement pub and pool table.

**Studs**, Götabergsgatan, off Engelbrektsgatan behind Vasa Church. This is the hub of Gothenburg student life, with a pub, bar and restaurant. The main advantage of the student bar is its prices. There's a two-for-one inducement on beer before 9pm every summer evening. If you haven't got student ID, friendly bluffing should get you in.

## Linne

**The Irish Rover**, Andra Långgatan 12. Run-of-the-mill Irish/English pub selling *Boddingtons* beer with other lagers, ales and cider on tap. There's also a wide range of bottled everything. Lamb, steaks and trout dishes for 59–95kr.

**1252**, Linnegatan. The first of the trendy places to be seen in, and the place that put the Linne area on the map. Reasonably priced food considering the location. Outdoor tables in summer.

# Clubs and live music

There are no outstanding **clubs** in Gothenburg. The classic nightclub is *Valand*, at Vasagatan 3, just off Avenyn. With three bars, it's where the clubby crowd strut their stuff. *Park Lane*, at Avenyn 36, is a hot, crowded club with three bars, a casino and live entertainment (☎20 60 58). *Yaki Da* is attached to *Gamle Port* (see p.135), and despite having three bars, a stage and a casino, it makes for a pretty depressing atmosphere; similarly *Bubbles Nightclub* at *Lipp* (see p.135) is a bit of a disappointment. Sweden's biggest dance floor (if that's a boast) is said to be at *Rondo*, the dance restaurant at Liseberg Amusement Park. There's always live bands, and people of all ages dance in a friendly atmosphere.

Gothenburg's **gay clubs** are thin on the ground. *RFSL*, at Esperantoplatsen 7 in the old town, run a bar and nightclub called *Touch*, frequented by a group of regulars who drink here on Wednesday nights and dance on Friday nights. *Bacchus*, at Bellmansgatan 7–9, is the only privately run club. Bigger than *Touch*, it is busiest on Saturday evenings and has a mixed (gay/straight) crowd on Sundays. *Delicious*, in the *NK* department store (weekends only), is a new mixed club.

## Live music

Gothenburg's large student community means there are plenty of **local live bands**. The best venue, with the emphasis on alternative and dance music, is *Kompaniet* on Kungsgatan. The top floor is a pub/bar, while downstairs there's dancing to Eurotechno stuff. Very few tourists head for *Kompaniet*, so it's ideal for meeting locals. Another selling point is the fact that the drinks are half-price between 8pm and 10pm, and the place stays open until 3am daily in summer (winter Wed–Sat only). Other bars worth checking out are *Klara*, Vallgatan 8, which has wannabe poets by day and, on Monday nights, a diverse range of indie and rock bands; and *Dojan*, Vallgatan 3, a small, smoky and crowded rock pub, with a mix of ages, and live bands every night.

Jazz enthusiasts should head for the trendy *Neffertiti* **jazz club** at Hvitfeldtsplatsen 6 (Mon–Sat from 9pm) – you may have to queue. *Jazzhuset*, Eric

Dahlbergsgatan 3 (Wed–Sat 8pm–2am), puts on trad, Dixieland and swing, but is more middle-aged and something of an executive pickup joint.

For **international bands**, there are some sizable stadia in the city, notably *Scandinavium* (☎81 84 00), which hosts some big-time acts, as does the new, colossal arena, *Ullevi Stadium*. Both are off Skånegatan to the east of Avenyn; take tram #1, #3 or #6.

## Classical music, cinema and theatre

**Classical music** concerts are performed regularly in the *Konserthuset*, Götaplatsen, and the *Stora Theatre*, Avenyn. Get hold of programme details from the tourist office.

There are plenty of **cinemas** around the city, and English-language films (which make up the majority) are always subtitled in Swedish, never dubbed. The most unusual cinema is *Bio Palatset*, on Kungstorget. Originally a meat market and then a failed shopping mall, this ten-screen picture house has an interior painted in clashing fruity colours, and the foyer has been scooped out in an excavation project to reveal flood-lit rocks studded with Viking spears. Another multi-screen is *Filmstaden*, behind the cathedral at Kungsgatan 35.

**Theatre** in Gothenburg is unlikely to appeal to many visitors. Not only are all productions in Swedish, the city's council-run theatres put on plays that would make Strindberg look like farce – the lack of audience is not a big concern. Commercial theatres such as the *Lorensberg*, on Lorensbergsgatan off Götaplatsen, go for light comedy shows in Swedish only and, like many other theatres in Sweden, is closed during the summer months.

# Listings

**Airlines** *British Airways,* at the airport (☎020/78 11 44); *Finnair,* Fredsgatan 6 (☎020/78 11 00); *KLM,* at airport (☎94 16 40); *Lufthansa,* Fredsgatan 1 (☎80 56 40); *SAS* at airport (☎020/91 01 10).

**Airport** General information at Landvetter airport on ☎94 10 00.

**American express** Taken care of by *Ticket,* Östra Hamngatan 35 (☎13 07 12).

**Banks & exchange** Most banks are open Mon–Fri 9.30am–3pm and are found on Östra Hamngatan, Södra Hamngatan and Västra Hamngatan. There are four *Forex* exchange offices, which accept *American Express, Diners Club, Finax* and travellers' cheques: Central Station (daily 8am–9pm; ☎15 65 16); Avenyn 22 (daily 8am–9pm; ☎18 57 60); *Nordstan* shopping centre (9am–7pm; ☎15 75 30); and Kungsportsplatsen (daily 9am–7pm; ☎13 60 74).

**Buses** Reservations are obligatory for buses to Stockholm, Helsingborg and Malmo, but once booked, a seat is guaranteed. Book at *Bussresebyra,* Drottninggatan 50 (☎80 55 30).

**Car rental** *Avis,* Central Station, (☎80 57 80) and at the airport (☎94 60 30); *Budget,* Kristinelundsgatan 13 (☎20 09 30), at the airport (☎94 60 55); *Europcar,* Stampgatan 22 D (☎80 53 90), at the airport (☎94 71 00); *Hertz,* Stampgatan 16A (☎80 37 30), at the airport (☎94 60 20).

**Doctor** *Medical Counselling Service and Information* (☎41 55 00); Sahlgrenska Hospital at Per Dubbsgatan (☎60 10 00). A private clinic, *City Akuten,* has doctors on duty 8am–6pm at Drottninggatan 45 (☎10 10 10).

**Emergency services** Ambulance, police, fire-brigade on ☎90 000.

**Ferry companies** If you want to book from Gothenburg to Britain or Amsterdam on *Scandinavian Seaways,* use the booking office at Östra Larmgatan 15 (☎17 20 50); for general information at Skandiahamn ferry terminal call ☎65 06 00. *Stena Line* have no walk-in offices; call ☎775 00 00 for information and bookings. *SeaCat* also runs day-trips from Gothenburg to Frederikshavn (1hr 45 min; 70kr, the Gothenburg Card allows two for the price of one); again there are no walk-in offices; call ☎775 08 10.

**Laundry** At *Nordstan Service Centre* (see below).

**Left luggage** at *Nordstan Service Centre* (see below) or Central Station.

**Newspapers** International newspapers from *Press Centre* in *Nordstan* shopping centre or Central Station – or read them for free at the City Library, Götaplatsen.

**Nordstan Service Centre** In the shopping centre near Central Station (Mon–Fri 10am–6.30pm, Sat 10am–4pm). You can leave luggage (10kr), take a shower here (20kr) and use the laundry service (95kr).

**Pharmacy** *Apoteket Vasen*, Götagatan 10, in *Nordstan* shopping centre, is open 24 hours a day, every day (☎80 44 10).

**Police** Headquarters at Ernst Fontells Plats (☎61 80 00); open Mon–Fri 9am–2pm.

**Post offices** Main post office for *poste restante* is in Drottningtorget (Mon–Fri 10am–6pm, Sat 10am–noon; ☎62 31 62). Others are on Avenyn (Mon–Fri 10am–6pm, Sat 10am–12.30pm); and at the *Nordstan* shopping centre (Mon–Fri 9am–7pm, Sat 10am–5pm).

**Public telephones** Mostly operated by cards, bought at *Pressbyrån* and *Ja* kiosks. In hotels/cafés and older public boxes, put in a minimum of two 1kr coins for a local call.

**Record stores** Gothenburg has a wide selection of **secondhand record stores**, all within walking distance of each other. *Bengans Records*, Stigbergstorget, is the biggest and most impressive – it even has its own café; *Skivhugget*, Masthuggstorget 2, has a section with many rare British and American LPs and CDs.

**Swimming** The biggest and best pool is the 1950s *Valhallabadet*, next to the *Scandinavium* sports complex, on Skånegatan.

**Trains** All trains arrive at Central Station (☎020 75 75 75; international train information ☎80 77 10).

**Travel agents** *KILROY travels*, Berzeliigatan 5 (Mon–Fri 9.30am–5pm; ☎20 08 60).

# AROUND GOTHENBURG

North of Gothenburg, the rugged and picturesque **Bohuslän coast**, which runs all the way to the Norwegian border, attracts countless Scandinavian and German tourists each summer. The crowds don't detract, though, from the wealth of natural beauty – rocks, coves, islands and hairline fjords – and the many dinky fishing villages that make this stretch of country well worth a few days' exploration. The most popular destination is the island town of **Marstrand**, with its impressive fortress and richly ornamental ancient buildings, but there are several other attractions further up the coast that are also worth visiting, not least the big centre for Bronze Age **rock carvings** at **Tamunshede**, near Strömstad.

Northeast of the city, the county of **Västergötland** encompasses the southern sections of Sweden's two largest lakes, **Vänern** and **Vättern**. Here the scenery is gentler, and a number of attractive lakeside towns and villages make good bases from which to venture out into the forested countryside and onto the **Göta Canal**. The waterway connects the lakes to each other (and, in its entirety, the North Sea to the Baltic), and there are a number of ways to experience it, from cross-country cruises to short, evening hops on rented boats or organized ferry rides. With energy and time to spare, **renting a bike** offers a great alternative for real exploration of Västergötland using the canal's towpaths, countless cycling trails and empty roads. Nearly all tourist offices, youth hostels and campsites in the region rent out bikes for around 80kr a day and 400kr a week.

# The Bohuslän coast

A chain-mail of **islands** linked by a thread of bridges and short ferry crossings make up the county of **Bohuslän** and, despite the summer crowds, it is still easy enough to find a private spot to swim or bathe. Sailing is also a popular pastime among the Swedes, many of whom have summer cottages here, and you'll see yachts gliding through the water all the way along the coast. Another feature of the Bohuslän landscape you can't fail to miss is the large number of **churches** that fill the county. Although church crawls may not be everyone's idea of a holiday, for long stretches these are the only buildings of note. The county has a long tradition of religious observance, fuelled in the early nineteenth century by the dogmatic Calvinist clergyman Henric Schartau, who believed that closed curtains were the sign of sin within – even today many island homes still have curtainless windows. The churches, dating from the 1840s to 1910, are mostly white, simple affairs, and look like windmills without sails. They are almost all built 1.3km from their villages, and are all surrounded by graveyards. Once you've seen inside one, you've seen most, but a few are exquisite or unusual and have been highlighted in the text. They are usually open between 10am to 3pm, but the clergyman invariably lives next door and will be happy to open up.

Travelling up the coast by public transport is possible by **train**, with services from Gothenburg through industrial Uddevalla and on to **Strömstad** (the most northern town of any size before Norway), but you are limited to the main towns. Although **buses** do run, services are sketchy and infrequent (on some routes there is only one bus a week). If you really want to explore Bohuslän's most dramatic scenery and reach its prettier villages, you need a car. From Gothenburg, the E6 motorway is the quickest road north, with designated scenic routes leading off it every few kilometres.

## Kungälv and the Bohus Fortress

Just under 20km north of Gothenburg on the E6, the quaint old town of **KUNGÄLV**, overshadowed by the fourteenth-century ruins of Bohus Fortress, is a gem of a place to stop for a few hours. Rebuilt after the Swedes razed it in 1676 to prevent the Danes finding useful shelter, the town now consists of pastel-painted wooden houses, all leaning as if on the verge of collapse, and sprawling cobbled streets. The **tourist office** (☎0303/992 00, fax 171 06), in the square below the fortress, will provide you with a useful walking-tour map detailing the history of almost every seventeenth-century property.

The main reason most people visit the town, though, is to see the remains of **Bohus Fortress**. The first defensive wooden fort was built here by the Norwegian king in the fourteenth century, on what was then Norway's southern border. This was replaced by a solid stone building, surrounded by deep natural moats, which became known as the strongest in the country. After withstanding six Swedish attacks in the 1560s, the colossal stronghold was rebuilt to contain a Renaissance palace. When the area finally became Swedish in 1658, Bohus had a breathing space, but during the next twenty years, a further fourteen sieges saw some spectacular bombardment by the Danes: records show that 15,000 men fired 30,000 red-hot cannon balls at the unfortunate fortress, which somehow managed not to fall. Where attack failed, Swedish weather has succeeded, how-

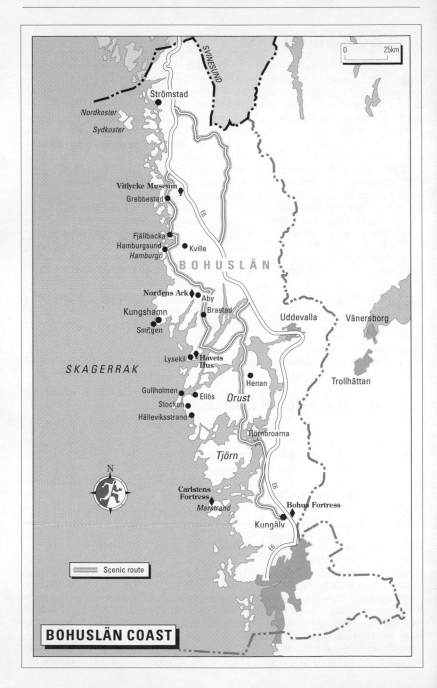

**BOHUSLÄN COAST**

ever, and today the building is very much a ruin. The fortress is open from May to September, with guided tours, concerts and opera performances in July and August – for full details call the tourist office; see p.139.

Once you've seen the fortress and wandered round the village, there is little else to do here, but if you want to stay, there's an *STF* **youth hostel** a stone's throw from the fortress at Farjevagen 2 (☎0303/189 00; fax 19 295; 100kr).

# Marstrand

To the west of Kungälv (about 25km), the island town of **MARSTRAND** buzzes with summer activity, as holiday-makers come to sail, bathe and take one of the highly entertaining historical tours around its impressive castle, Carlstens Fästning. With ornate wooden buildings lining the bustling harbour, Marstrand is a really delightful place to visit and a very accessible day-trip from Gothenburg – it shouldn't be missed.

The town's colourful history – as so often in Sweden – mainly revolves around fish. Founded under Norwegian rule in the thirteenth century, it achieved remarkable prosperity through herring fishing in the following century, when the ruling king, Haakon of Norway, obtained permission from the pope to allow the town's fishermen to fish even on holy days. Rich herring pickings, however, eventually led to greed and corruption, and Marstrand became known as the most immoral town in Scandinavia. The murder of a cleric in 1586 was seen as an omen – soon after the whole town burned to the ground and the herring mysteriously disappeared. The fish – and Marstrand's prosperity – eventually returned in the 1770s. Around this time, the king announced an open-door policy, or Porto Franco, for Marstrand, which for the first time allowed foreigners to settle in Sweden. In effect this meant an influx of Jewish people onto the island. Unfortunately, the fish disappeared again in 1808 and never came back. In his anger, the king removed Porto Franco, forcing the Jewish community to move to Gothenburg (pressure from the East India Company had brought a change in the law allowing Jews to settle in the city). Meanwhile, the town, without its main source of income, fell behind Gothenburg and Kungälv in importance. By the 1820s, the old herring salting houses had been converted into bath houses, and Marstrand had become a fashionable bathing resort.

## The Town
From the harbour, it's a lovely walk up the cobbled lane, past the Renaissance-style *Grand Hotel*, to a small square surrounded by exquisite wooden houses, painted in pastel shades. Boules is played by the locals here beneath the shade of a huge, ancient tree. Across the square is the squat, white **St Maria kyrka**, named after Maria, a girl who was shipwrecked in the twelfth century. The church was originally called Maria Strand (Maria's Beach), hence the name of the island. Inside, it is simple and unremarkable. From here all the streets lined with wooden villas climb steeply to the castle.

**Carlstens Fästning** (June–Sept daily 11am–6pm; 25kr) is an imposing sweep of stone walls solidly wedged into the rough rock. You could easily spend half a day clambering around the walls and down the weather-smoothed rocks to the sea, where there are always plenty of places to bathe in private. The informal **tours** take an hour and, though none are officially in English, guides are happy to oblige. The most interesting tales are told down in the prison cells: Carlstens's most noted prisoner-resident was **Lasse Maja**, a thief who got rich by dressing as a woman and seducing rich farmers. A sort of Swedish Robin Hood, Maja was known for giving his spoils to the poor. Once incarcerated here, Maja ingratiated himself with the officers by using his cooking skills in a kitchen not renowned for its cuisine. After 26 years, his culinary expertise eventually won him a pardon; when the new king visited, Maja had the foresight to serve him French food – the monarch was reputed to hate Swedish cooking.

In Maja's cell you can view the neck, waist and ankle shackles that prisoners wore for years on end. More unnerving, though, are the experimental cells, just two metres by three metres and pitch dark; a prisoner would stand inside until he invariably lost his sanity and eventually died. In 1845, one prisoner was chosen for the experiment because he was the least observant Christian in the town. Records show that he was allowed to speak to a pastor just once a year on Christmas Eve. His drawings in his own blood are still visible, as is the dip in the barred window sill where his hand tapped constantly until his death.

For 40kr extra, you can take one of the special tours that are run three times a week and lead up through the 1658-built, 100m-high towers. The views from the top are stunning, but you have to be fit to get there; the steep, spiral climb is quite exhausting. Once a year, around July 20, the fortress hosts a huge **festival**, with an eighteenth-century-style procession and live theatre. It's a colourful occasion and well worth catching.

On your way back down you can take a detour and visit the remains of **Fredriksborg**, one of the original twelve fortresses on the island, reduced now to a neat wall around the shore. Walking down Villagatan, before you get to the shore there's a small gateway on the right that leads to a house, covered with black, wooden tiles. Here the friendly owner will allow you (if you ask first) to walk along his garden path to a vault in the old fortress wall. Inside the vault, which was originally used to fire cannons at enemy boats, are the dusty remains of Scandinavia's soon-to-be-restored first synagogue. To get back to the town centre carry on down Villagatan to the shore and walk along the path till you reach Långgatan, which leads back to the main square.

## Practicalities

With a Gothenburg Card, a two-for-one ticket cuts the normal cost of a day-trip by boat from Gothenburg in half (down to 80kr). Boats leave from Lilla Bommen at 9.30am, arriving in Marstrand at 12.30pm, and operate on selected dates in May and June, but then go daily until the end of August. To save time, **bus** #312 runs from Nils Ericsonsplatsen, and if you buy a 100kr carnet at *Tidpunkten*, next to the bus terminal (press "5" on the ticket machines on the bus for each person), it's half the cost of buying a ticket on the bus and includes the two-minute ferry journey from the mainland.

The **tourist office** at the harbour (June–Aug daily 9am–4pm; rest of the year Mon–Fri 10am–4pm; ☎0303/600 87, fax 600 18) will book **private rooms** for a minimum of two people from 370kr (no booking fee) in an old barracks, where there's a small kitchen.There are also more pleasant en-suite rooms with kitchens in private homes or cottages (450kr for two people). The island's **youth hostel** (open all year; June to mid-Aug 200kr, April–May 140kr, Sept–March 100kr; ☎0303/600 10, fax 606 07) is wonderfully set in an old bath house, which looks out onto idyllic islands. There's a sauna, washing facilities, a swimming pool and a restaurant (see opposite).

Of the several very pleasant **hotels** on the island, the 1892-built *Grand Hotel*, at Paradis Parken (☎0303/603 22, fax 600 53; ④), is a real classic, just 50m from the tourist office and left through the park. Recently refurbished, this very fine hotel lives up to its name. *Hotel Alphydden*, at Långgatan 6 (☎303/610 30, fax 612 00; ③/②), has much more basic rooms though a lovely setting surrounded by water and sailing boats. It also provides budget rooms for not much more than the cost of a youth hostel room in summer.

About the most interesting place to **eat** on the island is the *American Bar*, close to the harbour, which has an authentic, worn feel of 1940s' America and serves excellent food in huge portions: chicken and cheese salad for 88k, or brie and bacon salad for 67kr – though coffee is a steep 20kr. In the evening, it's worth trying the home-made burgers. Very pleasant lunches or dinners are also served in the restaurant connected to the youth hostel: daily pasta dishes at 49kr and meat and seafood meals at 90–130kr. Eating outside affords delightful views, but inside retains all the old style of the bathing days, with stripped floors and painted tongue-and-groove walls. For a daytime coffee, the most atmospheric place is the café in the old officers' mess at the fortress.

At night, the *American Bar*, or neighbouring *Oscars*, are good **drinking** haunts. *Oscars* became Sweden's first discotheque in 1964, and today it's a **nightclub** playing disco and popular rock music to a 25- to 50-year-old age group.

# North to Strömstad

Aside from picturesque scenery and pretty villages, the highlights along this stretch of the coast are the exceptional **marine-life museum** at **Lysekil**, several nature reserves, a wildlife sanctuary and, at **Tanumshede**, an extensive array of Bronze Age **rock carvings**. If you have your own transport, you'll be able to follow the designated **scenic routes**, which lead off the E6; otherwise bus connections from Gothenburg are limited to a few of the main towns. If you have a car, it's easy enough to drive to Strömstad in a day, stopping off at a couple of sights on the way. Although there are plenty of hotels and hostels along the coast, this is one of the most popular parts of the country for **camping** and caravaning, with loads of sites all the way to Strömstad.

## Orust and Gullholmen

The first scenic route begins 23km north of Kungälv (take Road 160 off the E6). Once off the main road, you'll soon reach **Tjornbroarna**, a five-kilometre linkup of three graceful bridges connecting the islands of Tjörn and Orust and affording spectacular views over the fjords. **Orust**, a centre for boat building since Viking times, is geographically like a miniature Sweden, with westerly winds stripping it of trees at the coast yet with forest right to the sea on its eastern shores. **Henan**, the largest village, is unremarkable; you are much better off heading west in the direction of Ellos. Just outside the village of **STOCKEN** is the splendidly situated *STF* **youth hostel** (open all year; ☎0304/503 80; 100kr); a 1770-built wooden manor in huge grounds, it's a wonderful base from which to explore. A fine example of an unspoilt fishing village is on the island of **Gullholmen**, reached by a ferry crossing. Red-and-white wooden homes huddle around a substantial church, while the rest of the island is a nature reserve, where birds nest undisturbed beneath smooth, granite rocks.

## Lysekil

The largest coastal town in this area is **LYSEKIL** (two hourly express bus #840 from Gothenburg; or Road 162 from the E6 at Uddevalla), and though not as immediately attractive as other coastal towns, it does have plenty to recommend it. From the **tourist office** (June daily 9am–7pm; July Mon–Fri 9am–9pm, Sat & Sun 9am–7pm; rest of the year Mon–Fri 9am–5pm; ☎0523/130 50, fax 125 85), at Södra Hamngatan 6, it's just five minutes' walk to **Havets Hus** (daily 10am–4pm; ☎ 0523 165 30; 40kr), an amazing museum of marine life. The chief attraction here is an eight-metre-long glass tunnel with massive fish swimming over and around you. This sea-diver's view is a little distorted, however, as looking through the curved glass is a bit like gazing through someone else's glasses. Fish delighting in such names as Father Lasher, Picked Dogfish and Five Bearded Rockling feature along with varieties usually associated with lemon-wedges in restaurants; children can enjoy feeling the texture of slimy algae or starfish in a touch pool.

The intricately carved villas en route to Havets Hus are worth a look, too. These ornate houses are a reminder of last century when Lysekil was a popular and genteel bathing resort, and the rich and neurotic would come to take the waters. Today, nude (segregated) bathing and fishing are popular pastimes and much of the shoreline has been turned into a **nature reserve**, with over 250 varieties of plant life – for guided botanic and marine walks in summer, ask at the tourist office. Walk up any set of steps from the waterfront and you'll reach the town's **church** (daily 11am–3pm), hewn from the surrounding pink granite with beaten copper doors and windows painted by turn-of-the-century artist Albert Eldh.

If you want to **stay** in Lysekil, try the reasonably priced and central *Hotel Lysekil* at Rosikstorg 1 (☎0523/61 18 60, fax 155 20; ③/②).

## Nordens Ark

A diversion after Lysekil is to head back along the 162 and turn left for Nordens Ark **wildlife sanctuary** near Åby (about 25km). On the way you'll pass a couple of notable churches, in particular the one at **Brastad**, an 1870s' Gothic building, with an oddly haphazard appearance – every farm in the neighbourhood donated a lump of its own granite, none of which matched.

Don't be put off by the yeti-sized blow-up puffin at the entrance to **Nordens Ark** (open all year; call for times on ☎0523/522 15) on the Åbo fjord. Here is a unique wildlife sanctuary for endangered animals, where animal welfare is prioritized over human voyeurism. Red pandas, lynx, snow leopards and arctic foxes are among the rare animals being bred and reared at the sanctuary, where the mountainous landscape of dense forest and glades is kept as close as possible to the animals' natural surroundings. The enclosures are so big, and the paths and bridges across the site so discreet, that you may be disappointed to not see any animals at all. Your best bet for a glimpse is to follow behind the little truck that trundles around at feeding times. A full English guide is available in the fine eighteenth-century Åby manor house.

## Fjallbacka

If time allows for only one picture-perfect setting, **FJALLBACKA** is an ideal choice. Nestling beneath huge, granite boulders, all the houses are painted in fondant shades, with a wealth of intricate gingerbreading known in Swedish as *snickargladje* (carpenter's joy). As you enter Fjallbacka (from Åby you can either go back to the E6 and then take the 163 – around 35km – or follow a more wind-ing route along the coast), it will immediately become apparent that a certain cel-ebrated actress holds sway in the little town. The **tourist office** (June–Aug erractic hours; ☎0525/321 20) is in a tiny, red hut on **Ingrid Bergman's Square**; here a statue of the big-screen idol looks out to the islands, where she had her summer house, and the sea over which her ashes were scattered. There's not a lot to do in Fjallbacka, but steps behind Bergman's statue lead to a dramatic ravine between some cliffs, known as Kungskliftan (King's Cliff). In 1887, Oscar II etched his name into the rock and started a trend for bizarre graffiti.

There are plenty of **camping** opportunities in Fjallbacka, and an island **youth hostel** (May–Sept; ☎0525/312 34; 100kr), though its pretty setting is more frustrat-ing than romantic when the ferry man is too busy to carry visitors to the mainland.

### Tanumshede

The town of **TANUMSHEDE** (on the E6) has the greatest concentration of **Bronze Age rock carvings** in Scandinavia, with four major sites not far away in the surrounding countryside. Between 1500 and 500 BC, Bronze Age artists scratched images into the ice-smoothed rock, and at Tanumshede you'll see some fine examples of the most frequent motifs: the simple cup mark (which accounts for most), boats, humans and animals. When you reach town, it's well worth head-ing straight for the **tourist office** (June to mid-Aug Mon–Sat 10am–6pm; rest of the year Mon–Thurs 9am–4.30pm, Fri 9am–3pm; ☎0525/204 00, fax 298 60), oddly sited in a *Texaco* filling station, which will provide you with English book-lets (10kr) detailing the types of images at the four sites. The carvings appear mostly on sloping, smooth rock surfaces (these are very slippery when wet) and, being outside, it's best to view them when the sunlight is good. There is also a **rock carving museum** at nearby Vitlyckehallen (May to mid-Sept; 20kr), which explores the meaning of the various images. Interpretations are wildly liberal and often contradictory; take, for example, the celebrated Fossum Woman, who is var-iously described as "giving birth to the egg of life", "a male trophy" or "displaying nether-region jewellery."

The E6 express **bus** takes two hours from Gothenburg to Tanumshede and runs five times a day. There is a smattering of restaurants and nightlife opportu-nities at the caravan/camping mecca of **GREBBESTAD**, just a few kilometres southwest of Tanumshede.

## Strömstad and the Koster Islands

Once a fashionable eighteenth-century spa resort, **STRÖMSTAD** still has an air of faded grandeur. From its pretty train station, everywhere of interest is easily accessible, and with ferry connections to Sandefjord, Fredrikstad and Halden in Norway, the town makes a good breathing space before heading north. Aside from its close proximity to the Koster Islands (see p.147), Strömstad itself has a couple of quite remarkable public buildings that are well worth a look. Although you wouldn't guess it from its run-of-the-mill exterior, inside Strömstad's **church**, a few minutes' walk from the train and bus stations, there's an eclectic mix of unusual decorative features, including busy frescoes, model ships hanging from the roof, gilt chandeliers and 1970s hotel-style brass lamps. The church hosts con-certs and social occasions, and choreographer Ivo Cramér has set up a symbolic dance workshop here – visitors are very welcome to attend events.

The town's most bizarre building, however, is the massive, copper-roofed **Stadshus**, the product of a parent-fixated millionaire recluse. Born to a Strömstad jeweller in 1851, Adolf Fritiof Cavalli-Holmgren became a financial whizz kid, moved to Stockholm and was soon one of Sweden's richest men. When he heard that his poor home town needed a town hall, he offered to finance the project, but only on certain conditions. The town hall had to be situated on the spot where his late parents had lived, and he insisted on complete control over the design. By the time the mammoth structure was completed in 1917, he was no longer on speaking terms with the city's politicians, and he never returned to see the building he had battled to create, which was topped with a panoramic apartment for his private use. Much later, in 1951, it was discovered that in obsessive devotion to his parents he had designed the entire building round the dates of their birthdays and wedding day – January 27, May 14 and March 7. The dimensions of every room – and there are over one hundred – were a combination of these dates in metres, as were the size of every window, every flight of stairs and every cluster of lamps. Further, in all the years of correspondence with city officials, he only ever responded or held meetings on these days. Built entirely from rare local apple granite, the town hall is open to the public, but to view the most interesting areas you have to arrange a free private tour. You can see Adolf's portrait – dated falsely to include his favourites – in the main council chamber.

## Practicalities

Strömstad is reached by **train** from Gothenburg or by the E6 express **bus** between Gothenburg and Oslo; by car, take Road 176 off the E6. Both the train and bus stations are on Södra Hammen, opposite the **ferry** terminal for services to Sandefjord in Norway (*Scandi Line;* ☎0526/150 70). Ferries to Fredrikstad and Halden leave from Norra Hamnen, 100m to the north on the other side of the rocky promontory, Laholmen, as do the ferries to the Koster Islands (ask at the tourist office for full details of ferry times).

The **tourist office** on the quay (June–Aug daily 8am–9pm; Sept–May Mon–Fri 8.30am–5pm; ☎0526/130 25, fax 121 85) will help with **private rooms**, which cost from 125kr per person (plus a 50kr booking fee), and advise about renting **cabins**. The *STF* **youth hostel** is at Norra Kyrkogatan 12 (mid-April to mid-Oct, ☎0526/101 93; 100kr), a kilometre or so from the train station along Uddevallavägen; there's also an independent hostel, *Gastis Roddaren Hostel*, at Fredrikshaldsvagen 24 (open all year; ☎0526/602 01; 125kr), ten minutes' walk along the road fronting the Stadshus – breakfast, lunch and supper cost extra.

For a regular, central **hotel** try *Krabban* on Södra Bergsgatan 15 (☎0526/142 00; ②), or the modern, low-built *Hotel Laholmen* (☎0526/12 400, fax 100 36; ②), which is nothing to look at in itself but juts into the sea and enjoys wonderful views across the water. There is **camping** a kilometre from the train station, along Uddevallavägen, near the youth hostel, or at Dafto, 4km south in tiny triangular-shaped cottages.

As befits a resort town, there is no shortage of places to **eat and drink**, most of them easily found by just wandering around near the harbour area. The best of the bunch are *Backlund's*, a locals' haunt, with sandwiches at 18kr; *Café Casper*, on Södra Hamngatan, which does lunch specials for 35kr; and *Kaff Doppet,* a more characterful konditori by the station. **Nightlife** in Stromstad is, unsurprisingly, not too hot; the only place that really comes alive on a summer evening is *Skagerack*. A wedding cake of a building once used by the Stockholm elite, it is now very loud, very young and the place for big-name bands to play, if they hit the Bohuslän coast at all. An older crowd fills the more sedate (and expensive) terraces of *Hotel Laholmen* (see opposite).

### The Koster Islands

The local **Koster Islands** are Sweden's most westerly inhabited islands (population 400) and enjoy more sunshine hours than almost anywhere else in the country. **North Koster** is the more rugged, with a grand nature reserve, and takes a couple of hours to walk around. **South Koster** is three times as big, but with no vehicles allowed on the island, **renting a bike** (ask at the Strömstad tourist office) is the best way to explore its gentler undulating landscape. Both Kosters are rich in wild flowers, and there is plenty of good bathing to be had in warm waters, as well as bird and seal viewing expeditions during the sumer. Outside high season, it's vital to take an early-morning ferry to North Koster (80kr); if you leave later, the only way of making it across onto the south island is to hitch a lift in a local's boat. **Taxi boats** to the islands cost 500kr and can work out cheaply if there is a group of you; they are the only choice if you miss the last ferry back at 9.30pm.

Camping on North Koster is restricted to *Vettnet* (☎0526/204 66), though there are several sites on South Koster and a **youth hostel** (May–Sept; ☎0526/20 125; 100kr), 1500m from the ferry stop at Ekenäs. Before you get there, though, expect to be inundated by people prepared to rent out their **apartments** for 250–300kr a night, excellent value if there are three or more of you.

# The Göta Canal, Trollhättan and Vänersborg

The giant waterway known in its entirety as the **Göta Canal** flows from the mouth of the River Göta to Sweden's largest lake, **Lake Vänern**, via the **Trollhättan Canal**, then cuts across into the formidable **Lake Vättern** and right through southeastern Sweden to the Baltic Sea. If you don't have your own transport then some of the easiest places to see from Gothenburg are the few small towns that lie along the first stretch of the river/canal to Lake Vänern, in particular **Trollhättan**, where the canal's lock system tames the force of the river to dramatic effect. A few kilometres north of Trollhättan, **Vänersborg**, at the southernmost tip of Lake Vänern, provides a useful base for exploring the natural beauty of nearby hills, the home of Sweden's largest herd of elks. From Gothenburg, there are regular trains stopping at Trollhättan, or if you have a car take Road 45; the area is even closer at hand from Uddevalla in Bohuslän on Road 44.

## The Göta Canal

Centuries ago it was realized that lakes Vänern and Vättern, together with the rivers to the east and west, could be used to make inland transport easier. A continuous waterway from Gothenburg across the country to the Baltic would provide a vital trade route, a means of both shipping iron and timber out of central Sweden and avoiding Danish customs charges levied on traffic through Öresund. It was not until 1810 that Baron Baltzar Von Platten's hugely ambitious plans to carve a

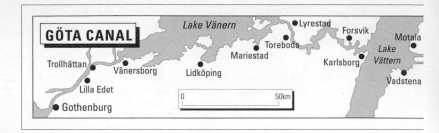

route to Stockholm were put into practice by the Göta Canal Company. Sixty thousand soldiers spent seven million working days over 22 years to complete the mammoth task. The canal opened in 1832, shortly after Von Platten's death.

Although the Trollhättan Canal section is still used to transport fuel and timber – the towns on Vänern having their lakeside views blotted by unsightly industrial greyness – this section and the Göta Canal proper, between Vänern and Vättern, are extremely popular tourist destinations, and there's a wide range of canal trip deals on offer.

If cost is not an issue, **Göta Canal Cruises**, Rederiaktiebolaget Göta Kanal, Hotellplatsen 2, Gothenburg (☎031/80 63 15, fax 15 83 11), offer what are dubbed "golden dollar" cruises aboard historic steamers for four-, six- or eight-day jaunts across the country to the Baltic. The emphasis is on glamour and sophistication, with dressing for dinner encouraged and baskets of fruit and bathrobes thrown in for "A" category cabins (13,500kr for four days); downstairs on the main deck prices are cheaper (8200kr). To cut down on expense and time, **day-trips** can take in a selection of locks, and any tourist office in the region will help organize the practicalities. You can also **rent a boat** or use your own. Tourist offices (see "Mariestad", p.155) will advise on fees and mooring places and on **renting a bike**, which is about the cheapest way to enjoy the canals, the towpaths being particularly picturesque.

## Trollhättan

Seventy kilometres northeast of Gothenburg, **TROLLHÄTTAN** is the kind of place you might end up staying for a couple of days without really meaning to. A small town, it nevertheless manages to pack in plenty of offbeat entertainment along with some peaceful river surroundings. Built around the fast river that for a couple of hundred years powered its flour mills and sawmills, Trollhättan remained fairly isolated until 1800, when the Göta Canal Company successfully installed the first set of locks to bypass the town's furious local waterfalls. River traffic took off and better and bigger locks were installed over the years. To take full advantage of all Trollhättan's watery activity, the best time to visit is during the **Fallensdagar** in July (usually the third week for three or four days), a festival of dancing and music based around the waterfalls. The summer is the only time when the sluices are opened and you can see the falls in all their crashing splendour (May & June Sat & Sun 3pm; July & Aug Sat Sun & Wed 3pm).

The locks and the steep sides of the falls are the main sights in town, and there are **paths** along the whole system as well as orientation maps. As you stroll south along the path towards the Insikten Energy Centre, the ordered network of canal

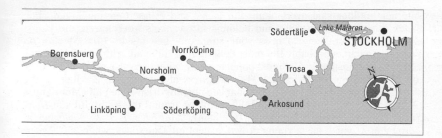

locks are to your left and the beautiful winding river to your right – it's a splendid half-hour walk, passing on the way a grand, English-style church perched on rocks between the waterways.

**Insikten Energy Centre** (mid-June to late Aug daily 10am–6pm; April & May, Sept & Oct Sat & Sun noon–4pm; free entry) is considerably more enjoyable than you might imagine, with none-too-scientific explanations of the workings of the nearby **hydro-electric power station** (June–Aug daily guided tours 10am–5pm), a fine 1910 building with thirteen massive generators, and of the environmental advantages of hydro-electric power over coal and oil burning. The centre also explains the extraordinary salmon and eel ladders outside the power station. On their way from the sea to lake Vänern, the migrating fish would die in the falls or at the power station were they not hoisted out of the water in spring, deposited in Vänern by lorry, and returned with extra reserves from breeding stations in autumn, just in time to make the seaward trip.

A little further down at the upper lock, the **Canal Museum** (mid-June to mid-Aug daily 11am–7pm; rest of year Sat & Sun noon–5pm; 5kr) puts the whole thing in perspective, with a history of the canal and locks, model ships, old tools and fishing gear. Crossing the canal and heading into the town's industrial hinterland, you'll soon reach the **Saab Museum** (June–Aug daily 10am–6pm; Sept–May Tues–Fri 1–4pm; call to arrange a tour on ☎0520 843 44). Every model of Volvo's arch rival is lined up, from the first 1946 bullet-shaped coupé to the Monte Carlo winning sports model, and to show safety standards, a simulated elk is depicted running into a saloon.

## Practicalities

The central **tourist office** (June–Aug Mon–Sat 9am–5pm, rest of the year Mon–Fri 10am–4pm; ☎0520/140 05, fax 872 71), at Gardhemsvagen 9, sells the Trollhättan **Tourist Card** (valid June 10–Aug 18; 20kr), which allows free entrance to most of the town's sites and gives discounts in restaurants, at the swimming pool and on boat trips. The tourist office can also book **private rooms** from 130kr. The former youth hostel overlooking the river is now a **hotel**, *Stromsberg* (☎0520/129 90, fax 133 11; ④/③); the nearest youth hostel is at Hunneberg (see p.151). You can find out about a range of central hotels, costing from 450 to 800kr in summer and on weekends throughout the year (550–1100kr at other times) from the tourist office. There's a **campsite**, close to the centre by the river (June–Aug; ☎0520/306 13), with a heated swimming pool, bike rental, tennis and golf.

The best **cafés** are mostly along Strandgatan by the canal. These include *Bikupan*, a lovely café with a terrace and sandwiches from 20kr; *Sluss Caféet*, a summer outdoor café overlooking the locks; and *Pingst Café* on Strandgatan, which does lunch from 39kr and belongs to Sweden's free church, the Pingst Church, a fact unlikely to miss your attention once inside. *Café Smulan* on Foreningsgatan is probably the most delightful of them all, with excellent cakes and a cosy atmosphere. The most popular **pubs**, which are also good for evening meals, are *Harry's* at Storgatan 44, and *Cheers* at Kungsgatan 24. Just up the street, *Butler's*, at no. 35, is a traditional late-opening Irish-style pub (Mon–Thurs till 1am, Fri 2am, Sun 11pm). Nightlife revolves around the **nightclubs** at *Hotel Swania*, entrance in Strandgatan (till 2am), and *KK's Bar & Nightclub* at Torggatan 3, which has a young crowd, except on Thursdays, when 25- 30-year-olds hit the dance floor. Trollhättan's **gay** community life is organized through *RFSL Trestad* (☎0520/41 17 66). From June to August, there are **boats** up the canal to Vänersborg; the four-hour round-trip costs 100kr. Otherwise, **buses** #600 or #605 regularly ply the route.

# Vänersborg and around

Dubbed "Little Paris" by the celebrated local poet Birger Sjoberg, **VÄNERSBORG**, on the tip of Lake Vänern 14km north of Trollhättan, doesn't quite live up to the comparison, but is, nonetheless, a charming little resort town. Its main sites are the nearby twin hills of **Hunneberg** and **Halleberg** (see opposite), both of which are of archeological interest and support a wide variety of wildlife.

In Vänersborg itself, the old town is compact, pivoting around a central market square, and it's pleasant to stroll past the numerous grand buildings – though all are overlooked by the bleak old prison at the end of Residensgatan. **Skracklan Park**, just a few minutes from the centre, is a pretty place to relax, with its 1930s' coffee house and promenade. The bronze statue of Sjoberg's muse, Frida, always has fresh flowers in her hand – even in winter, when the lake is solid ice, locals brave the sub-zero winds to thrust rhododendrons through her fingers.

Although Vänersborg's **museum**, behind the main square (June–Aug Tues noon–9pm, Wed, Thurs, Sat & Sun noon–4pm; Sept–May Tues noon–7pm, Sat & Sun noon–4pm; 20kr), has more cases of stuffed creatures and lifeless artefacts than most of Sweden's provincial museums, if you have an hour to spare the excess makes for fascinating viewing. It's the oldest such museum in the country, and the gloomy interior and the collections have hardly altered since the doors first opened to the public in 1891. The biggest collections are of African birds, perched in massive glass cases beneath a hand-painted ceiling. Also worth a glance is the caretaker's apartment, preserved in all its 1950s' gloom, and a reconstruction of Birger's home, which is darker still.

## Practicalities

The **tourist office**'s summer premises have been due to move for several years, but at the time of writing were still at Kungsgatan 15 (June–Aug Mon–Sat 9am–8pm, Sun 10am–6pm; ☎0521/27 14 00, 27 14 01). For the rest of the year, the office is on the first floor at Sundsgatan 6b (Mon–Fri 8am–5pm; ☎0521/27 14 02). Apart from the **youth hostel** at Hunneberg (see opposite), the cheapest **B&B** is the friendly and central *Hoglunds* at Kyrkogatan 46 (☎0521/71 15 61; 400kr, plus 25kr for breakfast). **Hotels** include the *Strand* at Hamngatan 7 (☎0521/138 50, fax 159 00; ②). You can **camp** at the lakeside *Ursands Camping* (☎0521/18 666, fax 686 76); get there on **bus** #661, which is really more of a taxi, making six journeys a day and requiring a call an hour before on ☎020/71 97 17. A great place to **eat** is *Konditori Princess* at Sundsgatan, a pleasant bakery with a café full of locals, or make the 2km journey to Värgon's top hotel restaurant (see below). **Nightlife** is pretty limited, the only options being *Club Roccad* on Kungsgatan 23 and *Strommarn*, open till 2pm on Saturday. To avoid a parking ticket from overzealous wardens, buy a two-hour **parking permit**, available for 10kr from kiosks and the tourist office.

### Halleberg and Hunneberg

The five-hundred-million-year-old twin plateaux of **Halleberg** and **Hunneberg**, just a few kilometres east of Vänersborg, are difficult to get to without your own transport, but well worth the trouble (see below). Crossing the Göta river, you'll first reach **VÄRGON**, home to a renowned, ultra-chic restaurant and hotel, *Ronnums Herrgord* (☎052/22 32 70; set lunch 11.30am–2pm, 187kr; a double room in summer 900kr). Alternatively, you can save your krona and get a good pizza and salad for 29kr at *Pizzeria Roma* at Nordkroksvagen 1 (☎0521/22 10 70).

After Värgon, the road cuts through the hills. Curious and tree topped, these ancient places – early human remains have been found here, as well as the traces of an old Viking fort – are best known as the home of Sweden's biggest herd of elks. **Elk safaris** run from late June to mid-August from Vänersborg's central square (150kr), but the old practice of offering money back if no sightings are made has been dropped since a disease has reduced the stock to just 120. Oscar II began shooting elk here in 1872, and the Royal Hunt continues to claim elk lives: the present king shoots a maximum of fifty during two days at the beginning of October (new animals are then brought in to keep the number steady). Without bothering with a safari, the easiest way of spotting the elks, and a splendid experience, is to drive or walk up the 5km lane around Halleberg at dawn or dusk. The elks are well worth the trouble. Leggy and long-faced, these massive creatures have no qualms about eating apples from your hand.

There are regular **buses** from Vänersborg, which are replaced in summer by a **taxi** service for the same price; there are just three a day and you need to give one hour's notice (☎020/71 97 17). Also bus #619 runs from Trollhättan straight to Hunneberg, while bus #62 goes to Värgon. The excellent **youth hostel** at Bergagårdsvägen 9 (open all year except Dec 17–Jan 12, reception daily 8am–10am & 5–9pm; ☎0521/22 03 40, fax 684 97; 95kr), at the foot of Hunneberg, dates from 1550 and was used by Danish soldiers to drive the Swedes into the hills. Following their line of retreat up Hunneberg brings you to the **Naturskola Nature Centre** (Mon–Fri 10am–4pm, Sat 10am–2pm, Sun 10am–3pm; ☎0521/22 37 70; free), with a **café** and lots of information about the wildlife in the hills. There is also a web of nature trails, including special trails for wheelchair users, that begin outside the centre.

# Between the lakes: Västergötland

The county of **Västergötland** makes up much of the region **between lakes Vänern and Vättern** – a wooded, lakeland landscape that takes up a large part of the Gothenburg-to-Stockholm train ride. The most interesting places lie on the southeastern shore of Lake Vänern, notably the pretty town of **Mariestad**, easily reached from Gothenburg, while with more time you can cut south to the western shore of Lake Vättern, and in particular to the colossal fortress at **Karlsborg**.

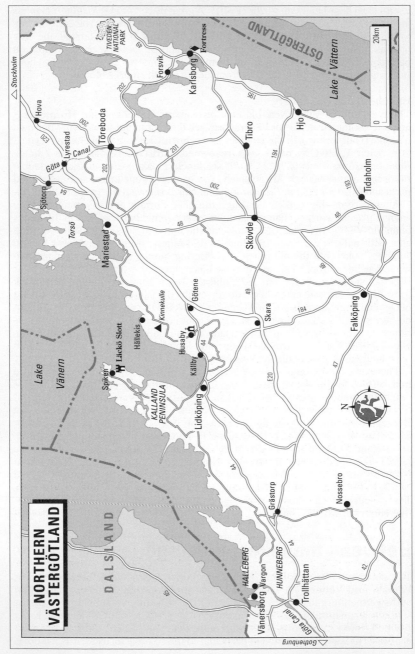

In between the lakes runs the **Göta Canal**, which along with the **Tiveden National Park** is the main regional target for Swedes taking their holidays in July and August.

# Lidköping and around

Although it flanks a grassy banked reach where the River Lidan meets Lake Vänern, **LIDKÖPING**, around 140km northeast of Gothenburg, falls short in charm compared to the rest of the region. The old town square dating from 1446, on the east bank, faces the new town square, founded by Chancellor Magnus de la Gardie in 1671, on the west, and both enjoyed a perfect panorama of Vänern until an unsightly concrete screen of coal storage cylinders and grain silos was plonked just at the water's edge. Despite this, it is pleasant enough to wander round the squares. The new one, Nya Stadens Torg, is graced with a wood hunting lodge, brought from de la Gardie's estate, and inside is the tourist office (see below).

The town's claim to fame is the **Rorstrand Porcelain Factory** (Mon–Fri 10am–6pm, Sun noon–4pm; guided tours June & Aug only; 15kr); Europe's second oldest, it is situated at the heart of the bleak industrial zone near the lake. The museum here is pretty uninspiring, but there are some pleasing classical designs on sale at supposedly bargain prices.

Though Lidköping itself has little to offer, it does make a good base for visiting picturesque **Läckö castle** on the Kalland peninsula, a finger of land pointing into Vänern to the west of the town that's brimming with scenic routes and a number of other architectural gems.

## Practicalities

Getting to and from Lidköping is easy by **train**; the station is by the old square. If returning to Gothenburg, you have to change trains at Herrljunga. If heading back towards Trollhättan, **bus** #5 is quicker, while bus #1 runs directly to Karlsborg (see p.156) in just under two hours. By **car**, Lidköping is on Road 44, 53km from Vänersborg. The **tourist office** in Nya Stadens Torg (June to mid-Aug Mon–Sat 9am–7pm, Sun 2–7pm; mid-Aug to May Mon–Fri 9am–5pm; ☎0510/835 00, fax 221 99) will help with **private rooms** (from 135kr per person). The cheapest option is the **youth hostel**, close by at Nicolaigatan 2 (☎0510/664 30; 100kr). For a really lovely and inexpensive **hotel**, *Park Hotell* (☎0510/243 90; ②/①, the price doesn't include meals) at 24 Mellbygatan – which runs south from Nya Stadens Torg – is a pink-painted 1920s' villa, with huge rooms and original features. Alternatively, *Edward Hotell* is at Skaragatan 7 (☎0510/22 110; ②, or ① if you provide your own sheets), or for more traditional luxury, try the *Stadthotel* (☎0510/220 85; ④/②) on Nya Stadens Torg.

For **snacks** and sandwiches, *Garstroms Konditori* at Mellbygatan 2, just opposite the tourist office, has been serving cakes and coffee since 1857. The confection-piled counter is original, though the decor is somewhat twee. For proper **restaurant** food, try *Gotes Festvaning* across the river at Östra Hamnen (☎0510/217 00), or *Madonna*, at Torggatan 6, off the main square, for kebab-type food.

If you are **changing money** in Lidköping, it's best to check the rates at the string of banks in Nya Stadens Torg, which will probably give better deals than the fixed rate at the shop adjoining the tourist office.

## North to Läckö castle

Almost everyone heads for Läckö castle, 25km north of Lidköping at the tip of the Kalland peninsula. Officially on its own island, but surrounded by water on just three sides, Läckö is everyone's idea of a fairy-tale castle – all turrets and towers and rendered in creamy white. The castle dates from 1290, but was last modified and restructured by Lidköping's chancellor, de la Gardie, when he took it over in 1652. Inside there is a wealth of exquisite decoration, particularly in the apartment that belonged to de la Gardie's wife, Princess Marie Euphrosyne. There are celebrated annual art exhibitions (ask at tourist office) and guided tours (May–Aug daily 10am–4pm, Sept daily 11am–1pm; 30kr). Be warned, however; Läckö's charms are no secret, and if you visit during summer, be prepared for the crowds. **Bus** #132 from Lidköping travels out here every hour during summer (20kr), via the tiny village of **SPIKEN**, 3km south of Läckö, which is a haven for lovers of smoked fish.

With your own transport, it's worth taking in some of the little-visited sights along the way to Läckö, notably **Riddargardskvarnen**, a perfect, mid-nineteenth-century windmill around 14km south. A remarkable structure, it was worked as a flower mill until its owner died in 1978, and is now maintained by the local people – the public are free to wander round. Opposite, the sign "Gravfalt" marks a huge **Viking burial site** – rather less to pick out in graves than sheep droppings, but a beautiful setting all the same. For a real trip into the past, though, follow the small lane marked "Froslunda" to a potato farm, from where it's a couple of kilometres walk to the avenue that leads to the secluded **Stola Herregard**, one of Sweden's finest Carolean estates (May–Sept tours by appointment, just turn up and arrange a time). A private estate since the Middle Ages, the present manor was built in 1713. Still in private hands, the house's authentic Rococo interior is a wonderful example of faded grandeur, and with a memorial park just outside, the whole area has changed very little in several hundred years.

## East to Kinnekulle

Twelve kilometres east of Lidköping and the first train stop on the *Kinkullebanan* route, **KALLBY** has an ancient burial site (turn left at the road junction), where two impressive stones face each other in an Iron Age cemetery, one carved with a comical, goblin-like figure supposedly the God Thor. Not far beyond, **Husaby** is a tranquil diversion with great religious and cultural significance. It was here in 1008 that Saint Sigfrid, an English missionary, baptized Olof Skotkonung, the first Swedish king to turn his back on Viking gods and embrace Christianity. The present, three-towered church was built in the twelfth century, and just to the east is the well where the baptism is said to have taken place.

**Kinnekulle**, the "Flowering mountain", is a couple of kilometres on (all the trains from Kallby will take you here), an area of woods and lakes all interwoven with paths and boasting hundreds of varieties of flowers, trees, birds and other animals. The strange shape of the plateau is due to its top layer of hard volcanic rock, which even four hundred million years of Swedish weather has not managed to wear down, and which makes for something of a botanical and geological treasure trove. There's an *STF* **youth hostel** (open all year; 100kr or 195kr with breakfast) and **campsite** combined at **HELLEKIS** (Råbäck station). The hostel has en-suite shower rooms and provides clean towels.

# Mariestad and Gullspång

Smaller, prettier and more welcoming than Lidköping, lakeside **MARIESTAD**, with its splendid medieval quarter and harbour area, is just an hour's train ride north and an excellent base for a day or two's exploration. The compact centre is brought to life by either the self-guided walking tour (pick up a map from the tourist office, see below) or the free guided tour laid on by the tourist office in summer (mid-June to mid-Aug Mon & Thurs). What lifts the town beyond post-card status is the extraordinary range of building styles crammed into the centre – Gustavian, Carolean, Classical, Swiss chalet style and Art Nouveau – like a living museum of architectural design. It's also worth taking a look at the now bishopless **cathedral**, on the edge of the centre, which was built out of spite at the end of the sixteenth century. Duke Karl (who named the town after his wife, Maria of Pfalz), jealous of his brother, King Johan III, built the cathedral in the likeness of the king's Klara kyrka in Stockholm, and filled it with over-the-top Baroque features, and some odd niceties – note the painted insects in every piece of stained glass.

Once you have toured Mariestad's fine architecture, there is little else to do in town – the clutch of seven folk museums in the vicinity aren't up to much. Instead, why not head to the nearby island of **Torso**, which now has a bridge connecting it with the mainland and offers good fishing and bathing opportunities (fishing equipment available on request at the tourist office). Perhaps best of all, Mariestad is also an ideal base from which to cruise up Lake Vänern to the start of the Göta Canal's main stretch at **Sjotorp**. There are 21 locks between Sjotorp and Karlsborg (see overleaf), with the most scenic section up to **Lyrestad**, just a few kilometres east of Sjotorp and 20km north of Mariestad on the E20. Lake and canal **cruises** cost 170kr for the whole day, however long you stay on the boat (contact the tourist office for details).

## Practicalities

The **tourist office**, by the harbour on Hamngatan (June–Aug Mon–Fri 8am–7pm, Sat & Sun 9am–6pm; Sept–May Mon–Fri 8am–4pm; ☎0501/100 01, fax 708 19), is opposite the hugely popular *STF* **youth hostel** (open all year but book in advance mid-Aug to mid-June; ☎0501/104 48; 100kr). Built after the fire of 1693, the hostel is a former tannery and, with galleried timber outbuildings and an excellent garden café, it's a great place to stay and close to all the sites. The most olde worlde **hotel** is the 1698-built *Bergs Hotell* in the old town at Kyrkogatan 18 (☎0501/103 24; ①). Other good-value central hotel options include *Hotell Viola*, Viktoriagatan 15 (☎0501/195 15; ①), and the imposing *Stadtshotellet* on Nya Torget (☎0501/138 00; d/②), just five minutes' walk away in the modern centre. The nearest **campsite** is *Ekuddens*, 2km down the river (May–Sept; ☎0501/106 37); alternatively you can stay on Torso at *Torso Camping* (May–Sept ☎0501/213 02).

Mariestad's trendiest **eating** hang-out is *Café Stroget* on Österlånggatan in the new town area, a very laidback place that's popular with young locals, who come to chat and flirt (sandwiches from 20kr). The liveliest **pub/restaurants** are *Buffalo* at Österlånggatan 3 and *Hjorten* at Nygatan 21; the latter also has occasional live music. **Nightlife** includes the disco at *Stadtshotellet* (see above) on Friday and Saturday nights, and there is year-round live music and dancing at

*Ohman's* – also owned by the *Stadtshotellet* – at Nygatan 16. In summer time, *Folkparken* at the harbour has a live band and dancing on a Saturday, and discos for the over-30s.

### Gullspång

Buses head 40km north from Mariestad to **GULLSPÅNG**. Between here and Torved, to the south runs 20km of abandoned railway track, now used for self-propelled trips on Western-style pump-action buggies, which carry one or two people and cost 200kr a day. The route lies alongside the eminently swimmable Gullspång river, and though you have to return the buggy to wherever you rented it, you can do so the next day if you want to camp out overnight. Gullspång is the more convenient end to rent a buggy, since there's an *STF* **youth hostel** there (open all year; ☎0551/207 86; 100kr) – book ahead outside the summer season.

## Karlsborg and around

Despite the great plans devised for the fortress at **KARLSBORG**, around 70km southeast of Mariestad on the western shores of Lake Vättern, it has survived the years as one of Sweden's greatest follies. By the early nineteenth century, Sweden had lost Finland – after six hundred years of control – and had became jumpy about its own security. In 1818, with the Russian fleet stationed on the Åland Islands and within easy striking distance of Stockholm, Baltzar Von Platten persuaded parliament to construct an inland fortress at Karlsborg, capable of sustaining an entire town and protecting the royal family and the treasury – the idea being that enemy forces should be lured into Sweden, then destroyed on home territory. With the town pinched between lakes Vättern and Bottensjön, the Göta Canal – also the brainchild of Von Platten and already under construction – was to provide access, but while Von Platten had the canal finished by 1832, the fortress was so ambitious a project that it was never completed. It was strategically obsolete long before work was finally abandoned in 1909, and the walls were not strong enough to withstand attack from new weaponry innovations. However, parts are still in use today by the army and air force, and uniformed cadets mill around lending an authenticity to your visit.

The complex, which is as large as a town, appears austere and forbidding, but you are free to wander through and to enter the **museum**, where you'll find endless military uniforms. A **guided tour** with special sound and smoke effects is a must for children, but not everyone's idea of a good time. For further information contact the tourist office (see below).

### Practicalities

There is no train service to Karlsborg and you'll have to come on one of the regular **bus** services from either Lidköping or Mariestad; by road take the 202 from Mariestad. The **tourist office**, right by the Göta Canal (June–Aug 9am–5pm; rest of the year Mon–Fri 9am–4pm; ☎0505/173 50, fax 125 91), can book **private rooms** for around 135kr per person. Both the **youth hostel**, 1km to the south (June–Aug; ☎0506/449 16, fax 125 91; 100kr), and the **campsite** (June–Sept; ☎0505/119 16), 500m to the north of the tourist office, are conveniently located on the banks of Lake Bottensjön. The tourist office can also tell you more about access to and accommodation in Tiveden National Park (see below).

## Forsvik

As far back as the early 1300s, the Karlsborg area maintained an important monastic flour mill, 8km north at **FORSVIK** (the monastery was founded by Sweden's first female saint, Birgitta). Using the height differential between lakes Viken and Bottensjon, first over waterwheels and later through power-generating turbines, a sizable industry emerged, working all manner of metal and wood products. During the Reformation, Forsvik was burnt down, but the creation of the Göta Canal gave the place new life, and it once again became a busy industrial centre. Its paper mill continued to operate until the 1940s, and its foundry until the Swedish shipyard crises in the 1970s. Today the mill is a **museum** (June–Aug noon–6pm; free), which has been restored to its 1940s' condition and provides a stimulating picture of Forsvik's industrial past. A bus runs from Karlsborg fairly frequently in summer.

## Tiveden National Park

Between Karlsborg and Askersund, 47km away, **Tiveden National Park** is a vast expanse of forest, lakes and ice-age boulders. One of southern Sweden's few remaining areas of virgin land, the park has never been inhabited – though charcoal has been produced at the edges of the area since the seventeenth century. The park, unlike more managed forests, aims to maintain an environment close to that of a primeval forest, with no human intervention, and the old or dead trees throughout Tiveden provide the right habitat for a number of rare birds and animals. There are 25km of **trails** passing though some spectacular scenery, with organized hikes tailored for differing abilities (ask at Karlsborg tourist office for details). The Tiveden wilderness is also the site used by the Karlsborg **Survival Training Centre** (Mon–Fri 8am–2.30pm; booking and information on ☎505/173 49). The courses here are for one to three days and are aimed at giving participants a sense of their ability to survive in conditions most travellers would prefer not to think about.

## travel details

### Trains

**From Gothenburg** to Kalmar (Mon–Fri 3, Sat 2, Sun 2; 4hr 20min); Karlskrona (Mon–Fri 2, Sat & Sun 1; 4hr 40min); Malmö (Mon–Fri 12, Sat 8, Sun 9; 3hr by X2000, 3hr 50min by intercity); Stockholm (Mon–Fri 13, Sat 9, Sun 12; 3hr 15min by X2000, 4hr 30min by intercity); Strömstad (Mon–Fri 9, Sat 8, Sun 7; 2hr 40 min); Trollhättan (Mon–Fri 15, Sat 12, Sun 8; 40min); Vänersborg Mon–Fri 10, Sat 4, Sun 4; 1hr 5min).

**Oslo-Copenhagen** trains involve changing at Gothenburg. There are two trains daily.

### Buses

**From Gothenburg** to Borås (Mon–Fri 13, Sat 3, Sun 8; 55min); Falun/Gavle (Mon–Thurs & Sat 1, Fri & Sun 3; 10hr 30min); Halmstad (Fri & Sun 3; 2hr); Karlstad (Mon–Thurs & Sat 3; Sun 4, Fri 5; 4hr); Linköping/Norrköping (Mon–Thurs & Sun 3, Fri 4, Sat 1; 4hr 35min); Mariestad (Mon–Fri & Sun 5, Sat 4; 3hr); Oslo (Mon–Fri 5, Sat & Sun 4; 4hr 45min); Oskarshamn (Fri & Sun 2; 5hr 20min); Tanumshede/Strömstad (Mon–Fri 5, Sat & Sun 4; 2hr 30min); Trollhättan (Mon–Thurs & Sun 5, Fri & Sat 2; 1hr 5min);

Varberg/Falkenberg (Fri & Sun 2; 50min/1hr 20min).

**From Strömstad** to Svinesund (Mon–Fri 5, Sat & Sun 4; 20min).

**From Mariestad** to Gävle (Mon–Fri 1; 7hr 30min); Örebro (Mon–Fri 2, Sat & Sun 1; 1hr 30min); Skövde/Jönköping (Mon–Thurs & Sun 3, Fri 4, Sat 1; 1hr 30min/2hr 10min).

**From Gullspång** to Mariestad (Mon–Thurs & Sun 2, Fri 3; 40min).

**From Lidköping** to Vånersborg/Trollhättan (Fri & Sun 2; 45min/1hr).

**Ferries**

**From Gothenburg** to Harwich (2 weekly; 24hr); 24hr); Frederikshavn (4–8 daily; 3hr 15min; by catamaran 3–5 daily; 1hr 45min); Keil (1 daily; 14hr); Newcastle (1 weekly June to mid-Aug.

**From Stömstad** to Fredrikstad (mid-June to mid-Aug Mon–Sat 5 daily; 1hr 15min); Halden (mid-June to mid-Aug Mon–Sat 3 daily; 1hr 15min); Sandefjord (mid-June to mid-Aug 2 daily; 2hr 30min).

# CHAPTER THREE

# THE SOUTHWEST

T here is a real historical interest to the **southwestern** provinces of **Halland**, **Skåne** and **Blekinge**, not least in the towns and cities that line the coast. The flatlands and fishing ports south of Gothenburg were almost constantly traded between Denmark and Sweden, counters won and lost in the fourteenth to seventeenth centuries. Several fortresses bear witness to the region's medieval buffer status.

**Halland**, a finger of land facing Denmark, has a coastline of smooth sandy beaches and bare, granite outcrops, punctuated by a number of small, distinct towns. Most charismatic is the old society bathing resort of **Varberg**, dominated by its tremendous thirteenth-century fortress; also notable is the small, beautifully intact medieval core of **Falkenberg**; while for extensive sands with nightlife, too, the regional capital, **Halmstad**, is a popular base.

Further south in the ancient province of **Skåne**, the coastline softens into curving beaches backed by gently undulating fields. This was one of the first parts of the country to be settled, and the scene of some of the bloodiest battles during the medieval conflict with Denmark. Although Skåne was finally ceded to Sweden in the late seventeenth century, the Danish influence died hard and is still evident today in the thick Skåne accent, often incomprehensible to other Swedes, and in the province's architecture. The latter has also been strongly influenced by Skåne's agricultural economy, the wealth generated by centuries of profitable farming leaving the countryside dotted with **castles** – though the continued income from the land means that most of these palatial homes are still in private hands and not open to the public.

Skåne has a reputation for fertile but mainly flat and uniform countryside; however, it takes only a day or two to appreciate the subtle variety of the landscape and its vivid beauty – blocks of yellow rape, crimson poppy and lush-green fields contrasting with the region's castles, charming white churches and black windmills. One of the best areas for **walking** and **cycling** is the **Bjäre peninsula**, the thumb of land to the west of the glamorous tennis capital of **Båstad**, where forested hill ranges, spectacular rock formations and dramatic cliffs make for some beautiful scenery. To the south, both **Helsingborg**, with its laidback, cosmopolitan atmosphere, and Sweden's third city, bustling **Malmö**, are a stone's throw from Denmark, with frequent ferries making the journey in just twenty minutes. Between these two centres, and in contrast to Malmö's industrial and Social Democratic heritage, the university town of **Lund** has some classic architecture and a unique atmosphere – a must for anyone travelling in the south.

As the countryside sweeps east towards the pretty medieval town of **Ystad**, the southwest corner of Skåne boasts excellent beaches around some minor resorts. Moving east, you enter the splendid countryside of **Österlen**. Unmasked by for-

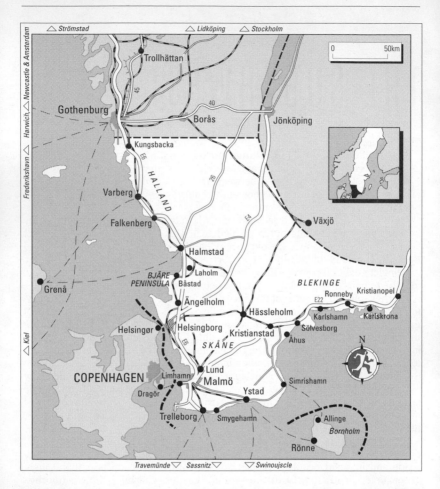

est, the pastoral scenery is studded with Viking monuments such as the Swedish Stonehenge at **Ales Stennar**, and, lined with brilliant white beaches backed by several nature reserves, it also offers some of Sweden's most enjoyable cycling. Edging north, the land becomes green and more hilly, the coast featuring a number of interesting little places to stop, such as **Kivik**, with its apple orchards and Bronze Age cairn, and the ancient and picturesque resort of **Åhus**. At the northeast of the county, **Kristianstad**, built as a flagship town by the Danes, retains its fine, Renaissance structure.

Beyond here to the east, the ledge of land running to the Baltic is **Blekinge**. Among the province's many small, not particularly distinguished resorts, **Karlskrona** stands out. Centred around a number of islands forming a small archipelago, Sweden's second city in the eighteenth century still exudes an air of regal and naval grandeur.

---

**ACCOMMODATION PRICES**

The pensions and hotels listed in the guide have been price-graded according to the scale outlined below; the number indicates the price for the least expensive double room. Many hotels offer considerable reductions at weekends (year round) and during the summer holiday period (mid-June to mid-Aug); in these cases the reduction is either noted in the text or, where it falls into another price band, given after the full price. Single rooms, where available, usually cost between 60 and 80 percent of a double.

① under 500kr   ② 500–700kr   ③ 700–900kr   ④ 900–1200kr   ⑤ over 1200kr

---

### Getting around

The national **train** network follows the coast south of Gothenburg, with frequent trains stopping at all towns as far as Ystad, from where it cuts northeast to Kristianstad. The comfortable, Danish-built *Kustpilen Express* trains run east/west across the country linking Malmö, Helsingborg and Lund with Kristianstad and Karlskrona. However, some of the most beautiful and less-frequented areas are not covered by the train network, and the **bus** service is skeletal at best, especially along the south coast. There are also certain transport anomalies to look out for: there are trains but no buses between Malmö and Ystad; between Ystad and Kristianstad the train service is very limited, making buses the more efficient option; and, more generally, some train and bus services stop early in the day. It's a good idea to equip yourself with timetables, and the best places to pick them up are the train and bus stations and tourist offices in Gothenburg and Malmö.

With no really steep hills, the southwest is wonderful country for **cycling**, and bike rental outlets (many listed in the text) are numerous; most tourist offices, youth hostels and campsites also rent out bikes. There are several recognized **walking trails**, all of which are referred to in the text.

# Kungsbacka and Tjolöholm

Just beyond the southernmost suburbs of Gothenberg, the small town of **KUNGSBACKA** is a residential backwater that's of no particular interest to travellers, unless you time your trip to arrive on lively market day (the first Thursday of the month). Although Kungsbacka dates from the thirteenth century, when it shared growth and prosperity with many other Hanseatic towns along the south coast, there is no real focus to the place. The town was razed by fire in 1846, and now just two houses stand as testament to its past. It's altogether better to use the town simply as a means of reaching the splendid and unique manor house on the coast at Tjolöholm, 15km south.

## Tjolöholm

The dream home of Scottish merchant and horse-breeder James Dickson, the manor house at **TJOLÖHOLM** (pronounced "chewla-home") was the subject of a grand design competition in the 1890s. Enormously wealthy, Dickson wanted a unique house to reflect the mélange of his British ancestry, the then current Swedish fascination for Romanticism and the latest comfort innovations of the day. The winner of the competition was the 27-year-old architect Lars Israel Wahlman, and the result of his work is a stunning Elizabethan-style stately home. Dickson, however, never saw Tjolöholm completed. A man accustomed to glamour, he died shortly after he opened a bottle of vintage champagne – cutting his finger on the bottle, he fatally poisoned himself by wrapping the lead cap around the wound.

In 1901, a village was built around the house, and its little red and white wooden cottages, with just one room and a kitchen, have been immaculately preserved. When Wahlman suggested that three-room cottages would be more comfortable, Blanche Dickson retorted, "If they [the estate workers and their families] have more than one room, they would just lock them up." Walking up the main driveway, you pass the huge stables and indoor riding track, which have been converted into an airy café (mid-June to mid-Aug Tues–Fri 11am–5pm; April to mid-June & mid-Aug to Oct Sat & Sun 11am–5pm) – try the delicious Swedish roast beef and potato salad for 55kr. The stables were finished long before the house, and Dickson ran a school for coachmen here. It's worth peeking inside the carriage museum in the next building (same opening times as the house; see below), where among the many stylish carriages and London-built Hansom cabs, the most bizarre exhibit is an amazing four-wheeled, cab-sized electric horse-drawn vacuum cleaner. Horses gave the carpets a not-so-quick once over from outside by means of a 40m hose, hoisted up through the windows.

The interior of the house (June–Aug daily 11am–4pm; Sept & Oct Sun only 11am–4pm; 45kr) deserves a good hour or so, and the excellent room description pamphlets available free at reception make it easy to guide yourself (official tours in English have to be pre-booked). Among the many highlights of the finely detailed interior are the billiard room, where the walls are lined with Belgian marble and punctuated by hot-air vents (part of the avant garde central heating system), and the sophisticatedly regal study, which was oak panelled by Liberty's of London. Sweeping through Blanche Dickson's red boudoir and her four fabulous bathrooms, delicately coloured in green, pink, orange and blue, and all with sunken baths and showers – which sprayed Mrs Dickson from above, below and the sides – you're led on to the Charles Rennie Mackintosh-inspired children's nursery, with its simple, white motifs.

Once you've seen the interior, the grounds and nearby beach are wonderful places to while away a warm summer's afternoon. The landscape here marks a noticeable change; the dramatic rocky cliffs of Bohuslän make way for the open beaches of Halland. This move from rough to smooth became one of the subject matters for the Varberg group of painters (see p.165). On sunny days, the grass-fringed beach beyond the gardens is a popular and relaxed spot for sunbathing, or if you prefer, meander through the ash and oak woods around the manor.

### Practicalities

To reach Tjolöholm, take the **local train** from platform 15 at Gothenburg's Central Station to Kungsbacka (journey time 20min). A special bus runs from here to the house at 11am year round (the bus gets you back in plenty of time for trains back to the city; if you miss that, bus #732 (within the cost of the train ticket) goes to within 3km, from where you'll have to walk or hitch. In July and August, there's a special *SJ* **bus** right to Tjolöholm from Nils Ericsonsplatsen by

Gothenburg station (Sat, Sun & public holidays). By car, turn off the E6 highway just south of Kungsbacka at Fjärås and follow the signs to Åsa for 2km, from where there are signs for Tjolöholm.

Kungsbacka has a **youth hostel** (mid-June to mid-Aug; ☎0300/194 85; 95kr), which is 2km from the train station, on the road to Sarö – turn left from the station, then right onto the main road. **Private rooms** at 150kr per person can be booked at the **tourist office** opposite the station (May to late June Mon–Fri 9am–6pm, Sat & Sun 11am–3pm; late June to mid-Aug Mon–Sat 9am–7pm, Sun 11am–3pm; mid-Aug to April Mon–Fri 10am–4pm; ☎0300/345 95, fax 131 34). There is a 25kr fee if the booking is for outside Kungsbacka itself. The only central **hotel** is *Hotel Halland* at Storgatan 35 (☎0300/775 30; ④/②), almost next to the tourist office. It's a bland but reasonable place, and all rooms have a TV, shower and toilet. The nearest **campsite** (June–Aug ☎0300/148 29; Sept–May ☎0300/346 48) is 3km away at the *Kungsbacka Sportscenter*. Buses to the centre only run during school term times (Oct–May).

# Varberg

More atmospheric than any other town in Halland, the fashionable little nineteenth-century bathing resort of **VARBERG** boasts surprisingly varied sights – its imposing fortress the most obvious one – a laidback atmosphere and plenty of good places to eat. Bathing and windsurfing opportunities are also plentiful.

## Arrival and accommodation

Varberg is a handy entry point to southern Sweden; a year-round **ferry** service (90kr one-way, 150kr return; 3hr 45min) links it with Grenä in **Denmark**. Regular **trains** run down the coast from Gothenburg, and local **buses** cover the 45km trip south from Kungsbacka (bus #732 changing to #615 at Frillesås). From the train and bus stations, turn right down Vallgatan, and the town centre is off to the left and the fortress to the right. The central square is dominated by the grand *Warbergs* bank; opposite is the **tourist office** (mid-June to mid-Aug Mon–Sat 9am–7pm, Sun 3–7pm; ☎0340/887 70, fax 111 95), where you can pick up a free map of the town.

Varberg is easy to walk around, but if you want to explore the coast around the town, you can **rent a bike** from *Team Sportia* (☎0340/124 70; 75kr a day) in front of the tourist office or the expensive *Cykelhus* (☎0340/61 10 60; 95kr a day) at the harbour. In spring and summer, **Strandpromenaden**, a path that runs south along the coast, is a pleasant walk and popular with cyclists, roller skaters and wheelchair users.

### Accommodation

It's worth booking well in advance for the fortress prison **youth hostel** (open all year ☎0340/887 88; 120kr); outside the summer season you have to book through the tourist office (see above). Aside from being spotlessly clean, the prison is much as it was, with original cell doors, complete with spy-holes (each has its own key). The cells are arranged on two floors, the upper one around a central gallery. Cell 24 on the upper gallery has been preserved without redecoration; push the door open for a chilling glimpse of past conditions. If you do want to stay, ask for

Cell 13, the only one with a full-sized (although barred and curtainless) window and a great sea view. If full (July is the busiest month) there is an *STF* **hostel** (April & Sept; ☎0340/410 43; 100kr) 8km south at **HIMLE** – bus #652 from the bus station runs down E6 to within a kilometre.

The cheapest **hotel** is *Hotel Bergklinten*, close to the station at Västra Vallgatan 25 (☎0340/61 15 45; ①); it's a shabby, rather dilapidated old hotel with a spartan wartime feel, but it is clean. The most interesting and luxurious hotel, *Hotel Fregatten* (☎0340/770 00, fax 61 11 21; ④/②), is in a former cold storage warehouse, overlooking the harbour and within a few steps of the fortress; it's a modern stylish place, with simple decor, a jacuzzi, a sauna and beer on tap. The similarly priced *Stadshotell*, Kungsgatan 24–26 (☎0340/161 00; ④/②), is a more traditional hotel with some Art Nouveau features; it also has a good restaurant, barcum-nightclub and jacuzzi. For **B&B**, *Nils Mårtensgård* (☎ & fax 0340/408 37; 195kr per person) is fifteen minutes' drive east, just off the E6 towards Sibbarps, in a comfortable old farm house surrounded by woodland, and serving homemade bread with their excellent breakfasts.

There are a number of **campsites**, the nearest being *Apelvikens Camping* (April–Oct; ☎0340/141 78; July & Aug 137kr per tent; June & Sept 110kr), which is 3km south of the fortress along Strandpromenaden; there is just one cabin (sleeps three; 337kr). *Getteröns Camping* is near the nature reserve area 5km to the north (☎0340/168 85, fax 104 22; 137kr per tent, plus 30kr for electricity). Three-person cabins cost 335kr, but in July to early August you can only book for the week at 2300kr. Alternatively, there are plenty of places to put up a tent for free beyond the nudist beaches.

# The Town

All of Varberg's sights are concentrated along or near the seafront. The thirteenth-century moated **fortress** set on a rocky promontory in the sea is Varberg's most obvious attraction. It was home to the Swedish king Magnus Eriksson, and important peace treaties with Denmark were signed here in 1343. The great bastions were added for protection by Danish king Christian IV in the seventeenth century, just in time for him to see it become permanently Swedish in 1645. Standing outside, it's easy to imagine how impenetrable the fortress must have appeared to attackers in the past – and, due to the lack of signposting, may still seem today. It is entered on the sea-facing side by either climbing uneven stone steps to a delightful terrace café (June–Sept noon–10pm), or approaching through the great archways towards the central courtyard.

Although tours in English (daily 10am–7pm year round, tours hourly in July & Aug, children's tours 1.30pm & 2.30pm daily; 20kr, children 10kr) take you into the dungeons and among the impressive dark-cocoa painted buildings that make up the inner courtyard, it's the **museum** that deserves most of your attention (mid-June to mid-Aug daily 10am–7pm; rest of the year Mon–Fri 10am–4pm, Sat & Sun noon–4pm; 30kr in summer, 10kr rest of year). The most unnerving exhibit is **Bocksten Man**, a six-hundred-year-old murder victim who was garrotted, drowned, impaled and buried in a local bog, until 1936 when a farmer dug him up while planting crops. His entire garb preserved by the acid bog, Bocksten Man sports the Western world's most complete medieval wardrobe made up of a cloak, a hood, shoes and stockings. His most shocking feature is his thick, red ringletted hair, which cascades around his puny skull. To ensure that his spirit never escaped to seek out his murderers, three stakes were thrust through his body.

In the neighbouring room, a great deal is made of a small **brass button**. Couched in velvet, spot-lit and constantly revolving, the button not only matched those on the uniform of King Karl XII, but fitted exactly the hole in his regal cranium where he was shot dead while attacking a Norwegian castle in 1718. Convinced that the king had special powers, his assailants believed his life could only be ended by something that belonged to him and, having stolen the button, had it filled with lead. An oil painting of the rather unattractive king lets you see whose life they were so keen to end. The rest of the museum is for the most part dispensable, with sections on farming and fishing in Halland from the 1750s and some southern Swedish peasant wall hangings. A room devoted to the sensitive work of the so-called **Varberg School** is, however, worth viewing. A small colony of artists – Richard Bergh, Nils Kreuger and Karl Nordström – linked up in the last years of the nineteenth century and developed a *plein air* national painting style reflecting the moods and atmosphere of Halland, and particularly Varberg. Night scenes of the fortress beneath the stars show a strong Van Gogh influence, but in other paintings, the misty colours create a melancholy effect, evoking the atmosphere of the time.

Overlooking the sea and painted in custard and cream, the 1850-built **fortress prison** looks like a soft option in the shadow of the looming fortress. The first Swedish prison built in the American style of individual cells, it housed life sentencers, until the last one ended his days here in 1931. Today you can stay in a private youth hostel in the fortress, which has been carefully preserved to retain most of its original features (see p.163).

A couple of fine remnants from Varberg's time as a spa resort are within a minute of the fortress. Just behind it, and facing the town, is the grand **Societeshuset** set in its own small park. A bridal-like confection of white and pink carved wood, this was where upper-class ladies took their meals after bathing in the splendid **Kallbadhuset** (cold bath house), just to the north of the fortress and overlooking the harbour. Somewhat battered by time and the sea-wind, but shortly to be renovated (due to open in 1998), this dainty bath house has separate-sex naked-bathing areas and is topped at each corner by Moorish cupolas, lending it an imperial air. While in the harbour area, take a look inside the busy **Konsthall** (Tues–Fri noon–6pm, Sat & Sun noon–5pm), in a fine old warehouse building, where glass-blowers, silversmiths and several ceramic artists sell their wares.

## The beaches

Although the Halland coastline is still a little rocky around Varberg, there are several excellent spots for bathing; for the best ones head down Strandpromenaden. After about five minutes, two well-known **nudist beaches** are signposted, with not very private fencing marking the separate-sex areas. Called "Goda Hopp" (for men) and "Kärringhålan" (for women), these translate, somewhat provocatively, as "Good Hope" and "Pit of Bitches". Alternatively, a few kilometres further north at **Getterön**, a fist of land jutting into the sea, there's a nature centre and extensive bird reserve (for details of guided tours ask at the tourist office). There are regular **buses** to Getterön, where you can bathe in secluded coves and among the wild flowers that fill the rock crevices in early summer.

## Eating and drinking

There are plenty of good places to eat in Varberg, mostly along Kungsgatan running north of the main square. The best **café** in town is *Otto's Skafferi*, Kungsgatan 12 (Mon 7.30am–8pm, Tues–Thurs 7.30am–10pm, Fri & Sat 7.30am–1pm, Sun noon–5pm), a pleasure as much for the decor as the sumptuous sweet-and-savoury pies and big sandwiches. One room is decorated in eighteenth-century costume prints, another full of old settees and posters advertising chocolate, another crammed with 1950s' kitsch. Popular with a young crowd, it's a great place for breakfast. *Ny Fiket* at no. 18 (Mon–Thurs 8am–9pm, Fri & Sat 8am–1pm) is a pleasant, regular café; in contrast, the big eating place next door, *Harry's Pub & Restaurant*, has a rather jumbled identity. Its dark interior is adorned with chandeliers and statuettes of Liberty and Hiawatha, while it serves a range of pastas all named after English football teams (75kr). With a popular happy hour (4–7pm), there's a wide selection of malt whiskies and beers. Opposite is *Scruphy Murphy's*, part of the Irish-style pub chain; this one insists that the late Mr Murphy emigrated to Varberg during the Irish potato famine. For a more genteel lunch, it's worth spending a little extra at the *Societen* in Societets Park, directly behind the fortress, where steaks and fish dishes are served for moderate prices (11.30am–1.30pm). The place comes alive on Thursday and Saturday evenings with foxtrots on the ground floor and a disco in the basement. If you're out bathing along Strandpromenaden, *Kärleksparkens Servering* (10am–6pm) is a small café through the trees, with filled baguettes at 30kr and ice cream.

# Falkenberg

It's a twenty-minute train ride south from Varberg to the well-preserved medieval town of **FALKENBERG** (falcons were once hunted here, hence the name). With some lively museums and a long beach, it's a likable little town that really comes alive in July and August. It also has a long-standing reputation as a centre for fly-fishing.

In the 1820s, Sir Humphrey Davy, the inventor of the mining safety lamp, visited the town, having heard about the excellent **fly-fishing** to be had on the River Ätran that runs through it. Soon after came a succession of wealthy **English countrymen**, their numbers swelling as Falkenberg's reputation for good salmon fishing spread. One such devotee, London lawyer William Wilkinson, went so far as to write a book, *Days In Falkenberg* (1894). The well-to-do visitors stayed at what Wilkinson described as "an ancient inn with a beautiful garden leading down to the river". One of the few buildings to have missed every town fire, it now houses *Falkmanska Caféet*, the best café in town (see "Eating and drinking"). These upper-class Englishmen brought considerable wealth with them, and had a tremendous influence on the town. Predictably enough, they made no attempt to adapt to local culture; as a result Falkenbergers had to learn English for the first time, and throughout the latter half of the nineteenth century, baby boys were named Charles instead of the Swedish Karl, while the most popular girls' name was Frances, after Wilkinson's daughter. Even today, there is a classic British telephone box near the post office, given by the English twin town of Ostletwistle. Another legacy of the English connection is the current low fish stocks; the waters have been so overfished that it now costs relatively little to try your hand in the permitted 2km stretch of river from the splendid 1756-built stone Tullbron toll bridge. The tourist office (see below) will sell you a licence that allows you to catch up to three fish a day (March–Sept; 80kr).

## Arrival, information and accommodation

Regular **buses** and trains drop you close to the centre on Holgersgatan, from where it's a couple of hundred metres along to the **tourist office** in Stortorget (mid-June to Aug Mon–Sat 9am–7pm, Sun 3–7pm; Sept Mon–Fri 9am–5pm, Sat 10am–2pm, Oct to mid-June Mon–Fri 9am–5pm; ☎0346/174 10, fax 145 26). The tourist office will book **private rooms** from 120kr per person, plus 30kr booking fee. The comfortable and well-equipped *STF* **youth hostel** (June to mid-Aug; ☎0346/171 11; 100kr) is in the hamlet of **NÄSET**, 4km south of town, accessible by local buses #1 and #2, but only till 7pm. It is just a few minutes' walk through the neighbouring **campsite** (☎0346/171 07) to the southern end of the beach.

The cheapest **hotel** is *Hotel Steria*, a ten-minute walk away from the river up Arvidstorpsvägen (☎0346/155 21, fax 101 30; ① or ② with en-suite shower); it's plain but the price includes breakfast. In the town centre, the smart *Grand Hotel* (☎0346/144 50, fax 829 25; ④, no summer reductions, but weekends ③) overlooks the historic Tullbron bridge. Its upmarket restaurant offers classic but pricey meals, while the bar and disco are popular night-time haunts for the young. Rather more interesting, and just as central, the riverside *Hvitan* (☎0346/820 90, fax 597 96; ③, weekends ② including breakfast) is a picturesque open courtyard of low-built houses dating from 1703, which has a fine restaurant and a pub. Best located for the beach is *Nya Hotel Strandbaden* (☎0346/58 000, fax 161 11; ④/③, price includes breakfast and free entry to *Klitterbadhuset* – see overleaf); a plush modern hotel, it lacks any design niceties but does have an excellent sea-viewing lounge and is only 2km from the old town centre (follow Strandvägen to the beach).

## The town and around

Other than fishing, Falkenberg's pleasures are quite distinct. The **old town**, to the west of the curving river, comprises a dense network of low, wooden cottages and cobbled lanes. Nestling among them is the fine twelfth-century **St Laurentii kyrka**, its interior awash with seventeenth- and eighteenth-century wall and ceiling paintings. An electronic box by the door lets you choose a taped commentary in a range of languages; if you press the wrong language, there's no way to rectify it, and you'll be regaled with information at a frightening volume for twenty minutes in the wrong tongue. It is hard to believe that this gem of a church also spent time as a shooting range, a cinema and a gymnasium; however, after the building of the solid neo-Gothic "new" church at the end of the nineteenth century, its secular usage saved it from demolition. When it was reconsecrated in the 1920s, its sixteenth-century font and silverware were discovered (and recovered) from all over northern Europe.

Bypassing the pedestrian County Museum on St Lars Kyrkogatan, with its collections tracing the town's history until 1900, head straight for the **new museum** (June–Aug Tues–Fri 10am–4pm, Sat & Sun noon–4pm; Sept–May Tues–Fri & Sun noon–4pm; 20kr) in an old four-storey grain store near the main bridge. Although there are the usual archeological collections, the enthusiastic curator has chosen to devote most of the museum to the 1950s, considering the decade to be the most interesting and educational. The fact that Falkenburg had over one-hundred dance bands up until the 1970s provides the basis for one of the permanent exhibitions, and, along with original interiors of a shoe repair shop and stylized café (complete with jukebox), it's worth a look – though labelling in English is minimal.

The town also boasts a rather unusual **Fotomuseum** (late June to mid-Aug Tues–Thurs 1–8pm; rest of year Tues–Thurs 5–8pm, Sun 2–6pm). At present the museum is housed in the owner's home at Karl Salomonssons Vägen 9 (ring for directions on ☎0346/803 93); it's a fifteen-minute drive away and there's no public transport, but in July 1997 it's moving to Sandgatan 13, the home of Falkenberg's oldest purpose-built cinema (1907 – the first films were shown in St Laurentii's). There are over one thousand cameras and a remarkable collection of cinematic paraphernalia, including some superb local peasant portraits, taken in 1898 for the Nordic Museum in Stockholm by Axel Aurelius, and Sweden's first colour photographs, which Aurelius took of his wife, a native of the town. The oldest pictures on show are English and date back to the 1840s. There's also an impressive section on Sweden's well-loved author Selma Lagerlöf – her portrait appears on all 20kr banknotes – at her celebrated home in Mårbacka.

Less demanding is a tour of the local **Falken Brewery** (July & Aug Mon–Thurs 10am & 1.15pm; 20kr; book through the tourist office); Sweden's most popular beer, *Falken*, has been brewed here since 1896 and is readily available for sampling at the end of the tour.

### Skrea Strand and Klitterbadhuset

Over the river and fifteen minutes' walk south, **Skrea Strand** is a fine, 4km stretch of sandy beach. At the northern end, a relaxing diversion is the large bathing and tennis complex of **Klitterbadhuset** (Tues & Thurs 6–9am & noon–8pm, Wed noon–8pm, Fri noon–3pm OAPs only & 3–7pm over-16s only, Sat 9am–5pm, Sun 9am–3pm), which has a 50m pool (with a shallow children's pool nearby), a vast sauna, jacuzzi and steam rooms all for 30kr. If you walk all the way down past the busy wooden holiday shacks at the southern end of the long beach – and you may have to if you're staying at the youth hostel (see p.167) – there are secluded coves, and in early summer the marshy grassland is full of wild violets and clover. It's a great place for **birdwatching**: ungainly cormorants nest here, while oyster-catchers, shell ducks and plover are also thick on the ground.

# Eating and drinking

In this, the birthplace of *Sia Glass* – a popular ice cream made by Sweden's oldest family firm, established in 1569 – and *Falcon* beer, eating and drinking can certainly be a pleasure, although the variety of food on offer is small. About the best place is the *Falkmanska Caféet*, Storgatan 42 (Mon–Fri 10am–6pm, Sat 10am–2pm). With a stripped wood floor, mellow furnishings and a lovely garden, it has a terrific atmosphere and serves huge baguettes along with decadent home-made cakes. Other agreeable cafés include *Pokalen Café* on Ågatan, by the river, for salads and snacks, and *Folkes Café* on the main square (Mon–Thurs 9am–9pm, Fri & Sat 9am–midnight, Sun 3–9pm). A basic place, usually full of older teenagers, it doubles as a solarium at 50kr a go. For American food, the friendly *D.D.* on Hotelgatan 3 (June to Aug daily 11am–2am; rest of the year Wed–Sat only) is a smallish restaurant and club, with old cart wheels made into lamps. Lunch (daily 11.30am–2pm) is 55kr, and at night a dance floor is opened up for a 20- 30-year-old crowd (40kr cover charge on Sat only). Mixing American and British influences, *Harry's Bar* on the main square (noon till late) is a busy eating place and pub. The poshest restaurant is *Gustav Bratt*, Brogatan 1, near the main square (11.30am–2pm & 6pm–midnight). Built as a grain warehouse in 1860, and looking like the museum, this is where people go to indulge themselves, but the à la carte menu is a disappointingly ordinary selection of fish and pizza dishes. Lunch costs around 150kr.

# Halmstad

The principal town in Halland, **HALMSTAD**, was once a grand walled city and important Danish stronghold. Today, although most of the original buildings have disappeared, Halmstad has a couple of cultural and artistic points of interest – most notably the works of the Halmstad Group, Sweden's first Surrealists – extensive, if rather crowded, beaches not far from town and a wide range of really good places to eat . All in all, it's a sound choice for a day or two's relaxation.

In 1619, the town's **castle** was used by the Danish king Christian IV to entertain the Swedish king Gustav Adolf II; records show that there were seven days of solid festivities. The bonhomie, however, didn't last much longer, and Christian was soon building great stone and earth fortifications, all surrounded by a moat with four stone gateways into the city. Soon after, however, a fire, rather than the Swedes, all but destroyed the city; the only buildings to survive were the castle and the church. Undeterred, Christian took the opportunity to create a modern Renaissance town with a gridwork of straight streets. The high street, Storgatan, still contains a number of impressive merchants' houses from that time. After the final defeat of the Danes in 1645, Halmstad lost its military significance, and the walls were torn down. Today, just one of the great gateways, Norre Port, remains, while Karl XIs Vägen is the road running directly above the filled-in moat.

## Arrival, information and accommodation

From the **train station** (it takes 25min from Falkenberg by train) follow Bredgatan to the Nissan river, and just by Österbro (East Bridge) is the tourist office; across the bridge is the main square. The helpful **tourist office** (June & Aug Mon–Fri 9am–6pm, Sat 10am–3pm, Sun 1–3pm; July Mon–Sat 9am–7pm, Sun 3–7pm; ☎10 93 45, fax 15 81 15) will book **private rooms** from 120kr per person, plus a booking fee of 25kr if you visit the office, 50kr if you telephone. It also sells the five-day **Halmstad Card** (50kr), which provides free museum entry, twenty percent off taxi fares, free designated parking, 100kr off family day excursions to Denmark on *Lion Ferry* and some restaurant discounts.

A good way to get to the beaches or the Mjållby Arts Centre is to rent a **bike**. There is currently only one outlet, *Arvid Olsson Cykel*, Norra Vägen 11 (Mon–Fri 9.30am–6pm, Sat 9.30am–1pm; ☎21 22 51), which charges a steep 95kr per day for a five-speed bike; trailers are 75kr extra.

The telephone code for Halmstad is ☎035.

## Accommodation

The new, central **youth hostel** (mid-June to mid-Aug; 4-bed rooms 125kr per person, 2-bed rooms 160kr; ☎12 05 00) is at Skepparegatan 23, 500m to the west of St Nicolai church, and has showers and toilets in all rooms. The best central **hotel**, the very comfortable old *Norre Park Hotel*, is at Norra Vägen 7 (☎21 85 55, fax 10 45 28; ④/③), which is through the Norre Port Arch north of Storgatan, and overlooks the beautiful Norre Katt Park. The price includes saunas, use of the fitness room and an excellent buffet breakfast. The long, low *Hotel Tylösand* on the Tylösand beach (☎305 00, fax 324 39; ④/①) has been bought by Per Gessle, better known as the singer/songwriter from the Swedish rock duo *Roxette,* who hail from the town, and plans are afoot to revamp the place for a younger market. It has a big, international restaurant with shows and a casino, plus a pool, sauna and solarium. **Camping** is a popular option here, the best site being *Hägons Camping* at Östra Stranden, about 3km from the centre (☎12 53 63, fax 12 43 65; 140kr plus 30kr for electricity per family in caravan in summer); there are also **cabins** (up to 5 people 3100kr per week, or 4500kr with shower and toilet). The site is next to the nature reserve to the east of the town centre. There are hamburger restaurants at the site (see also p.172).

# The town and around

At the centre of the big and lively market square, **Storatorg**, is Carl Mille's *Europa and the Bull*, a fountain with mermen twisted around it, all with Mille's characteristically muscular bodies and ugly faces. Flanking one side of the square is the grand **St Nikolai kyrka** (8.30am–3.30pm). It dates from the fourteenth century, and its monumental size attests to the town's former importance. Today, the only signs of its medieval origins are the splodges of bare rock beneath the plain, brick columns. Adjacent to the church, the **Tre Hjartan** (Three Hearts) konditori is a vast, proud building of cross beams; it's worth taking your coffee and cake upstairs, where the beams and ceiling are beautifully handpainted, and historical photographs of nineteenth-century Halmstad adorn the walls. Three hearts make up the town's emblem, Christian IV having granted this crest to the town's citizens in gratitude for their loyalty to Denmark. Today, the image is overused, the big bulging heart lending historical sites a saucy postcard feel whenever it appears. Not far from Österbro bridge, **Halmstad Castle** is a mellow, red-stone affair half hidden by trees. A private governor's residence, it is closed to the public, but in front is moored *Najaden*. Built in 1897, this small, fully rigged sailing ship was used for training by the Swedish navy; tours below deck are free (July & Aug Tues & Thurs 5–7pm, Sat 11am–3pm).

Leading north from the square, pedestrianized **Storgatan**, which until the 1950s was the old E6 highway, is the main thoroughfare for restaurants and nightlife (see p.172). It's a charming street with some creaking old houses built in the years following the 1619 fire. The great stone arch of **Norre Port** marks the street's end. Walking straight through, to the right is the splendid **Norre Katt Park**, a delightful, shady place, with mature beech, copper beech and horse chestnut trees sloping all the way to the river, where great weeping willows drip into the water. The town's most serene spot is at the park's centre, where above a bridged water-lily pond is an old ornate band-stand café, which serves waffles at 15kr (June & Aug Mon–Fri 1–5pm, Sat & Sun noon–8pm, July daily 10am–10pm).

## The Halmstad Museum and Hallandsgården

At the northernmost edge of the park by the river is a fine **museum** (early June to late Aug daily 10am–7pm, Wed till 9pm; rest of the year 10am–4pm, Wed till 9pm; 20kr, half-price in winter). The archeological finds and basement collections are unlikely to set many pulses racing, but the first-floor displays (rooms 6, 7 & 8) are a lot of fun. You can wander through home interiors from the seventeenth, eighteenth and nineteenth centuries, with some exquisitely furnished dolls' houses and a room of glorious Gustavian harps and square pianos from the 1780s. It's not at all stuffy and none of the exhibits is roped off. The shipping room avoids the usual nautical maps and bits of old boats and instead shows a charismatic collection of ghoulish figureheads from ships wrecked off the Halland coast. The museum is known for its southern Swedish tapestry paintings; these won't excite everyone, but the full English commentary amusingly explains the pictorial stories. The top floor is devoted to the work of the **Halmstad Group**; if you don't intend seeing the full collection of their work at Mjållby Arts Centre (see below), this is a fair sample, together with some contemporary sculptures – arresting pieces using glass and prismic forms to intriguing effect.

Close to here, on so-called Gallows Hill, is a small collection of Halmstad's older houses moved to the site to form a mini-outdoor museum, **Hallandsgården** (early June to late Aug 11am–5pm, guided tours 2pm each day; other times by arrangement on ☎11 03 74; free).

## Mjållby Arts Centre

A few kilometres north from the town centre (near the small airport, and on the way to Tylösand), is **Mjållby Arts Centre** containing the largest collection of works by the **Halmstad Group**, a body of six local artists from the 1920s who championed Cubism and Surrealism in Sweden. The group, which consisted of brothers Eric and Axel Olson, their cousin Sven Jonson and three others, is reputedly the only one of its type in the world to have stayed together in its entirety for fifty years. Strongly influenced by Magritte and Dalí, their work caused considerable controversy in the 1930s and 1940s, and, almost unheard of in Swedish art, they sometimes worked on a single project as a group. A good example of one of these group pieces is at the Halmstad City Library, where a 14m, six-section work hangs impressively above the shelves. If Viveka Bosson, the daughter of Eric Olson, is around, you may get a free guided tour around Mjållby. To get there, take bus #350 or #351 to the airport, from where it is a 1km walk to the arts centre down the road on the right.

## Martin Luther Church

For a completely different church to any other you may have visited in Sweden, the gleamingly 1970s' **Martin Luther Church** (9am–3pm) is on Långgatan, one of the main roads out of town, 1km east of the centre. The first church in Scandinavia to be assembled entirely of steel – it is known by locals as the Tin Factory – this unique creation has an Art Deco/Futuristic style, looking from the outside like an unsuccessfully opened sardine can, with jagged and curled edges and stained glass. Inside is just as unusual; all the walls are a rusted orange version of the outer skin, and there are some striking ornaments. It's famed for its acoustics, and there are concerts here on Sunday evenings in summer and a seven-day music festival held during the first week of July (☎15 19 55 for details).

## The beaches: Tylösand and Östra Stranden

Eight kilometres west of the town centre, Halmstad's most popular **beach** is at **Tylösand** (buses run regularly from town), which in July and August becomes packed with bronzing bodies; by night the same bodies fill the surrounding bars and restaurants. There's a smuggler's cove to wander in at **Tjuvahålan**, directly off the beach, and plenty of excellent spots for bathing, including **Svårjarehålan**, a little further north, where a bathing beach has been adapted for the disabled. If you're not too keen on body-to-body sunbathing, the strip of coast to the north is a better bet.

The best beach to the east of town is at **Östra Stranden**, where there is also a large, well-equipped campsite (see p.170). It's reached by crossing the river from Stora Torg and heading along Stationgatan past the train station, then turning southeast for a couple of kilometres down Stälverksgatan. The long beach – deep, sandy and less crowded than at Tylösand – is excellent for children as the waters are particularly shallow here. Further south is **Hägon**, a secluded **nudist beach**, where privacy is afforded by the deep hollows between the dunes; behind it is a nature reserve.

# Eating, drinking and nightlife

For **eating**, **drinking** and **nightlife** people congregate in the restaurants, bars and clubs along cobbled, pedestrianized **Storgatan**, lined with trendy, stylish and fun eating places. Prices can be steep, but there are also plenty of cafés and light meal options. **Tylösand beach** is a separate night-time spot for the beach crowd, with most of the action concentrated on *Hotel Tylösand* (see "Accommodation").

## Cafés and restaurants

**Gamla Rådhuskällaren**, Storgatan. Carnivores can choose from fine Swedish steaks sold by weight, in the candle-lit, vaulted cellars of this seventeenth-century law court. A large entrecôte will cost around 135kr. Big wine list. Tues–Sat 6–11pm.

**Konditoria**, Norregatan, next to *Norre Park Hotel*. Traditional bakery and coffee house with a relaxed atmosphere, overlooking the park and serving mouthslavering cakes and plates of white chocolate truffles. A coffee and sandwich is 40kr. Open till 10pm.

**Nygatan**, Nygatan 8, off Storatorg. Quite ordinary check-tablecloth café-diner, but good-value three-course dinner at 129kr. Mon–Sat 9am–midnight, Sun 6pm–midnight.

**Pia & Co**, Storgatan. Half the restaurant is a coffee shop, the other half is for more serious eating. A lovely place, where the speciality is steaks served on wooden planks with clouds of mashed potato at 169kr.

**Skånska Hembageriet**, Bankgatan 1. Wonderful seventeenth-century cake shop and konditori just off Storgatan. Upstairs is all uneven floors and some interesting antique furniture. Mon–Fri 8.15am–5.30pm, Sat 9am–1.30pm.

**Tre Hjartan**, Storatorg. Cakes, sandwiches and light meals are all served within this impressive konditori (also see p.170).

**Ulle's Café**, Brogatan 7. Café serving the usual snacks and sandwiches. Surreal ceiling paintings and great little garden at back. Mon–Fri 9am–6pm, Sat 9.30am–2.30pm.

## Bars and discos

**Daltons**, Storgatan. An alternative-music bar offering Swedish music on one floor and dancing on the main floor, with a bar open to the sky in summer. Entry through a small doorway next door but one to *Pia & Co* (see above).

**Harley's**, Storgatan. A stylish, lively hang-out with wacky photos on bare brick walls. The food is Mexican and very good (meals from 80kr), but it's more a place to drink than eat. The basement bar is devoted to Elvis, with the walls covered in rare poses of the King and a screen showing Elvis film footage. Daily 6pm–2am, except Fri 4pm–2am.

**Ladan** (opposite *Harley's*). A stylish restaurant, pub and casino with a wild west theme and buffalo-hide bar. Meat and fish main courses at 120kr. Tues–Sat from 6pm.

**John Bull's Pub**, Lilla Torg, a step away from Storgatan. Very popular, English-style bar with live music. 1960s' sounds on Mon nights. Mon–Fri 11.30am–1am, Sat & Sun noon–midnight.

# Laholm and Mellbystrand

Just 10km south of Halmstad by train, **LAHOLM** is the oldest, smallest and most southerly town in Halland. It is also the most underrated and undermarketed place on Sweden's west coast and consequently is often ignored. Yet Laholm is a pleasant little resort, and its chief attraction is its proximity (6km) to the out-standing beach at **Mellbystrand**.

Established in the twelfth century, Laholm ping-ponged between the Danes and the Swedes until 1645, when all the fortifications were torn down on the orders of Karl XI. Today it has a villagey feel to its centre, and there are some delightful strolls to be taken around the lanes of half-timbered houses that lead off **Stortorget**, with its small, colourful daily fish and flower market. However, the most remarkable thing about Laholm is the number of witty contemporary **sculptures** that are dotted around the town and its park. The 28 official works that adorn the tiny centre were all funded by Axel Malmqvist, who wrote and staged 36 outdoor productions in the 1930s to fund the restoration of Laholm Castle. So successful were the plays that the leftover money was enough to pay for all the art work. A self-guided tour is available at the tourist office (see overleaf), but you'll stumble across the majority without it. One of the most amusing is *Women Picking Potatoes*, in the little square near the tourist office. Great fun, yet entirely omitted from all tourist information, is an unofficial collection of quirky wood sculptures in the park up behind the youth hostel (see overleaf). Created as part of an eco-logical project by local unemployed people, the sculptures form a children's play-ground. Wooden slides and roundabouts with finely carved animal images stand among the trees, while other pieces bob up and down on springs.

If you enjoy fishing, Laholm has plenty to offer. Ranged almost entirely around the southern shore of the River Lagan, **salmon fishing** has been a big activity here since the sixteenth century. Unlike at Falkenberg (see p.167), salmon breed-ing programmes were developed in Laholm back in the nineteenth century, so fishing is still a rewarding pastime. The salmon hatchery, centrally situated by the power station in Lagavägen, operates surprisingly interesting summer tours (details from the tourist office) showing each stage of the life cycle. The tourist office can provide you with a licence for the **salmon fishing** season (March 8–Dec 31); fishing is allowed from the power station to the estuary of the river, a distance of eight kilometres. If you catch the season's biggest salmon, you win the much-sought-after title King – or Queen – of Salmon and a seasonal fishing licence.

Other river activities include a **steamboat trip** (July & Aug; 75kr, tickets from the tourist office) on the tiny 1888-built wooden steamer *Sofiero*, which is owned and run by the local brewery of the same name. You're never far from the steam pipes, however, so on a hot day the boat is like a sauna and the two-hour trip is rather too long. If you are interested you can go on one of the tours of the old brewery itself (July Tues & Thurs 9.30am); the factory is a fifteen-minute walk east from the town centre (ask at the tourist office for details).

## Mellbystrand

A beach holiday mecca, **Mellbystrand**, just a few kilometres from Laholm, is a 12km stretch of wide beaches, fringed by dunes and scrubland, behind which are endless campsites for caravans, tents and cabins. There are a couple of restaurants here, mainly pizza places attached to the campsites. Popular with Swedes, Mellbystrand gets very crowded in summer. Nude bathing sections are indicated by signs showing the back view of a family with taught triangular buttocks.

# Practicalities

The new **train** station is an inconvenient 3km from Laholm; although there are buses to take you to the disused old station in the heart of town (11kr), you have to be quick, as they don't hang around once the train has arrived. Mellbystrand is something of a public transport oversight, with no train service and infrequent buses, and, with **taxis** (☎713 10) costing 100kr, **bike rental** is a good option. In Laholm there's *Blåkulla Cykel*, Angelholmsvägen 11 (☎0430/132 50; 75kr per day or 160kr per week), while at Mellbystrand, you can try the very cheap *Sturesson* at Tärnvägen 13 (25kr per day or 100kr per week). There are cycle paths all the way to Mellbystrand. The **tourist office** is on the central square, close to the old station (mid-June to Aug Mon–Fri 10am–6pm, Sat 10am–3pm, other times Mon–Sat 10am–2pm; ☎0430/154 50), and, in summer, another information point is at *Maxi*, a café in Mellbystrand (☎0430/278 44).

If you want to stay in town, the STF **youth hostel** at *Parkgårdens*, Tivolivägen 4 (open all year except mid-Dec to mid-Jan; ☎0430/133 18, fax 153 25; 100kr plus 40kr for breakfast) is a good, friendly place ideally situated beneath the park and a few metres from Stortorget. Otherwise, the tourist office will book **private rooms** for around 130kr. A good, central **hotel** is the stately white-stuccoed *Stadshotellet* (☎0430/128 30; ② including breakfast). **Camping** is the most popular accommodation at Mellbystrand. *Marias Camping* (☎0430/285 85; Aug 140kr per person, otherwise 100kr – plus 30kr for electricity) is the best, with excellent roomy cabins, though you can pitch tents here, too. The *Strand Hotel*, 200m from the beach, is no longer a hotel but a busy restaurant, pizzeria and grill for neighbouring campsite users.

There are some fine cafés around the main square for **daytime eating**: *Conditori Cecilia* serves a wide range of scrumptious cakes in its down-to-earth café area; while *Phoenix Konditori* (Mon–Fri 8am–6pm, Sat 9am–5pm) is the most appealing, with a 1950s jukebox, hand-painted ceiling and cakes to lose sleep over. For **evening meals** and **nightlife** your choice is restricted to three venues – most people head off to Mellbystrand or Halmstad. *Annabelle's,* on Hästtorget off Stortorget (Mon–Fri 11am–2pm & 5–10pm, Sat & Sun 4–10pm), is a restaurant serving meat and pizzas, but best is the shrimp salad, which comes on a massive plate with mounds of fresh vegetables and fruit like melon, cherries, kiwi and peppers, all at 62kr. There's also a popular and inexpensive pizza restaurant on the square, *RD's*. From either of these, the locals move on to *Bakfickan*, a regular pub next door to *Annabelle's*.

# Båstad and the Bjäre peninsula

Although tourist information tends to lump the classic tennis centre of **Båstad** with the attached **Bjäre peninsula**, their qualities are so completely at odds, they really should be considered separately. Båstad is geared towards the chic lifestyle pastimes of yachting, golfing and tennis; the Bjäre peninsula, on the other hand, is a lot less manicured – with both rugged coastlines and pretty meadows, it's an area of outstanding natural beauty.

## Båstad

It is only a seven-minute train ride south from Laholm into **BÅSTAD**, the most northern town in the ancient province of Skåne, yet its character is markedly different from other towns along the coast. Cradled by the Bjäre peninsula, which bulges westwards into the Kattegat (the waters between Sweden and Jutland), Båstad is Sweden's elite **tennis centre**, where the Swedish Open is played at the beginning of July (tickets cost 100–200kr). The rest of Båstad boasts sixty other tennis courts, five eighteen-hole golf courses and the *Drivan Sports Centre*, one of Sweden's foremost sports complexes. It's all set in very beautiful surroundings, with a horizon of forested hills to the south. There is a downside, though, which can blunt enthusiasm for the place. Ever since King Gustav V chose to take part in the 1930 tennis championships and Ludvig Nobel (nephew to Alfred of the Nobel Prize) gave financial backing to the tournaments, retired wealthy Stockholmers and social climbers from all over Sweden have flocked to bask in the social glow. The result is an ostentatious smugness reflected in the clothes boutiques and overpriced oriental antique specialists that line Köpmansgatan, the main thoroughfare. Despite all this, Båstad isn't a prohibitively expensive place to stay and makes a good base from which to explore the peninsula.

Running east from the train station, it's a half-hour walk down **Köpmansgatan** to the central, old square and tourist office (see "Practicalities"– a lot of accommodation is signposted along the way). The street's architecture is unusual for Sweden and somewhat reminiscent of provincial France, with shuttered, low-level shops and houses, and due to the town's mild climate – afforded by the protection of the hills surrounding the town – some have vines growing up the walls. If you want to stop for a coffee, *Continental Café* (June–Aug daily 7am–6pm, rest of year Fri–Sun only) is a comfortable old place run by the same family since 1923 and full of old portraits of Swedish royalty. It's the only real café in Båstad; most people prefer to be seen in the showier waterside brasseries at the harbour (15min walk from the centre). To reach **the beach**, head down Tennisvägen, off Köpmansgatan, through a glamourous residential area till you reach Strandpromenaden, where you can take a lovely evening stroll as the sun sets on the calm waters. To the west, the old 1880s' bath houses have all been converted into restaurants and bars, beyond which the harbour is thick with bobbing masts.

### Practicalities

There are around twenty **trains** a day from Laholm (7min journey). Båstad's **tourist office** on the main square (mid-June to mid-Aug daily 10am–6pm; rest of year Mon–Sat 10am–4pm; ☎0431/750 45, fax 700 55) will book **private rooms** at 140kr per person and rent out **bikes** at 60kr per day. Accommodation in Bästad is plentiful, but finding somewhere to stay during the tennis tournament is almost impossible; you need to book months in advance. The *STF* **youth hostel** (☎0431/759 11, fax 717 60, Sept–May call ☎710 30; 100kr) is next to the *Drivan Sports Centre* at Korrödsvagen, signposted off Köpmansgatan. It's open all year, but tends to be reserved for groups in winter; popular with sports-playing youngsters, it is one of the noisiest places to stay.

The cheaper **hotels** are mostly close to the station end of town, and unlike the rest of Sweden, prices are likely to increase dramatically during the summer due to the tennis tournament. *Hotel Pension Enehall* at Stationsterrasen 10 (☎0431/750 15, fax 724 09; ② in summer) is a modern, standard hotel just a few metres from the train station. A pleasant, traditional wooden house, *Pensionat Malengården* is at Åhusvägen 41 (☎ & fax 0431/695 67; from 195kr per person in summer), the same turning off Köpmansgatan as the youth hostel; you can also **rent bikes** here. *Hotel Pension Furuhem*, Roxmansvägen 13 (☎0431/701 09, fax 701 80; ① in summer), close to the train station, is the town's oldest pension; it's an appealing old place that was once used as a posh boarding school. For a harbour-side setting *Hotel Skansen* (☎0431/720 50, fax 700 85; ② in summer including breakfast) is in a century-old cream-brick bathing house that contains a restaurant, *Slamficken* (see below). For real glamour, *Hotel Buena Vista* on Tarravägen 5 (☎0431/760 00, fax 791 00; ④ in summer) doesn't look so good from the outside, but has a splendid interior. This vast villa, built out of Cuban stone by a wealthy Cuban émigré, has two grand dining rooms – one overlooking Laholm Bay, the other with Art Nouveau decor. **Camping** is not allowed on the dunes – locals can be stuffy if you try; you are better off heading to the Bjäre peninsula.

**Eating and drinking** is as much a pastime as tennis in Båstad, and most of the waterside restaurants and hotels both here and on the peninsula join in a 99kr two-course-dinner offer; there's different food at each venue, and menus change weekly. *Pepe's Bodega* at the harbour (Mon–Thurs 7pm–1am, Fri 7pm–2am, Sat & Sun noon–1am) is a swish pizza place, with a pizza-for-two offer at 98kr; while next door is *Fiskbiten*, a busy fish restaurant, set in a turn-of-the-century bathing house. *Slamficken*, in a neighbouring old bathing house, has a popular grill from 6pm, and is also open for breakfast (7.30–10am) and lunch. If you fancy eating waffles in a pretty setting, *Solbackens* waffle bakery, on Italienskavägen off the Torekov road (2km from town), dates from 1907 and serves outside in summer. Although there are a few **nightclubs**, Båstad is much more geared up for wine sipping in restaurants; only the very young fill the naff clubs along Köpmansgatan. You could try *Titanic*, attached to *Brasserie Fenix*, or *Crazy Horse* just opposite (Mon & Thurs 6pm–11pm, Wed 6pm–1am, Fri 6pm–2am, Sat 1pm–2am, Sun 1–8pm). If you want to get involved in any sports activities, ask at the tourist office for information on booking tennis courts or renting out sports equipment.

## The Bjäre peninsula

The highlight of the entire region, the **Bjäre peninsula**'s natural beauty has a magical quality to it that deserves a couple of days' exploration. Its varied scenery includes wide fertile fields, where potatoes and strawberries are grown (the potatoes are sold in Båstad at up to 200kr a kilo on New Potato Day in June), splintered red-rock cliff formations and remote and seal-ringed islands thick with birds and historical ruins. To help you find your way around, it's best to buy a large-scale map of the area from Båstad tourist office (40kr). The well-known **Skåneleden walking trail** runs around the entire perimeter, but it's also great to cycle along (a few gears helps as it can get hilly). **Public transport** around Bjäre is adequate, with buses connecting the main towns and villages. Bus #525 leaves Båstad every other hour for Torekov (Mon–Fri; 20min trip; 16kr) and runs through the centre of the peninsula, stopping at the small hamlets of Hov and Karup, on the peninsula's southern coast, which is useful if you've walked this far round and want to connect with the buses to Båstad or Torekov. On the weekend you must call *Båstad taxi* (☎0431/696 66) an hour before you want to leave for Torekov (charges the same as the bus; make sure to book it back on the outward trip). If you want to move on to Ängleholm, bus #523 leaves regularly from Torekov (6 daily; 50min). **Staying on** the Bjare peninsula is no problem; there are plenty of spots to pitch a tent for free, several official camping places (see below) and plenty of good hotels in the main towns.

## The northern coastline

Heading north out of Båstad along the coast road, it's just a couple of kilometres to **Norrvikens Gardens** (May to mid-Sept daily 10am–6pm; 35kr), a paradise for horticulturists and lovers of symmetry. With the sea as a backdrop, these fine gardens were designed by Rudolf Abelin at the end of the nineteenth century; he is buried in a magnificent hollow of rhododendrons near the entrance. The best walk is the "King's Ravine", ablaze in late spring and early summer with fiery azaleas and blushing rhododendrons and leading to the finest Japanese garden. At the centre of the grounds there's a villa with a café-restaurant.

Two to three kilometres further, past *Norrvikens Camping Site* for caravans (April–Oct ☎0431/691 70), is **KATTVIK**. Once a village busy with stone-grinding mills, it is now largely the domain of wealthy, elderly Stockholmers, who snap up the few houses as soon as they appear on the market. Kattvik achieved its moment of fame when Richard Gere chose a cottage here for a summer romance. Otherwise, it contains little more than the friendly *Delfin Bed & Breakfast* (☎0431/731 20; ①), an idyllic base for exploring the region, with vegetarian gourmet cooking and breakfast under the apple trees. There are plans for 1998 to expand it into a retreat with horse riding, mountain climbing, boat rental and guided excursions into the surrounding forests. A few minutes' walk out of town off the Torekov road (follow the sign "*rök fisk*") is *Kai's* fish smokery, an old farm where a seasoned fisherman smokes fish in little furnaces over sawdust from the nearby clog factory. You can buy here – and have a taste of – the very best smoked fish; as well as the usual mackerel and salmon, you can sample *horngadda*, a scaly fish with bright green bones, and *sjurygg*, an extraordinarily ugly, seven-crested fish with oily, flavoursome flesh.

Heading north on the coast road or the walking trail, the undulating meadows and beamed cottages have a peculiarly rural English feel. If you've taken the trail from Kattvik, then at the T-junction follow the path for **Hovs Hallar** nature reserve to continue along the coast (around a 20min walk). Wandering across to the reserve from the car park, you can clamber down any of paths towards the sea. The views are breathtaking – screaming gulls circling overhead (particularly unnerving if you've just bought fish) and waves crashing onto the unique redstone cliffs. Overlooking the cliffs, *Hovs Hallar Värdhus* (☎0431/651 09) is a fine restaurant serving à la carte and lunch specials. There are pretty, four-bed **cabins** just behind the restaurant, each with a toilet, shower and TV (June–Aug from 470kr for the cabins, rest of the year from 200kr per person per night; cheaper if rented by the week).

## Torekov and Hallands Väderö

The sleepy village of **TOREKOV**, just a couple of kilometres from Hovs Hallar, lies on the peninsula's western coast, and from its little harbour old fishing boats leave for the nature reserve of Hallands Väderö (see below). The notoriously dangerous waters off the coast were once a ship graveyard, and for centuries wrecks were washed up along the shore. Torekov is named after a little girl, later known as Saint Thora, who, so the story goes, was drowned by her wicked stepmother. Her body was washed ashore and given a Christian burial by a blind man, who miraculously regained his sight. There's precious little to do here, other than have a look-in at the rather irreverent cut-in-half sailing ship **museum** (free). The **tourist office** is at Hamnplan 2, by the harbour (June–Aug Mon–Sat 9am–6pm, at other times contact the Båstad office; ☎0431/631 80, fax 645 53). One odd sight is the daily ritual of elderly men in dressing gowns wandering along the pier – so sought after and expensive is the property here, these old gents promenade in bathrobes as proof of residency.

There are regular boats to **Hallands Väderö** (June–Aug hourly; rest of year every 2 hours; 15min; 55kr return); the last one back leaves at 4.30pm, so it's well worth setting off early (first boats at 9am) and giving yourself a full day to take in the island's awesome beauty. You can buy a map (30kr) of Hallands Väderö from Torekov harbour ticket office before you leave. The island is a scenic mix of trees and sun-warmed bare rocks, with isolated fishing cottages dotted around its edges, while above countless birds – gulls, eiders, guillemots, cormorants – fly noisily across the sky. One particularly beautiful spot is at its southernmost tip, where weather-smoothed skerries stand out in the tranquil turquoise waters. If you're lucky, you may be able to make out the seal colony, which lies on the furthest rocks; there are organized seal safaris (noon & 6pm; 100kr; ask at Torekov tourist office). On the south of the island, the English graveyard, surrounded by mossy, dry-stone walls, holds the remains of English sailors who were killed here in 1809, when the British fleet were stationed on the island in order to bombard Copenhagen during the Napoleonic Wars. Torekov church would not have them buried on its soil as the sailors' faith was, strangely, considered unknown.

There is no camping on the island (heads are counted on return trips in case anyone tries), so if you do want **to stay** over night you have to rent one of the two idyllic cottages by the northern lighthouse (ask at Torekov tourist office for details). Back on the mainland, you can **camp** at *Kronocamping* (open all year; ☎0431/645 25), 1.5km from Torekov on the Båstad road. In Torekov itself, on its pretty, cobbled main street is the century-old *Hotel Kattegat* (☎0431/630 02; ③); this fine old building has en-suite rooms with TVs (room no. 9 has the finest view) and a lovely frescoed dining room. Just opposite, *Svenson's* glass-roofed **restaurant** (Tues, Thurs & Sun 6–11pm, Fri & Sat 6pm–1am) serves good fish dishes and has vines growing up its walls; while *Hamn Krogan* restaurant by the harbour has a bar with à la carte meals (80–180kr). Alternatively, you can buy smoked fish and baguettes (filled with fish, meat and salads for 18kr) from the harbour fish shop.

# Ängelholm

The best aspects of peacefully uneventful **Ängelholm** are its 7km of popular golden beach and its proximity to elsewhere – Helsingborg is just thirty minutes away by train, and the Bjäre peninsula beckons to the north. With a range of accommodation and some agreeable restaurants, its not a bad base at all; there is also surprisingly lively nightlife for a young, club crowd. Ängelholm's efforts to sell itself, however, concentrate not on its beaches but on the town mascot, a musical clay cuckoo – unglazed and easily broken versions of the bird are sold everywhere – and UFOs. The latter have been big business here since 1946, when a railway worker, Gösta Carlsson, convinced the authorities that he had encountered tiny people from another world in a discus-shaped craft. A piece of stone harder than diamond and a strange other-worldly ring together with the supposed landing imprints of the spaceship made the now elderly Carlsson a rich man. Today Ängelholm hosts international UFO conferences, and the tourist board, recognizing the potential, runs tours to the mysterious site throughout the summer.

The town itself has a small historic core – the result of orders from the Danish king Christian II ("the Good" to the Danes, "the Tyrant" to the Swedes), who forced the people of nearby Luntertun to relocate here in 1518 – which is pleasant enough to wander around but has little to detain you. From the train station, it's just a few minutes' walk over the Rönneå river to the main square (where you'll find the tourist office; see below). Not far from here, up Kyrkogatan, is a **handicrafts museum** (May–Aug Tues–Fri 1–5pm, Sat 10am–2pm; 10kr). Housed in what used to be the town prison, the museum has a rather unexciting collection of tannery and silversmith artefacts, eighteenth-century peasant furniture and a ceramics collection dominated by pottery cuckoos. Should you want to see more of the town, the least strenuous way is a **boat trip** up the river from the harbour (June 8–Aug 11, 4 daily 40min trips, 45kr; or daily 2hr return trips, 60kr, ☎0431/203 00). For more freedom of movement, *Skåne Marin*, which runs the tours, also rents out boats and canoes.

If none of this appeals, head for the **beaches**, 2–3km away from the town centre. You can take the free bus – there are no regular buses – that runs from the main square in summer (late June to mid-Aug every hour 10am–4pm), or walk: from the main square, head down Järnvägsgatan, and turn left onto Havsbadsvägen; this soon turns into Råbockavägen, from where several overground paths lead to the beaches. There are no official demarcations, but the most southerly beach is nudist (both sexes), to the north is a section for the style gurus and body beautifuls, and a little beyond is the best family beach; while thirty-something singles seem to gravitate even further north to the last stretch of sand nearest the town.

## Practicalities

There are regular **trains** from Båstad (17 trains a day; 25min), and **buses** from Båstad and Torekov. It's a short distance from the train station to the **tourist office** in the main square (June–Aug Mon–Fri 9am–7pm, Sat 9am–4pm, Sun 1–5pm; Sept–May Mon–Fri 9am–4pm; ☎043/821 30, fax 192 07). It is easy to walk around central Ängelholm, but one useful bus route is the #50, which runs from the train station to the square and on to harbour. For **bike rental**, *Hotel Lergöken*, opposite the train station, is half the price of other rental places (35kr a day, plus 10kr insurance), or ask at the tourist office.

If you want to stay, the tourist office can also book hotels (20kr fee) or **private rooms** (from 110kr with a 30kr fee). There is an *STF* **youth hostel** (April–Oct; ☎0431/523 64; 95kr) at Magnarp Strand, 10km north of the train station and beyond the beaches detailed above (local buses ply the route). For a good-value, friendly **hotel**, try *Hotel Lilton* (☎0431/44 25 50, fax 44 25 69; ③/②) at Järnvägsgatan 29, just a few steps from the square. The hotel, with its breezy atmosphere and big rooms, is a favourite with visiting musicians and singers, who play at the clubs (below); the names of the best known – The Sweet and Catrina & The Waves – appear on the walls. There's also a great garden café here (June & Aug noon–6pm; July till 8pm), tucked away beneath a cluster of beech trees near the river. Down the side of the hotel to the left, it's worth a quick browse in *Strot & Korn* (Tues–Fri noon–6pm, Sat 10am–2pm), which sells collectables from the 1930s to 1960s. Other central hotels include *Hotel Continental* at Storgatan 23 (☎0431/127 00, fax 127 90; ②) and *Riverside Hotel* at Östergatan 27–29 (☎0431/41 10 02, fax 827 44; ②/①). There are several **campsites**; the most convenient for the beach is at the end of Råbockavägen, *Råbocka Camping* (☎0431/105 43, fax 832 45; 110kr per person). Just opposite is *Klitterbyn*, a large, leafy holiday village of wooden chalets and apartments (☎0431/586 00, fax 195 72; around 130kr per person).

The best place for **food** is at the harbour. *Hamn Krogen* (daily April to mid-Aug 11am–1am) doesn't look anything special from the outside, but within, there's a cosy, marine feel with lots of old auction-bought furniture and knick-knacks. Here you can eat the best fish dishes in Ängelholm, with starters from 23kr, main courses from 85kr – their speciality is Toast Skagen, shrimps and red caviar on toast. Once the pride of the town, *Klitterhus* is a fish restaurant set in a peeling old wooden bathing house right on the beach (just north of the family beach and south of the harbour). A few metres up the beach, in a whitewashed wartime bunker, is *Bunken* restaurant and bar (Mon–Fri 6pm–1am, Sat & Sun noon–1am). Serving a diverse choice of eats from fish and chips (35kr) to lavish fish and seafood dishes, including shark (140kr), it's a new and buzzing place, with local and imported beers and regular live music.

The most popular **nightclub** is the stylishly cavernous *Club Esther* on Nybrovägen 3, off Industrigatan, which is a continuation of Järnvägsgatan (Fri & Sat 10pm–2am; minimum age men 22, women 20; 40kr). It's in a big warehouse, and there's a mix of new and old music and a big open barbeque area attracting a 20–35 age group. Next door, *Factory* is for a younger crowd. A hundred metres up the road is *Rönneå River*, an equally popular outdoor club and summer bar.

# Helsingborg and around

It is sometimes joked by locals that the most rewarding sight in **HELSINGBORG** is Helsingør, the Danish town whose castle, Hamlet's celebrated Elsinore, is clearly visible, just 4km over the Öresund (The Sound). This has less to do with any failings the bright and pleasing town of Helsingborg might have, and much more to do with Denmark's cheaper alcohol outlets. Trolley-pulling Swedes converge on Helsingborg from all over the country both to stock up on beer and to

The telephone code for Helsingborg is ☎042.

spend entire nights on the ferry-laden waters, becoming increasingly drunk for fewer kronor than they could on land.

In the past the links between the two towns were less convivial; in fact Helsingborg has a particularly bloody and tragic history. After the Danes fortified the town in the eleventh century, the Swedes conquered and lost it again on six violent occasions, finally winning out in 1710 when led by Magnus Stenbock. By this time, the Danes had torn down much of the town and on its final recapture, the Swedes razed its twelfth-century castle, except for the 5m-thick walled keep (kärnen), which still dominates the centre. By the early eighteenth century, war and epidemics had reduced the population to just seven hundred, and only with the onset of industrialization in the 1850s did Helsingborg wake up to a new prosperity. Shipping and the railways turned the town's fortunes round, evidenced by the formidable late nineteenth-century commercial buildings in the centre and some splendid villas to the north overlooking the Öresund.

Today, a constant through traffic of Danes, Germans and Swedes spend only the time it takes to change trains, which is a pity, as there is a youthful, Continental feel to this instantly likable town with its warren of cobbled streets, its cafés, historical sights and enjoyable day excursions.

## Arrival, information and transport

Unless approaching by car on the E6, chances are you will arrive at the harbourside **Knutpunkten**, the vast, glassy expanses of which incorporate all **car**, **train** and **passenger ferry** terminals. On the ground floor behind the main hall is the **bus** station for all destinations outside Helsingborg, while tickets offices and transport enquiries are in front, opposite the tourist office (see below). Below ground level is the combined **train station** for the national *SJ* trains and the lilac-coloured local *Pågatåg* trains, which run south down the coast to Landskrona, Lund and Malmö. One floor up brings you to a *Forex* **currency exchange** office (daily 8am–9pm). The *Sundsbussarna* passenger-only ferry to Helsingør uses the quayside at Hamntorget, 100m away. For ferry ticket details, see "Ferries to Helsingør" on p.187; for bus and train information, see "Listings".

By the entrance to Knutpunkten, the **tourist office** (June–Aug Mon–Fri 9am–8pm, Sat & Sun 9am–5pm; Sept–May Mon–Fri 9am–6pm, Sat 10am–2pm; ☎12 03 10, fax 12 78 76) gives out free maps and *Helsingborg This Month*, with sections in English; or for 10kr you can buy the excellent English-language *Helsingborg Guide for Tourists*. A huge wall map outside the tourist office has every sight you may want to see lit up at the press of a button, including camping sites, hostels and museums.

Central Helsingborg is all in easy walking distance, but for the youth hostel, the gardens of Sofiero and surrounding sights to the north (see p.185), or Råå to the south (p.187), you'll need a **bus**. Tickets bought on board are 12kr and valid for two changes within an hour; if you intend to stay, bus **passes** are a good idea for one, two, three or five days (25kr, 35kr, 50kr or 60kr). **Bike rental** is an enjoyable option, as all the best sights are within 5km. The tourist office is the obvious outlet, but if you are heading north of the centre, *Pålsjöbaden* (see p.185), the old bathing house on Drottninggatan, 3km north of the centre, is the best bet, while for excursions south, try *Stadscykeln*, Cindergatan 13 (Mon–Fri 8am–4pm; ☎10 73 83). Before booking a bike, it's worth checking whether it has handbrakes or gears – bikes from the tourist office have neither and may take some getting used to. All outlets charge 30kr per day, 120kr per week, and most open from June.

# Accommodation

The tourist office will book **private rooms** from 125kr per person plus a steep 70kr booking fee; if staying over three days, the booking fee is 200kr. The *STF* **youth hostel** at Dag Hammarskjöldsväg (open all year; ☎21 03 84, fax 12 87 92; 100kr), 2.5km north of the town centre, is called *Villa Thalassa* and is in a superb setting. The main villa was built in 1903 by Von Dardel, a courtier to King Gustav Adolf (the present king's grandfather), who lived at nearby Sofiero castle. Breakfasts at 40kr are served in *Thalassa*'s dining room, with wonderful views over the Öresund. It's a little disappointing that the accommodation is actually in cabins behind the villa, with showers an unwelcome trek away, but there are also more comfortable holi-day cottages (350kr per double). Bus #7 runs north from Knutpunkten (every 20min) to *Pålsjöbaden*, from where it's another 1km walk through really beautiful forest; after 7pm, bus #44 follows the route twice an hour till 1am.

### Hotels

There are plenty of central **hotel** options, too. The most glamorous are around Stortorget, while cheaper, but still good-standard ones are opposite Knutpunkten and the roads leading off it. All the following include breakfast in the price.

**The Grand**, Stortorget 8–12 (☎12 01 70, fax 11 88 33). Although new ownership has meant the loss of *The Grand*'s old exclusivity, the big summer reductions make its good rooms affordable. ⑤/②

**Kärnen**, Järnvägsgatan 17 (☎12 08 20, fax 14 88 88). Opposite Knutpunkten, this comfort-able, recently renovated hotel prides itself on "personal touches", including ominous English-language homilies on each room door; room no. 235 reads: "He who seeks revenge keeps his wounds open". There's a small library, cocktail bar, sauna and special golf packages. ④/②

**Linnea**, Prästgatan 4 (☎21 46 60, fax 14 16 55). Very cheap (55kr in summer) and central, this hotel has recently been remodelled in a simple, pleasing style. ②/①

**Marina Plaza**, Kungstorget 6 (☎19 21 00, fax 14 96 16). A big, modern and well-equipped hotel right at the harbour side next to Knutpunkten. With a popular restaurant, *Hamnkrogen*, the *Marina* nightclub, and much-frequented *Sailor Pub*, this is a lively, less austere top hotel. ④/③

**Mollberg**, Stortorget 18 (☎12 02 70, fax 14 96 18). Every bit a premier hotel, with a grand nineteenth-century facade, elegant rooms and a salubrious brasserie. ④/②

# The town centre

The most obvious starting point is on the waterfront by the copper statue of Magnus Stenbock on his charger. With your back to the Öresund and Denmark, to your left is the **Rådhus** (town hall), a heavy-handed, neo-Gothic pile complete with turrets and conical towers. The extravagance of provincial nineteenth-centu-ry prosperity, and the architect's admiration for medieval Italy, make it worth see-ing inside (July & Aug Mon–Fri; 40min tours at 10am) – in particular for the many fabulous ecclesiastical-style stained glass windows, which tell the entire history of the town. The ones to look out for are those in the stairway hall, depicting Queen

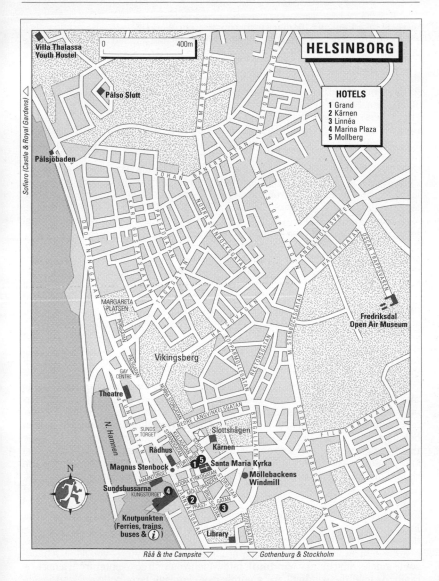

Margaretta releasing her rival Albert of Mecklenburg in Helsingborg in 1395, and the last window in the city-council chamber, showing John Babtiste Bernadotte arriving at Helsingborg in 1810, having accepted the Swedish crown. When he greeted General Von Essen at the harbour, farce ensued as their elaborate gold jewellery and medals became entangled in the embrace. The windows were all donated by the town's wealthiest industrial magnates, and such is their value, they were all taken out and hidden for the duration of World War II. The original wall and ceiling frescoes – deemed too costly to restore and painted over in 1968 – are currently being uncovered.

The town hall marks the bottom of **Stortorget** – the central "square" so oblong that it's more like a boulevard – which slopes upwards to meet the steps leading to the remains of the medieval castle (there is a lift to the side; June–Aug daily 10am–8pm, Sept–May Mon–Fri & Sun 10am–6pm; 5kr, free for children & wheelchair users). At the top, the massive castellated bulk of **kärnen** (keep) is surrounded by some fine parkland. Shaped simply as a huge upturned brick, it's worth climbing (June–Aug daily 10am–7pm; April, May & Sept daily 9am–4pm; Oct–March daily 10am–2pm; 15kr) more for its views than the historical exhibitions (descriptions in English). The keep and St Maria kyrka (see below) were the sole survivors from the ravages of war, but the former lost its military significance once Sweden finally won the day. In the mid-nineteenth century, it was due for demolition, only surviving because seafarers found it a valuable landmark. What cannon fire failed to achieve, neglect and the weather succeeded in bringing about, and the keep became a ruin until restoration began in 1894.

From the parkland at the keep's base, you can wander down a rhododendron-edged path, *Hallbergs Trappor*, to the **St Maria kyrka** (Mon–Sat 8am–4pm, Sun 9am–6pm), which squats in its own square by a very French-looking avenue of beech trees. The square is surrounded by a cluster of quaint places to eat and some excellent food shops for picnics, notably *Maratorgets* on the south side of the square, selling fresh fruit, and the adjacent *Bengtsons Ost,* a specialist cheese shop. The church itself, begun in 1300 and completed a century later, is Danish Gothic in style and resembles a basilica. Its rather plain facade belies a striking interior, with a clever contrast between the early seventeenth-century Renaissance-style ornamentation of its pulpit and gilded reredos and the jewel-like contemporary stained-glass windows.

Walking back to Stortorget you get to **Norra** and **Södra Storgatan** (the streets that meet at the foot of the stairs to kärnen), which were Helsingborg's main thoroughfare in medieval times and are lined with the town's oldest merchants' houses. As you head up Norra Storgatan, the 1681 **Henckelska house** is hidden behind a plain stuccoed wall; once you have pushed your way through the trees that have grown over the entrance archway, you'll see a rambling mix of beams and windows, with a fine little topiary garden hidden beyond a passage to the right. This garden was laid out in 1766 to please the future wife of King Gustav III, who was to spend one night at the beautiful eighteenth-century **Gamlegård house** opposite. As you head south along Södra Storgatan, the museum that used to be here has been closed down – many of the exhibits are currently at Fredriksdal (see opposite) until the new harbour-side museum opens in 2000 – however, if you take the opening to the left of the sign for the old museum, a real historic gem awaits you. After a fairly arduous climb of 92 steps, you'll find a handsome nineteenth-century **windmill**, into which you're free to enter from a narrow ramp. Around the windmill are a number of exquisite farm cottages, and inside the short (1.2m) doors is a treasure trove of eighteenth-century peasant interiors with straw beds, cradles and hand-painted grandmother clocks. A further reward for your climb is the fact that at one 1763-built house, brought to this site in 1909, there's been a waffle servery, *Möllebackens Våffelbruk* (May–Aug daily noon–8pm) since 1912. They still use the original recipes, and you can enjoy your snack sitting on an eighteenth-century settee, or outside beneath the windmill.

If you want to see some of the city museum's exhibits take bus #2, #3 or #5 from outside the Rådhus for the 2km trip to **Fredriksdal** (May–Sept 10am–6pm; rest of the year more limited hours; ☎10 59 81; 20kr). Here a large, open-air museum is set around a fine eighteenth-century manor house; there's plenty to look at, with parks, peasant homes and extensive botanical gardens.

## North of the centre: the Royal Gardens of Sofiero

The best local excursion – and one it would be a shame to miss – is to the **Royal Gardens of Sofiero** (May to mid-Sept 10am–6pm; 30kr); take bus #252 from Knutpunkten or cycle the 4km north along the coast. Built as a summer residence by Oscar II in the 1860s, the house is not particularly attractive, looking more like an elaborate train station – the architect was in fact the designer of many of Sweden's stations. The thrill here is in seeing the gardens, given by Oscar to his grandson, Gustav Adolf, when he married Crown Princess Marghareta in 1905. Marghareta created a horticultural paradise, and, as she was a granddaughter of Queen Victoria, the gardens are strongly influenced by English country-garden design. Although Marghareta died aged 38 in 1920, the king's second wife Louise continued her work and the English theme. Even if gardens are not your thing, the rhododendron collection is really something special, one of Europe's finest, a stunning array of ten thousand plants with over five hundred varieties spreading a blanket of rainbow colours down to the Öresund.

The area between Sofiero and the town centre also contains some pleasing diversions. Even if you're not staying at the youth hostel 2km south of Sofiero, it's a lovely walk to the nearby **Pålsjö Slott**, an immaculate eighteenth-century toy-town palace. While the building has nothing to see inside – it's been converted into offices – the public are free to wander behind to its gardens. Walking through a long, narrow avenue of gnarled beech trees, which have knotted together overhead, and on towards the Öresund you'll come to a beautiful pathway, *Landborgspromenade*, which to the left (direction of town) passes some large, Art Nouveau villas in fine gardens. At the end of the path (where bus #7 runs into town) stands **Pålsjöbaden**, a classic 1880-built bath house on stilts (Mon, Wed & Thurs 9am–7.30pm, Tues 6.45am–9pm, Fri 6.45am–6.30pm, Sat & Sun 8am–5pm; 25kr).

## Eating, drinking and nightlife

Helsingborg has a good range of excellent **restaurants** which can, predictably, be expensive. During the day there are some great **cafés** and konditori, but at night café life is non-existent, and when locals recommend "taking the boat to Helsingør", the entertainment is the boat itself, not landing in Denmark (see p.187). There are, however, some happening **clubs** for a young crowd.

### Cafés and restaurants
**Café Annorledes**, Södra Storgatan 15. The best home-baked cakes and tarts in town in this friendly café with a 1950s' atmosphere. Very popular with young, chatty crowd. Mon–Fri 9am–6pm, Sat 10am–4pm.
**Café Mmmums**, Södra Storgatan, behind St Maria kyrka. The owners, returned from Canada, have created this hip, stylish café serving huge glass bowls of healthy salads (42kr), big sandwiches and pasta. Daily 9am–7pm.

**Fahlmans**, Stortorget. This original, classic bakery/café has been serving elaborate cakes and pastries since 1914.

**Grafitti**, Knutpunkten, 1st floor. The ideal place if you're hungry, skint and it's past 9pm. Generously filled baked potatoes or baguettes with a young, sometimes rowdy crowd.

**Gröna Tallriken**, Södra Storgatan 13. A large, bright vegetarian restaurant, also selling health-food products. Californian-style health drinks (15kr), soup (23kr) and meals (48kr).

**Ida's**, Norra Storgatan. An informal fish and meat restaurant serving the likes of grilled ostrich, kangaroo and great home-made ice cream with hot cloudberry cream. Meals around 150kr. Tues–Fri noon–2pm, also Tues & Wed 7–10pm & Thurs–Sat 7–11pm, Sun 2–9pm.

**Oasen**, Bruksgatan 25 (☎12 80 74). A packed-out, excellent fondue restaurant with meat, fish, cheese and red wine or oriental fondues (150kr). Booking always necessary; Tues–Sat 6pm–midnight, Sun 5–10pm.

**Oscar's**, Sundstorget at the harbour (☎11 25 21). This posh and expensive fish restaurant has simple decor but is really designed for expensive accounts. Mon–Sat till 11pm.

**Pålsjökrog**, attached to the lovely old bath house 2km north of the centre (see p.185; ☎14 97 30). This fine place is run by an architect who designed it to feel like a Swedish country eating house. It's a special-occasion place with traditional, well-presented Swedish food (main courses 150kr). Walls are covered with old pictures of veteran Swedish comic actor Edvard Personn.

**Utposten**, Stortorget 17. Very stylish decor – mix of rustic and industrial – at this great, varied Swedish-food restaurant beneath the post office at the steps to kärnen (2 courses 140kr). Try the delicate and filling seafood and fresh salmon stew at 80kr.

## Bars and clubs

**Cardinal**, Södra Kyrkogatan 9. A piano bar and nightclub with a meat-oriented restaurant (6pm–1am). The first floor is a popular disco; on the second is a quieter piano bar and roulette table (9.30pm–3am). Cover fee is 70kr on Sat, 60kr other nights. Age limit for nightclub is 25 (mostly it's a 30s and 40s age group). The food speciality is char-grilled steaks at 150kr, three-course specials at the same price.

**Jazz Clubben**, Nedre Långvinkelsgatan 22. Sweden's biggest jazz club and well worth a visit on Wed, Fri and Sat evenings, this is where to come for live jazz, Dixieland, blues, Irish folk and blues jam sessions.

**Marina**. A Continental atmosphere at this new entry to the club scene located at *Hotel Marina* by the harbour (also see *Sailor's Inn* below). It gets very crowded, and the lower age limit is 24. Thurs–Sat 10pm–3am.

**Sailor's Inn**, part of the *Hotel Marina* at the harbour. This is a pre-disco or post-dinner drinking spot and extremely popular, too. Regular troubadour on Fri nights. Mon–Wed 3pm–midnight, Thurs & Fri 3pm–1am, Sat 2pm–1am.

**Telegrafen**, Norra Storgatan 14. A long-term favourite, this cosy pub, bar and restaurant is full of oddities such as stuffed animals wearing sunglasses. Good lunches at 52kr, lively atmosphere. 11.30am–midnight.

# Listings

**Airport** Nearest airport is at Ängelholm, 30km north of town; for domestic departures take the bus from Knutpunkten (1hr before flight departure). For international services, you'll need Copenhagen's Kastrup airport – take the *Kustlinjen* bus from Knutpunkten (2hr journey).

**Buses** For Stockholm the daily bus leaves from Knutpunkten; reservations essential (☎0625/240 20), but buy the ticket itself on the bus (260kr). For Gothenburg buses leave Fri & Sun only (190kr), no reservations (seat guaranteed); tickets must be bought from the bus information section at the train booking office.

---

**FERRIES TO HELSINGØR**

If you want a taste of what the locals do for fun, and to avoid expensive restaurants and bars, buy a **ferry** ticket from Knutpunkten (1st floor) to Helsingør. *Scandlines* ferries run every twenty minutes (32kr return; children 6–11 half price), as do *Sundbussarna*'s (20kr one-way, 30kr return, children 6–14 half price); while *Tura* offer back-and-forth ferry trips (32kr). Try and get one of *Scandlines's* Swedish boats (*Aurora, Regula* or *Ursula*), as they have better restaurants and bars than the Danish ones (*Princess Elizabeth* and *Tycho Brahe*). The idea is to go back and forth all night; the only reason to get off at Helsingør, apart from taking a closer look at **Helsingør Castle** (Hamlet's Elsinore and less thrilling than you may imagine), is to buy duty-free drink not for sale on the boat. If you do want to visit Denmark with a car, car ferries cost 495kr for up to five people; to book call ☎18 61 00.

---

**Car rental** Arranged at the tourist office, or direct through: *Avis*, Garnisonsgatan 2 (☎15 70 80); *Budget*, Gustav Adolfsgatan 47 (☎12 50 40); *Europcar*, Muskötgatan 1 (☎17 01 15); *Hertz*, Bergavägen 4 (☎17 25 40).

**Exchange** *Forex* in Knutpunkten (1st floor) or Järnvägsgatan 13 (June–Aug 7am–9pm; rest of year 8am–9pm); maximum 20kr fee.

**Ferries** See "Ferries to Helsingør" above for details.

**Gay centre** Pålsgatan 1 (☎12 35 32), close to the concert hall, ten minutes' walk from Knutpunkten. *RFSL*-run café and pub/bar and occasional discos.

**Left luggage** Lockers at Knutpunkten (20kr) and at the *Sundsbussarna* terminal (5kr).

**Library** *Stadsbiblioteket* at Bollbrogatan 1 (June–Aug Mon–Fri 10am–7pm, Sat 10am–2pm; Sept–May Mon–Fri 10am–7pm, Sat 10am–3pm). Read international newspapers here, listen to music or use the café.

**Pharmacy** *Björnen*, Drottninggatan 14. Open shop hours.

**Post office** Stortorget 17 (Mon–Fri 9am–6pm, Sat 10am–1pm). You can exchange money here but it costs 35kr per transaction.

**Shopping** Helsingborg has a good smattering of unusual little antique, bric-a-brac and curiosity shops. Try *Kuriosaboden*, Möllegränden, at the corner of Södra Strandgatan (Mon, Tues, Thurs & Fri, 2–6pm, Sat 11am–2pm), or *Möwe Grändens Kuriosa*, Koppurmöllegatan 19B (Mon–Thurs 2–6pm, Fri 11am–6pm, Sat 10am–2pm), which has lots of 1950s' ephemera and some antique clothes. *Magasinet Antik & Design*, Södra Storgatan 21, is another wacky place for inexpensive old silver plate and glass.

**Trains** The *Pågatåg* trains from Knutpunkten require a ticket bought from an automatic machine on the platform; international rail passes are valid. The machines take 100kr, 50kr and 20kr notes and 10kr, 5kr and 1kr coins: it's 50kr one-way to Lund and 60kr one-way to Malmö. Fare dodging invites a 600kr spot fine.

## Around Helsingborg: Råå, Ven and Ramlösa Spa

It's just 7km south of Helsingborg to the pretty, if sleepy, fishing village of **Råå**. You can take bus #1A or #1B from the Rådhus, or cycle along the cycle lanes if you don't mind the industrial mess of Helsingborg's southern suburbs. Råå's main street, **Rååvagen**, is a subdued place. Signs indicate the twelfth-century **Raus kyrka** (left up Lybecksgatan, over the highway and along Rausvägen), but it's nothing special. If you are heading that way, take a rough track to the right of the train line and you find an **ostrich farm**, which has the poor bemused-looking birds running in panicked circles every time a train goes past.

Råå's main attraction is its **harbour**, dense with masts (ferries leave from here to Ven; see below); it is uncommercialized and more attractive than many other such harbour sides. The **Maritime Museum** here is run by a group of Råå's residents and shows a comprehensive collection of seafaring artefacts. Next door, the long-established *Råå Wärdshus* serves pricey fish dishes at around 150kr, with lighter snacks and lots of salad choices for around 50kr. To the left of the museum, *Råå Hamnservering* (8.30am–midnight) is the best bet for a less expensive lunch. The lunch buffet at 58kr is excellent and, unlike at the *Wärdhus*, which faces inland, here you get plenty of sea views; the restaurant is built on the pier and has water on three sides. A fascinating, although somewhat stomach-churning, sight at the harbour is that of eel sorting: the giant, squirming, spaghetti-like creatures are slopped into an appropriately coffin-shaped box with a trap door at one end through which they slide, to be separated into sizes by fishermen using claw-shaped pincers.

If you want to **stay** you're limited to *Råå Camping Site* (☎10 76 80, fax 26 10 10; 90kr per tent, 105kr if with car plus 25kr for electricity), which is advertised as being "waterfront". It is, but its most obvious views to the north are of Helsingborg's industrial smog.

## Ven

Little ferries regularly make the 35-minute trip from Råå to the local island of **Ven** (9.30am–5.30pm; every 2hr). With a population of about 350, Ven, apart from being a beautiful island, is where the celebrated and impossibly tempered astronomer Tycho Brahe built his sixteenth-century observatory. The son of a Danish nobleman, Brahe discovered a new star, which he proved to be beyond the moon, contradicting Aristotle's theory that nothing beyond the moon could move. Brahe was known for his irascible nature; the tip of his nose was cut off in a dual following one of his fits of rage, and he spent the rest of his life with an artificial nose made of gold. Although nothing now remains of the observatory, funded by an impressed Frederick II, it was by all accounts an exquisite Dutch Renaissance-style creation. Brahe worked here for over twenty years, but after another row in 1597, this time with the king, he left Ven and Sweden and settled till his death in Prague. You can rent a **bike** cheaply (25kr) when you arrive, or wander around the sites, which are all about Brahe – a museum, remains of his observatory, and his attractive, now partly restored, garden.

## Ramlösa Spa

Just a kilometre or so northeast of Råå on the way back to Helsingborg, **Ramlösa Brunnspark** offers a delightful hour or so of meandering beneath huge horse chestnut trees and among the shocking pink rhododendrons of early summer. This nineteenth-century park is also full of elegant, wooden pavilions with carved verandas and balconies. Although private now, the houses were originally built for the wealthy characters who came to take the waters here, after Dr Johan Döbelius discovered two springs, one high in iron, the other in calcium, and set up a health spa in 1707. People flocked to the park, apparently undeterred by the unappealing look of the iron-filled orange water in which they had to douse themselves. Rather more appetizing are the waffles served down by the water pavilion (May–Aug), from where you can trace the shady "Philosophical walk", an exercise encouraged by the doctor. The spa guests clearly took time out from philosophizing to carve their names on the trees in a seemingly acceptable bout of nineteenth-century vandalism.

# Lund

A few kilometres inland and 54km south of Helsingborg is **LUND**, whose status as a glorious old university city is well founded. A sea of students on bikes will probably be the first image to greet you, and like Oxford in England – with which Lund is usually and aptly compared – there is a bohemian, laidback eccentricity in the air. With its justly revered twelfth-century Romanesque **cathedral**, its medieval streets lined with a variety of architectural styles and its wealth of cafés and restaurants (some fearfully expensive), Lund is an enchanting little city that could well captivate you for a couple of days. There is also a wide range of **museums** that may seem daunting in their scope, but with the exception of two excellent ones, they are largely of minority interest and can be bypassed. Cultural attractions aside, it is the mix of architectural grandeur and the buzz of student life that lends Lund its unique charm among Swedish cities.

## Arrival, information and accommodation

**Trains** arrive at the western edge of town, with everything an easy walk from the station. Regular buses from Helsingborg stop outside the train station. If you're **flying** into Sturup airport to the east of Malmö you can catch the hourly *Flygbuss* (Mon–Fri 5.30am–7.30pm, Sat 6.30am–5.30pm; 40min; 60kr). There is also a regular *Intercitybuss* (#999; 65kr) connecting Lund with Copenhagen via Malmö and the Limhamn-Dragör ferry (also see p.234). The **tourist office** (June–Aug Mon–Fri 10am–6pm, Sat & Sun 10am–2pm; Sept & May Mon–Fri 10am–5pm, Sat 10am–2pm; Oct–April Mon–Fri 10am–5pm; ☎35 50 40, fax 12 59 63) is opposite the Domkyrkan at Kyrkogatan 11 and provides maps and *I Lund*, a monthly diary of events with museum and exhibition listings (the June-to-August edition has English translation).

While all the sights are no more than ten minutes' walk away from one another, if you plan to do a lot of cycling around the region, the frequent sales of military **bikes** offer excellent value. Large, sturdy and khaki green, the bikes are almost indestructible. The tourist office has details of where the sales are on, or try Harry's *Cykelaffar*, Banvaktsgatan 2 (☎211 69 46).

There is a decent range of **accommodation** on offer in Lund – nearly all of it in the centre – and all the hotels have good summer reductions. The tourist office will book **private rooms** for 120–150kr per person, plus a 50kr booking fee. If you want to stay at the town's STF **youth hostel**, *Tåget,* at Vävaregatan 22 through the tunnel behind the train station (open all year; ☎14 28 20, fax 32 05 68; 100kr), you're in for a bit of a surprise: it's housed in the carriages of a 1940s' train. The novelty soon wears off, however, when you're crammed in three-deep bunks with rope hoists – furthermore, the kitchens and showers are rudimentary. A hostel alternative is *La Strada*, at Brunnshögsvägen (open all year; ☎32 32 51, fax 521 39; 1-, 2-, & 4-bed rooms 125kr per person, breakfast 40kr). It's a bit far out, though: take bus #4 from west of Martens Torget 4km to Klosterängsvägen, then follow the bicycle track under the motorway for 1km.

The telephone code for Lund is ☎046.

## Hotels

**Ahlström**, Skomakaregatan 3, just south of the Domkyrkan (☎211 01 74). Old-fashioned, very central cheapie with the option of en-suite rooms. ②/①

**Concordia**, Stålbrogatan 1, a couple of streets southwest of Stortorget (☎13 50 50, fax 13 74 22). The *Concordia* was a student hostel until the 1960s, and although tarted up, it still shows. Just across the street, August Strindberg spent his time vainly trying to produce gold before his rather more successful writing career took off. ④/②

**The Grand**, Bantorget 1 (☎211 70 10, fax 14 73 01). A grand nineteenth-century hotel, this pink-sandstone edifice straddles an entire side of a small, stately and central square. Without any of the pomp associated with premier hotels, the bedrooms are comfortable, well decorated but unrenovated. The breakfast buffet in the lovely dining room is enormous, varied and unusual. ④/③

**Petri Pumpa**, St Petri Kyrkogatan 7 (☎13 55 19). An exclusive hotel that is best known for its exquisite restaurant (see p.193). ⑤/③

# The Town

Lund is a wonderful town to just wander around, with its cobbled streets festooned with climbing roses. Its crowning glory is its cathedral; just 100m north of **Stortorget**, the surprisingly dull "central square", and only a short walk east from the station, the Domkyrkan is the obvious place to begin.

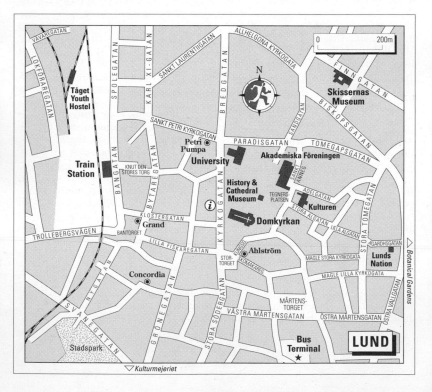

## The Domkyrkan

The magnificent **Domkyrkan** (Mon, Tues & Fri 8am–6pm, Wed & Thurs 8am–7.15pm, Sat 9.30am–5pm, Sun 9.30am–7.30pm; guided tours 3pm) is built of storm-cloud charcoal and white stone, giving it an imposing monochrome appearance. Before going inside, have a look round the back of the building. On the way you'll notice the grotesque animal and bird gargoyles over the side entrances, their features blunted by eight centuries of weathering; while at the very back is revealed the most beautiful part of the exterior, the three-storey apse above the crypt, which is crowned with an exquisite gallery.

The majestic interior is surprisingly unadorned, an elegant mass of watery-grey, ribbed stone arches and stone-flagged flooring. One of the world's finest masterpieces of Romanesque architecture, the cathedral was built in the twelfth-century when Lund became the first independent archbishopric in Scandinavia, laying the foundation for a period of wealth and eminence that lasted until the advent of Protestantism. There are several striking features to admire, such as the elaborately carved fourteenth-century choir stalls depicting Old Testament scenes and the grotesque carvings hidden beneath the seats. The most vividly coloured feature is just to the left of the entrance, an amazing astronomical clock dating from the 1440s, which shows hours, days, weeks and the courses of the sun and moon in the zodiac. Each day at noon and 3pm, the clock also reveals its ecclesiastical Punch and Judy show, as two knights pop out and clash swords as many times as the clock strikes, followed by little mechanical doors opening to trumpet-blowing heralds and the three wise men trundling slowly to the Virgin Mary.

The dimly lit and dramatic **crypt** beneath the apse has been left almost untouched since the twelfth century, and should not be missed. Although the thick smattering of tombstones are actually memorial slabs brought down to the crypt and so without bodies beneath, there is one tomb with remains – that of Birger Gunnarsson, Lund's last archbishop. A short man from a poor family, Gunnarsson chose the principal altar-facing position for his tomb, and dictated that his stone effigy above it should be tall and regal. Two pillars are gripped by stone figures – one of a man, another of a woman and child. Legend has it that Finn the Giant built the cathedral for Saint Lawrence; in return, unless he could guess the giant's name, Finn wanted the sun, the moon, or his eyes. The saint was just preparing to end his days in blindness when he heard Finn's wife boasting to her baby, "Soon Father Finn will bring some eyes for you to play with." The relieved saint rushed to Finn declaring his name. The livid giant, his wife and child rushed to the crypt to pull down the columns and were instantly turned to stone. Even without the fable, the column-hugging figures are fascinating to view.

## The museums and Botanical Gardens

Just behind the cathedral on Sandgatan, the **History and Cathedral Museum** (Tues–Fri 11am–1pm; free) is for the most part rather dull unless you have specialist interests, but the statues from Scånian churches in the medieval exhibition do deserve a look, mainly because of the way they are arranged – a mass of Jesuses and Marys bunched together in groups. The crowd of Jesuses hanging on crosses have a Hitchcockesque ominousness, while in the next room all the Madonnas are together with all the baby Jesuses.

A few minutes' walk north on Tegnerplatsen is the town's best museum, **Kulturen** (May–Sept daily 11am–5pm, Thurs till 9pm; Oct–April daily noon–4pm,

Thurs till 9pm; 40kr). Although this privately owned open-air museum has no English-language translations (except for a book on all exhibits that costs 100kr), it's still easy to spend the best part of a day just wandering around this virtual town of perfectly preserved cottages, farms, merchants' houses, gardens and even churches, brought from seven regions around Sweden and from as many centuries. Together they make a fascinating collection.

Walking further north from the square along St Annegatan, it's worth stopping on the corner of Tomegapsgatan to have a look at *Larsson's Sweet Shop* (May–Sept noon–5pm); opened in 1814, it still has all its original fixtures. Continuing north along Sandgatan, and then taking a right onto Finngatan, you'll soon find another rather special museum, **Skissernas Museum** (Museum of Sketches), Finngatan 2 (Tues–Sat noon–4pm, Sun 1–5pm; free). Inside is a fascinating collection of preliminary sketches and original full-scale models of artworks from around the world. One room is full of work by all the major Swedish artists, while in the international room are sketches by Chagall, Matisse, Leger, Miro and Dufy, and the best-known sculptural sketches are by Picasso and Henry Moore.

As an antidote to museum fatigue, the **Botanical Gardens** (mid-May to mid-Sept 6am–9.30pm, mid-Sept to mid-May 6am–8pm, greenhouses noon–3pm), a few minutes' stroll further southwest down Finngatan (turn left at the end of the street into Pålsjövägen and right into Olshögsvägen), are as much a venue for picnicking and chilling out as a botanical experience – on hot summer days, clusters of students congregate and stretch out beneath the trees. The greenhouses and rock gardens are the best areas to view; the Far Eastern paper mulberry and huge tulip trees, with their mass of flowers in June, are the rarest sights.

# Eating, drinking and nightlife

There are plenty of great places to eat and drink in Lund, an awful lot of them associated with the university – certain **cafés** are student institutions and a number of the better **restaurants** are attached to student bodies or museums. This student connection keeps prices low, especially for beer; however, Lund also boasts a couple of nationally celebrated restaurants that are so expensive only business accounts can afford them. If you want to buy your own provisions, the market at Mortenstorget, *Saluhallen*, sells a range of fish, cheeses and meats, including Lund's own tasty speciality sausage, *Knake*. Next door to the *Espresso House* (see opposite) on Sankt Petri Kyrkogata, *Wilderbergs Charkuteri* is a long-established foodie shop brimming with cooked meats and baguettes for the ultimate picnic.

For **nightlife**, it's worth knowing that the university is divided into "Nations", or colleges, named after different geographical areas of Sweden and with strong identities. Each nation has its own bar that's active two nights a week, and there are also regular discos. *Lund Nation* is, unsurprisingly, the biggest. It's based in the big red-brick house on Agardhsgatan, and the bar is cheap. *Småland's Nation* on Kastanjatan, off Mortenstorget, is the hippest, socialist nation. Both are known as the music nations and host all the best bands and regular live music. Another lively place on the alternative music scene is the bright lilac-painted **Majeriet** at the end of Stora Södergatan, which runs south from the main square. Converted into a music and cultural centre in the 1970s, this one-hundred-year-old dairy is now a "cultural dairy", with a stylish café and concert hall, attracting artists as diverse as Iggy Pop and the Bulgarian Women's Choir; it also contains an arts cinema (concert information on ☎12 38 11; cinema details on ☎14 38 13).

## Cafés and restaurants

**Café Ariman**, Kungsgatan, attached to the Nordic Law Department. A nineteenth-century brick café, this deliberately shabby place is a classic left-wing coffee house and a place for wannabe writers – posey beards, ponytails and blond dreadlocks predominate. Cheap snacks and coffee. Mon–Fri 11am–6pm, Sat 11am–4pm, Sun 1–5pm.

**Café Baguette**, Grönegatan. A simple, Mediterranean-style central café, with baguettes from 20kr and fish and meat meals for 70–90kr.

**Café Borgen** at the Botanical Gardens. A pleasant café with a basic selection of food, in a castellated building overlooking the waterlily pond in the gardens. June–Aug daily 10am–6pm.

**Café Credo**, behind the cathedral. This 500-year-old monks' dining room serves coffee and snacks; the food is nothing special, but the setting is very peaceful. Mon–Fri 10am–5pm, Sat 10am–3pm.

**Café Stortorget**. Stortorget. In this National Romantic-style former bank, staff don't bother too much with service and the prices are high, but it's crowded all the same with tables spilling out onto the street. The food is good, if it ever arrives.

**Conditori Lunagård**, Kyrkogatan. *The* classic student konditori. A delightful institution with excellent caricatures of professors adorning the walls. Justly famous for its apple meringue pie.

**Espresso House**, Sankt Petri Kyrkogata 5, opposite the library. Great atmosphere at this new, stylish coffee and bagel house. A big range of delicious coffees for 12–20kr, and mellow music sets the mood. Daily 8am–11pm.

**Fellini**, opposite train station (☎13 80 20). Stylish and popular Italian restaurant. All dull chrome and stripped wood. Two-course meals for 135kr. Mon–Thurs 11.30am–midnight, Fri & Sat till 2am, Sun till 10pm.

**Gloria's**, Sankt Petri Kyrkogata, near the *Espresso House*. Serving American food, *Gloria's* is very popular with students and tourists of all ages. Local bands play Fri & Sat nights, and there's a big, lively garden area at the back. Mon 11.30am–midnight, Tues–Thurs 11.30am–1am, Fri & Sat 11.30am–2am, Sun 1pm–midnight.

**Kulturen**, just in front of the Kulturen museum. Beneath a giant copper beech and facing ancient runestones, this is a lovely, busy café, bar and restaurant. A great place to people watch, with a 20s–30s crowd drinking cheap beer (28kr). Good lunch with vegetarian choice (54kr).

**Lundia**, Knutenstorestorg. Serves good lunches in ugly, 1980s' surroundings (also a nightclub; see overleaf). Mon–Thurs 11.30am–midnight, Fri & Sat 11.30am–1am, Sun 1–10pm.

**Petri Pumpa**, St Petri Kyrkogatan 7 (☎13 55 15). With an extremely expensive, international menu served in cool, elegant surroundings, this restaurant is known as "the second finest in Sweden".

**Stadpark Café**, in the popular park at the end of Nygatan. This old, wooden pavilion, fronted by a sea of white plastic garden furniture, is busy with families munching on snacks. Big baguettes fill you up for 35–40kr.

**Tegnes Terass**, in the building of the same name next to the student union (Akademiska Föreningen – also see below). Forget any preconceptions about student cafés being tatty, stale sandwich bars. Lunch for 55kr (49kr with student card) is self-service and means as much as you like from a choice of delicious, gourmet meals. The main hall is resplendent with gilded Ionic columns and Scandinavian-wood tables; sit inside or on the terrace. Daily 11.30am–2.30pm.

## Bars and clubs

**Easy**, in Tegnes Terass building next to the student union. A new student nightclub (Thurs nights 7pm–3am; free entry till midnight, then 20kr). It also has a restaurant (Thurs 7pm–3am). With a student card, 18-year-olds and upwards can get into the club; otherwise there's a strict over-23 age limit.

**John Bull Pub**, Bantorget, adjacent to *Grand Hotel*. English-style, shabby traditional pub, with Art Nouveau details on the exterior.

**Lundia**, Knutdenstorestorg. Filled with tourists, the atmosphere in this club is rather soulless. Wed–Sat 11pm–3am.

**Petri Pumpa Bar**, next to *Gloria's*. A glamorous place serving beer from an imported French bar and excellent Continental lunches at 60–70kr. The sort of bar that has roasted hazelnuts rather than peanuts.

# Malmö

Founded in the late thirteenth century, **MALMÖ** became Denmark's most important city after Copenhagen. The high density of herring in the sea off the Malmö coast – it was said that the fish could be scooped straight out with a trowel – brought ambitious German merchants flocking to the city; the striking fourteenth-century St Petri kyrka is heavily influenced by German styles. Eric of Pomerania gave Malmö its most significant medieval boost, when, in the fifteenth century, he built the castle, with its own mint, and gave Malmö its own flag – the gold and red griffin of his own family crest. It wasn't until the Swedish king Karl X marched his armies across the frozen belt of water to within striking distance of Copenhagen in 1658 that the Danes were forced into handing back the counties of Skåne, Blekinge and Bohuslän to the Swedes. For Malmö this meant a period of stagnation, cut off from nearby Copenhagan and too far from its own uninterested capital. Not until the full thrust of industrialization, triggered by the tobacco merchant Frans Suell's enlargement of the harbour in 1775, did Malmö begin its dramatic commercial recovery. In 1840, boats began regular trips to Copenhagen, in the same year the great Kockums shipyard was opened, and not long after an extensive train network was set up.

Today the attractive medieval centre, a myriad of cobbled and mainly pedestrianized streets, full of busy restaurants and bars, paints a false picture of economic wellbeing – Malmö, Sweden's third city, is facing commercial crisis. Since its industrial heyday between the first and second world wars, the city's standing has plummeted. A series of miscalculations on top of the industrial decline felt throughout the country has stripped Malmö of its wealth, a fact apparent from the carcasses of industry left scattered around its environs. At Limhamn, where the car ferry from Denmark pulls in (see "Arrival, information and transport" opposite), the huge concrete works are now a dormant waste ground and the great limestone quarry just a massive gaping hole. If you arrive here, then your first sight of Malmö is a bizarre blend of industrial decay and the magnificent villas that front the long stretch of sandy beach, which runs all the way to the city centre (Malmö means "sand mound"). The city also invested heavily in the shipping industry just at the time of the great shipping decline in the 1970s, and even the state-of-the-art SAAB car plant, into which vast sums of money were poured, has failed here, too.

For tourism, this means that desperate measures are being taken to salvage Malmö's worn-out image. A wild scheme to create a huge artificial lake with an island in the old Limhamn quarry is just one idea, but as yet no backing has been found; building a massive theme park on the old concrete works is another. A further aggravating sore is the love-hate relationship that exists between Malmö and Lund. Students at Lund both scorn and crave the bright, brash neon

of Malmö, while Malmö council is keen to pull down the classic Kockums shipyard crane – a mascot of the city – and build a big university. The hottest
current issue is the construction of a 17km bridge between Malmö and
Copenhagen (see p.203).

Whatever its problems, Malmö makes for a worthwhile visit. Although you
won't need more than a day to get a feel for the compact centre, there are also
delightful parks, a long and popular beach and some interesting cultural diversions
south of the centre. The city's lively nightlife is another inducement to stay a while.
One VIP who does hang around is the current prime minister, who lives here
despite having an extensive official residence in Stockholm. The first ever to refuse
to live in the capital, he flies there by private jet each morning from Malmö.

# Arrival, information and transport

All passenger-only **ferries** and **catamarans** from Copenhagen dock at the various terminals along the conveniently central Skeppsbron docks (ticket details are
given under "Listings"). This route to the city gives the best initial vantage point,
with grand facades reflecting Malmö's proud industrial heritage. Just up from
here is the central **train station**. As well as the *SJ* national trains, the Danish-built
(and much more comfortable) *Kustpilen* trains run hourly from here to Denmark
(change at Hässleholm) and east to Kristianstad, Karlskrona and through to
Linköping. The frequent local *Pågatåg* trains to and from Helsingborg/Lund and
Ystad use platforms 9–13 at the back. To get to the square outside, Centralplan,
either walk through central station or use the separate exit/entrance (which is
marked as *Lokal stationen*). In the square is the main **bus terminal**. Frequent
buses to and from Lund, Kastrup airport (in Denmark), Kristianstad/Kalmar and
Ystad all stop here. Buses from Stockholm, Helsingborg and Gothenburg arrive
at Slussplan, east of Central Station just over Slussbron at the end of Norra
Vallgatan. If you're **flying** into Sturup airport to the east of Malmö, the hourly
*Flygbuss* runs to the city centre (Mon–Fri 5.30am–7.30pm, Sat 6.30am–5.30pm;
40min; 60kr). The other possible arrival point is the **Dragör-Limhamn car
ferry**, 3km west of the city (see p.206). Bus #82 runs from here up Strandgatan
and right up to Central Station. The *Intercitybuss* #999 (Mon–Sat 4 daily
8.30am–5.35pm; 2 on Sun) leaves from Norra Vallgatan via Limhamn and Dragör
to Copenhagen's Central Station (50kr).

## Information and discount cards

The **tourist office** (June–Aug Mon–Fri 9am–8pm, Sat 9am–5pm, Sun 10am–5pm;
Sept–May Mon–Fri 9am–5pm, Sat 9.30am–2pm; ☎30 01 50, fax 23 55 20) is inside
Central Station. Here, you can pick up a wealth of free information, including several good maps and an events and listings brochure, *Malmö This Month*. You can
also buy the very useful **Malmökortet** (Malmö Card; available for 1, 2 or 3 days;
175kr for a 3-day card), which gives free museum entry, car parking, a guided bus
tour and up to eight bus journeys, plus various other discounts on transport, cinemas, concerts and trips around the city, including fifty percent off day tickets to
the *Aq-Va-Kul* indoor waterpark (see p.205 for full details) and both Sibbarps and
Ribersborgs open-air bath houses and saunas (see p.197 and p.202). A useful and

---

The telephone code for Malmö is ☎040.

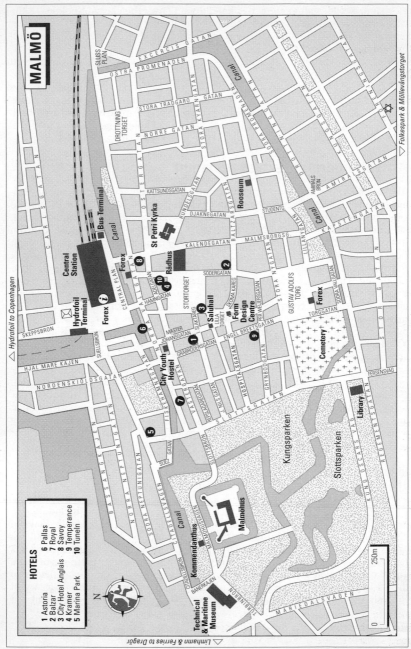

△ *Hydrofoil to Copenhagen*

▷ *Folkespark & Möllevångstorget*

**MALMÖ**

SLUSS PLAN

EXCERCIS GATAN

ÖSTRA PROMENADEN

STORA TRÄDGÅRD

NORRE GATAN

DROTTNING TORGET

STORA KYRANGATAN

KATTSUNDSGATAN

St Petri Kyrka

DJAKNEGATAN

Rooseum

STUDENTG

KALENDEGATAN

MALMSBORGSG

Bus Terminal

Central Station

Forex

Rådhus ■ 8

SÖDERGATAN

STORTORGET

GUSTAV ADOLFS TORG

Forex

Hydrofoil Terminal

Forex

i CENTRAL PLAN

SKEPPSBRON

 HAMNGATAN

Saluhall ■ 3

LILLA TORGET

Form Design Centre ■ 9

ENGEL BREKTSGATAN

TORGGATAN

HJALMARE KAJEN

NORDENSKIÖLDSGATAN

City Youth Hostel ■ 1

MASTER JOHANSGATAN

GRÅBRÖDERSGATAN

HOSPITALSGATAN

GRYNBODGATAN

FERSENSVÄG

Cemetery

Library

Kungsparken

Slottsparken

Malmöhus

Kommendanthus

Technical & Maritime Museum

MARIEDALSVÄGEN

250m

0

**HOTELS**

1 Astoria          6 Pallas
2 Balzar           7 Royal
3 City Hotel Anglais 8 Savoy
4 Kramer           9 Temperance
5 Marina Park     10 Tuneln

N

△ *Limhamn & Ferries to Dragör*

good-value two-day ticket is the **Öresund Runt** (Round the Öresund; 145kr, children 70kr), which takes you whichever route you choose (or any part of it) by ferry, train and hydrofoil to Lund, Helsingborg, Helsingør and across to Copenhagen. There are *Forex* **money exchanges** just opposite the tourist office in Central Station (daily 8am–9pm), on Norra Vägen 60 (7am–9pm) and Gustav Adolfs Torg (9am–7pm).

### City transport

Although the city centre is easy to walk around, its central squares and streets all interlinked, you'll need to use the city **bus** service to reach some of the sights and some accommodation. It costs 12kr a ride (tickets valid for 1hr); a 100kr magnetic card is also available, which reduces bus fares and can be used by several people at the same time. All tickets are sold on the bus. If you want to use **taxis**, it's worth comparing rates (several will ask you how much you can manage). A rough idea of costs is: Malmö centre to the airport 225kr; Central Station to the soccer stadium 65kr, and to the Limhamm ferry 80kr. A one-hour guided **sightseeing tour** (11am & 1pm; 80kr; free with Malmö Card) leaves from the tourist office, but it's pricey and is conducted in Swedish, English and German, so progression through the streets is necessarily slow. Alternatively you can do your own guided tour on standard city bus #20, which also leaves from outside the tourist office (several buses an hour; both the bus ride and brochure are free with the Malmo Card). The tourist office will sell you a specially designed brochure that points out areas of interest for 12kr.

## Accommodation

There are some really good and surprisingly affordable **hotels** in Malmö; the city is eager to attract tourists, and competition between the hotels can be fierce. Also the tourist office sells a **Malmö Package**, providing visitors with a double room in a central hotel with breakfast and a Malmö Card thrown in, too. The scheme – along the lines of those in Stockholm and Gothenburg – runs from June to late August and weekends only for the rest of the year and costs from 365kr to 650kr per person, depending on the hotel. It's a good deal, although the usual summer reductions at many non-participating hotels may prove even better value. All the hotels listed overleaf participate in the scheme, except for the cheapest, *Hotel Pallas*.

Malmö has two **youth hostels**. The central *City Youth Hostel,* Västergatan 9, is student accommodation let out as a hostel over suumer (June–Aug; ☎ & fax 23 56 40; single rooms 125kr per person, dorms 100kr) and is friendlier and more convenient than the *STF* hostel (see below). It's worth getting your own room (ask for no. 24, the best furnished and the only one with a sea view), as the dormitories are in the basement and crammed with beds. Upstairs, however, is well equipped with kitchens. The *STF Vandrarhem*, Backavägen 18 (open all year except mid-Dec to mid-Jan; ☎822 20; 100kr) is 5km from the city centre and pushed up against the E6 motorway; only go for this if *City Youth Hostel* is full or closed. To get there, take bus #21A from Centreplan to Vandrarhemmet, cross over the junction past traffic lights and take first right; the hostel is signposted to left. The nearest **campsite**, *Camping Sibbarps* at Strandgatan 101 in Limhamn (open all year; ☎34 26 50), is currently in a picturesque spot; however, the new bridge to Copenhagen is being built nearby (see p.203). It is also convenient for **Sibbarps Saltsjöbad**, a fine, open-air bath house with a wood-fired sauna (take bus #82).

## Hotels

**Astoria**, Gråbrödersgatan 7, a few minutes from the train station across the canal (☎786 60, fax 788 70). Upgraded in past few years, it's a good, plain hotel. ③/②

**Balzar**, Södergatan 20 (☎720 05, fax 23 63 75). Very central hotel between the two main squares. A swanky, traditional place, the decor all swags and ruches, some rooms with superb painted ceilings. None of it is remotely Swedish in style. ④/②

**City Hotel Anglais**, Stortorget 15 (☎714 50, fax 611 32 74). A grand, turn-of-the-century hotel in the best central position. Tasteful rooms and recently renovated, this is a fine choice on the premiere square. ④/②

**Kramer**, Stortorget 7 (☎20 88 00, fax 12 69 41). Beautiful, white-stuccoed, turretted hotel from the 1870s, this was once the top hotel. A very luxurious, beautifully preserved classic. ⑤/③

**Marina Park**, Citadellvagen (☎23 96 05, fax 30 39 68). Five minutes' walk to the right from the train station, in the direction of Malmöhus. Its comfortable, pleasant interior is belied by the facade, which looks like a 1950s' apartment tower and overlooks the tall pink cylinders of a factory. Price includes a good breakfast and free parking; 690kr drops to 590kr in summer. ②

**Pallas**, Norra Vallgatan 74 (☎611 50 77, fax 97 99 00). A deceptively pretty, ornate old building that's rather tatty inside. A hotel/hostel cross. Same price all year; breakfast 30kr. ①

**Royal**, Norra Vallgatan 94 (☎97 63 03, fax 12 77 12). Just up from the train station, this is a small, family-run hotel and part of the Sweden Hotels group. Price includes breakfast taken in a pleasant back garden. ③/②

**Savoy**, Norra Vallgatan 62 (☎702 30, fax 97 85 51). No longer prohibitively priced, this is the essence of style, with splendid furnishings and excellent Swedish and international food served in the historical elegance of the *Savoy Dining Rooms*. Attached is the *Bishop's Arms* pub, an all English-style cosy place for a drink and inexpensive light meal. ④/③

**Temperance**, Engelbrektsgatan 16 (☎710 20, fax 30 44 06). A pretty, central hotel with fairly standard decor. Price includes sauna, solarium and a big buffet breakfast. ③/②

**Tuneln**, Adelgatan 4 (☎10 16 20; fax 10 16 25). The finest small hotel in Malmö. Very central and dating from the Middle Ages (it was built as a mansion in the 1340s); the rooms are either Gustavian style pastel or dark cherry. It's beautifully furnished – note the marble stairs. No summer reduction but price goes down to 565kr on the weekends. ③

# The city centre

Walking away from the heavy-handed nineteenth-century opulence of the train station, with its curly-topped pillars and red-brick ornate arches, the **canal** in front of you, which was dug by Russian prisoners, forms a rough rectangle encompassing the old town directly to the south and the moated castle to the west. The castle is also surrounded by a series of lovely and interconnecting parks including the Kungspark, Slottspark and Mariedals Park. First off, though, head down Hamngatan to the main square. On the way you'll pass the striking sculpture of a twisted revolver, a monument to non-violence, that stands outside the grand 1890s former Malmö Exchange building.

## Stortorget and St Petri kyrka

**Stortorget**, the proud main square, necessitated the tearing down of much of Malmö's medieval centre when it was laid out in the mid-sixteenth century. Among the elaborate sixteenth- to nineteenth-centuries buildings, the 1546-built **Rådhus** draws the most attention. It's a pageant of architectural fiddling and crowded with statuary: restoration programmes last century robbed the building of its original design, and the finicky exterior is now in Dutch Renaissance style.

It's impressive, nonetheless, and to add to the pomp, the red-and-gold Scånian flag, of which Malmö is so proud, hangs from the eaves. There are occasional tours of its more original interior, but check with the tourist office for the ever-changing times. The cellars, home to *Rådhus Källaven Restaurant* (see "Cafés and restaurants"), have been used as a tavern for more than four-hundred years. To the right of the town hall, have a look inside **Apoteket Lejonet** (Swedish pharmacies are always named after creatures of strength, *lejonet* meaning "lion"). The outside is gargoyled and balconied, and the inside is a busy mix of inlaid woods, carvings and etched glass. From here, **Södergatan**, Malmö's main pedestrianized shopping street, leads down towards the canal. At the Stortorget end, there's a jaunty troupe of sculptured bronze musicians; further down, a rake of lively cafés and restaurants. On the opposite side of the square, the crumbling, step-gabled red-brick building was once the home of sixteenth-century mayor and Master of the Danish Mint, Jörgen Kocks. Danish coins were struck in Malmö on the site of the present Malmöhus castle (see overleaf), until irate local Swedes stormed the building and destroyed it in 1534. In the cellars of Jörgen's pretty home, you'll find the *Kockska Krogan* restaurant, the only entry point for visitors today. In the centre of the square, a statue of Karl X, high on his charger, presides over the city he liberated from centuries of Danish rule.

If you head a block east, behind the Rådhus, the dark, forbidding exterior of the Gothic **St Petri kyrka** on Göran Olsgatan (Mon–Fri 8am–6pm, Sat 9am–6pm, Sun 10am–6pm) belies a light and airy interior. The church has its roots in the fourteenth century, and, although Baltic in inspiration, the final style owes much to German influences, for it was beneath its unusually lofty and elegantly vaulted roof that the German community came to pray – probably for the continuation of the "sea silver", the herrings that brought them to Malmö in the first place. The ecclesiastical vandalism of whitewashing over medieval roof murals started early at St Petri; almost the whole interior turned white in 1553. Consequently your eyes are drawn to the two most impressive items: the pulpit and a four-tiered altarpiece, both of striking workmanship and elaborate embellishment. The only part of the church left with its original artwork was a side chapel, the **Krämare (merchant's) Chapel** (from the entrance turn left and left again). Added to the church in the late fifteenth century as the Lady Chapel, at the Reformation it was considered redundant and was sealed off, so protecting the paintings from the zealous brush of the reformers. The paintings on the vaulted ceiling are in better condition than those on the walls and depict mainly New Testament figures surrounded by decorative foliage, including the boy Jesus with a parrot and a fig. Beneath you, the chapel floor is a chessboard of tombs in black, white and a few in redstone. Unfortunately, the paintings in the rest of the church were scraped away in nineteenth-century restorations.

## Lilla Torg

Despite the size of Stortorget, it still proved too small to suffice as the sole main square, so in the sixteenth century **Lilla Torg**, formerly marshland, was sewn on to the southeast corner. Looking like a film set, this little square with its creaky old half-timbered houses, flower pots and cobbles is everyone's favourite part of the city. During the day, people congregate here to take a leisurely drink in one of the many bars and wander around the summer jewellery stalls. At night, Lilla Torg explodes in a frenzy of activity, the venues all merging into a mass of bodies who converge from all over the city and beyond (also see "Eating and drinking").

It's worth walking through an arch on Lilla Torg to the **Form Design Centre**, built into a seventeenth-century grain store and a centre for Swedish design in textiles, ceramics and furniture, although the title is rather more ambitious than the contents. The courtyard entrance contains several small trendy boutiques, and the Form Design Centre itself is crisply modish, with blond, minimalist wooden furniture contrasting with the beams supporting the ancient structure. A simple café serves not very much for not very much, but it's all well presented, if a little pretentious. From the turn of the century until the 1960s, the whole of Lilla Torg was a covered market, and the sole vestige of those days, **Saluhallen**, is diagonally opposite the Design Centre. Mostly made up of specialist fine food shops, *Saluhallen* is a pleasant, cool retreat on a hot afternoon.

## Rooseum

A few streets out of the general line of sights, but well worth a visit if you're interested in contemporary art, is **Rooseum** (daily except Mon 11am–5pm, guided tours Sat & Sun 2pm; 30kr, free with a Malmö Card) on Stora Nygatan. It's an imaginative use of space in an elaborately designed building from 1900 that was originally used to house the Malmö Electricity Company's steam turbines. The main turbine hall is the central gallery, with experimental installations and interesting photographic works. There are regular new exhibitions and a fine little café (see "Cafés and restaurants").

## Malmöhus

Take any of the streets running west from Stortorget or Lilla Torg and you soon come up against the edge of **Kungsparken**, within striking distance of the fifteenth-century castle of **Malmöhus** (June–Aug daily except Mon 10am–4pm, rest of year noon–4pm; 40kr, free with the Malmö Card). For a more head-on approach walk west (away from the station) up Citadellsvägen; from here the low castle with its grassy ramparts and two circular keeps is straight ahead over the wide moat.

Following its destruction as Denmark's mint by the Swedes in 1534, the Danish king Christian III built a new fortress two years later, only to be of unforeseen benefit to his enemies who, once back in control of Skåne, used it to repel an attacking Danish army in 1677. For a time a prison (the Earl of Bothwell, Mary Queen of Scots's third husband, its most notable inmate), the castle's importance waned once back in Swedish hands, and it was used for grain storage until becoming a museum in 1937. Today the large, modern museum complex obliterates views of most of the inner castle walls.

Pass swiftly through the natural history section – a taxidermal Noah's ark with no surprises; the most rewarding part of the museum is upstairs, where an ambitious series of furnished rooms move through most modern styles from the mid-sixteenth-century Renaissance period through Baroque, Rococo, pastel-pale Gustavian and Neoclassical. A stylish interior from the Jugend (Art Nouveau) period is also impressive, while other rooms have Functionalist and post-Functionalist interiors, with some wacky colour and texture combinations. It's a fascinating visual feast – but would be considerably improved by labelling in English. Other sections of the historical exhibition include a display of medieval skeletons from Malmö's churchyards, showing contemporary diseases like leprosy and tuberculosis – less gruesome than you might imagine. It's more interesting to head into the castle itself with its spartan but authentic interiors.

Just beyond the castle to the west along Malmöhusvagen is **Kommendanthuset** (Governor's House), containing the strange marriage of a military and toy museum. The military section is a fairly lifeless collection of neatly presented rifles and swords and the usual dummies sporting eighteenth- and nineteenth-century uniforms. The most interesting exhibit is an 1890 ambulance carriage. Upstairs, along with cases of glittering military decoration, are some fine portraits of military heroes. The toy museum is more fun, the link between the two museums-in-one being a bridgade of toy soldiers, oddly of the British army. A little further west running off Malmöhusvagen is a tiny walkway, **Banerkajen**, lined with higgledy piggledy fishing shacks, selling fresh and smoked fish – a rare little area of traditional Malmö that contrasts with the lively pace of the rest of the city. Just beyond the lane is the **Technical and Maritime Museum** (same times as the Malmöhus; 15kr). The technical section has displays on transport (planes, roads), power (steam, wind, water) and local industries (sugar, cement); while upstairs in the science section the main display is a model of Tycho Brahe's observatory on the island of Ven (see p.188).

Once you've had your fill of museums, the castle **grounds** are good for a stroll, peppered with small lakes and an old windmill. The paths lead all the way down to Regementsgatan and the City Library in the southeastern corner of the park. You can continue walking through the greenery as far as Gustav Adolfs Torg by crossing Gamla Begravnings Platsen, a rather pretty graveyard.

## South of the city

Tourists rarely head further south of the city than the canal banks that enclose the old town. If you have a few hours to spare, however, the buildings and areas leading off Amiralsgatan give an interesting insight into Malmö's mix of cultures and its Social Democratic roots, which played such a major role in the city's development. A few hundred metres down Amiralsgatan, the splendid copper-domed Moorish building standing out on Föreningsgatan is the restored **Malmö Synagogue**. Designed and built by the same architect as the neighbouring Betania kyrka in 1894, the synagogue is decorated with concentric designs in blue and green glazed brick. Strict security measures mean that to see inside you have to telephone the Jewish Community offices (the tourist office will help). The unrenovated interior is rather fine, with the original German-inspired octagonal wooden ceiling, ark and enormous dull brass chandelier. There's a separate women's gallery, this synagogue serving an Orthodox community, who came mostly from Germany in the latter part of the last century and the 1930s.

Back on Amiralsgatan, it's a ten-minute walk to **Folkespark**, a quiet garden area at the centre of which stands **Moriskan**, an odd, low building with Russian-style golden minarets topped with sickles. This is Sweden's oldest existing working people's park and was once the prize of the community. Now rather shabby, Folkespark contains a basic amusement park, and the *Moriskan*, a ballroom. Both, however, are now privately owned, a far cry from the original aims of the park's Social Democratic founders. Severe carved busts of these City Fathers are dotted all over the park. Malmö has always been at the forefront of left-wing politics, and the city was central to the creation and development of the Social Democratic Party. The Socialist agitator August Palm made his first historic speech here in 1881, which marked the beginning of a 66-year period of unbroken Social Democratic rule.

More interesting than the twirling giant tea-cup fun rides in the park is the multicultural character of the city south from here. Arabic, Asian and Balkan émigré families predominate and, strolling from the park's southern exit down Möllevången to **Möllevångstorget**, you enter an area populated almost entirely by non-Swedes, with Arabic and Urdu the main languages. The vast Möllevångstorget is a haven of cafés (see "Cafés and restaurants") and exotic food stores, along with shops selling pure junk. On a hot summer afternoon it would be easy to forget you were in Sweden at all, the more makeshift and ramshackle atmosphere contrasting with the clean, clinical order of an average Swedish neighbourhood. It's worth taking a close look at the provoking **sculpture** at the square's centre. Four naked, bronze men strain under the colossal weight of a huge chunk of rock bearing effigies of Malmö's smoking chimneys, while two naked women press their hands into the men's backs in support. It's a poignant image of toiling and sweating in a city founded on limestone quarrying and the Social Democratic vision of the working man struggling beneath the burden of his life.

# The beaches and Limhamn

Separated from the city centre by the delightful **Öresund park**, Malmö's long stretch of sandy beach reaches all the way to Limhamn, and alongside it runs the **Ribersborgs Recreation Promenade**. Fringed by dunes and grassland, the beach area is enjoyed by groups of young people who hold barbeques, light fires, smoke and play music throughout the summer months. A classic Malmö experience at the town end of the beach is the **Ribersborgs kallbadhuset** (mid-April to mid-Sept Mon–Fri bath house 8.30am–7pm, sauna from 11am, Sat & Sun bath house 8.30am–4pm, sauna from 9am; mid-Sept to mid-April Mon–Fri for both noon–7pm, Sat & Sun 9am–4pm; 28kr, with Malmö Card 14kr), a cold-water bath house with a sauna and café. All the beaches along this stretch are favoured by young families as the water remains shallow for several metres; there is one bathing area further west (a couple of kilometres from town) that is specially adapted for people with disabilities. Grand old villas set in glorious gardens overlook the Öresund, and the whole stretch is known as the Golden Coast because of the wealth of its residents.

## Limhamm
**LIMHAMN** (limestone harbour), 3km to the southwest of the city, has an unusual history and one which will become very apparent if you're staying at the *Sibbarps* campsite or using the Limhamn car ferry to Dragör in Denmark (as for the town itself, it's not particularly attractive, and there's no real reason to visit). Once a quiet limestone-quarrying village, Limhamn was taken by storm by a local man with big ambitions called Fredryk Berg. At the end of the nineteenth century, he had a train line built between the village and Malmö, and, by winning the support and later affiliation of rival firms, he built up the huge cement works known first as Cementa and later as Euroc. Berg also founded the international construction and engineering giant Skansen. Heading down Limhamnsvägen (the road runs parallel with the beach) to Limhamn (or take bus #82), the island of **Ön** will come into view. With glamorous, if isolated apartment buildings, it's another one of Berg's creations; he had it built out of waste concrete, and on it constructed houses for factory workers and a couple of churches. His politics

## THE MALMÖ-COPENHAGEN BRIDGE

Just beyond *Sibbarps* campsite is an area called Lernacken from where a contro-versial 17km bridge over to Copenhagen is now being built – it's due for comple-tion in 2002. Under discussion for the past forty years, this colossal construction project involves building two levels, one for road traffic and one beneath for trains. The idea is that for the first time Sweden will be physically linked with Denmark, and so increase contact with Norway, and it will be possible to drive straight through to the Continent. Of the many arguments against – in Malmö's Stortorget lobbyists holding "Make love not bridges" placards are a regular sight – the most powerful is that the bridge will cause major environmental damage, during its con-struction and from the subsequent increase in car fumes. More sentimentally, nos-talgia plays a part, too; like the Helsingborg-to-Helsingør ferry, the Malmö-to-Copenhagen trip is integral to Malmö's social life. Traditionally, a good night out means spending an evening on board eating and drinking, sometimes to oblivion – a pastime that could well come to an end.

were, unsurprisingly, at odds with the flourishing Social Democratic movement, and when the workers attempted to strike, he became the first Swedish employ-er to lock them out. A strongly religious man, he was fond of saying that the two best things in life were making corporations and attending church, earning him the nickname "Concrete Jesus".

# Eating and drinking

Most of Malmö's **eating places** are concentrated in and around its three central squares (Lilla Torg attracting the biggest crowds; also see "Bars"), and among them you'll find some interesting interiors – check the industrial *Espresso Rooseum* – and fine food. By day, several cafés serve good lunches and sumptu-ous cakes and at night, although the range of cuisines isn't that wide, there are a couple of top places to eat, notably the Italian *Spot Restaurant*. If you want a change of scene why not head south of the centre to Möllenvångstorget, the heart of Malmö's immigrant community, for cheaper eats and a very un-Swedish atmos-phere. Alternatively to cut costs, *Saluhallen*, at the corner of Lilla Torg, is an excellent indoor market that's cheap and sells wholefoods; there are also special-ist food stores here, like *Krydboden*, which stocks herbal and fruit teas, coffees and crystallized fruits.

## Cafés and restaurants

**Bageri Café Saluhallen**, corner of Lilla Torg. Excellent bagels, baguettes, sweet pies and health foods – with outside eating, too. Mon–Fri 8am–6pm, Sat 10am–4pm.

**Bro's Jazz Café**, Södra Vallgatan 3 (by the canal south of Gustav Adolfs Torg). Good-value, big, filling sandwiches named after jazz greats. Long-winded menus in English perused by a young, friendly crowd. Mon–Fri 10am–1am, Sat & Sun noon–1am.

**Café Europa**, Södergatan 1. Does good à la carte lunch menu for a reasonable 55–70kr. In a splendid red-stone building and looking out onto the even fancier *Handelsbank*. Mon–Thurs & Sun 9am–10pm, Fri & Sat 9am–midnight.

**Café Siesta**, Ostindiefararegatan (turn right at end of Landbygatan, on the first corner on the left). A fun little café specializing in home-made apple cake. Mon 10am–6pm, Tues–Fri 10am–midnight, Sat 10am–6pm, Sun noon–6pm.

**Conditori Hollandia**, Södra Förstadsgatan (south of canal at Drottninggatan). Classic, pricey konditori with a window full of melting chocolate fondants. Inside is sedate – Klimt prints cover the walls. Speciality is strawberry cheesecake. Mon–Fri 8.15am–7pm, Sat 9am–5pm, Sun 11am–6pm.

**Cyber Space Café**, Engelbrektsgatan 13, just east of Stortorget. A new computer and internet café. Screens in front of each bar stool in this stylish, blue-painted bar. Surf the net while sipping coffee or soda and eating baguettes and pastries. All drinks 10kr. Half an hour surfing the net costs 20kr. Daily 2–10pm.

**Espresso Rooseum**, Gasverksgatan 22. Within the contemporary art museum set in the fine old electricity and gas works; it's worth going just for the superb chocolate cake. A giant generator takes up most of the room, with seats around the edge. Tues–Sun 11am–5pm.

**Golden Restaurant**, corner of Södra Parkgatan & Simrishamnsgatan to the south of the city. In the main immigrant area, this spartan place serves cheap crepes, pizza and kebabs.

**Gustav Adolfs**, Gustav Adolfs Torg. Popular spot, open late at weekends, serving coffee (18kr) in grand, white-stuccoed building with seating outside. Also a morning coffee and snacks menu.

**Johan P Fish Restaurant**, *Saluhallen* (also accessed from Landbygatan). Black-and-white chequered, this place serves only fairly pricey fish dishes in stylishly understated fishmonger- style restaurant.

**Kockska Krogan**, corner Stortorget & Suellgatan (☎703 20). A very fine old cellar restaurant – but rather overpriced – in the former home of Malmö's sixteenth-century mayor Jörgen Kock. Mon–Fri 11.30am–11pm, Sat 5–11pm.

**Pelles Café**, Tegelgårdsgatan 5. In a quaint period house, this simple café does really big, cheap baguettes, bottles of cold chocolate milk and plays jolly, dated music. Also has a popular leafy area for outside eating. Mon–Fri 7am–7pm, Sat & Sun 9am–7pm.

**Rådhus Källaven**, beneath the town hall on Stortorget. In this gloriously decorative building, main dishes cost 200kr, but there's a daily economy meal at 65kr that's well cooked and beautifully served. Outside eating in summer. Mon–Fri 11.30am–11pm, Sat 3–11pm, Sun 3–9pm.

**Rinaldo's**, *Saluhallen* (also accessed from Landbygatan). Restaurant serving big, fresh rainbow-coloured salads and some wicked desserts.

**Spot Restaurant**, Stora Nygatan 33 (☎12 02 03). A chic Italian restaurant with attached Italian charcuterie (*Spot's Deli*, selling fresh pasta, meats and cakes is due to open next door). All ingredients imported direct from Italy. During the day, light meals based on ciabatta and panini breads are served. There's an evening menu of fish, cheese and meats. Not too expensive, this is a really great place to eat. Mon 9am–6pm, Tues–Sat 9am–midnight.

## Bars

Lilla Torg is *the* place to go in the evenings. The square buzzes with activity, as the smell of beer wafts between the old, beamed houses, and music and chatter fill the air. It's largely a young crowd, and the atmosphere is like a summer carnival – yellow-jacketed bouncers keep the throng from suffocating. It doesn't make a huge difference which of the six or so bars that you go for – expect a wait to get a seat – but as a basic pointer, *Mellow Yellow* is for the 25-plus age group, *Moosehead* for a younger crowd, and *Victors* even younger and more boisterous, although all are fun. On Möllenvångstorget, south of the centre in the immigrant quarter, *Pub 27* is a popular, laidback place to drink.

# Entertainment: music and sport

It used to be that the only entertainment in Malmö was watching rich drunks become poor drunks at the blackjack table in the Central Station bar. Now, if you know where to look, there are some decent **live music** venues and **discos**, most of which are cheaper to get into than their European counterparts. The best venues are the very popular *Haket Bistro*, at the *Hotel Temperance*, Engelbrektsgatan, where live music – jazz, salsa or reggae – can be heard from Thursday to Sunday, and *Matssons Musikpub*, Göran Olsgatan 1, behind the Rådhus. This is the best place to see live music, with a variety of Scandinavian R&B and rock bands (open nightly 9.30pm–2am). Check out *Malmö This Month* for the latest nightclubs and "what's on" information.

Classical music performances take place at the *Concert Hall*, Föreningsgatan 35 (☎34 35 00; two for the price of one with Malmö Card), home of the Malmö Symphony Orchestra, and at *Musikhögskolan*, Ystadvägen 25 (☎19 22 00); check with the tourist office for programme details. If that doesn't appeal there's one of Europe's finest **soccer** teams based in the city, as well as a range of other sporting and not so sporting pastimes (see below), including two annual **festivals**. The **Folkfesten** takes place in early June and is devoted to progressive and classic rock. Begun in the early 1970s and now enjoying a renaissance in popularity, it is held in Kungsparken near Malmöhus; young people, tie-dyed and beaded, attend this mini-Woodstock. A far more all-encompassing event is the **Malmö Festival** in August, which mainly takes place in Stortorget. Huge tables are set out and crayfish tails are served (free), revellers bringing their own drinks. In Gustav Adolfs Torg, the stalls are all set up by the immigrant communities, with Pakistani, Somali and Bosnian goodies and dance shows; while at the canal, rowing competitions take place.

### Top soccer action – and other sports and pastimes

**Malmö FF** is the only professional soccer club in Sweden, league champions on several occasions and former finalists in the European Cup. The team plays at Malmö Stadium, John Erikssons väg; bus #20 from the centre. Tickets cost from around 60kr (☎34 26 81 for information).

**Swimming** is not a problem, either at *Aq-va-kul*, Regementsgatan 24 (Mon noon–9pm, Tues–Fri 9am–9pm, Sat 9am–6pm, Sun 10am–6pm; 10kr), an adventure pool with waves and chutes; or at the beaches and pools in Sibbarp (bus #11A), by Limhamn (May–Aug Mon–Fri 8am–7pm, Sat & Sun 8am–4pm). If you've got children to amuse, then you could try **Malmöparken** (mid-April to mid-Sept), an amusement park at Amiralsgatan 35; take any one of buses #32 and #36–38. More unusually, you can go **fishing** from the city on boats leaving from Hjälmarekajen, opposite the hydrofoil terminal. The tourist office has details; you'll be able to rent fishing gear, and there's a small discount with the Malmö Card.

## Listings

**Airlines** *British Airways*, Sturup airport (☎020/78 11 44); *Finnair*, Baltzarsgatan 31 (☎020/78 11 00); *KLM*, Sturup airport (☎020/50 05 30); *Lufthansa*, Gustav Adolfs Torg 12 (☎717 10); *SAS*, Baltzarsgatan 18 (☎35 72 00).

**Airport buses** Hourly *Flygbuss* #109 to Kastrup airport (daily 5am–10pm; 100kr) from Centralplan; hourly *Flygbuss* #110 to Sturup airport (Mon–Fri 5.25am–7.20pm, Sat 6.15am–7.25pm, Sun 8.25am–7.25pm; 60kr).

**Buses** From Centralplan to Lund (#130), Kristianstad/Kalmar (#805) and Ystad (#330). From Norra Vallgatan, an *Intercitybuss* (#999; 50kr) runs to Copenhagen via the Limhamn–Dragör ferry.

**Car rental** *Avis*, Skeppsbron 13 (☎778 30); *Budget*, Baltzarsgatan 21 (☎775 75); *Europcar*, Mäster Nilsgatan 22 (☎38 02 40); *Hertz*, Jorgenkocksgatan 1B (☎749 55). Agencies also inside the *SAS* hovercraft terminal on Skeppsbron and at Sturup airport.

**Consulate** British Consulate at Gustav Adolfs Torg 8c (☎611 55 25).

**Doctor** On call daily 7am–10pm; ☎33 35 00; at other times ☎33 10 00.

**Exchange** Best rates are at *Forex*, Norra Vallgatan 60 (June–Aug daily 8am–7pm), Gustav Adolfs Torg 12 (shorter hours) and at the train station (same hours); or try the Central Station post office (Mon–Fri 8am–6pm, Sat 9.30am–1pm).

**Ferries and catamarans** *Flygbåtarna*, Skeppsbron (catamaran; 85kr one-way to Copenhagen, 50-percent discount with Malmö Card; ☎10 39 30); *SAS*, Skeppsbron (hovercraft direct to Kastrup airport; 475kr one-way; ☎35 71 00); *Scandlines*, Limhamn–Dragör ferry crossing (35kr one-way, children half-price; car plus passengers 350kr one-way, 525kr return; ☎16 20 70); *Pilen* (catamaran to Copenhagen; 29kr one-way; ☎23 44 11).

**Left luggage** Lockers in Central Station are at the entrance to platforms 3–6 and are graded in three sizes (10, 15 or 20kr); the largest takes any size of case or backpack.

**Pharmacy** 24-hour service at *Apoteket Gripen*, Bergsgatan 48 (☎19 21 13).

**Post office** Skeppsbron 1 (Mon–Fri 8am–6pm, Sat 9.30am–1pm).

**STF** Hiking and youth hostel information from an office inside the post office.

**Taxis** *City Cabs* (☎71 000); *Limhamn taxi* (☎13 00 00). Typical prices are: Malmö to Sturup airport 225kr; the train station to Dragör ferry 80kr; Malmö to Lund 200kr; the train station to the soccer stadium 65kr.

**Telephone office** *Televerket*, Storgatan 23 (Mon–Fri 8am–9pm, Sat 9.30am–3pm).

**Trains** *Pågatåg* information office inside the *Lokalstationen* (Mon–Fri 7am–6pm, Sat 8am–3pm, Sun 9am–3pm). Tickets to Lund cost 25kr one-way.

---

# Southeastern Skåne: from Malmö to Ystad

The local *Pågatåg* train and the E6 and E14 highways cut directly east towards Ystad, missing out some picturesque, minor resorts, a couple of the region's best beaches, along Sweden's most southwesterly tip, and an extensive Baltic amber workshop at Kämpinge, set in picture-perfect countryside. If you have time to explore, and particularly if you have your own transport, this quieter part of the south makes for a delightful few days' exploration.

With a car, it's worth taking the old coast-hugging E6 road in the direction of Trelleborg, to the village of **VELLINGE** (alternatively take bus #150 from Malmö's Centreplan). Opposite the old town hall, which is well disguised as a fairy-tale cottage, with a deep thatched roof and perfectly preserved court-yard, is one of Sweden's oldest inns, a gastronomic landmark called *Hvellingegästgifvaregård* (Mon 11.30am–3pm, Tues–Thurs 11.30am–10pm, Fri 11.30am–11pm, Sat 1–11pm, Sun 1–6pm). Skåne's rich soils and farmland have justifiably earned it the reputation for the country's best dairy and cereal products – the region is frequently referred to as Sweden's bread-basket. Genuine **Scånian inns**, revered by locals, are deceptively basic in appearance and well worth seeking out. This one dates from the early seventeenth century and offers such delights as beer-cooked eel with scrambled eggs (80kr), Scånian duck in port (225kr) and *äggakaka*, a Scånian egg pancake with lingonberries(150kr); there is also a good-value 65kr daily lunch option. Moving on (by car or bus #150), you cross an expanse of heathland to which birdwatchers flock every autumn to spot nesting plovers and terns, as well as millions of migratory birds fleeing the Arctic for the Stevns peninsula, south of Copenhagen.

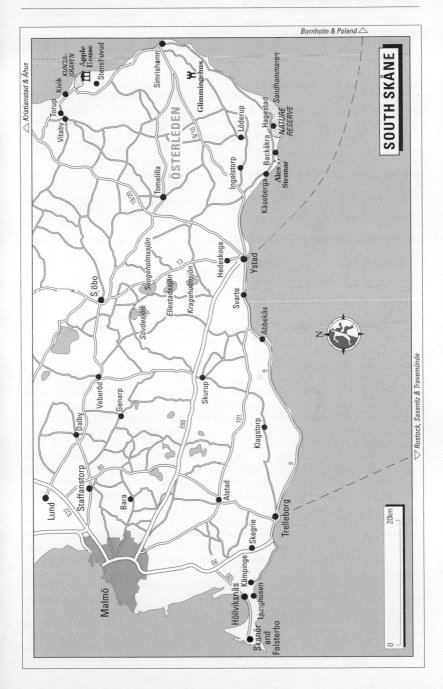

SOUTH SKÅNE

# Skanör, Falsterbro and Kämpinge

A few kilometres on, at the fan-shaped southwest tip of the country, lie the bathing resorts of Skanör and Falsterbro. Crossing a canal, which was dug by Swedes during World War II to provide a transport alternative to occupied Danish coastal waters, you arrive in the early-medieval town of **SKANÖR**. Founded as part of the Hanseatic commercial system, due to the abundance of herring off this stretch of the coast, the town was an important commercial centre. In the first years of this century, Skanör and its neighbour Falsterbro (see below) became fashionable bathing resorts for rich Malmö families and, although both have since gone in and out of vogue, they are once again desirable destinations for much the same set. There's not much to see in Skanör – its castle ruin no more than a grassy hill – but its beaches are superb: long ribbons of white sand bordering an extensive bird and nature reserve. From the beach, you can see across the reserve to Skanör's two-sectioned church, built in two eras, half medieval, half High Gothic. When the herring swam on to new waters in the sixteenth century, the town lost its importance, and the church never received its intended updates, making it all the more appealing. From the little harbour, it's a pleasant walk to the town square and the lovely old cottages lining Mellangatan. At the corner of Dykengatan is another classic Scånian inn, *Gästgivaregården* (March–Sept Mon & Wed–Fri 5–10pm, Sat 1–11pm, Sun 1–6pm). The only thing to do here is admire the pretty houses, but if you want to **stay**, and the beach is worth it, *Hotell Gässlingen* (☎040/47 30 35, fax 47 51 81; Sept–April ④, weekends outside summer ③), at Rådhustorget 6, is a lovely, simple place. If you're **camping**, there are plenty of places to throw down a tent for free, but be careful not to pick a protected bird reserve area.

## Falsterbro

**FALSTERBRO**, just 2km south, is also very picturesque, attracting the yuppie coterie of Swedish society. Along with its castle ruin, eighteenth-century lighthouse and church, it also boasts really fine beaches and is slightly livelier than its sister town. A couple of restaurants worth trying are *Kaptensgården,* Stadsalleyn (Mon–Sat 5pm–midnight, Sun 1–10pm), an elegant establishment with a garden terrace and occasional live jazz, and, just a few steps up the road, the new *Café Restaurant Allen.* Here the happy hour stretches from noon to 5pm, and the after-beach menu (2–5pm) comprises light snacks for 35kr, such as good sweet-herring salad, ice cream and cakes. Falsterbro's train station (which closed down when tourism declined) is now a gallery for contemporary art exhibitions.

## Kämpinge

The hamlet of **KÄMPINGE** (5km east of Falsterbro on Road 100 or bus #182 from Vellinge) is home to a remarkable **amber workshop and museum** (mid-June to mid-Aug 10am–6pm; at other times call ☎040/45 45 04); isolated among fields of yellow rape, the museum is signposted "Bärnstenssnideri 500 metres". After heavy storms, dull yellow nuggets of rough Baltic amber are regularly washed up on the shores around this part of the southwest, and particularly at Skånor beach. This remarkable centre was set up by one man, Leif Bros, who is dedicated to studying the fossilized pine-tree resin. The most valuable pieces on show are those with insects trapped inside (known as inclusions); the most striking examples are of mating couples and insects caught in a web with a spider captor. In the early 1990s, Bros's collections drew the attention of the makers of

**Jurassic Park,** who descended on the place to research how DNA from dinosaur blood could be enclosed in the stomach of mosquitoes caught in the sticky resin millions of years ago and preserved with the DNA intact. Regular tours, in English, give you a full run-down on amber and all its uses – in ancient times, it was worn to guard against baby swapping. For today's market, the raw material, milky and pale beneath its rough crust, is put under intense pressure and heat to create the much-sought-after translucent cognac glow. If you're interested, you can find out how to tell the real from the fake stuff – bakelite from the 1920s, and plastic from present-day North Africa: hold a heated needle to amber and the smell of the prehistoric resin should immediately become apparent.

# Trelleborg

Following the south coast heading east, the rolling fields are punctuated by World War II concrete bunkers, some now converted into unlikely looking summer houses. **TRELLEBORG**, around 15km from Kämpinge, greets road traffic with a curtain of low-level industry blocking all views of the sea – although this won't bother you too much if you're taking one of the ferries over to the German towns of Rostock, Sassnitz or Travemünde. Yet behind the graceless factories there's a busy little town; its main attractions are the inspired reconstruction of a recently discovered Viking fortress and a gallery of works by the sculptor Axel Ebbe.

From the ferry terminals on the sea front, walk up Kontinengatan, past the tourist office (see "Practicalities" for details), which supplies a good free leaflet, *A Couple of Hours in Trelleborg,* a realistic view of how long most people will stay. A few minutes' further on is the **Axel Ebbe Gallery** in a compact, 1930s' Functionalist building that once was the local bank. Ebbe's superb sculptures make for a powerful collection of sensual nudes, all larger than life and in black or white stone. At the turn of the century, Ebbe's gently erotic work was celebrated in Paris, though in Copenhagen, his graceful, sprawling female, *Atlas's Daughter,* caused an outcry. Embracing much of the new styles of the era – Art Nouveau, Neoclassical and National Romanticism – his sculptures are elegant, rhythmic and romantic. The exhibition also includes distinctive, goblin-like figures that provide a lighter touch but are less interesting. A few steps into the **Stadsparken**, opposite, is Trelleborg's main square, which is dominated by Ebbe's *Sea Monster,* a fountain comprising a serpentine fiend intertwined with a characteristically sensual mermaid.

The main shopping promenade is **Algatan**, running parallel with the sea front. Walking up the street from the ferry terminal end, you'll soon come to **St Nicolai's kyrka**, which has some bright ceiling paintings, elaborate sepulchral tablets, and monks' chairs from a Franciscan monastery destroyed at the Reformation. A couple of minutes' stroll from here is Trelleborg's most dramatic new attraction, the **Trelle Fortress** (open all year; free), which cancels any need to visit the less impressive run-through of local Viking life at the town museum (Östergatan 58). Surrounded by a moat, the original circular fortress, dating from around 980AD, was built by King Harald Blue Tooth around a seventh-century settlement of pit houses and was made entirely of earth and wood. Archeologists have made comparisons with four almost identical forts in Denmark and, using a certain amount of guesswork, have built an impressive structure with split oak logs. By the eleventh century, the fortress's days were over, Vandals – the original kind – had raged along the Scånian coast and the inhabitants had fled inland.

## Practicalities

The train station is close to the ferry terminal; three **trains** a day run from Malmö to Trelleborg, timed to connect with the Sassnitz ferry. **Buses** stop at the bus terminal behind the main square. **Ferry** departures to Germany are daily and pretty regular – check "Travel details" at the end of the chapter for schedules.

The **tourist office**, just off Kontinengatan at Hamngatan 4 (mid-June to mid-Aug Mon–Fri 9am–8pm, Sat 9am–6pm, Sun 1–6pm; rest of year Mon to Fri 9am–5pm; ☎0410/533 22, fax 134 86) is tucked in behind a hot dog stand, but boasts its own pleasant café, *Garvaregården*. If you do want to **stay**, the tourist office will book **private rooms** for 130kr plus a 35kr booking fee. There is a dismal looking pre-fab **hostel-cum-hotel**, *Night Stop* at Östergatan 59, but it's clean inside (single rooms 190kr, doubles at 290kr, triples at 390kr). Open all night, it's ideal for late ferry arrivals. To get in, walk back to the phone box on the corner of Johan Kocksgatan and dial ☎15*. The cheap *Hotel Standard*, Österbrogatan 4 (☎0410/104 38, fax 71 18 66; ③), is central and although shabby, the rooms are big and better than the entrance suggests. At the other end of the spectrum, *Hotel Dannegården,* Standgatan 32 (☎0410/71 11 20, fax 170 76; ⑤/③), is a beautiful 1910 villa surrounded by scented bushes, with just five double rooms in original Art Nouveau style.

Even if you don't stay here, *Hotel Dannegården* is the finest place for a romantic meal (Mon–Fri noon–2pm & 6–10pm, closed July). Three courses will set you back 275kr and the gourmet menu is dearer still at 495kr, but it's excellent food and a lovely ambience. On Algatan, a couple of reasonable konditori **cafés** include the verandahed *Billings*, and *Palmblads*. If you have to wait for a bus, a pleasant place for a coffee is the 1912, National Romantic water tower behind the bus station. Just 50m from the Axel Ebbe Gallery is a **swimming pool**, which also offers saunas (18kr), turkish baths (45kr) and a solarium (30kr), plus massage for men (Tues) and women (Thurs). One wall of the pool is covered by a remarkable 1940s' mosaic. For **money exchange**, there's a *Forex* exchange at Friisgatan 1, just outside the Rostock ferry terminal (Mon–Fri 7am–7pm, Sat 7am–1pm, Sun 10am–7pm).

# Smygehamn and Smygehuk

Around a third of the way from Trelleborg to Ystad along coast Road 9 (bus #183), the hamlet of Smygehamn prides itself on being Sweden's most southerly point. Half a kilometre before you reach this tiny harbour village, neighbouring **SMYGEHUK** has little to it except a particularly cosy **youth hostel** (for details see opposite), which is part of a range of pretty old wooden houses clustered around a quaint **lighthouse**, dated 1883 (it's now superseded by an automatic offshore beacon). Climbing the lighthouse's spiral stairs affords a panoramic sea view, and at its base is **Captain Brincks' Cabin**. This old lighthouse laundry is crammed with seafaring artefacts from the travels of the old sea captain, who lives in another little cottage nearby and who is more than happy to regale you with nautical tales. The bus stops right outside the hostel.

Walk through the richly flowered, and even more richly nettled, undergrowth along the coast and you'll soon reach **SMYGEHAMN**. The tiny harbour is surrounded by a few summer-time restaurants, a café and a particularly fragrant smoked-fish shop (10am–6pm), which sells excellent salmon marinated in cognac, together with bread and cutlery, for a cheap picnic. The only other shop sells all that is twee, and is full of wooden magic geese. Sweden's best-loved children's author, **Selma Lagerlöv** (whose face appears on all 20kr notes), created a magic goose on which her young hero, Nils Holgersson, flew the length and breadth of Sweden, his travels beginning on the Scånian coast. The harbour itself was built out of a limestone quarry, and, from Smygehamn's heyday in the mid-nineteenth century until the 1950s, lime burning was big business here. The area is still dotted with lime kilns, odd, igloo-like structures with cupola roofs. If the fancy takes you, crawl on all fours inside the oldest one, just a few metres from the harbour, where the limestone was burned at a thousand degrees. Back from the harbour, Axel Ebbe's *The Embrace* is a good example of his Romantic style – a female nude, embracing the elements, rises up from the scrubland (for more on Ebbe, see p.209).

### Practicalities

The **tourist office** in Smygehuk is by the harbour (June–Aug daily 10am–6pm; ☎0410/240 53), inside a fine, early nineteenth-century corn warehouse, which was originally used to store smuggled goods during the British blockade of the Napoleonic Wars. The amiable tourist office staff have few suggestions once you've seen the local megalithic tombstones (for which they give directions), but the building is worth a visit if only for the very cheap coffee (8kr including refills). If you want to stay in the area – and it is a peaceful haven – aside from Smygehuk's **youth hostel** (see opposite; mid-May to mid-Sept; ☎0410/245 83, fax 245 09; 100kr), which is in the lighthouse keeper's house and has a big kitchen and homely living area full of books, the tourist office can book **private rooms** from just 90kr per person, plus 35kr booking fee. The nearest **hotels** are in Trelleborg, 13km away, but *Smygehus Havsbad*, an old bathing house (☎0410/243 90, fax 293 43) just 500m away, has four-bed cabins for 850kr, including breakfast. There's a **restaurant**, sauna and swimming pool here, too. If the Smygehuk hostel is full, a **private hostel**, *Hedmansgården* (☎0410/234 74), 3km inland at Bösteläge, has rooms at 190kr per person including breakfast.

# Ystad

An hour by *Pågatåg* train from Malmö, the medieval market town of **YSTAD** is exquisitely well preserved – its core of quaint cobbled lanes lined with cross-timbered cottages and its chocolate-box central square ooze rural charm (though the prettiness of the centre may come as a surprise if you've arrived at the train station down by the murky docks). With the stunningly beautiful coastal region of Österlen stretching northwest from town in the direction of Kristianstad (see p.220) and some excellent walking to the north of town (see p.214), Ystad is a splendid place to base yourself for a day or so. It is also where **ferries** depart for the Danish island of Bornholm and to Poland.

## Arrival, information and accommodation

From the **train station**, cross the tracks to St Knuts Torg where the **tourist office** (mid-June to mid-Aug Mon–Fri 9am–7pm, Sat 11am–7pm, Sun 1–7pm, rest of year Mon–Fri 9am–5pm; ☎0411/772 79, fax 55 55 85) is next to the art gallery. St Knuts Torg is also where buses from Lund (#X300), Kristianstad (*Skåne Express*) and Simrishamn (#572) will drop you off, and where buses leave for destinations along the coast and into the rest of Skåne. There are no buses, however, from Malmö to Ystad. You have to either take a *Pågatåg* local train from Malmö, or bus #183 from Trelleborg/Smygehamn to Skateholm and then bus #330 to Ystad. There are also no trains from Ystad to Kristianstad; to go by train you have to return to Malmö and take the inland train. The **ferry** terminal is behind the train station, signposted "Till Färjorna" – turn left and walk for ten minutes along the quayside to the ticket office and departure hall. Tickets to Poland cost from 220kr one-way (9hr crossing), or you can buy a 420kr ticket, which covers a return trip if made within four days. To get to Borgholm costs 135kr one-way (2.5hr crossing); if you return on the same day, it's the same cost as a single ticket. **Bike rental**, a great way to see the surrounding cycle-friendly landscape, is available from the tourist office (60kr per day, 300kr per week).

## Accommodation

There are several good and reasonably priced **hotels** (see below) in town and one at the beach. The **youth hostel** is close to the *Saltsjöbaden*, on the beach at Sandskogen (open all year; ☎0411/665 66; 95kr) – take bus #572 or #304 – but it's limited to groups from September to May. There is a neighbouring **campsite** (mid-April to mid-Sept; ☎0411/192 70) with cabins for rent (from 110kr per person).

*HOTELS*

**Bäckagården**, Bäckagården 36 (☎0411/198 48, fax 757 15). More a guest house than hotel in a converted home just behind the tourist office. Price includes breakfast. ②

**Continental**, Hamngatan 13 (☎0411/137 00, fax 332 21). A fine, classic hotel touted as Sweden's oldest; its substantial stuccoed facade opens onto a grand lobby of Corinthian topped pillars, marble and crystal chandeliers. Bedrooms are modern, Italian style. The breakfasts are a treat (see p.214). ④/③

**Prins Carl**, Hamngatan 8 (☎0411/737 50, fax 665 30). A mid-range place with rooms reserved for non-smokers, others adapted for people with disabilities or allergies. ③/②

**Saltsjöbaden**, Saltsjöbadsvägen 6 (☎0411/136 30, fax 55 58 35). Renowned for its beach-side position, just east of town, this large, 100-year-old hotel has endless modern corridors tacked on. There's a sauna and summer-only pool, and a restaurant in the original salt-water bathing house. ④/③

**Sekelgården**, Stora Västergatan 9 (☎0411/739 00, fax 189 97). A charming, small, family-run hotel in the heart of Ystad. A former merchant's house from 1793, this friendly, informal hotel features a cobbled courtyard garden dripping with scented flowers beneath a huge willow. Rooms, all en suite, in both the main house and the lovely old tannery at the back. Excellent breakfast included. ③/②

**Tornväktaven**, Stora Östergatan 33 (☎0411/129 54, fax 729 27). Plain and cheap, with breakfast buffet included, this is a reasonable choice if *Sekelgården* (above) is full. No summer reduction. ②

# The Town

Turning left from the station and ferry terminals and right up Hamngatan leads to the well-proportioned **Stortorget**, a grand old square around which twist picturesque streets. The thirteenth-century **St Maria kyrka** is a handsome centrepiece, with additions from nearly every century since it was begun. In the 1880s, these rich decorative features were removed, as they were thought "unsightly," and only the most interesting ones were returned during a restoration programme forty years later. Inside, the Baroque early seventeenth-century pulpit is worth a look for the fearsome face carved beneath it and, opposite, the somewhat chilling medieval crucifix, which was placed here on the orders of Karl XII to remind the preacher of Christ's suffering. The figure of Christ is wearing a mop of human hair – last century, a local parishioner sacrificed all his own in an attempt at realism. Notice also the green box pews at either side of the entrance, which were reserved for women who hadn't yet been received back into the church after childbirth.

If you stay in Ystad, you'll soon get acquainted with a tradition that harks back to the seventeenth century: from a room in the church's watchtower, a night watchman blows a haunting tune on a bugle, every fifteen minutes from 9.15pm to 3am, as a safeguard against the outbreak of fire. The idea was that if one of the thatched cottages went up in flames, the bugle would sound repeatedly for all to go and help extinguish the blaze. The sounding through the night was to assure the town that the watchman was still awake; until the mid-nineteenth century, if he slept on duty he was liable to be executed. The melancholic bellowing continues today; in fact, it only ceased during World War II, and then the residents complained they couldn't sleep in the unbroken silence.

From Stortorget, it's a short stroll up Garvaregränd, past art and craft workshops – *Krukmakaren* on the right is in a remarkably higgledy-piggledy house – up Klostergatan to **Ystadbygdens Museum** (Mon–Fri 11am–6pm, Wed till 8pm, Sat & Sun noon–4pm; 30kr, under 16s free). Set in the thirteenth-century Gråbröder (Greyfriar's) Monastery, the contents comprise the usual local history collections, but are given piquancy by their preserved medieval surroundings. After the monks were driven out during the Reformation, the monastery declined and was used as a hospital, then a poorhouse, a distillery and finally a dump. A decision to demolish it in 1901 was overturned, and today its mellow setting is worth a visit; outside there's a small lake alive with ducks and geese.

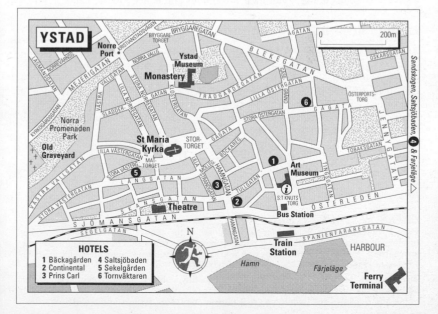

---

**WALKING AROUND YSTAD**

The forested lake region 20km north of Ystad provides plenty of hiking possibilities, either along organized trails or in undeveloped tracts where you can camp
rough. Take any bus north in the direction of **Sjöbo** (by car take Road 13), and
you'll link with the **Skåneleden** trail (or the "Long Trail"), which takes a hundred-
kilometre circular route from just outside Ystad. The tourist office (see p.211) can
provide route plans as well as details on where to find places to eat and stay en
route. You can also head north on foot from Ystad to Hedeskoga and then follow
trails through a bracelet link of forest-fringed **lakes**, Krageholmsjön, Ellestadssjön
and Snogeholmssjön, up to Sövdesjön (a 20km hike).

---

If you want to explore more of the old town, it's still possible to use a map of
Ystad from 1753, supplied by the tourist office, to guide yourself around the
streets. Lilla Västergatan was the main street in the seventeenth and eighteenth
centuries, and if you stroll down from Mattorget, a small square behind St Maria
kyrka, you'll see the best of the Lilliputian cottages. Not far from the church, up
Lilla or Stora Norregatan, is Norra Port, the original northern entrance to the
town. More appealing, though, is a stroll through nearby **Norra Promenaden**, a
strip of mature horse-chestnut trees and surrounding parkland. Here you'll find
*Café Promenaden* (also see "Eating, drinking and nightlife"), a white pavillion built
in the 1870s to house a genteel café and a dance hall for the brass band. Inside, it
retains its charm, with original velvet settees and silver samovar. The café is
something of a favourite spot for funeral teas (the small park borders on a graveyard), with many of Ystad's older residents wanting to be remembered at the
place where most of them met their loved ones and danced to the band.

# Eating, drinking and nightlife

There is a fair selection of places to eat in Ystad, with some atmospheric **cafés** and
fine **restaurants** (see below); most of the latter are on Stortorget. To start the
day, even if you are not staying there, you can stuff yourself at the *Continental*'s
huge **breakfast buffet** (Mon–Fri 7–10am, Sat & Sun 8–10.30am; 60kr), ideal if
you've just come off a morning ferry. Aside from the bar-cum-restaurant *Prince
Charles Pub* (listed opposite), **nightlife** is pretty minimal – the only trendy club
being *Starshine* at Osterportstorg, east from Stortorget (follow Stora Östergatan,
on some maps referred to only as Gågatan, meaning "pedestrianized street").
There's a disco and bar here (age limit 18 on Thurs, 20 on Sat), and just once a
month, "Stardust" is an evening for 35s and over (although the lower age limit is
25). Otherwise, locals tend to take a bus thirty minutes north to **Tingballa**, where
there are a couple of dance halls.

## CAFÉS, RESTAURANTS AND PUBS

**Café Promenaden**, in Norra Promenaden, north of the centre. An excellent café serving
luscious fruit pies with coffee and a range of beers. There's also a good restaurant menu,
specializing in salmon, with lunches at 52kr and good-value evening meals for 70–90kr.
June–Aug 11am–10pm.

**The English Book Café**, on Gäsegränd. Down a tiny, cobbled street off Stora Östergatan
and inside this precariously leaning eighteenth-century wooden house, it's all old English
china and books to read while you're eating home-baked scones and tea. The gardens

are also a treat, kept to their 1778 shape and with the original water pump. 10am–5pm most days.

**Lotta's,** on Stortorget. The most (justifiably) popular restaurant in town, it gets packed each evening in summer with locals eating good food and enjoying friendly service. Mon–Fri 5–11pm.

**Prince Charles Pub** on Hamngatan next door to the *Prins Carl Hotel.* A maroon velour, English-style pub and restaurant serving a big meat and fish menu, with live music on Fri and Sat nights. July daily noon–1am, rest of year Mon–Sat 4pm–1am, Sun noon–10pm.

**Rådhuskälleren,** in the cellars of the Rådhus. Rather more sedate than *Lotta's* opposite, with candle-lit lunch (55kr) and dinners (200kr), this multivaulted 700-year-old prison is romantic, but the service can be less than convivial. Mon–Fri 11.30am–2pm & 6–10pm, Sat 5–11pm.

**Saltsjöbad,** at the beach. The hotel's restaurant does daily lunches (50kr) and a wide à la carte menu for all tastes (main dishes 80–200kr); in July there are special menus and live music.

# Österlen and the coast to Åhus

It's easy to see how the landscape of the southeastern corner of Skåne, known as **Österlen**, has lured writers and artists to its coastline and plains. Here sunburst-yellow fields of rape stand out against a cobalt-blue sky and are punctuated only by white cottages, blood-red poppy fields and the odd black windmill. However cynical you might be about tourist office blurbs, these ones don't exaggerate. Along with the vivid beauty of the countryside, Österlen has a number of engaging sights, notably the Viking ruin, **Ales Stennar**, pretty villages and plenty of smooth, sandy beaches. Moving further northeast are the orchards of Sweden's apple region, **Kivik**, with its fragrant and surreal Apple House museum and a nearby Bronze Age cairn. **Åhus**, a fairly low-key resort famous for smoked eels, ends this stretch of the coast.

Unfortunately, **getting around** this part of the country isn't so easy; the only major road, Road 9 to Kristianstad via Simrishamn, cuts out the main corner of Österlen. The whole area is poorly served by buses, and the only train service is the *Pågatåg* train from Ystad to Simrishamn; the last one leaves at 6.30pm, so if you want to get to Kristianstad on the connecting bus, it's worth leaving mid-afternoon. If you haven't got a car, the best way to get around is to combine walking and cycling with public transport.

## The coast to Ales Stennar

There are two ways to get to Ales Stennar from Ystad: either take bus #322 (20min) or rent a bike and follow the coast cycle track for the 20km journey. The track runs through an area of pine forest opening onto white sandy beaches with excellent bathing opportunities. From here (following signs to Kåseberga), you'll pass through a thick wedge of attractive, but uneventful, rolling fields that stretch for several kilometres; when you get to the sign for Ingelstorp, you'll find a very simple but idyllically set cottage and stable. Built into the hills, with a private beach just 400m behind, and crammed with old furniture and its own rudimentary kitchen, the cottage is not for luxury seekers, but a perfect base if you feel like communing with nature (☎0411/222 25; double rooms go for 150kr per person).

Four kilometres on is **Ales Stennar**, near the hamlet of **KÅSEBERGA**. An awe-inspiring Swedish Stonehenge, it is believed to have been a Viking meeting place and consists of 56 stones forming a 67m-long boat-shaped edifice, prow and stern denoted by two appreciably larger monoliths. The site was hidden for centuries beneath shifting sands, which only cleared in 1958. Even now the sight is buried several metres into the sand, and it's difficult to imagine how these great stones, not native to the region, were transported here. Ales Stennar stands on a windy, flat-topped hill, and despite the inevitable tourists snapping away at the ancient site (most of whom don't bother to climb up), there's a magestic time-lessness at the top that more than rewards your climb.

To reach the site from the nearby car park, you pass a string of low, white cottages; if you're hungry, it's well worth filling up at one of them, *Café Solståndet* (the owners live here, so opening hours are flexible). You can buy baguettes (40kr), cakes and piles of chocolates, and if you're camping rough, they serve breakfast (8–10am). They also do **B&B** (☎ & fax 0411/272 73; 135kr per person, 30kr for sheets & towels, plus 45kr for a good breakfast). Down by Kåseberga's harbour, below the stones, the sense of enchantment is instantly lost, amid bus-loads of tourists who spend their time at the tourist stalls and the fish smokery, the scent of which is the only appealing thing about the place.

# Backåkra and the Hagestad Nature Reserve

Five kilometres further is **BACKÅKRA**, a small village surrounded by three nature reserves, the best of which is the Hagestad Nature Reserve, originally set up by a former United Nations secretary-general, Dag Hammarskjöld, whose home is now a museum. The reserve offers some gentle walks and the best beach in Skåne. If you're not taking the #322 bus, there's a worthwhile detour on the way to Backåkra to a particularly good antique shop called *Antikhandel*, in an ancient thatched cottage a little way off the rough single-lane road (about 2km from Ales Stennar at the signpost for Grimshög, walk through the fields for 10min). Although fairly expensive, it sells genuine Swedish glass, ceramics and wooden furniture from the past three centuries, much of it easy to carry (☎0411/261 38 for changing opening times). A little further, just before you get to Backåkra at **Löderups Strandbad** is a beautifully situated **campsite**, with a café and restaurant; while in the village itself is a well-equipped *STF* **youth hostel** in an old school house (mid-May to Aug; Sept–April book in advance at Ystad tourist office; ☎0411/260 80; 100kr per person in a double, 70kr for a dormitory bed; breakfast 40kr). There's a bus stop outside the door and you can rent **bikes** from the hostel at 35kr per day, perfect for exploring the nature reserves.

### Hagestad Nature Reserve and the Dag Hammarskjöld Museum

For a day in really splendid natural surroundings, it would be hard to beat **Hagestad Nature Reserve**, just a few minutes from the youth hostel. Thousands of pines were planted here in the eighteenth and nineteenth centuries to bind the sandy earth, and, together with oaks and birches, they make up a densely forest-ed area; the clumps of gnarled and stunted oaks are particularly distinctive. It's especially beautiful in mid-summer when the orchids and heathers colour the for-est floor; if you're lucky, you may also see elk, badgers and roe deer, while buz-zards and golden orioles are often sighted above.

In the midst of the nature reserve, uphill on heathland towards Backåkra is an old farmstead bought by Dag Hammarskjöld, a secretary-general to the United Nations in the 1950s. His love of the Scånian coast led him to buy the farm and the sur-rounding sixty acres in order to save it from developers. Hammarskjöld was killed in a plane crash in 1961, but he willed the farm and its range of intriguing contents, including collections of art from all over the world, to *Svenska Turistföreningen* (Swedish Touring Club), which now runs the house as a **museum** (opening times vary; call Mr August Trulin on ☎0411/260 10 or 261 51; 25kr). Today, the heathland character of the land is preserved by not allowing cars up to the farm itself, but it's worth the walk to view such diverse works as an ancient Egyptian painting of the jackal-headed god Anubis, Greek bronzes from 200BC, oriental ivories and original contemporary pieces by Barbara Hepworth, Picasso and Matisse.

Hagestad Nature Reserve is also the home of the most glorious **beach** in Skåne. Walking through the trees and you'll soon reach a bright white ribbon of sand – called **Sandhammaren** on maps – backed by steep dunes and lapped by turquoise waters.

## Simrishamn and Glimmingehus Castle

There's not much to the little fishing town of **SIMRISHAMN** (about 25km north of Backåkra), although its old quarter of fondant-coloured tiny cottages and a church, orginally built as a twelfth-century fishers' chapel, are certainly pretty enough. The nearby, unexceptional **museum** is full of the usual archeological finds and bits and pieces of farm and fishing equipment. There is, however, a **summer catamaran** service to the Danish island of **Bornholm** from the town's pleasant harbour (see "Travel details"). *Hotell Kockska Garden*, Sturgatan 25 (☎0414/41 17 55, fax 41 19 78; ③), is a comfortable **accommodation** option, housed in a renovated tavern. For **bike rental**, ask at the **tourist office**, Tulhusgatan 2 (mid-June to mid-Aug Mon–Fri 9am–8pm, Sat noon–8pm, Sun 2–8pm; rest of the year Mon–Fri 9am–5pm; ☎0414/41 06 66).

One impressive sight, just off Road 9, a few kilometres inland from Simrishamn, is the uncompromising brick-shaped thirteenth-century **Glimmingehus Castle** (June–Aug daily 10am–6pm; April, May & Sept daily 9am–5pm; 20kr). Standing like a fist in the flat landscape and visible for miles around, Glimmingehus lacks any of the aesthetic niceties of most of Sweden's castles, but it is remarkably well preserved. One of the few projections on its flat facade is an oriel from which missiles could be dropped, clear evidence of its role as a fortification. In fact, the architect Adam Van Duran was drafted in to dream up as many impenetrable features as possible, and he certainly did the owners proud, combining 2m-thick walls, slits instead of windows and a deep cellar in the event of a siege – the only concession to comfort was an ingenious heating system spreading warmth from the kitchen upwards. Ironically, this was one castle that was never attacked; the only threat to its existence was Karl XI's desire to demolish Glimmingehus in order to avoid Danish guerillas getting hold of it once Skåne had became a Swedish province.

## Kivik and around

Almost halfway from Simrishamn north along the coast to Åhus (take Road 118 for about 20km), **Kivik** is Sweden's **apple region**, the dark forests and hilly green fields giving way to endless orchards. In springtime there's a snow of blossom and in the autumn a sensational mass of burnt colour and sweet smells. The village of **KIVIK** has no real centre, but the bus stops outside *Kivik Vardhus* hotel (see "Practicalities" overleaf). The uncommercialized harbour is just a few minutes away down Södergatan, and within a couple of kilometres are a number of sights:

Sweden's most notable Bronze Age remains, **Kungsgraven** (King's Grave); a cider factory with an **Apple House** that has to be seen to be believed; and **Stenshuvud National Park**, which offers fine walks. In all, it makes for a day of enjoyable sightseeing and meandering. Kivik also hosts one of the country's biggest **markets** for two days each July (around the middle of the month), an enormous event with stalls and family entertainment centred around the main square.

### Kungsgraven

**Kungsgraven** (May–Aug daily 10am–6pm; 10kr), just 500m from the bus stop, is a striking 75-metre Bronze Age cairn, an upturned saucer of rocks that lay hidden until discovered by a farmer in 1748. At its centre, a burial cist is entered by a banked entrance passage, and inside are eight flood-lit, three-thousand-year-old runic slabs showing pictures of horses, a sleigh and what looks like dancing seals. It's an impressive sight, though the bronze entrance hall makes it feel more like a designer bar than an ancient monument. For coffee and cake in a gorgeous setting, try *Café Sågmöllan*, in the old thatched mill cottage by the stream next to the ticket kiosk.

### Kiviksmusteri and the Apple House

Two kilometres from the grave through hills of orchards (follow the signs), **Kiviksmusteri** is a cider factory, with a shop selling apple juices, sauces, ciders, dried rings and wines by the crate. You can't tour the factory, but more entertaining is the newly opened **Apple House** (9am–6pm, tours 40kr, children under 16 free). A non-profit-making venture, the Apple House is aimed at making visitors as obsessed with apples as its dedicated workers, who are dressed in flowing apple-printed smocks. In a new building painted in apple greens and reds, there is an entire apple museum, each room infused with a different smell. A room devoted to great apples in history (Adam and Eve's, Newton's etc) smells of cider, while a room detailing attempts to create an insect-resistant industrial apple smells of apple pie. Other less sane exhibitions concentrate on such topics as the symphonic soul of apples, while an internet facility allows addicts to send apple-related messages to one another around the world.

### Stenshuvuds National Park

Just 200m beyond the Apple House, **Stenshuvuds National Park** is a perfect place to come back to reality. The hill is almost 100m-high, and the view from the top – which is covered with walking trails – is superb, particularly over Hanöberg to the east. Sand lizards and smooth snakes have lived here for eight thousand years. Although you're unlikely to see any reptiles, you can take a self-guided walk that leads around remnants of an ancient fortress. There are also special wheelchair-accessible paths that lead through the beautiful forested hillsides.

### Practicalities

The frequent *Skåne Express* **bus** runs from Simrishamn to Kivik (30min) and from Kristianstad (55min). If you want to stay, the *Kivik Vardhus*, a lovely nineteenth-century vine-strewn farmhouse opposite the bus stop, is both a **hotel**, with pleasant rooms (open June–Aug; 0414/70074, fax 71020; ②), and a restaurant. Lunches cost 55kr; the speciality for dinner is local venison (11.30am–9pm). For cheaper accommodation, the *STF* **youth hostel** is in its own attractive gardens, just north of the harbour at Tittutvägen and only five minutes' walk from the bus stop (open all year; ☎0414/711 95; 100kr).

Another good **place to eat**, *Kärnhuset,* is at the Apple House (see opposite). It serves only local produce such as fish, chicken and vegetables with an inevitable emphasis on apple deserts and exceptionally good fresh-pressed cider. Back near the harbour, *Café Gallite* on Eliselundsvägen offers coffee, cakes and Scånian *spettekaka*. If you've yet to try this somewhat overrated crisp meringue-like confection that's whisked up into a half-metre-high sugary mountain and eaten all over the county, this is a good place to indulge yourself as it's sold in bite-size pieces for 4kr. The café is named after Gallite, a character created by local writer and wannabe pirate Fritzhof Nilsonn, who lived in the adjoining house. A witty sculpture of him stands close by, and his grave in Kivik's little churchyard reads, "Here lies one who put off everything until tomorrow until the day he died – which he did on time." There's also an excellent harbourside fish smokery called *Bahres* (daily 10am–6pm), where you can taste a dozen varieties of pickled herring and smoked eel. **Bikes**, a great choice for the local sights, especially the orchards, can be rented at the harbour kiosk (mid-June to mid-Aug 10am–10pm; 75kr per day).

# Åhus

Once a major trading port, and in medieval times a city of considerable ecclesiastical importance, **Åhus**, 55km north of Simrishamn, today relies on holidaying Swedes for its income. The town is famed for its eels, which appear on menus all over the country, smoked and usually served with scrambled eggs, and for its popular but unexceptional ice cream. There are three areas of possible interest: the old centre with its bulky and impressive church, the harbour and the River Helge, and, finally, to the northwest of town, the beaches.

From the tourist office (see "Practicalities" overleaf), it's a short walk up Köpmannagatan to the beautiful old cobbled main square. The **museum** (mid-June to mid-Aug daily 1–6pm; Sept Mon–Fri 1–6pm; free) is in the strawberry-painted old Rådhus, but holds no surprises. The twelfth-century **St Maria kyrka** behind the museum is more appealing and wonderfully preserved, its sheer size attesting to the town's former eminence. There's a lively-looking altarpiece and high-ended pews painted a rather surprising shade of turquoise, but it's one of the gravestones in the graveyard that really raises eyebrows. Take a look at the headstone of Captain Måns Mauritsson, which stands between the church and the museum. According to the inscription, the captain's wife, Helena Sjöström, was 133 years old when she died, and her daughters were born when she was 82 and 95 years old respectively. The captain only lived to 101. At nearby Västerport (walk to the end of Västergatan from the centre) is **Tobaksmonopolets Lada** (free to enter), a building that contains tobacco labels and all the paraphernalia of tobacco processing. For 250 years, the weed was very important in Åhus; every household had a tobacco patch in their gardens, until the government cancelled their contract with the growers in 1964 and the industry here finally came to an end.

Beyond this, there's little more to do than cut through from the main square down Västra Hamngatan to the waterside, where small pleasure yachts line the harbour, a pretty spot if you avert your eyes from the industrial hinterland to the left. For the **beach**, head out on Järnvägsgatan, behind the tourist office, past a run of old train carriages – there are no trains running now – and left up Ellegatan, following signs for **Åhus Strand**.

## Practicalities

Unless you're driving, it's easiest to aproach by bus from Kristianstad (there are also sightseeing boat trips between the two towns; see p.223), 20km to the north-west (#551; 25min). The bus stops at the **tourist office**, Köpmannagatan 2 (June–Aug Mon–Fri 9am–7pm, Sat 9am–6pm, Sun 2–6pm; Sept–May Mon–Fri 9am–5pm ; ☎044/24 01 06, fax 24 38 98). The **youth hostel** (open all year – book through tourist office Sept–May; ☎ 044/24 85 35; 100kr) is at Stavgatan 3, just a few metres away. Alternatively, you can stay on the bus for an extra few minutes to the beach, where there are plenty of hotels and campsites. If you want **hotel** accommodation in Åhus itself, *Gästgivaregåten*, by the lakeside at the harbour, has pricey rooms (③), all with exposed beams and waterside views, but is otherwise fairly standard and offers no summer reductions. At the beach, *Hotel Åhus Strand* (☎044/28 93 00, fax 24 94 80; ②, small summer reduction) is reasonable, if plain, and convenient for the beach. Nearby, *Sports Hotel* is owned by the *Åhus Strand* (book rooms through them) and is very cheap at 260kr for a double, but dismal to look at and really a hostel. Åhus **campsite** is in the forest near the beach and has a heated open-air pool and a restaurant (open all year; ☎044/24 89 69).

There's a **bike rental** shop on Ellegatan (on the way to the beach) that also rents out double-pedalled buggy bikes at 40kr per hour. If you don't take the local bus out to the beach, the twenty-minute walk takes you past some weather-worn but fine old suburban houses.

There are some lovely **places to eat** in Åhus. Down by the harbour, the genteel *Gästgivaregård* specializes in Baltic fish dishes (Mon–Fri 11.30am–2pm, Sat 4–10pm, Sun 1–5pm), but for the most enjoyable and relaxed place, walk 200m along the waterside to *Ostermans* (May–Sept daily 3.30–10.30pm) at Gamla Skeppsbron. At this small wooden restaurant at the water's edge, Greenland prawns are the only item on the menu, and you buy your meal by weight – a kilogram costs 180kr, and most people manage half a kilo with bread, sauces and beer. For a cheap but delightful café-restaurant, head back up Västra Hamngatan where at *Gallericaféet* (June–Aug daily noon–6pm) is a small art gallery and garden restaurant, which again specializes in local seafood. Try sandwiches filled with smoked eel, warm smoked salmon or herrings in dill (30–38kr), and the main meals of herring and sour cream or salmon fillets (50–90kr). The café is built over the twelfth-century cemetery of the old cloistered monastery. Every July, there's a joint **jazz festival** with Kristianstad; ask at the tourist office for details.

# Kristianstad

Twenty kilometres inland, eminently likable **KRISTIANSTAD** (for its correct pronunciation, try a gutteral "Krwi-chwan-sta") is eastern Skåne's most substantial historic centre – a Renaissance town created by Christian IV, Denmark's seventeenth-century "builder-king". Dating from 1614 (during the brief 44-year period of Danish rule over Kristianstad), it's a shining example of the king's architectural preoccupations, beautifully proportioned central squares and broad gridded streets flanking a wide river. It's the earliest and most evocative of Christian's Renaissance towns (there are several others in Scandinavia) he nurtured plans to make this modern fort one of Denmark's most important, and it wasn't until the mid-nineteenth century that the fortifications were finally levelled and the town spilled beyond the original perimeters. The late nineteenth-century Parisian-style boulevards, which are so pleasant to wander in today, earned the town the name "Little Paris".

## Arrival, information and accommodation

Local **buses** from Ystad (1hr 30min), Simrishamn (1hr 30min) and Åhus (30min) all stop in Kristianstad outside the central bus station on Östra Boulevarden, although the quickest way here is by **train** (the journey from Malmö takes 1hr 16min) on the ultra-comfortable Danish-built *Kustpilen Express* running regularly between Malmö on the west coast to Karlskrona on the east. The **tourist office** (June to Aug Mon–Fri 9am–8pm, Sat 9am–5pm, Sun 2–6pm; Sept–May Mon–Fri 10am–6pm; ☎044/12 19 88, fax 12 08 98) down Nya Boulevarden (right out of the train station then second left; from the bus station turn right then left) rents out **bikes**, though the centre is easily walkable. It also books **private rooms** from 125kr plus a 40kr fee, or you can check the list on the door and book yourself. There is a **campsite** with attached **youth hostel** at *Charlottsborg Camping* (open all year; ☎044/21 07 67; 100kr), 2km away (bus #22 or #23; Fri & Sat nights bus #17 to Vä from Busstorget, close to Lilla Torget). Campers can use all the hostel facilities such as the TV and lounge room.

All but one of Kristianstad's **hotels** are side by side, just a few steps from the train station. The cheapest is the very comfortable *Hotel Turisten*, Västra Storgatan 17 (☎044/12 61 50; ③/①), an old building with a friendly atmosphere, good breakfast and sauna. It's also the only hotel in town with baths in some of its bathrooms (the rest have showers only). Right of the *Turisten* is the lovely *Lillemors B&B* at no. 19 (☎044/21 95 25, mobile 070/521 68 00; ②, small summer reduction); built in the 1790s, this cosy hotel has exposed beams, a bright country-style attic dining room and big bedrooms. At no. 15 to the left of the *Turisten*, the modern and modest-looking *Grand Hotel* (☎044/10 36 00, fax 12 57 82; ⑤/②) cuts its prices by half in summer and offers excellent friendly service and well-equipped en-suite rooms, with supremely comfortable beds. A rather splendid place to spend the night is *Hotel Christian IV*, Västra Boulevarden 15 (☎044/12 63 00, fax 12 41 40; ⑤/③), just 200m south from the main run of hotels. A grand, castle-like confection built at the turn of the century in the old *Sparbank* building, it has beautifully renovated features like original fireplaces and parquet floors; the old bank vaults are now a washroom and a wine cellar.

## The Town

The most obvious starting point is the **Trefaldighetskyrkan** (Holy Trinity Church; daily 9am–5pm) right opposite the train station. It stands as a symbol of all that was glorious about Christian's Renaissance ideas. The grandiose exterior has seven magnificent spiralled gables, and the high windows allow light to flood the white interior. Inside, the most striking feature is the height of the elaborately carved pew ends: each is over 2m tall and no two are the same. Notice also the wonderful 1630-built organ facade.

Diagonally across from the church, the main square **Storatorg** contains the late nineteenth-century **Rådhus**, itself an imitation of Christian's Renaissance design. Inside the entrance, a bronze copy of the king's 1643 bust is something of a revelation; Christian is sporting a goatee beard, one earring, a single dreadlock

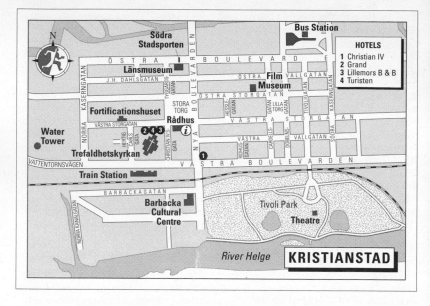

and one exposed nipple decorated with a flower motif. Opposite the town hall, the 1920s' post office and the old *Riksbank*, the latter now home to a popular steak-house and pub (see "Eating, drinking and entertainment"), offer a marked archi-tectural contrast; while the adjacent 1640s' Mayor's House is different again, with a Neoclassical yellow-stuccoed facade. The square also boasts Palle Pernevi's splintered *Icarus* fountain, which depicts the unfortunate Greek soul falling from heaven into a scaffolded building site.

Behind the post office and old bank is the **Länsmuseum** (June–Aug Mon–Fri 10am–5pm; Sept–May Mon–Fri noon–5pm; year round Wed till 8pm; free); before going inside, it's worth glancing at the building in which it is housed. It was built by Christian in 1616; he intended it to be a grand palace, but work got no further than the low buildings – the stables were turned into an arsenal as soon as they were built. Ammunition for the Danish partisans was stored here during the bloody Scånian wars, and there are exhibitions about the *Snapphare* (from the German *schnappen*, to snatch or steal), the name given to pro-Danish partisans. Aside from its historical context, the museum also has some inter-esting textiles and art collections on the top floor. If you've time on your hands, it's a pleasant stroll up Nya Boulevarden to Östra Boulevarden, where you can see **Södra Stadsporten**, the 1790s' southern town gate, one of the few bits of fortification saved before the great demolition. There's a park close by, but it's considerably duller than the lovely Tivoli Park to the south (see opposite), and it's more fun to peep in at a beautiful hidden courtyard at No. 8 JH Dahlsgatan, one block south of the town gate and to the right, a gorgeous muddle of narrow outhouses framing a courtyard around a Renaissance merchant's home. If you want a panoramic overview of both the town and the local lakes of Hammarsjön and Aradövssjön, connected by the River Helge, it's just a couple of minutes' walk west to the **water tower** (Mon–Sat 10am–6pm, Sun noon–6pm; free).

There's a small lift up the 42 floors (the stairs are kept locked) and a café at the top with wall maps for orientation.

Walking back through the town centre, a few minutes east of the Storatorg, the **Film Museum**, Östra Storgatan 53 (Tues–Fri & Sun 1–4pm; free), is heralded by a bronze, early twentieth-century movie camera outside the door. This is Sweden's oldest film studio, where the country's first films were recorded between 1909 and 1911; early flickering works are now viewable on videotape inside. Wander down any of the roads to the right and you'll reach **Tivoli Park**, where you can stroll beneath avenues of horse chestnut trees, in the centre of which is a fine Art Nouveau **theatre**, a stylish white building with characteristically curving lines of green paintwork. Its architect, Axel Anderberg, who was born in Kristianstad, also designed the Stockholm Opera (see p.92). **Sightseeing boats** (*Vattenriket*) splash their way between Kristianstad and Åhus from behind the theatre (June–Aug 3 daily; 65kr, book at the tourist office). At the northern edge of Tivoli Park, there's an art gallery, showing temporary exhibitions and housing the **Barbacka Cultural Centre**, which gives information about musical events around the town.

# Eating, drinking and entertainment

Kristianstad has a number of really good, stylish and fun places to eat. The loveliest **café** is in *Fornstuga House*, an elaborately carved Hansel-and-Gretel lodge built in 1886 in the middle of Tivoli Park (daily 10am–5pm, later if there are concerts in the park). It serves waffles and coffee, and it's worth going just for the unique, original interior. A classic and central konditori is *Du Vanders*, Hesslegatan 6 (Mon–Fri 8am–7pm, Sat 8am–5pm, Sun 10am–5pm); while at *Grafitti Café*, Västra Storgatan 45, you can fill up cheaply on baked potatoes, but it closes early (Mon–Fri 6.30pm; Sat & Sun 2pm).

A classic old **restaurant** is *Restaurant Klipper*, Östra Storgatan, a block south of JH Dahlsgatan (lunch daily 11.30am–2pm; dinner Mon–Thurs 6–10pm, Fri & Sat 6–10.30pm). Dating from 1600, the eating area is beneath atmospheric original cellar vaults with crispbread drying from the ceiling. The specialities are steaks and fowl, but prices are high, with dinner at 250kr and lunches 140kr (lunch buffets are cheaper). Nearby, *Restaurant Roma*, Östra Storgatan 15, is an inexpensive Italian restaurant worth trying for its big pizzas at 65kr. The two trendiest eating places are owned by the same people and are a must if you're interested in food. *Godsfikan* (Mon–Fri 11am–11pm, Sat 6–11pm; ☎044/11 05 20) is in the pretty red- and cream-brick station building. The kitsch decor, including pony-skin stools, hubcaps and jelly moulds, is popular with an informal "in" crowd. The food is biggish at reasonable prices (lunch 49kr; dinner 115–150kr). It's worth booking as the place packs out at weekends. *Westermanns*, Tivoligatan, is the more up-market sister restaurant, serving fine, European-style food in stylish but relaxed surroundings. For the best Swedish home cooking at very reasonable prices, it's worth jumping on the *Kustpilen Express* train 2km west to Vinslöv, where outside the station to the left you'll find *Vinslöv Gästgiveri,* a real shirt-sleeves place that makes superb food for local workers.

### Pubs, clubs and festivals

One of the most frequented pub-restaurants, *Stänken Pub and Steakhouse*, is in the old *Riksbank* on Storatorg (Mon, Tues & Thurs 11.30am–11pm, Wed till 1am, Fri till 2am, Sat noon–2am) and has a massive range of around 250 beers. For an alternative **pub**, try *Bitte Eine Bit*, opposite *Du Vanders* on Hesslegatan (Mon–Fri 11am–2pm & every night till late except Mon). This German-owned little pub serves German food (schnitzels, sausages, potato salad and soup at 37kr), German beers and plays German folk music – an acquired taste; the walls, however, are covered with pictures of Old Kristianstad. For a 30s crowd and loud rock music, try *Harry's Bar*, Östra Storgatan (not one of the southern Sweden *Harry's Bar* chain); it's crowded, small and has a very popular beer garden. In the *Grand Hotel* on Västra Storgatan, a traditional Irish-style pub, *O'Keefe's*, fills with locals of all ages on the weekends, but isn't much to get excited about; there's also a traditional à la cart menu here (Mon–Thurs 5pm–midnight).

The hippest **nightclub** is *G Punkten* (g-spot) upstairs from *Godsfkan* at the train station. It's a blaze of coloured lights and varied music attracting a young (18–25) age group. *Grands Nightclub* (Thurs 8pm–2am, Fri & Sat 9pm–1am) in the basement of the *Grand Hotel*, is a glitzy joint with old-time dance nights (Thurs) and dated rock and rave discos. The town hosts two annual festivals: **Kristianstadsdagarna**, a huge seven-day cultural festival in the second week of July (during which the tourist office stays open till 10pm), and the annual **Kristianstad and Åhus Jazz Festival** around the same time; ask for details at the tourist office.

# East into Blekinge

The county of **Blekinge** is something of a poor relation to Skåne in terms of tourism. Tourist offices here pump out endless glossy brochures calling the region "the garden of Sweden", and each town is, predictably, the "heart" or "pearl" of that garden. The reality is that there are some good beaches, plentiful fishing, fine walking trails and enough cultural diversions to make Blekinge enjoyable for two or three days. The landscape is much the same as in northeastern Skåne: forests and hills with fields fringing the sea. There are, however, a number of islands and a small archipelago south of Karlskrona that are picturesque destinations for short boat trips. If you only have a day or two in the region, it's best to head to the handsome and lively town of **Karlskrona**, the county capital, from where the tiny, fortified hamlet of **Kristianopel** is just 30km away and a splendid contrast.

**Public transport** in Blekinge requires some careful timetable studying to avoid being stranded from early evening onwards. Most locals drive, and on weekend evenings there are likely to be no trains or buses between the towns. This fact is keenly observed by taxi drivers who charge, for example, 250kr to take you between Ronneby and Karlshamn, while hitching is nigh on impossible here. The *Kustpilen Express* train runs from Malmö/Lund to Karlskrona and stops at all the towns detailed below.

### Mörrum

Around 50km east of Kristianstad (40min train journey), **MÖRRUM** is Sweden's high-class **angling centre** and consists of very little else. Licences for a day's salmon and trout fishing here run from 220kr to 950kr; the latter price buys you the chance of catching the big fish at the start of the season on April 1. The river's rapids and leaping salmon are incentive enough for non-enthusiasts, too, while an

**aquarium** (April–Oct daily 9am–5pm; 35kr) lets you view the river fish through a series of underwater windows. There's a small café by the waterside, which, unsurprisingly, specializes in fish and seafood. Signs point you to the river from all over town, and you can buy fishing licences from the aquarium.

# Karlshamn

A more rewarding place for a day's exploration is **KARLSHAMN**. The town was destroyed by fire in 1763, and wealthy merchants then built ever-more grand houses for themselves as replacements; some are still standing. The town saw its heyday in the nineteenth century, when it manufactured such goodies as punch, brandy and tobacco. Today, margarine and ice-cream factories flank the harbour, but don't be put off. Karlshamn also has some beautiful little streets of pastel-painted houses, a clutch of museums, including a really splendid eighteenth-century merchant's house, a couple of summer-time festivals that transform the town into a mini-Woodstock, and offshore islands (see p.228) that offer a wooded retreat and some clean-water swimming.

From the train station, turn left onto Eric Dahlbergsvägen and right down Kyrkogatan, which is lined with old, wooden houses painted pale yoghurt shades. Karl Gustav kyrka, an unusual late seventeeth-century church, squats at the junction with Drottininggatan. Walking down this street you are retracing the steps of many nineteenth-century emigrants on their way to "New Sweden" in America; for many this was the last bit of their homeland they would ever see. A grey house, on the left, its front door sided by two flights of stairs running to the left and right, is the former **Hotel Hoppet**, which was immortalized by Wilhelm Moberg's *The Emigrants*. Here the novel's idealistic peasant farmers, Karl and Kristina Oskar, spend their last night in Sweden. There's not much to see – it's now the offices of an architectural firm – but if you carry on to the harbour, a poignant memorial sculpture by the Halmstad Group's Axel Olson (a copy of which is at the House of Emigrants in Växjö, see p.252) depicts the husband staring out to sea and an unknown future, his wife glancing wistfully back for a final time at all she has known.

## The museums

The town's **museums** (10kr covers them all) are all close together at the other end of Drottininggatan at the junction with Vinkelgatan. The best of the bunch is the amazingly well-preserved eighteenth-century merchant's house. Built after the fire that effectively obliterated the town, and occupied until the 1940s, **Skottsbergska Gården**, on Drottininggatan (Mon–Fri 10am–5pm; free), deserves a visit. On the ground floor, the kitchen is of most interest, furnished in eighteenth-century style with an enormous open fireplace and all the pots and pans used over the centuries. These were last used to fry up breakfast for Hanna Lyunggren, the unmarried, final descendant of the original owner. She died in 1941, and her apartments on the ground floor remain as they were at her death. Upstairs there is some splendid Gustavian decoration, although, inexplicably, there don't appear to be any bedrooms; the wardrobes, which still have ancient clothes in them, are all in what seem to be living rooms. In the basement – which predates the great fire – is a preserved shop selling tobacco.

On the corner, the **Museum of Local History** (June–Aug daily except Mon noon–5pm, rest of year weekends only) is in Smithska House, built in 1765 by

Olof Berg, the town's richest man. Inside, there's the usual range of exhibits – painted chests, old domestic furniture, marine odds and ends – but if you take a door into the old courtyard, various buildings ranged about the square hold more interest (though there's no English translation of the explanatory notes). You can wander up creaking stairs to authentic interiors, including a tobacco-processing works, where there's a collection of tobacco packages and the pervasive smell of the weed. Leaving aside the uninspiring **art gallery** (June–Aug Tues–Sun noon–5pm) in an old warehouse at Vinkelgatan 9 (opposite the history museum), the only museum likely to fire enthusiasm is the **Punch Museum** (the same entrance and hours as the art gallery), which has free tours on demand and illegal servings of the liquor at 20kr. It's an intriguing place, containing all the workings and contents of Karlshamn Flaggpunch, the factory that blended the potent mixture of sugar, arrak and brandy, until it was closed down in 1917, when a state monopoly of all alcohol trade and distribution began. A non-alcoholic – and accordingly less celebrated – punch was made here until 1967.

## Practicalities

Karlshamn is an hour's **train** ride from either Kristianstad or Karlskrona and just nine minutes from Mörrum. A short walk from the station, the harbourside **tourist office** is on the corner of Ågatan and Ronnebygatan (mid-June to mid-Aug Mon–Fri 9am–8pm, Sat 10am–2pm & 5–8pm, Sun noon–7pm; rest of year Mon–Fri 9am–5pm; ☎0454/165 95, fax 842 45) and will book **private rooms** (100kr per person plus 40kr booking fee) and **private cottages** (850kr per week for two) anywhere in the region. A squeaky new *STF* **youth hostel** is next to the train station at Surbrunnsvägen lc (May–Sept; ☎0454/140 10; 100kr). The nearest **campsite** (May–Sept; ☎0454/812 10; 120kr per person, 320kr for 4-person cabins) is at **KOLLEVIK**, 3km out of town; take bus #312 from next to the train station or from Stortorget. It's well positioned by the sea with local beaches and a swimming pool close by. Another campsite 10km north (inland) is *Långasjönäs* (May–Sept; ☎0454/206 91; 120kr per person; 260kr for 4-person cabins); take bus #310 to within 3km, then walk.

The cheapest central **hotel** is *Bode Hotel*, Södra Fogdelyckegatan (☎0454/315 00; ① year round, breakfast 35kr), while for more luxury, *Hotel Carlshamn*, Varvsgatan 1 (☎0454/890 00, fax 891 50; ④/②), the bright hotel at the mouth of the harbour, has a grand atrium hall, a pleasant bistro and big summer discounts.

Karlshamn has an extraordinarily good **vegetarian restaurant**, *Gourmet Grön* at Drottninggatan 61 (Mon–Fri 11.30am–3pm & 6pm–1am, Sat noon–3pm), serving massive bowls of delicately flavoured gourmet dishes elegantly presented on a buffet table. As much as you can eat costs a remarkable 50kr during the day, 100kr in the evening. There's an Italian menu, too, and superb home-made desserts. Even dedicated carnivores will be impressed. *Terrassen Restaurant*, Ronnebygatan 12 (daily 11am–midnight), has a wide range of fish and meat dishes, with outside seating. The most popular **café** is *Christins* at Drottninggatan 65. Nothing special to look at, its location makes it a favourite local meeting place.

The annual – laidback but dated – **rock festival** (300kr), staged on the west bank of the river at Bellvue Park, occurs in mid-June, when the streets become littered with half-naked and more than half-inebriated revellers. The crowds get bigger each year and attract international groups such as Status Quo and Deep Purple. The **Baltic Festival** in the third week of July is far bigger, an impressive, all-consuming town celebration with lots of drinking and merriment among a wide age range.

# Ronneby

Much of **RONNEBY** has been destroyed by development. As you arrive by train, even the summer sun cannot disguise the banality of the buildings ahead. There is, however, a tiny **old town**, a few minutes' walk up the hill to the left, a brief testament to the fact that in the thirteenth century, this was Blekinge's biggest town and centre for trading with the Hanseatic League. Only when the county became Swedish in the four centuries later did Ronneby fall behind neighbouring Karlskrona. Today, the main attraction is the beautifully preserved collection of spa houses, a couple of kilometres over the river (turn right from the station) at **Ronneby Brunnspark** (see below), where there is also one of the area's best cafés and some good walks.

In the town itself, walk uphill to the left of the train station, and turn left again onto the main street, Kungsgatan. There is nothing much of interest here until you reach **Helga Korskyrkan** (Church of the Holy Cross). With its whitewashed walls, blocked-in arched windows and red-tiled roof, the church looks like a Greek chapel presiding over the surrounding modern apartment buildings. Dating originally from the twelfth century, this Romanesque church took quite a bashing during the Seven Years' War (1563–70) against the Danes. On the night of what is known as the **Ronneby Blood Bath** in September 1564, all those who had taken refuge in the church were slaughtered – gashes in the heavy oak door at the north wall made during the violence can still be seen. The seventeenth-century wood carvings on the pulpit and altar are impressive and, if you peer carefully through the gloom, you'll see a partly damaged Dance with Death wall painting on the south wall, each man and woman having a skeleton as a dancing partner.

## Ronneby Brunnspark

In 1775 the waters here were found to be exploitably rich in iron, and Ronneby soon became one of Sweden's principal spa towns, centred around **Ronneby Brunnspark**. Just fifteen minutes' walk from the train station up the hill and over the river (or bus #211), the park's houses stand proudly amid blazing rhododendrons and azelias. One such property is now a fine *STF* youth hostel (see overleaf for details). The neighbouring building is the wonderful café-bar **Wiener Café**, with bare floorboards and hand-painted abstract designs on the walls. Built in 1862 as a doctor's home, it later became a small hospital and during World War II was occupied by Danish resistance fighters. Today, it has live music and outside drinking (see overleaf). There are pleasant **walks** through the beautifully kept park, past a pond with half a dozen types of duck, and into the wooded hills behind, picking up part of the **Blekingeleden** walking trail. Also through the trees are some unexpected gardens, including a Japanese Garden. If you're interested in the local nature, another of the old spa houses contains **Blekinge Naturum** (June–Aug 11am–6pm), which can advise on the best walking in the surrounding countryside. The park is also the site of a giant **flea market** every Sunday morning (May–Sept), where genuine Swedish antiques can be picked up for not much alongside kitschy items and general tat. Tours of the area run every Sunday from June to August – ask at the tourist office for details.

## Practicalities

From Karlshamn, there are frequent **train** (34min) and **bus** services to Ronneby. The **tourist office** (June–Aug Mon–Fri 9am–7pm, Sat 10am–4pm, Sun

## ISLAND TRIPS FROM KARLSHAMN, RONNEBY AND KARLSKRONA

With a smattering of attractive **islands** punctuating the waters to the south of Karlshamn and Ronneby, there are a number of pleasant boat trips to choose from along this stretch of the coast – although at present military restrictions mean that certain islands are off-limits to non-Swedes. Before setting off for any of the islands you need to get a **permit**; if taking a boat from Karlshamn, you apply directly to the boat's captain (permits are free and don't take long to obtain), while in Karlskrona you can get an instant permit from Fisktorget, a finger of land close by to the west of the town centre, where the boats are moored.

The most popular island destinations from Karlshamn and Karlskrona are **Tjärö**, just off the coast at Karlshamn, and **Tärno**, a little further out to sea (to get to both from either town takes around 20min; 50kr). Cost cutting means there are no longer any boat trips to these islands from Ronneby, but ferries from **Järnavik** run six times a day to Tjärö (15min; 40kr), but to get to Järnavik involves a train ride to Bräkne-Hoby, and there's no public transport for the last 8km.

There's a very popular *STF* **youth hostel** in an old farm building at Tjärö (May to mid-Sept; ☎0454/600 63, fax 390 63; 140kr; 170kr for a bed in a double room); the connected **restaurant** is open to everyone, staying there or not. Tjärö has some great bathing areas among the rocks, and, if you have a tent, this is a good place to camp. However, the island comes alive from June onwards with partying Swedes, so finding a secluded spot may be difficult, and it's advisable to book at the youth hostel well in advance. A nature guide runs all summer if you're interested. This also needs pre-booking through the youth hostel. There is no accommodation on Tärno.

The only island trip now possible from Ronneby is to **Karön**, just 500m off the mainland; take the bus from Ronneby train station to Ekenas, from where an old boat regularly makes the short trip. It's a beautiful place to wander around during the day, with old wooden houses hiding among the trees, though the island is more popular as a night-time destination for a young crowd. *Restaurant Karön* serves lunches (daily except Mon noon–2.30pm) and has dancing four nights a week (Wed, Thurs, Fri & Sat). On Thursdays it's *Club 29* (9pm–2am), a disco with entry, food and bar drinks all costing 29kr each; Saturday is a regular 1960s/1970s night; while on Sunday there's cheap food from noon to 9pm. There are boats back to the mainland after the restaurant/nightclub closes.

noon–4pm; Sept–May Mon, Wed & Fri 9am–5pm, Tues & Thurs 9am–7pm; ☎0457/176 50, fax 174 44) is in the Kulturcentrum, close to the church in the tiny old town area. The Kulturcentrum has minor art exhibitions (same hours as the tourist office) and a bar and restaurant (Mon–Fri till 11pm). You can rent **bikes** here for 40kr per day, 250kr per week.

Without a doubt the best place to stay is at the *STF* **youth hostel** (open all year except Dec to early Jan; ☎ & fax 0457/263 00; 100kr) in Ronneby Brunnspark, with its balustraded balcony where you can eat alfresco (breakfast 40kr). In town, the owners of the hostel also run the inaptly named *Grand Hotel*, Järnvägsgatan 11 (☎0457/268 80, fax 268 84; ②, summer reduction to 500kr), an adequate place in a modern apartment building opposite the train station. Less central but better placed for Ronneby Brunnspark is *Strandgården*, Nedre Brunnsvägen 25 (①, including breakfast), a small, family-run pension past the youth hostel on the right.

For **eating and drinking** in town, try *Nya Wienerbageriet* on Västra Torgatan, off the main square, an old bakery converted into a bar and café with outside tables serving good, wholesome lunches, including a daily pasta dish, with coffee, salad and juice, for 50kr. At the back is a stylish new **bar** (Thurs–Sat 7pm till late) with occasional live music, mostly blues or jazz. Just off Stortorget is the best konditori, the *Continental*, a well-stocked bakery and the only place open on a Sunday morning to sit and have a coffee. There are also a few places near the station: *Restaurant & Pub Piaff,* on Karlskronagatan, is an established pizza restaurant, with tables outside on the veranda; a few steps away is an intimate, traditional pub, *Jojjes Pub Bar,* and on the ground floor of the *Grand Hotel* is a cheap pizza restaurant, *Pizzeria Milano,* selling basic pizzas at 30kr. *Wiener Café* in Ronneby Brunnspark has singing troubadores and is the place most people go to drink (Tues 6.30–11pm, Wed–Fri 6pm–midnight, Sat noon–1am, Sun noon–4pm).

# Karlskrona

Blekinge's most appealing destination, **KARLSKRONA** is the regal county capital and set on the largest link in a chain of breezy islands. Founded by Karl XI in 1680, who chose it as an ideal ice-free southern harbour for his Baltic fleet, everything about the town today revolves around its maritime heritage. The wide avenues and stately squares, which all survive intact, were built to accommodate the king's naval parades, and cadets in uniform still career around streets named after Swedish admirals and battleships. The most unusual of Karlskrona's three fine churches is **Admiralty Church**, and the biggest museum is, unsurprisingly, dedicated to Maritime History. Don't despair, though, even if you're not a naval fan, Karlskrona has plenty more to offer. There's a picturesque **old quarter** around the once-busy fishing port at Fisktorget and some short cruises around the islands in the archipelago; however, due to military restrictions no bathing is allowed on them. Instead there is good swimming off the nearby island of **Dragsö** or at the fine 1910 bath house in town. The port is also where **ferries** regularly leave for Gdynia in Poland.

Arriving by **train** (from Ronneby 23min) or **bus** – both stations are together – offers an encouraging first glimpse of the island network. The first island you'll pass is **Hästö**, once home to Karlskrona's wealthiest residents. It's just a few minutes further to the centre on the island of **Trossö**, connected to the mainland by the main road, Österleden (E22). Climb uphill past Hoglands Park, named after an eighteenth-century battle, to the main square, **Stortorget**, at the highest point and geographical centre of the island. It's a vast and beautiful square, dominated by two complementary **churches**; both were designed by Tessin the Younger and are stuccoed in burnt orange with dove-grey stone collonades. If you're honing down church visits head just for the circular domed **Trefaldighetskyrkan** (Mon–Fri 11am–3pm, Sat 9.30am–2pm; guided tours on request). Built for the town's German merchant community in 1709, the domed ceiling is its most remarkable feature, painted with hundreds of rosettes and brilliantly shaded to look three-dimensional. The altar is also distinctive, golden angelic faces peering out of a gilded meringue of clouds. In the crypt are the remains of two of Karlskrona's most revered men, Count Hans Wachtmeister, responsible for much of the building of the town in the late seventeenth century, and Johan Törnström, who made most of the fabulous ship figureheads on show at the Maritime Museum (see p.231). **Fredrikskyrkan** (Mon–Fri 11am–3pm, Sat 9.30am–2pm), a few steps away, is an elegant, light-flooded church with towers, but holds fewer surprises inside.

## The Admiralty Church

Between the churches, walk past the pseudo-medieval castellated waterworks – now a Greek café – down Södra Kungsgatan. The wide, cobbled street is divided down the centre by the boulder-like stone walls of a tunnel, where a disused train line once ran from the main station up to the harbour. The leafy square ahead is **Amiralitets Torget**, and perched at its centre is the huge, peeling wooden bell tower of the Admiralty Church. To see the church itself, head down Vallgatan on the left of the square, passing the symmetrical austerity of the Marine Officers' School, and just before you reach the harbour, the beautifully proportioned, entirely wooden **Admiralty Church** (Kungliga Amiralitetskyrkan) is up on the right. Built in 1685, this simple elegant structure is Sweden's biggest wooden church. Outside the entrance, take a look at one of the city's best-known land-marks: the wooden statue of **Rosenbom**, around whom hangs a sorrowful tale. Mats Rosenbom, one of the first settlers on Trossö island, lived nearby with his wife and twelve children and earned his keep in the shipyard. However, after a fever killed six of his children and left him and his wife too ill to work, he applied for and was granted a beggar's licence. One New Year's Eve while begging alms at the homes of leading townspeople, he became somewhat drunk from the fes-tive wine on offer and forgot to raise his hat to thank the wealthy German figure-head carver, Fritz Kolbe. When admonished for this, Rosenbom retorted, "If you want thanks for your crumbs to the poor, you can take my hat off yourself!".

Enraged, Kolbe struck him between the eyes and sent him away, but the beggar, unable to make it home, froze stiff and died in a snow drift by the church. Next morning, Kolbe found the beggar frozen to death and, filled with remorse, carved a figure of Rosenbom to stand at the spot where he died, designing it so that you have to raise his hat yourself to give some money.

## The harbour side and museums
From the waterside at the end of Vallgatan, the divide between the picturesque town and the continuing military presence is most apparent. To the left stands the old white lighthouse, looking out to sea and the archipelago, and the pink- and white-stuccoed County Governor's Residence. To the right, however, mud-coloured military vessels fill the old quayside and "Forbidden to Enter" signs abound. Boats leave from the nearby Aspö ferry terminal to the **Maritime Museum**, which has recently been moved to huge new premises on Stumholm Island, next to a new art gallery (times and entry fee to be decided; ask at the tourist office). Among its vast and graphic collections, the most striking include Johan Törnstrom's ship figureheads and a few intriguing items like a cat-o'-nine-tails in a naval punishment display.

For more of a feel of old Karlskrona, wander west past the military hardware towards the **Björkhomen** area. Here a couple of tiny, wooden, early eighteenth-century houses in little gardens survive, homes that the first craftsmen at the then new naval yard built for themselves. All the streets running north-south are named after types of ships while all those east-west are named after admirals. Nearby **Fisktorget** is pleasant for a stroll. Historically a fish market site, nowadays the boats here are mainly pleasure yachts, but there are a couple of pleasant cafés as well as the terminal for boats to Tjärö and Tärno (see p.228) and for river trips through town. You'll also find the dull **Blekinge Museum** (Mon–Fri 10am–4pm, Sat & Sun 11am–4pm; free), housed in the 1705 wooden home built for Count Wachtmeister – the pleasant summer-time café is more appealing than the exhibits on ship building and the like.

## Practicalities
The **tourist office** (June & Aug Mon–Fri 10am–6pm, Sat 10am–2pm; July Mon–Fri 10am–7pm, Sat 10am–4pm, Sun noon–6pm; Sept–May Mon–Fri 10am–5pm; ☎0455/834 90, fax 822 55) is in the library just off Stortorget. You can book **private rooms** here for around 125kr per person and rent cheap, green **military bikes** for 25kr a day – a popular option, especially if you intend to visit Kristianopel (see over-leaf). Local buses will carry bikes and without one, there's a six-kilometre walk at the other end. Bikes are also available from the harbourside kiosk near the Aspö ferry terminal. Student accommodation during most of the year, the new *STF* **youth hostel** at Bredgatan 16 (mid-June to mid-Aug; ☎0455/834 81; 100kr) is very central; while **camping** is out on Dragsö island (☎0455/153 54) around 2.5km away. Bus #7 leaves from the bus station to Saltö, the island before Dragsö, from where it's a 1km walk. The most appealing new **hotel** is *Hotel Carlskrona*, Skeppsbrokajen (☎0455/196 30; fax 259 90; ④/②), in a strikingly contemporary building, with mir-ror-windowed gable ends right next to the ferry terminal at Fisktorget. It serves a huge breakfast buffet (Mon–Fri 6.30–9.30am, Sat & Sun 8–10am; 55kr). If you fancy a traditional place, the 1890-built *Statt Hotel* (☎0455/192 50, fax 169 09; ④/②) is on the main shopping and restaurant street, at Ronnebygatan 37–39, and has the swish-est facade. Big summer reductions bring prices at this luxury hotel down to a rea-

sonable level. For cheaper, more basic places, *Hotel Conrad* on Västra Köpmangatan
(☎0455/823 35; includes breakfast, ②/①), halfway up the hill from the station to
Stortorget, is plain and reasonable. Owned by the same people and at the same price
is the still more central and slightly brighter *Hotel Aston*, Landbrogatan 1
(☎0455/194 70); while *Hotel Siesta*, Borgmästaregatan 5 (☎0455/801 80, fax 801 82;
②/①), is the ugliest but the most central of all, just off Stortorget.

Most of the town's **konditori** are indistinguishable, two exceptions being *Café
Tre G* on Landbrogatan, opposite Hoglands Park, which serves baked potatoes,
cakes and sandwiches in pleasant surroundings, and *Systrarna Lindkvists Café*,
Borgmästaregatan 3, across from the tourist office, where two sisters prepare coffee in fine old gilded china cups, with silver teaspoons and sugar tongs. The
majority of Karlskrona's **restaurants** are along central Ronnebygatan. None is
outstanding but the best of the bunch is the Italian-style *Ristorante Il Divino* at no.
29; while a few metres up, *Red Light* serves kebabs and light meals, and next door
is the new *English Pub*. A more unusual setting is in the *Old Water Works* (daily
11.30am–9pm), between the big churches on Stortorget, which offers light
Greek food and specializes in lamb kebabs. The most popular summer **pub** is
*Jolen*, Norra Kungsgatan 1, with outside terrace drinking. The rest of the year,
locals go to the *Kings Crown* on Stortorget for British-style supping.

**Ferries to Gdynia**, Poland, leave daily (10hr 30min); daytime tickets cost
320kr return and 180kr one-way, night-time 410kr and 230kr. In July, all trips are
at 8pm.

# Kristianopel

Arriving by road at the idyllic hamlet of **Kristianopel**, 30km northeast of
Karlskrona, there is not the slightest hint that this village of just 38 inhabitants
was once a strategically positioned fortification with a bloody history, or that
every July the place packs out with holiday makers and comes alive with an
atmosphere of summer revelry seldom found in the rest of Sweden.

Only when you've walked past the minute, untouched cottages in their tumbling, fragrant gardens and all the way to the tiny harbour do you see the two kilometres of three-metre thick **fortification walls** that surround the settlement. The
low, squat walls are actually a 1970s' reconstruction, but are built on the foundations of the original fortifications, erected in 1600 by Danish king Christian IV to
protect against Swedish aggression. The walls were finally raised by the Swedes
after the little town had spent 77 years changing hands with alarming regularity.
There is very little to see in Kristianopel; the only other sight worth a brief look
is the **church**, near the village shop; inside is an eye-catching altar, decorated
with vividly drawn trees. The present church replaced a medieval one, which in
1605 was the scene of great bloodshed: it was burnt to the ground, killing all the
village women, children and elderly, who were huddled inside for what they imagined was protection. They mistakenly believed that the then sixteen-year-old King
Gustav Adolf would respect it as a place of God. Today, it's just a grassy mound
near the campsite.

Although a charming place to visit at any time, Kristianopel is at its very best
during summer, when the population jumps to around two thousand. Nearly all the
visitors stay at the tiny ten-bed hostel and adjacent campsite (see opposite), tucked
inside the low walls and overlooking the sea. Every **July**, the two campsite restau-

rants are the focus for a wide range of **music** and **night-time entertainment**, beginning on Monday evening with country and western. Tuesday sees a bizarre night of Eurovision Song Contest favourites, Thursday favours Frank Sinatra and easy listening, while on Friday and Saturday live bands and troubadours play blues, jazz and rock 'n' roll. To finish, folk music takes over on Sundays. Even if some of the music doesn't grab you, the all-encompassing bonhomie and the wonderful setting make this a great social event that's well worth dipping into.

## Practicalities

Getting to Kristianopel is tricky by public transport. **Bus #120** from Karlskrona (to Kalmar) only runs along the main E22, stopping at Fågelmara, 6km from the village; however, once the school terms starts in September, bus #122 from Karlskrona stops at Kristianopel. Alternatively **bikes** rented in Karlskrona can be taken on the #120 bus at no extra cost, and **hitching** is easier here than in most places.

For accommodation in the village you are limited to the **youth hostel/campsite** (open all year; tents & caravans only: ☎/fax 0455/661 30; hostel 85kr), or the one **hotel**, a simple eighteenth-century farmhouse called *Gästgiferi* (April–Sept ☎/fax 0455/660 30; ③, including breakfast), which is set in beautiful gardens and found to the left of the main road into the village. Just outside **FÅGELMARA**, an old wooden farmhouse has rooms with a basic kitchen (call Marina Söderberg on ☎0455/643 06). It has a rather unusual atmosphere, with hens, horses and the household's four young children, but it's fun and very cheap at 100kr per person for up to six people. Guests can also arrange **horse riding** here. From the campsite you can rent a **rowing boat** (10kr per hour, 50kr per day) or – for those who prefer to shoot at wildlife rather than just admire it – go on seabird hunting trips to the local islands (Sept–Jan).

There are three **restaurants** in the village: at the hotel there's a small place with a pub, while the two others are run by the hostel/campsite. Just by the campsite, the basic and wooden *Värdshuset Pålsgården* (Fri 6–9pm, Sat noon–9pm, Sun noon–6pm) serves basic food and opens late every night in July as a pub. A few minutes away, *Restaurant Sjöstugan* is a slightly more upmarket pizza restaurant, with glorious views to the closest islands off this lovely coast. If you want to cater for yourself there are a couple of shops on the campsite, and another near the church (Mon–Fri 9am–6pm, Sat & Sun 9.30am–noon).

## travel details

### Express trains

Daily express trains operate throughout the region, in particular **Oslo–Copenhagen** (via Gothenburg, Varberg, Halmstad and Helsingborg) and **Stockholm–Copenhagen** (via Helsingborg). Both routes have a branch service through to Malmö. Despite complicated timetabling, the service is frequent and regular north or south between Gothenburg and Helsingborg/Malmö.

### Trains

**From Helsingborg** to Gothenburg (11 daily; 2hr 40min); Lund/Malmö (Mon–Fri 12, Sat & Sun 10; 40–50min).

**From Karlskrona** to Emmaboda for connections to Växjö, Stockholm & Kalmar (1–2 hourly; 40min).

**From Kristianstad** to Karlshamn (hourly; 50min); Karlskrona (hourly; 1hr 50min);

Mörrum (hourly; 40min); Ronneby (hourly; 1hr 20min).

**From Malmö** to Gothenburg (8–10 daily; 3hr 45min); Hässleholm/Kristianstad (4 daily; 47min); Karlskrona (hourly; 3hr 15min); Lund (3 hourly; 13min); Ystad (Mon–Fri hourly, Sat 5, Sun 5; 50min).

## Buses

**From Ängelholm** to Torekov (3–5 daily; 45min).

**From Båstad** to Torekov (5 daily; 30min).

**From Helsingborg** to Båstad (4 daily; 55min); Halmstad (6 daily; 1hr 50min).

**From Karlskrona** to Stockholm (Fri & Sun; 7hr 30min).

**From Kristianstad** to Kalmar (1 daily; 3hr); Lund/Malmö (1 daily; 2hr 30min/2hr 45min).

**From Malmö** to Gothenburg (Mon–Thurs 1, Fri & Sun 3; 4hr 25min); Halmstad/Falkenberg/Varberg (Fri & Sun 2; 2hr 25min/2hr 55min/3hr 20min); Helsingborg (Mon–Thurs 1, Fri & Sun 6; 1hr 5min); Jönköping (Mon–Thurs 1, Fri & Sun 3; 4hr 30min); Kristianstad/Kalmar (1 daily; 2–5hr 30min); Lund (hourly; 20min); Mellbystrand (Fri & Sun 1; 2hr); Stockholm (Mon–Thurs 1, Fri & Sun 3; 9hr); Trelleborg (hourly; 35min).

**From Ystad** to Kristianstad (Mon–Thurs 5, Fri 6, Sat & Sun 3; 1hr 55min); Lund (Mon–Fri 3; 1hr 15min); Malmö (3 daily; 1hr); Simrishamn (Mon–Fri 3, Sat & Sun 1; 50min); Smygehamn (Mon–Fri 5, Sat & Sun 2; 30min).

## Ferries, hydrofoils and catamarans

All the following services are to towns in Denmark unless otherwise stated.

**From Halmstad** to Grenå (2 daily; 4hr).

**From Helsingborg** to Helsingør (3 hourly; 25min).

**From Karlskrona** to Gdynia in Poland (1 daily; 10hr 30min).

**From Limhamn** (Malmö) to Dragör (14–18 daily; 55min).

**From Malmö** to Copenhagen (*Flygbåtarna* and *Pilen* hydrofoils hourly, 45min; *Shopping Linjen* hydrofoil 5 daily, 45min).

**From Simrishamn** to Allinge on Bornholm (summer only catamaran 3–4 daily).

**From Trelleborg** to Rostock (3 daily; 6hr); Sassnitz (5 daily; 3hr 45min); Travämunde (2 daily; 7–9hr).

**From Varberg** to Grenå (2 daily; 3hr 45min).

**From Ystad** to Rönne on Bornholm (3–5 daily; 2hr 30min); Swinoujscie in Poland (2 daily; 7–9hr).

# CHAPTER FOUR

# THE SOUTHEAST

A lthough a less obvious target than the coastal cities and resorts of the southwest, Sweden's **southeast** certainly repays a visit. You'll find impressive castles, ancient lakeside sites, and numerous glassworks amid the forests of the so-called "Glass Kingdom", while off the east coast, Sweden's largest Baltic islands offer beautifully preserved medieval towns and fairy-tale landscapes. Train transport, especially between the towns close to the eastern shore of Lake Vättern and Stockholm, is good; speedy, regular services mean that you could see some places on a day-trip from Stockholm.

**Småland** county in the south encompasses a varied geography and some stridently different towns. **Kalmar** is a very likable stop; a glorious historic fortress town, it deserves more time than its tag as a jumping-off point for the island of Öland suggests. Inland, great swathes of dense forest are rescued from monotony by the many **glass factories** that continue the county's tradition of glass production, famous the world over for its design and quality. Abundant wood fuel serviced a glass industry already flourishing in the eighteenth century, families living in small communities around the factories. By the mid-nineteenth century, however, Småland witnessed the mass emigration of hundreds of thousands of its people to America – the result of agricultural reforms and a series of bad harvests. In **Växjö**, the largest town in the south, two superb museums deal with the art of glass-making and the history of Swedish emigration. At the northern edge of the county and perched on the southernmost tip of Lake Vättern, **Jönköping** is known as Sweden's Jerusalem for its remarkable number of free churches; it is also a great base for exploring the beautiful eastern shore of Vättern. In the middle of the lake is the island of **Visingsö**, which is rich in royal history and historic sites.

The idyllic pastoral landscape of **Östergotland** borders the eastern shores of the lake and reaches as far east as the Baltic. Popular with domestic tourists, the small lakeside town of **Vadstena** is one of the highlights, its medieval streets dwarfed by austere monastic edifices, a Renaissance palace and an imposing abbey, brought into being by the zealous determination of Sweden's first female saint, Birgitta. The **Göta Canal** wends its way through the northern part of the county to the Baltic and a number of fine towns line the route, including **Linköping** (*köping* means "market"), with its strange open-air museum of Gamla "old" Linköping, where people live and work in a re-created nineteenth-century environment. Just to the north, **Norrköping**, a bustling and youthful town, grew up around the textile industry and today boasts Europe's best collection of preserved, and extremely handsome, red-brick and stuccoed factories.

Outside the fragmented archipelagos of the east and west coasts, Sweden's only two true islands are in the Baltic: Öland and Gotland, adjacent slithers of land with unusually temperate climates. They were domestic tourist havens for years, but now an increasing number of foreigners are discovering their charms – sun, beach-

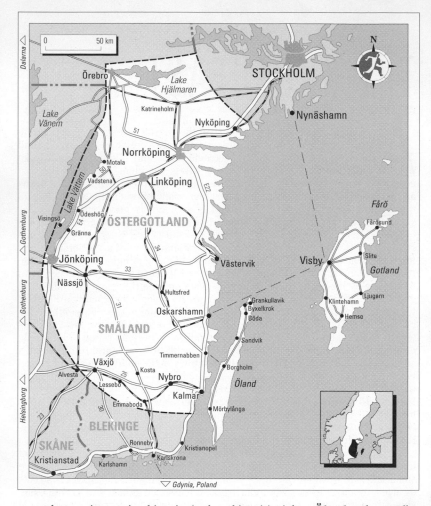

es and some impressive historic (and prehistoric) sights. **Öland** – the smaller island and closer to the mainland – is less praised than Gotland, but its mix of dark forest and flowering meadows makes it a tranquil and untouched spot for a few days' exploration. **Gotland** is known for its medieval Hanseatic capital, **Visby**, a stunning backdrop to the carnival atmosphere that pervades the town in summer, when ferry-loads of young Swedes come to sunbathe and party. The city is one of the most popular places for Swedes to celebrate **Midsummer's Night**. The rest of the island, however, is little visited by tourists, and is all the more magical for that. There are plenty of hotels in Visby – though they tend to fill quickly in summer – and numerous **campsites** dotted around the rest of the island and on Öland, though both islands are good places to exercise *Allemansrätten* and camp rough. The islands are also wonderful cycling country, and **bike** rental is available on both.

**ACCOMMODATION PRICES**

The pensions and hotels listed in the guide have been price-graded according to the scale outlined below; the number indicates the price for the least expensive double room. Many hotels offer considerable reductions at weekends (year round) and during the summer holiday period (mid-June to mid-Aug); in these cases the reduction is either noted in the text or, where it falls into another price band, given after the full price. Single rooms, where available, usually cost between 60 and 80 percent of a double.

① under 500kr    ② 500–700kr    ③ 700–900kr    ④ 900–1200kr    ⑤ over 1200kr

# Kalmar

Bright and breezy **Kalmar**, set among a huddle of islands at the southeastern edge of the county of Småland, has treasures enough to make it one of southern Sweden's most delightful towns – a fact sadly missed by most visitors with their sights on the Baltic island of Öland, separated from Kalmar by a 6km bridge. In the centre of the seventeenth-century **"New Town"**, surrounded by fragments of ancient fortified walls, the cobbled streets and lively squares are lined with some lovely old buildings, and within two minutes' walk of the train station is an exquisite fourteenth-century **castle**. Scene of the Kalmar Union, which united Sweden, Norway and Denmark as a single kingdom in 1397, the castle was fashioned two centuries later into what is recognized as Scandinavia's finest preserved Renaissance palace – its interior alone makes Kalmar worth visiting. Just a couple of minutes in the other direction, the **Länsmuseum** contains a fascinating exhibition of the **Kronan**, one of the world's three biggest warships that sunk off Öland over three hundred years ago. Even now, new finds are being discovered, helping to piece together the world's most complete picture of seventeenth-century maritime life.

## Arrival, information and accommodation

The **tourist office** at Larmgatan 6 (mid-June to mid-Aug daily 9am–9pm; early June & late Aug daily 9am–7pm; Sept–May Mon–Fri 9am–5pm; ☎0480/153 50, fax 174 53), at the junction with Ölandsgatan, is within spitting distance of the **train station** (5 trains a day from Gothenburg, 4hr 15min; several from Stockholm, 5hr) and **bus terminal**. Here you can get a decent map of Kalmar, though for English-language information on Öland, you'll have to cross onto the island itself. Kalmar can be explored easily on foot, but if you want to strike out into the surrounding countryside, you can rent a **bike** from *Team Sportia*, Södravägen 2, or at *Stensö Camping* site (see overleaf).

### Accommodation

The tourist office arranges **private rooms** from 175kr per person, 250kr for a double, plus a 50kr booking fee. Other cheap accommodation options include the **youth hostel**, Rappegatan 1c (open all year; ☎0480/129 28, fax 882 93; 100kr, breakfast 40kr), on the next island to the north, **Ängö**, a pleasant ten-minute walk.

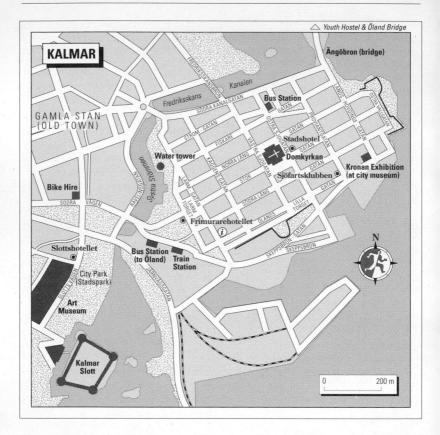

It's a well-equipped, busy hostel with clothes-washing facilities and a basic food shop. Staff also run the economy *Hotel Svarnen*, right next door, with double rooms at 410kr (including the hostel breakfast). *Sjöfartsklubben*, Ölandsgatan 45, which caters for naval students, is open to guests from June to August (double rooms at 250kr, book through the tourist office). The nearest **camping** is on Stensö island, 3km from the centre, where you can rent cheap cabins. Local buses head out this way; check with the tourist office.

There are several really attractive central **hotels**, with even more attractive summer discounts. The 1906-built *Stadshotel*, Stortorget 14 (☎0480/151 80, fax 158 47; ⑤/②), is in a lovely old building with a stuccoed facade. Prices are halved in summer and include an excellent buffet breakfast (available to non-guests at 55kr); it is also open 24 hours a day. Another fine place, on the popular Larmtorget, is *Frimurarehotellet* (☎0480/152 30, fax 858 87; ③/②, including breakfast). Built as a hotel back in 1878, this castle-like building is owned by the Freemasons. All the stylish rooms are en suite, some with a bath; the twin bed-rooms are smaller than doubles. Breakfast for non-residents is 50kr (7–9am). The prettiest, most costly and most regal hotel is the old *Slottshotellet* at Slottsvägen 7 (☎0480/882 60, fax 882 66; 1350kr, no summer reductions, but 1050kr if booked less than a week ahead, 950kr for a last-minute booking), which overlooks the castle across the bridge in the Old Town. The authentic interior is grand and extremely tasteful – breakfast is served in a pavillion. There's no restaurant, but facilities to cook; you can use the sauna and solarium.

# The Town

Beautifully set on its own island, just to the left of the train and bus stations, the first stones of **Kalmar Slott** (May–Sept Mon–Sat 10am–5pm; rest of the year shorter hours) were probably laid in the twelfth century. A century later, it became the most inpenetrable castle in Sweden under King Magnus Ladulås. The biggest event to take place within its walls was in 1397, when Danish Queen Margareta instigated the Union of Kalmar, which made her head of the realm over all Scandinavia. With such hatred between the Swedes and Danes, the union didn't stand much change of long-term success, and the castle was subject to eleven sieges, as the Swedes and the Danes took power in turn. The castle, surprisingly, remained almost unscathed. By the time Gustav Vasa became king of Sweden in 1523, Kalmar Slott was beginning to show signs of stress and strain, and the king set about rebuilding it, while his sons Eric XIV and Johan III took care of decorating the interior. Preserved in fantastic detail as a fine Renaissance palace, it well illustrates the Vasa family's concern to maintain Sweden's prestige in the eyes of foreign powers.

Today, if the castle doesn't appear to be defending anything in particular, this is due to a devastating fire in the 1640s, after which the town was moved to its present site on the island of Kvarnholmen – though the Old Town (Gamla Stan) beyond the castle still retains some winding old streets that are worth a look. Unlike many other southern Swedish castles, this one is storybook accurate: turrets, ramparts, a moat and drawbridge and a dungeon. The castle's fully furnished interior – reached by walking over an authentically copied wooden drawbridge and through a stone arched tunnel beneath the grassy ramparts – is great fun to wander through. Among the many highlights is King Johan's bedroom, known as the **Grey Hall**. His bed, which was stolen from Denmark, is decorated with carved faces on the posts, but, due to Johan's guilt, all their noses have been chopped off – he believed that the nose contained the soul and didn't want the avenging souls of the rightful owners coming to haunt him. The **King's Chamber** (King Eric's bedroom) is the most visually exciting – the wall frieze is a riot of vividly painted animals and shows a wild boar attacking Eric and another man saving him. Eric apparently suffered from paranoic attacks, believing his younger brother Johan wanted to kill him. To this end, he had a secret door cut into the extravagantly inlaid wall panels, with escape routes to the roof in event of fraternal attack. The adjoining **Golden Room**, with its magnificent ceiling, should have been Johan's bedroom, but sibling hatred meant he didn't stay here while Eric lived. As it happened, Eric didn't live that long, and Johan is widely believed to have poisoned him with arsenic in 1569 – putting Eric's paranoia into question. Johan took his old bedroom once again, keeping his mistress, Agda, in a room leading off from his; while his wife lived in her own Queen's chambers at a safer distance.

There are a couple of huge and intriguing portraits in the Golden Room. Gustav Vasa, despite his advanced age and wound-riddled body, appears young-looking with unseemly muscular legs – the royal artist had been ordered to seek out the soldier with the best legs and paint those before attempting a sympathetic portrayal of Vasa's face. In the portrait next to his, Queen Margareta's ghostly white countenance was acheived by the daily application of lead and arsenic. Isolated on another wall, King Eric's portrait measures less than one metre square and hangs much higher than the others; his family believed that the mental illness from which he supposedly suffered could be caught by looking into his eyes – or even images of them.

The tour guides reveal that the place is rattling with Renaissance-era ghosts, but for more tangible evidence of life during the Vasa period, the kitchen fireplace is good enough; it was built to accommodate the simultaneous roasting of three full-size cows.

## The Kronan Exhibition

Housed in a refurbished steam mill on Skeppsbrongatan, the awe-inspiring **Kronan Exhibition** is the main attraction of the **Länsmuseum**, Kalmar's county museum (mid-June to mid-Aug daily 10am–6pm; rest of year daily till 4pm; 40kr). The royal ship *Kronan*, built by the British designer Francis Sheldon, was one of the world's three largest ships; it had three complete decks and was twice the size of the *Vasa*, which sank off Stockholm in 1628 (see p.55). Fully manned, the *Kronan* went down in 1676, and the lives of 800 of its 842 crew were lost, their bodies preserved for more than three hundred years on the Baltic sea bed.

It wasn't until 1980, after thirty years of research, that super-sensitive scanning equipment detected the whereabouts of the ship, 26m down off the coast of Öland. A salvage operation began, led by the great-great-great-great-grandson of the ship's captain, Admiral Lorentz Creutz, and the amazing finds are displayed in an imaginative walk-through reconstruction of the gun decks and admiral's cabin, all with canon fire and screaming gull sound effects. While the ship's treasure trove of gold coins are displayed at the end of the exhibition, it's the incredibly preserved clothing – hats, jackets, buckled leather shoes and even silk bows and cuff links – which bring this exceptional show to life. Other rooms detail the political nature of the wars between the Swedes, Danes and Dutch at the time of the sinking.

The moments leading up to the disaster have been pieced together brilliantly – unlike the ship itself, which was blown out of existence in the explosion. Just before the *Kronan* sank, the Swedish fleet had been at battle with the Dutch in the waters between Öland's main town, Borgholm, and Trelleborg on the south coast. Admiral Creutz received a royal order to attack and recapture the Baltic island of Gotland, just to the north. Pursued by the Danish, Creutz, who had remarkably little naval experience – just one week at sea – was eager to impress his king and engage in combat. To this end, he ignored pleas from his crew and ordered the *Kronan* to turn and face the enemy. A gale caused the ship to heave, and water gushed into her open gun ports, knocking over a lantern, which ignited the entire gun-powder magazine. Within seconds, the explosion ripped this mammoth ship apart. Among the survivors, Anders Sparrfelt was blown over two enemy ships before landing safely in the sail of a Swedish vessel.

## The Konstmuseum and the Domkyrkan

Opposite the castle, Kalmar's **Konstmuseum** (June–Aug Mon–Fri 10am–5pm, Sat & Sun noon–5pm; Sept–May Mon–Fri 10am–5pm & 7–9pm, Sat & Sun noon–5pm; 30kr, children under 16 free) has changing exhibitions of contemporary art, with an emphasis on late 1940s' and 1950s' Expressionism, and a first-floor exhibition devoted to chair design throughout the ages. The top floor contains one largish gallery of nineteenth- and twentieth-century Swedish nude and landscape paintings.

It's far better to head back into the elegantly gridded Renaissance New Town, which is laid out around the grand **Domkyrkan** (daily 9am–6pm) in Stortorget. Designed in 1660 by Nicodemus Tessin the Elder (as was the nearby Rådhus), after a visit to Rome, this vast and airy church in Italian Renassiance style is today a complete misnomer: Kalmar has no bishop and the church no dome. Inside, the altar, designed by Tessin the Younger, shimmers with gold, as do the *Faith* and *Mercy* sculptures around it. The massive painting beneath the altar rather unusually depicts the practical details of Jesus being taken down from the Cross by men on ladders, his lifeless form winched down with ropes. The pulpit is also worth a look; its roof is a three-tiered confection crowned with a statue of Christ surrounded by gnome-like sleeping soldiers, below which angels brandish instruments of torture, while on the "most inferior" level, a file of women symbolize such qualities as maternal love and erudition.

# Eating & drinking

There's a generous helping of unusual and special places to eat in Kalmar. The liveliest night-time area is **Lärmtorget**, with restaurants, cafés and pubs serving Swedish, Indonesian, Chinese, Greek, Italian and English food. For daytime snacks, *Kullzenska caféet*, Kaggensgatan 26 (daily 10am–6.30pm), is a charming, classic **konditori**. Set upstairs in an eighteenth-century house, this was originally the living quarters of an unmarried brother and sister, named Kullzen, until their deaths in the early 1980s. Crammed with the family's eighteenth- and nineteenth-century mahogany furniture, sofas and Indian rugs, the café offers homemade cakes and sandwiches to eat either inside or out.

### Restaurants and bars

**Bamboo Restaurant**, on Lärmtorget. Of the several oriental restaurants, this is the best-located, though it offers mediocre Indonesian food (83–100kr) and Swedish dishes (65–135kr).

**Calmar Hamnkrog**, built right by the water on squat stilts. This place offers such delights as catfish, duck or lamb with classy sauces for 200kr.

**Ernesto Spaghetti & Cocktail Bar**, opposite *Krögers* on Lärmtorget. Serves a huge range of pizzas (50–60kr) and pastas (55–75kr), as well as traditional Italian salads, antipasti and meat courses (120kr) in quite upmarket surroundings. Daily 11am–midnight.

**Ernesto Steakhouse**, at the harbour. A glassy building similar in style to its Italian sister restaurant, this one serves more substantial and expensive meat and fish meals. Daily lunch is reasonable, though, at 55kr (11am–2pm).

**Krögers** on Lärmtorget. The most popular pub/restaurant, where a relaxed crowd eat light, Swedish meals like *Kottbullesmörgäs* (meatball sandwiches; 40kr) or rather less Swedish fish and chips (66kr), plus meat dishes and pastas. There's live music every Sunday from September to April. June–Aug daily noon–1am; rest of the year daily 4pm–1am.

**Lodbroks Café & Pub**, entered from Norra Långgatan 20. The romantic dining room is sophisticatedly rustic, and its short but unusual menu quite delicious: try the speciality, fried anchovies and parsley with cold sour cream (32kr), or the excellent spare ribs (58kr). *Lodbroks* also do a very good-value sandwich-coffee-and-juice breakfast (7am–1pm; 20kr).

**Ming Palace**, Fiskeragatan 7. The best Chinese restaurant in town, with a lunch special at 50–60kr. To find it, head towards the base of the castellated old water tower. Mon–Thurs 11am–10.30pm, Fri 11am–11pm, Sat noon–11pm, Sun 1pm–10.30pm.

**O'Keefe's**, part of the *Stadshotel*. A pub with a good atmosphere outside of Lärmtorget, it is full of bicycles and other oddities hanging from the ceiling. Mon, Tues & Thurs 11.30am–midnight, Wed & Fri 11.30am–2am, Sat 5pm–2am, Sun 5pm–midnight.

**Oscar Bar & Brasserie**, on Lärmtorget. A pleasant Greek-inspired place serving a three-course meal for 99kr and pan pizzas for 60kr; there's also a well-stocked bar. Mon–Fri 4pm–1am, Sat & Sun noon–1am.

**Pub Stocken**, connected to the Bamboo Restaurant on Lärmtorget. A regular bar doing light snacks and baked potatoes (30–50kr). Daily 5pm–1am.

# Öland

Linked to mainland Sweden by a 6km-long bridge, the island of **Öland** is the kind of place a Swedish Famous Five would come on holiday: mysterious forests and flat, pretty meadows to cycle through, miles of mostly unspoilt beaches, wooden cottages with candy-striped canopies, flower boxes, windmills and ice-cream parlours. Swedes have come here in droves for over a century, but since becoming popular with non-domestic tourists, too, it's now visited by fifty-five thousand people every July and August. Despite this onslaught, which clogs the road from the bridge north to the main town, **Borgholm**, this long, splinter-shaped island retains a very likable old-fashioned holiday atmosphere. The labyrinthine **walking trails** and **bicycle routes** wend their way past more than four-hundred old wooden **windmills**, which give the Öland a peculiarly Dutch air, and the bathing opportunities are among the best in Sweden.

As a royal hunting ground from the mid-sixteenth century until 1801, Öland was ruled with scant regard for its native population. Peasants were forbidden from chopping wood or owning dogs or weapons. While protected wild animals did their worst to the farmers' fields, Kalmar's tradesmen exploited the trade restrictions to force low prices from the islanders for their produce. Danish attacks on Öland (and a ten-month occupation in 1612) made matters worse, with seven-hundred farms being destroyed. A succession of disastrous harvests in the mid-nineteenth century was the last straw, a quarter of the population packing their bags for a new life in America. This century, mainland Sweden has become the new magnet for Öland's young, and, by 1970, the island's inhabitants numbered just 20,000.

Today, Öland's attractions include numerous ruined castles and Bronze and Iron Age burial cairns, runic stones and forts, all set amid rich and varied fauna and flora and striking geography. The geology of the island varies dramatically due to crushing movement of ice during the Ice Age, and the effects of the melting process, which took place 10,000 years ago. To the south is a massive limestone plain known as the **Alvaret**; in summer, its thin covering of surface soil is lit up by sweet-smelling, tiny flowers. Limestone has been used here for thousands of years to build runic monuments, dry-stone walls and churches. In central Öland, where the Ice Age left the limestone more hidden, the area is blanketed with forest, while to the north, the coastline is craggy and irregular with dramatic-looking *rauker* – stone pillars, weathered by the waves into jagged shapes. Along with rare flowers, like the delicate rock rose and the cream-coloured wool-butter flower that are both native to southeast Asia, the south contains a sensational **bird reserve**, where skylarks and lapwings join sea birds, waders and millions of migrating birds in spring and early autumn. Further north, the dense forests are characterized by some exotic, foreign plants and the twisted misshapen pine sand oaks in the romantically named **Trolls Forest**.

## Getting there

If you're driving, take the Ängö link road to Svinö (clearly signposted), just outside Kalmar, which takes you over the bridge to **Möllstorp** on Öland. A new rule forbidding **bikes** to be cycled over the bridge has something of a silver lining. There is now a free bus from Svinö especially for cyclists, dropping you off outside the island's main tourist office in Möllstorp. If you're **hitching**, you can try your luck with the free bus, too, citing the bridge's lack of a footpath as the reason to take a free trip. The **bus** timetable, available from Kalmar's bus or train station and tourist office, is impossible to decipher – not helped by bus numbers changing with the season. Buses #101 and #106 are safe bets, however, and run pretty well every hour from Kalmar bus station to Borgholm (50min). The evening service is more erratic, but continues in some form until 2am in summer. If you don't want to go to Borgholm, ask at the bus station for the buses that stop at **Färjestaden**, the bus network hub, a couple of kilometres south of Möllstorp.

There are two **ferry** services to Öland. The more popular car ferry takes you from Oskarshamn, 80km north of Kalmar, to **Byxelkrok** (in north Öland) twice a day at 1.30pm and 5.30pm, taking two hours (120kr per adult one-way, 160kr return; 190kr for a car with one adult, 490kr for a car with four adults; bikes 40kr). A passenger-only ferry also runs frequently from Timmerrabben, 40km north of Kalmar, to **Borgholm** (70kr per person one-way, bikes 30kr).

## Information and getting around

Öland's main **tourist office** is in a large pink building in **Möllstorp** next to the end of the bridge (April & May Mon–Fri 9am–6pm, Sat 10am–5pm, Sun 10am–4pm; June, Aug & Sept Mon–Fri 9am–7pm, Sat 10am–6pm, Sun 10am–4pm; July Mon–Sat 9am–7pm, Sun 10am–6pm; Oct–March Mon–Fri 9am–5pm; ☎0485/39 90 20, fax 390 10). Pick up a bus timetable (but don't expect an explanation) and the Öland *Karten* (49kr) – costly, but a really good map with clear road routes. While you're at the tourist office, take a look-in at the nature centre, *Naturum*, where an exact, model of the islands lights up to show all the areas of interest.

It's worth noting the shape and size of Öland before forming ambitious plans to cover it all by bike. Although the island is geared for cycling, with endless cycle tracks along the flat roads, if you want to explore it from north to south, you're looking at 130km. **Bike rental** is available from Kalmar, Borgholm and at most of the campsites, hostels and the odd farm with a sign outside. All outlets charge around 40kr per day, 200kr per week, and it's not hard to find tandems (80kr) or child seats. If you have a **car**, orientation could not be simpler. There is only one big road, the 136 that runs from the lighthouse at the island's northernmost tip to the lighthouse in the far south. The 136 is picked up directly from the bridge and runs parallel with the west coast, until it reaches Källa, where it swings to the east, before twisting west to run directly through to Byxelkrok. A smaller road (without a number) runs off the 136 down the east of the island south from Föra.

The **bus** network connects most places in Öland, but the service, though efficient, is infrequent, and you have to be prepared for a lot of waiting around, particularly in the south – time trips carefully to avoid being stranded. **Hitching** is possible in the south and most likely when you are heading north across the plain.

An exciting if short-lived introduction to Öland is to take one of the **around-the-island flights** (15min for 150kr, children 100kr) from one of two tiny airfields, one a kilometre south of Borgholm (☎0485/104 00), the other at Ölanda Airfield in a forest clearing, further north near Löttorp (☎0485/281 41 or mobile phone ☎0707/48 74 72). The tiny planes that carry a maximum of three passengers also make taxi flights to Visby on Gotland (500kr one way, 700kr return). Also at Ölanda Airfield are **go-karting** tracks; it's 60kr for a seven-minute speed around on a 65kph kart, or for children aged 5–8, 30kr for a slower, smaller version (June & Aug noon–6pm, July noon–8pm; same number as for flights).

# Borgholm

Walking the simple square grid of streets that makes up **Borgholm**, Öland's "capital", it's clear that tourism is the lifeblood of this villagey town. Although swamped well beyond its capacity each July by tens of thousands of visitors, cramming its pizzerias and bars and injecting a riotous carnival atmosphere, Borgholm is in no way the tacky resort it could be. Encircled by the flaking, turretted and verandahed villas, which were once the pride of the town during its first period as a holiday resort in the nineteenth century, most of the centre is a friendly, if bland, network of shops and restaurants leading to a very pleasant harbour.

The only real attraction here is just to the southwest of the centre, **Borgholms Slotts ruin** (May–Aug 10am–6pm; free). A colossal stone fortification with rows of huge arches and corridors open to the skies, it is reached either through a nature reserve, signposted from the town centre, or from the first exist south off Road 136. When the town was founded in 1816, with just 33 inhabitants, the castle, which gave the town its name (*borg* means "castle") was already a ruin. Built in the twelfth century, it was fortified four hundred years later by King Johan III, and given its present shape, with a tower at each corner, in the seventeenth century. Regularly attacked, the castle eventually fell into disrepair, and after a fire in 1806, it has spent nearly two hundred years being clambered over by tourists – evidenced today by some dangerously shaky masonry.

Just a few hundred metres to the south of the castle is the present Royal Family's summer residence, **Solliden Park**, an Italian-style villa built to a design specified by Swedish Queen Victoria (the present king's great grandmother) in 1903. A huge, austere red-granite bust of Victoria rises out of the trees at the entrance to the car park. The villa itself is private – the Royal Family always spend July here – but the gardens (mid-May to mid-Sept 1–6pm; 35kr) are worth a stroll if you like formal gardens. There's a very ordered Italian Garden, a colourful Dutch Garden and a simple English-style one. Alternatively, you could just head for the delightful café, *Kaffetorpet* (same hours as the garden), just near the car park. It was once a croft, and coffee has been served here since 1890. It serves light lunches, cakes, ice cream and waffles at reasonable prices, and there's a garden of irises and berry bushes growing from the thatched roof.

The only other minor diversion in Borgholm is **Forngard**, Köpmangatan 23 (mid-May to Aug Mon–Sat noon–6pm; 20kr), a museum of Öland life, which is best seen at the end of your visit, as the treasures on display are taken from the historical sites around the island. The ground-floor exhibition includes bits of ancient skulls, some Viking glass, Bronze Age jewellery and grave finds. The upstairs of this early nineteenth-century house has some attractive period rooms, but nothing outstanding; the outbuildings all contain quaint seventeenth- and eighteenth-century peasant interiors.

Just to the north of the town centre, **Blå Rör** is Öland's largest Bronze Age cairn, a huge mound of stones excavated when a coffin was discovered in 1849. In the 1920s, burnt bones indicating a cremation grave were also discovered, along with bronze swords and tweezers – common items in such tombs. The tourist office promotes it as a major site, but apart from the knowledge of its antiquity, there's nothing much to see.

## Practicalities

Set in quiet, park-like gardens, the large and stately *STF* **youth hostel** at Rosenfors (May to mid-Aug; ☎0485/107 56; 100kr) is a kilometre from the town centre – ask the bus driver to stop at *Q8* filling station just before Borgholm proper, from where the hostel is just 100m away. The dormitories and a big kitchen are in old stone outbuildings. The tourist office will book **private rooms** over the counter only, from 120kr per person, booking fee 25kr (50kr if 2–5 days). The local **campsite**, *Kapelludden's Camping* (☎0485/101 78, fax 129 44), is on a small peninsula five minutes' walk from the centre. Here you can pitch a tent for 140kr per person (plus 30kr electricity); there are no cabins. As with the rest of the island, there's no shortage of beautiful spots to camp rough.

Of the **hotels** in the centre of town, *Hotel Borgholm*, Trådgårdsgatan 15 (☎0485/770 60, fax 12 466; ③) has smart rooms; while the vast *Strand*

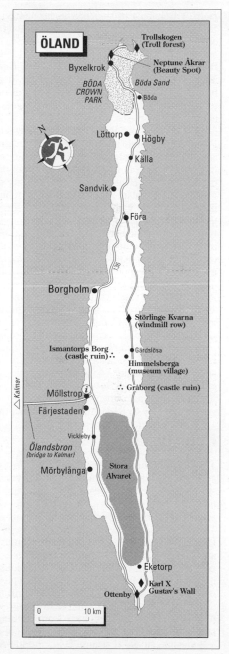

*Hotel,* Villagatan 4 (☎0485/888 88, fax 124 27; ③), straddles one side of the harbour. Styled like a modern Spanish sea-side hotel, its massive interior includes a small shopping mall, a disco and nightclub. Guests have free use of the indoor pool, sauna and solarium. Eight kilometres south of Borgholm on Road 136, one of the very few really fine hotels on the island, *Halltorps Gästgiveri* (☎0485/850 00, fax 850 01; ④, including a superb breakfast), is based in a beautiful eighteenth-century manor house. Its large annexe bedrooms are furnished with the understated luxury of contemporary Swedish design. There's an excellent gourmet restaurant; weekend packages, including meals, are available.

There is a pronounced summer-holiday feel to the town's **restaurants** and bars. Pizza places abound around Stortorget and down to the harbour. Nearly all offer terrace eating, simple furniture, white-plastic trellises and red-and-white-check tableclothes. Cashing in on the summer influx of tourists, pizza prices are fairly high, 65–85kr. *Mama Rosa* (mid-May to mid-Aug daily noon–1am), right at the harbour on Södra Långgatan, is smarter than most and has a more varied menu. As well as pizzas (66kr), they offer classic Italian dishes and a fair wine list. On the far side of the harbour, *Skeppet* (May–Sept daily noon–11pm) is a jolly little Italian restaurant, hidden quite alone behind 1940s' industrial silos. The special, with just about all the ingredients of all the other pizzas together, is a good choice at 70kr. For the finest food with matching prices head for *Backfickan* at *Hotel Borgholm* (daily 6–10.30pm), which has been an inn since 1861. The chef is Karin Fransson, something of a culinary celebrity in Sweden, and main courses come at a hefty 200kr. More fun (and less cost) is the restaurant-cum-pub *Båtan* (mid-June to Aug daily 2pm–2am). On a 1915-built pleasure boat, moored at the harbour (though out of season, *Båtan* chugs off to Vänersborg on Lake Vänern), it serves à la carte meals and a Tex Mex choice (50–80kr); cold dishes cost 45kr; and there's live music daily.

For **drinking**, *Pubben*, Storgatan 18 (daily 1pm–1am), is a cosy pub with old radios and crystal sets for decor. As well as lager, stout and bitter, this popular bar specializes in whisky – 46 varieties of malts and blends. The only **nightclub** worth checking out, *Rooky Bar* (daily 6pm–2am), is on Södralanggatan, 500m from the harbour. Built as a hospital for venereal diseases and later, becoming a church, you can boogie to R&B and house music; there are occasional live bands.

# North Öland

The north of the island makes for the most varied and interesting landscape, with some unexpected cultural and social diversions. Heading up the 136, there's no shortage of idyllic villages, dark woods and flowery fields. At **FÖRA**, about 20km north of Borgholm, there's a good example of a typical Öland church – it doubled as a fortress and was capable of withholding a considerable garrison in times of war. The windows are low enough to peer in at its medieval interior, if the doors are locked. To see a real feat of nineteenth-century engineering, it's well worth stopping at **SANDVIK**, which is dominated by Scandinavia's largest windmill, a Dutch-style construction, with eight floors and ingenious wooden workings. Built in the 1850s, it operated until 1955 and now contains a pleasant pizza restaurant. Sandvik's economy is still based around its stone-cutting factory, one of the few surviving non-tourism industries. Next door to the factory, the café and pizza restaurant (daily noon–midnight) has benefited from its neighbour; inside the benches, bar and tables are made of slabs of white marble cut at angles. It's not a bad place for pizza, lasagne and steaks at around 80kr, and has a range of beers and spirits.

## Källa kyrka

Proud, forlorn **Källa kyrka**, about 7km north, has been empty since 1888 and sits in splendid isolation, 2km outside town (not to be confused with the current church by the sign for **KÄLLA**). Surrounded by brightly flowering meadows, this tall, dull-white medieval church is bounded by dry-stone walls, and its grounds are littered with ancient, weathered tombs. Inside, the lofty interior has seen plenty of action: built of limestone in 1130 to replace an earlier tiny stave church, this one was regularly attacked by heathens from over the Baltic seas. It was modernized in the fourteenth century, when Källa was a relatively important harbour and trading centre, and stripped of its furnishings in the nineteenth century; a row of six models are the only interior features left. There's a fish smokery in the only other building close by.

Just over the main road, a low, deep-thatched spread of early eighteenth-century farm houses contains a restaurant, *Källagården* (daily 11am–11pm), which serves good-value lunch specials at 50kr and on Tuesdays (7–10pm) a *räk buffe* – as many prawns as you can eat for 85kr. There's an overpriced antique shop next door.

## Högby to Byxelkrok

**HÖGBY**, a few kilometres on, has the only remaining tied church houses on the island, relics of the medieval Högby kyrka nearby, but there's not a lot to see. For a most unusual, though somewhat pricey, dining experience, head for the village of **Löttorp**, off the 136, and follow the signs east for 4km down country lanes to the local institution, the *Lammet & Grisen* restaurant, housed in a Spanish hacienda (daily 5.30pm–midnight). The only dishes on the menu are salmon and spit-roasted lamb and pork (hence the restaurant's name), with baked poatoes, flavoured butters and sauces. You eat all the meat you can for 210kr or everything but the meat for 110kr – which isn't worth it. The smoked salmon costs 195kr. There is regular live music.

Continuing north and west off the 136 across the island (the 136 now runs up the eastern side of Öland), **Byrums Rauker** are a striking sight: solitary limestone pillars formed by the sea at the edge of a sandy beach. From here, the north of Öland is shaped like a bird's head, the beak facing east and with a large bite out of its crown. The best **beaches** are along the east coast; starting at Böda Sand, the most popular stretch is a couple of kilometres north at **Kyckesand**, and there's a nudist beach just to the north, marked simply by a large boulder in the sea. Small east coast roads run to the beaches, but the many campsites posted off 136 also lead on to the beaches.

There are some gorgeous areas of natural beauty to the far north. The nature reserve of **Trollskogen** (Trolls Forest), to the east – so-called because it is exactly the kind of place you would imagine trolls to inhabit, with twisted, gnarled trunks of ancient oaks all shrounded in ivy – offers some excellent walking. Around the western edge of the northern coast, the waters are of the purest blue, lapping against rocky beaches; on a tiny island at the tip stands *Långe Eric Lighthouse*, a handsome 1845-built obelisk and a good goal for a walk or cycle ride. **Neptune Åkrar**, 3km south on the western coast, is covered with lupin-like flowers forming a sea of brilliant blue to rival the real sea blue beyond. The name, given by Carl Von Linné, means Neptune's Ploughland, because the ridged land formation looks like ploughed fields. The only town in this region is **BYXELKROK**, a quiet place with an attractive harbour, where ferries dock from mainland Oskarshamn.

## North Öland practicalities

There's not much in the way of proper hotels north of the Borgholm area (see pp.245–46), but high-standard **campsites** abound, marked every couple of kilometres off the 136 and mostly beside a beach. The most extensive site is *Krono Camping* at Böda Sand (☎0485/222 00, fax 223 76), 50km north of Borgholm and 2km off the main road at the southern end of the beach. Camping is 160kr per space, plus 30kr electricity and 10kr for cable TV. Cabins range from 3000kr per week for four people, up to 4700kr with a water supply. Facilities are extensive, with a holiday village of shops, and à la carte and pizza restaurants with troubadour entertainment. There's also a bakery for early-morning oven-warm loaves.

The *STF* **youth hostel**, *Vandrarhem Böda* at Mellböda (open all year; ☎0485/220 38, fax 221 98; 100kr, plus 40kr for breakfast), is just south of Böda's campsite. A big, well-equipped hostel with a cosy kitchen, it has single rooms. For an unusual alternative, the nearby *Bödabaden Öland Square Dance Centre* (open all year; ☎0485/220 12 or 220 85, fax 220 07; 480kr including breakfast) is Europe's only square dancing theme park, with American square dancing tournaments and courses every day, both open air and in a barn. The cabins are quite upmarket, all en suite and more like basic hotel rooms. There's also a good pub decked out as an American saloon.

Just 6km northwest at **Byxelkrok**, *Solö Värdhus* (open all year; ☎0485/283 70; ②, plus 40kr for breakfast, 50kr for lunch) is a pleasant enough, low, white **hotel**. If you're looking for **nightlife** in the north of Öland, what there is mostly happens here at *Sjöstugan* (April noon–5pm, May noon–8pm, June–Aug noon–2am), a restaurant, pub and disco, right by the shore. The speciality is salmon (100kr) and flounder (80kr), but they also serve pizzas (55–85kr) in cardboard boxes, and one vegetarian dish (70kr). Troubadours sing downstairs every day in June, while Swedish dance bands are the thing in July, with discos every Thursday to Saturday.

# Central Öland

Cutting eastwards from Borgholm (take bus #102), following signs to **Räpplinge** leads to **Störlinge Kvarna**, a row of seven windmills by the roadside. A sign tells you this is the island's longest line of post-mill type windmills, but as you'll probably have already seen several windmills by now, there's no real inducement to stop. A couple of kilometres south, **GÄRDSLÖSA** has the island's best-preserved medieval church. The exterior has been maintained so well that it's almost too pristine, but inside is worth looking at, particularly its 1666-made pulpit and the thirteenth-century ceiling paintings; these were whitewashed over in 1781 but were discovered and uncovered in 1950.

The preserved village of **Himmelsberga** , a few kilometres further south, is an **open-air museum** (May to mid-Sept daily 10am–6pm; 30kr) in an idyllic setting. Since the decline of farming in the middle of this century, most of Öland's thatched farmhouses have been rather brutally modernized. Himmelsberga escaped this, however, and since the 1950s, two of its original farms have been open as museums. Subsequently, buildings were brought from all over the island, and it is now an extensive collection of crofters' farms, a smithy and a windmill. Due to a lack of available timber on Öland, as islanders were forbidden to cut their own lest it spoil the royal hunting, the peasants, rather bizarrely, had to buy entire oak houses from the mainland and reassemble them on the island; several of these you can see here. There's a café in the village, where tea and coffee are served in bright copper pots.

**Ismantorps Borg** (dating from around 450 AD), an ancient castle ruin east from Himmelsberga, only warrants a visit if you fancy a walk though a lovely wooded path. It's a huge, circular base of stones, and you can see the foundations of 88 rooms inside – if you try. **Gråborg**, passed by bus #102, another 10km south of here, is Öland's largest ancient castle ruin, with 640-metre-long walls. Built around 500 AD and occupied through the Middle Ages, when the Gothic entrance arch was built, today the walls encircle little more than a handful of hardy sheep.

# South Öland

Dominated by **Stora Alvaret**, the giant limestone plain on which no trees can grow, the south of the island is sparsely populated, and the main town is the rather dull **Mörbylånga**. Despite tourist literature references to "exposed rock", the landscape of the south is one of flat meadows, which boast, among other unusual plant life, some rare alpine strains that have stoically clung to life since the Ice Age. **Buses** run so infrequently here, you'll need to double check times at Färjestaden, just south of the bridge, where the few buses south start their journey. **Hitching** is possible – probably because drivers know that without their help, chances are you'll be stranded for long periods of time. Facilities are fewer than in the north, so if you don't have a car, it's worth stocking up before you head off. Despite the difficulties of travelling though the south, its great advantage is that summer crowds thin out here, and you can peacefully explore the most untouched parts of the island – and visit Öland's most interesting fort at Eketorp.

## Vickleby

The prettiest village south on the 136 is **VICKLEBY**, equidistant between Färjestaden to the north and Mörbylånga to the south, where a remarkable art and design school, **Capella Gården**, was set up by Carl Malmsten early this century. A furniture designer and idealist, Malmsten struck out against the traditional system of teaching: his dream was to create a school that stimulated mind, body and soul – a sort of educational utopia that was criticized as unworkable by a shocked Stockholm society. In 1959, he bought a range of picturesque farmhouses at Vickleby and opened an art and design school for adults that still runs today. It's not for everybody – the atmosphere is more than a little intense – but courses attract people from all over the world, who live for a few weeks in a commune environment, woodcutting, textile weaving, gardening and making pottery. The results, including some lovely ceramic and wood pieces, are for sale in a big annual exhibition. If you do visit, it's best to call the studios first (☎0485/361 32), rather than just turning up.

## Eketorp and Ottenby bird station

Of all the forts on Öland, the one most worth a visit is at the village of **EKETORP**, reachable by bus from Mörbylånga. The site (May to mid-June & late Aug daily 9am–5pm, guided tours in English 1pm; 45kr, children under 14 free) includes an archeological museum. During a major excavation in the 1970s, three settlements were discovered, including a marketplace from the fourth century and an agricultural community dating from 1000. The result is a wonderful achievement in popular archeology, actual physical evidence being thin on the ground. A large encircling wall has been reconstructed on the plain, and by examining food waste in bone fragments found at the site, researchers have identified animal species once living here; today, the same animals – pigs, sheep and geese – wander around the fort to bring it to life. The best of the finds, such as jewellery and weapons; are on show in the museum, and there's a workshop where, if you feel inclined, you can have a go at leather work or "authentic" ancient cookery.

If you head south from here, a stone wall cuts straight across the island. Called **Karl X Gustav's Wall**, it was built in 1650 to fence off deer and so improve hunting chances. A strain of 150 fallow deer still roam about today at **Ottenby**, in the far south of the island. Öland's largest estate, built in 1804, this is now a bird-watcher's paradise, with a huge nature reserve and Ottenby **bird station**, which, since 1946, has been Sweden's centre for migrating birds. There are also two protected bird observation towers and a bird museum. You have to be keen on our feathered friends, who trill in their millions, for the area to hold much appeal – there's absolutely nothing else here.

### South Öland practicalities

The main **tourist office** at Möllstorp (see p.243) will book **private rooms** from 150kr per person per night, with a 25kr booking fee – more for longer stays. *Mörby Youth Hostel* (open all year; ☎ & fax 0485/493 93; ①), 15km south of the bridge, is a **hostel and hotel** combined, the only difference being that the hotel (400kr) includes sheets and breakfast, while the hostel at 250kr for a double does not. Bus #105 drops you off outside. *Top 12* is a kind of hotel, with a **campsite**, 10km south of the bridge at Haga Park; the beach here is a centre for windsurfing. In an oldish wooden house, the hotel offers no frills B&B: double rooms, with en-suite shower, cost 400kr, plus 30kr for breakfast; four-bed family rooms with a kitchen and bathroom are 650kr per night; while the most basic dormitory accommodation is 110kr per bed. There's also a good, cheap restaurant, where meals like salmon and potatoes go for 60kr (5–10pm).

For a **regular hotel**, try *Hotel Kajutan* (☎0485/408 10; ③); built in 1860 by a vintner who produced wine from the garden, it's a pleasant old place at the harbour behind the bus station in **Mörbylånga**. At Vickleby, a more attractive location, *Hotel Bo Pensionat* (☎0485/360 01; ②), in a traditional row of village houses, is very popular; it's worth booking ahead in high season.

# Småland

Thickly forested and studded with lakes, **Småland County** makes up the southeastern wedge of Sweden, and although appealing at first, the uniformity of the scenery means it's easy to become blasé about its natural beauty. Småland is often somewhere people travel through – from Stockholm to the southwest, or from Gothenburg to the Baltic coast – yet beneath the canopy of greenery, there are a few vital spots of interest (apart from Kalmar, already covered on p.236), alongside opportunities for hiking, trekking, fishing and cycling.

Historically, Småland has had it tough. The simple, rustic charm of the pretty painted cottages bely the intense misery endured by generations of local peasants; in the nineteenth century, this lead to a massive surge of emigration to America. Subsistence farming had failed, and the people were starving; consequently a fifth of Sweden's population left the country – most of them from Småland. While their plight is vividly retold at the **House of Emigrants** exhibition in **Växjö**, which makes an excellent base from which to explore the region, the county's main tourist attraction is the myriad of **glass factories** hidden in forest clearings.

# Växjö

Founded by Saint Sigfrid in the eleventh century, **VÄXJÖ** (pronounced "vehquer") is by far the handiest place to base yourself if you are interested in the distinctive glassware produced in the region. Deep in the heart of Småland county (110km from Kalmar), the town itself boasts two superb museums: the newly renovated and extensive **Smålands Museum**, which is notable for being home to the **Swedish Glass Museum**; and the **House of Emigrants**, which explores the mass emigration from Sweden in the nineteenth and early twentieth centuries. There's also a particularly romantic castle ruin 4km north, and a cathedral that has been renovated almost as many times as it is centuries old – eight. Aside from these attractions, the town centre lacks any other buildings of interest, and its many shops are fairly standard.

## Arrival, information and accommodation

The **train** (hourly trains from Kalmar; 1hr 30min) and **bus stations** are side by side in the middle of town, from where it is a short walk to the tourist office. The helpful **tourist office** at Kronobergsgatan 8 (mid-June to mid-Aug Mon–Fri 9am–6pm, Sat 10am–2pm, Sun 11am–3pm; Sept to mid-June Mon–Thurs 9.30am–4.30pm, Fri 9.30am–3pm; ☎0470/414 11, fax 478 14) will book **private rooms** from 110kr, 25kr extra for sheets, plus a 50kr booking fee. The splendid *STF* **youth hostel** (open all year; ☎0470/630 70, fax 632 16; 100kr) at **EVEDAL**, 5km north of the centre, is among the most civilized and beautifully maintained in the country. If you normally don't stay in hostels, try this one. Set in parkland on tranquil Lake Helgasjön (it has its own beach), this eighteenth-century house was once a society hotel, and serves a good breakfast for 43kr (laundry facilities 30kr). To get there, take Linnegatan north, following signs for Evedal, or take bus #1C from the bus terminal to the end of the route (last bus is at 4.15pm, 3.15pm on Sat), or bus #1A, which leaves you with a 1500m walk, but runs daily till 8.15pm. Next to the hostel by the lake is a **campsite**, *Evedal Camping* (☎0470/630 34, fax 631 22), which has a decent shop for stocking up on food. Tents can be pitched for 115kr, plus 25kr for electricity; new four-person cabins are 450kr, or 550kr for six-person cabins, including electricity, kitchen and shower.

### HOTELS

**Esplanad**, Norra Esplanaden 21A (☎0470/225 80, fax 262 26). A reasonable, central hotel room with no frills. ②/①

**Statt**, Kungsgatan 6 (☎0470/134 00, fax 448 37). The usual executive-class hotchpotch of shiny marble, potted palms and terrible carpets, the hotel serves a generous buffet breakfast. Within the hotel is an Irish pub, *O'Keefe's*, and in summer, the *Lagerlunden Restaurant* (Mon–Thurs 6pm–1am, Fri & Sat till 2am). ④/③

**Teaterpark**, in the central *Concert Hall* building (☎0470/399 00, fax 475 77). Visually striking, this ultra-stylish, Functionalist hotel also has special bedrooms fully designed for the disabled guests. ④/②

**Tofta Strand Hotel**, Lenhovdvavägen 72 in Sandsbro (☎0470/652 90, fax 614 02). Although some way out of town, this cheap hotel/pension is a fun place to stay. Delightful gardens lead down Lake Toft, where you can drive out on a bizarre motorized raft for coffee and home-made cake. To get to the hotel, take Road 23 in the direction of Oskarshamn, or hop on #bus 5 from Växjö bus terminal to Sandsbro; the hotel is 400m further on the right. ①

**Värend**, Kungsgatan 27 (☎0470/104 85, fax 362 61). Another standard hotel, this also does good-value triple rooms. ③/①

## Smålands Museum

The newly renovated **Smålands Museum**, behind the train station (June–Aug Mon–Fri 11am–6pm, Sat & Sun 11am–4pm; Sept–May Tues, Wed & Fri 11am–6pm, Thurs 11am–8pm, Sat & Sun 11am–4pm; 30kr), includes two perma-nent exhibitions: the less enticing, though intelligently displayed, history of Småland's manufacturing industries and the more interesting "400 years of Swedish glass". The latter shows sixteenth-century place settings, eighteenth- and nineteenth-century etched and simple coloured glass, and stylish Art Nouveau-inspired pieces, with subtle, floral motifs. The most visually appealing, though, are the displays of contemporary glass in the extension building, which are all mounted on white wood plinths. The range of exhibits is vast, with elegant classics, brash pop-art glass and other pieces that show just how inventive the glass-blower's rod can be in trained hands. The exhibition also explains how many of the smaller glassworks have been taken over or squeezed out by the *Kosta* and *Orrefors* giants.

## House of Emigrants

Directly in front of the Småland Museum, a plain building contains the inspired **House of Emigrants** (Open all year; Mon–Fri 9am–4pm, Sat 11am–3pm, Sun 1pm–5pm; 25kr), with its moving "Dream of America" exhibition. The museum presents a living picture of the intense hardship faced by the Småland peasant population from the mid-nineteenth century. Due to the agricultural reforms that denied the peasants access to village common ground and a series of bad harvests, between 1860 and 1930 a million Swedes emigrated to America – a sixth of the population – and most of them from Småland. Using creative tech-niques, including English-lanugage telephone narratives and extensive displays with English translations, the exhibition traces individual lives and recounts the story of the industry that grew up around emigration fever. Most boats left from Gothenberg and, until 1915, sailed with the British *Wilson Line* to Hull, where passengers crossed to Liverpool by train to board the transatlantic ships. Conditions on board were usually dire: the steamer *Hero* left Gothenburg in 1866 with five-hundred emigrants, nearly four-hundred oxen and nine-hundred pigs, calves and sheep sharing the accommodation.

By 1910, Chicago had a higher population of Swedes than Gothenburg, becom-ing known as Sweden's second city, and walking through the exhibition, past models of crofters' huts in Småland and a sizable model of the deck of an emigrant ship, you are finally led on to displays of life in America. There are stories about those who literally struck gold; one man, known as Lucky Swede, became America's most successful gold prospector in Klondyke, before losing it all to his chorus girl wife. There is also a section on women, who accounted for 52 percent of the emigrants called "Not Just Kristina", the exhibition refers to Kristina and Karl Oscar, the fictitious couple around whom Wilhem Möberg, one of Sweden's most celebrated writers, based his trilogy *The Emigrants*. On display is Moberg's writing cabin, which was given to the museum after his death in 1973. One of the saddest tales is of Mauritz Ådahl, who, like a fifth of those who left, returned to try and live again in his native land. Money pressure forced him to emigrate for a second time in 1912, and due to the English coal-miners' strike, which meant his ship could not sail, he took the much-publicized maiden voyage on the *Titanic*. Of the 1500 people killed in the *Titanic* disaster, several hundred were Swedish emigrants who, as third-class ticket holders, had no access to the deck until the lifeboats had all been taken. When he was discovered twelve days later in the sub-zero waters, his watch had stopped at 2.34am, just as the *Titanic* vanished beneath the waves.

The **Research Centre** (Mon–Fri 9am–4pm; ☎0470/201 24) charges 100kr per day to help interested parties trace their family roots, using passenger lists from ten harbours, microfilmed church records from all Swedish parishes and records of such bodies as the Swedish New York Society, Swedes in Australia and the Swedish Congo Veterans Association. It's worth booking ahead during the peak research season of May to mid-August.

### Other sights: the Domkyrkan and Kronoberg Castle

There's not much else to see in the centre, except a quick look at the very distinctive **Domkyrkan** (daily 8am–8pm, June–Aug guides 9am–5pm), with its unusual twin green towers and apricot-pink facade. Regular restorations, the most recent in 1995, together with a catalogue of sixteenth-century fires and a lightning strike in 1775 have left nothing of note except a unique 1775 organ. There are, however, some brilliant new glass ornaments by Göran Wärff, one of the best-known of the contemporary Glass Kingdom designers, including a wacky alternative font. The cathedral is set in **Linné Park**, named after Carl Von Linné, who was educated at the handsome adjacent school (closed to the public). Linnés likeness appears on all 100kr banknotes.

Set on a tiny island in Lake Helgasjön, the ruin of **Kronoberg Castle** lies 4km north of the centre in a beautiful and uncommercialized setting – follow signs for Evedal, or bus #1B from Växjö bus station (Mon–Fri every hour, less frequent on Sat). The bishops of Växjö erected a wooden fortress here in the eleventh century, but it was Gustav Vasa in 1540 who built the present one in stone. Entered over an old wooden bridge set at a narrow spot in the lake, it's a perfect ruin, leaning precariously and complete with rounded tower and deep-set lookouts. Some new brick archways and a couple of reinforced roofs, added in the 1970s, stop the whole thing collapsing. At the centre grows an ancient oak, beneath which is a well. Between the ruin and the grass-roofed centuries-old café *Ryttmästargården* (see overleaf), the old paddle steamer *Thor* makes regular excursions around Lake Helgasjön and up to Lake Asassjön – a delightful way to see the pretty lakeland scenery (see "Activities and sightseeing" for full details).

## Eating, drinking and activities

One of the pleasures of Växjö and its surrounds is the wealth of really good **eating** opportunities, though few of them come cheap. If you're interested in trying traditional Småland food, the endless forests and poverty associated with the region have created a cuisine based around woodland berries, potatoes and forest animals. **Isterband** is a flavoursome, spicy sausage, usually served with potatoes and a dill sauce, while **krösamos** are potato pancakes with lingonberry sauce. More expensive restaurants charge high prices for elk steaks, hare and venison, while the classic local dessert is a rich curd-cheese cake with warm cloudberry sauce. If you want to eat cheaply, there is a glut of pizza and Chinese restaurants and a *McDonalds*; the mobile street grills even do pasta lunches. **Drinking** in Växjö is mostly done in restaurant bars, as there are few actual pubs in town.

## Daytime cafés

**Broqvists**, Kronobergsgatan 14, just off Stortorget. Good cakes in this Växjö classic, but it can get smoky. Mon–Fri 8.30am–8pm, Sat 8am–7pm, Sun 8.30am–3pm.

**Café Momento** in Smålands Museum (open museum hours; p.252). The best of the daytime cafés, serving Italian panini and ciabatta with Italian pastes (35kr) and decadent desserts. The proprietors also run *Café Ryttmästargården* and *PM & Friends*; see below.

**Café Ryttmästargården**, overlooking Kronoberg Castle. The same food as *Café Momento* but in an eighteenth-century cottage in an idyllic lakeside setting – summer mosquitoes are a menace, though; you'll need your own transport in the evening. Open May–Aug daily.

**Tofta Strand Hotel** (see p.252), in a room at the back of the hotel. A great konditori. The owner's daughter is a wedding cake specialist, and the home-made pastries, meringues and tarts are wonderful, though the decor is on the tatty side. Mon–Sat 11am–7.30pm; June–Aug daily.

**Tomas Skåres**, Kungsgatan 13. A popular central konditori with coffee-and-cake specials for 20kr. Mon–Fri 7.30am–7pm, Sat 7.30am–6pm, Sun 10am–6pm.

## Restaurants

**Evedal Vardhus**, next door to the youth hostel on Lake Helgasjön (☎0470/630 03). The best food in Växjö is served in this eighteenth-century, lakeside former society restaurant. Swedish specialities include roast pike with crayfish, all fresh from the local lake. Two courses cost 260kr, but lunches are 55kr. Open daily 11.30am–2.30pm & 6–10pm.

**PM & Friends** ,Västra Esplanaden 9. Very popular, noisy and stylish – though it doesn't look like much from the outside. Lunch specials are 54kr and there's an extensive European wine list. Mon–Thurs 11.30am–2pm & 6pm–midnight, Fri till 1am, Sat 6pm–1am.

**Restaurant Teaterpark**, connected to *Hotel Teaterpark* in the new *Concert Hall* building. This beautiful restaurant has a good-value summer menu of grills – shark, salmon or meats – at 80–100kr (Mon–Sat 5–11pm). In winter, there's a more costly, wider menu and it opens for lunch (65kr).

**Spisen**, Norra Järnvägsgatan 8. Another gourmet choice, but only for real money spenders; lunch at 59kr will give a taster. Open daily 6–11pm.

## Activities and sightseeing

Aside from the few main sights in the town centre, you could easily spend a day exploring the surrounding countryside, which is riddled with forest **hiking routes**, designed for all levels of enthusiasm. The tourist office can supply information and maps. **Cycling** is very popular, too, though it's by no means flat country and the forest lanes are often pretty rough. **Bike rental** is available from *Cykeluthyrning* at the *Shell* filling station, Mörnersväg 60, in the centre (75kr per day, 100kr overnight, 400kr per week). There are also numerous **canoeing** opportunities on the still waters of the lakes, with special routes prepared. Among the dozens of places to rent canoes and get information, a good starting point is *Evedals Kanotuthyrning*, next to the youth hostel, a professional body supplying all canoeing equipment and advice (☎0470/639 93).

Vintage **steamer tours** on the classic boat *Thor* will take you on the "sluice trip" from Lake Helgasjön to Lake Asasjön in two and a half hours (100kr including coffee), or there's a one-hour trip for 75kr. Book at *Café Ryttmästargården*, opposite Kronoberg Castle. For a more glamorous dinner tour, take the boat across Lake Asasjön to Asaherregård, a country mansion (250kr, including dinner). Alternatively, try the grill-dinner trip to the sluice gates between the lakes for 200kr (takes 3hr 30min); book for both at Smålands Museum (☎0470/451 45).

# The Glass Kingdom

Within the dense birch and pine forests that, together with a thread of lakes, make up the largely unbroken landscape between Kalmar and Växjö, are the bulk of Småland's celebrated **glassworks**. The area is dubbed **Glasriket**, or the "Glass Kingdom", with each glassworks signposted clearly from the spidery main roads. This seemingly odd and very picturesque setting for the industry is no coincidence. King Gustav Vasa pioneered glass-making in Sweden when he returned from Italy in the mid-sixteenth century and decided to set up a glassworks in Stockholm. However, it was Småland's forests that could provide the vast amounts of fuel needed to feed the furnaces, and so a glass factory was set up in 1742 called Kosta, after its founders, Koskull and Stael von Hostein. Today, it is the largest glassworks in Småland.

## Visiting the glassworks

Of the twenty or so glassworks still in operation in Småland, thirteen of them have captivating glass-blowing demonstrations on weekdays, several have permanent

---

### GLASS-MAKING AND BUYING IN GLASRIKET

Watching the **glass-making process** is mesmerizing and worthy of study. The process involves a glass plug being fished out of a shimmering, molten lake (at 1200°C) and then turned and blown into a graphite or steel mould. In the case of wine glasses, a foot is then added, before the piece is annealed (heated and then slowly cooled) for several hours. It all looks deceptively simple and mistakes are rare, but it nevertheless takes years to become a *servitor* (glass-maker's assistant), working through the ranks of stem-maker and bowl-gatherer. In smaller works, all these processes are carried out by the same person. In many of Småland's glassworks, it's an amazing sight to see the bowl-gatherer fetching the glowing gob for the master blower, who then skilfully rolls and shapes the syrupy substance. When the blower is attaching stems to wine glasses, the would-be handle will slide off or sink right through if the glass is too hot; if too cold, it won't stick – and the right temperature lasts a matter of seconds.

If you want to **buy glassware**, which is marketed with a vengance – take a look at the hyberbole in the widely available *Kingdom of Crystal* magazine – don't feel compelled to snap up the first things you see. The same batch of designs appears at most of the glassworks, a testament to the fact that *Kosta Boda* and *Orrefors* are the main players nowadays; many of the smaller works have been swallowed up, even though they retain their own names. This makes price comparison easier, but don't expect many bargains; the best pieces go for thousands of kronor. You may find it useful to see the glassware exhibition in Väjxö's Smålands Museum first to get an idea of the various styles and where you can find them (see p.252).

exhibitions of either contemporary work or pieces from the firm's history, and without exception, all have a shop. **Bus** services to the glassworks, or at least within easy walking distance, are extremely limited, and without your own transport it is almost impossible to see more than a couple in a day – however, this should be enough. While each has individual design characteristics, the **Kosta Boda** (easiest from Växjö; see below) and **Orrefors** (its main rival and closer to Kalmar) works have extensive displays and, if your time is limited, these give the best picture of what is available. To get to *Orrefors* from Kalmar, take Road 25 to Nybro, then Road 31 or a train from Växjö to Nybro, then bus #138, #139 or #140 to the factory (June to mid-Aug; glass-blowing Mon–Fri 8am–3.30pm, Sat 10am–3pm, Sun 11am–3pm; exhibition Mon–Fri 9am–3pm, Sat 9am–4pm, Sun 11am–4pm).

## KOSTA BODA

The **Kosta Boda** and **Åfors** glassworks are all operated by the same team, and while two of Kosta's most celebrated designers, Bertil Vallien and Ulrica Hydman Vallien, have their studios at *Åfors*, the biggest collection is at *Kosta* (June to mid-Aug; glass-blowing Mon–Fri 10am–3pm, Sat 9am–3pm, Sun 11am–4pm). The historical exhibition here (Mon–Fri 9am–6pm, Sat 9am–4pm, Sun 11am–4pm) contains some of the most delicate turn-of-the-century glassware designed by Karl Lindeberg, while if you're looking for contemporary simplicity, Anna Ehrener's bowls and vases are the most elegant. In the adjacent shop (Mon–Fri 9am–6pm, Sat 9am–4pm, Sun 11am–4pm) you can buy large vases by her for around 2000kr and dishes for 1058kr. Current design trends, though, tend more towards what the *Kosta* blurb calls "playful disrespect for conventional form – a rhapsody of sensuality", which in reality means a lot of colourful high-kitsch. Ulrica Hydman Vallien's newest designs involve painted-on faces with glass noses stuck on. A single, traditional *akvavit* glass costs 89kr, and at the upper limit, new designer sculptural pieces go for astoundingly high prices. If you're eager to make a purchase, however small, designer egg cups are 250kr. To get to *Kosta* from Växjö, take Road 23 in the direction of Oskarshamn, then Road 31 southeast and on to Road 28. By public transport, bus #218 now goes direct from Växjö bus station to the glassworks. To get there and back in the day, take the 8.15am or 11.15am (one hour trip) returning at 2.50pm, 3.40pm or 4.40pm.

## OTHER GLASSWORKS

**Strömbergshyttan** glassworks near Hormantorp (June to mid-Aug; shop only Mon–Fri 9am–6pm, Sat 9am–4pm, Sun 11am–4pm) is the best bet for a local trip from Växjö; with both *Kosta* and *Orrefors* displays, it's more comprehensive than nearby **Sandvik**, an *Orrefors* company. Strömbergshyttan is south down Road 30 from Växjö, or take bus #218 (the *Kosta* bus; 40min), which runs more frequently here than to *Kosta*. If you like the distinctive, simple blue-rimmed glassware popular all over Sweden, this can be seen at **Bergdala** (mid-June to mid-Aug; glass-blowing Mon–Fri 9am–2.30pm, Sat 10am–3pm, Sun noon–4pm; shop Mon–Fri 9am–7pm, Sat 10am–4pm, Sun noon–4pm), 6km north of Hormantorp; there's no public transport. A small, traditional factory, it offers a more intimate look at the blowing process.

To the north, **Rosdala** is unusual in that it only produces glass for lampshades (mid-June to mid-Aug; glass-blowing Mon–Fri 8am–3pm, though closed most of

July). It's not too exciting, though, as most of the designs are staid floral patterns painted on the globes, and the *Rosdala* **museum** (Mon–Fri 9am–6pm, Sat 10am–4pm, Sun 11am–4pm) displays some of the ugliest 1970s' designs. The shop isn't bad value, with the smallest lampshades from 170kr (Mon–Fri 9am–6pm, Sat 10am–4pm, Sun 11am–4pm). A few kilometres further north on the same road, the 1905-founded **Lindshammar** works has mostly quite ordinary glassware, and some real tat, too; the few really good vases cost 3200kr. From Växjö, take Road 23 to Norrhult-Klavreström, then Road 31 north; there's no public transport to *Rosdala*.

**Johansfors** to the south of the region is small and set by a lake (exhibitions Mon–Fri 9am–6pm, Sat 10am–4pm, Sun noon–4pm; shop daily 9am–6pm); take Road 28 from *Kosta*; there's no bus service here. It specializes in stemware (wine goblets). Nearby **Skruf** has the most basic, jam-jar style collection, which is also about the cheapest, but is one of the few to charge (5kr) for its museum entry.

## Practicalities

All the glassworks have simple **cafés**. The bigger ones also have local **accommodation**; check availability with tourist offices at Växjö or Kalmar. One of the most enjoyable, though costly, eating experiences – and one that really can claim to be a Småland original – is the nightly **hyttsill**, a meal of herrings baked in the factory glass furnaces at 300°C using a glass-maker's rod. Five of the glassworks – *Kosta, Orrefors, Sandvik, Bergdala* and *Lindshammar* – cook up *hyttsill*, each on a different night but always at 7pm (check individual days with the tourist office). The herring comes with furnace-baked potatoes, Småland curd cake (a rich local cheesecake), coffee and beer. The standard price at all the participating glassworks is 240kr, and it's important to reserve a day or two in advance (*Bergdala* ☎0478/316 50; *Kosta* ☎0478/508 35 or 345 00; *Lindshammar* ☎0383/210 25; *Orrefors* ☎0481/300 59; *Sandvik* ☎0478/405 15).

# Jönköping

Perched at the southernmost tip of Lake Vättern, one of the oldest medieval trading centres in the country, **Jönköping** (pronounced "Yun-shurp-ing") won its town charter in 1284. Today it is famous for being the home of the matchstick, the nineteenth-century manufacture and worldwide distribution of which made the town a wealthy place. Matches are no longer made here, and the downfall of the industry was mainly due to one man, the 1920s' match magnate Ivar Kruger. Jönköping's most notorious twentieth-century figure, he lent vast amounts of money he didn't have to countries with large national debts in exchange for a monopoly on match sales. One of Sweden's wealthiest men, rather than become bankrupt he shot himself in Paris in 1932, signalling an end to the success of the industry. Despite the town's plum position at the tip of the great lake, too many high-rise offices and bland, central buildings ruin what could be a pleasant town. It does, however, have good accommodation and some excellent restaurants and bars, making it a viable, if not so pretty, lakeside base. Jönköpingers themselves head for the coast during the summer months, so if you are here between June and August you'll find it fairly quiet. The most interesting part to explore is the renovated historical core, focused around the match museum, in a quaint cobbled courtyard.

The biggest 1844-built match factory now houses **Tändsticksmuseet**, the match museum (May–Aug Mon–Fri 10am–5pm, Sat & Sun 11am–3pm; Sept–April Tues–Thurs noon–4pm, Sat & Sun 11am–3pm; 25kr) at Västra Storgatan 18. Inside, however, it isn't too thrilling, just a collection of matchbox labels and match-making machines and not much else. Opposite, the **Radio Museum** is a dream for airwave fanatics, with every type of radio from early crystal sets to Walkmans. A couple of metres away and set in an old match factory is **Kulturhuset**, a sort of trendy arts centre, with rooms for band rehearsals and antiquarian and alternative bookshops (Mon–Fri 5–7pm). During summer (June–Aug), the centre is converted into a private youth hostel (see below). There's also a good cheap café here and, next door is *Bio,* a stylish art-house cinema. From September to May, there's also a bustling early-morning Saturday market on the street outside the centre.

The only other museum to bother with is the **Länsmuseum** (daily 11am–5pm, Wed till 8pm; 20kr, under 18s free), on Dag Hammarskjölds Plats, on the other side of the canal between lakes Vättern and Munksjön. A mish-mash of oddities, with exhibits on garden chairs throughout the ages, bonnets, samovars and doll's houses, it is like wandering round a well-stocked junk shop – and there's no English labelling. The best part is the well-lit collection of paintings and drawings by **John Bauer**, a local artist who enthralled generations of Swedes with his Tolkeinesque representations of gnomes and trolls in the *Bland Tomtar och Troll* books. Bauer's work goes beyond this though, his sensual Ophelia-like depictions of women blending National Romantic and Art Nouveau styles.

Although there's little else to see in the town centre, it is remarkable for its numerous **free churches** – 23 in the immediate vicinity – and consequently Jönköping has been dubbed "Sweden's Jerusalem". As the traditional Church watches its congregations diminish, people are turning instead to these independent and fundamentalist churches. If you see a white #777 bus parked around town, it's a mobile café belonging to the Pingst, or Pentacostal Church, into which people are invited to sip coffee and listen.

### Arrival, information and accommodation

The **train** and **bus stations** are next to each other on the lake's edge. Just over the bridge, the **tourist office** is in the *Djurläkartoget* shopping centre (mid-June to mid-Aug Mon–Fri 8am–6pm, Sat 10am–1pm; mid-Aug to mid-June Mon–Fri 8am–4.30pm; ☎036/10 50 50, fax 12 83 00). The tourist office can assist with **private rooms** at 150kr per person, while the town's **youth hostel** (mid-June to mid-Aug; ☎036/19 05 85; 110kr) is just a few steps west of the train station. Outside of summer, the nearest youth hostel is 6km east in **HUSKVARNA**, Odengatan 10 (☎036/14 88 70, fax 1488 40; 95kr), a hundred metres from the station – take bus #4 from outside the tourist office. **Camping** is more accessible; the site at Rosenlund (open all year; ☎036/12 28 63), right on the lakeside, is 3km from the town centre, with several buses heading out that way. Most of the main **hotels** slash their prices in summer by up to half. The most prestigious is *Stora Hotel*, Hotellplan (☎036/10 00 00, fax 71 93 20; ④/②); built in the 1860s, this imposing place overlooks the lake, and the rooms are decorated in Gustavian-style pastels. For a rather stylish, yet surprisingly inexpensive, classic hotel, the *Grand Hotel*, Hovrättstorget (☎036/71 96 00, fax 71 96 05; ②/①, breakfast not included), was established in 1904. *Prize Hotel City*, Västra Storgatan 25 (☎036/71 92 80, fax 71

88 48; ②/①, plus 50kr breakfast), is very central, just three minutes' walk from the train station, and is a clean, standard hotel with a night-time reception.

## Eating, drinking and nightlife

Jönköping has plenty of good and lively places to **eat** and **drink**. However, some close for the summer when many of their regulars are away at the coast, while others are inexplicably closed on Fridays and Sundays. If you like eating food special to the area, go for **Arctic char** from the little mobile fish shop down by the harbour, or at any of the better restaurants. The char comes from Vättern; an unusually cold and deep lake, it is able to sustain fish normally only found in the Baltic Sea.

If you want to carry on after the bars close, the trendiest **nightclub** for a young crowd is the stylish *Gruvan* (50kr cover charge), in a former match factory by the match museum. It's packed on Friday and Saturday nights; an 18–23 age group use the big dance area or more relaxed bar area, which is kitted out with coal-mining paraphernalia.

### CAFÉS AND RESTAURANTS

**Anna-Gretas Matsal & Café**, Västra Torget. The oldest café in town, this is a lovely place with a friendly atmosphere. It opens so early on Saturday for the market traders, who set up stalls in the square outside. Mon 7am–6pm, Tues 7am–10pm, Wed–Fri 7am–11pm, Sat 6am–2pm & 6pm–midnight.

**Café Bla Bla**, on Smedjegatan. A laidback café-bar, with a stylish interior frequented by twenty-to-thirty somethings eating huge cinnamon rolls; try their superb chocolate balls (6kr). Mon–Fri 11.30am–5pm & 9pm–3am, Sat 11am–3pm & 9pm–3am.

**Mäster Gudmunds Källare**, Kappellgatan 2. A vaulted cellar restaurant serving good, traditional Swedish. Mon–Fri 11am–10pm, Sat noon–10pm, Sun & holidays noon–5pm.

**Svarta Börsen**, Kyrkogatan 4 (☎036/71 22 22). The best restaurant in town, in one of the only remaining classic buildings on the west side of the centre, is expensive but excellent – it's best to book. Lunch Mon–Fri 11.30am–2pm, dinner Mon–Thurs & Sat 6–11pm.

**Taj Mahal**, Kappellgatan 15. This is one of the best Indian restaurants, with a takeaway service selling lunch with coffee at 65kr.

**Trottoaren Restaurant**, connected to the grand *Stora Hotell* at Hotellplan. A wacky American-style diner, with a pink Vespa, US number plates and filling station pumps on a cobbled floor. The tables are surprisingly complete with crisp linen and silver candlesticks, and full menus are from 159kr.

### BARS

**Balzar's Bar & Brasserie**, which is part of *Hotel Klosterkungen*, Klostergatan 28. A quiet, pleasant place for a meal or a beer, with main courses at 100–150kr or light meals at 65kr. There's occasional live music, a mix of pop and old tunes (Fri & Sat). Happy hour 5–7pm.

**G och Company**, Smedjegatan 36. The town's most popular, lively venue. Heavy rock music means you can't really have a conversation on a weekend evening, but the Mexican food is good and there's a summer beer garden.

**Karlsonns Salonger**, Västra Storgatan 9. New to the scene, the bar gets very busy and the food is good. Mon & Tues 5pm–midnight, Wed–Sat 5pm–2am.

**Rignes**, attached to the *Hotel Savoy* at Brunnsgatan 13–15. A dark, candle-lit pub, serving Norwegian beer. The music is blues and rock and roll, mostly by bands. The set daily menu is mainly meat dishes though not expensive, and a daily lunch menu including salad, coffee and cake costs 40kr. Open till 2am at weekends, midnight on weekdays (closed Mon; 20kr cover charge on Fri & Sat).

# Along the shore of Lake Vättern to Vadstena

The road heading north along the eastern shores of **Lake Vättern** offers the most spectacular scenery and delightful historical towns in the region. Jönköping can be used as a base for excursions, but there are plenty of places to eat and stay along the way, including some lesser-known, idyllic hotels and restaurants. It's perfect for **trekking**, too, with several walking paths.

## Huskvarna

Six kilometres east of Jönköping on the E4 – initially called Östra Storgatan – is **HUSKVARNA** (10min bus trip), originally named after the 1689 arms factory Husquarna. The company still exists and today produces sewing machines and motorbikes. When you first arrive, Huskvarna appears very industrial, but if you press on to the old quarter and the preserved smith's village called **Smedbyn**, you'll find some quaint wooden cottages that now house art and craft galleries. Nearby, there's also a town museum in the old powder house, **Kruthuset** (May–Aug Sat & Sun 2–5pm; 15kr), and a musuem of local industry, **Husqvarna Fabriksmuseum** (May to mid-Sept daily 1–5pm; 15kr), based in the company's 1867-built musket barrel factory. Unless you are particularly interested in the town's history, it's altogether more rewarding to head north up either the E4 or the more picturesque *Grännavagen* (the old E4). There are no trains, but buses #120 and #121 make the trip to Gränna in around an hour (stopping at Hakarp and Röttle on the way), and there's a quicker express bus twice a day, too.

## Hakarp and Röttle

A few minutes on from Huskvarna, the crashing waterfalls that used to drive the town's industry come into view as the road winds. A couple kilometres further, the church of **HAKARP** (daily 9am–4pm; June–Aug till 6pm) is really special. The **church** is set in gardens, with a separate bell tower nearby, and it's interior is a riot of paintings that were clearly designed to terrify the peasant parishioners. There are graphic depictions of hell, with demons stabbing and torturing naked women. The image of Eden to the right of the entrance looks positively dull in comparison. Above, and obscured by the organ, the ceiling has interesting paintings of both the present church, built in 1694, and the medieval church before it, together with an interpretation of New Jerusalem, with more naked women climbing from their graves. Note, too, the pew backs, painted most bizarrely with leopard-skin spots, which look more 1970s than 1770s but are original. The place is packed with imagery and icons, including plaster figures suspended in mid-air above the pulpit.

One of the most idyllic goals for a few hours' wandering is the next hamlet of **RÖTTLE**. Its name derives from words meaning "roaring torrent", and industry existed here as early as 1297, when Rytlofors Mill established grinding rights. One of the oldest mills, called the Jerusalem Mill, which King Magnus gave to the Bishop of Linköping in 1330, still stands. The village was once owned by Per Brahe, one of Sweden's best-known aristrocrats (see "Gränna" opposite), and the trades here included glove manufacture, animal skin processers, coppersmiths and sword cleaning. Today, the ancient, red wooden cottages that sit snugly amid

# 100 Rough Guides*

# 100% Reliable

# Stay in touch with us!

ROUGH*NEWS* is Rough Guides' free newsletter. In three issues a year we give you news, travel issues, music reviews, readers' letters and the latest dispatches from authors on the road.

I would like to receive ROUGH*NEWS*: please put me on your free mailing list.

NAME . . . . . . . . . . . . . . . . . . . . . . . . . . . . . . . . . . . . . . . . . . . . . . . . . . . . . . . . . . . . . . . . . . . . . . . . . . . . . . . . . . . . . .

ADDRESS . . . . . . . . . . . . . . . . . . . . . . . . . . . . . . . . . . . . . . . . . . . . . . . . . . . . . . . . . . . . . . . . . . . . . . . . . . . . . . . . . . . . .

Please clip or photocopy and send to: Rough Guides, 1 Mercer Street, London WC2H 9QJ, England or Rough Guides, 375 Hudson Street, New York, NY 10014, USA.

# Travel the world
# HIV *Safe*

# Travel *Safe*

HIV, the virus that causes AIDS, is worldwide.

You're probably aware of the dangers of getting it from unprotected sex, but there are many other risks when travelling.

Wherever you're visiting it makes sense to take precautions. Try to avoid any medical or dental treatment, but if it's necessary, make sure the equipment is sterilised. Likewise, if you really need to have a blood transfusion, always ask for screened blood.

Make sure your travelling companions are aware of the risks and the necessary precautions. In fact, you should take your own sterile medical pack, available from larger high street pharmacies.

Remember, ear and body piercing, acupuncture and even tattoos could be risky, because they all involve puncturing the skin. And although you might not normally consider any of these things now, after a few drinks - you never know.

Of course, the things that are dangerous at home are just as dangerous when you travel. So don't inject drugs or share works.

Avoid casual sex and always use a good quality condom when having sex with a new partner (and each time you have sex with them).

And it's not just a gay disease' either. In fact, worldwide, it's most commonly transmitted through sex between men and women.

For information in the UK:

Ring for the TravelSafe leaflet on the Health Literature Line freephone 0800 555 777, or pick one up at a doctor's surgery or pharmacy.

Further advice on HIV and AIDS: National AIDS Helpline: 0800 567 123. (Cannot be reached from abroad).

The Terrence Higgins Trust Helpline (12 noon–10pm) provides advice and counselling on HIV/AIDS issues: 0171 242 1010.

MASTA Travellers Health Line: 0891 224 100.

**Travel** *Safe*

# Travel the world HIV *Safe*

emerald green grassland and silver birches are picturesque rather than industrial, and the sound of the water is now a gentle lull. Next to Röttle is **Västanå
Nature Reserve**, which runs all the way to the lake and is carpeted with
heathers, cowberries and delicate yellow, blue, and white wood anemones. A
splendid **walking trail** to take is the John Bauerleden, which wends its way from
Huskvarna northwards for 50km, but if you pick it up at Röttle, it makes for an
excellent easy walk.

# Gränna

A delightful target for a day-trip, **Gränna**, 40km north of Jönköping, is associated
with pears, striped candy rock and hot-air ballooning (see below). It's easy to
while away a whole afternoon in the cafés here, and if you want to stay, then apart
from some very good cheaper accommodation, a couple of really fine, historic
hotels make charming and romantic bases. Approaching from the south, the
beautiful Gränna Valley sweeps down to your left, with the hills to the right, most
notably the crest of Grännaberget, which provides a majestic foil to some superb
views over Lake Vättern and its island, Visingsö. Vättern is known not only for its
clean, deep waters, but its unpredictable nature. The lake's capriciousness ended
the lives of the artist John Bauer and his entire family, when their boat capsized
in the choppy waters in 1918.

Per Brahe, one of Sweden's first counts (see "Visingsö" overleaf), built the
town, using the symmetry, regularity and spaciousness in planning that he had
learnt while governor of Finland. If you arrive in late spring, the hills around
Gränna are a confetti of pear blossom, Per Brahe having encouraged the planting
of pear orchards – the Gränna pear is still one of the best-known varieties today.
The lively main street, **Brahegatan**, was widened to include space for gardens
fronting all the houses, while the other main roads were all designed so Brahe
could look straight down them as he stood at the windows of his now-ruined castle, **Brahehus**. The gardens along Brahegatan remain mostly intact, and until the
1920s, there were no additions to the original designs. Even now, there's very
much a village feel to the little town. The best starting point for a great view is to
head up behind the market square, where there's a statue of Brahe, to *Café
Stugan* (for details see p.263).

## S. A. Andree Museum

Next to the tourist office on Brahegatan is the fascinating **S. A. Andree museum** (mid-May to mid-June daily 10am–5pm; July–Aug daily 10am–6pm; other
times 10am–4pm; 20kr), dedicated to Salomon August Andree, the Gränna-born
balloonist who led a doomed attempt to reach the North Pole by balloon in 1897.
Born at Brahegatan 37, Andree was fired by the European obsession of the day to
explore and conquer unknown areas, and also by the national fervour sweeping
through the country. In 1895, he made a speech in Stockholm in which he rhetor-
ically asked: "Am I mistaken in the fact that, in the same way that we expect the
peoples of southern Europe to explore Africa, they expect us to explore the white
expanses of the north?" This atmosphere of zealous nationalism gained him and
his little team funding from Alfred Nobel, King Oscar and Baron Oscar Dickson;
with no way of really directing the balloon, however, the trip was destined for disaster from the start. After a flight lasting only three days, the balloon made a
forced landing on ice, and having flown more than 800km, it had landed just

470km from its departure point. The men attempted to walk towards civilization, but ice floes meant they made no progress, and after six weeks' trekking, they set up camp on an ice floe drifting rapidly southwards. Sadly, the ice cracked and their shelter collapsed, and with it their hopes. Finally they died from the cold, starvation and poisoning from trichinosis, after eating the raw meat of a polar bear they had managed to spear. It was 33 years before their frozen, preserved bodies and their equipment were discovered by a Norwegian sailing ship. They were reburied in Stockholm at a funeral witnessed by a crowd of forty thousand.

The exhibition is poignant because one of the crew, 25-year-old Nils Strindberg, kept a diary until October 7, a couple of days before his own death. Also preserved film taken by the team has been developed and makes for pitiful viewing: Andree and Strindberg are seen with the polar bear, and other sequences show the three hopelessly pulling their sledges across the ice sheets.

### Gränna rock

Gränna is also known, more happily, for striped candy rock, called **polkagris**, ever since Amalia Eriksson, a penniless widow, eked out a living producing the tooth-rotting red and white sugar tubes in the mid-nineteenth century. It's not the most pleasant thing to eat, but fun to watch in production, which is possible at one of the small factories, called **Cabbe Polkagrisfabrik**, 3km south of Gränna, just opposite the *Hotel Gyllene Uttern*. Behind the counter, displaying a hundred colours and flavours of the sweet, you can watch as the ingredients (comprising 99 percent sugar, a drop of dye and a drop of pure peppermint) are heated to 150°C, melted, poured, twisted, hardened and cut into the sweets.

### Visingsö

From Gränna, a twenty-minute **ferry** crossing (June–Aug half-hourly, otherwise hourly; 16kr on foot, 150kr return with a car – though there's limited availability) drops you on **Visingsö**. At the harbour, there's a lagoon for summer swimming that's warmer than the deeper waters of Vättern. There's also a fine smoked fish shop opposite the dock, selling mackerel, whitefish and salmon smoked with brandy.

During the twelfth and thirteenth centuries, Swedish kings often lived on the island, which is just 12km by 3km wide, and five medieval monarchs died there, including Magnus Ladulås in 1290. It was in the mid-sixteenth century, though, that Eric XIV decided that Sweden should follow the example of Continental monarchies and bestow titles and privileges on deserving noblemen. He created the title of Count of Visingsborg, whose lands included the island, and awarded it to Per Brahe the Elder. With the gift of additional lands from Queen Kristina, Per Brahe the Younger enjoyed a spate of castle building, including Västanå Slott, to the south, and the Visingsborg Slott, on the east shore of the island. However, after Brahe the Younger's death in 1680, the Crown took back much of the land, including the island.

Arriving at the dock, you're likely to be met by a horse and trap called a *rem-malag*, a tempting way to cover the three-kilometre trip (42kr return) to **Kumlaby** church, the oldest relic on the island, dating back to the twelfth century. With beautifully painted ceiling and walls, the church's truncated tower is the result of astronomy classes organized by Brahe the Younger, whose school was the first in the region to accept women. Between June and August, you can climb the steps of the tower for a fine view of the island (daily 9am–8pm). **Bikes** can be rented from near the dock to see the remains of **Näs castle**, at the southern tip of the island.

This was once a major power centre in Sweden, though there's little sign of its erstwhile glory. **Visingsborg Slott**, near the ferry terminal, is also an empty shell, its roof burned off by Russian prisoners celebrating the death of Karl XII in 1718.

## Practicalities

The **tourist office** is on Brahegatan, right beside the S. A. Andree Museum (June–Aug Mon–Fri 9am–6pm, Sat 10am–2pm; rest of the year Mon–Fri 10am–4pm; ☎0390/410 10, fax 102 75; free). Two **youth hostels** serve Gränna: the first is *Gränna Vandrarhem*, booked through the tourist office and situated nearby (mid-June to early Aug; 110kr per person for the first night, then 100kr). The second is right on the beach near the ferry (May–Sept; ☎0390/107 06; 120kr, breakfast 35kr). The tourist office will also book **private rooms** from 100kr plus a booking fee of 30kr.

If you want to stay in a really lovely **hotel**, the *Grand Hotel Ribbagården*, just off Brahegatan (☎ & fax 0390/108 21; ③/②), is a charming place, full of antiques. Once a farm, the building has been a hotel since 1922, when Baron Von Düben, who had worked as a masseur in London, set it up as a hostelry for a glamorous set. For 970kr, you can stay in the room Greta Garbo used, with lovely views from big windows. The other famed hotel in Gränna is *Hotel Gyllene Uttern*, or "Golden Otter" (☎0390/108 00, fax 418 80; ④/③, or annexe rooms ③/②), 3km south of town close to the main road. Although built in the 1930s, it looks like a medieval German castle, with stone castellations, a meadow of wild flowers growing on the sloping roof and a baronial interior. With its own chapel, the hotel is a favourite place for weddings.

There are several excellent **cafés** in Gränna, all of which are on Brahegatan, except for *Café Stugan* (June–Aug 10am–10pm, May 10am–9pm), a steep climb from the market square – it's also possible to drive up. Inside it's all stripped floors and country rugs, while eating outside affords a wide vista over the lake. Try their speciality shrimp sandwiches at 40kr or some Swedish cheesecake. Back in town, another pleasant place is *Café Allard*.Better, though, is *Café Amalia*, named after the queen of Gränna rock, which sells superb lingonberry ice cream and has a big terrace overlooking the rooftops and lake. A picture of Amalia shows her looking not unlike Queen Victoria, and if you wander back into the café, you'll see there's even an Amalia Eriksson Fan Club. A little further up the road is *Haglunds Konditori,* with a wide selection of delicious cakes and breads. Gränna only has one **pub** of note, *Gränna Pub* at *Café Hjorten*, also on Brahegatan, a very pleasing restaurant and bar with a beer garden and pizza parlour. Proper meals from 75kr are served on the sunny terrace, while you can eat cheap pizzas downstairs.

# Around Lake Tåkern

Following Lake Vättern's shoreline north, the land surrounding **Lake Tåkern** (just 10km south of Vadstena) offers some beautiful open landscapes, with excellent walking trails, a litter of medieval churches and the substantial remains of a twelfth-century monastery; also the lake itself is one of the country's best bird sanctuaries. All these sites are probably best visited as day-trips from one of the main towns, but if you're in a car, it would be a shame to hurry too quickly on to Vadstena. If you are relying on public transport, bus #610 runs between Ödeshög, Vadstena and Motala, with stops at every site (Mon–Fri 7 daily, Sat & Sun 2 daily). The express bus #840 between Gränna and Vadstena does not stop as frequently.

## Omberg and the Alvastra Monastery

**Omberg** is a 10km stretch of forested hill country, with several walking trails; Jhässatorget leads to its highest point, Hjässan, affording spectacular views over Vättern and the plains to the east. The **Naturum** (Nature Centre), near the southern end of Omberg, is only for real enthusiasts, but does have general tourist information. The ruins of **Alvastra Monastery**, just 2km off Road 50 at the southern tip of Omberg, is set amid unspoilt countryside, which in early to mid-summer is alive with colour: acid-yellow rape and blue, underripe corn fields against the duller blue of Vättern to the west. On the way, you'll also pass the Sverker Stone commemorating Sverker the Elder, king of Östergotland. The ruins here are perfect enough to be a film backdrop – all arches and jagged stones topped with grass, with Omberg looming up behind. The monastery was founded in 1143 when King Sverker invited a group of French Cisterian monks to Sweden. It went on to become a centre of considerable power, at one point owning nearly five-hundred local farms, and it was home to Sweden's first archbishop Steanis, who was the confessor to Saint Birgitta, Sweden's first and enormously influential female saint (see "Vadstena", opposite). The monastery was destroyed by Gustav Vasa in the sixteenth century, Vasa using its stones to help build his castle at Vadstena. Nowadays, summer midnight concerts are staged here, with mystical lighting effects through the arches; they're worth catching, though you'll need your own transport. The times change each year, so ask at the tourist office in Vadstena.

In the nearby village of **ALVASTRA**, *Ombergs Turist Hotel* (☎0144/330 02, fax 330 90; double room 550kr including breakfast in summer family rooms sleeping four for the same price) is a comfortable, genteel old **hotel** and, if you have a car, is a good alternative to the more expensive hotels in Vadstena. It's worth checking out the hotel restaurant (Tues–Sun 11am–6pm), where you can eat fish fresh out of Vättern, with à la carte meals costing 100–150kr; lunch is pricey but good at 85kr. There's also an *STF* **youth hostel** in the Omberg region at **STOCKLYCKE** (April–Sept; ☎0144/330 44; 100kr). It has cabins for two to six people, a café and sauna.

### Rökstenen

About 8km east off Road 50 (buses #664 & #665 from Alvastra Monastery; 10min) stands **Rökstenen**, regarded as the most remarkable of all Sweden's two thousand or so **runestones**. Standing by Rök kyrka, itself in neatly hedged isolation, the Rök Stone is beneath a specially made protective canopy. Dating from the ninth century, the four-ton lump of granite has over eight-hundred runes engraved into its surface, making it the world's longest continual runic inscription.Written by a father, Varin, in memory of his son, Vaemod, its translation makes for some pretty incomprehensible reading; it begins: "I tell the tale which the two war booties were, twelve times, both together from man to man" and so it goes on. Yet it is seen as the greatest insight into Swedish literature in antiquity, and accompanying boards explain all about the stanzas, narrative metre and rhythm.

### The lake

**Lake Tåkern**, formed around 7000 BC when the inland ice receded from Östergotland's plains, is not impressive in size but is one of the best in the country for birdwatching, with 260 species appearing here. There are also several walking trails for a tranquil half-day meander (from April 1 to June 30, you are restricted to specially marked trails clearly printed on signs all over the area). The **bird-**

**watching tower** is close to the car park, where the Tåkern Canal spills out of the lake, with another at Hor to the lake's eastern shore, which has been adapted for the disabled. In late summer, thousands of wading birds rest on the mud banks in front of the main tower, and if you're about in autumn, a large flock of geese fills the air – up to 45,000 bean geese migrate from Russia and Finland, using Tåkern as their resting point. Even later in the year, golden and sea eagles appear, too. If approaching from the north, take the sign for Strå, 7km off Road 50, for 2km and turn off just past the canal. For the southern visiting area, take the E4, turning off at the sign for Kyleberg, then left at Kyleberg. For the disabled access tower to the east, take Road 944 off the E4 and continue for 6km north of Väderstad.

# Vadstena and Motala

With its beautiful lakeside setting, **VADSTENA**, which once served as a royal seat and important monastic centre, is the most evocative town in Östergotland and a fine place for a day or two's stay. Sixty kilometres north of Gränna and just 16km southwest of **Motala**, the town's main attraction is a rather gorgeous moated **castle**, planned in the sixteenth century by Gustav Vasa as part of his defensive ring protecting the Swedish heartland around Stockholm. The cobbled, twisting streets, which are lined with cottages covered in climbing roses, also contain an impressive abbey, whose existence is the result of the passionate work of four-teenth-century **Saint Birgitta**, Sweden's first female saint.

Birgitta (1303–73) came to the village of Vadstena as a lady-in-waiting to King Magnus Eriksson and his wife, Blanche of Namur, who lived at Bjälbo Palace. Married at thirteen, and after giving birth to eight children, Birgitta had her first of many visions, while living at the palace. Such was the force of her personality, she persuaded her royal employers (to whom she was vaguely related) to give her the palace in order to start a convent and a monastery. Based on her revelations, the central theme for both was to be that of simplicity and poverty. In order to obtain papal approval to found the monastery, she set off alone for Rome in 1362, but luck was against her – the pope was in Avignon, France. She spent the next twelve years in Rome, having more visions, campaigning for his return and eventually succeeding, only to die before ever returning to Vadstena. She was canonized in 1391, a final vision having already told her this would be the case. Her daughter, Katarina, carried on her work and brought about the building of the monastery and abbey; she too became a saint in 1484. Although the convent closed to novice nuns in 1595 during the Reformation, many of the existing nuns came from influential families and were allowed to continue living there until 1618.

## Arrival, information and accommodation

From Gränna, express **bus** #840 (the Jönköping express) runs to Vadstena in fifty minutes (90min if setting off from Jönköping). During the week, it leaves Gränna at 8.40am or 5.10pm (Jönköping at 8am or 4.25pm), but there is no Saturday service; on Sunday, there's just an afternoon bus. Bus #610 runs regularly from Motala to Vadstena. By car, it's a straight run along the E4 and Road 50 north from Gränna or southwest on the 50 from Motala. While there are no longer any trains on regular lines, an old steam or diesel train does **sightseeing tours** to Fågelstra to the east (twice a day in July, late May & June at weekends only; 50kr). Tickets are available from the otherwise disused train station by the castle.

Vadstena itself is easily walkable, but for striking out into the Östergotland countryside, **bikes** can be rented (90kr per day or 300kr per week) from the quaint old **tourist office** at Rådhustorget (May Mon–Fri 9am–5pm, Sat 10am–noon; June & Aug Mon–Fri 10am–6pm, Sat 10am–1pm, Sun 4–7pm; July Mon–Fri 10am–7pm, Sat 10am–1pm & 5–7pm, Sun 4–7pm; ☎0143/151 25, fax 151 29). You can also buy a **Vadstena Card** here for 60kr for free entry to the castle, the hospital museum, Mårtens House and a sightseeing tour; it's only worth it if you intend to see the lot.

## Accommodation

Vadstena's *STF* **youth hostel** at Skänningegatan 20 (open all year; ☎0143/103 02, fax 104 04; 100kr, breakfast 38kr) is close to the lake, just up from the abbey. Advance booking is essential outside the mid-June to mid-August period. The other *STF* hostels are both in fine locations and ideal if you're checking out the countryside to the south of Vadstena. One is in the Omberg mountain region (see p.264 for details), and the other prettily situated at Ödeshög (☎0144/107 00; 90kr), close to Lake Vättern just off Road 50. Alternatively, the tourist office will provide a list of **private rooms** (20kr fee), though it won't book them for you.

Set in converted historic buildings and catering for glamorous tastes, the main **hotels** are fairly expensive. The *Vadstena Kloster Hotel*, in the 1369-built nunnery next to the abbey (☎0143/315 30, fax 136 48; ③, or ④ for a lake view), is still very atmospheric, especially the old Kings Hall – from the original palace – where breakfast is served; the bedrooms are pleasant but ordinary. Non-residents can breakfast here for 50kr (Mon–Fri 7.15–9am, Sat & Sun 8.30–10am). *Vadstena Slottshotel*, Ayslen (☎014/103 25), opposite the castle, is built within a late nineteenth-century hospital. A grand, comfortable place, it is owned by the same company as the *Kloster* and rooms are much the same price. A rather pleasant and cheaper alternative, especially if you have your own transport, is *Ombergs Turist Hotel*, 10km south at Alvastra (see p.264 for details).

# The Town

While Vadstena boasts numerous ancient sites and buildings, each with an information plate (in English) – such as Sweden's oldest court house, the Rådhus, a distinctive fifteenth-century building – the two outstanding attractions are the castle and the abbey. If you have time to spare, there are also a couple of museums that are well worth visiting: the Mental Hospital Museum and one dedicated to a lesser-known twentieth-century sculptor, Gottfied Larsson.

## Vadstena Slott

If you've already visited the castle at Kalmar in Småland (see p.239), you'll be familiar with the antics of Gustav Vasa and his troubled family. The saga continues with gusto at **Vadstena Slott** (June & Aug 10am–1pm, July 10am–4pm; 35kr). With four seven-metre-thick round towers and a grand moat, it was originally built as a fortification to defend against Danish attacks in 1545, but was then prettified into a palace to serve as a home for Vasa's mentally ill third son, Magnus. His elder brother, Johan III, was responsible for its lavish decorations, but fire destroyed it all just before completion, and to save on costs the post-fire decor was simply paint-ed on the walls, including swagged curtains that can still be seen today.

Its last resident was Eleanor, the widowed queen of Karl X; after she died, the castle was regarded as hopelessly unfashionable and no royal would consider liv-ing there. Since the end of the seventeenth century, the building fell into decay and was used as a grain store; the original hand-painted wooden ceilings were chopped up to make into grain boxes. As a result, there wasn't much to see inside, but a recent drive to buy up period furniture from all over Europe has re-created something of the atmosphere. Portraits of the Vasa family have also been crammed in, displaying some very unhappy and ugly faces that make for enter-taining viewing. It's worth joining the regular English-language tours to hear all the Vasa family gossip, but if this doesn't fit in with your schedule, the most inter-esting area to aim for is the dark, vaulted towers, where 150 soldiers slept at a time. Each summer, a play is performed in one tower (ask at reception for times) recounting the story of Gustav Vasa's daughter, Catarine. While Catarine was honeymooning at the castle on her way to Germany, the homeland of her new husband, Catarine's sister Cecilia, who was famed for her beauty and defiance, chose to begin an affair with her new brother-in-law's brother. The couple were discovered at an indelicate moment, and the lover was carted off to prison, with the promise that when released he would never show interest in women again. According to contemporary records, he never did.

## The abbey

Saint Birgitta specified that the **abbey church** (May daily 9am–5pm; June & Aug daily 9am–7pm; July daily 9am–8pm) should be "of plain construction, humble and strong". Wide, grey and sombre, the lakeside abbey, which was consecrated in 1430, certainly fulfills her criteria from the outside, but inside it has been embell-ished with a celebrated collection of medieval artwork. More memorable than the crypts of various royals that are also inside is the statue, now devoid of hands, of Birgitta "in a state of ecstacy". To the right, the rather sad "Door of Grace and Honour" was where each Birgittine nun entered the abbey after being professed – the next time she entered through the door would be in a coffin on her funeral day. Birgitta's bones are encased in a red velvet box, decorated with silver and gilt medallions, in a glass case down stone steps in the monks' choir stalls. The altar-piece here is worth a glance, too. Birgitta, looking rather less than ecstatic, is por-trayed dictating her revelations to a band of monks, nuns and apostles.

Although now housing a restaurant and a hotel, the **monastery** and palace-turned **nunnery** on either side of the abbey are open for tours; the nunnery is more evocative of times past. A minute is all it takes to see the thirteenth-century Bjälbö Palace; the most interesting part is the Kings Hall, which was originally a banqueting hall, with an elegant lofty ceiling. On its conversion to a convent, Birgitta had the ceiling lowered to what she considered a more appropriate level for the nuns – and it remains so today.

## The Mental Hospital and Mårten Skinnares House

Just beyond the abbey graveyard gates, the Mental Hospital Museum (June–Aug daily 1–3pm; 20kr) and neighbouring Mårten Skinnares House are less adver-tised but still fascinating attractions. The **Mental Hospital Museum** is based in Sweden's oldest mental hospital, dating from 1757, which was called Stora Dårhuset – the Large Mad House. Inside, the exhibits of instruments of torture are harrowing enough, but what sets the museum apart are the photographs of the inmates from the last century (extensive research having been carried out to ensure that there are no surviving relatives). Among the range of terrifyingly inappropriate contraptions used to control and "cure" the inmates is a spinning chair, in which difficult patients were tightly strapped and spun until they vomited in submission, and a "compulsory chair" for really problematic cases. The victims were tied into a seat with a commode base for up to a week. Other contraptions include an iron bath in which patients were tied and scalded to relieve them of their madness, and a tub used until 1880 in which patients were held down among electric eels. Upstairs, among the neck irons and leather mittens, the case studies make shocking reading; one such study details the life of a 35-year-old maid, who, in 1833, "showed signs of nymphomania and sang indecent songs". She was prescribed and received the spinning chair and the eel bath until she vomited and passed out, which was perceived as a success. Also on the first floor, the most poignant displays are of the excellently drawn satirical pictures by the patients, depicting the tortures inflicted on them.

Next door, the **Mårten Skinnares House** only demands five minutes of your time. Mårten was a wealthy furrier who had this exquisite little house built in 1520. It has just two rooms, though there are hidden treasure-store cellars and, most oddly, the earliest of indoor lavatories – an upstairs commode seat set over the back of the house, quite open to what used to be the pig sty beneath.

### Gottfied Larsson Museum and the glassworks

The **Gottfied Larsson Museum**, Skänningegatan 9, just a few metres from the abbey (daily 11am–3pm; 10kr), houses a collection of powerful human figures by an underrated contemporary of Sweden's better-known twentieth-century sculptor, Carl Milles. The figures, some of which are set in the gardens behind the seventeenth-century museum building, are mostly large studies of naked male manual workers, and some fine, female heads. There are also modern temporary sculpture exhibitions.

Close to the castle, Vadstena's 1985-founded **glassworks** (glass-blowing Mon–Fri 8am–4pm; shop Mon–Fri 9am–5pm, Sat noon–3pm) is called *Vas Vitreum* and produces some refreshingly simple designs, along with more traditional pieces. The seconds shop, in one of the two old wooden grain stores outside the castle, has the same items as the factory for forty percent less.

## Eating and drinking

Eating in Vadstena is expensive. The pick of the **cafés** is extremely busy *Gamla Konditori* (Mon–Fri 9am–7pm, Sat 9am–6pm, Sun noon–6pm) on Storgatan just up from the tourist office. It sells great cakes and sandwiches; there's a smoky backroom and a smoke-free front room. The best **restaurant** in town is *Vadstena Valven*, Storgatan 18, with a lunch special at 55kr (11.30am–3pm) and fine dinners (Mon–Sat 6.30–11pm, Sun 2–10pm; closed Sundays outside summer). The speciality is Vättern char in white wine sauce, but you won't find it on the menu, as the restaurant's own fisherman can only get it when the waters are warm enough, so it's worth asking. Also try the smoked whitefish with artichoke (67kr). The restaurant at *Vadstena Kloster Hotel* (Mon–Sat 11.30am–3.30pm) in the monastery by the abbey looks from the outside like a flaking reform school, and inside, despite high-vaulted corridors and flagged stone floors, this stylish restaurant is not at all what Saint Birgitta ordered. It serves meat and fish at around 175kr a course, desserts for a hefty 60–80kr. Much more friendly is *Restaurant Rådhus Källeren,* in the cosy cellars of the sixteenth-century court house on Rådhustorget (Mon–Wed & Fri noon–11pm, Thurs & Sat noon–midnight, Sun 1–10pm). Here, smoked whitefish from Vättern is 129kr. It's also a **pub** and where Vadstena locals hang out on Thursday and Saturday evenings; the music gets louder then, too. A younger crowd head for *Sjömagasinet* at Lilla Hamnamen, on the far side of the castle. The bar and **disco** here are the liveliest place in this otherwise staid town. For a good pizza, try *Pizza Firenze* at Storgatan 13 (Mon–Wed 11am–11pm, Thurs & Fri 11am–1am, Sat noon–1am, Sun noon–10pm). It's also a pub and nightclub of sorts, but it's best known for a good choice of food in basic surroundings.

## Motala

At **Motala**, 16km north of Vadstena, the Göta Canal tumbles into Lake Vättern through a flight of five locks. One of the most popular spots on the canal, the town was designed by the waterway's progenitor, Baltzar Von Platen: where lake and canal meet, a promenade cuts a smooth arc around the bay, while Motala fans out behind. You'll pass Von Platen's grave, beside his statue, on the canal-side walk. Pleasing though strolling around the lake is, the best thing to do in Motala is to cruise down a stretch of the canal, something that's easiest during the peak summer season (mid-June to mid-Aug), though not impossible at other times of the year. In summer, **boats** run along the canal to Borensburg, 20km east, leaving Motala at 10.30am and taking around five hours for the round-trip (150kr, lunch on board 80kr). Alternatively, you could cover the same journey, or any other, by **bike**; the tourist office can advise about boat tickets and bike rental places. If you're here in June, you might consider joining the fourteen-thousand-strong field in what is claimed to be the world's biggest friendly cycle race, around the lake.

The town itself is, for the most part, rather bland. An exception, however, is the new **Motor Museum** (May–Sept daily 10am–8pm; 40kr) at the harbour edge, which is much more entertaining than its name implies. Far from the expected parking lots of shiny vehicles, this is a really museum of style, and great fun even if you have no particular interest in cars. Each of the unusual, rare and wacky motors is displayed in context, with music appropriate to its era blaring from radio sets, and models, ranging from 1950s' American classics to old Jaguars and the occasional Rolls Royce. It's a hive of activity, with piles of old televisons, telephones and crystal sets amid the cars and motorbikes. Among the highlights is a 1931 Chrysler Imperial limousine, which was owned by the local Nobel prize-winning poet Verner von Heidenstam. There's a painted background of his manor house – which you can visit, 10km north – and a tape recording of his poetry. On the hill behind the town, there is also a small **Radio Museum** (June–Aug daily 11am–4pm; 10kr), recalling the days when "Motala Calling" was as redolent to Swedes as "This is London" is to avid BBC World Service listeners.

Just up from the Motor Museum is the **Canal and Navigation Museum** (May Mon–Fri 9am–4pm; June & Aug Mon–Fri 8am–6pm; July daily 8am–8pm; 20kr), which details the canal's construction and demonstrates the operation of a lock. Just outside, at the point where the lake and canal meet, a plaque and maps show the striking similarities between the Göta Canal and its official "twin", Scotland's

Caledonian Canal. Both waterways linked the east and west of their respective countries, and the men behind them, Von Platen in Sweden and Thomas Telford in Scotland, were born and worked at the same time.

An ambitious new project intended (perhaps optimistically) to generate tourism for Motala is **Locomotiv 2000** (July–Sept Mon & Fri–Sun 10am–6pm, Tues & Thurs 10am–8pm; 25kr). Set in the old workshop buildings at Motala Verkstad, on the narrow strip of land to the east of the centre, between the waterways of Göta Canal and Motala Ström, its regularly changing exhibitions are aimed at creating a "smithy for ideas", a sort of museum of environmental history with an emphasis on future technological breakthroughs. Not exactly a recipe for relaxation, but it can be teamed up with a pleasant water trip. To get to the centre, you can take a boat up Motala Ström or bus #322; bus #301 stops 1km short.

Just 3km west of the centre, **Varamon Beach** claims to be Scandinavia's largest inland bathing beach, with a kilometre of golden sand. Although the claim isn't true, it does have the warmest waters in Lake Vättern, as Varamon Bay is the most shallow area, and the beach is thick with bronzing bodies on hot summer days. It's also popular for windsurfing.

## Practicalities

**Trains** pull in parallel with the canal about a kilometre from the centre. For the **tourist office** (June–Aug daily 10am–6pm; Sept–May daily 10am–5pm; ☎0141/22 52 54, fax 521 03) at Fokes Hus, turn left along Östermalmsgatan, right along Vadstenavägen and left into Repslagaregatan. This will lead past the central Storatorget and the **bus station**; the tourist office is on the right close to the harbour. A second, summer-time tourist office is at the harbour (June to mid-Aug daily 8am–8pm) and **rents** out bikes (60kr per day, 250kr per week).

**Private rooms** can be booked through the main tourist office at around 180kr; while the *STF* **youth hostel** at Varamon (☎ & fax 0141/57436 or mobile 0103/871 28; 95kr, breakfast 38kr) is right on the beach – take bus #301 from Storatorget. There's a popular summer café here, too. The hostel does not accept any credit cards, so if necessary change money at any of the banks in Storatorget. There's also a well-located and equipped **campsite** on the beach called *Z-Parkens Camping* (☎0141/21 11 42), which has what it calls *Varamon Chalet Colony* – pretty wooden cabins overlooking the lake and bookable through the tourist office.

The main town-centre **hotels** are entirely business oriented, but are the only option if you value en-suite bathrooms. *Stadshotellet* on Storatorget (☎0141/21 64 00, fax 21 46 05; ④/②) has worn but big rooms; *Palace Hotel,* Kungsgatan 1, just off Storatorget (☎0141/21 66 60, fax 57 221; ④/③) is much the same. A fresher and better choice if you don't mind sharing bathrooms is the new *Hotel Urban Hjarne* at Bispmotalagatan 11 (☎0141/23 52 00, fax 21 75 45; ①, including breakfast), run by the Salvation Army. The cosy and clean double rooms all have a TV and telephone. You can make food in the hotel's kitchen, too. No smoking is allowed in the hotel.

Most of Motala's **restaurants**, grouped around Storatorget, are non-descript and do daily lunches at around 50kr. For a pleasant **café**, try *Teatercaféet*, next to the tourist office (Mon–Thurs 9am–8pm, Fri 9am–midnight, Sat 9am–5pm, Sun 1–8pm), for sandwiches, cake and coffee in a typical theatre-foyer atmosphere of bare brick walls and strewn magazines. Most of the **pubs** cater for a very young crowd (under 22), but a really good alternative for food and drink all day is *Hallen* (daily 11am–2pm & 6pm–1am), just off Storatorget near the *Stadshotellet*. Built in

1924 as a food market, it retains the original glazed brick interior, and the serving area and bar are designed like the original stalls. A good daily lunch for 55kr always offers a choice of fish or meat; the night menu is more extensive, specializing in Vättern fish. Fifty beers – mostly British and German – are served. It's busiest on Tuesday, Friday and Saturday nights, when the *Stadshotellet* has dancing and a strict 23-plus age limit.

# North to Örebro

Beyond Motala, Lake Vättern runs out of decent-sized towns and it isn't until **Örebro** – 60km north of Vättern – that you reach a signficant settlement. Its light industrial hinterland promises little, and even Örebro's proudest boasts are anticlimactic: it's Sweden's sixth most populous city, lying on the shores of Hjälmaren, the country's fourth largest lake. Yet the heart of Örebro comes as a pleasant surprise, the much fortified thirteenth-century **castle** forming a magnificent backdrop for the cultivated contours of the water-lily studded **River Svatån**, which meanders around elegant Art Nouveau buildings and through parkland to the **Wadköping open-air museum**. Aside from the town's attractions, **Lake Tysslingen**, a few kilometres west, makes for a good afternoon excursion by bike. In spring, several thousand whooper swans settle here on their way to Finland and make spectacular viewing from observation towers. You can also take a **boat trip** on Lake Hjälmaren.

Örebro's development was dictated by its important strategic position. The main route from southwest Sweden to Stockholm – currently Route E20, which bypasses the town – was called King Eric's Way and ran right through the centre, where a build-up of gravel made the river fordable. The name Örebro means "gravel bridge".

## Arrival, information and accommodation

Örebro is just three hours from Stockholm on the main east-west **train** line. The very helpful and knowledgeable **tourist office** is inside the castle (June–Aug Mon–Fri 9am–7pm, Sat & Sun 10am–5pm; Sept–May Mon–Fri 9am–5pm, May also open Sat noon–4pm; ☎019/21 21 21, fax 10 60 70). To reach the castle, turn right from the train station, or left from the bus station opposite, walk a few metres along Östra Bangatan, and a crescent of elegant, wrought-iron balconied apartments opens out to the right. Follow it around and the castle is immediately ahead, sitting four-square on its island. The town centre is easy to see on foot, but if you want to see some of the surrounding countryside, renting a **bike** is a good idea; at the Technical Museum, Hamnplan, or at any Pressbyrån, bikes cost 40kr per day, including overnight, or 180kr per week. There are also tandems and child seats available. Another way of sightseeing is to take a **boat trip** around nearby **Lake Hjälmaren** on *M/S Linnea* or *M/S Gustav Lagerbjelke*. Shorter, two-hour sightseeing trips cost 60kr, better value than three-hour trips at 200kr. There are also popular prawn-eating evenings for 200kr, including food but not beer (book in advance for prawn evenings for *M/S Linnea* on ☎019/18 23 51 or *M/S Lagerbjelke* on ☎019/10 71 91).

The tourist office can book **private rooms** for 130kr per person, plus a 25kr booking fee. The *STF* **youth hostel** has recently moved to new premises at

Fanjunkarevägen 5 (☎019/31 02 40, fax 31 02 56; 100kr), an old army barracks just to the north; take bus #31 to Rynninge, getting off one stop before the end of the line. Accommodation ranges from dormitories to rooms with their own toilet and shower. The nearest **campsite** is 2km south of town at **GUSTAVSVIK** (mid-May to Aug; ☎019/19 69 50, fax 19 69 90), entry to some facilities at the nearby Leisure complex.

Of Örebrö's rather uninspiring **hotels**, the most swish and glossy is the central *Stora Hotellet*, Drottninggatan 1 (☎019/12 43 60, fax 611 78 90; ④/②). The oldest hotel in town, built in 1858, it is supposed to be haunted by the ghost of a young woman and her mother; late last century, the girl hanged herself because her mother forced her into an unrewarding marriage. Mother and daughter are known as the Black and White ghosts. *City Hotel,* Kungsgatan 24 (☎019/10 02 00, fax 13 74 46; ③/②), and *Hotel Continental,* opposite the train station at Järnvägsgatan 2 (☎019/11 95 60, fax 11 73 10 43; ④/①), are very similiar mid-range hotels; while *Hotel Gullvivan*, Järnvägsgatan 20 (☎019/611 90 35, fax 18 94 50; ③/①), is cheaper still. Recently renovated, it looks better inside than out. You can take a budget double room supplying your own sheets for 360kr in summer; a double with a sauna costs 650kr. The cheapest, but quite adequate, hotel is *Hotel Linden*, Köpmangatan 5, with double rooms without toilet or shower from 330kr double (275kr in summer).

# The Castle

Ever since a band of German merchants settled here in the thirteenth century, attracted by rich iron mining, a fort was built to defend the little town. It was enlarged by King Magnus Eriksson, who lived here with his French wife, Blanche (in Swedish Blanka). Gustav Vasa added fortifications, and his son Karl IX did what Vasa's sons invariably did and turned it into a splendid Renaissance castle, raising all the walls to the height of the medieval towers and plastering them in cream stucco. After the town lost its importance, **Örebro Castle** fell into disuse and was saved by becoming a store house and a prison. Prisoners of war and political strife were locked up here, and you can still see, in the former prison on the fourth-floor, words scratched in the walls by Russian inmates. Another room was used to hold suspected witches and was furnished by King Karl as a well-equipped torture chamber: at the time, fear of witchcraft was reaching fever pitch, and over four hundred women lost their heads after failing to drown in the nearby river. Today the torture chamber serves as a rather macabre theme restaurant (see p.274).

The fairy-tale exterior you see today is the result of renovation in the 1890s. Architects, influenced by the National Romanticism of the day, carefully restored it to reflect both its medieval and Renaissance grandeur. The same cannot be said for the interior, where valiant **tour guides** (May–Sept 5 daily; English tour at 2pm; 50kr) face a real challenge: there is no original furniture, many of the rooms are used for conferences and others are home to the county governor. It's all sold as a "living castle" to make up for what it lacks, and, naturally, it's riddled with ghosts, from Queen Blanka, who is said to be in torment for murdering her son, to Engelbrecht, who became a national hero when he stormed the castle in 1434 and led a riot to win liberty for farmers oppressed by harsh taxes. Engelbrecht's own head was chopped off two years later. If you do join a tour, the few features of interest are some finely inlaid doors and floors dated just from the 1920s, depicting historical events at Örebro, and a large family portrait of Karl XII and

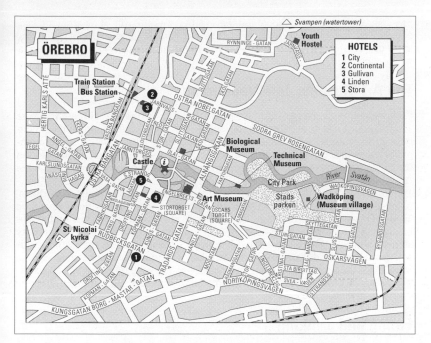

his family, all their faces painted to look the same – an imagined ideal, though all have popping eyes, the result of using arsenic to whiten their faces.

The top floors of the castle now hold the historical exhibits from the old Länsmuseum; it's a mainly local collection, specializing in ecclesiastical artefacts, altarpieces and tapestries.

## St Nicolai kyrka and the Biological Museum

Nearby, **St Nicolai kyrka**, at the top of the very oblong Stortorget, dates from 1260, but extensive restoration in the 1860s robbed it of most of its medieval character. Although recent renovations have tried to undo the damage, today the contemporary art exhibitions on show here are more striking. However, the church is historically significant. It was here in 1810 that the unknown figure of Napoleon's marshal, Jean Baptiste Bernadotte, was elected successor to the Swedish throne. The descendants of the new King Karl Johan, who never spoke a word of Swedish, are the current royal family. Engelbrecht was also supposed to be buried here after his murder, but when his coffin was exhumed in the eighteenth century, it was empty, and his bones have never been recovered.

For a charismatically dilapidated museum, the **Biological Museum** (mid-June to mid-Aug daily 11am–2pm; 10kr), in the grand old Karolinska School by the castle, is interesting in that its musty and fearful occupants – stuffed polar bears, ostriches, bison and lynx – are not behind glass, but lean over the narrow walkway, harking back to nineteenth-century museum design. Most unusual is the vast number of badly stuffed sparrows on display – late last century the

Swedish equivalent of an apple for the teacher was the gift of an amateur taxidermal experiment. Up the rickety spiral staircase, the gallery level has uncased stuffed everything from lions and ocelots to tortoises and some gruesome bottles of pickled marine life.

# The Art Museum and Wadköping

Following the river eastwards leads to the **Art Museum** (June–Aug Mon 11am–4pm, Tues–Sun 11am–6pm; Sept–May Tues–Sun noon–4pm; 25kr), housed in what was the Länsmuseum. It's a surprisingly spacious series of galleries, with temporary and permanent collections. Much of it is mediocre, the best room showing a collection by the late nineteenth-century local artist Axel Borg.

A little further up the river, past the appealing Stadspark, stands **Wadköping** (May–Aug 11am–5pm, Sept–April 11am–4pm; shops and exhibitions closed on Mon). This is an entire village of centuries' old wooden cottages and shops brought to the site as a living open-air museum. It's all extremely pretty but very staged. Some of the cottages have been reoccupied, and the twee little shops sell pastel-coloured wooden knick-knacks. There's an unambitious School Museum – little more than some old desks – and a very good bakery and café; the bakery sells delicious cakes and breads, the smell of which alone make the visit worthwhile.

# Eating and drinking

There are plenty of atmospheric cafés and **restaurants** to enjoy a wide range of good Swedish food around town, together with some popular **pubs**. If you're here in July, though, be prepared for some of the smaller restaurants to be locked for the holidays. For a fine **daytime café** in beautiful surroundings, head for *Café Stadsträdgården* in the greenhouses at the entrance to Stadpark (Mon–Fri 11am–6pm, Sat & Sun till 5pm). All the delicious cakes, pies and sandwiches are home-baked, using organic ingredients with plenty for vegetarians; there are good-value lunches at 45kr. Or for a very scenic afternoon tea, head north of town to the 58m-high mushroom-shaped water tower **Svampen**, which provides sweeping views of the surrounding plain and Jyälmaren Lake, and has a reasonable café and restaurant inside.

## Restaurants and bars

**Bishop's Arms**, next door to the *Slottskällaren*. Hugely popular for outdoor drinking, and serves the likes of fish and chips for 55kr.

**Björnstugan**, on Kungsgatan. The most trendy pub in town and extremely busy.

**Ett Rum Och Kök**, at Ringgatan 30, about ten minutes' walk from the castle. With simple primary-colour decor and really good food: meat dishes (120–140kr) and lighter salads (50kr). It has a bar called *Garage* made out of half a red Volvo Amazon, the classic 1950s' sports saloon. Mon–Thurs 11.30am–2pm & 5.30–11pm, Fri till midnight, Sat 1pm–midnight, Sun 2–11pm.

**Medeltidspuben, Drottning Blanka** (*Queen Blanka's Medieval Pub*) in the castle's torture chamber. A fun place to eat, it serves dishes such as wild boar and spare ribs with stone flagons of mead. Main courses and a drink cost around 80k; desserts include almond pie and a rather disappointing rose-flavoured blancmange.

**Slottskrogen Restaurant**, in the castle above *Queen Blanka's Medieval Pub*. It's nicer eating outside, as the formal interior lacks the atmosphere you'd expect, despite a painting of the anti-Catholic King Karl screaming abuse at a young Catholic boy. There's a cheap grill menu, from chicken at 35kr to tuna grilled with basil-flavoured creme fraiche at 85kr. Pike-perch is the restaurant's speciality, but best-value for a light meal is the *brännvinbord* – herring, sausage and cheese for 60kr, and you bring your own schnapps (evenings only). Open June–Aug daily 10.30am–2am.

**Slottskällaren Restaurant & Bar**, opposite the castle in the *Stora Hotellet* building. Despite translating as "castle-cellar", it is neither, but still a long-standing, very popular restaurant. Main courses cost upwards of 150kr, but there are also cheaper, light meals like the classic *pytt i panna* for 59kr. Daily 6pm–midnight.

**Wärdshuset Gyllen Oxen**, Ringgatan 19. For a superb pizza in this upmarket meat and pasta place try the "special" pizza at 59kr. Open daily noon–2am.

# East to Linköping

Sixty kilometres east of Lake Vättern, **Linköping**, in the county of Östergötland, has an appealing character, its nine-hundred-year-old history apparent in a range of pleasing buildings. The architectural highlights are the remarkable Domkyrkan and an entire living village caught in a late nineteenth-century time-warp, called **Gamla Linköping**, a few kilometres to the west. Linköping's best-kept secret, however, missed by all but a handful of visitors, is a unique art exhibition, hidden in a faceless office building, which reveals more about eighteenth-century Swedish society than any number of preserved dwellings could hope to do. It's also well worth looking at the art collection in the Länsmuseum and at the town's other hidden treasure: the basement excavations at the often overlooked twelfth-century St Lars kyrka.

## Arrival and information

All **trains** and **buses** arrive at and leave from **Resecentrum** (travel centre) in the north of the town centre. Linköping is easy to walk around, and if you do get lost, the Domkyrkan spire is rarely out of sight. The main **tourist office** (open all year Mon–Fri 9am–6pm; June–Aug also Sat & Sun 9am–3pm; ☎013/20 68 35 or 31 46 00, fax 14 21 55) in the airy *Concert and Congress Hall*, is just a few minutes' walk west from Resecentrum – cross Järnvägsgatan and head down Järnvägsavenyn, and it's on the left. A helpful, though less extensive, **evening office** is based at the *Ekoxen Hotel*, Klostergatan 68 (open all year Mon–Fri 6–10pm; June–Aug Sat & Sun 3–10pm) – from Järnvägsavenyn turn right down Klostergatan, and it's at the far end on the right.

## Accommodation

Linköping is not a popular holiday destination for many Swedes, and several of the smaller **hotels** (see overleaf) close for July. The plus side is that some of those that stay open drop their prices dramatically. The tourist office will book **private rooms** from 150kr per person and, unusually, make no booking charge. The *STF* **youth hostel**, Klostergatan 52A (☎013/14 90 90, fax 14 83 00; 100kr), apart from being very central, is very well appointed; every room has its own mini-kitchen and en-suite shower and toilet. There are also "comfort rooms" available (480kr for a double), including bed linen and a buffet breakfast. For a good, modern **campsite**, with four-bed cabins, *Glyttinge Camping* is 3km east of town at Berggårdsvägen (mid-April to Sept; ☎013/17 49 28); take bus #201, which brings you right to the site.

## Hotels

**Du Nord**, Repslagaregatan 5 (☎013/12 98 95). Looks the prettiest from the outside, a pink-painted detached house wedged between two dull apartment buildings, just 200m from the station. It's less lovely on the inside, though its modern rooms all have en-suite facilities and satellite TV. Tends to close in July. ③/②

**Ekoxen**, Klostergatan 68 (☎013/14 60 70, fax 12 19 03). More than halving its rate in summer, this is a good, well-equipped hotel: sauna, swimming pool, solarium, massage and gym facilities, 24-hour delicatessen and an international menu at its bistro. ⑤/②

**Frimürarehotellet**, St Larsgatan 14 (☎013/12 91 80, fax 13 95 44). With a grand, National Romantic facade from 1912 and elegant columns supporting its dining hall, this hotel is only spoiled by the 1970s' interiors. It contains the *Metropole Beer Bar and Barbeque* (see "Eating and drinking"). ④/③

**Park**, Järnvägsgatan 6 (☎013/12 90 05, fax 10 04 18). Dates from the turn of the century, and serves a good buffet breakfast. ③

**Östergyllen**, Hamngatan 2 (☎013/10 20 75, fax 12 59 02). The cheapest and best-value hotel in town. It's family-run and comfortable, with a good breakfast included, but, the most economical rooms do not have en-suite shower or toilet. The hotel also operates **cycling and canoeing packages**, the latter for trips down the Kinda Canal and Stångan river, opposite the hotel. Three nights in a double room including bike rental, route maps and four days of lunch boxes costs 890kr per person (1390kr for 6 days); four days of canoe rental plus a river/canal map costs 950kr. Canoes alone can be rented for 170kr per day. ①

# The town and around

With its soaring, 107m-high spire, the elegant **Domkyrkan** (June & July Mon–Sat 9am–7pm, Sun 9am–6pm; Aug–May 9am–6pm, Sun 10am–6pm), set in a swathe of greenery, dates from 1232 – though the bulk of the present, sober building was completed in around 1520 – and is built entirely of local hand-carved limestone. Stonemasons from all over Europe worked on the well-proportioned building and, with a belfry and the west facade added as late as 1885, it incorporates a number of styles from Romanesque to Gothic. Of particular note is the restored south portal, with biblical carvings above its Moorish-influenced, geometrically worked doors. The venerable old buildings around the Domkyrkan include the much rebuilt thirteenth-century castle which, like so many others, was fortified by Gustav Vasa and beautified by his son Johan III.

Five minutes' wander down Ågatan in the direction of the Stångån river, the town's most unexpected cultural diversion is in the unlikely setting of the **Labourers' Educational Association** (ABF) at Snickaregatan 22. On the fourth floor is a priceless collection of 85 brilliantly executed pictures by the celebrated artist Peter Dahl, illustrating all the *Epistles of Bellman*. Carl Michael Bellman was an eighteenth-century poet/songwriter who exposed the hypocrisies of contemporary Swedish society. His epistles tell of life in pubs, of prostitutes and of the wild and drunken sexual meanderings of high society men and women, all set against fear of the Church and final damnation. Oslo-born Peter Dahl is a Swede by adoption, and although previously the head of the Stockholm Art School, he is better known for these pictures, some of which are shot through with vibrant colour, others in sepia and finely sketched. The collection was bought by the ABF in the early 1980s, and though it's much admired by those who have seen it, you won't find many who know of its existence in Linköping. Officially, the ABF closes for July, but if you walk round the corner onto Storgatan and to the left of the *Spar Bank*, another set of elevators leads to a second entrance, where someone should let you in.

Just one block back on St Larsgatan, **St Lars kyrka** (Mon–Thurs 11am–4pm, Fri 11am–3pm, Sat 11am–1pm) is often bypassed as it stands within a few metres of the great Domkyrkan; however, inside is another hidden attraction. The church was consecrated by Bishop Kol in 1170, and the present interior has had too many face lifts to show many signs of its great age. It was a ground reinforcement plan, though, which led to the discovery of twelfth-century engraved stone and wood coffins. Again there are no signs to direct you, but beneath the church, in candle-lit half-light, complete twelfth-century skeletons – including one without a head – lie in new glass coffins, alongside remarkably preserved wood coffins and the explosed remains of the original church, rebuilt in the 1730s. To see it all, just ask whoever is selling postcards to unlock the door leading to the basement.

If you have some spare time, the **Länsmuseum** (May–Sept Mon–Wed & Fri–Sun noon–4pm, Thurs till 9pm; Oct–April Tues–Thurs noon–9pm, Fri–Sun noon–4pm; 30kr) has an interesting art collection, ranging from a fifteenth-century, surprisingly vivid Swedish representation of Adam and Eve to 1980s' post-modernist work. A group of impressive turn-of-the-century paintings includes several that beautifully evoke the stoical character of toiling men and women. Many Nordic painters of the time excelled at this subject matter and style, and here, of particular note, are Johan Krouthen's *Goldsmith's Home Interior* and August Hagborg's more free-spirited *Pulling the Boat*. There are some minor works by Munch, and John Bauer's Ophelia-like *Freja*. Among the contemporary collections Roy Friberg's Surrealistic painting is eye-catching, as is Staffan Hallström's bright-yellow *Pyramid of Skulls*, painted the year he died.

## Gamla Linköping

Just 3km west of Linköping proper, **Gamla Linköping** (Mon–Fri 10am–5.30pm, Sat & Sun noon–4pm; free) is a living open-air museum and a real must. An entire town of houses, shops and businesses have been brought here from Linköping, along with streetlighting, fences, signs and even trees, to re-create the town as an identical copy of its nineteenth-century incarnation; even the street plan is exactly the same. Fifty people actually live here, and there's a massive waiting list for eager new tenants, despite the drawbacks of not being allowed to alter the properties and the fact that tourists trundle through year round. Craftsmen work at nineteenth-century trades, and most shops are open every day, including a small chocolate factory, gold- and silversmiths, a woodwind workshop and linen shops. An eighteenth-century farm house from southern Östergotland is now a very pleasant cafeteria, and there's an open-air theatre, with performances throughout the summer. Buses #203 and #205 run (Sept–May; every 20min) from Resecentrum.

## Canal and lock trips

Linköping is riddled with waterways and if you want to see a lot of locks in close proximity, this is your chance. The **Göta Canal** is the most obvious one to choose, wending its way from Motala through Borensberg to the seven-sluice

Carl Johan Lock at Berg, just north of Linköping, where it meets Lake Roxen. South of the city, the less well-known **Kinda Canal** has a manually operated triple lock at Tannefors, and you can head south for 35km through a mix of canal and river to Rimforsa.

There are endless combinations of canal and river trips, with mystifying cost options, from a basic Göta Canal trip for two adults or an adult and children for 210kr, to a more glamorous spree on the *M/S Nya Skärgården* to Söderköping (35km east) and back in a 1915, classic steamer (bookings call direct ☎070/637 17 00). For a less ambitious trip, boats also head down the Kinda Canal/Stångån river to a pleasant outdoor café at Tannefors. For the least expensive and probably just as enjoyable canal experience, you can rent canoes or bikes along the old towpath at *Hotel Östergyllen* (see p.276).

# Eating and drinking

Linköping is a likable spot to spend an evening, and the liveliest and most appealing places to eat and drink after dark are all on **Ågatan** running up to the Domkyrkan. Some of these are open during the daytime, too. A couple of **café-konditori** around Storatorget serve the best cakes and sandwiches: *Lind's*, on the edge of the square, is better than its neighbouring rivals, while *Gyllen* on Lilla Torget is a very popular, with outside seating for people-watching. The only daytime café that also stays open beyond 9pm is *Café Absalon* (Mon & Tues 9am–9pm, Wed & Thur 9am–midnight, Fri & Sat 9am–4am, Sun 1–9pm) at Ågatan 55; it attracts a young, friendly post-pub crowd. For a **gay** bar, the *RFSL*-run *Joy Café*, Nygatan 58, has a daytime café (1–4pm) during summer; for entry to the popular Friday-night pub (8pm–midnight), Linköping Commune's licensing laws dictate that you have to be a member of *RFSL*, the national gay organization, so there are consequently few non-locals.

## Restaurants and bars

**B.K. (Bar & Kök)**, Ågatan. A cosy, stylish place with a fun atmosphere, a huge cocktail bar and a small, elegant restaurant serving unusual and well-presented dishes, such as crocodile, kangaroo and frogs' legs (90–139kr). Try chicken in sweet chilli cream.

**Gula Huset**, Ågatan. With a long tradition of serving an extensive vegetarian buffet until 3pm (5pm on Sat; 55kr), and big portions of Swedish meat and fish dishes and pan pizzas (74kr) later on, this place is justifiably popular. The evening speciality is plank steaks (155kr). A good-value, summer-time barbeque menu is served outside for 110kr, and the beer is the cheapest in town at 20kr for medium-strong. Mon 5pm–midnight, Tues–Thurs 11am–midnight, Fri & Sat 11am–1am.

**Harry's Bar & Restaurant**, a couple of doors down from *B.K.* This ever-popular chain restaurant/bar is always crowded; its warm, dark interior sports the usual American/British look and chandeliers. Mon & Tues 11am–11pm, Wed–Fri 11am–1am, Sat 1pm–1am, Sun 1pm–11pm.

**Metropole Beer Bar and Barbeque**, *Frimürarehotellet*, St Larsgatan 14. Serves good-value steaks, ribs and baked potatoes. Outside the summer season, a pricier à la carte menu takes over. Thurs–Sat.

**Veranden Restaurant and Benny Hill pub**, *Stora Hotellet*, Storatorget. This grand, pompous hotel pulls a sizable crowd to its restaurant and bar; both open daily till 2am, Fri & Sat till 3am.

**Överste Mörne**, Storatorget, next door to *Stora Hotellet*. Busy outside drinking at this traditional, spacious, candle-lit pub.

# Norrköping and around

It is with good reason that the dynamic, youth-oriented town of **NORRKÖPING** calls itself Sweden's Manchester. Like its British counterpart, Norrköping's wealth came from its textile industry, which built up in the eighteenth and nineteenth centuries – coincidentally, the Swedish for corduroy is "Manchester". The legacy from this period is the town's most appealing feature: it is one of Europe's best-preserved industrial urban landscapes, with handsome red-brick and stuccoed mills reflecting in the waters of Motala Ström.

It was this small, rushing river that attracted the Dutch industrialist Louis De Geer to the town in the late seventeenth century. He was called the father of Norrköping, and his paper mill, which still runs today, became the biggest factory, followed by many wool, silk and linen factories. Today many buildings are painted a stong, tortilla-chip yellow, as are the trams – De Geer favoured the colour, and it has become symbolic of the town. Textiles kept Norrköping booming until the 1950s, when foreign competition began to sap the market. The last big textile mill closed its doors in 1992. In the past couple of decades, the parallel with Manchester has become even more apparent: Norrköping has become a nucleus for music-inspired youth culture. Popularized in the 1970s and 1980s by one of Sweden's most famous singer-songwriters, Ulf Lundell, the town was also home to the country's best-known working-class rock band, *Eldkvarn*.

Norrköping has one of the highest immigrant populations in Sweden. The first to come here were the Jews in the mid-eighteenth century. Today's immigrant communities are mostly from Asian and Arabic countries, and in the past few years the most noticeable influx has been from the former Yugoslavia.

## Arrival, information and accommodation

The helpful **tourist office** at Drottninggatan 11 (June–Aug Mon–Fri 9am–7pm, Sat & Sun 9am–3pm, Sept–May Mon–Fri 9am–5pm; ☎011/15 15 00, fax 16 08 78) is five minutes' walk from the **train** (it's 30min by train from Linköping) and **bus** terminals. You can buy a range of cards and packages that are really good value for sightseeing and accommodation. The **Norrköping Runabout Card** (295kr, children up to 13 free) is valid for three days and gives free admission to Kålmorden Djurpark and Löfstad Manor, free museum entry (though it's only the Art Museum which charges anyway), and a range of odd freebies like boat trips and tours. The more ambitious **Östergötland County Card** (325kr, 7- 13-year-olds 50kr) adds more trips and throws in a Vadstena Card (see p.266); while a **Runabout Package** (mid-June to mid-Aug) makes for cheaper accommodation (all the town's hotels participate), with a Runabout Card included, it costs 498kr per person for two nights in an available four-bed room. The tourist office will also explain tram routes and times for the 1902 **vintage tram**, which circles around on a sight-seeing tour during summer. The ordinary, yellow trams run on two lines all over the town centre, costing a flat 15kr, including any tram changes within the hour.

### Accommodation

The tourist office will book **private rooms** from 130kr per person, plus a 60kr booking fee, or provide a free list for you to book yourself. There are two *STF* **youth hostels**: *Turistgården* (open all year; ☎011/10 11 60, fax 18 68 63; 90kr),

Ingelstadsgatan 31, is just a few hundred metres behind the train station; and there's also a much more picturesque hostel at Abborreberg, 5km east of town (see p.283). The closest **campsite** is by the rock carvings at Himmelstalund, *City Camp* (☎011/17 11 90, fax 17 09 82) on Utställningsvägen. Either walk west along the river, or take bus #118 from the bus station.

The cheapest central **hotel**, *Hotel Centric,* Gamla Rådstugugatan 18–20 (☎011/12 90 30, fax 18 07 28; ②/①), close to the train station and parallel with Drottninggatan, has the shabbiest entrance, but this fourth-floor hotel (with lift) is quite reasonable, with a striking wall fresco by Gothenburg artist Lars Gillies, brilliantly depicting all Norrköping's central areas. More upmarket is the classic, turn-of-the-century *Grand Hotel*, Tyska Torget 2 (☎011/19 71 00, fax 18 11 83; ⑤/②) bang in the centre. The *President Hotel*, just as central and next door to the fine theatre at Vattengränden 11 (☎011/12 95 20, fax 10 07 10; ⑤/③), has a few special touches like adjustable beds; its very small, French-style *Teater Bar* restaurant is renowned for its pepper steaks. For a calm and pleasant alternative, *Södra Hotellet*, Södra Promenaden 42 (☎011/18 99 90; ④/②), stands on an elegant avenue, south of the centre, which was favoured by the textile mill owners; this 1920s' house has bean sympathetically updated.

# The Town

From the train station to the north of the town, Drottninggatan runs as a straight north-south central artery, crossing Motala Ström. Just a few steps down from the station, the small but pretty **Carl Johans Park** is unusual in that it has 25,000 cactii, which are formally arranged in thematic patterns. Over the river and following the tram lines up cobbled Drottninggatan (the tourist office is on the left), a right turn into Repslagaregatan leads into **Gamla Torget**, overlooked by a charismatic sculpture of Louis De Geer by Carl Milles. From here, the modern and stylish riverside **Concert Hall** is fronted by trees, providing a lovely setting for the café, *Kråkholmen Louis De Geer* (see "Eating and drinking"). It's worth stepping inside the *Concert Hall* for a moment, as its apparent modernity belies the fact that this was once one of De Geer's factories. You can also pick up information on the symphony orchestra's weekly concerts. Through the impressive, eighteenth-century paper mill gates to the left, and across a wooden bridge behind the hall, is **Arbets (Work) Museum** (11am–5pm daily; free), housed in a triangular, yellow-stuccoed factory from 1917. Known as "The Iron" – though its shape and colour are rather more a wedge of cheese – the building was described by Carl Milles as Europe's most beautiful factory. It's a splendid place, with seven floors of exhibitions on living conditions, workers' rights and day-to-day life in the mills. The highlight is the seventh-floor "Women of the World" exhibition – the only permanent one – which shows striking photographs of women working to support families and build self-esteem. Although there is a lift, take the stairs down to see a touching exhibition in the stairwell about the life of one woman, Alva, who spent 35 years as a factory worker here. If you're here in spring or autumn, the first floor holds Tuesday evenings of jazz and blues.

Next door, over another little bridge is the excellent **Stadsmuseum** (Tues, Wed & Fri 10am–4pm, Thurs 10am–8pm, Sat & Sun 11am–5pm; free). Set in an interconnecting (and confusing) network of old industrial properties, the most

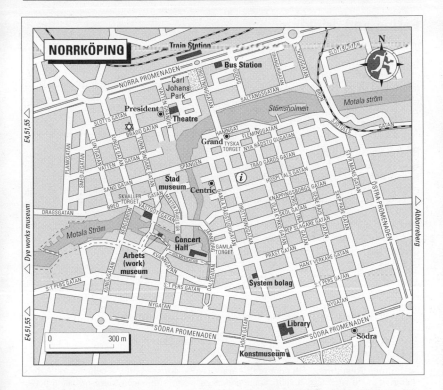

rewarding of the permanent exhibitions is a trade street: a little road with a milliner, confectioner, chimney sweep and, in a backyard, a carriage maker. All are cleverly designed and worth wandering through.

Back across the river and following the bank west leads to an idyllic country-side setting in just ten minutes; here the **Färgargården**, an open-air dyeworks museum (May–Aug Tues–Sun noon–4pm; free), is ranged in a huddle of wooden nineteenth-century houses. A better reason to come here than the exhibitions and garden, with herbs and plants for dyeing, is the oudoor café, open whenever the weather is good during summer.

If you're interested in Swedish art, Norrköping's **Konstmuseum**, at the south-ernmost tip of Drottninggatan (Tues–Sun noon–4pm, Wed till 8pm; 30kr), is full of some of the country's best-known modernist works. Founded by a local snuff manufacturer at the turn of the century, the galleries offer a fine, well-balanced progression from seventeenth-century Baroque through to up-to-the-minute twentieth-century paintings. Coming out of the art museum, the bunker-like, con-crete building to the right is the town **library**; more interesting and user friend-ly than most, it has a jukebox with headphones and a big range of national news-papers from all over the world. Many immigrants come to read the news from the old country. There is also free use of the Internet.

# Eating and drinking

There is a fair selection of **eating places** in Norrköping, and most double as **bars**. It's a town custom to drink at home before heading out, so the town only starts coming alive from 10pm; but from then onwards, the numerous new establishments that have opened up since the early 1990s get very busy. If you want to carry on after the bars close, the most popular **nightclub** and restaurant is *Tellus* (Wed, Fri & Sat 9pm–3am), beneath *Pub Vasa* at Kungsgatan 38; the food here is basic and cheap.

## Restaurants and bars

**Bishop's Arms Pub** at the *Grand Hotel*, Tyska Torget 2. Just up Drottninggatan from the station, this is a long-standing, traditional, English-style pub.

**Cromwell House** just over the road from *Pub Wasa* (see below) and under the same management. More upmarket than the *Wasa*, it serves light meals like fish, chips, calamari, omelettes and chicken wings for around 85kr. The best main course dish is perch fillet, and the ice cream with warm cloudberry and punch is a delight at 52kr. Lunch 11.30am–2pm (except July); dinner Mon–Thurs 5–11pm, Fri & Sat 5pm–1am.

**Guskelov**, Dalsgatan 13. Far and away the best restaurant and bar in terms of decor, friendly service and food. At the opening to the industrial area and next door to the *Concert Hall*, this Art Deco-style restaurant specializes in fish dishes; try the seafood chowder with aïoli (95kr) or the great gazpacho with almonds (39kr). It also does hundreds of cocktails – *guskelov* translates as "Thank God" and is a common Östergötland saying. The restaurant is open Mon–Fri 11.30am–2.30pm & 5.30pm–midnight, Sat 5.30pm–midnight; the bar Mon–Thurs 5.30pm–1am, Fri & Sat 5.30pm–3am.

**Kråkholmen Louis De Geer**, outside the *Concert Hall*. With the crashing water of Motala Ström beside you, the daily lunch menu serves the likes of beef casserole at 45kr. Open 11am–mid-afternoon, depending on the weather.

**Laxholmen Restaurant**, 6th floor of the Arbet (Work) Museum; open same hours. A daily changing menu such as fish soup, apple pancakes, pasta with bacon sauce or baked potato with tuna filling and coffee for 44kr. They also do warm, filled baguettes like salmon and prawn for 35kr.

**O'Leery's**, Drottninggatan. American and Mexican classics such as black bean soup and cajun chicken, but service is painfully slow.

**Pub Wasa**, Kungsgatan 38. Shaped and decked out as the interior of a great ship (hence the name), this busy and unusual riverside pub is complete with little cannons pointing out of the porthole windows. There's **live music** daily except Wed, with rock on Thurs evenings; unusually, no food is served.

**Restaurant La Mansion**, Södra Promenaden 116. A sedate but charming lunch or dinner option in the preserved former home of a textile mill manager. Dinner menus, like venison and wild mushrooms and salmon and seafood mousse, are 150kr. Two-course lunch is a steep 135kr. Mon–Fri 11.30am–2.30pm & 5.30–11pm, Sat noon–midnight; shorter hours in July.

# Around Norrköping: Abborreberg, Löfstad Manor and Kolmården Djurpark

The following are all easy trips from Norrköping; even closer to the centre are the rock carvings at **Himmelstalund**, a couple of kilometres west of the centre. Norrköping's present appearance belies its far more ancient origins; these carvings date from around 1500 BC and show with unusual clarity ships, weapons, animals and men; while burial mounds, though nothing much to look at, attest to Iron Age and Viking settlements in the area. To get there take bus #118 from Norrköping.

## Abborreberg
The splendid old wooden villas at **ABBORREBERG**, 5km east of Norrköping, are weathered but charmingly authentic early nineteenth-century summer residences and make a delightful lakeside setting for coffee and cake. Passing through the affluent suburb of Lindö, Abborreberg looks out onto Lindö Bay from a forested setting. The collection of small, verandahed villas and cottages all retain their lived-in look, but the drawing room of the main Seaside Villa should be the target of your visit. Although the views from the lovely old windows are fine enough, it's the wallpaper that takes the limelight. Hand-printed and brought in the 1870s from Paris, it is one of only four such papers and depicts in gloriously unrealistic detail a panoramic scene called "The Banks of the Bosporus". If you ask at the **café** (open 11am–5pm or whenever the weather is good during summer), they will unlock the larger villa, now used for weddings, which has a wonderful atmosphere of faded gentility, with fancy woodwork and old furnishings. One of the old residences is now used as an *STF* **youth hostel** (mid-June to mid-Aug; ☎011/31 94 24; 80kr); although it is an idyllic spot, with new and efficient showers and toilets, they're in a separate building and the kitchen is more primitive than most. To reach Abborreberg, take bus #111 from outside the *Domino Store* on Repslagaregatan, just off Drottninggatan in the town centre, to Lindö; ask the driver for the nearest stop to *STF Vandrarhem*. After 6pm, take bus #101 from outside the library.

## Löfstad Manor
Just 10km southwest of town, **Löfstad Manor** (May Sat & Sun only; June to mid-Aug daily; tours hourly on the hour noon–4pm; 30kr) is a fine country home dating from the 1650s, but rebuilt a hundred years later after a fire destroyed all but its shell. The same family owned Löfstad until the last, unmarried daughter, Emily Piper, died in 1926. She willed the house, its contents and the whole estate to the Museum of Östergötland, which has kept it untouched since her death. Generations of ancestors before Emily all added their mark, and there's a splendid collection of eighteenth- and nineteenth-century Baroque and Rococo furniture and pictures, though presented in a rather more stiff and formal way than the description "as she left it" implies. Her most notable ancestor was Axel Fersen, who, during the French Revolution, tried in vain to save King Louis XVI and Queen Marie-Antoinette. His motives may not have been entirely political – he was rumoured to have been the queen's lover, and it's thought that the portrait of Marie Antoinette's daughter in the drawing room is a portrait of his daughter, too. The areas with the most authentic, lived-in feel are the kitchen and servants' quarters; in the scullery there's an elaborate candle-maker and a machine for twisting metal into bed springs – the house was designed to be self-sufficient. In the servants' quarters is Emily Piper's bathroom, with her ancient bathrobe still hanging from the door. The tour guide whisks you round pretty quickly and sometimes, if there are a lot of visitors, won't give English translations; it's best to ask before the tour gets underway, as you're not allowed to wander around on your own.

**Bus** #481 runs from Norrköping bus terminal to the Löfstad (just ask for Löfstad Slott). Getting back can be a problem, especially on weekend afternoons.

If you haven't got your own transport, it's an idea to make friends with someone on the tour, as almost everyone passes Norrköping when they leave. There's a pleasant **restaurant** in one wing of the house, *Löfstad Värdhus* (11am–11pm), which serves traditional Swedish food at standard restaurant prices and *Dagens Rätt* for 65kr. For a less formal and very enjoyable cold lunch, a café in the stables does delicious smoked beef with mounds of potato salad for 55kr (11am–5pm).

### Kolmården Djurpark

In the other direction, 28km northeast of Norrköping, **Kolmården Djurpark** is one of the country's biggest attractions. A combined zoo, safari park and dolphinarium, it's understandably popular with children, who have their own zoo as well as access to a gaggle of other diversions and enclosures. If your views on zoos are negative, it's just about possible to be convinced that this one is different; there are no cages, but instead sunken enclosures, rock barriers and moats to prevent the animals from feasting on their captors. There's certainly no shortage of things to do either: there's a cable-car ride over the safari park, a tropical house, working farm and dolphin shows.

If you're interested in just one or two specific attractions in the park, it might be as well to ring first (☎011/24 90 00); the safari park only opens when the weather is calm and the temperature above -10°C degrees. Generally, though, most things are open daily (10am until around 4–6pm); the dolphinarium has between one and four shows a day for most of the year. The entrance price varies according to what you want to see, but a combined ticket for everything runs from 160kr to 200kr, depending on the season. If you don't have your own transport, take bus #432 from Norrköping bus terminal (hourly; 50min). There's an expensive **hotel**, the *Vidmarkshotellet* (☎011/15 71 00; ④/②), at the park; alternatively, you can **camp** close by at the water's edge at *Kolmården Camping* (☎011/39 82 50).

# Nyköping and around

The county of Södermanland – known as Sörmland – cuts diagonally to the northeast of Norrköping above Bråviken bay. Its capital, the very small historic town of **NYKÖPING**, has seen a lively past, but today is used by most visitors simply as a springboard for the picturesque coastal islands to the east. This is a pity, as its underrated charms include an excellent museum, in and around the ruins of its thirteenth-century castle, and a harbour that bustles with life in summer.

A late twelfth-century defensive tower, built to protect the trading port at the estuary of the Nyköping river, was converted into a fortress by King Magnus Ladulås, and it was here in 1317 that the infamous **Nyköping Banquet** took place. One of Magnus's three sons, Birger, invited his brothers Erik and Valdemar to celebrate Christmas at Nyköping and provided a grand banquet. Once the meal was complete, and the visiting brothers had retired to bed, Birger had them thrown in the castle's dungeon, threw the key into the river and left them to starve to death. It wasn't until the nineteenth century that the key was found by a boy fishing in the river; though whether the rusting item on display is really the one last touched by Birger, no one knows. Gustav Vasa fortified the castle with gun towers in the sixteenth century, and when he died, his ten-year-old son Karl became Duke of Södermanland and later converted it into one of Sweden's most regal Renaissance palaces. In 1633, the body of Karl's son, King Gustavus Adolphus, was brought here after he was killed at the Battle of Lützen, and it stayed festering in state for eleven months, while his mortuary chapel was being built in Stockholm. A fire thirty years later reduced all lesser buildings to ash and gutted the castle. With no money forthcoming from the national coffers, it was never rebuilt; only the King's Tower was saved from demolition and used as a granary.

Today, the riverside tower and connected early eighteenth-century house built for the county governor form a **museum complex** (July daily noon–4pm, rest of year closed Mon; 20kr). Wandering through the original gatehouse beneath Karl's heraldic shield, you reach the extensively restored **King's Tower**. Climbing up to the first floor you'll pass carefully stacked bits and pieces excavated from Karl's palace – most notably, some spectacular Ionic column tops. On the first floor, a stylish job has been done of rebuilding the graceful archways that lead into the Guard Room. Here a model of the fortress fronted by a dashboard of buttons allows you to follow the events of the Nyköping Banquet – complete with gory details. There's also a collection of twelfth- and thirteenth-century shoes in a cabinet. The top floor has some evocative exhibits, too, including a bizarre 3-D cameo, which is viewed through a window and depicts the dead King Gustavus Adolfus, lying in state, with his widow, twisted in misery, and six-year-old Queen Kristina looking on. It's the old **Governor's Residence**, however, that has the most exquisite collections. Downstairs is the original kitchen, shiny with copper pots and utensils, and a surprisingly tasteful souvenir shop, which sells expensive medieval-style clothes for both sexes. It costs nothing, and is rather more fun, to climb the stairs, lined with menacing portraits, to an exceptional run of magnificently decorated rooms from each stylistic period. Among the highlights, and there are many, is the red-silk bed in the Baroque room, a copper steam bath in a nineteenth-century bedroom, and best of all, the Judgend room – about the finest example you'll see in Sweden. Amid the stylish finery are some splendid portraits by twin brothers Bernard and Emil Österman, who were famous for their passionate and sensual style. There's also a modern museum building nearby with temporary art installations.

Once you've seen the castle and museum, Nyköping offers a pleasant walk along the river bank, which is lined with people fishing, to the popular harbour and marina, a regular goal for the Stockholm yachting set – the capital being just 100km away by road or train; the flat water inside the 1500m-long breakwater is also an important venue for canoe racing.

## Around Nyköping

There are hundreds of **islands** that are accessible from Nyköping, and there are regular boat trips from town. The most popular is to the nature reserve on Stendörren; from here boats carry on to the idyllic little coastal town of Trosa. **Stendörren**, around 30km west of town, offers some fine walking between the islands, which are connected by foot bridges. **Trosa** (also reachable by road, 40km along the E4) is ideal for tranquil riverside walks, forested trails and the picture-perfect, red, wooden cottages around the old centre.

*M/S Labrador* leaves the dock at Nyköping for Stendörren and then on to Trosa at 9am (mid-June to mid-Aug Thurs & Fri). It costs 80kr to get to Stendörren,

120kr for Trosa; the return boat leaves at 3.20pm. Alternatively you can stay on Trosa in the *STF* **youth hostel** (June to mid-Aug; ☎015/65 32 28; 85kr), based in an old school. If you don't want to return to Nyköping, you can take bus #702 from Trosa bus terminal to Liljeholmen (1hr) and connect up with public transport to Stockholm (see opposite for full details). **Camping** near Trosa is possible at *Nynäs Camping* (mid-April to mid-Oct; ☎015/64 10 09). There's only one cabin, so it's worth booking well in advance.

## Practicalities

The **train station** (buses stop outside) and harbour are at opposite ends of town, though still easily walkable. The central **tourist office** is on Rådhus Storatorget (June to mid-Aug Mon–Fri 8am–5pm, Sat & Sun 10am–5pm, mid-Aug to May Mon–Fri 8am–5pm; ☎0155/ 24 82 00, fax 24 88 00) and will book **private rooms** from 125kr (no booking fee). The delightful *STF* **youth hostel**, Brunnsgatan 2 (May to mid-Sept, rest of the year groups only; ☎0155/21 18 10; 100kr in a 2-bed room, dormitory bed 70kr), is in an eighteenth-century former hospital set in the castle grounds and overlooking the King's Tower. There are also two **camping sites**: the closest to town is *Oppeby Camping* (May–Sept; ☎0155/21 13 02), 2km northwest of the centre near the E4, which has cheap cabins. *Strandvikens* is 6km south on the Baltic coast (mid-May to mid-Sept; ☎0155/ 978 10).

The most stylish, good-value and well-positioned **hotel** is the *Kompaniett* on Folkungavägen by the harbour (☎0155/28 80 20, fax 28 16 73; ⑤/②); the price includes breakfast, afternoon tea and a buffet dinner. The rooms are big, the service is friendly and, as part of the individualistic Home Hotel chain, it has its own museum of pictures showing Swedish furniture design and displays on the Swedish car industry. The cheap and basic *Hotel Wictoria,* Fruängsgatan 21 (☎0155/21 75 80, fax 21 44 47; ②/①, including breakfast) is quite adequate and close to the town's picturesque theatre. More glamorous, but out off the E4, *Blommenhof Hotel*, Blommenhovsvägen (☎0155/20 20 60, fax 26 84 94; ④/②), has private saunas, a warm pool and a stylish restaurant.

Most of the **eating and drinking** is, unsurprisingly, done at the harbour, but for the best daytime **café**, head for *Café Hellmans* on Västra Trädgårdgatan 24 (Mon–Fri 7.30am–6pm, Sat 9am–4pm, Sun 10am–4pm), just off Storatorget. In a converted grain warehouse with a summer-time courtyard at the back, it attracts a young, relaxed crowd and serves great sandwiches, fresh-fruit flans and big mugs of good coffee. *Tova Stugen*, behind the castle grounds close to the harbour (Mon–Fri 11am–5pm, Sat & Sun noon–5pm), has an historic setting. Light sandwich meals – try a cold fried fish and sour cream sandwich called *Inlagd Strömming* (35kr) – are served in low, grass-roofed fifteenth-century cottages brought here from around Södermanland, one with unique medieval wall paintings; for full meals, like steaks or lasagne, you can eat outside or in other dark, low buildings, though these smell strongly of their antiquity. If you're in a car you might like to try *Åstugan*, a café-antique shop with a riverside setting on the old E4 past Svarta (mid-June to mid-Aug daily noon–8pm; Sept–May Sat & Sun only); it offers fine pastries and a relaxed atmosphere.

For a bright and fun **restaurant** and **bar** scene head for the old wooden storage buildings along the harbour side. *Restaurant Hamn Magasinet* in a handsome eighteenth-century grain store is very popular; two-course meals cost

166kr, with a vegetarian option, and the speciality is sweet chilli shrimps (56kr as starter or 156kr as a main course). The most laidback place for a young, casual crowd is *Lotsen* (daily 11am–2pm), in a picturesque wooden house serving similar food – but cheaper – than *Hamn Magasinet*. On cooler summer nights, the stylishly nautical, candle-lit interior is a pleasant place to drink and listen to regular live music.

If you're leaving Nyköping for Stockholm by **car**, it's a straight run on the E4; by public transport, the **train** is very quick (1hr 15min). The **bus** route is convoluted, involving one of five buses to either Trosa or Vagnhärad, then bus #782 to Liljeholmen followed by a subway trip to the city centre.

# Gotland

The rumours about good times on **Gotland** are rife. Wherever you are in Sweden, one mention of this ancient Baltic island will elicit a traditional Swedish sigh followed by an anecdote about what a great place it is. You'll hear that the short summer season is an exciting time to visit; that it's hot, fun and lively. Largely, these rumours are true: the island has a distinct youthful feel as young, mobile Stockholmers desert the capital for a boisterous summer spent on its beaches. The flower-power era makes its presence felt with a smattering of elderly VW camper vans lurching off the ferries, but shiny Saabs outnumber them fifty to one. During summer, bars, restaurants and campsites are packed, the streets swarm with revellers, and the sands are awash with bodies. It's not everyone's cup of tea: to avoid the hectic summer altogether, come in late May or September when, depending on your bravado, you can still swim.

Gotland itself, and in particular its capital, **Visby**, has always seen frenetic activity of some kind. A temperate climate and fortuitous geographical position attracted the Vikings as early as the sixth century, and the lucrative trade routes they opened, through to Byzantium and western Asia, guaranteed the island its prosperity. With the ending of Viking domination, a "Golden Age" followed, with Gotland's inhabitants sending embassies, maintaining trading posts and signing treaties with European and Asian leaders as equals. However, by the late twelfth century their autonomy had been undermined by the growing power of the Hanseatic League. Under its influence, Visby became one of the great cities of medieval Europe, as important as London or Paris, famed for its wealth and strategic power. A contemporary ballad had it that: "The Gotlanders weigh their gold with twenty pound weights. The pigs eat out of silver troughs and the women spin with golden distaffs."

This romantic notion of the island's prosperity remained popular until this century, when Gotlanders began relying on tourism to prop up the traditional industries of farming, forestry and fishing. Twentieth-century hype makes great play of the beaches and the sun, and with good reason: the roses that give Gotland its "Island of Roses" tag have been known to bloom at Christmas. It's not all just tourist brochure fodder, though. Nowhere else in Scandinavia is there such a concentration of unspoilt medieval country churches, all built

The telephone code for Gotland is ☎0498.

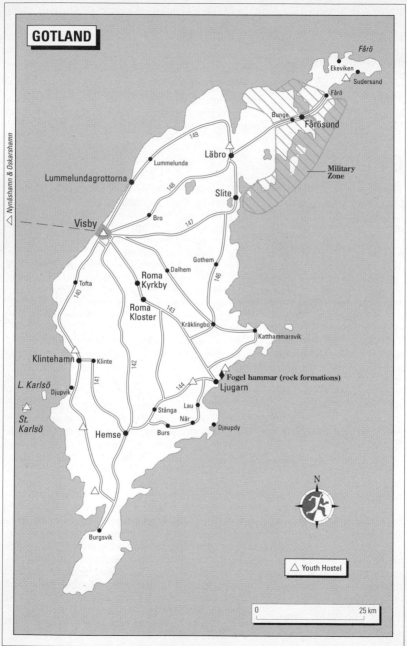

GOTLAND

*Fårö*

Ekeviken

△ Sudersand

Fårö

Bunge

Bunge Fårösund

149

Lummelunda

Läbro

Military Zone

△ Nynäshamn & Oskarshamn

Lummelundagrottorna

148

Slite

Visby

Bro

147

Gothem

Dalhem

146

Roma Kyrkby

Tofta

140

Roma Kloster

143

Kräklingbo

Katthammarsvik

Klintehamn

Klinte

142

*L. Karlsö*

Djupvik

△ St. Karlsö

141

144

Fogel hammar (rock formations)

Ljugarn

Stånga

Lau

När

Hemse

Burs

Djaupdy

N

Burgsvik

△ Youth Hostel

0        25 km

before the end of the fourteenth century. Today 93 of them are still in use, displaying a unique Baltic Gothic style and providing the most permanent reminder of Gotland's ancient wealth.

## Getting there: ferries and planes

**Ferries** to Gotland are numerous and, in summer, packed, so try and plan well ahead. *Gotlandslinjen*, the ferry line, has booking centres in both Nynäshamn and Oskarshamn. Or, in Stockholm, call into *Gotland City* (☎08/23 61 70, fax 411 79 65), Kungsgatan 57, which can provide plenty of information and sell advance tickets. One-way fares cost around 135kr during high season (June to mid-Aug), 175kr on Friday, Saturday and Sunday; and there are student discounts (30 percent) on all crossings. The night sailings in summer are packed out – with bodies sleeping in every available space – so you may well think it worthwhile to take one of the very comfortable, en-suite cabins; a return ticket for two costs 1016kr. Taking a bicycle costs 35kr. See "Travel Details" for a full run-through of ferry schedules and frequencies.

The nearest port to Stockholm is **NYNÄSHAMN**, which has a **youth hostel** (open all year; ☎08/520 208 34), not far from the train station at Nickstabadsvägen 17 – advance booking is essential from September to May. From Gothenburg or the southwest of the country, **OSKARSHAMN** may well be the easier port (a succession of local and national train links means you can cross from Gothenburg to Oskarshamn by train in little over six hours; ask at any main train station for the print-out of times). If you've arrived at Oskarshamn with time to spare before the ferry, the place boasts one charming restaurant-bar, *Peterssons*, Skeppsbrodelen 13 (Mon, Tues, & Thurs 7pm–midnight, Wed, Fri & Sat 7pm–2am, Sun 7pm–1am) just 500m beyond the terminal on the left of the main road; it serves great cold roast beef in baguettes (52kr) and baked potatoes with a mountain of prawns (58kr). If you're taking the six-hour night crossing, it's worth bearing in mind that the very limited food available on the ship is expensive and its shop only sells chocolate, so stock up before you leave.

Recently prices between the two airlines servicing the island have made **flying** a competitive option – at least for under-24s. One-way fares from Stockholm can be as little as 296kr standby. Local tourist offices can provide up-to-date prices.

# Visby

Undoubtedly the finest approach to **VISBY** is by ship, seeing the old trading centre as it should be seen – from the sea. If you sail on one of the busy summer night-time crossings, it's good to get out on deck for the early sunrise. By 5am the sun is above the city, silhouetting the towers of the cathedral and the old wall turrets. Gliding in on the morning tide, the heady experience is – much as it must have been for thirteenth-century traders – welcoming and reassuring.

## Arrival and information

Visby **airport** is 3km from town, a five-minute ride on the airport bus (30kr). A **taxi** into the centre will cost around 65kr. All the huge **ferries** serving Visby dock in the same terminal, just outside the city walls (and off our map). Just turn left and keep walking for the centre. Alternatively, a short way to the right along the harbour front will bring you to *Gotlandsresor* at Färjeleden 3, which has a room-booking service (see "Accommodation", overleaf).

The main **tourist office** is within the city walls in Donnersplats (mid-April to May Mon–Fri 8am–5pm, Sat & Sun 10am–4pm; June to mid-Aug Mon–Fri 7am–7pm, Sat & Sun 10am–7pm; mid-Aug to mid-April Mon–Fri 9am–4pm; ☎20 17 00, fax 27 89 40). Here you can buy the excellent *Turistkarta Gotland* (25kr), a map marking and describing all the points of interest, or take one of the free Visby guides. There's also a selection of **tours** available, some of which are worth considering if time is short: a walking tour of Visby (May–Aug daily at 11.30am; 70kr) and separate day-long tours of the south and north of the island by bus (May–Aug 1–2weekly; 300kr). It's worth checking about day tours in good time, as even those advertised on blackboards outside the tourist office only run when enough people are interested.

## Getting around

Visby itself is best **walked** around. Despite its warren-like first appearance, it's a simple matter to get the hang of the narrow, crisscrossed cobbled streets. The main square, **Storatorget**, is signposted from almost everywhere, and early arrivals will be rewarded by the smell of freshly baked bread from the square's bakery (open from 5am but with a better choice a couple of hours later). Modern Visby has spread beyond the limits defined by its old city walls, and today the new town gently sprawls from beyond **Österport** (East Gate), a few minutes' walk up the hill from Storatorget. From here, in **Östercentrum**, the **bus terminal** serves the rest of the island; the tourist office has free timetables.

For getting around the island, it's hard to resist the temptation to rent a **bike**. Most ferry arrivals at Visby are plagued by people hustling bikes, and if you don't have one you might as well succumb here. Apart from just outside the ferry terminal, bike rental is also possible on Korsgatan or, as a last resort, at Österport, though this is the least friendly. Most cost around 50kr a day, and if you want to try a tandem, it's best to arrive early as they are unusually popular. If you intend striking out into the countryside beyond Visby – a real joy and left undiscovered

---

### CYCLING TIPS

- Gotland is flat but even so cycling can get tiring and it's worth renting a slightly more expensive **3-speed** model.

- **Luggage** can usually be left at the rental office, although a few kronor more gets you baskets or bicycle trolleys.

- Most places offer **bike insurance** (around 25kr a day) and the choice is yours; the built-in rear wheel lock should be enough to deter most joyriders, but if you are worried, an extra chain and padlock will do the trick. Be warned, though, that if your machine goes walkabout when insured, you'll still be liable for the first 200kr. A replacement, on the other hand, will cost about 3500kr.

- Check if you can return the bike the morning after your rental period finishes. Most rental places are down by the ferry terminals, and it's fairly standard practice to let you keep the bike overnight to ride down to the harbour the next morning. Otherwise early ferry departures mean a long walk from the youth hostel or campsites.

- You can take bikes on the island's buses for a flat fee of 20kr.

- A cycle route circumnavigates almost the entire island, signposted out of Visby. You can pick up a free route map from the tourist office.

by most of the young summer crowd – it's worth knowing that bikes can easily be rented, and for less, at various towns to the south of Visby, though Gotland's bike outlets like to appear vague about this possibility.

## Accommodation

Finding **accommodation** in Visby should seldom be a problem; the abandoned-looking souls wrapped in sleeping bags and collapsed in the parks are only there through alcoholic excesses the night before, not homelessness. There are plenty of hotels (though few are particularly cheap; see below), several nearby camp-sites and cabins, and a youth hostel. The *Gotlandsresor* office at Färjeleden 3 (☎20 10 20, fax 20 12 70), and the tourist office (see opposite) can help with **private rooms** from 120kr per person, as well as **cottages**. More information and help is available at *Gotlands Turist Service* at Österport (open all year; Mon–Fri 9am–6pm; ☎20 60 00, fax 24 90 59), which has better access to accommodation information than the tourist office.

The **youth hostel**, *Gotlands Ice Hockey Federation Youth Hostel* (open all year; ☎24 82 02, fax 24 82 70; 150kr per person), is 3km from Visby centre, behind the city's ice hockey hall (ask the bus driver to drop you at *Isall* – ice hall). Set in forest surround-ings, this big, well-equipped place has chalets and rooms, with laundry facilities and a huge TV lounge (meals for groups only). If you don't have your own transport, hitching is easy from the main road, but a taxi back will cost around 80–90kr.

Chiefly, though, Gotland is a place for **camping**. After the success of Ulf Lundell's youth-culture novel *Jack* (after Kerouac), which extolled the simple plea-sure of getting wasted on a beach, Gotland (handy for Stockholmers) became the place to go for wild summer parties: at many campsites, the most exercise you'll get is cycling to and from the *Systembolaget*. The closest campsite, *Nordenstrands* (May–Sept; ☎21 21 57), is 1km outside the city walls – follow the cycle path that runs through the Botanical Gardens along the seafront.

### HOTELS

**Borgen**, Adelsgatan 11 (☎27 99 00, fax 24 93 00). The most attractive smaller, family hotel in the middle of the action, yet with lovely, peaceful gardens. All en-suite rooms; there's a sauna and solarium. ③/④

**Donnersplats**, Donnersplats 6 (☎21 49 45, fax 21 49 44). A popular, central hotel that is pleas-ant enough; also has economical 2–3-bed apartments for 950kr. Essential to book in July and August, especially during Medieval Week. ④/③

**Gute**, Mellangatan 29 (☎24 80 80, fax 24 80 89). A very central, reasonably comfortable hotel with the possibility of reduced rates if you appear at the last minute. ③/④

**Hamn**, Färjeleden 3 (☎20 12 50, fax 20 12 70). Opposite the harbour, this is by far the most convenient hotel (only open May–Sept) for early-morning ferries back to the mainland. All rooms have TV, shower and toilet; breakfast is included in the price and served from 5am. ②

**Solhem**, Solhemsgatan 3 (☎27 90 70, fax 21 95 23). Just outside the city walls at Skansporten, this is a large, comfortable hotel, but considerably shabbier than its grand price suggests. Only an option if all other central hotels are full. ④

**Strand**, Strandgatan 34 (☎21 26 00, fax 27 81 11). A rather glamorous place in a delightful street in the heart of town, with a sauna, steam bath, indoor pool and a bright, stylish atmos-phere. ⑤/④

**Wisby**, Strandgatan 6 (☎20 40 00, fax 21 13 20). The loveliest hotel in town, this splendid place dates to the Middle Ages; it was a grain store until 1850. Mellow rooms, fine breakfasts (open to non-residents for 65kr) and very central – though in May, June & Aug the price goes up to 1410kr. ⑤

## The City

Visby is much older than its medieval remnants suggest. The name derives from its status as a Stone Age sacrificial site – "the settlement", *by*, at "the sacred place", *vi* – but it's the medieval trappings that give the city its distinctly Mediterranean air. The magnificent **defensive wall** is the most obvious manifestation of Visby's previous importance, a 3km circuit enclosing the entire settlement. It was hardly a new idea to fortify trading centres against outside attack, although this land wall, built around the end of the thirteenth century, was actually aimed at isolating the city's foreign traders from the island's own locals.

Annoyed at seeing all their old trade monopolized, the Gotlanders saw something sinister in the wall's erection and didn't have to wait long to be vindicated. In 1361, during the power struggle between Denmark and Sweden, the Danish king, Valdemar III, took Gotland by force and advanced on Visby. The burghers and traders, well aware of the wealth of their city, shut the gates and sat through the slaughter outside. Excavations this century revealed the remains of two-thousand bodies, more than half of them women, children and invalids. **Valdemar's Cross**, a few hundred metres east of Söderport (South Gate), marks their mass grave. Erected by the survivors of the carnage, it reads factually and pathetically: "In 1361 on the third day after St James, the Goths fell into the hands of the Danes. Here they lie. Pray for them."

Back inside the city walls, the merchants surrendered, and a section of the wall near Söderport was broken down to allow Valdemar to ride through as conqueror. Valdemar's Breach is recognizable by its thirteen crenellations representing, so the story goes, the thirteen knights who rode through with the Danish king. Valdemar soon left clutching booty and trade agreements, and Visby continued to prosper while the island's countryside around it stagnated, its people and wealth destroyed.

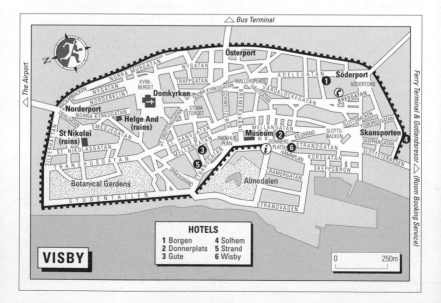

The old **Hanseatic harbour** at Almedalen is now a public park, and nothing is much more than a few minutes' walk from here. Pretty **Packhusplan**, the oldest square in the city, is bisected by curving Strandgatan, which runs southwards to the fragmentary ruins of **Visborg Castle**, overlooking the harbour. Built in the fifteenth century by Erik of Pomerania, the castle was blown up by the Danes in the seventeenth century. In the opposite direction, northwest, Strandgatan runs towards the sea and the lush **Botanical Gardens**, just beyond which is the **Jungfrutornet** (Maiden's Tower), where a local goldsmith's daughter was walled up alive – reputedly for betraying the city to the Danes.

**Strandgatan** itself is the best place to view the impressive merchants' houses looming over the narrow streets, with storerooms above the living quarters and cellars below, notably **Burmeisterska house** (June–Aug 11am–6pm; free). One of the most picturesque buildings is the old pharmacy, **Gamla Apoteket** (June–Aug Mon–Fri 2–6pm, Sat 10am–1pm; 10kr), a lofty old place with gloriously higgledy-piggledy windows. The small **Natural History Museum** (June–Aug daily 11am–5pm; free) on Strandgatan has little in the way of English translation, and its none too thrilling exhibits are very missable. However, the **Gotlands Fornsal Museum**, next door, is well worth a visit (see below).

Strolling around the twisting streets and atmospheric walls is not something that palls quickly, but if you need a focus, aim for **Norra Murgatan**, above the cathedral, once one of Visby's poorest areas. At the end nearest Norderport is the best view of the walls and city rooftops, and there'a rare opportunity to climb on to the ramparts. The dark, atmospheric tower on Strandgatan, **Kruttornet** (June–Aug daily 10am–6pm), affords more grand views; while the roof of the **Helge And** church ruin (May–Sept daily 10am–6pm), which has been reinforced to allow access to the second floor, provides another central vantage point. Or head for the water's edge, where **Studentallén** is a popular late-evening haunt and the sunsets are magnificent – brilliant fiery reds, glinting mirrored waters and bobbing sailing boats in the middle distance.

## *GOTLANDS FORNSAL MUSEUM*

A really fine museum with some brilliantly laid-out exhibitions, **Gotlands Fornsal Museum** (mid-May to Aug daily 11am–6pm; Sept to mid-May Tues–Sun noon–4pm; 30kr, under 16s free) is at Strandgatan 14. The superb guide book in English costs 20kr. Housed in a mid-eighteenth century distillery, there are five storeys of exhibition halls covering eight thousand years of history, plus a good café and bookstore. Among the most impressive of the exhibitions is the **Hall of Picture Stones** in Room 1. Dating mostly from the fifth to seventh centuries, these large, keyhole-shaped stones are richly ornamented. The earlier ones are covered in runic inscriptions; but the older ones are more intriguing, with vivid depictions of people, animals, ships and houses. The **Hall of Prehistoric Graves** is also fascinating; here skeletons dating back six thousand years are displayed in glass cases, and red arrows in one box point out where a flint arrowhead lodged in its occupant's ancient hip and killed him. In another, a twenty-year-old woman from 2500 BC lies with the decorative pins she once used to fix her hair. Other rooms devoted to Gotland's prehistory are not so immediately appealing, whereas those further on (9 to 13) are more relevant, tracing the history of **medieval Visby**. In Room 9, you can see a trading booth, where the burghers of Visby and foreign merchants dealt in commodities – furs, lime, wax, honey and tar – brought from all over northern Europe.

The years **1500 to 1900** are cleverly represented in a series of **tableaux**, which make a historical and stylistic progression through the centuries. Starting with Eric of Pomerania, the first resident of Visborg Castle, it leads on through the years of Danish rule to the Peace of Brömsebro, when Gotland was ceded to Sweden. The central feature of the eighteenth-century section is a depiction of Carl Linnaeus, later knighted von Linné, who came to explore the remarkable flora and fauna on the island. This century also saw Gotland's first boom in industry for centuries, and the trading house headed by the Donner family became one of the largest in Sweden. There's a wax model of Anna Margareta Donner, who by the 1750s was a widow who was so shrewd and forward in business that on the correspondence preserved from the time she is referred to as "Mrs Donner, Sir". You'll notice the Donner name all over the centre of the city, notably the square in which the tourist office stands and the café set in her beautiful home (see opposite). The straight lines and right angles of the Gustavian period are linked in the next scene with the Russian invasion of the island in the early nineteenth century. By this century Gotland had won its first tourists, the beginning of boom which has snowballed to the present day.

## VISBY'S CHURCHES

At the hight of its power, Visby maintained sixteen **churches** and while only one, the Cathedral of St Mary, is still in use, the ruins of eleven others – very often only their towers or foundations – can be seen. The **Domkyrkan** (Sun–Fri 8am–9pm, Sat 8am–6.30pm) was built between 1190 and 1225 and as such, dates from just before the great age of Gothic church building on the island. Used as both warehouse and treasury in the past, it's been heavily restored, and about the only original fixture left is the thirteenth-century sandstone font inside. Most striking are its towers, one square at the western front and two slimmer eastern ones, standing sentry over the surrounding buildings. Originally each had spires, but since an eighteenth-century fire, they've been crowned with fancy Baroque cupolas, giving them the appearance of inverted ice cream cones. When inside, have a look beneath the pulpit, decorated with a fringe of unusually hideous angels' faces.

Seventeenth- and eighteenth-century builders and decorators found the smaller churches in the city to be an excellent source of free limestone, tiles and fittings – which accounts for the fact that most are today in ruins. Considering the number of tourists clambering about them, the smaller church ruins manage to retain a proud yet abandoned look. Best of what's left is the great **St Nicolai** ruin, just down the road from the Domkyrkan, once the largest church in Visby. Destroyed in 1525, its part-Gothic, part-Romanesque shell hosts a week-long **chamber music festival**, starting at the end of July; tickets range from 100kr to 300kr and are available from the tourist office – which also sells a rather disappointing guide, *The Key to all of Gotland's Churches*.

## Eating, drinking and nightlife

For **eating**, the usual *Dagens Rätt* deal applies in most restaurants, and the centre is small enough to wander around and size up the options. More specifically, **Adelsgatan** is lined with cafés and snack bars, Wallersplats and Hästgatan are busy at lunchtime, while **Strandgatan** is the focus of Visby's evening parade. For good, cheap food all day, try *Saluhallen,* the market opposite the harbour. Here you can buy fresh baked bread, fish and fruit and eat it at tables overlooking the water. Visby's restaurants and bars see plenty of life during the day, but at night they positively heave with young bodies – many of them drunk. **Donnersplats**, opposite the tourist office, is also alive at night, with lots of takeaway food stalls.

For a different style of youthful **nightlife**, head down to the **harbour**, where forests of masts make a pretty backdrop to the loud, happy beat of music and revellers grooving away on the dance floors. *Anton's Pub* is about the loudest, with old rock hits and folk music, while *Skeppet* is a frenzy of activity next door. A couple of boats are also bars: *Graceland* is popular, unsurprisingly playing Elvis hits and serving drinks from the Priscilla Bar. Note that many of Visby's discos and clubs open in the late afternoon, from around 4pm onwards, for "After Beach" sessions of relatively cheap beer.

Gotlanders also enjoys a unique licence from the state to brew their own **beer**, the recipe differing from household to household. It's never for sale, but summer parties are awash with the stuff – be warned, it is extremely murky and strong.

## DAYTIME CAFÉS

**Café Björkstugan**, Späksgränd. In a fabulous, lush garden on the prettiest central cobbled street, with climbing roses, this little café serves savoury and sweet pies and coffee amid a rainbow of flowers.

**Café Ryska Gården**, Storatorget. Amid fine rustic decor, *saffranspanskakka*, a saffron-yellow rice pie, rather stronger in colour than taste, is served along with Gotland's own salmberry (a sweet, hybrid berry) jam and cream.

**Café Strandporten**, just outside Almedalen park near the harbour. Serves *saffranspanskakka* under a massive horse chestnut tree. It opens later than the rest. June–Aug daily 9am–10pm.

**Madame Donners Café**, Donnersplats. A splendidly picturesque café with a glorious rose bush and tree-filled garden; inside the tables were once owned by the venerable Mrs Donner (see "Gotland Fornsal Museum", opposite). There are regular art exhibitions, and a menu in five languages explains the main courses, including cod with almonds at 50kr and open sandwiches for 20kr.

**Skafferiet**, Adelsgatan. A lovely eighteenth-century house turned into a cosy café boasting a lush garden at the back. Serves baked potatoes and great cakes in a place dripping with character.

## RESTAURANTS AND BARS

**Acacia Restaurant**, opposite Fornsal Museum on Strandgatan. Not the most sophisticated of places, but very popular café and kebab place catering to a young, chatty crowd.

**Bakfickan**, corner St Katarinegatan & Storatorget. A quiet, relaxed little restaurant, with a tiled interior. It's a good place for a drink.

**Barbeque Garden**, Strandgatan 15. On the site of Visby's medieval town hall, this is a huge garden pizza restaurant, with indoor and extensive outdoor seating. Lots of cocktails, and a bright if not so trendy atmosphere.

---

### MEDIEVAL WEEK

During the first week of August, Visby becomes the backdrop for a boisterous re-enactment of the conquest of the island by the Danes in 1361. **Medieval Week** sees music in the streets, medieval food on sale in the restaurants (no potatoes – they hadn't yet been brought to Europe) and on the first Sunday a procession re-creating Valdemar's triumphant entry through Söderport to Storatorget. Here, modern-day burghers are stripped of their wealth and then the procession moves onto the Maiden's Tower – all good touristy fun with a genuine carnival atmosphere to boot.

**Burmeister**, Strandgatan. One of the hot venues. A full à la carte menu offers starters at around 80kr, pasta (90kr) and main courses at 160kr. Pricey pizzas appear at 95kr. Busy bar; expect long queues.

**Café Boheme**, Hästgatan 9. A mellow place, candle-lit, young and lively without being frenetic, it serves inexpensive salads, sandwiches and pizzas and lots of cakes, including a rather good *kladdkaka* (gooey chocolate pie). June–Aug daily 11am–11pm – sometimes till 1am; rest of the year shorter hours and closed Sun & Mon.

**Friheten**, Donnersplats. A lively pub attached to *Wisby Hotel*. Loud, live bands reverberate on a Fri & Sat evening. Daily 11.30am–2am.

**Gutekällaren**, Lilla Torggränd, just a couple of steps up from *Henry's Bar* (see below). This quiet fish and meat restaurant has an uncharacteristically sober atmosphere; à la carte and grill menu and cheaper bar food for around 50kr.

**Henry's Bar**, corner of St Hansgatan & Lilla Torggränd. One of the busiest joints, with a big, traditional pub, dancing and a steady queue to enter. Burgers, ribs and wok-cooked chicken and salads are served with the beers; all food around 60–90kr.

**Munk Källeren**, Lilla Torggränd, opposite *Gutekällaren* . Massively popular, vaulted and *the* place to be seen – and be pushed against someone else in the crowd. There's an extensive à la carte menu, all in English.

**Nunnan Restaurant and Pub**, Storatorget. A lively, crowded, sit-down eating place attracting a mixed-age group.

## Listings

**Banks and exchange** Östercentrum has the largest concentration of branches for changing money; the tourist office also has fairly good rates.

**Car rental** *Avis*, Donnersplats.

**Ferries** Buy tickets down at the terminal buildings or at the travel agency on Södergatan.

**Market** Fruit, veg and souvenirs in Storatorget Mon–Sat throughout the summer.

**Post office** Main office for poste restante at Norra Hansegatan 2 (Mon–Fri 9am–6pm, Sat 10am–noon).

**Systembolaget** in Storatorget and at Östervägen 3. The other off-licences on the island are at Hemse, Slite, Klintehamn, Färösunds and Burgsvik.

**Telephones** Make international calls from the telephone office on Adelsgatan (May–Aug Mon–Fri 8.30am–3.30pm), though it's cheaper from the IDD phones you'll find all over the island.

# The rest of the island

There is a real charm to the rest of Gotland – rolling green countryside, forest-lined roads, fine beaches and small fishing villages, and everywhere the rural skyline is dominated by churches, the remnants of medieval settlements destroyed in the Danish invasion. Yet perhaps because of the magnetic pull of Visby, very few people bother to go and explore. Main roads are pleasingly free of traffic and any minor roads are positively deserted – cycling is a joy. The **south** of the island, in particular, boasts numerous wonderful and untouched villages and resorts; while the **north**, though pretty, is more a target for a day-trip from the capital. As you go, keep an eye out for the waymarkers erected in the 1780s to indicate the distance to *Wisby* (the old spelling). They are calculated in Swedish miles (ie 10 km) and appear every quarter-mile, though the mile markers are the most ornate.

Gotland's **buses**, though regular, are very few indeed. Outside Visby, they tend to run only twice daily – morning and evening. **Hitching**, however, is an accepted means of transport, and locals expect it, so unless you have a specific destination, the general attractiveness of the countryside, especially in the south, means it's often just as well to go wherever the driver is heading.

## The south: from Hemse to Burs

The so-called "capital" of the south, **HEMSE**, around 50km from Visby (buses ply this route), is little more than a main street, but there are a couple of banks and a good local café, *Bageri & Conditori Johansson* on Storgatan – if you're camping or without your own transport, this is where to stock up with food. You can rent **bikes** from two places on Ronevägen, off Storgatan: *Hemse Krog* is a general rental shop with bikes, while next door, *Ondrell's* (☎48 03 33) is the cheapest place you'll find (40kr per day, 20kr each day after or 160kr per week); it also rents trailers. There's not a lot else to Hemse, except a **swimming pool** (June–Aug Mon–Thurs 2–8pm, Fri 5–8pm; 35kr, solarium 40kr), signposted "simhall", off Storgatan at the north end of the town. Hemse **bus station**, parallel with Storgatan (head down Ronevägen for one block and turn left), is oddly in a boarded-up and vandalized house.

Taking Road 144 west, signposted Burs, the countryside is a glorious mix of meadows, ancient farms and dark, mysterious forest. A sign for "museum" leads into a wooded area, where a cluster of old buildings display wood cuttings and old direction signs (June–Aug Mon & Wed–Fri 1–5pm; 10kr). It's rather more fun, though, to head a kilometre or so on to *Studioglass Ronny Carlsson*, a small glass and ceramics works at **FLORSBURS**. Here you can watch the experts glassblowing simple semi-opaque blue glassware. One of the most charming villages just a couple of kilometres further, **BURS** has a gorgeous thirteenth-century saddle church, so-called because of its low nave and high tower and chancel. There's a fabulously decorated ceiling, medieval stained-glass windows and ornately painted pews. For a really friendly, local's café, the nearby *Burs Café* (June–Aug daily noon–10pm; rest of the year 4–9pm & closed Mon) serves cheap, filling meals like beef stroganoff or hamburgers made with Gotland beef for just 30kr (25kr to takeaway).

## När and Lau

Turning right from Burs, following signs to När, the scenery is a paradise of wild, flowering meadows and medieval farm holdings, all untouched by the centuries, with ancient windows and carved wooden portals. The tranquil and pretty hamlet of **NÄR** is notable for its church, set in an immaculate churchyard. The tower originally served as a fortification in the thirteenth century, but more arresting are the bizarre portraits painted on the pew ends right the way up the left-side of the church. All depict women with demented expressions and bare, oddly placed breasts.

A couple of kilometres north and just beyond the village of **LAU**, *Garde* **youth hostel** (open all year, pre-book outside summer; ☎49 11 81, fax 49 11 81; 95kr) provides some of Sweden's strangest accommodation: the cluster buildings are situated right by the local football pitch, and the bathroom facilities (in a building on their own) are clean and spacious, but shared with anyone doing football practice. There's a food shop (daily 9am–7pm) around the corner from the hostel reception. For a delightful daytime café, art gallery and evening bar try *Svinhuset* at Lau (Tues–Sun 11am–6pm; pub June–Aug till 9pm, otherwise Sat & Sun only). Once a pig farm, it is set in lovely countryside, and the stark, white gallery shows changing exhibitions of contemporary paintings. In the pub, the place's mascot, a cross-bred Asian and Vietnamese pot-bellied pig, wanders around while you drink. Heading east towards the coast on Road 144, it's well worth stopping at *Meieret* (Mon–Fri 11am–6pm, Sat & Sun noon–3pm), a stylish conversion of an old dairy into an artistic centre full of textiles, ceramics and paintings. Cool, white light floods the spacious, lofty interior, where tasteful pottery and sweaters made of Gotland wool go for high prices.

## Ljugarn

For beaches, and the nearest thing Gotland has to a resort, the lively and charming town of **LJUGARN** makes a good base. The **tourist office** (May & mid-Aug to mid-Sept daily 11am–4pm; June daily 9am–6pm, July to mid-Aug daily 8am–7pm) is just off the main road as you approach town and has plenty of information about the southeast of the island. Ljugarn, though full of restaurants and obviously aimed at tourists, retains an authentic feel and is famous for its *rauker* – tall limestone pillars rising up from the sea. Claudelinska Huset, on Storgatan, is an **art gallery** (open 2–7pm; free) in someone's rather fine if battered drawing room, complete with old Gustavian furniture and Indian silk carpets, and it's these that appeal rather than the moslty dull landscape paintings. It's only 100m to the sea from here, with popular, sandy beaches. A delightful cycle or stroll down Strandvägen follows the coast line through woods and clearings carpeted in *blåeld,* the electric-blue flowers for which the area is known. The *rauker* stand like ancient hunched men, their feet lapped by the waves.

This is one place where it's easy to find a range of eating places to suit most tastes, and accommodation, unlike most of the island outside Visby, is not restricted to camping or hostels. "*Rums*" are advertised in appealing-looking cottages all over the little town, and Ljugarn **youth hostel** (open all year; ☎49 31 84; 95kr), on Strandridaregården, has two- to six-bed rooms. The tourist office will book **private rooms** from 100kr (30kr booking fee). Gotland's oldest **B&B**, *Badpensionatet*, is here, too (☎49 32 05; ②, including breakfast); it opened its doors in 1921. All rooms have toilet, shower and telephone; there's also a restaurant (the only one in town opened all year; daily noon–10pm), with lunch at 52kr (noon–5pm) and evening meals ranging from one to three courses for 100–150kr. Cheap but perfectly functional rooms are for rent at *Storvägen 91* (both its name and address: ☎49 34 16). Rooms with shower and toilet are 100kr per person, plus 50kr for sheet; **bike** rental costs 35kr per day.

For a splendid **café**, *Café Espegards* (daily 9am–8pm) on Storvägen is a must. Serving some of the best cakes you could find anywhere in Sweden – try the almond tart – it's very popular, so expect a queue. Further down Storvägen, on the corner of Claudelinsvägen, the best fish **restaurant** in town is *Kråkan* (daily 5pm–1am), a lovely, relaxed place, with a big list of cocktails, long drinks and a fair wine list (starters 65kr, main courses 120–170kr); there are plenty of meat options, too. If you wander a few steps further down the street, *Brunna Dorren* (Mon–Thurs & Sun noon–midnight, Fri & Sat noon–1am) is a pleasant old stuccoed house now home to a pizza place, with a big garden where beer is served overlooking the sea and ideal for a post-beach eat (pizzas 60kr, other light meals 35–65kr). A surprisingly genteel place for a tasty snack is *Strandcafé* (daily 10am–10pm) on the beach itself; it's done up like a country kitchen and has luscious cakes, as well as salads, hamburgers, pies; you can also sit out on a popular wooden terrace looking over the sea.

## Stånga

Heading back west from Ljugarn, Road 144 passes through **LYE**, a charming if sleepy hamlet with an antique shop and café, where several rooms are filled with inexpensive, but unimpressive curios, but the atmosphere is congenial thanks to the friendly owner, who drifts about serving vegetarian paté sandwiches and coffee. **STÅNGA** is just a few kilometres on. Its fourteenth-century church is worth visiting for the extremely unusual sculptured wall tablets running down the facade and attributed to Egypticus, a sculptor whose exact identity has never been discovered, but who shows strong Egyptian influences. Inside this atmospheric church, which has little in the way of windows, is a single, heavily carved stone pillar beneath a vaulted roof decorated with a grotesque gargoyle. Likewise, the twelfth-century font has fanged monsters devouring frog-like creatures around its base.

By the golf course outside, is *Gumbalda Golf* (☎48 28 80, fax 48 2 884; ①, including breakfast), a fine **place to stay** at a very reasonable price. It's a perfect base for exploring the south, and the beautiful grey wooden hotel in old farm stables is stylishly done out in simple, Swedish design. It has special golf packages on offer; the green fee for this eighteen-hole course is 200kr per day.

## Stora and Lilla Karlsö

The two islands of **Stora Karlsö** and **Lilla Karlsö**, lying over 6km off the southwest coast, have been declared nature reserves, and both have bird sanctuaries where razorbills, guillemots, falcons and eider duck breed relatively undisturbed. It's possible to reach Stora Karlsö from Klintehamn: tickets are available from the harbour office for sailings at 9am and 11am (150kr return; 45min). Lilla Karlsö is reached from Djupvik, 7km south of Klintehamn (no buses); return tickets, from the harbour office there, cost 120kr. There is a restaurant on Lilla Karlsö, where lunch and dinner are served, as well as breakfast for anyone staying overnight in the hostel-style accommodation (☎24 10 19; 100kr). It is necessary to book meals.

The only **accommodation** on Stora Karlsö is at the *STF* **youth hostel** (☎24 500, fax 24 52 60) in tiny fishermen's huts, which sleep up to four people; as picturesque as it sounds and, at 100–200kr a night per hut, it is economic, it's also extremely basic, with no showers. Any other kind of camping is not allowed on the islands.

## The north: from Visby to Slite

Thirteen kilometres north of Visby are the **Lummelundagrottarna** (May–Aug daily 9am–6pm; Sept daily 9am–4pm; 40kr), limestone caves, stalagmites and stalactites that form a disappointingly dull and damp stop. There's a more interesting natural phenomenon 10km to the north, where you'll see the highest of Gotland's coastal **limestone stacks**. These are the remnants of reefs formed over four-hundred million years ago: the fact that they're well above the tide line is proof of earlier, higher sea levels. This stack, 11.5m high and known as **Jungfruklint**, is said to look like the Virgin and Child – something you'll need a fair bit of imagination to deduce.

Instead of taking the coastal road from Visby, you could head inland towards **BRO**, which has one of the island's most beautiful churches. Several different building stages are evident from the Romanesque and Gothic windows in the tower, but the most unusual aspect is the south wall with its flat-relief picture stones, carved mostly with animals, that were incorporated from a previous church that once stood on the site.

On the whole, though, it's far better to press on further into the eminently picturesque north, where many of the secluded cottages are summer holiday homes for urban Swedes. Much of the peninsula north of **Lärbro** is prohibited to foreign tourists due to the army's presence; just the main road corridor to Fårösund is open to reach the lovely **Fårö island** beyond (see below). You can go as far as **BUNGE** without special permission, and it's worth making the journey to visit its bright fourteenth-century fortified church and open-air museum (mid-May to mid-Aug daily 10am–6pm; 30kr). **SLITE**, just to the south of Lärbro and open to everyone, is the island's only really ugly place – the day-trip buses pass right through its cement factories, quarries and monumentally dull architecture. Beyond this, though, Slite has a sandy beach and good swimming. If you don't mind paying for your camping, then the campsite (May–Sept ☎22 08 30), right on the beach, isn't a bad choice.

## Fårö

The tourist office in Visby arranges special day-long bus trips (June–Aug Tues & Thurs; 300kr) to **Fårö** (Sheep Island), although it's also possible to travel independently, taking a bus to the town of **FÅROSUND** and making the half-hourly ferry crossing from there (daily every 15min; free). There's a down-at-heel but surprisingly good café in town, *Färösund Grill*, which serves excellent sandwiches (25kr) and moist almond tart (10kr), with good, cheap coffee. Just opposite is *Bungehallen*, a very well-stocked supermarket (daily till 10pm).

Most of Fårö island is flat limestone heath, with shallow lakes and stunted pines much in evidence. In winter (and sometimes in summer, too) the wind whips off the Baltic, justifying the existence of the local windmills – and of the sheep shelters, with their steeply pitched reed roofs, modelled on traditional Fårö houses. Examples of both line the road as you leave the ferry.

The best place to head for (and where most of the Swedish holidaymakers are going) is the five-kilometre white sand arc at **SUNDERSANDSVIKEN**; much of the rest of the swimming is done at **EKEVIKEN**, on the other side of the isthmus. The rest of the coastline, though, is rocky, spectacularly so at **LAUTERHORN** and, particularly, **LANGHAMMARS**, where limestone stacks are grouped together on the beach. At Lauterhorn you can follow the signs for Digerhuvud, a long line of stacks leading to the tiny fishing hamlet of **HELGUMANNEN**, which has no more than a dozen shacks on the beach, now used as holiday homes. Continuing along the same rough track brings you to a junction; right runs back to the township of Fårö; left, a two-kilometre dead-end road leads to Langhammars.

## travel details

### Trains

**From Hallsberg** to Gothenburg (hourly; 2hr 40min); Stockholm (hourly; 1hr 30min).

**From Jönköping** to Falköping (change for Stockholm & Gothenburg; hourly; 45min); Nässjo (change for Stockholm & Malmö; hourly; 35min).

**From Kalmar** to Emmaboda (16 daily; 35min); Gothenburg (5 daily; 4hr 15min) plus more frequent local trains from Emmaboda and Växjo; Malmö (8 daily; 3hr 40min); Stockholm (5 daily; 6hr 30min); Växjo (10 daily; 1hr 15min).

**From Motala** to Hallsberg (for Örebro, Stockholm & Gothenburg; 6 daily; 45min);

Mjöbly (for Malmö & Stockholm; 2 daily; 15min).

**From Norrköping** to Linköping (1 or 2 hourly; 25min); Malmö (11 daily; 3hr 15min); Nyköping (5 daily; 40min); Stockholm (hourly; 1hr 40min).

**From Örebro** to Gävle (6 daily, some changing at Falun; 3–4hr); Hallsberg (change for Stockholm & Gothenburg; 1 or 2 hourly; 20min); Motala (6 daily; 1hr 30min); Stockholm (7 daily; 3hr 10min).

**From Oskarshamn** to Gothenburg (3 daily; 5hr 30min); Nässjo (3 daily; 2hr 25min); Jönköping (3 daily; 3hr 20min).

**From Växjo** to Kalmar (6 daily; 1hr 40min); Karlskrona (2 daily; 1hr 30min); Tothenbureg (8 daily; 3hr 20min).

**Buses**

**From Jönköping** to Gothenburg (Mon–Fri 2, Sun 3; 2hr 15min); Gränna/Vadstena/Motala/Örebro (up to 2 daily; 30min/1hr 20min/1hr 40min/3hr 5min); Växjo (Fri & Sun 1; 1hr 20min).

**From Kalmar** to Gothenburg (1 daily; 6hr); Lund/Malmö (1 daily; 5hr 30min/5hr 45min); Oskarshamn/Västervik/Stockholm (3 daily; 1hr 25min/2hr 35min/6hr 50min).

**From Motala** to Norrköping/Stockholm (Fri & Sun 2; 1hr 35min/3hr 25min).

**From Norrköping** to Löfstad Manor (every 2hr; 20min); Kolmården Djurpark (5 daily; 1hr); Linköping/Jönköping/Gothenburg (6 daily; 30min/2hr 40min/4hr 55min); Kalmar (5 daily; 4hr 15min); Stockholm (5 daily; 2hr 10min).

**From Växjo** to Jöpöping/Linköping/Norrköping/Stockholm/Uppsala (Fri & Sun 1; 1hr 20min/3hr 30min/4hr/6hr 30min/7hr 30min).

**Ferries**
*GOTLAND*

**From Nynäshamn** to Visby (mid-June to mid-Aug 2–3 daily; 5hr day, 6hr night).

**From Oskarshamn** to Visby (mid-June to mid-Aug 2 daily; 3hr day, 6hr night).

*Throughout the rest of the year, the service between Visby and Nynäshamn or Oskarshamn is usually night boats only and is much less frequent.*

*ÖLAND*

**From Oskarshamn** to Byxelkrok (3 daily, mid-June to mid-Aug).

**From Timmernabben** to Borgholm (3 daily, mid-June to mid-Aug).

# CHAPTER FIVE

# THE BOTHNIAN COAST: GÄVLE TO HAPARANDA

S weden's east coast forms one edge of the **Gulf of Bothnia** (*Bottenhavet*), a corridor of land that, with its jumble of erstwhile fishing towns and squeaky-clean contemporary urban planning, is quite unlike the rest of the north of the country. The coast is dominated by towns and cities; the forest, so apparent in other parts of the north, has been felled here to make room for settlements. Almost the entire coastline is dotted with towns and villages that reveal a faded history. Some, like **Gävle** and **Hudiksvall**, still have their share of old wooden houses, promoting evocative images of the past, though much was lost during the Russian incursions of the eighteenth century. If you can, take plenty of time to amble up the coast; they are attractive and relaxed places to visit. Today, though, cities like **Sundsvall**, **Umeå** and **Luleå** are more typical – modern, bright and airy metropolises that rank as some of Sweden's liveliest and most likable destinations.

Throughout the north you'll find traces of the religious fervour that swept the region in centuries past; **Skellefteå**, **Piteå** and **Luleå** all boast excellently preserved *kyrkstäder* or parish villages, clusters of knarred old wooden cottages dating from the 1700s, where villagers from outlying districts would spend the night after making the lengthy journey to church in the nearest town. If you're working your way up the coast on the long train ride to Kiruna and Riksgränsen, it's worth breaking your trip at one or two of these places.

The highlight of the Bothnian coast is undoubtedly the stretch known as the **Höga Kusten**, or the High Coast, between Härnösand and Örnsköldsvik – for peace and quiet, this is easily the most idyllic part of central Sweden. Its indented coastline is best seen from the sea, with shimmering fjords reaching deep inland, tall cliffs and a string of pine-clad islands that make it possible to island-hop up the

---

### ACCOMMODATION PRICES

The pensions and hotels listed in the guide have been price-graded according to the scale outlined below; the number indicates the price for the least expensive double room. Many hotels offer considerable reductions at weekends (year round) and during the summer holiday period (mid-June to mid-Aug); in these cases the reduction is either noted in the text or, where it falls into another price band, given after the full price. Single rooms, where available, usually cost between 60 and 80 percent of a double.

① under 500kr    ② 500–700kr    ③ 700–900kr    ④ 900–1200kr    ⑤ over 1200kr

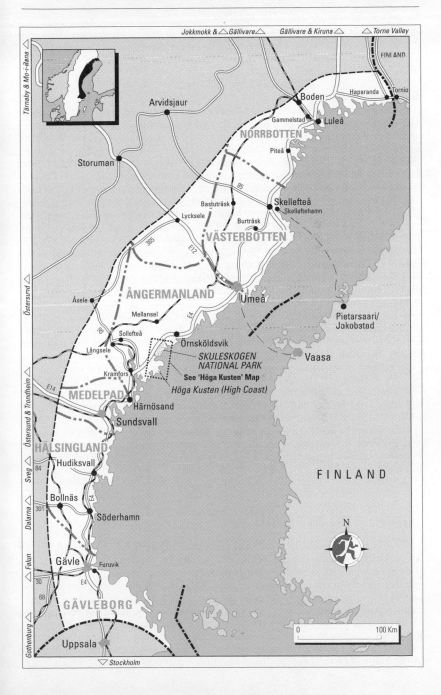

coast. There's also good **hiking** to be had here in the **Skuleskogen National Park**. The weather may not be as reliable as further south, but you're guaranteed clean beaches – often to yourself and ideal for nude bathing – crystal clear waters and some of the finest countryside for walking.

## Getting around

The **train** route hugs the coast until just beyond Härnösand, where intercity services terminate. From here a branch line swings inland, joining up in Långsele with the main line north to Kiruna and on to the Norwegian port of Narvik. There are regular services between Stockholm and Sundsvall, stopping at Gävle, Söderhamn and Hudiksvall; from Sundsvall a handful of trains continue onto Härnösand, sometimes with a direct connection from Stockholm. There's also a handy train and bus connection to Sundsvall from the inland town of Östersund (see "Travel details" at the end of the chapter). After Härnösand things get more tricky; there are currently only two trains a day (also three buses that accept train tickets and passes) via Kramfors and Sollefteå to Långsele, where you can connect onto the two night trains up to Luleå and Boden, Gällivare and Kiruna. To avoid waiting around at night at Långsele station, it's easier to continue north by **bus** from Härnösand up the High Coast towards Örnsköldsvik and on to connect with the main train line at Boden or Luleå. Island-hopping through the High Coast via Högbonden, Ulvön and Trysunda (ferry tickets are reasonable; see p.322 for details) is a wonderful way to make your way north and to take in one of northern Sweden's most beautiful regions. The High Coast also offers good **cycling**; contact local tourist offices for advice on renting bikes. From Örnsköldsvik north, there are frequent bus services via Umeå, Skellefteå and Piteå to Luleå and Boden. Remember also that there are several bus services running inland from Örnsköldsvik, Umeå and Skellefeå, which can whisk you up into the mountains if you tire of the coast. Between Härnösand and Luleå, the only coastal town with a direct train link to Stockholm is Umeå routed via Vännäs. Various bus companies offer discount tickets and passes for regional travel, but they're not worth it unless you intend to visit every town and village in a particular area.

Over recent years the number of **ferry services** between the Bothnian coast and **Finland** has shrunk dramatically. The only remaining year-round service operates between Umeå and Vaasa (journey time 4hr). The future of the crossings between Skellefteå and Pietarsaari and Kokkola is uncertain. Ticket details are given in the text.

# Gävle and around

It's only two hours north by train from Stockholm to **GÄVLE** (pronounced "Yervle"), principal city of the county of Gästrikland and the southernmost in Norrland, the region which makes up two-thirds of Sweden and to all intents and purposes covers everything north of Uppsala. Gävle is an old city – its town charter granted in 1446 – although this knowledge doesn't prepare you for the modern centre: large squares, broad avenues and proud monumental buildings. The city was almost completely rebuilt after a devastating fire in 1869, and its layout reflects the heady success of its late nineteenth-century industry, when Gävle was the export centre for locally produced iron and timber. Today the city is more famous as the home of *Gevalia* coffee (the old Latinized name for the town), which you'll

The telephone code for Gävle is ☎026.

no doubt taste during your time in Sweden. If you're heading for Höga Kusten, Gävle makes a good stop en route – if instead you're travelling further north into Lapland, you'd do better to crack on with the journey and stop somewhere further north like Sundsvall or Umeå.

# Arrival, information and accommodation

The city centre is concentrated in the grid of streets spreading southwest from the **train station** on Stora Esplanadgatan. You'll find left-luggage lockers (15kr) on the main platform. For the **bus station**, use the subway under the train tracks to the other side of the station; here you'll find the departure point for both local and long-distance services. The tiny **airport** is west of town near Sandviken. There are currently weekday flights to Stockholm and Hudiksvall with *Holmstroem Air Sweden*.

The **tourist office** is in Berggrenska Gården at Norra Kyrkogatan 14 (June–Aug daily 9am–6pm; rest of the year Mon–Fri 9am–4pm; ☎14 74 30), where there's also a summer-time open-air café, serving, amongst other things, the best home-made bread in town.

The tourist office will book private **apartments** from 170kr per person per night (cheaper by the week or month); it's not necessary to book in advance. Gävle has two **youth hostels** – one is superbly located in the old quarter at Södra Rådmansgatan 1 (open all year; ☎62 17 45, fax 61 59 90; 100kr); the other is on the coast at Bönavägen 118 in **ENGELTOFTA**, 6km northeast of the city (May–Aug; ☎961 60, fax ☎960 55; 100kr). To get there take bus #5 from Rådhuset (12 daily). Gävle's **campsite** is out at *Furuvik Amusement Park* (see p.309); the park is a bus ride away on either #821, #838 or #832, which leave roughly every half-hour. Much better to make use of *Allemansrätt* and camp rough somewhere on the outskirts of town.

## Hotels

**Aveny**, Södra Kungsgatan 31 (☎61 55 90, fax 65 15 55). A small and comfortable family-run hotel south of the river. ③/①

**Boulogne**, Byggmästargatan 1 (☎12 63 5, fax 12 63 52). Cosy basic hotel with breakfast on a tray. Close to Boulognerskogen park. ②/①

**Grand Central**, Nygatan 45 (☎12 90 60, fax 12 44 99). One of the smartest hotels in town, with old-fashioned style en-suite rooms. ④/③

**Nya Järnvägshotellet**, Centralplan 3 (☎12 09 90, fax 10 62 42). The cheapest hotel in Gävle, with toilet and shower in the corridor but quite okay. ②/①

**Winn**, Norra Slottsgatan 9 (☎17 70 00, fax 10 59 60). Another smart hotel with its own pool, sauna and sunbeds. ④/③

# Gamla Gefle

**Gamla Gefle** escaped much of the fire damage and today passes itself off as the authentic old town, but unfortunately there's not much left of it. If you stay in the youth hostel, you'll be right on the edge of the few remaining narrow cobbled streets – notably Övre Bergsgatan, Bergsgränd and Nedre Bergsgränd – complete with their pastel-coloured wooden cottages, window boxes overflowing with summer flowers and old black lanterns. It's very attractive and quaint, even if a bit of a fraud – the juggled lanes now house the odd craft shop and a café or two. For another glimpse of social conditions a century ago, visit the **Joe Hill-Gården** at Nedre Bergsgatan 28 (June–Aug daily 10am–3pm; free; other times by arrangement on ☎61 34 25). Joe Hill, born in the house as Johan Emanuel Hägglund in 1879, emigrated to the United States in 1902, Americanized his name and became a working-class hero – his songs and speeches became rallying cries to comrades in the International Workers of the World; but, framed for murder in Salt Lake City, he was executed in 1915. The syndicalist organization to which he belonged runs the museum, a collection of standard memorabilia – pictures and belongings – given piquancy by the telegram announcing his execution and his last testament.

On the other side of Gamla Gefle at Södra Strandgatan 20 (near the train station) is the **Länsmuseum Gävleborg** (Tues, Thurs & Fri 10am–4pm, Wed 10am–9pm, Sat & Sun 1–5pm; 25kr, under 20s & students free), a thoughtful county museum that's a cut above the usual fare. The extensive displays of artwork by most of the great Swedish artists from the 1600s to the present day, including Nils Kreuger and Carl Larsson, are unusual for a provincial museum and attract visitors from across the country. Work from local man Johan-Erik Olsson (popularly known as "Lim-Johan"), whose vivid imagination and naive technique produced some strange childlike paintings, can also be seen. There are also displays on ironworks and fisheries in the area.

## The rest of the city

The modern city lies over the river, its broad streets and avenues designed to prevent fires from spreading. From the sculpture-spiked **Rådhus** up to the beautiful nineteenth-century theatre, a central slice of parks, trees and fountains neatly splits the city. All the main banks, shops and stores are in the grid of streets on either side of the central avenue, while the roomy **Storatorget**, sporting a phallic monolith, has the usual open-air market (Mon–Sat from 9am), which is worth patronizing for fruit and veg.

Gävle's other main sights – none of them major – are out of the centre but close enough to reach on foot. Back at the river by the main double bridge, **Gävle Slottet**, the seventeenth-century residence of the county governor, lost its ramparts and towers years ago and now lurks behind a row of trees like some minor country house. It's not possible to get inside for a poke around, although with an appointment you can visit the **Fängelsemuseum** (Prison Museum) on the premises, if that appeals; speak to the tourist office.

From Gävle Slottet a short walk following the river leads to a wooden bridge, across which is Kaplansgatan and the **Heliga Trefaldighets kyrka**, the Church of the Holy Trinity, a seventeeth-century masterpiece of wood-carved decoration. Check out the pulpit, towering altarpiece and screen – each the superb work of a German craftsman, Ewardt Friis. Cross back over the river and take a stroll down picturesque Kungsbäcksvägen, a narrow street lined with brightly painted wooden houses, for fifteen minutes or so till you reach **Silvanum** (open all year Tues, Thurs & Fri 10am–4pm, Wed 10am–9pm, Sat & Sun 1–5pm; free) at Kungsbäcksvägen 32. Northern Europe's largest forestry museum, it's interesting only if you're keen to learn more about the unforgiving forest that you'll soon become well acquainted with as you travel further north. Continue and you'll

CENTRAL GÄVLE

Teatern
STAKENGATAN
Grand Central
Bus Station
Train Station
NORRA SLOTTSGATAN
NORRA SKEPPARGATAN
N. CENTRALGATAN
STAKETGATAN
NORRA RÅDMANSGATAN
NYGATAN
CENTRAL PLAN
DROTTNINGGATAN
KAPLANSGATAN
NORRA KUNGSGATAN
RUDDAMMSGATAN
Winn
KYRKOGATAN
Nya Järnvägshotellet
STORTORGET
Radhus
Boulogne
NYGATAN
DROTTNINGGATAN
S. STRANDGATAN
S. CENTRALGATAN
Boulognerskogen
Pharmacy
KYRKOGATAN
Lansmuséet Gävleborg
BYGGMÄSTARGATAN
Silvanum (Forestry Museum)
N. STRANDGATAN
GAMALA GEFLE
Hel. Tref. kyrka
SLOTTSTORGET
NEDRE BERGSGATAN
Gävle Slott
Systembolaget (Off-Licence)
Youth Hostel
N
HAMILTONGATAN
SÖDRA KUNGSGATAN
Ferry
SÖDRA RÅDMANSGATAN
0       250 m
BUNNSSGATAN
Avery
SÖDERMALM -STORG
Railway Museum

come to the rambling **Boulognerskogen**. It opened in the mid-nineteenth century and still provides an oasis of trees, water and flowers just outside the city centre – a good place for a picnic and a spot of sunbathing. There's also music pavilions, mini-golf, an open-air café and a sculpture by Carl Milles of five angels playing musical instruments.

On a rainy day you may find yourself contemplating the **Sveriges Järnvägsmuseum**, *Swedish Railways'* museum at Rälsgatan 1 (open all year Tues–Sun 10am–4pm; 30kr, free with *InterRail*) – walk from the train station along Muréngatan. In what used to be Gävle's engine shed, it's a train enthusiast's paradise, stuffed to the gills with about fifty locomotives – sixteen are over one-hundred years old and five are still in full working order – and other paraphernalia. The café in the museum is in one of the 1950s' carriages. On weekends in summer, a veteran **steam train** travels to Furuvik (see p.309) three times a day. As you head out past the station, you'll see the old dock-side warehouses, off Norra Skeppsbron just by the river, a reminder of the days when ships unloaded coffee and spices in the centre of the Gävle. Today, with the company names fading on the red, wooden fronts of the empty buildings, the area feels more like a Hollywood movie set than a Swedish town.

## Eating, drinking and nightlife

There's a fair choice of **eating places** in Gävle, but for the best options stick to the central grid of streets around Storatorget and spots up and down the central esplanade between Rådhuset and the theatre. Nearly all cafés and restaurants double as **bars**, and some also combine **nightclubs**, too. If you want to go dancing, *Heartbreak Hotel* and *O'Leary's* are fun and always very busy. As elsewhere in Sweden, the theatre has no English-language productions. To see a film, which are always subtitled rather than dubbed, there are two **cinemas** on Norra Slottsgatan, *Filmstaden* and *Sandrew*.

### Cafés, restaurants and bars

**Arken**, on a boat moored alongside Norra Skeppsbron. Has a great atmosphere on a summer's evening; two courses of fish or seafood for 125kr, three courses 150kr.

**Brända Bocken**, Storatorget. Young and fashionable, with outdoor seating in summer. Beef and pork dishes, hamburgers and salmon around 80kr. Also a popular place for a drink.

**Café Artist**, Norra Slottsgatan 9. Another trendy hang-out offering fish and meat dishes for around 140kr, smaller dishes such as *pytt i panna* for 60–70kr; in the evenings this is a relaxed place for a beer or two on cosy sofas.

**Heartbreak Hotel**, Norra Strandgatan 15. Pub, bistro-style bar and nightclub. This place has recently improved, since the teenyboppers moved on; it now attracts a slightly older crowd – worth checking out.

**Kungshallen**, Norra Kungsgatan 17. Next to the theatre and with mammoth-sized pizzas for 44–60kr. Beer at 29kr is a steal.

**O'Leary's**, Södra Kungsgatan 31. Incredibly busy and catering for a young crowd, this is *the* place to do your boozing and boogying.

**Skeppet**, in the *Grand Central Hotel* at Nygatan 45. Fine fish and seafood in a grand maritime atmosphere – with prices to match. Lunch menu of pasta for 75kr.

**Tennstoppet**, Nygatan 38. Cheap and cheerful hamburger restaurant: sausage and chips 40kr, egg and bacon 49kr, mixed grill 50kr.

**38°**, Norra Kungsgatan 7A. A once popular bar, but now losing its clientele. Still an okay place for a bite to eat and a drink.

**Österns Pärla**, Ruddammsgatan 23. Fairly standard Chinese restaurant, serving all the usual favourites for 80–90kr.

## Listings

**Airport** *Gävle-Sandvikens flygplats*, Rörberg, Valbo (☎323 40).

**Bank** *Nordbanken* with cash machine, Norra Kungsgatan 3–5.

**Bus information** Local buses operated by *Länstrafiken* (☎91 01 09); long-distance buses operated by *Swebus* (☎14 40 00).

**Car rental** *AVIS* (☎51 57 50); *Budget* (☎51 48 20); *Hertz* (☎51 18 19); *Statoil* (☎12 01 12).

**Gay Gävle** The *RSFL* centre is at Fjärde Tvärgatan 55 (☎18 09 67); switchboard Sun 7–9pm; café Wed 6.30–9pm; parties second Sat in the month 9.30pm–2.30am.

**Pharmacy** Nygatan 31 (☎10 02 46).

**Post office** Drottninggatan 16 (☎12 13 90).

**Systembolaget** at Södra Kungsgatan near Gävle Slottet.

**Taxi** *Gävle Taxi* on ☎12 90 00 or ☎10 70 00.

**Travel agent** *Ticket*, Drottninggatan: ferry tickets with *Silja Line* and *Stena Line* as well as student and young person's flights.

## Around Gävle: beaches, Limön and the Furuvik Amusement Park

If the sun's shining, you'll find locals catching the rays at the nearby sandy beach of **Rullsand**, which stretches for about 3km. Bus #838 should go there in the morning and return in the evening, but it's worth checking with the tourist office for the latest details. If you miss the bus you could head out instead for the beaches at either **ENGELTOFTA** (near the youth hostel) or **ENGESBERG**; take bus #5 from Rådhuset (12 daily). From here the bus continues to **BÖNAN**, where there's an old lighthouse that now holds a museum; at the time of writing the lighthouse was being renovated, so check current opening times with the tourist office. There is also more good swimming to be had here. Other enjoyable beaches are on the island of **Limön**, reached by summer ferry from Skeppsbron (three daily; 30kr), with one departure making a stop in Engeltofta on the way. Limön is a pleasant place for some gentle walks, with paths criss-crossing the island.

In the other direction is the **Furuvik Amusement Park** (May to late-June Mon–Fri 10am–4pm, Sat & Sun 10am–5pm; July daily 10am–6pm; early Aug daily 10am–5pm; adults 95kr, children 55kr); ride coupons cost 12–24kr a time, or you can buy a pass for everything (*Åkband*) for 95kr. You'll find a zoo, fairground, parks and playgrounds – probably the cheapest entertainment in Gävle. Buses #821, #838, #832 leave roughly every half-hour from the bus station. There's also a **campsite** near the zoo; you can rent cabins as well as pitch your tent here (for more information call ☎980 28 or 19 90 00).

# Söderhamn and Hudiksvall

On the first leg of the coastal journey further into Norrland, the train line sticks close to the coast and the onward trains are frequent enough. If you are in no great rush to reach the bigger towns and tourist centres further north, **Söderhamn** and **Hudiksvall** both suit a leisurely stop. Hudiksvall's wood panel architecture gives it the edge over Söderhamn, though this pint-sized town does boast the most northerly butterfly house in the world. Out of the main tourist season, it's best to avoid Sundays – or you'll be the only person in the streets.

## Söderhamn and around

It's easy to see that **SÖDERHAMN** was once much more important than it is today. It was founded in 1620, and its glory days came several decades later; the seventeenth-century **Ulrika Eleonora kyrka** that towers over the Rådhus gives hints of the wealth the city once had, which was earned primarily from fishing. Relics from an earlier church that stood on the same spot are kept in **Söderhamns Museum** (late June to early Aug daily noon–5pm; 10kr), halfway up Oxtorgsgatan from Rådhustorget, the main square. The museum is housed in what was once a rifle manufacturing workshop, a reminder of the days when Söderhamn supplied the weapons that helped Sweden to dominate northern Europe.

A number of devastating fires took their toll on the town; the largest, on July 22, 1876, destroyed virtually everything in its path. As a result the modern town is built on a grid pattern, with space for central parks and green spaces. The familiar mix of pedestrianized shopping streets and parkland gives the town a likable air, and it's inviting enough to while away some time at a pavement café. However, the wide-open spaces don't give a true impression of the area, as a climb up the white, 23m-tall **Oskarsborg tower** (June–Aug daily 9am–9pm) will demonstrate; follow the path signposted from down by the train tracks. From the top, the surrounding forests that hem the town in stretch away as far as the eye can see.

If you like **butterflies** then you'll be in seventh heaven in **Fjärilshuset** (May–Sept daily 9am–5pm; Oct–April daily 10am–3pm); you can watch the brightly coloured creatures from the Philippines and Malaysia flutter around in a near rainforest environment. The Butterfly House is in the village of **INA** on the road to Bollnäs, which the bus to the youth hostel passes (10min journey; see below). If going **walking** is more your thing, you'll find a series of paths striking out from near the hospital; head up Kyrkogatan, from under the railway bridge near Rådhustorget, and continue up the hill onto the footpath, turn left into Krongatan and on towards the hospital past the helipad, then turn right into the forest.

Another option would be to take a **boat trip** out into Söderhamn's **archipelago**, which is made up of about five hundred islands; the largest, **Storjungfrun**, literally "The Great Virgin", gave its name to the stretch of coast around Söderhamn and Hudiksvall – *Jungfrukusten* or "The Virgin Coast". For information about trips out to the islands onboard *M/S Strömskär* ring ☎026/12 77 66 or mobile phone ☎010/295 91 69. Boats leave from the opposite end of town to Rådhustorget – walk down the main street and along the canal for about fifteen minutes until you come to the jetty.

## Practicalities

The **tourist office** is out of town on the way to the Butterfly House (June to early Aug Mon–Fri 9am–7pm, Sat & Sun noon–5pm; rest of the year Mon–Fri 9am–4pm; ☎0270/753 53); it has information on boat trips and hiking routes. **Staying** in Söderhamn doesn't exactly overwhelm you with choices. In town, the central *First Hotel Statt*, Oxtorgsgatan 17 (☎0270/414 10, fax 135 24; ④/②), is a swanky **hotel**, though in summer the prices drop considerably. If money is tight, a much better choice would be to stay at the wonderfully situated **youth hostel** (June–Aug; ☎0270/452 33, fax 453 26; 100kr) at **MOHED**, 13km west of town in a deep pine forest. The hostel is right by a lake and occupies an old sanatorium, which was built here so that patients could benefit from Mohed's famous clean air. Ask about swimming, boat rental, fishing, horse riding and mini-golf, which are all available. There's a year-round **campsite** here, too. To get to Mohed, take the hourly buses #64 and #100; the #100 continues to **Bollnäs**, about thirty minutes' ride away and handy for the mainline trains north to Boden, Luleå, Gälivare and Kiruna.

Eating and **drinking** establishments in Söderhamn have come on in leaps and bounds in recent years, and there's now a fair number vying for your custom. For **daytime** coffee and cakes try *TeWe's Konditori* on the main pedestrian street, Köpmangatan; it is also open on Sundays. Most restaurants are to be found along the same thoroughfare: Indian food can be had at *Restaurang Tandoori* at the Rådhus end of the street; while, next door, at *Mosquet Restaurant*, you'll find pizzas for 40–50kr, pasta for 55kr and fish dishes for 100–120kr. The Chinese restaurant, *Mandarin Palace*, in Köpmantorget next to the bus station, has *Dagens Rätt* for 53kr; either Chinese or Swedish delicacies are available. À la carte eating starting at 100kr is enjoyed at *Restaurang Faxe* on Kungsgatan; upmarket food is also served at the *Stadsrestaurang*, inside the *First Hotel Statt* on Oxtorgsgatan. **Drinking** is best done at *Dino* at Oxtorgsgatan 17, where beer costs 29kr during Happy Hour, *Bryggeriet* at Dammgatan 3 or at the Irish pub *Tigern* at Västra Storgatan 20 (under the railway bridge from Rådhustorget and turn left); the latter two charge 25–29kr for beer and do food. You can also lay your hands on cheap beer at the *King's Road Café* on Kungsgatan.

# Hudiksvall

The oldest town in Sweden north of Gävle, **HUDIKSVALL** has had its fair share of excitement over the years. Due to the land rising, at the beginning of the seventeenth century Hudiksvall was forced to move location. The first settlement, around the bay of Lillfjärden at the mouth of the river Hornån, was by then several hundred metres away from the sea. The old bay is now a lake, connected to the sea by a canal. An important commercial and shipping centre, it then bore the brunt of the Russian attacks on the northeast Swedish coast in 1721: its church is still pockmarked with cannon holes. The whole of Hudiksvall, with the exception of the church, was burnt to the ground. The area with the oldest, post-1721 buildings – the most interesting part of the city – is split into two main sections. Turn right out of the train station and cross the narrow canal, Strömmingssundet, or Herring Sound, and you'll soon see the small old **harbour** on the right; this area is known as **Möljen**. Here the wharf side is flanked by a line of red, wooden fishermen's cottages and storehouses, all leaning into the water; it's a popular place for locals to while away a couple of hours in the summer sunshine, with a beer or two and dangling their feet into the water. The back of the warehouses hide a run of bike and boat repair shops, interesting handicraft studios and the tourist office (see overleaf).

More impressive and much larger than Möljen, **Fiskarstan** (Fishermen's Town), beyond *First Hotel Statt* down Storgatan, contains neat examples of the so-called "Imperial" wood panel architecture of the late eighteenth and nineteenth centuries. It was in these tightly knit blocks of streets, lined with beautiful wooden houses and fenced-in plots of land, that the fishermen used to live during the winter. Take a peek inside some of the little courtyards – all window boxes, summer flowers and cobblestones. The history of these buildings is put into context in the excellent **Hälsinglands Museum** (open all year Tues, Thurs, Fri 9am–4pm, Wed 9am–8pm, Sat & Sun 11am–3pm; 20kr, free on Sat and for students and children) on Storgatan, which traces the development of Hudiksvall as a harbour town since its foundation in 1582. Have a look at the paintings of **John Sten** upstairs: born near Hudiksvall, his work veered strangely from Cubism to a more decorative fanciful style.

The best time to visit Hudiksvall is in the middle two weeks of July, when the town hosts the **Musik vid Dellen**, a multifarious cultural festival, including folk music and other traditional events; information and tickets are available from the tourist office. For a day-trip head out to the beautiful and unspoilt **Hornslandet**

**peninsula** and its quaint fishing villages, **Hölick** and **Kuggörarna**. The whole area is rich in flora and fauna, as well as being ideal for swimming, fishing and walking; ask at the tourist office for more details. To get there, take bus #37, which runs from the bus station to both villages twice daily from mid-June to mid-August.

## Practicalities

Arriving in Hudiksvall couldn't be easier: the **train** and **bus stations** are opposite each other, and it's just two minutes' walk along the main road to the centre around Möljen. There's a **tourist office** (mid-June to mid-Aug Mon–Fri 9am–7pm, Sat 10am–6pm, Sun noon–6pm; rest of the year Mon–Fri 9am–4pm; ☎0650/191 00), close by behind the old warehouses, which hands out free maps of the town and general bumph.

The **youth hostel** (open all year; ☎0650/13260; 100kr) is out at the Malnbaden **campsite**, 3km from town; bus #5 runs there hourly in summer (10am–6pm), but other than that you'll have to fall back on taxis available from the bus station (opposite the train station) costing 80kr each way. It's sited on the bay and has a large sandy beach, jogging tracks on the opposite side of the road and offers bike rental; there are also cabins for rent. For **hotel** accommodation *Hotell Temperance* (☎/fax 0650/31107; ②/①) is a cheapish place at Håstagatan 5, near the train station. *First Hotel Statt* at Storgatan 36 (☎0650/150 60, fax 960 95; ④/②), built in 1878, is the swishest hotel in town. It was here that the barons of the timber industry did their best to live up to the town's reputation as "Glada Hudik" (Happy Hudiksvall), a phrase coined in the first half of the nineteenth century, when the people here became known for their lively social life and generous hospitality.

Today, oddly enough, Hudiksvall has fewer **eating and drinking** opportunities than smaller Söderhamn to the south. A popular restaurant is *Bolaget* at Storgatan 49, where main dishes cost around 85kr and pizzas 45kr. Alternatively, try the smarter *Le Bistro* on Hamngatan, which has Happy Hours for food and drinks from 3pm to 11pm. The poshest place in town is *Bar o Kök*, the restaurant attached to *First Hotel Statt* on Storgatan. The one and only bar is the *Tre Bockar* at Bankgränd, opposite the fishermen's warehouses at Möljen; at lunchtime the *Dagens Rätt* and a beer go for 69kr; there is occasionally jazz of an evening. **Nightlife** is to be found at the club and bar *Bakfram* on Hamngatan, from where most people emerge in tune with the name of the joint – back to front.

# Sundsvall

The capital of the tiny province of Medelpad, **SUNDSVALL**, known as "Stone City", is immediately and obviously different. Once home to a rapidly expanding nineteenth-century sawmill industry, the whole city burned to the ground the day after Midsummer in June 1888. A spark from the wood-burning steamboat, *Selånger*, set fire to a nearby brewery and the rest, as they say, is history – in fact so much so that the interjection "that hasn't happened since the town burned down" is now an established Sundsvall saying. Nine thousand people lost their homes in the blaze, and the offending steamboat was promptly dubbed "The Arsonist". The work of rebuilding the city began at once, and within ten years a new centre was constructed entirely of stone. The result is a living document of turn-of-the-century urban architecture, designed and crafted by architects who were involved in rebuilding Stockholm's residential areas at the same time. Wide

The telephone code for Sundsvall is ☎060.

streets and esplanades that would serve as firebreaks in the event of another fire formed the backbone of their work. These thoroughfares are home to 573 residential buildings, all of which went up in four years, and the centrepiece is the house that dominates the main square, Storatorget.

The reconstruction, however, was achieved at a price: the workers who had laboured on the city's refurbishment became the victims of their own success. They were shifted from their old homes in the centre and moved out south to a poorly serviced suburb – the glaring contrast between the wealth of the new centre and the poverty of the surrounding districts was only too obvious. When Nils Holgersson, a character created by the children's book author Selma Lagerlöf, looked down from the back of his flying goose (see the picture on 20kr notes), he remarked: "There was something funny about it when you saw it from above, because in the middle there was a group of high stone houses, so impressive that they hardly had their equal in Stockholm. Around the stone houses was an empty space, and then there was a circle of wooden houses, which were pleasantly scattered in little gardens, but which seemed to carry an awareness of being of lesser value than the stone houses and therefore dared not come too close."

# Arrival, information and accommodation

From the **train station**, it's a five-minute walk to the city centre; turn left and go under the subway. The helpful **tourist office** (mid-June to mid-Aug Mon–Wed & Fri 9am–8pm, Sat & Sun 10am–8pm; rest of the year Mon–Wed & Fri 11am–5pm, Thurs until 6pm; ☎61 42 35) is in the main square, Storatorget, where you can collect a free map and plenty of advice about the surrounding area. The **bus station** is at the bottom of Esplanaden, though if you want information or advance tickets for the express bus (Thurs–Mon only) south to Stockholm or north to Örnsköldsvik or Sollefteå (also inland to Östersund), visit *Y-Bussen* at Trädgårdsgatan 13 (☎17 19 60). For other bus information contact the tourist office. The **airport** is 20km north of town on the way to Härnösand and is linked to Sundsvall by an airport bus whenever a Stockholm flight is leaving or arriving; there are currently direct flights to Gothenburg, Gällivare, Kiruna, Luleå, Stockholm, Umeå, Örnsköldsvik and Östersund.

The tourist office has a limited supply of **private rooms** for between 125kr and 150kr per person, plus a 60kr booking fee. Other cheap options include the youth hostel and a number of hotels that have rooms at the bottom end of the range in summer and at weekends throughout the rest of the year. The **youth hostel** (open all year; ☎61 21 19, fax 61 78 01; 100kr) is out of town at Norra Stadsberget, the mountain overlooking the city (take bus #72 or #73), and is a bit grotty, with accommodation in minuscule cabins. You are better off going for one of the **low-budget central hotels**.

### Hotels

The cheapest hotel in Sundsvall is *Hotel Ritz*, Esplanaden 4 (☎15 08 60), with doubles at 450kr reduced to 295kr. Otherwise, the following three are all small, basic hotels, with around ten rooms each and nothing much to choose between them: *Lilla Hotellet*, Rådhusgatan 15 (☎61 35 87; ②/①); *Hotell Continental*, Rådhusgatan 13 (☎61 26 07; ②/①); *Hotell Svea*, Rådhusgatan 11 (☎61 16 05; ②/①). *Good*

*Morning*, Trädgårdsgatan 31–33 (☎15 06 00, fax 12 70 80; ②/①), is worth trying if the others are full. Other hotels in Sundsvall include:

**Baltic**, Sjögatan 5 (☎15 59 35, fax 12 45 60). Centrally located near the *Kulturmagasinet* and the harbour, with perfectly adequate rooms. ④/②

**First Hotel Strand**, Strandgatan 10 (☎12 18 00, fax 61 92 02). The smartest hotel in town; there are 200 rooms, an indoor pool and a wicked breakfast buffet. ⑤/②

**Grand**, Nybrogatan 13 (☎15 72 05, fax 61 64 84). Not a bad choice if you get the summer or weekend reduction. ③/②

**Scandic**, Esplanaden 29 (☎17 16 00, fax 12 20 32). This international hotel boasts eight cinemas, saunas, sunbeds and a golf simulator, with prices to match the opulence. ⑤/③

**Stenstan**, Sjögatan 11 (☎15 07 20, fax 12 34 56). Renowned for its sandwiches if not its rooms, with Finnish-speaking staff. ③/②

**Södra Berget**, on the southern hill (☎12 30 00, fax 15 10 34). With fantastic views, and popular in winter for skiing. ⑤/③

# The City

The sheer scale of the rebuilding is clear as you walk in from the train station. The style is simple, uncluttered limestone and brick, the size often overwhelming. Most of the buildings functioned as offices as well as residences, and the four- and five-storey houses are palatial structures. As you stroll the streets you can't help but be amazed by the tremendous amount of space that surrounds you even in the heart of the city; Sundsvall is unique in this respect, yet is conversely the most densely populated metropolis in northern Sweden. **Esplanaden**, a wide central avenue, cuts the grid of streets in two, itself crossed by **Storgatan**, the widest street. **Storatorget**, the central square, is a delightfully roomy shopping and commercial centre and home to various impromptu exhibitions and displays as well as a fresh fruit and veg market (Mon–Sat from 9.30am).

Several of the buildings in the centre are worth a second look, not least the sturdy bourgeois exterior of **Sundsvalls Museum** (Mon–Thurs 10am–7pm, Fri 10am–6pm, Sat & Sun 11am–4pm; free), which is housed within four late nineteenth-century warehouses, down by the harbour. The buildings stood empty for twenty years before a decision was taken to turn them into what's now the **Kulturmagasinet** (Culture Warehouse) comprising museum, library and café. The old street, Magasinsgatan, complete with its train tracks, still runs between the warehouses, providing a glimpse of the days when coffee and rice were transported along its length to the harbour for export. The museum deserves a quick look and does its best to depict the history of Sundsvall and the province of Medelpad – despite display titles such as "Sun, Mountain, Water". Upstairs, the art exhibition also warrants ten minutes of your time: the works of twentieth-century Swedish artists are on show and, in particular, those of the local artist Carl Frisendahl. Continue along the main pedestrian street, Storgatan, and at the far end you'll come across **Gustav Adolfs kyrka** (June–Aug daily 10am–4pm; Sept–May 11am–2pm), which marks one end of the new town, a soaring red-brick structure, whose interior looks like a large Lego set.

Beyond the city's design, the most attractive diversion is the 3km climb to the heights of **Gaffelbyn**, the northern hill that overlooks the city; walk up Storgatan, cross over the main bridge and follow the sign to the youth hostel, which is also up here. If you want to spare your legs, buses #4, #72 and #73 will cover much of the uphill slog for you and leave from the bus station at regular

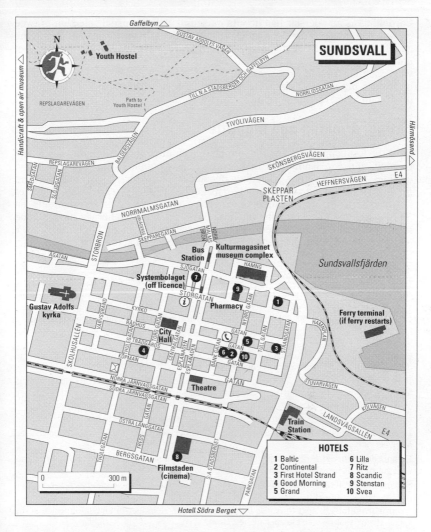

Gaffelbyn △

**SUNDSVALL**

**Youth Hostel**

N

Handicraft & open air museum △

GUSTAV ADOLFS VÄG

TILL N:A STADSBERGET OCH GAFFELBYN

NORRLIDSGATAN

Härnösand △

Path to Youth Hostel

REPSLAGAREVÄGEN

TIVOLIVÄGEN

BALDERSVÄGEN

SKÖNSBERGSVÄGEN

E4

REPSLAGAREVÄGEN

HEFFNERSVÄGEN

SMEDSGATAN

SLÖJDGATAN

NORRMALMSGATAN

**SKEPPAR PLASTEN**

STORBRON

SKEPPAREGATAN

*Sundsvallsfjärden*

ÅGATAN

**Bus Station**

**Kulturmagasinet museum complex**

SJÖGATAN

HAMNG

**Systembolaget (off licence)**

⑦

**Gustav Adolfs kyrka**

ⓘ

⑨

**Pharmacy**

①

**Ferry terminal (if ferry restarts)**

KYRKO

NORRA

NYRK GATAN

HAMNGATAN

VÄRVSGRÄND

RÅDHUS

**City Hall**

GATAN

STRANDGATAN

SKOLHUSALLÉN

TRÄDGÅRDS

CENTRALGATAN

ESPLANADEN

ⓒ

⑤

④

THULEGATAN

ESPLANADEN

BANKGATAN

⑥②⑩

③

STUVARVÄGEN

KÖPMAN

GATAN

NORRA JÄRNVÄGSGATAN

SÖDRA JÄRNVÄGSGATAN

GATAN

LANDSVÄGSALLÉN

KÖLVÄGEN

**Theatre**

ÖSTRA LÅNGGATAN

FREDS

**Train Station**

E4

BERGSGATAN

⑧

THULEGATAN

S:A STADSBERGET

PARIGATAN

LANDSVÄGSALLÉN

**Filmstaden (cinema)**

| 0 | 300 m |

| **HOTELS** | |
|---|---|
| 1 Baltic | 6 Lilla |
| 2 Continental | 7 Ritz |
| 3 First Hotel Strand | 8 Scandic |
| 4 Good Morning | 9 Stenstan |
| 5 Grand | 10 Svea |

Hotell Södra Berget ▽

intervals each hour until 10pm; alternatively book a *turisttaxi* from the tourist office for a fixed rate of 50kr. The view from the top on a clear day is fantastic and gives a fresh perspective on the city: not only of its planned structure but also of the restrictive nature of its location, hemmed in on three sides by hills and the sea. From here you can see straight across to **Södra Berget**, the southern hill, with its winter ski slopes. Ask in the restaurant if you want to get a slightly better view from the nearby viewing tower – though at the time of writing it was closed, after a gang of local lads blew it up. The nearby **Norra Bergets Hantverks och Friluftsmuseum** (June–Aug Mon–Fri 9am–6pm, Sat noon–4pm, Sun 11am–4pm; rest of the year Mon–Fri 9am–4pm; free; Activity

Card 40kr) is an open-air handicrafts museum, with the usual selection of twee old wooden huts and assorted knick-knacks. It does, however, also offer you the chance to try your hand at baking some *tunnbröd*, the thin bread that's typical of northern Sweden and looks something like pitta bread. The idea is to roll out your dough extra thin, brush off as much flour as you can, slip the bread into the oven on a big wooden pizza-type scoop, and count to five. The bake-your-own offer is included on the museum's Activity Card.

# Eating, drinking and nightlife

Over the last couple of years, the number of **restaurants** in Sundsvall has mush-roomed, and you'll now find that there's a good choice of places to eat and cuisines to choose from, including unusual options such as Vietnamese and Egyptian – something you may want to make the most of if you're heading further north. There are a handful of inexpensive pizza places and restaurants on Storgatan, most offering daily lunches. **Bars** in the city generally have a good atmosphere, and there are several places serving cheap beer. **Nightclubs** are a bit thin on the ground; the best one to head for is *Seaport* at the *First Hotel Strand*, Strandgatan 10, where over-23s gather to shake their stuff to the latest sounds.

### Cafés and restaurants

**Athena restaurang och pizzeria**, Köpmangatan 7. All your Greek favourites from tzatziki to souvlaki as well as pizzas – all around 100kr.

**Café Charm**, Storgatan 32 & Köpmangatan (near the post office). A good choice for coffee and cakes, with free refills and naughty but nice cream concoctions; attracts a young crowd but closes at 6pm.

**China Restaurant**, Esplanaden (near bus station). Chicken dishes for 72kr, meat 76kr and duck 93kr to eat-in, or takeaway at cheaper prices.

**Fem rum och kök**, Östra Långgatan 23. A tastefully designed restaurant comprising five different rooms and offering northern Swedish delicacies such as reindeer and elk; reckon on 150kr for a main dish.

**Kairo**, Köpmangatan 13. Authentic Egyptian atmosphere and food – dishes from 80kr.

**La Spezia**, Sjögatan 6. Bargain-basement pizzas but perfectly acceptable for 35kr; also a take-away service.

**Restaurang Seaport**, Strandgatan 10 in the *First Hotel Strand*. A chi-chi international brasserie, with gourmet dishes and accompanying clientele. Reckon on at least 200kr for dinner.

**Saigon Palace**, Trädgårdsgatan 5. Vietnamese restaurant with some good prices – chicken in peanut sauce for 87kr.

**Skeppsbrokällaren**, next to *Hotell Baltic* on Sjögatan. Reindeer in cinnamon sauce is the speciality for 185kr – also cheaper dishes.

### Bars

**Dublin**, Nybrogatan 16. Irish pub with a broad selection of different beers, Irish music and darts: beer at 39kr – or try the Irish soup for the same price.

**Hoagy's**, Strandgatan 10 in the *First Hotel Strand*. A tasteful piano bar, where well-oiled locals can be found rounding off an evening's boozing – open till 3am, with beer at 25kr during Happy Hour (8–11pm).

**Jop's**, Trädgårdsgatan 3. The most popular and fashionable restaurant and bar in town, with an Irish atmosphere and wackily designed menu. Meat and fish dishes from around 100kr, burgers for 60kr. Local bands at weekends.

**Macken**, Sjögatan 25. Done out as a 1950s'-style filling station with beer on tap from gas pumps – Happy Hour 5–9pm, when beer is 28kr.

**Mercat Cross**, Esplanaden 27. Scottish pub with staff in kilts. One of the most expensive places for beer – at 44kr and 48kr, the 4kr extra is for the stronger stuff.

**O'Bar**, Bankgatan 11. A good lively bar; if your pocket can take the pace, try the excellent cocktails.

**Skippers**, Storgatan 40. Known for its huge selection of beers and buzzing atmosphere. Happy Hour Mon–Thurs & Sat 5–8pm, Fri 4–8pm, with beer for 29kr. Also a lively place for lunch (57kr); choose from pork, lasagne, burgers or salads.

## Listings

**Airport** Information and bookings on ☎18 80 00 or ☎19 75 20.

**Banks** *Handelsbanken*, Storgatan 23; *Nordbanken*, Kyrkogatan 15; *SE-Banken*, Storgatan 19.

**Bus station** On Sjögatan (☎15 31 00).

**Car rental** *Bilbolaget*, Bultgatan 1 (☎18 08 90); *Budget,* at the airport (☎57 80 06); *Shell*, Bergsgatan 114 (☎61 60 51).

**Cinema** *Filmstaden* at the far end of Esplanaden over the train lines.

**Foreign newspapers** Sundsvall library in the *Kulturmagasinet*; or buy them from *Sundsvalls Tobaksaffär*, Storgatan 20B.

**Gay Sundsvall** The *RSFL* center is in a basement on the corner of Skolhusallén and Östra Långgatan (☎17 13 30). Switchboard Thurs 8–10pm (☎15 77 78); café Wed & Sun 7–10pm; pub Fri 10pm–2.30am; disco 2nd and last Sat of the month 10pm–2.30am.

**Hospital** Lasarettsvägen 19 (☎18 10 00).

**Pharmacy** Storgatan 18, open Mon–Fri 9am–6pm, Sat 10am–3pm (☎18 11 17); also at hospital (☎18 11 17).

**Police** Storgatan 37 (☎18 00 00).

**Post office** Köpmangatan 19 (☎19 60 00).

**Systembolaget** Torggatan 1, open Mon–Wed & Fri 9.30am–6pm, Thurs 9.30am–7pm (☎61 36 69).

**Taxi** *Taxi Sundsvall* (☎19 90 00); *City Taxi* (☎12 00 00).

**Train station** Parkgatan (☎18 30 00).

**Travel agent** *Ticket*, on the corner of Rådhusgatan and Esplanaden; open Mon–Fri 9am–6pm, Sat 10am–1pm.

## Alnö

The island of **Alnö** is within easy striking distance of Sundsvall and makes a good day-trip. Take the regular local bus #1 (4 daily) from the bus station over the arched Alnöbron bridge onto the island; in winter, the water in the channel below freezes, allowing people to nip across by snow scooter. Alnö's empty roads and tranquil scenery are particularly popular with **cyclists** (ask at Sundsvall tourist office for bike rental information), who come to cruise the narrow country lanes that wind their way past pine forests, sandy coves and the odd farmstead. The main place to head for is the tiny, pretty fishing village of **SPIKARNA** in the southeast corner of the island (change buses in main village of Vi and take #116). Red, wooden fishermen's cottages snuggling round a tiny bay for protection from the wind and snow that sweeps in from the Gulf of Bothnia are evidence of a long fishing tradition, which is still going strong today. You'll see nets laid out to dry on frames all around the village. To get into the centre – if it can be called that – cross the wooden bridge and continue along the footpath. In summer, you can buy smoked whitefish from small huts by the side of the path, while to the right there's a cluster of rocks that are good for sunbathing. Once a week in summer there are jazz evenings by the side of the fishermen's cottages – a wonderful way to enjoy the light nights, sitting on the waterfront and listening to music as the sun goes down. If Alnö appeals and you want to stay longer, contact the tourist office back in Sundsvall, which has cottages for rent for 2000–2500kr per week, though these get snapped up very quickly. Alternatively, you can camp rough.

# Härnösand and around

From Sundsvall it's an hour's train trip north along the coast to **Härnösand**, a pleasant little place at the mouth of Ångerman river. Founded in 1585, the town has had its fair share of disasters: two great fires in 1710 and 1714, only to be followed by a thorough ransacking by invading Russians in 1721. Yet despite this, Härnösand is full of architectural delights and is definitely worth a stop on the way north. The town marks the beginning of the stunningly beautiful county of **Ångermanland** – one of the few areas in Sweden where the countryside resembles that of neighbouring Norway. The coast here, north from Härnösand to Örnsköldsvik, is known as **Höga Kusten** (the High Coast), with craggy coastlines, long fjords that reach far inland and low mountains. This is the most scenic coastal stretch in northern Sweden and a wonderful route further north from Härnösand. Alternatively, you can go inland to **Sollefteå** and on to Långsele to connect up with the main-line train north (see below for more on transport details).

## Härnösand

For such a small provincial place, **HÄRNÖSAND** – the centre is on the island of **Härnön**, from which it takes its name – reeks of grandeur and self-importance, each of its proud civic buildings a marker of the confidence the town exudes. The main square, **Stora Torget**, was once declared by local worthies as the most beautiful in Sweden. From the square take a stroll up Västra Kyrkogatan to the heights of the Neoclassical **Domkyrkan** (daily 10am–4pm), which dates from the 1840s, though bits and bobs have been incorporated from earlier churches on the site – the Baroque altar is from the eighteenth century, as are the VIP boxes in the nave. The cathedral holds two records: it's the smallest in Sweden and the only white cathedral in the country. From the Domkyrkan turn right and follow the road round and back down the hill until you come to the narrow old street of Östanbäcksgatan, with its pretty painted wooden houses from the 1700s. For a taste of the town's architectural splendour take a walk up the main street, Nybrogatan; the grand building at no. 15, which houses the county council offices and *Mitt Sverige Turism* (a good source of information on the High Coast; see opposite), is particularly beautiful, with its facade of orange pastel. From the top of this hilly street, there are good views back over the town and the water.

### Around Härnösand: beaches and Murberget

The long sandy **beaches** in nearby **Smitingen** are generally regarded as some of the best in Norrland. Sloping gently down to the sea, they are ideal for children;

there's also an asphalt ramp to help wheelchair users. To get to Smitingen take the four-times daily **bus #14** (15min) that leaves from the bus station, just over the bridge from the train station and on the left. Pebble beaches are within walking distance from the town centre near the Sälsten campsite.

If you continue round the coast from here you'll eventually reach the impressive **open-air museum** (June–Aug daily 11am–5pm; 40kr) at **MURBERGET**, which is the second biggest in Sweden after Skansen in Stockholm. You can also take bus #2 and #52 (every hour) from the bus station. The first building to take up its location here was a bell tower, which was moved from the village of Ullånger (further north) to its current position in 1913. There are around eighty other buildings, most notably traditional Ångermanland farmhouses and the old Murberget church, a popular place for local weddings. The nineteenth-century *Spjute Inn* is still a restaurant and also holds a skittle alley, dating from 1910, where you can have a game – skittles came to Sweden from Germany in the Middle Ages. In the nearby **Länsmuseum** (County Museum; open all year daily 11am–5pm; 25kr), there are worthy exhibitions showing how people settled the area two thousand years ago, as well as very dull displays of birds' feet, silver goblets and spectacles from more modern times. If you're interested in armoury then you're in luck: the museum also has a collection of hunting weapons, peasants' weapons and army weapons from the seventeenth, eighteenth and nineteenth centuries.

## Practicalities

For information about the town and free maps head for the **tourist office** (June–Aug Mon–Fri 10am–5pm; ☎0611/881 40), close to the train station inside the building marked "Spiran" at Järnvägsgatan 2. If you're travelling further afield in Ångermanland and, in particular, up to the High Coast, you should head for the excellent *Mitt Sverige Turism* office (same hours as the main office; ☎0611/290 30) at Nybrogatan 15, where helpful staff will give you endless brochures as well as advice about transport and accommodation in the area. Staying in Härnösand is cheapest at the **youth hostel** (mid-June to early Aug; ☎0611/104 46; 100kr), a fifteen-minute walk from the centre of town up Nybrogatan and then left. It's located in a kind of student village, *Statens Skola För Vuxna*, at Volontären 14; staying here generally means your own flat complete with kitchen and bathroom. The nearby **campsite**, *Sälstens Camping* (☎0611/181 50), is around 2km from the town centre and next to a string of pebble beaches; it also has a small selection of four-bed cabins for 250kr per night and will **rent out bikes** if you're staying there. Of the town's three **hotels**, *Hotell Royal*, close to the train station at Strandgatan 12 (☎0611/204 55; ②/①), and *Hotell City* at Storgatan 28 (☎0611/277 00; ③/①) are cheapest, with little to choose between them. The *Scandic Hotell* at Skeppsbron 9 (☎0611/105 10; ④/③) is much bigger and a bit plusher than the other two hotels, but not really worth the money.

The most popular **restaurant** and pub all rolled into one is *Kajutan* on the pedestrianized Storgatan, which links Stora Torget and Nybrogatan. There are occasional special eat-as-much-as-you-dare deals for 89kr; otherwise reckon on 80kr for burgers, chicken or meat dishes – in summer the price of a beer drops to 30kr. If you feel like splashing out and sampling traditional northern Swedish delicacies such as reindeer and Arctic cloudberries with ice cream, *Restaurang Apothequet*, Nybrogatan 3, is the place: reindeer will cost around 180kr, cloudberries 70kr; otherwise two-course set meals cost 149kr, three courses 179kr. The restaurant is in an old pharmacy, which dates from 1909, and on the ground floor

## MOVING ON: NORTH INTO LAPLAND AND APPROACHES TO HÖGA KUSTEN

The coastal train line expires at Härnösand, and although it's still possible to take the train up to **Långsele** to join the main line, you'll have to time your departure carefully, as there are currently only two train services daily on this stretch; three daily buses also make the journey and their times are posted up at the train station. From Långsele trains run north via Boden to Luleå, Gällivare and Kiruna as well as south via **Bräcke** back to Stockholm; by changing trains at Bräcke you can also travel west to Östersund and east to Sundsvall, though the connections are in the middle of the night. There's currently only one train south a day from Långsele at 2.45am to Bräcke; arriving at 4.30am; it connects with the night train to Östersund coming up from Stockholm. If you're heading the other way to Sundsvall, then stay on the train till the next station down the line, Ånge, where there's a shorter, though still lengthy, wait of around ninety minutes for the early-morning connection across to Sundsvall.

A much more picturesque way of heading for Långsele is to take a boat trip up the Ångerman river on board the *M/S Ådalen III* as far as **Sollefteå** (late June to early Aug; single trip 120kr), from where there are buses and trains the short distance to Långsele. Departures are from Skeppsbron, but times vary from year to year (generally once or twice a week; for information call ☎0612/505 41, mobile ☎010/250 25 01). Although the river trip is well worth fitting in if you can, it is much more rewarding to continue your journey along the coast to take in the beauty of **Höga Kusten**. There are two options. One is to take one of the express *E4-bussarna* (or *E4-bus*) from the bus station for Örnsköldsvik; these pass through the tiny villages of Ullånger and Docksta (which are good jumping-off points for the island of Ulvön; see p.323) and skirt round the Skuleskogen National Park. Much better, though, is to take the *E4-bus* bound for Luleå, which leaves Härnösand at around midday for Bönhamn (changing at Lunde and Nordingrå: latest details from *Mitt Sverige Turism*). From here a small boat leaves for the island of Högbonden, and you can begin island-hopping up the coast – see the Höga Kusten section opposite for full details.

there's also a bar, where locals ask for a glass of "medicine" at the pharmacist's counter. Other places to eat include the neighbouring *Restaurang Nybrokällaren* (lunch 11am–2pm), the popular pizzeria, *Matverkstaden*, at Storgatan 5, and the *Rutiga Dukan Café* near the cathedral at Västra Kyrkogatan 1, where lunch goes for 50kr, and good home-baked pastries and apple pie are also on the menu. In summer, a refreshing place to sit with a coffee or a beer is *Café Skeppet & Restaurang*, the boat moored on Skeppsbron, by the bridge over to the train station. For **nightlife**, try the disco at *Restaurang Nybrokällaren* at Nybrogatan 5 (June–Aug Wed & Fri; rest of the year Sat).

# Sollefteå

After Härnösand the train line swings inland, slowly winding its way 80km northwest to **SOLLEFTEÅ** (you can also get here by boat; see above), an appealingly peaceful little town, beautifully sited on the banks of the Ångerman river. Once you've walked the one main pedestrianized street, Storgatan, and seen its parks and gardens, there's nothing much left. It's an easy stroll to the single attraction, the unassuming **Sollefteå kyrka** (June–Aug daily 7am–4.30pm; rest of the year daily 8am–dusk), on a small hill overlooking the river just outside town. The eighteenth-century church encompasses bits of the original medieval building within its shell; the separate wedding-cake bell tower is a later addition. Inside you'll find an eighteenth-century Rococo pulpit and a carved altarpiece. Across the main road, the curious **Regiment Museum** (open all year Mon–Fri noon–3pm; July also Sat & Sun noon–3pm & Tues 6–8pm; free) contains, amongst other more mundane exhibits, a stuffed regimental horse.

The **tourist office** (June to mid-Aug Mon–Fri 9am–7pm, Sat 10am–3pm, Sun noon–6pm; rest of year Mon–Fri 8am–4pm; ☎0620/825 36) is at Torggatan 4 and has useful information on the whole province of Ångermanland and on local hiking trails; it also has a few rooms and cabins for rent – ask for the latest details and prices. The **youth hostel** (open all year; ☎0620/158 17; 100kr) is associated with the *Hundhotellet* (☎0620/158 17; ①) in ÖVERGÅRD – from the train station it's about a 2km walk; turn right and follow the road, cross the train tracks and turn left at the next T-junction. Nearby is the **Statens Hundskola** (Swedish Dog Training School), where sniffer dogs and guide dogs are taught the tricks of the trade; the school is open to visitors, and the puppies are extremely cute. Back in town, another decent, fairly inexpensive hotel is *Hotell Appelberg* (☎0620/121 30; ②) at Storgatan 51. For the town's **campsite**, walk just five minutes from the centre to the beautifully situated *Sollefteå Camping* (☎0620/173 70 or 145 71), right on the river; there are also water slides and outdoor heated swimming pools on site. It's open all year round and has twelve four-bed cabins for around 250kr per cabin.

There's a rash of pizzerias in the centre of town around Storgatan; for good pizza at reasonable prices try *La Betola*. At lunchtime the best deals are to be had at *Appelbergs* **restaurant** in the hotel of the same name (see above); *Dagens Rätt* goes for around 50kr, and there's also a good buffet for slightly more. The **pub** and restaurant, *Old House,* is worth checking out for a beer or two and its agreeable atmosphere.

# Höga Kusten – the High Coast

**Höga Kusten**, or the High Coast, is the stretch of coast between Härnösand and Örnsköldsvik and is of striking elemental beauty: rolling mountains and verdant valleys plunge precipitously into the Gulf of Bothnia, and the rugged shoreline is composed of sheer cliffs and craggy outcrops, as well as gentle sandy coves. Offshore are dozens of islands, some no more than a few metres square in size, others much larger and covered with dense pine forest. It was on these islands that the tradition of preparing the foul-smelling *surströmming* is thought to have begun (see p.325). The coastline is best seen from the sea, and a trip out to these islands gives a perfect impression of the scale of things: the High Coast is, unsurprisingly, the highest coastline in Sweden. However it's also possible to walk virtually the entire length of the coast on the **Höga Kusten Leden** (see p.326), a long-distance **hiking path** that stretches the 130km from the new bridge across the mouth of the Ångerman river just north of Härnösand.

The excitement that surrounds the building of the High Coast **suspension bridge** (due for completion in 1997) is quite remarkable. Although it is stunning, the bridge doesn't quite live up to the tourist-brochure description of it as a world-class attraction. The highest construction in Sweden, reaching 180m over the water and with a span of 1210m, it will be the seventh longest suspension bridge in the world behind the Golden Gate Bridge in San Francisco, which was its inspiration.

# Island-hopping up Höga Kusten

A trip out to the islands off Höga Kusten has to rank as the highlight of any trip up the Bothnian coast. Using a combination of buses and boats you can make your way to three of the most beautiful islands in the chain: **Högbonden**, **Ulvön** and **Trysunda**. Högbonden only has connections to the mainland, which means doubling back on yourself a little to take the bus up the coast to reach the boat that sails out to Ulvön from **DOCKSTA**. There are **youth hostels** on all the islands, but other useful mainland hostels are at Docksta (open all year, Sept to mid-May advance bookings only; ☎0613/130 64, fax 403 91; 95kr) and at **KÖPMANHOLMEN** (mid-May to end-Aug; ☎0660/334 96; 100kr), where the ferry from Trysunda puts in.

## Högbonden

After just ten minutes' boat ride from the mainland, the steep sides of the tiny round island of **Högbonden** rise up in front of you – a wonderfully deserted haven of peace and scenic beauty. There are no shops (bring all provisions with you) and no hotels on the island; in fact the only building here is a lighthouse, situated at the highest point on a rocky plateau, where the pine and spruce trees, so

---

### GETTING TO THE ISLANDS

**HÖGBONDEN** Take the 11.55am *E4-bus* for Luleå from Härnösand to Bönhamn (changing at Lunde and Nordingrå), from where *M/F Högbonden* (mid-June to mid-Aug daily every two hours 10am–6pm; book ahead at other times; 60kr return) makes the ten-minute trip out to the island. Tell the bus driver you're taking the boat over to Högbonden, and he'll ring the skipper to ask him to wait for the bus; the same applies on the trip back to the mainland, when you can ask the ferry man to let the bus driver know of your arrival. More information from the skipper, Karl-Erik Molin on ☎0614/179 54 or mobile ☎010/254 90 50.

**ULVÖN** If you're coming from Högbonden, take the bus from Bönhamn via Nordingrå to Lunde, where you can connect onto the frequent buses that run between Sundsvall and Umeå (for the latest bus times call ☎0660/21 12 00 or ☎0612/71 14 00); get off at **Docksta**. If you're coming directly from Härnösand, there are frequent direct buses to Docksta. From here *M/S Kusttrafik*, operated by *Höga Kusten Båtarna* (June–Aug; ☎0613/105 50; 75kr single), leaves daily at 10.15am arriving in **Ulvöhamn** at 11.30am, returning at 3pm. The boat begins its journey in Ullånger, but the jetty is a long way from the village and difficult to find – it's much easier to catch the boat in Docksta, where the bus stops next to the jetty. It's also possible to reach Ulvön from the north by taking *M/S Otilia II* (late-June to early Aug; ☎0660/12537; 70kr single) from Örnsköldsvik; the boat leaves once daily at 9.30am, returning from Ulvöhamn at 3pm.

**TRYSUNDA** From Ulvöhamn you can island-hop by *M/F Ulvön* (☎010/254 2108; 30kr single) to the delightful island of Trysunda; this service operates all year. Although departures vary from day to day, they are roughly twice daily on weekdays, once daily at weekends; the journey takes roughly an hour. This boat continues from Trysunda to **Köpmanholmen** back on the mainland (25kr single; 45min), from where there are regular buses into Örnsköldsvik (for bus information call ☎0660/844 55).

prominent elsewhere, have been unable to get a foothold. The lighthouse has now been converted into a **youth hostel** (mid-May to end-Sept, groups only outside mid-June to mid-Aug; ☎0613/230 05; 100kr) run by an endearing woman in her seventies, Rut Lindström. The youth hostel only has 27 beds, so the island never gets overcrowded. The views out across the Gulf of Bothnia are stunning, and on a sunny day you could easily imagine you're in the middle of the Mediterranean. You'll only get to know the special charm of Högbonden if you stay a couple of nights and take time to explore the island, with its narrow gorge running north-south across it, forested hillsides and a shoreline where eider ducks glide by with their young. Besides the pine and spruce, Högbonden is home to rowan, sallow, aspen and birch trees, as well as various mosses that struggle for space with wild bilberries. When evening comes head for the traditional wood-burning **sauna** down by the sea; afterwards, it's an idllyic spot to take a swim in the cool waters of the Gulf of Bothnia and watch the sun set.

## Ulvön

**Ulvön** is really two islands, Norra and Södra Ulvön, and the largest in the chain. However, the southern island is uninhabited, separated from its northern neighbour by a narrow channel. Ulvön used to be home to the High Coast's biggest fishing community, but after World War II, when the industry started to decline, many islanders moved to the mainland. Today there are only around forty permanent residents. Ulvön is famous for its production of **surströmming** or fermented Baltic herring. Although the last salthouse closed in 1983, it's still possible to buy the stuff in the island's shops (for more on *surströmming* see p.325).

All boats to the island dock at the main village, **ULVÖHAMN**, a picturesque one-street affair with red and white cottages and tiny boathouses on stilts snuggling up to each other eave to eave. Walk a short distance to the left of the quay, where the *M/S Kusttrafik* from Docksta puts in, and you'll come to a tiny wooden hut that functions in summer as the **tourist office** (mid-June to mid-Aug daily but erratic hours; ☎0660/340 93). You can **rent bikes** here for 60kr per day and pick up information about the *Ulvön Regatta*, a big annual celebration that takes place in July. The island's only **hotel**, *Ulvö Skärgårdshotell* (☎0660/340 09, fax 340 78; ③), is to the right of the jetty at the very end of the street. Walking along the waterfront, you'll pass more painted wooden houses and the fisherman's chapel, which dates from the 1600s; inside its walls are covered with flamboyant eighteenth-century murals. The road that leads up the hill to the right, just beyond the chapel, will take you to the **youth hostel** (June–Aug; ☎0660/340 68; 95kr), about 2km from the harbour.

At the other end of Ulvöhamn's main street, you'll find the village shop, which is good for picnic treats; *M/F Ulvön* to Trysunda and Köpmanholmen leaves from the quay outside. A stone's throw further on the other side of the visitors' jetty is the berth for *M/S Otilia II*, which arrives from Örnsköldsvik. The shop also hands out keys and limited information about the pine **cabins** (with cooking facilities) that are available on the island; there are four four-bed cabins just by the shop, with fantastic views out over the harbour and the bay, and ten four-bed cabins up the hill behind the harbour at **FÄBODVALLEN** (for more information and bookings ☎0660/310 13, fax 305 17; June–Aug 560kr per night, 2280kr per week, Sept–May 350kr per night, 1480kr per week). For **eating and drinking**, it's best to buy your own from the village shop, though you could always try the pizzeria

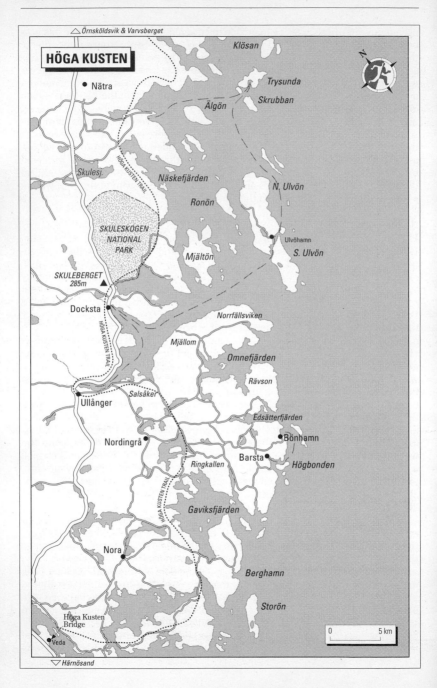

△Örnsköldsvik & Varvsberget

**HÖGA KUSTEN**

N

• Nätra

Klösan

Trysunda

Skrubban

Älgön

Skulesj.

HÖGA KUSTEN TRAIL

Näskefjärden

N. Ulvön

Ronön

SKULESKOGEN
NATIONAL
PARK

Mjältön

Ulvöhamn

S. Ulvön

SKULEBERGET
285m ▲

Docksta

HÖGA KUSTEN TRAIL

Norrfällsviken

Mjällom

Omnefjärden

Rävson

Ullånger

Salsåker

Edsätterfjärden

Nordingrå •

Bönhamn

Ringkallen

Barsta

Högbonden

HÖGA KUSTEN TRAIL

Gaviksfjärden

Nora •

Berghamn

Storön

Höga Kusten
Bridge

0        5 km

• Veda

▽ Härnösand

---

## SURSTRÖMMING

Mention the word *surströmming* to most Swedes and they'll turn up their noses in disgust. It's best translated as "fermented Baltic herring" – though to the non-connoisseur the word "rotten" would seem more appropriate. The tradition of eating the foul-smelling stuff began on the islands off the High Coast at a time when salt was very expensive; as a result just a little was used to start the fermentation process, thereby allowing the fish to be kept longer. Today, it's made in flat-shaped tins, which, over the course of the year's fermentation process, blow up into the shape of a football under the pressure of the odious gases produced inside. Restaurants refuse to open the tins on the premises because of the lingering stink that's exuded — the unpleasant job has to be done outside in the fresh air. *Surströmming* is eaten with the yellow, almond-shaped variety of northern Swedish potatoes and is washed down with beer or *akvavit*; alternatively it's made into a sandwich and is rolled in a piece of *tunnbröd*, the thin unleavened bread traditional to this part of the country.

---

near the **tourist office** hut, the restaurant at *Ulvö Skärgårdshotell* or *Café Måsen*. For **beaches** follow the sign marked "Strandpromenaden" from the village shop; it's about ten minutes by bike past small sandy coves to the entrance of the harbour and a promontory of red rocks, beyond which lie several sandy stretches.

If you continue on the road out of town that leads to the youth hostel, you'll pass Ulvön's churchyard on a tiny island in the middle of a lake. About 4km further is the island's second village, **SANDVIKEN**; although not a long bike ride from the main village, the journey across the island does involve some steep climbs. A fishing village for around three hundred years, it's now a tiny holiday resort – *M/S Otilia II* to Örnsköldsvik sometimes puts in here after Ulvöhamn, which can save you the trek back. With a long sandy beach, Sandviken is certainly the place to come if you want to get away from it all.

## Trysunda
**Trysunda** is just an hour's boat ride from Ulvön, and its tiny village is hemmed in around a narrow U-shaped harbour. The best-preserved fishing village in Ångermanland, it really is a charming little place, with forty or so red and white houses right on the waterfront. The chapel in the village dates from the seventeenth century and, like the church on Ulvön, is decorated with some colourful murals inside.

The island's gently shelving rocks make it ideal for bathing, and you'll find plenty of secluded spots; there's a sand **beach** at **Björnviken** — either walk up along the path over the hill, Kapellberget, or round it to get there. If you want to do more walking, Trysunda is criss-crossed with walking paths, leading through the forests of dwarf pine that cover the island – many of which have become knarled and twisted under the force of the wind. As you leave Trysunda by boat, you might be lucky enough to catch a glimpse of the elk on the neighbouring volcanic and uninhabited island of **Skrubban**. Every year hunting takes place here — as in the rest of Sweden — to kill some of the animals and prevent unnecessary suffering from starvation. If you want to stay on Trysunda, you'll find Sweden's smallest **youth hostel** (early June to end-Aug; ☎0660/430 38; 95kr), with just eight beds — and a sauna. There's also a shop in the village for those bare necessities, including fresh and smoked fish.

# Höga Kusten Leden and Skuleskogen National Park

It's possible to walk the entire length of the High Coast along **Höga Kusten Leden**, or the High Coast Trail, which stretches 130km from **Veda** near Härnösand to **Varvsberget**, virtually in the centre of Örnsköldsvik. The trail is divided into thirteen stages, which vary in difficulty and are between seven- and fifteen-kilometres long. At each stage break, there is accommodation, mostly free overnight cabins (see below for details). The route takes in the magnificent **Skuleskogen National Park**, which is noted for its dense forests, coastal panoramas and sharp-edged ravines. The Skuleskogen is home to a rich mix of **flora and fauna**, including many varieties of bird – the rare whitebacked woodpecker, capercaillie, hazel and black grouse, wren, coal tit and crested tit – and numerous forest animals such as elk, lynx, ermine, marten, mink, mountain hare and squirrel. You'll also see the unusual long beard lichen *(Usnea longissima)* which grows on spruce trees. Leading inland through the park, there are a number of well-marked paths aside from the trail that will take you past some wonderful countryside.

You can also go **mountain climbing** in Skuleskogen; trails up **Skuleberget** (285m), near Docksta, afford stunning views from the top, and anyone in normal shape can make it safely to the summit. If you're out to do some serious climbing you can rent equipment at Skule Naturum (see below) and get sound advice from

## STAGES IN THE HÖGA KUSTEN LEDEN

**VEDA-SÖR-LÖVVIK** (9.3km; demanding). Cabins with kitchen at Sjöbodviken.

**LÖVVIK-FJÄRDBOTTEN** (9.6km; average). Four wooden cabins at Fjärdbotten by the promontory at Häggnäset.

**FJÄRDBOTTEN-GAVIK** (12.8km; demanding). Cabin Nipstugan Lidnipan for a maximum of 5-6 people.

**GAVIK-LAPPUDDEN** (11.5km; easy). Six cabins available in Lappudden on the edge of the Vågfjärden.

**LAPPUDDEN-ULLÅNGER** (15km; demanding). *Hotell Erikslund* (☎0613/104 75).

**ULLÅNGER-SKOVED** (10.5km; average). Cabins on the beach at Lake Mäjasjön; no cooking facilities.

**SKOVED-SKULE NATURUM** (6.8km; easy). Youth hostel in Docksta at Dockstavägen 47 (open all year, Sept to mid-May advance bookings only; ☎0613/130 64, fax 403 91; 95kr).

**SKULE NATURUM-KÄL** (9.2km; average). Cabins at Bergsbodarna, 5km north of Skuleberget mountain; a path leads there from Skule Naturum.

**KÄL-NÄSKE** (8.5km; demanding, passes through wilderness). Simple hut by Lake Tärnettvattnet in Skuleskogen National Park.

**NÄSKE-KÖPMANHOLMEN** (7km; easy). Youth hostel in Köpmanholmen (mid-May to mid-Aug; ☎0660/334 96; 100kr) by the ferry quay.

**KÖPMANHOLMEN-SANDLÅGAN** (12.3km; demanding). One cabin at Bodviken in the Balesudden nature reserve.

**SANDLÅGAN-SVEDJEHOLMEN** (12km; average). Restored farm store house at Småtjärnarna.

**SVEDJEHOLMEN-VARVSBERGET** (5.5km; easy). Accommodation in Örnsköldsvik (see p.328).

experts. If you only want to do part of the trail, it's worth noting that the buses between Härnösand and Örnsköldsvik stop very close to several stages along the way: Lappudden, Ullånger, Skoved, Skule Naturum and Köpmanholmen. For more **information** contact *Mitt Sverige Turism* in Härnösand (☎0611/290 30), which sells the *Small Map Book for the High Coast* for 40kr, or the tourist office in Örnsköldsvik (see below). For more general guidance on the dos and don'ts of walking in Sweden, see p.396.

# Örnsköldsvik

About 120km north of Härnösand beyond the High Coast lies the port of **ÖRNSKÖLDSVIK** (usually shortened to Ö-vik), a busy, modern city stacked behind a superbly sheltered harbour. Örnsköldsvik began life in 1842 – when it was known as Köping – and became a city in 1894. The town's present name comes from the county governor, Per Abraham Örnsköld – the ending *vik* simply means "bay". Although the harbour side is a pleasant place to eat or drink, the city itself holds little of appeal; the brassy slogan that heads the tourist propaganda – "We discovered Örnsköldsvik" – is nothing to boast about. The city's only saving grace is its **museum** at Läroverksgatan 1 (Tues & Thurs–Fri 10am–4pm, Wed 10am–8pm, Sat & Sun 11am–4pm; 10kr). From the bus station walk up the steps on the other side of Strandgatan, which will bring you out on Storgatan, and continue east along either Läroverksgatan or Hamnagatan to get to the museum. Ignore the typical collections of prehistoric finds and nineteenth-century furniture and ask to be let into the adjacent workshop, which conceals a sparkling documentation of the work of locally born artist **Bror Marklund**. Most of his art was commissioned by public bodies and goes unnoticed by travellers who brush against it all the time: his *Thalia*, the goddess of the theatre, rests outside the City Theatre in Malmö, and his figures adorn the facade of the Historical Museum in Stockholm. Inside the workshop look for the jester plaster casts, brilliantly executed and one of Markland's most easily identifiable motifs.

The only other thing to do here is to take a stroll along the harbour side, past the impressive culture and business centre, known as *Arken*, and the old warehouses. If it's raining when you visit Ö-vik, you might want to visit the indoor **swimming complex**, *Paradisbadet*, off Centralesplanaden near the bus station, with a 25m pool for serious swimmers, two massive water slides, jacuzzis, steam room and an outdoor pool heated to 25°C.

## Practicalities

If you've opted to come to Ö-vik by **train** you'll have to alight at **Mellansel** on the main line from Stockholm to Kiruna, about 30km to the northwest; to get into the city book a *tågtaxi* (train-taxi) at the station (or on ☎0660/120 70); special rates are available which will take you to the **bus station** on Strandgatan. It is much easier to take the bus, and the bus station is also a stop-off point for the so-called **E4-buses**, which run the entire length of the coast from Sundsvall and Luleå, as well as services from Sollefteå and Östersund (for more information call ☎0660/21 12 00). You can pick up a bus here for the **airport** (☎0660/863 10) an hour before flight departures; there are five direct flights daily to Stockholm with

*SAS*. **Boats** to and from Ulvön (see p.322) dock at the *Arken* quay in front of the bus station along Strandgatan.

The **tourist office** (June to late Aug Mon–Fri 9am–7pm, Sat 10am–2pm, Sun 10am–3pm; late Aug to May Mon–Fri 10am–5pm; ☎0660/125 37, fax 880 15) is at Nygatan 18 and has free town maps, bus and boat schedules and accommodation lists for both the city and Höga Kusten islands. The **youth hostel** (open all year; ☎0660/702 44; 100kr) is in **ÖVERHÖRNÄS**, 7km to the southwest – take the bus marked "Köpmanholmen" and tell the driver where you're going. There's no bus stop as such so simply flag the bus down. There's only one cheapish **hotel**: *Strand City Hotell*, right in the centre at Nygatan 2 (☎0660/106 10, fax 21 13 05; ③/①), is a cheap and cheerful hostel-like establishment. Rather more agreeable rooms are to be found both at the swanky *First Hotell Statt* (☎0660/101 10, fax 837 91; ④/②) at Lasarettsgatan 2 and the plain and functional *Hotell Focus* up the hill at no. 9 (☎0660/82100, fax 838 67; ④/②).

## Eating and drinking

During the day, open sandwiches and cakes are available from *Café UH*, which is attached to the *Hotell Focus* (see above). The city centre also has a number of pizza **restaurants**; the best are *Il Padrino* on Läroverksgatan, just off Stora Torget, with pizzas for around 55kr and pasta at 75kr, and *Restaurangen Mamma Mia* on Storgatan. Here you can have a good *Dagens Rätt* for 60kr, as well as a two-course business lunch for 150kr; in the evenings there's pizza, pasta and other meat and fish dishes for around 150kr – in summer, you can also play boules here in the yard. Off Stora Torget, between Hemköp and the Sparbanken, is the *China Tower Restaurangen*, which is also a pub; dishes start at 100kr. For more stylish eating and drinking head for the lively **harbour side**, where restaurants with outdoor tables offer good views out over the water of Örnsköldsviksfjärden. A brasserie-style place, *Arkenrestaurangen*, next to the harbour, offers a lunch deal, including soup, for 85kr and main dishes for around 120kr. Next door the *Arken* pub charges a reasonable price for beer. If you want to splash out and indulge yourself, *StrandKaj 4* serves up local delicacies, including whitefish for 145kr, and nearby *Fina Fisken* has fish dishes from 110kr in a cosy interior decked out as a wooden cabin – a nice place to eat.

*The* place to do your **drinking** is in one of the two bars at the *First Hotell Statt* at Lasarettsgatan 2; one of the bars is a piano bar. On the corner of Viktoriaesplanaden and Strandgatan there's *Hamncompaniet*, a bar and **disco** popular with 18- to 25-year-olds.

# Umeå

**UMEÅ** is the biggest city in the north of Sweden, with a population of around one hundred thousand. There's a young feel to the city, borne out by a stroll round the airy modern centre. Those who aren't in pushchairs are pushing them, and the cafés and city parks are full of teenagers. Demographically it's probably Sweden's most youthful city; the average age here is just 35 – a stunningly low figure influenced by the Norrland University and its twenty thousand students. Umeå is an appealing metropolis, with its fast-flowing river and wide, stylish boulevards, and it would be no bad idea to spend a couple of days here sampling some of the bars and restaurants – the variety of which you won't find anywhere else in Norrland.

The telephone code for Umeå and Holmön is ☎090.

## Getting to Umeå

If you're continuing up the coast from Ö-vik, the next stop on the regular **E4-bus**, which runs between Sundsvall and Luleå, is **Umeå** (journey time 1hr); there's only one **train** a day from **Mellansel** (the nearest station to Ö-vik), and it currently leaves at 5.15am. Useful bus routes if you're travelling from central Sweden are Vilhelmina-Umeå, Dorotea-Åsele-Umeå and Sorsele-Umeå). Also buses (with connections from Mo-i-Rana in Norway) have now replaced trains on the Storuman-Lycksele-Umeå route, which once linked the city to the *Inlandsbanan*.

If you're travelling directly to Umeå by **train** from Stockholm or Gothenburg you have two options: either take the coastal train route to Sundsvall and then continue by the E4-bus, or take the overnight services that depart from Stockholm and Gothenburg and include through cars to Umeå routed via Vännäs. Both options also apply if you're leaving the city for all points south; there is one sleeper a day from Umeå to Stockholm and Gothenburg.

It's possible to **fly** directly to Umeå from the regional airports in Gällivare, Kiruna, Luleå, Skellefteå, Sundsvall and Östersund, usually with *Skyways*, as well as from Stockholm with *SAS* and *Transwede*. If you're travelling to Sweden from Finland, Umeå is currently the only port with regular year-round **ferry** services arriving from Vaasa – note that Swedes spell this with one "a", and in Finland Umeå is Uumaja.

# Arrival and information

It's a ten-minute walk from either the **train** or **bus station** down one of the many parallel streets, which lead in the general direction of the river, to the city centre. The bus station will also be your point of arrival if you come to Umeå by ferry from Vaasa; *Silja Line* dock at nearby Holmsund, from where connecting buses run inland to Umeå. A good first stop is the **tourist office** (mid-June to mid-Aug Mon–Fri 8am–8pm, Sat 10am–5pm, Sun 11am–5pm; rest of the year Mon–Fri 9am–6pm, Sat 11am–2pm; ☎16 16 16) in Renmarkstorget, an ugly concrete square at odds with its romantic name, which means "Reindeer-country square". The staff here are very helpful and dish out assorted bumph, including a free newspaper with detailed listings.

Although Umeå is a reasonably large city, the centre is easy to **get around on foot** and many of the streets, including the main drag, Kungsgatan, are pedestrianized. Everything of interest is north of the River Ume.

# Accommodation

The tourist office will book **private rooms** for you from 150kr per night, booking fee 25kr. The **youth hostel** (open all year; ☎77 16 50, fax 77 16 95; 100kr), centrally located at Västra Esplanaden 10, is another jewel in the *STF* crown. Open as a hotel until 1975, the building then became a drop-in centre for alcoholics and unemployed people, until it was completely renovated and turned into a youth hostel in 1996: bright, airy and modern, it is one of the best deals in Umeå. The nearest **campsite** is *Umeå Camping Stugby* (☎16 16 60, fax 12 57 20), 5km out of town by the side of a lake on the E4 at **NYDALA**. Open all year, it also has **cabins** for four to six people for 560kr, individual double rooms in other cabins for 225kr and *trätält* (tiny two-bed huts) for 160kr per night; washing machines and **bike rental** are also available. To get there, take buses #6 and #7, which run together providing a three-hourly service on weekdays – #69 is twice-hourly at weekends only – and get off at Nydala and walk for around five minutes towards Nydalabadet.

## Hotels

**Björken**, Patientvägen 1 (☎10 87 00). A hotel used by hospital patients, but with rooms of good quality. ③/②

**First Hotel Grand**, Storgatan 46 (☎77 88 70, fax 13 30 55). Newly renovated and rather chic, right in the heart of town. ④/②

**Pilen**, Pilgatan 5 (☎14 14 60). One of the cheaper smaller hotels with clean and basic rooms and weekend and summer doubles for 500kr. ②

**Strand**, Västra Strandgatan 11 (☎12 90 20, fax 12 18 40). Another low-budget but perfectly adequate hotel. ③/②

**Tegs**, Verkstadsgatan 5 (☎12 27 00, fax 13 49 90). The cheapest hotel in town – in summer a double is down to 390kr – but south of the river and some way from the action. ②/①

**Umeå Plaza**, Storgatan 40 (☎17 70 00, fax 17 70 50). The best hotel in Umeå, very smart with marble washbasins and loudspeakers in the bathroom; superb views from the sauna suite on the fifteenth floor. Good-value weekend and summer deals. ⑤/②

**Uman Home**, Storgatan 52 (☎12 72 20, fax 12 74 20). Home from home, with evening coffee and newspapers for all guests. ⑤/②

**Wasa**, Vasagatan 12 (☎77 85 40, fax 77 85 49). A comfortable hotel in a lively central location. ③/②

**Winn**, Skolgatan 64 (☎12 20 20, fax 12 54 28). Close to the city bus station and good for nearby restaurants and bars. ④/②

# The city and around

Umeå is known as the "City of Birch Trees", named after the trees that were planted along every street after a devastating fire in 1888. Most of the city was burnt to the ground in the blaze, and two-thirds of the town's then three-thousand inhabitants lost their homes. Rebuilding soon began apace, and two wide esplanades were constructed to act as fire breaks and help prevent such a disaster happening again. A decree was handed down stating that the birch was the most suitable tree to add life to the town's new modern streets – even today the city council provides free birch saplings every spring for anyone who wants them. You'll be hard pushed to find any of the original wooden buildings, but around the little park near the river, in front of the **Rådhus**, lingering bits of turn-of-the-century timber architecture still look out over the water. The sound of the rapids along the River Ume give the city its name: *uma* means "roar".

As well as the accommodating ambience that you'll find here, Umeå has one terrific museum complex, **Gammlia**, which merits a good half-day's attention. The original attraction around which everything else developed is the **Friluftsmuseum** (mid-June to mid-Aug daily 10am–5pm; free), an open-air group of twenty regional buildings, the oldest the seventeenth-century gatehouse on the way in. The country setting is fun to wander around – past, among other buildings, a windmill, a church, two threshing floors and a smoke house for pork – and exchange a few words with the people dressed in period costume, who are very willing to tell you more about life in the mock town. At the bakery, you can see how Umeå people used to cook and bake their thin unleavened bread, *tunnbröd*, while for children, the farm buildings and yards are home to cows, pigs, goats, sheep and geese, and there's the chance to take a ride in a horse-drawn carriage. The indoor **Västerbottens Museum** (mid-June to mid-Aug Mon–Fri 10am–5pm, Sat & Sun noon–5pm; rest of the year Tues–Fri 9am–4pm, Sat noon–4pm, Sun noon–5pm; free) houses the main collection: three basic exhibitions that canter through the county's past from prehistory (including the oldest ski in the world – it's over five thousand years old) to the Industrial Revolution. It's all good stuff, well laid out and complemented by an array of videos and recordings with a useful English guidebook available.

Linked to Västerbottens Museum is the **Bildmuseum** (mid-June to mid-Aug daily noon–5pm; rest of the year Tues–Sat noon–4pm, Sun noon–5pm; free), a pictorial museum that houses the university art collection, highlighting contemporary Swedish work by artists such as Carl Larsson and Anders Zorn and a cobbled-together set of old masters. Back outside, county history continues in a sep-

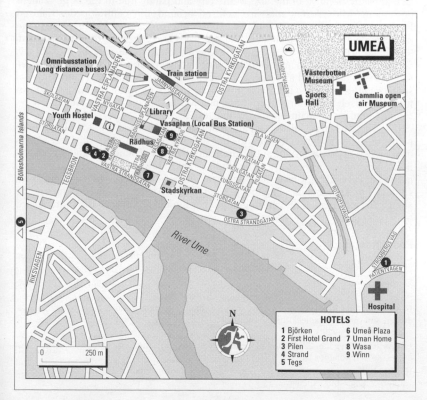

arate **Fiske och Sjöfartsmuseum** (mid-June to mid-Aug daily noon–5pm; rest of the year Tues–Sat noon–4pm, Sun noon–5pm; free), which does its best to be a maritime museum – a small hall clogged with fishing boats.

## Norrfors and Bölesholmarna

If you have a bike (see "Listings" for rental details), it's a gentle day's work to cycle the river's length along the **cycle path**, Umeleden, to **NORRFORS** and its five-thousand-year-old rock carvings in the former river bed. Back down the southern side of the river, the cycle path leads past a massive hydroelectric station and **Bölesholmarna**, two islands that can also be reached easily on foot from the city centre (a fifteen-minute walk). The islands are an ideal spot for picnics and barbecues as well as a quick dip in the small lake in the middle of them. Both the cycle path and the route to the islands are detailed on a free map available from the tourist office.

# Eating, drinking and entertainment

**Eating** and **drinking** possibilities are varied and generally of a high standard in Umeå, partly because of the size of the city and partly due to the large student population. Most restaurants are centred around the central pedestrianized Kungsgatan or Rådhusesplanaden. The best **café** is *Konditori Mekka*, close to the train station at Rådhusesplanaden 17; its pastries and cakes are delicious and coffee refills are free. Other snack food can be had at the café in the library, *Stadsbiblioteket*, amid an intellectual-looking young crowd, with goatees and thick-rimmed spectacles, and also at *Nya Konditoiriet* on Kungsgatan. A more unusual spot for coffee and cake is on board the *Vita Björn*, the white boat moored down from Rådhuset, a popular student hang-out. Market food – mostly fruit and veg – can be found in the main square, Rådhustorget.

Umeå's youthful population means that the city buzzes at night, and there are plenty of stylish and friendly **bars** to choose from, most of them British-style pubs or brasserie-style bars. A lot of the **nightlife** revolves around the student population, and Umeå is liveliest when the students are in town; there are usually discos in the union building, Universum, on term-time weekends. Strictly you must be a student, but it's worth hassling to try to get in or befriending a Swede who's going along. For information on what's going on at the university, call the switchboard on ☎16 50 00.

## Restaurants

**China Hall**, Kungsgatan 60. Reasonably priced Chinese and Japanese food with the option to fry your own at your table.

**Eurasia**, Renmarkstorget 12. Chinese food, pizzas and steaks. Perfectly okay food but somewhat bland.

**K-A Svenssons kök och matsalar**, Vasaplan. In an old, blue wooden building with 1960s' design and chequed tablecloths. Small dishes for 59kr, fish, seafood or meat for 150kr. The service and the quality of food varies.

**Lottas Krog**, Nygatan 22. A good place for lunch; the pub's menu includes a 65kr special of entrecote and potatoes (also see "Bars and nightlife").

**Rådhuskällaren**, under the *Grand Hotell* at Västra Rådhusgatan 1. Top-notch food under a vaulted ceiling – but expensive.

**Restaurang Charlotta**, corner of Nygatan & Rådhusesplanaden. Probably the priciest place in town: reindeer, sole, lamb, lobster, salmon for around 400kr per head. The interior is mostly wood, with heavy tablecloths, delicate lighting and soft music.

**Skytten**, near the train station at Järnvägstorget. Two restuarants in one, an upmarket place and a brasserie. Good choice of food and reasonable prices.

**Teater Cafeet**, Vasaplan. Grill specialities and light dishes. Three courses for 139kr or very good *gravad lax* for 109kr. Service not always so good; also see "Bars and nightlife".

**V&R**, inside the *Plaza Hotell* at Storgatan 40. Very smart and chi-chi; everything from vegetarian lasagne for 69kr to fillet of lamb for 159kr.

## Bars and nightlife

**Brasseriet Skytten**, Rådhusesplanaden 17. *The* place to be seen and to do the seeing – always packed out.

**Krogen**, Ålidhems Centrum beside the Ålidhem student campus, 40min walk or take bus #8. Popular with students in term time, with eating, drinking and dancing.

**Lottas Krog**, Nygatan 22. Eighty different beers with everything from McEwans to Marstons bitter; thirteen on tap, including Guinness. Good atmosphere; darts available.

**Mucky Duck**, Vasaplan. Forty-seven types of beer; attracts an older crowd.

**Scharinska Villan**, Storgatan 65. East of the centre near the church in a beautiful pink building; drink, dance and listen to jazz Wed–Sat only.

**Scruffy Murphy**, Norrlandsgatan 5. A popular Irish pub with traditional fittings and atmosphere. Also has a cheap and good buffet.

**Teater Cafeet**, Vasaplan. With outdoor seating in summer and Happy Hours every day 3–6pm bringing the price of a beer down to 30kr.

# Around Umeå: Holmön

Thirty kilometres northeast of Umeå are the sunniest islands in the whole of Sweden, **Holmön**. Reports from the islands' weatherstation over the last 150 years have shown that this part of the country gets the most sunshine and least precipitation. To get to the main island, take the bus to the tiny port of **Norrfjärden** (current bus details from the tourist office), the departure point for the **free ferry** to the islands (June–Aug Mon–Thurs & Sat–Sun 2 daily, Fri 3 daily; also morning & afternoon sailings back to the mainland; Sept–May reduced service), though in winter ice may affect departure times (latest details on ☎77 49 48).

The Gulf of Bothnia is at its narrowest between Holmön and the Finnish island of Björkö, and consequently the sea route between the two sets of islands was used for centuries for transporting goods, people, soldiers and mail. Sweden and Finland were one country until 1809, and there are still strong links between the two communities; every summer, the *postrodden* is held, when a number of boats row and sail their way over to Björkö just as the mail boats used to do.

The best way to get around the islands is by bike; you can rent one from the **tourist office** (June–Aug daily 10am–5pm; ☎551 81 or mobile ☎010/256 07 69), near where the boat puts in, and pick up a map of the island. Cycling is a wonderful way to see the small farmsteads, flower meadows and pine forests that fill the landscape. There are proper bathing facilities at *Holmö Havsbad*, but it's also easy to find your own secluded little nook. If you're around at the time, check out the Sea Jazz Festival at the end of June and the Holmöns Visfestivalen (Song Contest) in late July. If you want to stay over, try *Bäckströms* **B&B** (☎090/550 84; ②), not far from the tourist office.

## Listings

**Airlines** *SAS*, Renmarkstorget 15 (☎18 30 08); *Transwede* at the airport (☎10 62 80).

**Banks** *Föreningsbanken*, Renmarkstorget 9; *Handelsbanken*, Storgatan 48; *Nordbanken*, Rådhusesplanaden 3; *SE-Banken* with cash machine, Kungsgatan 52; *Sparbanken Norrland*, Rådhustorget.

**Beaches** *Nydala* at Umeå campsite; *Bettnesand*, 20km south of town; *Bölesholmarna*, 15min walk from the centre along the south bank of the river.

**Bike rental** *Cykel & Mopedhandlar'n*, Kungsgatan 101, open Mon–Fri 9.30am–5.30pm, Sat 10am–1pm (☎14 01 70); *Oves Cykelservice*, Storgatan 87, open Mon–Fri 8am–5pm (☎12 61 91). Count on around 50kr per day – less per day if you rent for longer.

**Buses** Bus station, Järnvägstorget 2 (☎13 20 70). City buses at Vasaplan (☎16 22 40) – single ticket 12kr, strip of five for 58kr, ten for 100kr.

**Cinemas** *Filmstaden*, Östra Rådhusgatan 2D; *Saga*, Kungsgatan 46; *Sandrew*, Skolgatan 68; *Spegeln*, Storgatan 50.

**Ferry tickets** *Silja Line* in Renmarkstorget; Mon–Fri 9am–5pm (☎14 21 00).

**Gay Umeå** Contact *RFSL* at Box 38, S-901 02, Umeå. *Club Feliz*, Östra Esplanaden 5, first floor, café on Wed 7–10pm; first and third Sat in the month disco 9pm–1am; switchboard Wed 7–10pm (☎77 47 10).

**Newspapers** English-language newspapers at the library, *Stadsbiblioteket*, at Rådhusesplanaden 6.

**Pharmacy** Renmarkstorget 6 or at the hospital, Norrlands Universitetssjukhus.

**Police** Götgatan 1 (☎15 20 00).

**Post office** Vasaplan also has cash machine; Mon–Fri 8am–6pm, Sat 10am–2pm (☎15 05 00).

**Swimming pools** Indoor at *Umeå simhall* at Rothoffsvägen 12 (☎16 16 40); outdoor at *Nydalabadet* by the campsite.

**Systembolaget**, Kungsgatan 50A, open Mon–Thurs 9.30am–6pm, Fri 8am–6pm; Vasagatan 11, open Mon–Wed & Fri 9.30am–6pm, Thurs 9.30–7pm.

**Taxi** *City Taxi* (☎14 14 14); *Taxi Umeorten* (☎13 20 00); *Umeå Taxi* (☎14 10 00); *Lillebil* (☎441 44).

**Train station** Järnvägsallén 7 (☎15 58 00).

**Travel agent** *Ticket*, Kungsgatan 58; Mon–Fri 10am–6pm, Sat 10am–3pm.

## Leaving Umeå

If you are continuing travelling further north, the **E4-buses** leave from the bus station in Järnvägstorget roughly every two or three hours; the next stop two hours up the road is Skellefteå (92kr), followed by Piteå and Luleå. Alternatively, there's a bus operated by *Länstrafiken* that leaves at 6am for Vännäs, with a train connection on from there to Luleå, Gällivare and Kiruna.

For those travelling on to **Finland** or if you fancy a day-trip, *Silja Line* operate a year-round service between Umeå and Vaasa, with a crossing time of around 4hr. Out of season a day return goes for as little as 95kr, in season (mid-June to mid-Aug) for 195kr. For a day-trip, typical departure times in summer are 8am from Umeå returning on the 10pm sailing from Vaasa. For those staying longer in Finland, standard single fares are 210kr; a standard return is double. Boats sail from the port of **Holmsund**, southeast of Umeå; buses leave from the bus station an hour before departure. Tickets and information from *Silja Line* in Renmarkstorget (see "Listings" for full details).

# Skellefteå

"In the centre of the plain was Skellefteå church, the largest and most beautiful building in the entire north of Sweden, rising like a Palmyra's temple out of the desert", enthused the nineteenth-century traveller Leopold von Buch, for there used to be a real religious fervour about **SKELLEFTEÅ**. In 1324 an edict in the name of King Magnus Eriksson invited "all those who believed in Jesus Christ or wanted to turn to Him" to settle between the Skellefte and Ume rivers. Many heeded the call, and parishes mushroomed on the banks of the Skellefte river. By the end of the eighteenth century, a devout township was centred around the monumental church, which stood out in stark contrast to the surrounding plains and wide river. Nowadays more material occupations support the town, and the tourist office makes the most of modern Skellefteå's gold and silver refineries – as well as being disarmingly honest in its attempts to sell the town: "Don't go to Skellefteå because it seems remarkable – it isn't. The best part of Skellefteå is that it is nice and cosy." There is little to see in the centre; instead concentrate on the nearby *kyrkstad* or parish village.

On your way to the parish village you'll pass the **Nordanå Kulturcentrum**, a large and baffling assortment of buildings that's home to a theatre, a twee period grocer's store (*Lanthandel* – the Swedish word for a country grocer's ) and a dire **museum** (Mon noon–7pm, Tues–Thurs 10am–7pm, Fri–Sun noon–4pm; free) containing three floors of mind-numbing exhibitions on every-

## PARISH VILLAGES IN NORRBOTTEN AND VÄSTERBOTTEN

Parish villages are common throughout the provinces of Västerbotten and Norrbotten. The *kyrkstad* consists of rows of simple wooden houses grouped tightly around the church. After the break with the Catholic Church in 1527, the Swedish clergy were determined to teach their parishioners the Lutheran fundamentals. By 1681, church services had became compulsory, but there was one problem – the population in the north was spread over considerable distances, making weekly attendance impossible. The clergy and the parishes agreed a formula: it was decreed that those living within 10km of the church should attend every Sunday, those between 10km and 20km every fortnight and those between 20km and 30km every three weeks. The compromise worked and within a decade parish villages had appeared throughout the region to provide the travelling faithful with somewhere to spend the night after a day of praying and strong sermons. The biggest and most impressive is at Gammelstad near Luleå (see p.339), which is to be added to the UNESCO World Heritage List; another good example, aside from the one in Skellefteå, is at Öjebyn, near Piteå (see p.338). Today, they are no longer used in the traditional way, but people still live in the old houses, especially in summer, and sometimes even rent them out to tourists.

thing from the region's first settlers to swords. Tucked away to the side of the grocer's store is *Nordanå Gårdens Värdshus*, a pleasant restaurant with outdoor seating in summer.

Skellefteå's **church** and **parish village**, *Bonnstan*, are within easy striking distance of the centre: head west along Nygatan and keep going for about fifteen minutes. First of all you'll come to the **kyrkstad** – it's five long rows of weather-beaten log houses, with battered wooden shutters, make an evocative sight. The houses are protected by law and all renovations are forbidden, including the installation of electricity. Take a peek inside but bear in mind that they're privately owned. To the right of the parish village you'll find the **kyrka** (Sept to mid-June daily 10am–4pm; mid-June to end Aug daily 10am–6pm), a proud white Neoclassical building with four mighty pillars along each of the four walls supporting the domed roof. Inside there's an outstanding series of medieval sculptures; look out too for the eight-hundred-year-old *Virgin of Skellefteå*, a walnut carving near the altar – it's one of the few remaining Romanesque images of the Virgin.

Before you head back into town, the outdoor café (late May to Aug) on the nearby island of **Kyrkholmen**, in the Skellefte, is handy for a cup of coffee and simple sandwiches, and is a pretty place to sit and while away an hour or two. From the church you have two options of walking paths back to the centre: either take Strandpromenaden along the river's edge, interrupted by barbecue sites and grassy stretches, or cross the wooden bridge, Lejonströmsbron, below the church and stroll along the south side of the river back to Parksbron, past the occasional boat and silent fisherman. The bridge dates from 1737 and was the scene of mass slaughter, when Russian and Swedish forces clashed there during the war that started in 1741.

Back in town, there is one museum that deserves a visit, the **Anna Nordlander Museum** on Kanalgatan (inside the library). Born in 1843, Anna Nordlander's first love was art; even early in childhood she began to show a remarkable skill and talent for painting. She went on to become one of the few successful women artists of her time and her work, mostly landscapes and portraits, is displayed in the museum. It is one of only three museums dedicated to women artists in the world; the other two are in Boston and Bonn.

## Practicalities

The small centre is based around a modern paved square flanked by Kanalgatan and Nygatan; at the top of the square is the **bus station** and the summer-time **tourist office** (end June to early Aug Mon–Fri 10am–7pm, Sat & Sun 10am–3pm; ☎0910/73 60 20), which will provide all the usual information and help with accommodation. The main tourist office is at Kanalgatan 56 (Aug–May Mon–Thurs 8am–5pm, Fri 8am–4pm; same number as above) and handles enquiries out of season.

The **youth hostel** (mid-June to mid-Aug; ☎0910/372 83; 100kr) is well worth seeking out at Elevhemsgatan 13: a newly renovated yellow building by the southern bank of the Skellefte river, half an hour's walk from the centre. Head east on either Storgatan or Nygatan, turn right onto Viktoriagatan, cross the river over Viktoriabron and take the first left, Tubölegatan, to its end, then keep to the gravel path rather than the main road and the hostel is on the left. Otherwise, there are four central **hotels**; the cheapest is *Hotell Viktoria* at Trädgårdsgatan 8 (☎0910/174 70; ②/①), a family-run establishment on the top floor of one of the buildings on the south side of the main square. Virtually next door at Torget 2,

*Hotell Malmia* (☎0910/77 7 300, fax 77 88 16; ④/②) has perfectly adequate rooms and is the centre of Skellefteå's nightlife (see below). Nearby at Stationsgatan 8, *Skellefteå Stadshotell* (☎0910/141 40, fax 126 28; ④/②) specializes in dark and dingy rooms (and a breakfast room to match) and charges the same as the *Malmia*. The smartest hotel is *Scandic Hotel* (☎0910/383 00; ④/③) at Kanalgatan 75, next to the library, but despite the plusher surroundings, it's not worth the money. For **campers**, *Skellefteå Campingplats* (☎0910/188 55) is about 1500m north of the centre on Mossgatan, just off the E4. It also has **cabins** for 250kr per night as well as a heated outdoor **swimming pool**, wave machine, jacuzzi and dozens of holidaying Norwegians, who drive down the Silver Way (the E95), to spend their summer holidays on the Bothnian coast.

### Eating, drinking and nightlife

For all its contemporary go-ahead industry – largely computers and electronics – modern Skellefteå is quiet and retiring, its restaurants will barely whet your appetite and there are few interesting bars. For proper **cafés**, try *Café Carl Viktor* at Nygatan 40, or the popular and twee *Lilla Mari* at Köpmangatan 13 – both are good for a afternoon break. The tastiest **restaurant** in town is *Kulturkrogen*, just by the bus station on Södra Järnvägsgatan, with beef and salmon for around 150kr. The restaurant on the veranda at the *Scandic Hotel* offers northern Swedish food for around 150kr and is the place to head for if you want reindeer and cloudberries. As for pizzerias, *Pizzeria Pompeii* at Kanalgatan 43 serves pizzas for 60kr, and meat dishes for 80–90kr, and *Pizzeria Dallas* at Köpmangatan 9 has fourteen different pizzas for 35kr each. Cheap Chinese food is available at the *Golden Palace* in the main square – lunch costs 56kr, and in the evening dishes start at 35kr. For **lunch**, you won't do better than *Urkraft* at the corner of Nygatan and Tjärhovsgatan; the *Dagens Rätt* goes for 60kr and the clientele are young and friendly – though the opening times are limited (lunch daily 11am–1pm, evening meals Tues–Thurs 4pm–10pm, Fri & Sat 6pm–midnight). **Drinking** is best done at *MB* at *Hotell Malmia* in the main square; in summer there's outdoor seating, where people gather to listen to music and catch the last rays before the sun disappears below the tall buildings on the other side of the square – during Happy Hour a beer is only 24kr. Much quieter, but still worth a look, is *Eriks Pub*, nearby on Storgatan. The oddly named *Restaurant Etage* inside the *Malmia* is actually a **disco** and is the best one in town, although in summer *Mollys Nightclub*, also at the hotel, puts up stiff competition and stays open until 3am.

## Moving on from Skellefteå

The easiest way to continue north from Skellefteå is by one of the frequent **E4-buses** which stop in Piteå, before terminating in Luleå. The nearest **train stations** are at Bastuträsk (Mon–Fri two daily) and at Jörn (Mon–Sat two daily, one on Sun); both on the main line north. Unfortunately, the bus times from Skellefteå don't connect with the train times north at either of the two stations; if you're heading for Gälivare and Kiruna, it's best to take the *E4-bus* to Luleå and change onto the train there. If you want to travel south by train, take the afternoon bus from Skellefteå to Bastuträsk, where you'll have a couple of hours to kill before the night train to Gothenburg leaves, and a bit longer for the sleeper to Stockholm.

At the time of writing, the future of **ferry** sailings from nearby **Skelleftehamn** (reached by connecting shuttle bus from the bus station) to Pietarsaari in

Finland (note the town's name in Swedish is Jakobstad) is uncertain. For the latest information ask at *Båtiken*, Kanalgatan 65 (Mon–Fri 9am–5pm; ☎0910/141 60) or contact the tourist office in Skellefteå. If you need to get to Finland and there are no boats, either continue by bus up to Haparanda and cross there over to Tornio or double back to Umeå and take one of the regular year-round sailings to Vaasa. Skellefteå is also connected by **air** to Sundsvall and Umeå with *Skyways* and to Stockholm with *SAS*; airport buses call at *Stadshotellet* on Stationsgatan and *Scandic Hotel* on Kanalgatan about an hour before Stockholm planes depart; for airport information call ☎0910/832 10.

# Piteå and around

The next stop for the **E4-bus** is the small town of **PITEÅ**, located in Sweden's most northerly county, Norrbotten. The town's history goes back to the beginning of the fourteenth century, when the village was situated at nearby Öjebyn, and it is here that you'll find one of northern Sweden's oldest parish villages (see box on p.335). Granted its town charter in 1621, Piteå was still situated 20km west of its current location, but later fire destroyed much of the town, and it was decided to up sticks and move to the coast. Today, modern Piteå is a mix of pedestrianized shopping streets and anodyne squares, as well as the home of one of Sweden's biggest paper producers, *AssiDomän*.

**Öjebyn's kyrkstad** is centred around a fifteenth-century medieval stone church on Kyrkovägen; inside, the carved pulpit is the work of a local craftsman, Mils Fluur, and the Baroque altar was brought from Stockholm. The small wooden cottages here are privately owned and most of them still have no electricity; there is a small museum and tearoom in the parish house. The debate continues as to whether this parish village is the oldest in Sweden – a title also claimed by nearby Luleå. To get to Öjebyn, take bus #1 (hourly till 4.15pm) from the bus station at the end of the pedestrianized Prästgårdsgata.

There is very little else to do in Piteå, so once you've seen the parish village, it is much more rewarding to escape the concrete grey of the centre and head out to the superb beaches and swimming complexes at **PITE HAVSBAD**. Renowned for its long hours of sunshine, Pite Havsbad is one of the most popular summer resorts in Sweden. There are open-air pools with water slides, as well as an indoor Tropical Bath, with jacuzzis and saunas, waterslides and waterfalls. The long sandy beaches here, including a separate official nudist beach – quite a rarity in Sweden given that you can sunbathe nude more or less anywhere you choose away from the crowds (follow signs for the "Naturistbad") – are well looked after, friendly and not as crowded as you might expect. It is easy to reach Pite Havsbad; bus #1 (in the other direction to Öjebyn's *kyrkstad*) leaves hourly until 8pm and the **E4-bus** also stops here on the way to and from Skellefteå.

## Practicalities

The **tourist office** at Noliagatan 1 (June–Aug daily 8am–8pm; rest of the year Mon–Fri 8am–5pm; ☎0911/933 90) can fix up **private rooms** for 200–600kr per person per night (there are also a couple available for just 100kr). The **youth hostel** is 6km out of town at Öjebyn (bus #1 goes within 400m of the hostel) in a former agricultural college (mid-June to mid-Aug; ☎0911/963 85; 95kr). It's also worth noting that the buses to Älvsbyn (on the main train line and the nearest station to Piteå) pass through Öjebyn. Of the town's two **hotels**, the oldest and biggest is the comfortable *Stadshotellet* at Olof Palmes Gata 1 (☎0911/197 00, fax 12 92; ④/③), with smart rooms with an olde-worlde character. Otherwise, there's *Time Hotell* at Uddmansgatan 5 (☎0911/910 00, fax 194 00; ③/②) off the main square; it's cheaper but with less character. There's a **campsite** at Pite Havsbad, if you choose to stay close to the beach, with cabins to rent as well as a more expensive hotel (contact all three on ☎0911/327 00, fax 328 00).

Most **restaurants** in Piteå serve up *pitepalt*, a local speciality made from potato and flour rolled up into a dumpling-shaped ball and stuffed in the centre with meat. The *palts* are eaten with butter, and if you're in Piteå in the middle of July there's a good chance they'll be served up for free along Storgatan – for no reason in particular. Aside from trying *pitepalt*, eating choices in Piteå are pretty limited. Your best bet is *Pentryt* at Sundsgatan 29 (closed Fri), with lunch deals for around 50kr – it serves food until 8pm, when it turns into a bar and disco. Another reasonable choice is *Pigalle* across the road at Sundsgatan 36, renowned for its big portions; a main meat dish will cost 100–200kr. The best pizzeria is *Ängeln* at Källbogatan 2, with pizzas and pastas from 45kr. **Drinking** dens can be found downstairs at the *Stadshotellet* in the *Cockney Pub*, but the beer is expensive. Another popular spot, especially on Friday evenings with 18- to 25- year-olds, is the bar in the *Time Hotell* , where beer costs slightly less.

## Moving on from Piteå

The **E4-bus** to Luleå is the easiest way to continue your journey north. Taking the **train** is more tricky; the nearest station is Älvsbyn, from where trains head north to Boden, Gällivare and Kiruna – and to all points south. To get to Älvsbyn for the northbound train take the daily (except Sun) early-morning bus. There's also a daily afternoon bus from Piteå that connects with the sleeper south to Gothenburg and Stockholm, as well as a later one (not Sat) for the second train south to Stockholm.

# Luleå

Twenty-five minutes down the train line from Boden, **LULEÅ** lies at one end of the *Malmbanan*, the iron-ore railway, built in 1888, that connects the ice-locked Gulf of Bothnia with the ice-free Norwegian port of Narvik in the Norwegian Sea. The wide streets and lively, friendly atmosphere make Luleå immediately likable, and if you're heading north for the wilds of the Torne valley, Gällivare and Kiruna, or to the sparsely populated regions inland, it's your last chance to enjoy a range of restaurants and bars before entering the forest and wilderness that spreads north and west from here. Watch the weather, though; Luleå is built on a peninsula which takes the full brunt of the northerly winds.

Luleå was founded in 1621, with the medieval church and **parish village** (see p.342) in nearby **Gammelstad** (Old Town) at its centre. Even in those days trade with Stockholm was important, and ships loaded and unloaded their goods in the Old Town's tiny harbour; but as business expanded the harbour proved too small, and the settlement was moved to its present site by royal command in 1649 – only

The telephone code for Luleå is ☎0920.

the church and parish village remained. Until the end of the eighteenth century, Luleå was still little more than a handful of houses and storage houses. Sweden's famous botanist, Linnaeus, passed through in 1732 on his Lapland journey and drank water from the spa in Gammelstad, and he described Luleå as a village, albeit a beautiful one. In the nineteenth century, the town became a shipbuilding centre. However, it wasn't until the construction of the rail line that Luleå's fortunes really started to flourish – its port was vital for lucrative iron exports (the main ironfields were around Kiruna and Malmberget). Today the city's population stands at around 45,000 and, although shipping is still important, over recent years Luleå has become *the* hi-tech centre of the north, specializing in metallurgy, and with an important university.

# Arrival, information and accommodation

The **train** and **bus stations** are at one end of the string of parallel streets that make up the centre, and it takes about five minutes to walk between the two. The **tourist office** is a good ten-minute walk away in the *Kulturcentrum Ebeneser* at Storgatan 43B (mid-June to mid-Aug Mon–Fri 9am–7pm, Sat & Sun 10am–4pm; rest of the year Mon–Fri 10am–7pm, Sat 10am–4pm; ☎29 35 00). Ask about the **free army bikes** on offer in Luleå; painted red, white and blue, the bikes are unlocked, and the idea is that you just take one and leave it wherever you choose. It also has information about Luleå's **midsummer carnival**, *Sjöslaget*, a week of music, dancing and street theatre centred around the open-air pavilion in Storgatan.

The tourist office can fix up **private rooms** for about 200kr per person, but there are only around ten of them, and they can only be booked in person. The **youth hostel** (open all year; ☎523 25, fax 524 19; 100kr) is out at **GÄDDVIK** (Pike Bay), and unfortunately suffers from being close to the main E4 – the drone of heavy lorries penetrates the thin walls of the tiny cabins all through the night. To get there, take hourly bus #6 from right outside the main door of the train station (journey time 10–15min) and tell the bus driver where you want to go; get off at the stop, just after the bridge over the Lule river, and take the riverside footpath. Once you have passed under the motorway bridge, cut up to the right through the trees to the red buildings of the hostel. After 8.30pm, buses to and from the hostel have to be booked at least thirty minutes before departure (☎23 55 97); pick up a timetable at the tourist office. The nearest **campsite** (☎500 60) is another five minutes on from the youth hostel and can also be reached on bus #6.

## Hotels

**Amber**, Stationsgatan 67 (☎102 00). A small and cosy family-run place, with summer doubles at the lower end of the range. ④/②

**Arctic**, Sandviksgatan 80 (☎109 80). A smart little hotel with en-suite rooms and very handy for the train station. ⑤/③

**Aveny**, Hermelinsgatan 10 (☎22 18 20). Another small and comfortable hotel, with reasonable prices in summer. ④/②

**Luleå Stads**, Storgatan 15 (☎670 00). The oldest and smartest of the city's hotels, with tasteful old-fashioned style rooms and right in the centre of town. The reduced price is for weekends only. ⑤/④

**Park**, Kungsgatan 10 (☎211 49). The cheapest of Luleå's hotels; basic but perfectly fine. Shower and toilet in the corridor. ①

**SAS Luleå**, Storgatan 17 (☎940 00). A modern hotel with heavy colours and gloomy wooden interiors. Closed at weekends in winter. ⑤/③

## The City

There's really only one main street, the long **Storgatan**, to the south of which by the main square, Rådhustorget, is the **Domkyrkan**. The medieval version disappeared centuries ago, and the latest model, built in 1893 and standing on the same spot, is a modern barrage of copper chandeliers hanging like Christmas decorations. Walking west up Köpmangatan you'll find **Norrbottens Museum** (June to mid-Aug Mon–Fri 10am–7pm, Sat & Sun noon–7pm; mid-Aug to May Mon 1–5pm, Tues–Fri 9am–4pm, Sat & Sun noon–4pm; free) at Storgatan 2, which, although it contains the usual rather dull resumé of county history, is worth a look for the good displays and exhibitions on the *Sami* life and culture that begins to predominate northwest of Luleå (see the following chapter). There's also a pleasant **café** in the museum. Just south of the Domkyrkan, **Konstens Hus** at

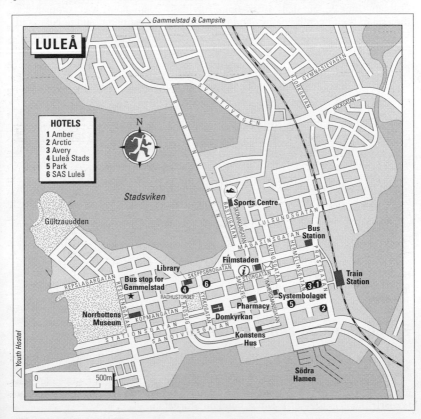

Smedjegatan 2 (Tues & Thurs–Fri 11am–6pm, Wed 11am–8pm, Sat & Sun noon–4pm; free) is worth a look, with interesting displays of work from local and not-so-local artists and sculptors. If the weather's good, the next stop should be the oddly named **Gültzauudden**, a wooden promontory that has a great beach; it was named after the German shipbuilder, Christian Gültzau, who helped to make Luleå a shipbuilding centre. On warm days, you'll find the rest of Luleå here. If you would like more space to stretch out, take the *M/S Stella Marina* out to the island of **Klubbviken**, where there's an enormous sandy beach. This is the prettiest of the score of tiny islets that lie in the **archipelago** offshore – for more on boat trips to the archipelago, see p.344.

## Gammelstad

The original settlement of Luleå, **GAMMELSTAD**, is 10km northwest of the current city centre. When the town moved to the coast a handful of the more religious stayed behind to tend the church, and the attached **parish village** remained in use. One of the most important places of historical interest north of Uppsala, the site is due to be added to the UNESCO World Heritage List. The **church** (June & Aug daily 10am–6pm; July daily 10am–8pm) was completed at the end of the fifteenth century and is one of the largest of its kind in Norrland. Church artists from far and wide worked on the building, and on the outside are decorative brick and plaster gables and an opening above the south door through which boiling oil was generously poured over unwelcome visitors. The high altar was made in Antwerp and is adorned with finely carved biblical scenes; the decorated choir stalls and ornate triptych are other medieval originals. Have a close look at the sumptuous 1712 pulpit, too, a splendid example of Baroque extravagance, its intricacies trimmed with gilt cherubs and red and gold bunches of grapes. Around 450 **church cottages** are gathered around, making it the biggest parish village in Sweden; they're still used today in much the same way as in days gone by, though now they're only occupied during important religious festivals.

The **tourist office** (mid-June to mid-Aug daily 9am–6pm; ☎543 10) is in one of the cottages and organizes guided walks around the village. Down the hill from the tourist office is **Friluftsmuseet Hägnan** (June to early Aug daily 11am–5pm; rest of August & early Sept Sat & Sun noon–4pm), an **open-air heritage park**, whose main exhibits are two old farmstead buildings from the eighteenth century. During summer, there are displays of rural skills such as sheep-rearing, the making of traditional wooden roof slates and the baking of northern Sweden's unleavened bread, *tunnbröd*. Gammelstad is readily reached by **bus** from Luleå: bus #8 and #9 every half-hour weekdays, #32 at weekends and weekday evenings, from Hermelinsparken, at the west end of Skeppsbrogatan; the last one back is at 10pm (30min).

## Eating, drinking and entertainment

The most lively and interesting **places to eat** are all found along Storgatan; prices are a little higher here, but there is generally a better atmosphere than in the quieter places on the sidestreets where, though cheaper, you might find you are eating alone. **Drinking** is also done at all the main restaurants listed opposite, particularly those in the *Luleå Stads* hotel on Storgatan.

Although summer can be busy, Luleå is culturally more lively in the winter when the students are around; try the small **theatre**, *Lillian*, behind the library for music concerts and its fine café. But the best bet all year round is the *Kulturcentrum Ebeneser*, upstairs from the tourist office in Storgatan; this is the biggest concert hall in Luleå and is where music recitals and theatre productions are held (information about events from the tourist office); there's also another good café downstairs. There are two **cinemas** in town: *Filmstaden* at Timmermansgatan 19 (☎109 20) and *Sandrews* at Nygatan 1 (☎21 10 15). **Clubbing** is done at the *Cleo Nightclub*, Storgatan 17, while live bands and discos happen at the *Lueå Stads* hotel on Storgatan.

## Restaurants and bars

**Ankaret**, Köpmangatan 16, near the Domkyrkan. Good fish dishes for around 100kr, but fairly quiet.

**Bryggan**, inside *Stads Hotell* at Storgatan 15. Reindeer and other northern Swedish food is the speciality – it's expensive, though: main courses are upwards of 150kr.

**Cook's Krog**, inside *SAS Luleå Hotel* at Storgatan 17. The best place for steak in Luleå – at around 150kr.

**Fiskekyrkan**, in Södra Hamnen. One of the cheaper restaurants in town, with pasta and other simple dishes for below 100kr. Popular with all ages. In summer, the bar with outdoor tables looks out onto the harbour side and is always busy.

**Pasta Restaurangen**, tucked away in a side street at Magasinsgatan 5. Hefty pizzas from around 60kr but reckon on the place being pretty empty.

**Pimpinella**, Storgatan 40. This is the liveliest and trendiest bar in town with tables out in the street during summer catering to a young crowd.

**Restaurang Corsica**, Nygatan. Good for a change, with traditional Corsican dishes. Entrecote for 89kr.

**Tallkotten**, inside the *Luleå Stads* hotel at Storgatan 15. Trendy place decked out in blue and yellow, serving everything you could imagine, including ostrich, but specializing in northern Swedish dishes. Count on between 100–150kr; lunch for 60kr.

**Waldorf**, inside the Wasa City shopping centre at Storgatan 33. Renowned for its pizzas, also Chinese and Japanese food. Pizzas from 60kr upwards, more substantial dishes over 100kr.

**WillGott**, Storgatan 11. Lunch buffet, also pasta for 70kr and meat and fish dishes for 120kr – trendy and smart.

**Ängeln**, corner of Nygatan & Storgatan. Simple place with pizza and pasta for under 100kr.

# Listings

**Airlines** *SAS* in the bus station on Storgatan; open Mon–Fri 9am–6pm, Sat 10am–2pm (☎24 31 00). For *Aeroflot* contact the airport.

**Airport** Kallax airport (☎24 30 08), 10km from the city; buses from the bus station. Direct flights to Kiruna, Stockholm, Sundsvall, Umeå, Östersund with *Skyways* and *SAS*; also direct to Rovaniemi in Finland, Murmansk and Arkhangelsk in Russia with *Aeroflot*.

**Banks** *Handelsbanken*, Storgatan, between the *Luleå Stads* hotel and tourist office; *Nordbanken*, Köpmangatan near the pharmacy.

**Bus station** Kvarteret Loet (☎890 85).

**Car rental** *Avis*, Kallax airport (☎22 83 55); *Biluthyrning i Luleå*, Varvsgatan 35 (☎121 87); *Budget*, Robertviksgatan 3 (☎131 11); *Dahlgrens Biluthyrning*, Sandviksgatan 72B (☎21 10 30); *Hertz*, Gammelstadsvägen 23 (☎22 56 00 or 22 56 10); *Europcar*, Kallax airport (☎101 65);*Luleå minibuss*, Trossvägen 5 (☎22 55 00); *Englunds Hyrcenter*, Hummergatan 8 (☎22 68 18).

## THE ARCHIPELAGO

The **archipelago** off the coast is made up of hundreds of tiny islands, most of which are uninhabited and unexploited. Several of the islands are accessible by **boat services** from Luleå, leaving the southern harbour (Södra Hamen). The main services are as follows:

- *M/S Favourite* goes to **Uddskär, Hindersön, Rödkallen, Altappen, Junkön, Smäskär** and **Kluntarna**. Departures vary from day to day; latest information from the tourist office.

- *M/S Laponia* makes trips out to **Småskär, Altappen** and **Brändöskär**; more information on ☎120 84 or mobile ☎070/530 33 44.

- *M/S Stella Marina* day-trips (June–Aug) out to the island of **Klubbviken**, renowned for its fantastic sandy beaches; information on mobile ☎010/225 07 61.

Two of the most popular islands are **Uddskär,** with its art gallery and church, and **Rödkallen,** with its important lighthouse. In the outer archipelago, Rödkallen offers fantastic sea and sky views. There are also a few island **cabins** on Klubbviken, which you can book at the tourist office; reckon on 450kr for four people per night.

**Gay Luleå** Information by post from Box 95, 971 04 Luleå (☎22 61 66); gay switchboard Sun 7–10pm (☎170 55).

**Hospital** Luleå Lasarett, Repslagaregatan 6–8 (☎710 00).

**Pharmacy** Köpmangatan 36c; open Mon–Fri 9am–6pm, Sat 9am–2pm, Sun 1–4pm (☎22 03 95).

**Police** Skeppsbrogatan 37 (☎29 50 00).

**Post office** Storgatan 53 (☎840 00).

**Swimming pool** *Pontusbadet*, Bastugatan 6–8 (☎29 32 72).

**Systembolaget** Köpmangatan; open Mon–Wed & Fri 9.30am–6pm, Thurs 9.30am–7pm.

**Taxi** *Taxi Luleå* (☎100 00); *6:ans Taxi* (☎666 66).

**Travel agent** *Ticket*, open Mon–Fri 9am–6pm, Sat 10am–1pm.

# Boden

Twenty-five minutes down the train line from Luleå, **BODEN** is a major transport junction for the entire north of the country; from here trains run northwest to Gällivare and Kiruna and eventually onto Narvik in Norway and south to Stockholm and Gothenburg. The branch line east to Haparanda (and on to Tornio in Finland, which once provided Sweden's only direct rail link with its eastern neighbour) has suffered the same fate as other branch lines in the north. Falling passenger numbers and increasing costs during the 1980s resulted in *SJ* pulling the plug. Travellers heading for Haparanda can now only make the journey by bus (*InterRail* cards valid). Boden's strategic position means that its tiny train station is often full of backpackers in summer; if you've got time to kill, venture outside – the town is a pleasant surprise.

Boden is roughly halfway along the coast of Norrbotten at the narrowest bridging point along the Lule river, which incidentally produces one-eighth of Sweden's electricity. Today it is Sweden's largest military town, and everywhere you look you'll see young men kitted out in camouflage gear and badly fitting black boots strutting purposefully (if somewhat ridiculously) up and down the streets; there are infantry, tank, artillery and air corps here. At the turn of the century, with the railway opening up the north, it was deemed necessary to defend the area against invasion. The first garrison was established in 1901 and a fortress was constructed by 1907. The army soon needed a hospital, and the one built in 1910 grew to be one of the biggest in the northern Sweden – but is soon to be replaced by a new hospital being built between Boden and Luleå. About 3km southeast of the centre and a forty-minute walk from the train station is the fort, **Svedjefortet** (June–Aug daily 11am–7pm; 10kr), which sits atop a hill offering good views of the town. Blasted out of the hill is an underground fortress, where you can view the old canons from 1894 and 1917 as well as a selection of military uniforms. For more military attire through the ages, head for the **Garnisonsmuseum** or Garrison Museum (June–Aug daily 11am–4pm; 10k), at the southwestern edge of town; it houses the largest collection of uniforms north of Stockholm.

Closer to the centre, **Överluleå kyrka** (mid-June to end June & early Aug daily except Sat 1–5pm; July daily except Sat 1–7pm) and its **parish village** were founded in 1826. The church is a twenty-minute walk from the train station, down the modest main street, **Kungsgatan**, over the bridge and right along Strandplan. Pleasant enough in itself, the church benefits considerably from its location: perched on a hillock, surrounded by whispering birch trees and overlooking the water. The surrounding cottages and stable of the parish village once spread down the hill to the lake, Bodträsket, lining narrow little alleyways. The cottages are rented out as superior **hostel accommodation** during the summer (see below for details).

## Practicalities

The summer-time **tourist office** is at the train station (June & Aug daily 9am–6pm; July daily 9am–9pm; ☎0921/624 10); the main office is at Färgaregatan 5, which is open the rest of the year (Mon–Fri 8am–5pm; ☎0921/623 14). You can rent the **parish cottages**, although these usually book up months in advance, so it's always worth checking availability (☎0921/198 70). The cottages cost around 345kr for two per night in July (265kr in June and Aug), and 390kr for three or four people in July (315kr in June and Aug). The cheap and cheerful *Hotell Standard* at Stationsgatan 5, right outside the train station (☎0921/160 55, fax 175 58; ①, in summer 395kr for a double), is handy for early departures; the **hotel** also offers dormitory beds for 90kr per person if you're between 15 and 35, and is in effect Boden's youth hostel. For more comfort and style, there's *Hotell Bodensia* in the centre of town at Kungsgatan 47 (☎0921/177 10, fax 192 82; ④/②). The **campsite** (☎0921/624 07) is a few minutes' walk from the church following the path along the lake side; here you can also **rent canoes** cheaply (30kr an hour, 150kr a day) and **bikes** (50kr a day) for a paddle or cycle round the woods and gardens of the town.

**Eating** in Boden is plain and simple; there are very few restaurants in town, but the best of the bunch is *Panelen* at the station end of Kungsgatan. It's an old wooden building with wood panelled walls inside and fake cacti; orders are taken at the counter, and meat dishes start at 75kr. For pizza, head for *San Marino* at Garnisonsgatan 41, where they cost 50–60kr and pasta 70–80kr, or *Restaurang Romeo* in the pedestrianized centre, with similar prices. Your best bet for a good lunch is *Café Ollé* at Drottninggatan 4 (opposite *Restaurang Romeo*), where the *Dagens Rätt* goes for 50kr; this place is also good for open sandwiches. Chinese food can be had from *Ming Palace* in the square on Drottninggatan, with lunch and pizzas for 55kr; other Chinese dishes go for 80–90kr. As for **drinking**, *Olivers Inn* just before Kungsbron bridge on Kungsgatan is decent enough, but beer is a hefty 49kr; you're better off visiting the *Systembolaget* at Drottninggatan 8 (Mon–Wed & Fri 9.30am–6pm, Thurs 9.30am–7pm), where a bottle of beers costs just 17kr – though watch out for the local drunks, who hang out outside the shop shouting and leering at passers-by.

# Haparanda and around

Right by the Finnish border and at the very north of the Gulf of Bothnia, **HAPARANDA** is hard to like. Trains no longer run up here (nearest stations are Boden in Sweden and Kemi in Finland), but the defunct train station sets the scene – a grand-looking building that reflects Haparanda's aspirations to be a major trading centre after World War I. That never happened, and walking up and down the streets around Torget is a pretty depressing experience. The destination signpost near the bus station reinforces the fact that you're a very long way from anywhere: Stockholm 1100km, the North Cape 800km and Timbuktu 8386km.

The key to Haparanda's grimness is the neighbouring Finnish town of Tornio (Torneå in Swedish). From 1105 until 1809 Finland was part of Sweden and Tornio was an important trading centre, serving markets across northern Scandinavia. But things began to unravel when Russia attacked and occupied Finland in 1807; the Treaty of Hamina followed, forcing Sweden to cede Finland to Russia in 1809 – thereby losing Tornio. It was decided that Tornio had to be replaced and so in 1821 the trading centre of Haparanda was founded – on the Swedish side of the new border, which ran along the River Torne. However, the new town was more than an upstart compared to its neighbour across the water. And so the situation remained – until recently. With both Sweden and Finland now members of the European Union, Haparanda and **Tornio** have declared themselves a **Eurocity** – one city made up of two towns from different countries. The inhabitants of Haparanda and Tornio are bilingual and both currencies change hands in both towns; roughly half of the children in Haparanda have either a Finnish mother or father. Services are also shared between the two; everything from central heating to post delivery is centrally coordinated. If a fire breaks out in Tornio, for example, Swedish fire crews from Haparanda will cross the border to help put out the flames. A regional council, the Provincia Bothiensis (a neutral name – neither Swedish nor Finnish) was set up to help cooperation.

There are only two real sights in town: the train station building, which was built in 1918 and was Sweden's only link eastwards, with two track widths (Finnish trains run on the wider Russian gauge), and the peculiar copper-coloured **Haparanda kyrka**, a monstrous modern construction that looks like a cross between an aircraft hangar and an apartment building. When the church was finished in 1963, it caused a public scandal and even won the prize for being the ugliest church in Sweden.

## Practicalities

There are no border formalities and you can simply walk over the bridge to Finland and wander back whenever you like. It used to be the case that Tornio was much cheaper than Haparanda, but prices are now roughly the same, although drinking is a little less expensive in Finland. It's worth remembering that Finnish time is one hour ahead of Swedish time and that Haparanda and Tornio have different names in Swedish (Haparanda and Torneå) and Finnish (Haaparanta and Tornio).

The **tourist office** (June–Aug Mon–Fri 9am–8pm, Sat & Sun 10am–2pm; rest of the year Mon–Fri 9.30am–5pm; ☎0922/615 85) can be found in the bus station off Norra Esplanaden, near the bridge to Finland. The nearby **youth hostel** (open all year; ☎0922/611 71; 100kr) is a smart riverside place at Strandgatan 26 and has the cheapest beds in town, with good views across to Finland. Alternatively, the cheap and cheerful pension, *Resandehem*, in the centre of town at Storgatan 65B (☎0922/120 68), charges per person per night: 150kr for one, 250kr for two, 300kr for three. *Haparanda Stadshotel* is the only **hotel** in town, at Torget 7 (☎0922/614 90, fax 102 23; ④/②). The **campsite**, *Sundholmens Camping* (☎0922/618 01 or 100 03) is at the opposite end of town from the youth hostel at Järnvägsgatan 1 – walk along the river down Strandgatan, take a right onto Storgatan, cross the train lines and follow the signs. There are four-bed cabins here, too, for 270kr per day.

As far as eating, drinking and nightlife go you're better off in Tornio in every respect. Do what the Swedish locals do at the weekends and head over the river. Friday nights are wild, the streets full of people trying to negotiate the return leg over the bridge – meanwhile, Haparanda sleeps undisturbed. For **eating** without trekking over to Finland your cheapest and best option is the lunch served at the *Stadshotel* in the main square – a help-yourself deal for 59kr. The *Dagens Rätt* is also available from the restaurant at the youth hostel and from the plastic-looking *Prix* restaurant at the bus station. Pizzas from 38kr and a beer from 25kr can be had from *El Paso Pizzeria* on Storgatan close to Torget. Pizzas are also served at the Chinese restaurant, *Lei-Lane* at Köpmangatan 15 (lunch 10am–3pm), as well as a range of Chinese dishes. *Nya Konditoriet* on Storgatan is good for coffee and cakes, and for open sandwiches try *Café Rosa* in the Gallerian shopping centre on Storgatan – baguettes for 16–28kr depending on filling. For **drinking** in Haparanda head for the pub *Ponderosa* at Storgatan 82; Happy Hour (8–9pm) takes the price of a beer down to 20kr, or alternatively, try the *Gulasch Baronen* pub attached to the *Stadshotel*, which serves strong beer from noon to 9pm for 29kr, after 9pm for 35kr.

# Around Haparanda

Haparanda is a handy base for several side trips. Twenty-four kilometres south-west of town you'll find the island of **Seskarö**, a beachy refuge for windsurfers and swimmers. There's a **campsite** here (☎0922/201 50), with cabins available, as well as cycle and boat rental; there are three buses a day from town to Seskarö. South of Seskarö, the Haparanda archipelago begins and extends into the Baltic's northernmost arm; the two main islands, **Seskar-Furö** and the larger **Sandskär**, were declared a national park in 1995 and contain important fauna and flora, including the razorbill and little tern as well as the lesser butterfly orchid. There are no regular boat trips to the islands, but the best landing place for private boats is Kumpula harbour at the southern edge of Sandskär.

North of town, 15km away, the impressive rapids at **KUKKOLAFORSEN** are best seen during the *Sikfesten*, Whitefish Festival, held on the last weekend in July. The whitefish, a local delicacy grilled on large open fires, are caught in nets at the end of long poles, fishermen dredging the fast, white water and scooping the whitefish out onto the bank. The festival celebrates a sort of fisherman's harvest, centuries old, although it's now largely an excuse to get plastered with a beer tent, evening gigs and dancing the order of the day. It costs 100kr to get in on the Saturday, 60kr on the Sunday, although if you're staying in the adjacent **campsite** (☎0922/310 00), which also has cabins for 270kr per night, you should be able to sneak in for free. At other times check out the local **Fiskemuseum** (mid-June to mid-Aug daily 10am–6pm; free), which gives accounts of local fishing activities; there's also a freshwater aquarium, a working nineteenth-century mill and enormous salmon.

The Swedish Sauna Academy has declared the **sauna** at Kukkolaforsen the country's finest; after making use of the sauna, you can step out onto the veranda with a cool beer, breathe the crisp air heavy with the scent of pine, and, looking across the river to Finland, listen to the roar of the rapids. If you'd like to get out onto the water, **river rafting** down the rapids can be arranged through the tourist office in Haparanda or at the campsite at Kukkolaforsen – 180kr rents the gear, helmet and life jacket specifically, and pays for a short trip down river plus a certificate at the end.

## Moving on from Haparanda: bus routes

**Swedish buses** head north on the Swedish side of the border through the beautiful Torne valley to Pajala (Mon–Fri 3 daily, 1 bus on Sun), from where connections can be made to either Gällivare or Kiruna or by changing at Vittangi to Karesuando. Alternatively, if you are continuing your trip into Finland, Finnish-operated buses connect Haparanda with Tornio and Kemi roughly every hour. Times are posted up at the bus station in Haparanda. There's also a once-daily direct afternoon bus from Haparanda to Rovaniemi (journey time 3hr).

## travel details

### Trains

**From Boden** to Gothenburg (1 daily; 17hr 30min); Gällivare (3 daily; 2hr); Gävle (2 daily; 12hr 30min); Kiruna (3 daily; 3hr); Luleå (5 daily; 25min); Narvik (2 daily; 6hr 30min); Stockholm (2 daily; 14hr); Uppsala (2 daily; 13hr).

**From Gävle** to Boden (2 daily; 12hr 30min); Gällivare (2 daily; 14hr); Falun (5 daily; 1hr); Hudiksvall (8 daily; 1hr 30min); Härnösand (3 daily; 3hr 30min); Kiruna (2 daily; 15hr 30min); Luleå (2 daily; 12hr); Stockholm (hourly; 2hr); Sundsvall (8 daily; 2hr 30min); Söderhamn (8 daily; 50min); Umeå (1 daily; 9hr); Uppsala (hourly; 1hr); Örebro (6 daily; 3hr); Östersund (4 daily; 4hr).

**From Hudiksvall** to Gävle (8 daily; 1hr 30min); Härnösand (3 daily; 2hr); Stockholm (8 daily;

3hr 20min); Sundsvall (9 daily; 1hr); Uppsala (8 daily; 2hr 40min).

**From Härnösand** to Långsele (4 daily; 2hr); Sollefteå (5 daily; 1hr 40min); Stockholm (3 daily; 6hr); Sundsvall (8 daily; 1hr).

**From Luleå** to Boden (5 daily; 25min); Gothenburg (1 daily; 18hr); Gällivare (3 daily; 3hr); Kiruna (3 daily; 4hr); Narvik (2 daily; 7hr); Stockholm (2 daily; 14hr 30min); Uppsala (2 daily; 13hr 30min).

**From Sundsvall** to Gävle (8 daily; 2hr 30min); Hudiksvall (9 daily; 1hr); Härnösand (8 daily; 1hr); Långsele (3 daily; 2hr); Stockholm (7 daily; 5hr); Söderhamn (9 daily; 1hr 45min); Östersund (6 daily; 4hr 15min).

**From Söderhamn** to Gävle (8 daily; 50min); Hudiksvall (9 daily; 40min); Härnösand (3 daily;

2hr 45min); Stockholm (8 daily; 2hr 40min);
Sundsvall (9 daily; 1hr 45min); Uppsala (8
daily; 2hr).

**From Umeå** to Boden (1 daily; 5hr);
Gothenburg (1 daily; 14hr); Gällivare (1 daily;
8hr); Gävle (1 daily; 9hr); Kiruna (1 daily; 9hr);
Luleå (1 daily; 5hr 40min); Stockholm (1 daily;
11hr); Uppsala (1 daily; 10hr).

## Buses

**The E4 express buses**: Following the withdrawal of branch-line rail services to the
coastal towns north of Sundsvall (except
Umeå), the *E4-bus* runs four times daily
between Sundsvall and Luleå, generally connecting with trains to and from Sundsvall. The
buses are reliable and all have toilet facilities
onboard. Buy your tickets from the bus driver
before boarding. From Sundsvall, the buses
call at Härnösand (45min); Lunde (for connections to the High Coast; 1hr 35min); Ullånger
(1hr 55min); Örnosköldsvik (2hr 40min);
Skellefteå (6hr 30min); Piteå (7hr 45min) and
Luleå (8hr 45min).

**Other important routes**: Services run from
the coast into central northern Sweden, often
linking up with the *Inlandsbanan*. There's also
one service from Umeå to Mo-i-Rana in
Norway. For buses from Härnösand and Örnsköldsvik to the High Coast see p.320.

**Services to and from Stockholm**: The only
long-distance up the Bothnian coast is #887,
which is operated by *Swebus Express* – it only
runs as far as Bollnäs and Edsbyn, calling at
Gävle and Uppsala en route. For information

call *Swebus* on ☎020/640 640 or from abroad
on ☎08/655 00 90.

**From Boden** to Haparanda (6 daily; 2hr
15min); Luleå (6 daily; 30min).

**From Haparanda** to Boden (6 daily; 2hr
20min); Luleå (9 daily; 2hr 30min); Pajala (4
daily; 3hr 30min).

**From Luleå** to Boden (6 daily; 30min);
Gällivare (2 daily; 3hr 30min); Haparanda (9
daily; 2hr 30min); Jokkmokk (3 daily; 3hr);
Kiruna (2 daily; 5hr); Pajala (2 daily; 3hr 30min).

**From Skellefteå** to Arvidsjaur (2 daily; 2hr);
Bastuträsk (for main-line train connections; 5
daily; 1hr); Jörn (for main-line train connections; 2 daily; 1 hr).

**From Piteå** to Älvsbyn (for main-line train
connections; 6 daily; 1hr).

**From Umeå** to Dorotea (2 daily; 3hr 15min);
Mo-i-Rana (Norway; 1 daily; 8hr); Storuman (3
daily; 3hr 40min); Strömsund (2 daily; 4hr
30min); Tärnaby (3 daily; 5hr 30min); Vännäs (for
main-line train connections; 22 daily; 30min).

**From Örnsköldsvik** to Åsele (for connections
to Dorotea and Vilhelmina; 1 daily; 3hr);
Mellansel (for main-line train connections; 11
daily; 40min).

## Ferries to Finland

**From Skellefteå** to Pietarsaari (Jakobstad in
Swedish). Future of sailings uncertain. Check
with *Silja Line* on ☎090/14 21 00.

**From Umeå** to Vaasa (mid-June to mid-Aug
3–4 daily; rest of the year 1–2 daily; 3hr
30min).

# CHAPTER SIX

# CENTRAL AND NORTHERN SWEDEN

I n many ways the long wedge of land that comprises **central and northern Sweden** – from the shores of **Lake Vänern** up to the Finnish border north of the **Arctic Circle** – encompasses all that is most typical of the country. This vast area of land is really one great forest broken only by the odd village or town. Rural and underpopulated, this is the image most people have of Sweden: lakes, pine forests, wooden cabins and reindeer – and the image is true enough. Swedes across the country lived like this until just one or two generations ago and took their cue from the people of these central lands and forest, who were the first to rise against the Danes in the sixteenth century and who shared their land, uneasily, with the *Sami*, earliest settlers of the wild lands in the far north of the country.

Folklorish **Dalarna** county is the most intensely picturesque region. Even a quick tour around one or two of the more accessible places gives an impression of the whole: red cottages with white door and window frames, sweeping green countryside, summer festivals and water bluer than blue. Dalarna's inhabitants maintain a cultural heritage (echoed in contemporary handicrafts and traditions) that goes back to the Middle Ages. And Dalarna is *the* place to spend Midsummer, particularly Midsummer's Eve, when the whole region erupts in a frenzy of celebration.

The privately owned **Inlandsbanan**, the great Inland Railway, cuts right through central and northern Sweden and links virtually all the towns and villages covered in this chapter. Running from **Mora** to **Gällivare**, above the Arctic Circle, it ranks with the best European train journeys, an enthralling 1100km in two days. There are buses connecting the rail line with the **mountain villages** that lie alongside the Norwegian border, where the surrounding Swedish *fjäll*, or fells, offer some spectacular and unspoilt hiking. Marking the halfway point, **Östersund**, the only town of any size, is situated by the side of the Great Lake, which is reputed to be home to Sweden's own Loch Ness monster. From here trains head in all directions: west to Norway through the country's premier ski resort, **Åre**, south to Dalarna and Stockholm, east to Sundsvall on the Bothnian coast and north into Lapland.

**Lapland** is the heartland of the **Sami**, and this wild terrain makes for the most fascinating trip in northern Sweden. The omnipresent reindeer are a constant reminder of how far north you are, but the enduring *Sami* culture, which once defined much of this land, is now under threat. The problems posed by tourism are escalating, principally the erosion of grazing land under the pounding feet of hikers, making the *Sami* increasingly economically dependent on

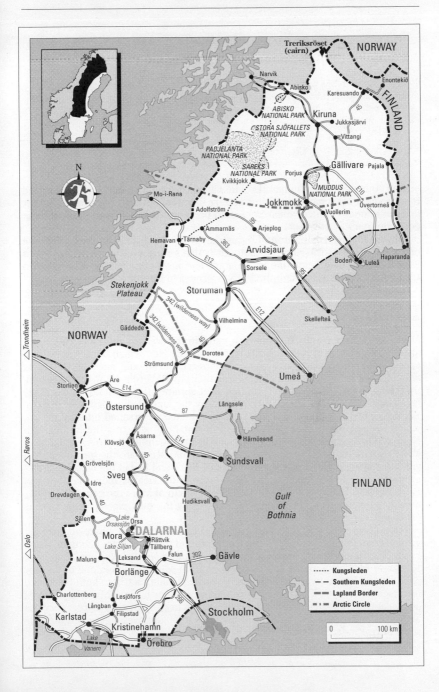

---

**ACCOMMODATION PRICES**

The pensions and hotels listed in the guide have been price-graded according to the scale outlined below; the number indicates the price for the least expensive double room. Many hotels offer considerable reductions at weekends (year round) and during the summer holiday period (mid-June to mid-Aug); in these cases the reduction is either noted in the text or, where it falls into another price band, given after the full price. Single rooms, where available, usually cost between 60 and 80 percent of a double.

① under 500kr    ② 500–700kr    ③ 700–900kr    ④ 900–1200kr    ⑤ over 1200kr

---

selling souvenirs and handicrafts. The Chernobyl nuclear accident in 1986 led to a fundamental change in living patterns; the fallout affected grazing lands, and even today reindeer meat in certain parts of the north is unfit for human consumption.

Moving further north, around industrial **Gällivare** (where the *Inlandsbanan* ends) and **Kiruna**, the rugged – potentially dangerous – **national parks** offer a chance to hike and commune with nature like nowhere else: the **Kungsleden trail** runs for 500km through the last wilderness in Europe.

# Dalarna

Dalarna is a large county that not only takes in the area around **Lake Siljan** but also the ski resorts of **Sälen** and **Idre** close to the Norwegian border. It holds a special misty-eyed place in the Swedish heart and should certainly be seen, although not to the exclusion of places further north. Verdant cow pastures, gentle rolling meadows sweet with the smell of summer flowers and tiny rural villages make up most of the county, backed by the land to the northwest of Lake Siljan (created millions of years ago when a meteorite crashed into the earth), which rises slowly to meet the chain of mountains that forms the border with Norway. One small lakeside town can look pretty much like another, so if time is short restrict yourself to one or two: **Leksand** and **Mora** are the best options. If you are staying in the area for a few days or more and tire of the lakeside area's predominantly folksy image and tourist crowds, the nearby industrial towns of **Borlänge** and **Falun** can provide light relief. North of Mora the county becomes more mountainous and less populous, and really the only place of note here is **Orsa** and its fascinating **bear park**.

**Trains** operated by *SJ* (the state company) call at Borlänge, where you can get a connection to Falun, and at all the towns around the lake, terminating in Mora. From Mora the privately owned and operated *Inlandsbanan* takes over, but Orsa, Sälen and Idre can only be reached by bus from Mora, which is one of the key points in the **bus** network in Dalarna. If you're planning a trip to both Sälen and Idre (see p.362), you'll be forced to retrace your steps back to Mora to get from one village to the other, adding about five hours to your journey. Direct services between the two villages were withdrawn due to falling passengers and the consequent rise in fares. Paradoxically, in summer when Dalarna is inundated with visitors, the bus system virtually shuts down; some places, like Idre and Sälen, are down to one bus a day. So if you want to leave the train line and strike out into the mountains, it's worth picking up a timetable from the tourist office and organiz-ing your route before you go – otherwise you could find yourself stranded with a very long wait. Alternatively, a good way to get about, especially around Lake Siljan, is to rent a **bike** from one of the tourist offices; there's no need to worry about **accommodation**; there are countless hotels, hostels and campsites around, generally catering for Swedish holidaymakers – the main ones are detailed in the text.

# Around Lake Siljan

Things have changed since Baedeker, writing in 1889, observed that "Lake Siljan owes much of its interest to the inhabitants of its banks, who have preserved many of their primitive characteristics.... In their idea of cleanliness they are somewhat behind the age." Today it's not the people who captivate but the scenery: **Lake Siljan** is what many people come to Sweden for, its gentle sur-roundings, traditions and local handicrafts weaving a subtle spell. There's a lush feel to much of the region, the vegetation enriched by the lake, which adds a pleasing dimension to what are essentially small, low-profile towns and villages. Only Mora stands out as being bigger and busier, with the hustle and bustle of holidaymakers and countless caravans in summer.

## Mora

If you've only got time to see part of the lake, then **MORA** (pronounced "Moo-ra") is as good a place as any to head for, and it's handy for onward trains on the *Inlandsbanan* (see overleaf) and for moving on to the ski resorts of Idre and Sälen (see p.362). At the northwestern corner of the lake, Mora's main draw is the work of artist **Anders Zorn** (1860–1920), who was most successful as a portrait painter, his subjects including American presidents Cleveland, Theodore Roosevelt and Taft. Sweden's best-known painter, he came to live in Mora in 1896, and his paint-ings are exhibited in the excellent **Zorn Museum** at Vasagatan 36 (Mon–Sat 9am–5pm, Sun 11am–5pm; 25kr) – look out for the self-portrait and the especial-ly pleasing *Midnatt* (Midnight) from 1891, which depicts a woman rowing on Lake Siljan, her hands blue from the cold night air. You might also want to wan-der across the lawn and take in his home, **Zorngården**, where he lived with his wife, Emma (Mon–Sat 10am–4pm, Sun 11am–4pm; 30kr). The other museum in town worth considering is the **Vasaloppsmuseet** (mid-Feb to end Sept; 30kr), also on Vasagatan but the other side of the church. The museum tells the history of the Vasaloppet (see p.363), a ski race that started years ago with the attempts of two Mora men to catch up with King Gustav Vasa, who was fleeing from the Danes on skis.

Once you've explored the museums, why not take one of the **cruises** on Lake Siljan on board the lovely old steamship *M/S Gustaf Wasa*; timetables vary from year to year, so check with the tourist office (see overleaf) or call for more infor-mation on the mobile numbers ☎010/252 32 92 or 204 77 24. Count on 120kr for a round trip to Leksand and back, which takes anything from two to five hours as cruise routes vary from day to day, or 80kr for a two-hour lunch cruise, including food, round a bit of the lake. Other trips out from town include the wonderful bear park near Orsa (see p.367) – take the bus (#118; 1hr).

## PRACTICALITIES

You should get off at the central Mora Strand **train station** (nothing more than a platform), rather than at the first station you come to, which is known simply as Mora – this is where the *Inlandsbanan* leaves from and where you'll find *SJ* train information, but it's a longer walk into town. The **tourist office** (mid-June to mid-Aug Mon–Fri 9am–8pm, Sat 10am–8pm, Sun 11am–8pm; rest of the year Mon–Fri 9am–5pm, Sat 10am–1pm; ☎0250/265 50), at Ångbåtskajen, down on the quayside and near Mora Strand station, has all the usual bumph, including a map of the *Vasaloppsleden* **hiking route**, which you can follow north from Mora to Sälen (also see p.363).

The **youth hostel** is at Fredsgatan 6 (open all year; ☎0250/381 96; 100kr), by the finishing line for the Vasaloppet. If you're coming straight here from the train, it's best to get off at Mora station (not Mora Strand), turn left and keep walking for about five minutes along the main Vasagatan. The biggest and best **hotel** is the *Mora Hotell* at Strandgatan 12 (☎0250/717 50, fax 189 81; ③/②) opposite Mora Strand station; choose either a modern or more old-fashioned room. *Hotell St Mikael* at Fridhemsgatan 15 (☎0250/159 00, fax 380 70; ②) is a small and sweet little place with tasteful rooms. Alternatively, *Hotell Kung Gösta* (☎0250/150 70, fax 170 78; ③/②), close to the main station, is handy for those early-morning departures on the *Inlandsbanan*; the hotel also has an annexe with prices about 100kr cheaper. If you're travelling with children your best bet is *Mora Parkens*

---

### INLANDSBANAN: PRACTICAL DETAILS

The *Inlandsbanan*, the great Inland Railway that links Dalarna with Lapland, is today a mere shadow of its former self. Spiralling costs and low passenger numbers forced *SJ* to sell the line, and the last state-run trains trundled down the single-line track in the autumn of 1992. Trains on the southern section between Mora and Kristinehamn had ceased running several years earlier, and part of the track has been dismantled. The railway was then sold to the fifteen municipalities that the route passes through, and the private company, *Inlandsbanan AB*, was launched. The line is now only operated as a tourist venture in summer – generally from mid-June to late August. Timetables are only approximate and the train will stop whenever the driver feels like it; maybe for a spot of wild strawberry picking or to watch a beaver damming a stream. Generally there are four-weekly trains from Mora at around 7pm (Tues, Wed, Fri & Sun), but this changes every year. In June and August the four stretches along the route (Mora–Östersund, Östersund–Vilhelmina, Vilhelmina–Arvidsjaur, Arvidsjaur– Gällivare) cost 150kr, 175kr in July. *InterRail* and *ScanRail* passes are not valid on the trains but do give 50-percent **discounts.** It's not possible to reserve seats in advance.

It's certainly a fascinating way to reach the far north of the country but not to be recommended if you're in a rush. Taken in one go the whole journey (1100km) lasts two days with an overnight stop in Östersund. Take it easy and make a couple of stops along the route and you'll get much more out of it (you can break your journey as many times as you like on one ticket). Special guides on the train are on hand with commentaries and information about places along the route. For **information** contact *Inlandståget AB*, Kyrkgatan 56, S-831 34 Östersund (☎063/12 76 95, fax 51 99 80) or call a free-phone information line (☎020/53 53 53). Starting at Mora, the first section of the *Inlandsbanan* route to Östersund is covered on p.353 and the second section, from Östersund north to Gällivare, on p.378. For a more detailed run-through of the route see "Travel details".

*Hotell* (☎0250/178 00, fax 185 83; ②) at Parkvägen 1, which is near the **campsite**, *Mora Camping* (☎0250/153 52). A ten-minute walk from the centre along Hantverkaregatan, which begins near the bus station, the campsite has a good beach and is near a small farm open for visits, as well as a lake for swimming.

In summer coffee and cakes can be enjoyed outside at two **cafés**, *Helmers Konditori* and *Mora Kaffestugan*, which are virtually next door to each other on the main shopping street, Kyrkogatan. For more substantial eating, all the hotels serve up a decent *Dagens Rätt* with little to choose between them. Of the **restaurants**, *Strandrestaurangen*, next to the tourist office on Strandgatan, serves any pizza you could imagine at cheap prices; while for bland Chinese *Dagens* or evening meals (three-dish set menu 129kr) try *China House* at the corner of Hamngatan and Moragatan near the church. The most popular place to eat is *Wasastugan*, a huge log building at Tingnäsvägen, between the main train station and the tourist office. Here you can have reasonably priced lunch and dinner (good meat and fish dishes from 80kr); at night, it's also a lively place to drink, with regular live music. It tends to attract a young crowd, especially to the discos. Although called a café, *Café Gabbis,* inside the *Mora Hotell* on Strandgatan, is in fact a **pub** and one of the liveliest places in the evening besides *Wasastugan*.

## Rättvik

At the eastern bulge of the lake, 37km from Mora, **RÄTTVIK** (pronounced "Rett-veck") is much smaller and quieter than Mora. In fact it's so small you hardly notice it's there – one tiny shopping street, a jetty out into the lake and an outdoor swimming pool and that's about the lot. The town may not have much in the way of sights but it does have plenty of wonderful countryside. Get out of the village as soon as you can and head up to the viewing point at **Vidablick** – it's about an hour's walk and quite a climb but the view is worth it; you can see virtually all of Lake Siljan, all the way to Mora, and the surrounding hillsides, covered in forests broken only by the odd farm – a truly idyllic rural scene. To get to the viewing point, walk along one of the marked trails through the forests above Rättvik: the tourist office (for details see below) can provide more information. The most appealing route is the well-signposted walk that begins at Bockgatan: head down the road towards the hotel at Lerdal, then follow signs for Tolvåsstugan by walking right along Märgatan and then right again up Werkmästargatan – take another right into the forest at the sign for Fäbodarstigen. Here there are a couple of information boards showing the different trails onwards from here – if you walk to Vidablick, there there's a small café and a shop to reward your efforts. The quickest way back down to Rättvik is to take the steep road down the hill (there are a couple of them so ask the staff in the shop to point it out for you), go left at the end onto Wallenkampfvägen and then right along Mårsåkervägen towards Lerdal again, all the time coming down the hill, and you'll see some of the most beautifully situated homes in Dalarna – all wood logs, flowers and views out over the lake.

## PRACTICALITIES

The **tourist office** is at the train station (mid-June to mid-Aug Mon–Fri 9am–8pm, Sat 10am–8pm, Sun 11am–8pm; rest of the year Mon–Fri 9am–5pm, Sat noon–4pm; ☎0248/702 00). The best place to stay in Rättvik is the **youth hostel** (open all year; ☎0248/105 66; 100kr) at Centralgatan (no number) – get to it along Domarbacksvägen, just 1km from the train station. The buildings have been constructed in the old Dalarna style and are made of large pine logs and surrounded

## THE DALA HORSE: THE SYMBOL OF SWEDEN

No matter where you travel in Sweden, you'll come across small wooden horses known as **Dala horses** (*dalahästar*). The Swedes love them, and it's virtually an unwritten rule that every household in the country should have a couple on display. For many outsiders, the horses' bright red colour, stumpy legs and garish floral decorations are high kitsch and rather ugly; Swedes, however, adore bright colours and the redder the better. **Nils** and **Jannes Olsson**, two brothers from the town of **Nusnäs**, just east of Mora on the lakeside, are responsible for the horses; in 1928, when they were just teenagers, they began carving them in their family's baking shed, creating what has become a symbol for the nation. If you're so inclined, you can visit the brothers' workshop in Nusnäs (mid-June to mid-Aug daily 8am–5pm; rest of the year Mon–Fri 8am–5pm, Sat & Sun 10am–2pm; free) by taking the #108 bus from Mora (Mon–Fri 4 daily; 20min).

by trees. When it comes to **hotels**, there's not much choice (all charge the same prices year round): the closest is *Hotell Lerdalshöjden* (☎0248/511 50, fax 511 77; ③), on Bockgatan with good views of the lake but rather average rooms; if you do stay here make sure you get a room with a view. The only other hotel worth considering is *Hotell Hantverksbyn* (☎0248/302 5, fax 306 60; ②), which is about 3km out of Rättvik – here pine cabins have been made into comfortable rustic apartments. There are two **campsites** in town; one is across the road from the youth hostel close to Räviksparken (☎0248/561 10), and the other is right on the lakeside behind the train lines (☎0248/516 91).

Rättvik has a dearth of good places to **eat and drink**; things are so bad that the local youth take off to Leksand and Mora of an evening in search of a decent pub or restaurant. The best of the bunch here is the small and twee *Restaurant Anna* on Vasagatan, with *Dagens Rätt* and pricey evening meals; they specialize in local dishes – how about elk and reindeer casserole for 138kr. The other main option is *Tre Krögare* on the pedestrianized mini-shopping street, Storgatan, which serves burgers and meat dishes at good prices; during its Happy Hour (Wed–Sun 3–8pm) a *storstark* costs 30kr. For cheap pizzas head for *Bella Pizza* at Ågatan 11.

## Tällberg

If you believe the tourist blurb then **TÄLLBERG** (pronounced "tell-berry") is Dalarna. A cutsey hillside village made up of wooden cottages draped in summer flowers between Rättvik and Leksand, Tällberg is a prime destination for middle-aged wealthy Swedes, who come to enjoy the good life for a few days, savour the delicious food dished up by the village's seven hotels and admire the fantastic views out over Lake Siljan. Tällberg first became famous in 1850, when the Danish writer Hans-Christian Anderssen paid a visit and wrote on his return to Copenhagen that everyone should experience its peace and tranquility and marvel at the wonderful lake views. Ever since hordes of tourists have flooded into the tiny village to see what all the fuss was about. Today Tällberg deserves a look if you're working your way round the lake, but prepare yourself for the crowds that unfortunately take the edge off what is otherwise quite a pretty little place. You can escape by walking down the steep hill of Sjögattu, past the **campsite** (☎0247/503 01) to the calm lapping water of the lake and a small sandy beach – keep going through the trees to find quieter spots for nude bathing. If you want to stay, avoid the expensive hotels and walk down Sjögattu to *Siljansgården* (☎0247/500 40), a wonderful old wooden farm building complete with cobbled courtyard and fountain. The rooms are youth hostel standard and not en suite; prices fluctuate, but reckon on around 200kr per night, making one of the best deals in Dalarna. Tällberg is on the main train line round Lake Siljan; the station is a ten-to-fifteen minute walk from the village. Alternatively, bus #58 (Rättvik to Borlänge) leaves every two to three hours and stops in the village.

## Leksand

**LEKSAND** is perhaps the most popular and traditional of the Dalarna villages and is certainly worth making the effort to reach at Midsummer, when festivals recall age-old dances performed around the Maypole. Incidentally and rather confusingly, Sweden's Maypoles aren't erected in May, unlike most other countries in Europe, but in June, because there are so few leaves on the trees in May and the ground can still be covered with snow. The celebrations culminate in the **church boat races**, an aquatic procession of sleak wooden longboats, which the locals once rowed to church every Sunday. Starting on Midsummer's Day in nearby **Siljansnäs** – take bus #84 from Leksand (Mon–Fri only) – and continuing for ten days at different locations around the lake, the races hit Leksand on the first Saturday in July and Tällberg on the first Tuesday after Midsummer. In general between twenty and twenty-five teams take part and, although the last race is usually held in Leksand, the starting point for the others changes from year to year, so ask for the latest details at the tourist office (see below).

Another event you should try to catch is **Musik vid Siljan** (Music by Lake Siljan): nine days packed with music from early morning to late evening performed in churches, on the lake side and at various locations out in the surrounding forest. The event is held during the first week of July and consists of chamber music, organ concerts, choir music, jazz, traditional folk songs and ditties, as well as danceband music.

If you miss the races and the festival, there's little else to do in Leksand other than to rest up and take it easy for a while. Stroll along the riverside down to **Leksands kyrka**, which enjoys one of the most stunning locations of any church in the land: set in a peaceful churchyard lined with whispering spruce trees and looking out over the river and the lake to the distant shore. The church, which is one of the biggest town churches in the country, has existed in its present form since 1715, although the oldest parts date back to the thirteenth century.

### *PRACTICALITIES*

There are seven **trains** a day between Mora and Börlange in both directions and all stop at Leksand (15min from Rättvik); from the station it is five minutes' walk up Villagatan, then left onto Sparbanksgatan to the **tourist office** on Norsgatan (mid-June to mid-Aug Mon–Fri 9am–8pm, Sat 10am–8pm, Sun 11am–8pm; rest of the year Mon–Fri 9am–5pm, Sat 10am–1pm; ☎0247/803 00).

The **youth hostel** in Leksand is one of the oldest in Sweden and is around 2.5km from the train station over the river at Parkgården (open all year; ☎0247/152 50; 100kr). For **hotels** go to the tourist office in the afternoon and check out the last-minute deals. *Hotell Moskogen* at Insjövägen 50 (☎0247/146 00, fax 144 30; ③) has comfortable and adequate rooms in log cabins that get cheaper the longer you stay. *Hotell Korstäppen* at Hjortnäsvägen 33 (☎0247/123 10, fax 141 78; ③) is a basic, standard hotel that has the same prices all year round. The tourist office can also book four-berth **cabins** in the surrounding vicinity (450–500kr per night, 2500–3000kr per week). For the **campsite**, it's a twenty-minute walk from the tourist office along Tällbergsvägen to *Leksands Camping* (☎0247/803 13 or 803 12) at Orsandbaden or 6km away over the bay at Västanvik (☎0247/342 01).

*Café Kulturhuset*, just up from the tourist office on Norsgatan – in summer there are outside tables in the garden at the back – should be your first choice for **lunch**; *Dagens Rätt* goes for 50kr. Alternatively, try *Bosporen*, a basic pizzeria in the tiny pedestrianized centre of town, which does lunch for 60kr. In the same ilk is *Bella Pizza* at Norsgatan 34. In the evenings both offer more substantial meat and fish dishes for around 100kr. For a **drink** head for the pub and disco, *Restaurant City*, which also does cheap pizzas, kebabs and pasta to eat in or to takeaway.

# Borlänge and around

In contrast with nearby Falun (see opposite), **Borlänge** is ugly and dull. As the biggest town in Dalarna, it developed as a steel and papermill centre, industries that still dominate today. Luckily there are a few saving graces, all lying in the centre: **Jussi Björling Museet**, not far from the tourist office (see below) at Borganäsvägen 25 (mid-May to mid-Sept Mon–Fri 11am–6pm, Sat 10am–2pm, Sun noon–5pm; Jan to mid-May & mid-Sept to Dec Tues–Fri noon–5pm; 20kr) commemorates the life and career of Borlänge's most famous son and world-famous tenor, with listening rooms where you can have Jussi sing for you at the flick of a button. It's a toss up as to which of the town's other two museums is marginally the more interesting: **Geologiska Museet** at Floragatan 6 (Mon–Fri 11am–2pm, Sat 11am–5pm; 10kr) has mind-numbing displays of rocks, minerals and fossils, whereas **Framtidsmuseet** at Jussi Björlingsvägen 25 (Mon 1–5pm, Tues–Fri 10am–5pm, Sat & Sun noon–5pm; 25kr) is a museum of the future; the best section is the planetarium.

If the museums hold no appeal, you could pass them over in favour of a stroll along the river; start at the open-air **Gammelgården** craft village, with its small collection of old wooden houses on Stenhålsgatan. To get to the village take the path over Siljansvägen, which begins just beyond Svea Torget, and follow it till you get to Kontorsvägen. From Gammelgården head away from the main road bridge to the left and follow the riverside path as far as the impressive power station built across the river – you can cross here and trace your steps on the opposite bank – all in all a pleasant walk of around an hour or so with plenty of places to stop for a picnic.

## Practicalities

From the central **train station** (7 daily trains from Leksand; 1hr) walk past the green Liljekvistska parken to the **tourist office** (mid-June to mid-Aug daily 9am–7pm; rest of the year Mon–Fri 10am–6pm; ☎0243/665 66) on Borganäsvägen.

If you do want to stay, the **youth hostel** (open all year; ☎0243/22 76 15; 100kr) is within easy walking distance from the centre at Kornstigen 23A. There are also several central and very samey **hotels** catering mainly for business people and offering modern, well-decorated rooms with wooden floors. The main ones are *Hotel Galaxen* (☎0243/800 10, fax 162 30; ④/②) at Jussi Björlingsvägen 25; *Hotel*

*Brage* (☎0243/22 41 50, fax 871 00; ④/②) at Stationsgatan 1; *Scandic Hotel Borlänge* (☎0243/22 81 20, fax 22 81 96; ④/②) at Stationsgatan 21–23; and the smaller and cheaper *Hotell Saga* (☎0243/21 18 40; ①) at Borganäsvägen 28. Only *Hotel Gustaf Wasa* (☎0243/810 00, fax 806 00; ④/②), at Tunagatan 1, has bath-tubs. The **campsite**, *Mellsta Camping*, is beautifully located by the river at **Mellstavägen** but is a bit of a trek from the centre; take bus #58.

The pick of the **cafés** is *Café 1896* in a wonderful old pink wooden house on Sveagatan – in summer, there are tables in the garden at the rear under the shade of a couple of trees. When it comes to **restaurants**, Borlänge holds the record for the number of pizzerias in any small Swedish town – 26. The best one is the romantic *La Pizza* on Tunagatan. For Greek specialities head for *En Liten Röd* on Vattugatan – try the lamb cutlets with garlic for 89kr. Chinese food from 80kr is best enjoyed at *Le Mandarin* in Svea Torget; and for Mexican and Cajun delights at around 100kr head for *Broken Dreams* inside *Hotel Gustaf Wasa*. The very best food, though, is served up in the smart *Stationsgatan 1*, the restaurant inside *Hotel Brage* – their flounder is legend. The intimate *Balders Krog*, on Målaregatan, serves traditional Swedish dishes; while inside the *Scandic Hotel Borlänge*, the *Tuna Krog* is also reputed to be good for home-style cooking (around 130kr for a main meal). The most popular **pubs** in town are the *Flying Scotsman*, which is in the same building as the Framtidsmuseet on Jussi Björlingsvägen, and *Rockfickan* inside *Hotel Brage* – don't raise your hopes too high, though.

## Torsång and Ornäs

There are a couple of places worth considering for a short visit once you tire of Borlänge. The idyllic village of **TORSÅNG** (bus #19 between Borlänge and Falun; Mon–Fri 5 daily) lies on Lake Runn, 8km east of town. There's not much here, except a medieval church from the 1300s, built out of stone and brick with a won-derful white vaulted ceiling and a separate wooden bell tower, which is used by the fire brigade to issue fire warnings. Take a seat in the summer café, *Torsångs Café*, by the water's edge and take it easy. Alternatively, head for the village of **ORNÄS** (bus #53 from the train station; daily every hour until 9pm), 8km to the northeast, and visit the fifteenth-century **Ornässtugan** (June–Aug Mon–Sat 10am–6pm, Sun 1–5pm; 15kr). The building is famous in Sweden as the place where King Gustav Vasa escaped from the approaching Danish army by jumping out of an upstairs sixteenth-century toilet window – his landing, needless to say, was somewhat softer than he might have imagined. Inside the ornate wooden structure, there's a Bible from the 1540s.

# Falun and Sundborn

Away from Lake Siljan, **FALUN** is essentially an industrial town – although a pleasant one at that – known for copper mining, which began here as early as the eleventh century. Without doubt the best time to visit is during the annual **International Folk Music Festival** (10–13 July), when the streets come alive to the sound of panpipes, bagpipes and every other type of pipes as folk musicians from around the world gather together. Falun is also known for a much more sobering event. In 1994, the town witnessed Sweden's worst case of mass murder, when a young soldier ran amok, jealous after seeing his girlfriend with another man, and shot dead seven local people.

## The copper mines and the Great Pit

Falun grew in importance during the seventeenth and eighteenth centuries when its **copper mines** produced two-thirds of the world's copper ore. Commensurate with its status as Sweden's second largest town (six thousand inhabitants), the town acquired grand buildings and a proud layout. Conditions in the mines, however, were appalling and were said by the botanist Carl von Linné to be as dreadful as hell itself. One of the most unnerving elements of eighteenth-century copper mining was the omnipresence of vitriol gases, which are strong preservatives. A recorded case exists of a young man known as *Fet Mats* (Fat Mats), whose body was found in the mines in 1719. He'd died 49 years previously in an accident and the corpse was so well preserved that his erstwhile fiancée, by then an old woman, recognized him immediately. The mines (May–Aug daily 10am–4.30pm, Sept to mid-Nov, March & April Sat & Sun only 12.30–4.30pm; 55kr) are at the out-of-town end of Gruvgatan, and **guided tours** lasting around an hour are organized on the site, beginning with a elevator ride 55m down to a network of old mine roads and drifts. It's quite cold down there, only around 6–7°C, so make sure you bring warm clothing and wear old shoes, as they're likely to come out tinged red. There's also a worthy **museum** on the site (May–Aug daily 10am–4.30pm, Sept–April 12.30–4.30pm; 10kr), which recounts the history of Falun's copper production. If the museum doesn't appeal, be sure not to miss peering into the **Great Pit** (Stora Stöten), just nearby, which is 100m deep and 300–400m wide. It appeared on Midsummer Day in 1687, when the entire pit caved in – the result of extensive mining and the unplanned driving of galleries and shafts. The few old wooden houses that survive – in 1761, two fires wiped out virutally all of central Faluncan – can be found in the areas of Elsborg (southwest of the centre), Gamla Herrgården and Östanfors (north of the centre) and are worth seeking out for an idea of the cramped conditions mine workers had to live in.

## The Dalarnas Museum, the National Ski Stadium and the beaches

For rainy days you could try the riverside **Dalarnas Museum** at Stigaregatan 2–4 (May–Aug Mon–Thurs 10am–5pm, Fri–Sun noon–5pm; Sept–May Mon, Tues, Thurs 10am–5pm, Wed 10am–9pm; 20kr), which has a reconstruction of the study where the author Selma Lagerlöf worked when she moved to Falun in 1897, and sections on the county's folk art, dresses and music.

If the weather is fine, it's well worth getting out of the centre and walking up Svärdsjögatan to **Lungnet** (a 25min walk), the hill overlooking the town and home to Sweden's **National Ski Stadium** (*Riksskidsstdion*), here you can take a lift 90m to the top of the ski jump. Close to the ski arena there are a couple of free outdoor **swimming pools** and a **nature reserve**, with the chance to sit undisturbed in a carpet of blue harebells. Alternatively, if you want to take a dip, you should head out north from the centre along Slaggatan for the **beach** at **Kålgårdsparken**, near the area of wooden houses at Östanfors; or take bus #702 or #703 to **Sandviken** where there are good sandy beaches. If you're staying at the youth hostel (see opposite), there's a pleasant bathing area at **Uddnäs**, which can be reached from the centre by bus #701.

## Practicalities

The **train** (7 daily from Börlange; 20min) and **bus stations** are to the east of the centre; if you walk through the bus station, then take the pass under the main road and head towards the shops in the distance, you'll soon come to Falun's **tourist office** in Stora Torget (mid-June to mid-Aug Mon–Sat 9am–7pm, Sun 11am–5pm; rest of the year Mon–Fri 9am–5pm, Sat 9am–1pm; ☎023/836 37), where you can get free maps of the town and useful advice on the folk festival.

The **youth hostel** (open all year; ☎023/105 60; 100kr) is about 3km out of town at Hälsinggårdsvägen 7, in **HARALDSBO**, and is housed in a couple of long low-rise modern buildings (#701 or #704 from the centre). The best **hotel** is up at **Lungnet hill**, *Scandic Hotell Falun* at Svärdsjögatan 51 (☎023/221 60; ④/②), which has fantastic views down over the town as well as ultra-modern rooms and a sauna complex and pool in the basement (the walk into town takes around 10–15min). In town the biggest hotel is the swanky, central *First Hotel Grand* at Trotzgatan 9–11 (☎023/187 00; ④/②), whose rooms are sumptuous to say the least. For a more home-from-home feel try *Hotell Bergmästaren* at Bergskolegränd 7, near the train station (☎023/636 00; ④/②). A cheap option, if you don't mind staying out of the centre, is *Pensionat Solliden* at Centralvägen 36, 6km away in **HOSJÖ**; a pleasant boarding house with its own restaurant and sauna (☎023/325 90; ③/②). The nearest **campsite** (☎023/835 63) is up at Lungnet by the National Ski Stadium.

There's a good choice of places to **eat** and **drink** in Falun (all of them in or around the main square) that far outstrips the selection in the other towns around Lake Siljan, not only in number but also in the quality of the food served. The most popular is the trendy *Banken Bar & Brasserie* at Åsgatan 41, which, as the name suggests, is housed in what used to be a bank – old notes still adorn the walls and linen cloths deck the tables. The food isn't cheap: burgers from 79kr and other meat dishes from 150kr – try the delicious salmon at 95kr. Next door is the slightly less expensive *Två rum och kök*, a small cosy restaurant that feels like you're eating in a friend's dining room. Another busy spot is *Rådhuskällaren*, under the Rådhus in Stora Torget in what looks to be a wine cellar; here you can indulge in delicious if somewhat pricey food – the cheapest bottle of wine will set you back 165kr. One of *the* places to be seen among Falun's young and trendy is the adjoining *Bakfickan* **bar** and restaurant. Other drinking establishments include the excellent *Pub Engelbrekt*, Stigaregatan 1, with its old wooden benches and the average British-style *King's Arms*, Falugatan 3. *De Niro*, opposite Dalarnas Museum and extremely popular with young people, is a pizzeria, restaurant and **nightclub** all rolled into one with bouncers on the door; it has regular special offers on set meals.

## Sundborn

In the nearby village of **SUNDBORN**, 13km from Falun, is one of Sweden's most visited tourist attractions: the home of the artist **Carl Larsson** and his wife Karin. The delightful **Carl Larsson-gården** (May–Sept daily 10am–5pm; 15kr) was first used as a summer cottage, but later the Larssons moved here permanently. At the turn of the century, the house represented an entirely new decorative style for Sweden; its bright and warm interior quite unlike the dark and sober colours used until this time. The artist added murals and portraits of his children to the interior decoration, while Karin decorated the house with her embroidery and tapestries. Carl Larsson is now buried in the churchyard in Sundborn and some of his paintings are displayed in the village church. To get there take bus #64 (Mon–Fri 5 daily, Sat & Sun 1 daily) from the train station in Falun.

# Sälen

SÄLEN is a major **ski resort** and in effect also encompasses the surrounding slopes and mountains of Lindvallen, Högfjället, Tandådalen, Hundfjället, Rörbäcksnäs and Stöten. Each site has its own slope but looks to the village of Sälen for shops and services – not least the *Systembolaget* (off-licence). Buses call at each resort in turn, terminating in Stöten. In summer there's just one bus a day from Mora to Sälen (#95; 1hr 40min); if you've missed it you may want to explore the possibility of taking the train from Borlänge to **Malung**, and from there bus #157 that takes just an hour. Alternatively, there's a direct daily service (#801) from Gothenburg via Mariestad, Kristinehamn and Filipstad. With no sights as such, your very first port of call should be the **tourist office** (late June to early Aug & Dec to late April daily 9am–6pm; rest of the year Mon–Fri 9am–6pm; ☎0280/202 50), which is on the one straggly main street that runs through the village. Sälen specializes in **outdoor activities** and during the summer the hills, lakes and rivers around the town will keep you busy for several days. Fishing, canoeing and beaver safaris are all available through the tourist office. If you don't fancy getting your feet wet, there's some fantastic **hiking** to be had in the immediate vicinity (see "Hiking around Sälen and Idre" opposite). During winter, Sälen – if all the different mountain resorts are counted as one – is the biggest ski centre in the Nordic area, with over a hundred pistes, and snow is guaranteed from November to May. For beginners there are special lifts and 36 nursery and easy slopes with tuition. There are plenty of intermediate runs through the densely forested hillsides and, for advanced **skiers**, there are twenty testing runs as well as an off-piste area. To get the best value for money, it's really worth buying a package rather than trying to book individual nights at local hotels; prices are high and in season they're packed to capacity (see *Basics* for more on package holidays).

**Summer accommodation** is best had at the wonderfully situated *Högfjällshotellet* (☎0280/870 00, fax 211 61; ④/②) at Högfjället – just on the tree line with good views of the surrounding hills (twice-daily bus from Sälen). There's a restaurant here and a bar with cheap beer – just 29kr – a large and superb steam and dry sauna suite in the basement and a swimming pool with whirlpool and jet streams. If you really want to be out in the wilds head for the **youth hostel** (open all year; ☎0280/820 40; 100kr) at Gräsheden near Stöten. Take bus #801 (June–Aug 1 daily); the hostel staff will pick you up from the bus in Stöten if you ring before you leave. Although there's a kitchen, meals can be ordered in advance; there's also a washing and drying room, electric heating for your car engine when the winter really starts to nip and a sauna.

# Idre

The twice-daily bus from Mora follows the densely forested valley of the Österdalälven on its near three-hour journey to one of Sweden's main **ski resorts** and its southernmost and smallest *Sami* village, officially called **Idrebua**, in the town of **IDRE**. However, if you're expecting wooden huts and reindeer herders dressed in traditional dress you'll be disappointed – the remaining six herding families live in normal houses and dress like everyone else (see "A brief look of the *Sami*" overleaf). Continuing up the mountain (take the twice-daily local bus; 20min), you'll come to the ski slopes at **Idrefjäll**. This

## HIKING AROUND SÄLEN AND IDRE

The little-known and excellent first part of the southern stretch of the **Kungsleden** (see p.397 for the northern section) starts at the *Högfjällshotellet* on **Högfjället**, one of the slopes near Sälen, and leads to **Drevdagen**, a thirty-minute drive west of Idre off Road 70, where it then breaks off (there are plans to join up both parts of the southern *Kungsleden* by construction of a path along the Norwegian border), starting again at Grövelsjön and continuing all the way north to **Storlien**. It's an easy path to walk, and the majority of the overnight cabins along its length are operated by *Svenska Turistföreningen* – however, there are no overnight cabins on the first stretch of the path, so from Sälen you are better off opting for the Vasaloppsleden to Mora (see below).

From **Idre** you can join the Kungsleden near the border at **Grövelsjön** (twice-daily bus from both the village and Idrefjäll), renowned for its stark and beautiful mountain scenery. There's also an **STF fell station** here (Feb–April, mid-June to Sept, Christmas & New Year; ☎0253/230 90; 195–380kr with 50kr discount for youth hostel members). From Grövelsjön the path goes over the reindeer-grazing slopes of Långfjället, skirts round Töfsingdalens National Park, crosses the county border from Dalarna to Härjedalen to the east of Slagufjället and continues ever northwards, passing Sweden's southernmost glacier on Helagsfjället on the way (the stretch from Grövelsjön to Helagsfjället is 124km). There are several overnight **cabins** along the way and three **fell stations** at the Storlien end of the path (see p.377). For more information, ask at the tourist office in Idre or from the fell station in Grövelsjön.

The **Vasaloppsleden** (90km) to Mora traces the route taken by skiers on the first Sunday in March during the annual **Vasaloppet race**, which marks King Gustav Vasa's return to Mora, after he escaped from the Danes on skis and was caught up with by two Mora men, who persuaded him to come back to the town in return for protection. The path starts just outside **Sälen** in **Berga** and runs uphill first to Smågan then downhill all the way to Mora via Mångsbodarna, Risberg, Evertsberg, Oxberg, Hökberg and Eldris. There are eight **cabins** along the route – it's also possible to get accommodation in a number of the hamlets on the way – look out for *rum* or *logi* signs. A detailed map of the route is available from the tourist offices in Sälen and Mora.

is still one of the most reliable places for snow (and hence rain in summer) in the entire country and, although not on the scale of Sälen, the ski resort is still one of the biggest in the Nordic area, with 32 lifts and 30 slopes. In winter the place is buzzing – not only with skiers but also with reindeer, who wander down the main street at will; they're attracted into town by the salt on the roads, which they lick for minerals.

Idrebua is a tiny one-street affair and is where you should stay if you come in summer. You'll find everything of any significance along its length, including a supermarket, bank and post office. The **tourist office** (mid-June to mid-Aug Mon–Fri 8am–7pm, Sat 8.30am–7pm, Sun 9am–7pm; rest of the year Mon–Fri 9am–5pm, Sat & Sun 10am–2pm; ☎0253/207 10) is at the far end of the main street when approaching from Mora. Like Sälen, Idrebua has plenty of **outdoor activities** to pursue, and the tourist office can help arrange fishing trips, horse riding, mountain biking, tennis, climbing and golf and will provide good advice about local hiking routes (see above). For **accommodation** in the village try

## A BRIEF LOOK AT THE SAMI

Among the oldest people in Europe, the **Sami** – better, but erroneously, known as "Lapps" to many – are probably descended from the original, prehistoric inhabitants of much of Scandinavia and northern Russia. Today, there are around 58,000 *Sami*, stretched across the whole of the northernmost regions of Norway, Sweden, Finland and Russia – while traces of their nomadic culture have been discovered as far south as Poland – and rather than Lapland (a region that covers the northwestern corner of Sweden), the *Sami* name for their lands is *Sápmi*. In Sweden itself, their region extends over half the country, stretching up from the northern parts of Dalarna, and, although the population is in decline, it still numbers around 17,000.

Their **language** is a rich one, based on a harmonious natural existence: there is no word for certain alien concepts (like "war"), but there are ninety different terms to express variations in snow conditions. One of the Finno-Ugric group of languages, which also contains Hungarian, the *Sami* language is divided into three dialects: Southern (spoken in southern parts of the *Sami* region), Central and Eastern (only spoken in Russia). Opposite is a brief glossary of some of the *Sami* words, many related to snow and reindeer, that you may come across while travelling in northern Sweden – also see p.385 for Lapland place names.

**Reindeer** have been at the centre of *Sami* life and culture for thousands of years, with generations of families following the seasonal movements of the animals. Accordingly the *Sami* year is divided into eight separate seasons: from early spring when they traditionally bring the reindeer cows up to the calving areas in the hills, through to winter when they return to the forests and the pastures. Many *Sami* families also settled close to the sea and made a living from fishing.

In the past, what characterized the *Sami* perhaps more than anything was a reluctance for their way of life to be disturbed by outsiders, yet for centuries Scandinavian adventurers treated them dreadfully. As early as the ninth century, a Norse emissary, Othere, boasted to Alfred the Great of his success in imposing a fur, feather and hide tax on his *Sami* neighbours.

Nevertheless, the *Sami* have managed largely to retain their own culture and identity in modern Sweden, though they were dealt a grievous blow by the Chernobyl nuclear disaster of 1986. This contaminated not only the lichen that feeds the reindeer in winter, but also the game, fish, berries and fungi that supplemented their own diet. Contamination of the reindeer meat meant the collapse of

the small and comfortable *Hotell Idregården* (☎0253/200 10, fax 206 76; ③/①) on the main road just as you come in from Mora. When it comes to **eating**, there's precious little choice: you can either go to the *Idregården*'s restaurant, which is famous for its ostrich and wild game, or *Kopparleden*, right at the other end of town near the tourist office, which, complete with plastic flowers, does simple fry-ups. The **bar** at the hotel is also the most popular spot at weekends. On Friday and Saturday evenings, you could try *Garaget*, which is attached to the *Kopparleden*.

Idrefjäll consists of one **hotel**, *Idre Fjäll* (☎0253/410 00, fax 401 58; ⑤/②), and the surrounding ski slopes and lifts. There are also snowboard areas, cross-country ski tracks, indoor swimming pools, saunas, jacuzzis, five hotel restaurants and a sports hall. All other facilities, such as banks, are down in the town. Room prices are fiendishly complicated and vary almost week to week through the season depending on when Stockholmers take their holiday. Don't just turn the export market to southern Scandinavia, Germany, America and the Far East; promises of compensation by the various national governments came late in the day and failed to address the fact that this wasn't just an economic disaster for the *Sami* – their traditional culture is inseparably tied to reindeer herding. However, perhaps as a consequence of the necessarily reduced role for reindeer in *Sami* life since Chernobyl, there has been an expansion in other outlets of *Sami* culture. Traditional arts and crafts have become popular and are widely available in craft shops, and *Sami* music (characterized by the rhythmic sounds of *joik*) is being given a hearing by fans of World Music.

## A glossary of Sami words

| | | | |
|---|---|---|---|
| *aahka* | grandmother, old woman | *lopme* | storm |
| *aajja* | grandfather, old man | *lopme-aajma* | snow storm |
| *aaltoe* | reindeer cow | *lopmedahke* | surface of the snow in autumn |
| *aehhtjie* | father | *lopme-moekie* | snow shower |
| *båtsuoj* | reindeer | *miesie* | reindeer calf |
| *daelvie* | winter | *nejpie* | knife |
| *geejmas* | black reindeer | *ruvveske* | water on the surface of the ice in spring |
| *giedtie* | reindeer pasture | | |
| *gierehtse* | sledge drawn by reindeer | *sarva* | reindeer bull |
| | | *saevrie* | loose, heavy snow that you can't walk on |
| *giesie* | summer | | |
| *gijre* | spring | *sahpah* | powdery wet snow that doesn't stick |
| *gåetie* | house, hut, tent | | |
| *jiengedahke* | autumn frost | *sieble* | slush |
| *klomhpedahke* | sticky snow surface | *soehpenje* | lasso |
| *klöösehke* | grey and white reindeer | *tjakje* | autumn |
| | | *tjidtjie* | mother |
| *kåta* | tent | *vielle* | brother |
| *lijjesjidh* | to snow lightly on bare (snowless) ground | *åabpa* | sister |

up here and expect to find a room – you won't. To save a lot of money, it's much better to book for a week or so; contact the tourist office down in the village for more details.

## Around Idre

It's worth noting that there are some good sandy beaches along the western shore of **Lake Idresjön**, a kilometre east of town; if you want to go canoeing you can rent a boat through the tourist office. If you have your own transport, it's well worth a trip to nearby **SÄRNA** (the only bus to the village is from Mora) to see the impressive **Njupeskär waterfall**, Sweden's highest with a drop of 125m. There's also a good and well-marked **walking route** that starts at the waterfall. To get here, you should take the main road to Särna, then turn right following signs for Mörkret and later for Njupeskärsvattenfall. If you're into **ice climbing** this is the place to head for it; in winter the waterfall freezes.

# Kristinehamn

South of Dalarna's tourist towns, the *Inlandsbanan* once began in **KRISTINE-HAMN**, a pretty harbour town on the northern fringes of Lake Vänern. Today, with the train route starting in Mora, there is little reason to come here, though if you are touring round Lake Vänern, Kristinehamn is easily accessible from Stockholm by train (10 daily; 2hr 45min). Now the bits of the *Inlandsbanan* track that still exist can by travelled along on special bicycles fitted with train wheels (contact the tourist office for more details; see below).

Kristinehamn has been an important port since the fourteenth century, when iron from the Bergslagen mines was shipped out from the town. Five hundred years later one of the country's earliest railways speeded up the process, when cars loaded with iron ore coasted downhill from the mines to the port. The empty cars were then pulled back to mines across the whole of the central mining area of Sweden, known as Bergslagen, by horses and oxen.

The town is proud, and rightly so, of its towering 15m-high Picasso sculpture, a sandblasted concrete pillar standing guard over the river entrance to the town. The striking piece is one of the *Les Dames des Mougins* series, based on Picasso's wife, Jaqueline, and was raised and decorated by the Swedish artist Carl Nesjar. Seeing as Picasso only provided a photograph of a model of the sculpture and never actually set foot in Sweden, the "Picasso sculpture" tag seems a little unfair to Nesjar. To get there – the sculpture is 6km from the centre – follow Presterudsvägen, out along the cycle track/footpath that skirts the river, past Kristinehamn's flotilla of garish private boats – right to the statue.

### Practicalities

From the **train station**, turn left and a five-minute walk brings you to the large main square, Södra Torget, and a river that branches its way through the centre. The **tourist office** is at Västerlånggatan 22 (June & Aug Mon–Sat 9am–6pm, Sun noon–6pm; July Mon–Fri 9am–8pm, Sat 9am–6pm, Sun noon–6pm; rest of the year Mon–Fri 9am–4pm; ☎0550/881 87); you can book **private rooms** here (from 100kr, plus a 25kr booking fee) and **rent bikes** for 75kr per day. The **youth hostel** (mid-May to end Aug; ☎0550/147 71; 85kr) and **campsite** are on same site in the village of **KVARNDAMMEN** (take Road 18 in the direction of Örebro); the campsite (☎0550/881 95) also rents out bikes at 100kr per day. The biggest hotel in town is *Stadshotellet* (☎0550/150 30, fax 41 12 35; ⑤) on Södra Torget. It's a lovely turn-of-the-century building with modern rooms and a restaurant. A cheaper option is *Hotel Fröding* (☎0550/151 80, fax 101 30; ③), at Kungsgatan 44. For **eating and drinking**, *Restaurant Sjöjungfrun*, at Vålösundsvågen 117 (open June–Aug), has top-quality fish and meat dishes on offer; it's right by the Picasso statue at Rönneberg. For lunch, the best place is *Roma Restaurant*, a busy pizzeria at Skaraborgsvägen 13; pizzas cost 50–60kr. The most popular place for a drink, *Arklow's* Irish **pub** and restaurant, is at Hamnbrogatan 18.

# Orsa to Östersund

The first stop for the *Inlandsbanan* on its long journey north from Mora (see p.354) is the tiny town of **ORSA**, 21km from Mora. Step off the train here and you are entering bear country – it's reckoned that there are a good few hundred huge brown bears roaming the dense forests around the town. Not surprisingly, the main attraction is the nearby **Orsa Grönklitt björnpark** (mid-May to early June & late Aug to mid-Sept daily 10am–3pm; early June to late Aug 10am–5pm; 55kr), the biggest **bear park** in Europe. The park is 13km from Orsa and can be reached by taking the once-daily bus #118 from outside the train station (or from Mora, where the bus starts); get off at the last stop (Toppstugan), and, once you've meandered through the park, catch the bus back at the entrance about an hour and a half later.

Despite their numbers, few sightings of the bears are made in the wild, except by hunters who cull the steadily increasing numbers each year. Visit the bear park, though, and they're out in force. Whatever your reservations about such places, think again: the bears are not tamed or caged, but wander around the nine hundred square kilometres of the forested park at will, hunting and living as normal. It's the humans who're caged, having to clamber up viewing towers and along covered-in walkways. Watching the bears throws all preconceptions out of the window: they are funny, gentle and vegetarian for the most part – occasionally they're fed the odd dead reindeer or elk that's been killed on the roads. The park is only open from early spring to late autumn because outside these times the bears hibernate in specially constructed lairs, which are monitored by closed-circuit television cameras. The king of the park is the enormous male bear called Micke, who weighs in at a staggering 450kilos. Micke has become something of a celebrity in recent years, after his teeth were fixed live on Swedish TV. In 1994 Grönklitt witnessed the birth of its first quintuplets – five little darlings, who drew record crowds. Trying hard not to be upstaged by the bears are two lynx and a couple of wolves – although you'll be lucky to see them – in fact, it's a good idea to bring along a pair of binoculars to help you pick out any rustlings in the undergrowth.

### Practicalities

The **train station** is in the centre on Järnvägsgatan. The **tourist office** is at Centralplan (mid-June to mid-Aug Mon–Fri 9am–8pm, Sat 10am–8pm, Sun 11am–8pm; rest of the year Mon–Fri 9am–5pm, Sat 9am–1pm; ☎0250/521 63). There's a beautifully located **youth hostel** (open all year except late April to mid-May & Nov; ☎0250/421 70; 100kr) by the side of Lake Orsa just 1km east of the centre on Moravägen, near the ice stadium. Or try *Strandvillan* **hotel**, Älvgatan 6 (☎0250/408 73; ③/②), 500m from the station. At the park there's another **youth hostel** (open all year; ☎0250/462 00; 100kr), just past the reception, with fine facilities: twin-bedded rooms plus breakfast, TV and a kitchen. Watch what you eat, though, in the nearby *Fyrksås Restaurang* – if it looks like pink roast beef it's bear meat. Sometimes an excess number of bears in the park means that one or two have to be killed.

# Härjedalen

A sparsely populated fell region with just 12,000 inhabitants, **Härjedalen** is an excellent area for **walking**. Stretching north and west to the Norwegian border, the county actually belonged to Norway until 1645, and the Norse influence is still evident today in the local dialect. The region got its name from the unfortunate Härjulf Hornbreaker, a servant to the Norwegian king, who mistakenly killed two of the king's men and was banished from the court and fled to Uppsala, where he sought protection from King Amund. After falling in love with Amund's cousin, Helga, and arousing the king's fury, he was forced to make another hasty exit. It was then he came across a desolate valley in which he settled and which he named after himself: Härjulf's dale, or Härjedalen as it's known today.

The county contains some of the best scenery in Sweden with more than thirty mountain tops reaching over 1000m. The main towns of **Sveg** and **Åsarna** make good bases from which to go walking – the latter is also a popular ski centre – while **Klövsjo** is reputedly the most enchanting place in all Sweden. The highest peak is **Helags** at 1797m (its icy slopes support Sweden's southernmost glacier). The nearest town to the mountain is **LJANGDALEN**, reached by bus #613 from Åsarna (Mon–Fri 2 daily, Sat & Sun 1 daily; 2hr). Härjedalen is also home to the largest single population of bears in the country, as well as a handful of shaggy musk oxen that have wandered over the border from Norway (ferocious creatures who can run faster uphill than downhill).

## Sveg

The main town in Härjedalen – and the first main stop on the *Inlandsbanan* after Orsa – is **SVEG** (pronounced "Svay-gg"), with a tiny population of just four thousand and site of a 1273 parliament called to hammer out a border treaty between Sweden and Norway. Since then things have quitened down considerably, and even on a Friday night in the height of summer you'll be pushed to find anyone in the wide streets lined with grand old wooden houses. Depending on your point of view, Sveg has nothing whatsoever to offer or as much as you could possibly imagine: there's a beautiful and very graceful river that runs right through the centre of town, and if the day's fine it's a delightful walk along the bank. Crossing the road and train bridge at the end of Fjällvägen, turn right into the forest over a little stream and head for the river's edge; if you look carefully, you'll come to a wonderful sweet-smelling open flower meadow hidden from the road by the trees. It's a gorgeous place for a picnic and for a spot of skinny-dipping in the river – but don't forget mosquito repellent.

*PRACTICALITIES*

The **train** (2hr 30min from Orsa) and **bus stations** (twice-daily *Inlandsexpressen*; 1hr 45min) are on Järnvägsgatan. Incidentally, you can reach Sveg direct from Stockholm by bus (Fri, Sat, Sun & Mon, 1 daily), but it's a seven-hour ride via Gävle and Bollnäs. The **tourist office** (☎0680/107 75 or 130 25) can be tricky to find; it's on an unnamed road at the campsite, near the river and behind the vicarage. Your best bet is to follow the green tourist information signs from the main street. It has useful leaflets, although in Swedish only, about the local walking path to **Ytterberg** and on other routes in the county.

If you're keen to **stay overnight**, try the ramshackle but very welcoming **youth hostel** (open all year but Oct–May by advance booking only; ☎0680/103 38; 100kr), a ten- to fifteen- minute walk from the station at Vallervägen 11, near the main square. It's run by Svea af Trampe, who unfortunately is rather hard of hearing. Next door but in the same building is *Hotell Härjedalen* (same telephone number as youth hostel; ①), with rather shabby rooms. More upmarket and just the other side of Torget at the corner of Fjällvägen and Dalagatan is the smart *Hotell Mysoxen* (☎0680/71 12 60, fax 100 62; ③/②). The **campsite** (☎0680/107 75) is open all year and is a stone's throw from the tourist office by the riverside.

The only places to **eat** that have regular clientele are the cramped *Kornan* pub, pizzeria and café, near the corner of Kyrkogatan and Dalagatan, and the *Knuten* pizzeria in the main square, which serves okay pizzas for around 50kr. For bargain-basement meals, try the greasy spoon *Inlandskrogen*, next to the train and bus stations on Järnvägsgatan, which offers fry-ups, burgers and pizzas; the food may not be excellent but there's a sporting chance you'll find people in there. All the above serve *Dagens Rätt* for around 50–60kr.

# Åsarna and Klövsjö

The region's ski slopes have produced their fair share of champions. At **ÅSARNA** (4 weekly trains from Sveg, 1hr 40min; 3 buses daily, 1hr 30min) four of them – Tomas Wassberg, Torgny Mogren, Jan Ottosson and Hans Persson – have clubbed together and set up a **ski centre**, open winter and summer, for organized skiing and advice on hiking. The centre is on the one and only main road a few minutes from the train station, and there's a **tourist office** in the same complex (June–Aug daily 8am–9pm; rest of the year daily 8am–7pm; ☎0687/301 93). If you have time on your hands you may want to check out the **ski museum** next to the tourist office desk (same hours; 15kr), which has worthy exhibitions of Olympic and World Championship medals taken home by Åsarna ski club as well as their skiing equipment, photographs of famous Swedish skiers and a couple of video displays. Much more interesting is the peculiar **Utedassmuseet**, or Outside Loo Museum, which is behind the main ski centre – entrance is free for this illuminating array of the alfresco pots and bowls graced by countless Swedish bottoms over the years. Wander down past the cabins to the river, turn right, and follow the age-old *Kärleksstigen*, Lover's Lane, along the water's edge for an evening stroll or an afternoon picnic in summer; you can cross the river over an old stone bridge further upstream by the rapids and return on the opposite bank along a minor road. Smooth low-lying rocks by the bridge are ideal for fishing and catching a few rays of sunshine.

While it's virtually impossible to stay in Åsarna in winter without an advance booking, in summer you can just turn up. Down by the river's edge, there's the ski centre's **youth hostel** (open all year; ☎0687/302 30; 100kr) and **campsite** (☎0687/302 30, fax 303 60), with a small bathing pool and a sauna. There are also three non-*STF* four-berth **cabins** for rent from 490kr per day. For those who've tired of conventional roof-over-head type accommodation, why not try a *Sami* tent or *kåta* in the grounds, complete with wood for your evening fire and reindeer skins to sleep on for just 50kr. If you don't fancy the ski centre, the *Åsarna Hotell* (☎0687/300 04; ②), opposite the train station, has smarter rooms and a proper restaurant and bar. It's also worth noting that there's a post office, filling station and a branch of *Sparbanken* in the village – but little else. For cheap meals the ski centre **restaurant** is hard to beat with breakfast for 35kr, *Dagens Rätt* for 55kr and evening meals around the 75kr mark (closes around 9pm).

## Klövsjö
Åsarna is well placed for a quick jaunt to **KLÖVSJÖ** (daily buses from Åsarna; 20min). A thoroughly charming place, with its log cabins set in rolling verdant pastures, it's gained the reputation of being Sweden's most beautiful village –

and with some justification – the distant lake and the forested hills that enclose Klövsjö on all sides give it a special other-worldly feeling. Ten farms still work the land in much the same way as they did in days gone by – ancient grazing rights still in force mean that horses and cows are free to roam through the village. Flower meadows, trickling streams, wooden barns and the smell of freshly mown hay drying on frames in the afternoon sun cast a wonderful spell. Once you've taken a look at **Tomtangården** (July to mid-Aug daily), a preserved seventeenth-century farm estate, there's not much else to do except breathe the bitingly clean air and admire the beauty. Unfortunately you can't stay here because there are no rooms to let, but the **tourist office** on the main road (mid-June to mid-Aug Mon–Sat 9am–7pm, Sun noon–7pm; rest of the year Mon–Fri 9am–5pm; ☎0682/212 50) has cabins to rent in the vicinity (375–500kr per day, 2000–2500 per week). The bus from Åsarna continues to **Vemdalen** and goes close (ask in the tourist office for exact details – there's about a 15min walk) to *Katarina Wärdshus* (☎0682/212 77, fax 212 72; ①), which also has **cabins**. This place is popular in winter with skiers, who make the most of the thirteen ski slopes nearby. It's worth noting that the three times daily #164 bus from the village back to Åsarna continues to Östersund.

# Östersund

Having reached **ÖSTERSUND**, which sits gracefully on the eastern shore of the mighty **Storjön** (Great Lake), it's worth stopping at what is the only large town until Gällivare inside the Arctic Circle. If you're heading north this is really your last chance to indulge in a bit of high life; the small towns and villages to the north have few of the entertainment possibilities or culinary delights available here. Gay travellers will be relieved to hear that the town has the only gay café in central northern Sweden. The town also has a number of interesting museums and a resident monster in the lake to rival that of Loch Ness. Furthermore Östersund is a major transport hub: the E14 runs through town on its way to the Norwegian border, the *Inlandsbanan* stops here, and trains run west to Åre and Storlien (with connections in Storlien to Trondheim in Norway), east to Sundsvall and south to both Stockholm and Gothenburg.

## Arrival, information and accommodation

From the **train station** (1hr 30min from Åsarna by train), on Strandgatan, it's a five-minute walk north to the town centre; the bus station is more central on Gustav III's Torg (6 buses daily; 1hr 20min). A couple of blocks north of the bus station, the **tourist office** (June and early to mid-Aug Mon–Sat 9am–7pm, Sun 10am–7pm; July Mon–Sat 9am–9pm, Sun 10am–7pm; rest of the year Mon–Fri 9am–5pm; ☎14 40 01), opposite the minaret-topped Rådhus at Rådhusgatan 44, is handy for a wealth of information and for the **Storsjökortet** (valid mid-May to mid-Aug; 100kr), a nine-day pass giving free bus rides, museum entry and fifty-percent discounts on bus and boat sightseeing trips.

The telephone code for Östersund is ☎063.

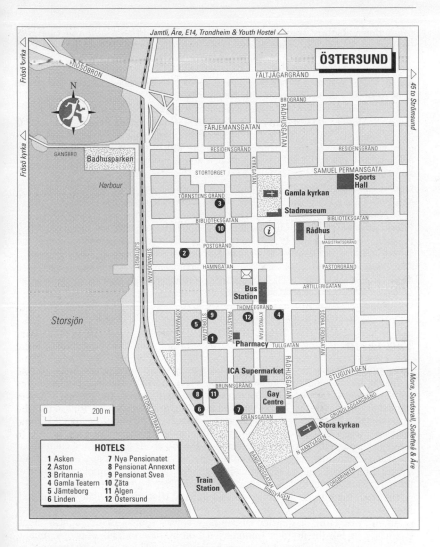

**HOTELS**

1 Asken      7 Nya Pensionatet
2 Aston      8 Pensionat Annexet
3 Britannia  9 Pensionat Svea
4 Gamla Teatern  10 Zäta
5 Jämteborg  11 Älgen
6 Linden     12 Östersund

## Accommodation

The modern and central *STF* **youth hostel** (mid-June to early Aug; ☎13 91 00; 100kr) is a ten-minute walk from the train station at Södra Gröngatan 34. More atmospheric, though, is a night spent inside **Jamtli**, a wonderful non-*STF* hostel amid the old buildings in the museum. You can phone direct (☎10 59 84), or the tourist office will book rooms there for a 40kr fee; it's a few kronor more to stay here, but you should be guaranteed free entry to the museum. **Campers** can stay either at *Östersunds Camping* (open all year; ☎14 46 15), a couple of kilometres south down Rådhusgatan, or over on the island of Frösön at *Frösö Camping* (June–Aug; ☎14 46 15) – take bus #3 or #4 from the centre.

## HOTELS AND PENSIONS

**Asken**, Storgatan 53 (☎51 74 50). Only eight rooms – all en suite but rather plain and simple – one room is for the use of people with allergies. ③/①

**Aston**, Köpmangatan 40 (☎51 08 51). A small hotel with plain rooms – some en suite. ①

**Britannia**, Prästgatan 26 (☎51 78 40). Garishly decorated tiny rooms, mostly en suite. ②/①

**Gamla Teatern**, Thoméegränd 20 (☎51 16 00, fax 13 14 99). Without doubt the best hotel in town, in an atmospheric turn-of-the-century theatre with sweeping wooden staircases, tall doorways and wide corridors. The main stage is now a restaurant. ③/②

**Jämteborg**, Storgatan 54 (☎51 01 01). Tasteless, drab and miserable. ②/①

**Linden**, Storgatan 64 (☎51 73 35). Cramped and basic rooms all with en-suite facilities. ③/①

**Nya Pensionatet**, Prästgatan 65 (☎51 24 98). Near the train station, this tastefully decorated house, dating from around 1900, has just seven rooms, with toilet and shower in the corridor. ①

**Pensionat Annexet** (☎10 74 73). A dingy place with thirteen well-appointed en-suite rooms. ②

**Pensionat Svea**, Storgatan 49 (☎51 29 01). Seven tweely decorated rooms with toilet and shower in the corridor. Discounted rates for long-term stays. ①

**Zäta**, Prästgatan 32 (☎51 78 60). Simple, plain but comfortable, with cable TV and a sauna. ③/①

**Älgen**, Storgatan 61 (☎51 75 25). Another small central hotel with plain yet comfortable en-suite rooms handy for the train station. ③/①

**Östersund**, Kyrkgatan 70 (☎12 45 00, fax 10 63 86). A massive modern hotel with 126 rooms; high on quality, with carpeted rooms and leather chairs, but low on charm. ④/②

# The Town

Östersund's lakeside position lends the town a seaside holiday atmosphere, unusual this far inland, and it's an instantly likable place in which to fetch up. The lake is home to Sweden's own Loch Ness monster and sightings are numerous, if unsubstantiated (see opposite). The town itself is made up of the familiar grid of parallel streets lined with modern quadruple-glazed apartment buildings designed to keep the winter freeze at bay (winter temperatures regularly plummet to -15°C to -20°C). Strolling through the pedestrianized centre, there's an air of contented calm about the place – take time out and sip a coffee around the wide open space of the main square, Stortorget, and watch Swedish provincial life go by, or amble along one of the many side streets that slope down to the still deep waters of the lake.

The main thing to do in town is to visit **Jamtli Historieland** (late June to mid-Aug daily 11am–5pm; 60kr, under-17s free when with an adult), an impressive **open-air museum**, a quarter of an hour's walk north of the centre along Rådhusgatan. For the first few minutes it's a bit bewildering, full of people milling around in traditional country costume, farming and milking much as their ancestors did. They live here throughout the summer and everyone is encouraged to join in – baking, tree felling, grass cutting. For children it's ideal, and adults would have to be pretty hard bitten not to enjoy the enthusiastic atmosphere. Intensive work has been done on getting the settings right: the restored and working interiors are authentically gloomy and dirty. In the woodman's cottage, presided over by a bearded lumberjack, who makes pancakes for the visitors, shoeless and scruffy youngsters snooze contentedly in the wooden cots. Outside even the roaming cattle and the planted crops are accurate to the period, while an old-fashioned local store, *Lanthandel*, has been set up among the wooden buildings around the square near

## THE GREAT LAKE MONSTER – STORSJÖODJURET

The people of Östersund are in no doubt. Storsjöodjuret (pronounced "stoor-shur-ooo-yoor-et) is out there. Eyewitness accounts – and there are hundreds of people who claim to have seen it – speak of a creature with a head like a dog, long pointed ears and bulging eyes that sweeps gracefully through the water, often several hundred metres away from the shore. In 1894, the hunt for this sinister presence began in earnest, when King Oscar II founded a special company to try to catch it. Norwegian whalers were hired, but the rather unorthodox methods they chose proved unsuccessful: a dead pig suspended in a metal clasp was dangled into the water as bait; specially manufactured large pincers were used to try to grip the creature and pull it ashore. Their tackle is on display in the Länsmuseet together with photographs of what is claimed to be the creature from the deep. Although several explanations have been given that dispel the myth – a floating tree trunk, a row of swimming elk, wake from a passing boat, a series of rising water bubbles – the people of Östersund still swear that there is a monster in the lake. It's taken so seriously that a protection order has now been slapped on it, with support of paragraph fourteen of the Nature Conservation Act. Thankfully, the commercialism that surrounds Scotland's Loch Ness monster is absent here.

If you fancy a bit of monster spotting why not take a **steamboat cruise** on the lake on board *S/S Thomée* – a creaking 1875 wooden steamship. Routes and timetables vary, but in general the boat does a two-hour trip (55kr) round the lake; a three-hour trip (65kr) out to the island of **Andersön**, with its nature reserve and virgin forests; a five-hour trip (75kr) to **Verkön**, where there's a turn-of-the-century castle; as well as a shorter one-hour trip (45kr) across the water to **Sandviken** and back; for more information contact the tourist office.

the entrance. The **Länsmuseet** on the site (late June to mid-Aug 11am–5pm; rest of the year Tues 11am–8pm, Wed–Sun 11am–5pm; 40kr, under-17s free when with an adult) shows off the county collections: a rambling houseful of local exhibits that includes monster-catching gear devised by lakeside worthies last century. The museum's prize exhibits are the awe-inspring Viking **Överhögdal tapestries**. Dating from the ninth to tenth centuries, most of them were discovered by accident in an outhouse in 1910, while another piece was rescued after being used as a doll's blanket – rumour has it the child had to be pacified with 2kr to hand it over. The tapestries are crowded with brightly coloured pictures of horses, reindeer, elk and dogs, but different types of dwellings are also depicted.

Back in the town centre, apart from the **Stadsmuseum** (Mon–Fri noon–4pm, Sat & Sun 1–4pm; free) – housing a crowded two hundred years of history in a building the size of a shoebox – next to **Gamla kyrkan** on Rådhusgatan (Mon–Fri 1–3pm), there's nothing much else to see. The **harbour** is a better bet; here a fleet of tiny boats bob about on the clean water. Immediately to the right of the harbour is the tiny **Badhusparken** – an extremely popular sunbathing spot.

### Across to Frösön

Take the foot or road bridge across the lake from Badhusparken and you'll come to the island of **Frösön**. People have lived here since prehistoric times; the island's name comes from the original Viking settlement and its association with the pagan god of fertility, Frö. There's plenty of good walking, as well as a couple of historical sights. Just over the bridge in front of red-brick offices, hunt for the eleventh-century **rune stone** that tells of a man called Östmadur (East Man), son of Gudfast, who was the first Christian missionary to the area. From here you can clamber up the nearby hill of Öneberget to the fourth-century settlement of **Mjälleborgen** – the most extensive in northern Sweden.

The beautiful **Frösö kyrka** (5km west along the main road and up the main hill; bus #3 from the town centre) is an eleventh-century church with a detached bell tower. In 1984 archeologists digging under the altar came across a bit of old birch stump surrounded by animal bones – bears, pigs, deer and squirrels – evidence of the cult of ancient gods, the *æsir*. The remains suggest that people have been attracted to this site of worship for almost two thousand years, and today the church is one of the most popular in Sweden for weddings – to tie the knot at Midsummer, you have to book years in advance.

From Frösön there are fantastic **views** across the lake back to Östersund, which appears to tumble down the hill towards the water. In **winter**, when the trees hang heavy under the weight of snow and ice, and the town's streetlights cast a soft glow into the dark sky, the view across the frozen lake to the streets buried deep under a fresh fall is one of the most romantic and beautiful in Sweden.

# Eating, drinking and nightlife

Gastronomically, there's more choice in Östersund than for a long way north, with good Swedish, Greek, Continental and even Indian food; most of the city's eating places, many of which double up as bars, are to the south of Stortorget. For **breakfast** (and several trains leave early in the morning), the train station café is good value and always busy. For **coffee and cakes** also try *Törners Konditori* at Storgatan 24 or better *Wedemarks Konditori* at Prästgatan 27, where you can make up your own sandwiches. *Brunkullans Krog* (see below) also opens as a daytime café. The *Lokalen* at Rådhusgatan 64, entrance round the corner in Gränsgatan (Mon–Fri noon–6pm; ☎13 19 00), is the one and only **gay café** in northern central Sweden (for more on gay Östersund see "Listings").

**Nightlife** can be found at *Källar'n* at Prästgatan 17, which attracts a young crowd and is the most popular **club** in town, opposite the *Systembolaget*. Alternatively, try *Saga Night Club* at Prästgatan 50, or *Magasinet/Levinska Villan* – a pub and club linked to each other with an entrance in the backyard approached through the black gates on Prästgatan.

## Restaurants and bars

**Athena**, Stortorget 3. An overpriced and pompous pizza restaurant.

**Brunkullans Krog**, Postgränd 5. Östersund's premier eating place, this old-fashioned, home-from-home restaurant, with polished lanterns and a heavy wooden interior, offers traditional Swedish dishes as well as more international fish and meat dishes. Expensive – although in summer there are tables in the garden at the rear with a cheaper menu.

**Captain Cook**, Hamngatan 9. A selection of delicious Australian-style grilled delights that really draws in the crowds – also one of the most popular places for a drink. Moderate.

**En Liten Röd**, Brogränd 19. Famous for its fondues, including a scrummy chocolate one, but very expensive.

**Kashmir**, Tegelbruksvägen 11. A fair trek on foot from the centre, but if you're longing for Indian food this is the place.

**Kvarterskrogen**, Storgatan 54. Linen tablecloth stuff and high prices to match, serving lamb, entrecôte, beef and sole.

**Ming Palace**, Storgatan 15. The town's best Chinese, with the usual dishes at moderate prices.

**Restaurang G III/O'Keefe's**, both inside the *Östersund* hotel, Kyrkgatan 70. A standard, fairly expensive à la carte restaurant, but right beside one of the town's popular drinking holes, *O'Keefes*.

**Restaurang Volos**, Prästgatan 38. Cheap pizzas and some good authentic Greek food. Look out for special offers on beer – sometimes around 30kr.

**Rydells Krog**, Storgatan 28. A popular drinking establishment offering a large beer in summer for 29kr. Also a simple and inexpensive menu.

**Skafferiet**, Stortorget 8. A delicious fish restaurant in the *Saluhallen* on Stortorget with an atmospheric interior. Good for lunch at 65kr, but closes around 6pm.

# Listings

**Airlines** *SAS* at the airport (☎15 10 10); *Nordic East* at the airport (☎430 10).

**Airport** on Frösön (free phone ☎61 62 63). Direct flights to Stockholm and Umeå. Buses (40kr) connect with all planes to and from Stockholm (information ☎0708/86 77 20).

**Banks** *Handelsbanken, Sparbanken, Föreningsbanken* are all on Prästgatan.

**Bike rental** *Cykelogen* at Kyrkogatan 45 (Mon–Sat; ☎12 20 80), with mountain bikes from about 100kr per day; *Cykelprojektet* (☎14 15 77) by the bus station with bikes from 30kr.

**Buses** *Swebus* operate all local buses within Östersund municipality (information & fares ☎16 82 61). The express bus, *Inlandsexpressen* (#45), leaves from the bus station south to Mora (2 daily; 5hr) and north to Gällivare (1 daily; 11hr) and also to Arvidsjaur (1 daily; 7hr). You can't book seats, just pay on board, but there is usually enough room – though it is always wise to get there early.

**Car rental** *Avis* at the airport (☎448 70) or at Bangårdsgatan 9 (☎10 12 50); *Budget,* Köpmangatan 25 (☎10 44 10); *Europcar,* Hofvallsgränd 1 (☎51 72 40); *Hertz,* Köpmangatan 25 (☎10 21 12); *Statoil,* Frösövägen (☎51 11 44), Hofvallsgränd (☎51 65 81), Krondikesvägen (☎12 39 75) and Mjällevägen (☎12 44 95).

**Cinemas** *Filmstaden,* Biblioteksgatan 14; *Filmstaden 78,* corner of Tullgatan and Prästgatan.

**Doctor** *Health Centre Z-gränd* (Mon–Fri 8am–5pm; ☎14 20 00; other times ☎13 44 00).

**Gay Östersund** Parties first Sat in the month at the *Lokalen* café (see "Eating, drinking and nightlife"); information from Box 516, 831 26 Östersund or the Switchboard (Mon–Fri 10am–6pm ☎10 06 68).

**Left luggage** Lockers at the train station for 15kr, 20kr and 25kr.

**Pharmacy** Prästgatan 51; Mon–Fri 9am–6pm, Sat 9am–4pm, Sun 11am–4pm.

**Police** (☎15 25 00).

**Post office** (free phone ☎020/23 22 21) .

**Systembolaget** Serve-yourself shop at Prästgatan 18, open Mon–Fri 9.30am–6pm; or Kyrkgatan 82, open Mon–Wed & Fri 9.30am–6pm, Thurs 9.30am–7pm.

**Taxi** *Taxi Östersund* (☎51 72 00).

**Trains** Information from the station on Strandgatan. The *Inlandsbanan* leaves daily Tues, Wed, Fri & Sun for Mora and Gällivare and Mon, Thurs & Sat for Arvidsjaur. All are early-morning departures.

**Travel agents** *Ticket,* Kyrkgatan, open Mon–Fri 9am–6pm, Sat 10am–1pm; *Z-Resor,* Samuel Permans Gata, open Mon–Fri 9.30am–5.30pm.

The second section of the *Inlandsbanan* from Östersund to Gällivare begins on p.378.

# West from Östersund

The E14 and the train line follow the course trudged by medieval pilgrims on their way to Nidaros (now Trondheim in Norway) over the border, a twisting route that threads its way through sharp-edged mountains rising high above a bevy of fast-flowing streams and deep, cold lakes. Time and again the eastern Vikings assembled their armies beside the holy Storsjön lake to begin the long march west, most famously in 1030 when King Olaf of Norway collected his mercenaries for the campaign that led to his death at the Battle of Stiklestad. The Vikings always crossed the mountains as quickly as possible and so today – although the scenery is splendid – there's no real attraction en route, other than the winter skiing and summer walking centres of **Åre** and **Storlien**.

## Åre

**Åre** (pronounced "Or-re"), two hours by train from Östersund, is Sweden's most prestigious ski resort, with 44 lifts and snow guaranteed between December and May. During the snowbound season rooms are like gold dust and prices skyhigh: if you do intend to come to ski, book accommodation well in advance through the tourist office or, better yet, take a package trip (see *Basics*). Equipment isn't so expensive to rent: downhill and cross-country gear costs 100–150kr per day and around 500kr per week – ask at the tourist office (see below).

In summer, although the Alpine village is quiet, it's a likable haven for ramblers, sandwiched as it is between the river and a range of craggy hills overshadowed by the mighty **Åreskutan mountain** (1420m). A network of tracks criss-crosses the hills or, for a more energetic scramble, the **Kabinbanan** (Sweden's only cable car; 75kr return) whisks you to the viewing platform and *Stormköket* restaurant some way up Åreskutan in just seven minutes, from where it's a thirty-minute clamber to the summit. Take sensible shoes with you and a warm pullover as the low temperatures are intensified by the wind, and it can be decidedly nippy. From the top the view is stunning – on a clear day you can see over to the border with Norway and a good way back to Östersund. If hunger strikes head for the tiny wooden café at the summit – long metal cables anchored into the ground put up a brave struggle against the brute force of the wind – which serves coffee and extortionately priced sandwiches. Even the shortest walk back (2hr) requires stamina; other longer paths lead more circuitously back down to the village. One word of warning: there are phenomenal **mosquitoes** and other insects up here in July and August, so make sure you are protected by repellent.

Back in the centre away from the killer mozzies, the **kyrka** (key hangs outside the door on a hook) just above the campsite (see opposite) is a marvellous thirteenth-century stone building: inside the simple blue decoration and the smell of burning candles create a peaceful ambience.

### Practicalities

There are four daily **trains** from Östersund (1hr 45min), but only one late-afternoon bus, #155 (1hr 30min). The **tourist office** (late June to late Aug & mid-Dec to late March daily 9am–6pm; rest of the year Mon–Fri 9am–3pm; ☎0647/177 20) is in the square 100m up the steps opposite the train station building. It has endless information about **hiking routes** in the nearby mountains and further afield

– ask for the excellent *Hiking in Årefjällen* booklet, which will tell you all you need to know and has detailed mountain maps. A popular route is the **Jämttriangle** from Sylarna via Blåhammaren to Storulvån, which takes in fantastic wilderness scenery close to the Norwegian border and involves two overnight stays in *STF* fell stations. If you fancy **mountain biking**, the mountains around Åre are as good a place as any to do it, and the tourist office can help sort out a bike for you.

There's plenty of **accommodation** in the village, packed in winter but with room to spare during the summer. The cheapest option is the unofficial **youth hostel** known as *Åre Backpackers Inn* (☎0647/177 31; 150kr) in the park below the square. The nearest *STF* hostel is at Brattlandsgården in **BRATTLAND** (all year but Sept to mid-June advance booking necessary & Oct–Dec groups only; ☎0647/301 38; 100kr), 8km to the east. There are weekday buses from Åre (details from the hostel), or a 4km hike from the train station at Undersåker, a stop on the train line from Östersund to Åre. It's also worth asking the tourist office about fixing up a **private room** from around 125kr per person per night in summer, almost all of them with kitchen, shower and TV. Alternatively there's the **campsite** (closed Sept–Nov; ☎0647/525 20), five minutes' walk from the station.

For **food**, Åre's not up to much, but there are several cheap places around the square: try the pie or sandwich lunches served at *Café Bubblan*, or the more substantial dishes at *Labands Krog Grill & Pizzeria*. At the bottom of the cable car, *Bykrogen* serves lunches at 50kr and reasonably priced main meals, but note the early closing time of 7pm. More palatable but very expensive fare can be sampled at *Villa Tottebo*, down by the train station, which cooks up local meat and fish for 200–250kr. Two winter-only restaurants are the upmarket *Bakfickan* at Åregården, and *Broken Dreams* at the *Diplomat Ski Lodge*.

## Storlien

Just six kilometres from the Norwegian border and a favourite biting spot for the region's mosquitoes, **STORLIEN** is an excellent place to stop if you are into hiking; the surrounding terrain is rugged and scenic. It is also prime berry-picking territory – the rare cloudberry grows here – and mushrooms can also be found in great number, in particular the delicious canterelle. There are regular **trains** (4 daily; 1hr) and **buses**, though the service is infrequent, from Åre, and the **tourist office** is in an old train carriage at the station (June–Aug daily 10am–5pm; rest of the year open for telephone inquiries on ☎0647/701 70). Aside from this, Storlien is little more than a couple of hotels and a supermarket amid the open countryside. The **youth hostel** (open all year but closed mid-June to mid-July; ☎0647/700 50; 100kr) is a four-kilometre walk across the tracks to the E14 and then left down the main road to Storvallen. If you're merely after a bed for the night then **ÅNN**, halfway between Åre and Storlien, is a good option. The youth hostel here (open all year; ☎0647/710 70; 100kr) is no distance from the station, and all trains running from Östersund and Åre to Storlien stop there. Of the **hotels**, *Hotell Storlien* (☎0647/701 51, fax 705 22) right by the station has megacheap rooms in summer – 95kr per person in a double room, 130kr per person per single room; bed linen costs 65kr extra. **Apartments** can be had at *Fjäl-lyor* (4-person 350kr; ☎0647/701 70), just to the right of the station, there's also a youth hostel-style section with beds at 125kr per night. Ten minutes away, *Storliens Högfjällshotell* (☎0647/701 70, fax 70 446; ③) is a luxury affair, with its own swimming pool and nearly two hundred well-appointed modern rooms and 35 individual cottages. **Eating** and

**drinking** opportunities are very limited. The best bet is *Le Ski* restaurant, night-club and bar at the station, which has cheapish eats for lunch and dinner (but beer is 43kr); or try *Café Storliengården* (Tues–Sun 9am–5pm), a two-minute walk left out of the station with coffee, waffles and sandwiches all year round.

**Moving on** from Storlien, two trains operated by Norwegian railways leave Storlien daily for Trondheim. In the opposite direction there are through trains to Stockholm and Gothenburg via Östersund, with sleeper services to both these destinations.

# North to Gällivare

After Östersund the **Inlandsbanan** slowly snakes its way across the remote Swedish hinterland, a vast and scarcely populated region where the train often has to stop for elk and reindeer – and occasionally bears – to be cleared from the tracks. Otherwise, if no station is in sight, it usually comes to a halt for a spot of berry picking, or for the guard to point out a beaver damming a nearby stream, while at the **Arctic Circle** everyone jumps off for photos.

Route 45, **Inlandsvägen**, sticks close to the train line on its way north to Gällivare. If you're not bound to the train this is the best road north; it's easy to drive and is well surfaced for the most part, although watch out for reindeer with a death wish – once they spot a car hurtling towards them they seem to do their utmost to throw themselves underneath it. You could drive from Östersund to Gällivare in a day if you left very early and put your foot down, but you are better off taking it in stages. The **Inlandsexpressen**, the daily bus service that runs from Östersund to Gällivare, follows Road 45 (see Östersund's "Listings" for details of departures and ticket buying). The bus isn't as much fun as the train, but it is faster and very comfortable.

## Strömsund

The first stop of any significance on the *Inlandsbanan* is the small waterside town of **STRÖMSUND** – an hour and a half up the line from Östersund. There's no train station here, so get off at nearby Ulriksfors and walk the 3km or so into Strömsund – a daily bus does cover the journey but doesn't connect with the train. The *Inlandsexpressen* **bus** stops in the town itself (1hr 30min from Östersund). The town is a centre for **canoeing**, and the **tourist office** (Mon–Fri 8am–4pm; ☎0670/164 03), in the Kommunhuset on Storgatan, can fix you up with canoes for 25kr per hour, 125kr per day or 615kr per week. The extensive network of **water-ways** that stretches northwest of the town is known as **Ströms Vattudal** and is excellent for messing about in boats. The tourist office can also provide information (plus maps, walking routes and details of places to stay) on the road known as the **Wilderness Way**, which starts here and leads through some wonderful scenery (see overleaf). There's a simple **youth hostel** in town at Verkstadsgatan 41 (mid-June to mid-Aug; ☎0670/108 05; 95kr) as well as a **campsite** (☎0670/164 10), just outside town on the way to Östersund. If you stay make an effort to get out to the **Stone Age rock paintings**, the *Hällmålningar*, ancient hunting stories painted in red ochre on the walls of the caves at **Brattforsen**, near Backe – unfortunately the paintings are hard to find; ask the tourist office for their detailed map and description of how to get there.

# Vilhelmina

Back on the main E45 and three and a half hours up the *Inlandsbanan* from Östersund, **VILHELMINA** is a pretty little town that once was an important forestry centre. Today the timber business has moved out of town and the main source of employment is a telephone booking centre for *Swedish Railways*. The town, together with its southerly neighbour Dorotea, is named after the wife of King Gustav IV Adolf, Fredrika Dorotea Vilhelmina, and is a quiet little place with just one main street. The principal attraction is the **parish village**, nestling between Storgatan and Ljusminnesgatan, whose thirty-odd wooden cottages date back to 1792, when the first church was consecrated. It's since been restored, and the cottages can be rented out via the tourist office (②).

The **tourist office** (mid-June to mid-Aug Mon–Fri 8am–8pm, Sat & Sun noon–6pm; rest of the year Mon–Fri 8am–5pm; ☎0940/152 70) is on the main Volgsjövägen, a five-minute walk up Postgatan from the **train station**, which also serves as the **bus** arrival and departure point (2 daily from Stömstad; 2hr 20min). The central **youth hostel** (mid-June to early Aug; ☎0940/141 65; 95kr) is in a school boarding house at Tallåsvägen 34; the tourist office deals with bookings placed before mid-June. There are two **hotels** in town; the posh and showy *Hotell Wilhelmina* (☎0940/554 20, fax 101 56; ④/②) at Volgsjövägen 16, and the simpler and friendly *Lilla Hotellet* (☎0940/150 59: ②) at Granvägen 1. The **campsite**, *Rasten Saiva Camping* (May–Oct; ☎0940/107 60), also has fourberth cabins for rent (200–450kr depending on size) and a great sandy **beach**; to get there walk down Volgsjövägen from the centre and take the first left after the youth hostel – allow about ten minutes. **Eating** and **drinking** doesn't exactly throw up a multitude of options: try the à la carte restaurant at *Hotell Wilhelmina* for traditional northern Swedish dishes, and *Dagens Rätts* for 60kr, or the plain *Pizzeria Quinto,* Volgsjövägen 27, for cheap pizzas. *Dagnys Café*, next to the parish village, serves coffee and sandwiches and has a reasonably priced lunch menu. In the evenings locals gravitate towards *Sven Dufvas Krog*, in the main square, for a drink or two.

# Storuman

**STORUMAN**, ninety minutes by the *Inlandsbanan* from Vilhelmina, is a transport hub for this part of southern Lapland. **Buses** run northwest up to E12 skirting the Tärnafjällen mountains to Tärnaby and Hemavan before wiggling through to Mo-i-Rana in Norway; in the opposite direction, the road leads down to Umeå via Lycksele, from where there are bus connections to Vindeln and Vännäs on the main coastal train line. A direct bus, **Lapplandspilen**, also links Storuman with Stockholm; there's lots of leg room onboard as the bus only carries 44 passengers and the seats give a 45° recline.

There's not much to Storuman: the centre consists of one tiny street that supports a couple of shops and banks. The **tourist office** (end-June to mid-Aug 8am–8pm; rest of the year Mon–Fri 9am–5pm; ☎0951/333 70 or 105 00) is in the **train station** and has a handy map of town and a few brochures. **Buses** stop outside the station (2 daily from Vilhemina; 50min). The **youth hostel** (mid-June to mid-Aug; ☎0951/104 28; 100kr) is 400m left of the station, and the luxurious **hotel**, *Hotell Toppen* (☎0951/117 00, fax 121 57; ④/②), with its pine and birchwood rooms, is a ten-minute walk up the hill from the station at Blå Vägen 238. In

### THE WILDERNESS WAY

Strömsund is the starting point for Road 342, the **Wilderness Way** (Vildmarksvägen), a narrow and winding road that strikes off northwest towards the mountains at Gäddede before hugging the Norwegian border and crossing the barren treeless Stekenjokk plateau. It then swings inland again rejoining the E45 at Vilhelmina. This route has to rank as one of the most beautiful and dramatic in Sweden: passing through great swathes of **virgin forest**, tiny forgotten villages and true wilderness, where the forces of nature have been left undisturbed. It's also the area in Sweden with the densest population of **bears**. If you're driving stop wherever you can, turn off the engine and listen to the deep silence broken only by the calls of the birds and the whisper of the forest. There are also plenty of **lakes** along the way ideal for **bathing** – you can choose whichever one you want to make your own; there'll be nobody else there. One of the best stretches of rocky beach is just south of the tiny village of Alanäs on the beautiful Flåsjön lake, before you get to Gäddede.

If you have your own transport (for information on travelling the route by bus, see opposite) you should turn left at **Bågede** and follow the minor road (the road surface is very rocky) along the southern shore of **Lake Fågelsjön** to reach **Hällsingsåfallet**, an impressive **waterfall** and Sweden's answer to Niagara Falls, complete with an 800m-long canyon that is getting longer every year.

The only town along the route is **Gäddede** (pronounced "Yedd-aye-de"), whose name means "the spot where the northern pike can no longer go upstream". The name may be cute but the place certainly isn't. Give it a miss and instead turn off the main road and follow the road signed "Riksgränsen" (National Border) for a few kilometres to the long and empty sandy beach of **Lake Murusjöen** – right on the border between the two countries: the beach is in Sweden, the water in Norway. You'll be hard pushed to find a more idyllic spot: the silence is total, the deep blue water still and calm, and the mountains in the distance dark and brooding.

Heading back towards Gäddede, take the left turn for **BJÖRKVATTNET**. The road to this tiny village is a 20km stretch with not one building along its entire length. The **youth hostel** (open all year, but mid-Nov to mid-Feb groups only; ☎0672/230 24; 100kr) is on the edge of the village. The hostel has information on some good local **hiking** trails and on a local bus that runs to **GÄDDEDE**, where there's a **tourist office** (June–Aug; ☎0672/105 00), a very grotty **hotel** (☎0672/104 20; ②) and a **campsite** (☎0672/100 35) on the lake shore.

From Björkvattnet, it's possible to rejoin the Wilderness Way by nipping briefly over the border into Norway, driving along the northern shore of **Lake Kvarnbergsvattnet** and taking a poorly surfaced minor road through dense forest to Jormlienand on to Åsarna (a different village to the one covered earlier).

the middle of the local **campsite** at Vallnäsvägen (☎0951/106 96), there's a church built in the style of a *kåta*, a traditional *Sami* hut. However, rather than hang around here, it's much better to head off into the mountains for some good **hiking** and **fishing** (ask at the tourist office for maps and information). If you do stay, the restaurant at *Hotell Toppen* should be your first choice for **food**, with a 60kr-lunch buffet; alternatively, the basic *Bel Ami Pizzeria* in the main square serves cheap *Dagens Rätts* and pizzas. Better is *Bettys Krog* opposite the station, which also has pizzas and lunch for the same prices. If you fancy good Greek food, take the twenty-minute walk down Blå Vägen, heading underneath the bridge on the road to Tärnaby, to *Grill 79*.

Lake Stora Blåsjön to the north is surrounded by blue mountains, and Stora Blåsjon is the last village before the road starts to climb above the tree line to cross the desolate boulder-strewn **Stekenjokk plateau** into the province of **Lapland**. The plateau is the temporary summer home of several **Sami** families, who tend their reindeer on the surrounding slopes, including the magnificent peak of **Sipmeke** (1424m) to the west of the road. After dropping into the minuscule village of **Klimpfjäll** (the stretch over the plateau between Lake Leipikvattnet and Klimpfjäll is only open mid-June to mid-Oct), the Way continues east. Taking the first turn to the left, you'll reach **Fatmomakke**, a fascinating **Sami parish village** made up of dozens of circular wooden huts, *kåtor*, gathered neatly around the church. The first church on the site was built in 1790, but the *Sami* met together here long before that for special religious celebrations. Look out for the *visningskåta*, the "snow house" near the church, and have a peek inside. The huts are made out of birch wood, with a hole in the roof to let the smoke out and birch twigs on the floor to sit on. Everything inside is orderly: the fireplace is in the middle, the cooking area at the back, and there's a strict code of behaviour – you must first wait in the entrance before being invited to enter. Nearby **SAXNÄS** has a **youth hostel** (June–Aug; ☎0940/700 44; 95kr) at Kultsjögården on the main road and a luxury **hotel** complex, *Saxnäsgården* (☎0940/700 80, fax 701 80; ③/②), which doubles up as a **health complex**. Complete with a divine 34°C saltwater swimming pool, herbal baths, massage facilities, fitness centre and sports hall, it is quite literally an oasis in the surrounding wilderness and a wonderful place to pamper yourself for a day. It also **rents** out mountain **bikes, canoes** and **boats**.

### Travelling the Way by bus

The #425 **bus** runs twice daily from Strömsund to Gäddede early in the morning (Fri also an afternoon bus; Sat & Sun 1 daily, in the morning and evening respectively). This means you can stock up with picnic delights in Strömsund, get off the bus wherever you like (just tell the driver to stop), and spend the day walking, or chilling out by the side of a lake, and then catch the evening bus onto Gäddede. From Gäddede the once-daily bus #472 runs to the village of Storviken and only stops at Lake Stora Blåsjön on Saturday. Unfortunately, there's no connection between here and Klimpfjäll, from where bus #420 runs four times daily down to Saxnäs and Vilhelmina (last bus from Klimpfjäll at 3.30pm). It may be possible to hitch between the two places – there are a lot of German and Dutch campervans on this stretch of the road who may be able to help out with a lift over the plateau.

# Tärnaby and Hemavan

Four **buses** daily make the two-hour drive northwest from Storuman to the tiny mountain village of **TÄRNABY**, the birthplace of Ingmar Stenmark, double Olympic gold medallist and Sweden's greatest skier. It's a pretty place: yellow flower-decked meadows run to the edge of the mountain forests, the trees felled to leave great swathes that accommodate World Cup ski slopes. At the eastern edge of the village as you approach from Storuman, the **Samegården** (end June to mid-Aug daily 10am–4pm; 10kr) is a pleasant introduction to *Sami* history, culture and customs. The museum recalls older times when, after a kill in a bear hunt, the gall bladder was cut open and the fluid drunk by the hunters. The **tourist office**, on the one main road (mid-June to mid-Aug daily 9am–8pm; rest of the year Mon–Fri 8.30am–5pm; ☎0954/104 50) can give advice about local **fishing**, which is reputed to be excellent, and give **hiking** trail information for the surrounding mountains. A popular walk is across nearby mountain **Laxfjället**, with its fantastic views down over the village – it can be reached by chair lift from either of the two hotels below. If it's sunny head for the beach at **Lake Laisan**, where the water is often warm enough to swim – take the footpath that branches off right from Sandviksvägen past the **campsite** (☎0954/100 09). There are several other inexpensive places **to stay**, including: the *Tärnaby Fjällhotell*, Östra Strandvägen 16 (☎0954/104 20, fax 106 27; ②/①), which also has four-bedded apartments for 395kr per day; and *Fjällvindens Hus* (☎0954/104 25, fax 106 80; ②/①) on Skyttevägen, which also rents out two- to six-berth cabins for 410kr per day.

## Hemavan

Buses continue on to **HEMAVAN**, which marks the beginning and the end of the 500km northern section of the Kungsleden trail (for more information on the trail and hiking in general, see "Hiking in the National Parks", p.395). The **youth hostel** (known as *FBU-Gården*; mid-June to Sept; ☎0954/305 10; 100kr) is on Blå Vägen, the main road as you come into the village from Tärnaby. If you have your own transport continue along the E12 for around fifteen minutes towards Norway to the gay-friendly *Sånninggårdens Restaurant & Pensionat* (☎0954/330 38, fax 330 06; ①), dramatically located next to a range of craggy mountains and renowned for its excellent food – try the mountain char with cream and chive sauce for 117kr. The pension is the last stop for the *Lapplandspilen* bus to and from Stockholm.

# Sorsele

**SORSELE** (pronounced "Sosh-aye-le") is the next major stop on the *Inlandsbanan* (also 2 daily buses from Storaman; 55min). A pint-sized, dreary town, on the **Vindelälven** (Vindel river), Sorsele became a *cause célèbre* among conservationists in Sweden, when activists forced the government to abandon its plans to build a hydroelectric power station and so regulate the river's flow. The river remains in its natural state today – seething with rapids – and is one of only four in the entire country that hasn't been tampered with in some way or other. During the last week in July (Wed–Sat), the river makes its presence felt with the **Vindelälvsloppet**, a long-distance race that sees hundreds of competitors cover over 350km from nearby Ammarnäs (see opposite) down to Vännäsby near Umeå. It's quite a spectacle – needless to say accommodation at this time is booked up months in advance. The other big event is the **Vindelälvsdraget**, a dog sleigh race held over the same course in the second week of March (Thurs– Sun).

If you're keen on **fly-fishing**, then Sorsele is an ideal base – the Vindelälven and other local river Laisälven are teaming with grayling and brown trout, and there are a number of local lakes stocked with char; for more details ask at the **tourist office** (end June to end Aug Mon–Fri 9am–8pm, Sat & Sun 10am–6pm; rest of the year Mon–Fri 9am–3pm; ☎0952/109 00) at the train station on Stationsgatan; buses stop outside. In the same building, there's a small **museum** (same opening times as the tourist office; 20kr) that details the life and times of the *Inlandsbanan* – although the labelling is in Swedish only. For **accommodation** there are four eight-berth **cabins** at the riverside **campsite** (☎0952/101 24; 285–550kr per day), as well as a small **youth hostel** (mid-June to early Aug; ☎0952/100 48; 95kr), just 500m from the station at Torggatan 1–2. The only **hotel** in town is *Hotell Gästis* (☎0952/107 20, fax ☎551 41; ④/②), a rather plain and drab affair at Hotellgatan 2. **Eating** choices in Sorsele are scant, although the food on offer is cheap, with nothing above 60kr: at lunchtime head for the hotel, which has simple dishes, or the drab pizzeria *La Spezia* on Vindelvägen. Other than that you're left with *Grillhörnan*, near the station, with its burgers and pizzas; there's a bakery in the same building for fresh bread. There are no **bars** here, like many of the villages in this part of Sweden, but you can find expensive beer at all the restaurants. The *Systembolaget* is over the river from the train station on the main shopping street.

# Ammarnäs

The tiny mountain village of **AMMARNÄS**, with a population of just three hundred, lies one and a half hour's bus ride northwest of Sorsele. Set in a wide river valley by the side of the **Gautsträsk lake** and at the foot of the towering **Ammarfjället mountains**, the village offers peace and tranquillity of the first order. This is reindeer country (one-third of the villagers here are reindeer herders), and for hundreds of years the local **Sami** are known to have migrated with their animals from the coast to the surrounding fells for summer pasture. The first settlement began here in 1821 when two *Sami* brothers, Måns and Abraham Sjulsson, were granted permission to settle at Övre Gautsträsk – when they failed to keep the terms of their agreement a new owner, Nils Johansson, took over. He eked out an existence by cultivating the land and is responsible for *Potatisbacken* or Potato Hill, by the river at the eastern end of the village, where the northern Swedish variety of sweet yellow potato is cultivated – unusual for a location so far north. With the founding of a postal station in 1895, the village changed its name to Ammarnäs – the foreland between the Tjulån and Vindelälven rivers.

The **Sami parish village**, near the hill on Nolsivägen, was built in 1850, moving to its present site in 1911. The dozen or so square wooden huts, which are perched on horizontal logs to help keep them dry, are still used today. Three

---

## HIKING AROUND AMMARNÄS

There's some excellent **hiking** to be had around Ammarnäs. The Kungsleden passes through the village (see p.384) on its way from Hemavan to Abisko, but for the less adventurous, **Mount Kaissats** (984m) is ideal for a day spent in the mountains; take the road at the western end of the village that leads to the lake of **Stora Tjulträsk**, from where a marked trail for Kaissats leads off to the right. Alternatively, a **chairlift** in the village ascends **Näsberget**, with trails leading back down into Ammarnäs again. Yet another route is along the road up to **Kraipe**, a small turning to the left before you reach Ammarnäs on Road 363, which is one of the steepest in Sweden; from the village you can easily reach the surrounding summits (if you take this route in September you may well encounter the marking and slaughtering of reindeer at Kraipe corrals). From any of these bare mountain tops, the spectacular views look out over some of the last remaining wilderness in Europe – mountains and dense forest as far as the eye can see.

times a year *Sami* families gather here, much as they did in days gone by, to celebrate important **festivals**: the Samefestivalen (Sun before Midsummer), Vårböndagshelgen (spring intercession day on the first Sun in July) and Höstböndagshelgen (autumn intercession day on Sept 30). The nearby **Samegården** on Strandvägen (Mon–Thurs 9am–2pm) has a simple display of *Sami* history and traditions.

The **Naturum**, which adjoins the tourist office on Tjulträskvägen (same opening hours, see below) has information about the local geology, flora and fauna, an unflattering selection of stuffed animals, including a lynx, and shows a 1940s' film of bears in the woods along the Vindelälven – just ask them to put it on. Also look out for the model of the surrounding mountains, which will give you an idea of just how isolated Ammarnäs is, locked in on three sides by mountains. The old name, Gautsträsk, a *Sami* word meaning "bowl", is an accurate description of the village's valley-bottom location.

## Practicalities

There are two **buses** daily from Sorsele (1hr 15min). The **tourist office** on Tjulträskvägen (mid-June to mid-Aug Mon–Fri 9am–7pm, Sat & Sun 1–6pm; ☎0952/601 32) has plenty of maps and brochures on the surrounding countryside (also see the Naturum above) and useful information on hiking, and can help with the renting of **Icelandic ponies**, **dog sledging** and **snow mobiles** in winter. For canoes, mountain bikes, fishing and camping equipment head for the shop below the tourist office called *Vägvisaren*.

The **youth hostel** (open all year; ☎0952/600 45; 100kr) is virtually opposite the tourist office, and is annexed to *Jonsstugan* (☎0952/600 45, fax 602 51; 325kr), a small and simple pension. Another very cheap alternative are the small wooden **cabins** with showers and toilets in a separate building at *Fridas Stugor* (☎0952/600 36; 250kr). The only **hotel** is the busy and popular *Hotell Ammarnäsgården* (☎0952/600 03, fax 601 43; ①), which has rather simple en-suite rooms aimed at hikers walking the Kungsleden – the fabulous sauna and pool complex, although in the basement, makes up for the lack of creature comforts in the rooms. For **eating** and **drinking** your only choice is the hotel bar and restaurant; if you're spending some time up here, it's a good idea to bring some beer with you from the nearest *Systembolaget*, 90km away in Sorsele.

**Travelling on** from Ammarnäs is quite tricky – all connections are via Sorsele. If you've walked the Kungsleden from Abisko and are ending here, the best way to Stockholm is to take the early-afternoon bus to Sorsele, change for the connection to Lycksele, change again for the evening bus to Vännäs, arriving in time for the night train to Stockholm. On Saturdays, there's a direct afternoon bus from Ammarnäs to Vännäs also connecting with the Stockholm train; more information on ☎020/91 00 19 or from the tourist office.

# Arvidsjaur and around

Back on the *Inlandsbanan* and an hour and a quarter north of Sorsele, **ARVIDS-JAUR** is by far the biggest place north of Östersund so far – although that's not saying much. Drab housing areas spread out either side of a nondescript main street, Storgatan. For centuries this was where the region's **Sami** gathered to trade and debate, their agenda hijacked by the Protestant missionaries, who established their first church here in 1606. The success of the Swedish settlement

### LAPLAND PLACE NAMES

Many of the names of places, lakes and mountains in Lapland come from the *Sami* language (also see "A brief look at the *Sami*" on pp.364–65). Below is a guide to some of the most common:

| | | | |
|---|---|---|---|
| *alla, gille* | western | *puolta, puolda* | hill |
| *jaure, jaur* | lake | *saivo* | small holy lake |
| *jokk; jokkuts* | creek, stream, river | *stuor; stuorab* | large; larger |
| *kaissats* | small pointed mountain | *tjuolta* | small mountain |
| | | *tjåkko, tjakke* | mountain, mountain top |
| *kaisse, gaise* | pointed mountain | | |
| *kaska* | middle | *unna, utse* | small, smaller |
| *kuoikka* | rapid, waterfall | *vagge* | wide mountain valley |
| *kåbbo* | hill | *vardo* | low mountain |
| *lule, lulle* | eastern | *vare* | mountain |
| *luspe* | lake outlet | *vuolle* | lower |
| *nuort, nuorta* | northern | *åive, åjja* | mountain |
| *paije, paje* | upper | *årje* | southern |

was secured when silver was discovered in the nearby mountains, and the town flourished as a staging point and supply depot. Despite these developments the *Sami* continued to assemble on market days and during religious festivals, building their own **parish village** of simple wooden huts at the end of the eighteenth century. About eighty have survived and are clumped unceremoniously towards the north end of town next to a modern yellow apartment building; the **Lappstaden** (officially open June–Aug 11am–5pm; 20kr, but at other times you can walk in for free) are still used today during the last weekend in August for a special **festival**, Storstämningshelgen, as well as for auctions and other events throughout the year. Of a total population of five thousand, there are still twenty *Sami* families in Arvisdjaur who make their living from reindeer husbandry. For a more hands-on experience of Sami life, visit the centre at Gasa, just west of town (see "Activities around Arvidsjaur" overleaf).

## Practicalities

There's no real reason to tarry, but if you want to stay, head for the **tourist office** (mid-June to mid-Aug daily 8.45am–7pm; rest of the year Mon–Fri 9am–5pm; ☎0960/175 00), at Garvaregatan 4, just off Storgatan and five minutes' walk from the station up Lundavägen. There are three daily buses from Sorsele (1hr 10min). The tourist office will fix you up with a **private room** for around 110kr, plus a booking fee of 25kr. There's also a cosy private **youth hostel**, *Lappugglans Turistviste*, conveniently situated at Västra Skolgatan 9 (☎0960/124 13; 100kr), or you could try *Camp Gielas* (☎0960/134 20), a few minutes' walk along Strandvägen and Järnvägsgatan from the tourist office, which has **cabins** for 495kr and sits beside one of the town's dozen or so lakes, Tvätttjärn, with its bathing beaches. There's a sports hall here, too, as well as a gym, sauna, tennis courts and mini-golf. You can rent a **bike with train wheels**, complete with camping equipment (each bike can carry two people), to cycle along the disued rail line southeast to **JÖRN** (100kr up to 4hr, 180kr for 24hr; ☎0960/108 90) – a jumping-off point for trains on the main coastal route. There are two **hotels** in town: *Hotell Laponia* at

Storgatan 45 (☎0960/555 00; ④/②) with comfortable, modern en-suite rooms and a swimming pool; and the more basic *Centralhotellet*, handy for the station, at Järnvägsgatan 63 (☎0960/100 98; ②/①). A cheaper option is the *Gästeriet* **pension** (☎0960/472 00; ①) at the top end of Stationsgatan, with modern rooms and apartments and fantastic views over the lake, Västra Ringlet; there's also a shared kitchen. Bear in mind that if you're in Arvidsjaur in winter much of the hotel accommodation will be full of test drivers from Europe's leading car companies, which come to the area to experience driving on the frozen lakes – book well in advance to secure a room.

For snacks and coffee try *Kaffestugan* at Storgatan 21, which also has cheap lunches, sandwiches and salads. Otherwise there's a small choice of **restaurants**: you can sit down to Italian food at *Athena*, Storgatan 10, with averagely priced lunches, pizzas, meat and fish dishes. Next door at Storgatan 8, *Cazba* serves up pizzas for the same price but has less atmosphere. For finer food and higher prices head for the restaurant at *Hotell Laponia*, where delicious á la carte meals include local reindeer. The **bar** here is the place to be seen of an evening but be prepared to shell out 45kr for a beer. Another popular spot is *Pegs Pub* at Skogsgatan 5, where prices are the same.

### Activities around Arvidsjaur

The **Båtsuoj Forest Sami Center** (June–Aug daily 1–9pm; at other times by advance booking on ☎0960/610 26 or 130 14), to the west of Arvidsjaur in the village of **GASA**, is a good place to get to grips with the everyday life of the *Sami*: you come face to face with a **reindeer** (*båtsuoj* in *Sami*) and meet real reindeer herders. They'll teach you how to milk a reindeer, the tricks of baking their traditional bread and about their religion and way of life. A half-day at Båtsuoj costs 350kr and includes dinner (of reindeer cooked over an open fire); a full day costs 550kr and includes an overnight stay in a *kåta* or tent; for children under twelve it's free. The centre arranges **cloudberry picking** expeditions for a pricy 600kr; the berries are rare and grow in the most inaccessible of northern Sweden's marshlands – hence the price. If you so desire you can also buy your own reindeer – and take it home with you quartered and frozen.

One of the other main attractions around Arvidsjaur is **river rafting** on Piteälven. The price (July–Aug 240kr, under 17s 110kr; minimum age 10) for a two-hour trip down some of the region's most exciting rapids – watch the video at the tourist office for an idea of how wet you'll get – includes rain clothes, helmets, boots and life jackets. Booking can be made at the tourist office, at the rafting centre, *Forsfärd på Piteälven* (☎0960/800 20), or at the Jokkmokk tourist office (see p.390), and trips leave from outside the Arvidsjaur office at 10.30am, 3pm and 6pm. There's a certificate for all those who make it back in one piece. It's possible to take the *Inlandsbanan* to nearby **Moskosel** and to head for the rapids from there – speak to the tourist office in Arvidsjaur for details or bus transfers.

# Arjeplog

The municipality of **Arjeplog** is roughly the size of Belgium but supports a population of less than four thousand – half of whom live in the eponymous lakeside town. It's one of the most beautiful parts of Sweden, with over double the number of lakes as people and vast expanses of mountains and virgin forests. Here the air is clear and crisp, the rivers clean and deep and the winters mighty cold – in 1989 a temperature of -52°C was recorded. January and February, in particular, are bitter, dark and silent months. However, it's during winter that Arjeplog is at its busiest: hundreds of test drivers from Korea, Australia, Germany, Britain, Italy, America and France descend on the town to use the winter test facilities that have been set up here. Cars are put through their paces in the freezing conditions and brakes and road holding are tested on the frozen lakes. In summer, Arjeplog is a likable little place away from the main inland road and rail routes, where **hiking**, **canoeing** and **fishing** are all popular activities, each offering the chance of blissful isolation, be it by the side of a secluded mountain tarn or in a clearing deep in the pine forest. In late July you can go cloudberry picking, and in the autumn, you can hunt for lingonberries, blueberries and wild mushrooms.

In **ARJEPLOG** town itself check out the yellow wooden building opposite the tourist office in the square: the **Silvermuseet** (mid-June to mid-Aug daily 9am–6pm; rest of the year Mon–Fri 10am–4pm, Sat 11am–3pm; 30kr) was founded by the Lapland doctor Einar Wallquist and is home to fascinating collections of *Sami* silver, including an ornate silver collar that was handed down from mother to daughter. If you're around in the first week of July make sure you see the **Laplands festspel** – an orgy of chamber music, folk and fiddle music and dancing.

## THE ARCTIC CIRCLE AND THE MIDNIGHT SUN

Just south of Jokkmokk (see p.389), the *Inlandsbanan* finally crosses the **Arctic Circle**, the imaginary line drawn around the earth at roughly 66° North, which marks the northernmost point that the sun can be seen on the shortest day of the year. This is occasion enough for a bout of whistle blowing as the train pulls up to allow everyone to take photos. However, the painted white rocks that curve away over the hilly ground, a crude but popular representation of the Circle, are completely inaccurate. Due to the earth's uneven orbit, the line is creeping northwards at a rate of about 14–15m every year. To the dismay of many tourists, the real Artic Circle is now around a kilometre further north. It won't be for another 10,000 to 20,000 years that the northward movement will stop – by which point the Circle will have reached 68° North – and then start moving slowly south again. If you find the godforsaken place appealing, there's a **campsite** here (contact the Jokkmokk tourist office for erratic opening times); a taxi into Jokkmokk (7km) will cost around 100kr.

Thanks to light refraction in the atmosphere, the **Midnight Sun** can be seen south of the Arctic Circle – Arvidsjaur marks the southernmost point in Sweden – for a few days each year. The further north you travel the longer the period when the phenomenon is visible, and conversely the longer the polar winter. The following is a list of the main towns and dates:

| | |
|---|---|
| Arvidsjaur and Haparanda | June 20 /21 |
| Arjeplog | June 12 /13 to July 28 /29 |
| Jokkmokk/Övertorneå | June 8 /9 to July 2 /3 |
| Gällivare | June 4 /5 to July 6 /7 |
| Kiruna | May 28 /29 to July 11 /12 |
| Karesuando | May 26 /27 to July 15 /16 |
| Treriksröset | May 22 /23 to July 17 /18 |

## Practicalities

There are three buses daily from Arvidsjaur (1hr 10min). The **tourist office** in the main square (mid-June to mid-Aug Mon–Fri 9am–7pm, Sat 10am–5pm, Sun noon–5pm; ☎0961/142 70) can help with local hiking trails, fishing tips (70kr per day for everything you need) and **cycles** (50kr per day, 150kr per week). The best-value **accommodation** is the central and palatial **youth hostel** (May to late Nov; ☎0961/612 10; 100kr), on Silvervägen, where every room sleeps a maximum of four and has en-suite facilities. The hostel is part of *Hotell Lyktan* (☎0961/612 10, fax 101 50; ④/②), which offers comfortable modern rooms of the highest standard. The accommodation at *Hotell Arjeplog* (☎0961/107 70, fax 614 26; ④/②), 1.5km up Öberget from the centre (a 30min walk), is dowdy but perfectly okay, with fantastic views over the village and surrounding lake. Ten minutes' walk along Silvervägen, the lakeside **campsite** *Kraja* (☎0961/315 00, fax 103 17) has simple **cabins** for 185–685kr per day depending on size – there's also a swimming pool here. If you're looking to get away from it all in your own private **cabin in the wilds**, speak to the tourist office: it has dozens for rent but generally out in **Jäkkvik** or **Adolfström** (both on the Kungsleden), or for complete isolation at **Vuoggatjålme** – tucked right up in the mountains close to the Norwegian border.

Bear in mind that in winter accommodation is booked months in advance by the likes of BMW, Mercedes and Porsche.

**Eating** and **drinking** in Arjeplog is not a joy. There are two cut-price options: the grotty *Mathörnun* on Drottninggatan, which serves up moderately priced reindeer, Arctic char and traditional Swedish home cooking amid hideously tacky decor, while the downstairs bar attracts the town's hardened drinkers; the other is *Pizzeria Verona* opposite, which, with its equally dingy 1970s' interior, offers salads and pizzas at similar prices. If you're longing for gourmet food head for *Kraja Wärdshus* at the campsite (evening only), where you can tuck into fillet of elk or saddle of reindeer; there's also a pub and disco here (Wed & Fri). Fine food, including Arctic char and salmon, is also served in *Hotell Arjeplog*'s light and airy restaurant, complete with open fire. For a coffee in summer head out to the island of Skeppsholmen, behind the tourist office, where a *Sami* café is hidden away in a traditional *kåta*.

# Jokkmokk

During his journey in Lapland, the botanist Carl von Linné said, "If not for the mosquitoes, this would be earth's paradise"; his comments were made after journeying along the river valley of the Lilla Luleälven during the short summer weeks when the mosquitoes are at their most active. The town's *Sami* name comes from one particular bend (*mokk*) in the river (*jokk*), which runs through a densely forested municipality the size of Wales, with a minuscule population of just six thousand five hundred; needless to say, **JOKKMOKK** is a welcome oasis, although not an immediately appealing one. At one time *Sami* winter quarters, a market and church heralded a permanent settlement by the beginning of the seventeenth century. Today as well as being a well-known handicraft centre, the town functions as the capital of the *Sami* and is home to the only further education college, Sameras Folkhögskola, teaching handicraft making, reindeer husbandry and ecology in the *Sami* language. Jokkmokk's fascinating **Ájtte museum** – *ájtte* means storage hut – is a brief walk east of the centre on Kyrkogatan, off the main Storgatan (mid-June to late Aug Mon, Tues, Thurs & Fri 9am–6pm, Wed 9am–8pm, Sat & Sun 11am–6pm; rest of the year Mon–Fri 9am–4pm, Sat & Sun noon–4pm; 40kr), and is the place to really mug up on the *Sami*. Displays and exhibitions recount the tough existence of the original settlers of northern Scandinavia and show how things have slowly improved over time – today the modern *Sami* are more dependent on snow scooters and helicopters to herd their reindeer than on the age-old methods employed by their ancestors. There are also imaginative temporary exhibitions on *Sami* culture and local flora and fauna; the museum staff can arrange day-trips into the surrounding marshes for a spot of mushroom picking (and mosquito squatting). Close to the museum on Lappstavägen, the **Alpine Gsarden** (mid-June to mid-Aug daily noon–7pm; other times by arrangement on ☎0971/170 70; 25kr) is home to moor-king, mountain avens, glacier crowfoot and other vegetation to be found on the fells around Jokkmokk.

Have a look, too, at the **Lapp kyrka**, off Stortorget, a recent copy of the eighteenth-century church on the site. The octagonal design and curiously shaped tower represent *Sami* styles, but the surrounding graveyard wall is all improvisation: the space in between the coarsely hewn timbers was used to store coffins during winter, waiting for the thaw in May when the *Sami* could go out and dig graves again. The temperatures in this part of Sweden regularly plunge to -30°C and below.

## The winter market and other activities

The four-hundred-year-old great **winter market**, known simply in Swedish as Jokkmokk's **marknad**, is held on the first Thursday to Sunday of each February, when thirty thousand force their way into town – ten times the normal population. It's the best and coldest time of year to be here: with lots of drunken stallholders trying to flog reindeer hides and other unwanted knick-knacks to even more drunken passers-by – there's a Wild West feeling in the air. Held on the frozen Talvatissjön lake behind *Hotell Jokkmokk* (see below), the **reindeer races** can be a real spectacle as man and beast battle it out on a specially marked-out ice track – although the reindeer often have other ideas and every now and then veer off with great alacrity into the crowd, sending spectators fleeing for cover. A smaller and less traditional autumn fair at the end of August (around the 25th) is an easier, but poorer, option.

During summer, Talvatissjön is the preferred spot for catching Arctic char and rainbow trout, although to **fish** here you need a **permit** (*fiskekort*), available from the tourist office. There's a cleaning table and fireplace laid on, should you catch anything. It's also possible to go **white-water rafting** on the Pärlälven river just to the west of town. You can choose from two different routes, one for beginners and a more turbulent stretch of water for those who live life in the fast lane – safety equipment is included in the price; for more information contact *Äventyrarna* (adults 350kr, under-15s 175kr; ☎0971/126 96).

## Practicalities

If you're coming up by train from Stockholm, get off at **Murjek**, from where bus #254 run west to Jokkmokk (4 daily). It's a four-hour journey on the *Inlandsbanan* from Arvidsjaur, or just over two hours on the *Inlandsexpressen* bus. Jokkmokk **tourist office** (mid-June to mid-Aug daily 9am–7pm; during winter market daily 8am–6pm; rest of the year Thurs–Sun 8.30am–4pm; ☎0971/121 40), Stortorget 4, is five minutes' walk from the train station along Stationsgatan. They've got all sorts of printed information, useful if you're considering hiking in the region.

**Accommodation** in town is plentiful enough, but if you want to stay here during the winter market it means booking up a good year in advance, although some **private rooms**, which you can arrange through the tourist office (100kr; booking fee 10kr), do become available in the autumn before the market. The **youth hostel** (open all year; ☎0971/559 77; 100kr) is in a wonderful old house at Åsgatan 20 and is especially delightful in winter, when the garden is deep with snow and the trees outside the windows heavy with ice. Otherwise, the convenient **hotel**, *Hotell Jokkmokk*, has an attractive lakeside setting at Solgatan 45 (☎0971/553 20, fax 556 25; ④/②), although its en-suite rooms are dull and the restaurant a 1970s' nightmare. The other hotel, *Hotell Gästis*, at Herrevägen 1 (☎0971/100 12; ②/①), is nothing to write home about – simple en-suite rooms with modern decor. The **campsite**, *Jokkmokks Turistcenter* (☎0971/123 70), is 3km southeast of town on the Lule river off the main Road 97, from Jokkmokksvägen to Boden and Luleå; the best way to get here is to **rent a bike** from the tourist office for 50kr per day.

Jokkmokk has a limited number of **eating** and **drinking** possibilities. At the cheap and cheerful *Restaurang Milano*, on Berggatan, lunch is 50kr and pizzas at other times 60kr. The rather nicer *Restaurang Opera*, Storgatan 36, offers lunch and pizzas for the same prices, plus there's the usual range of meat and fish à la carte dishes. If you're after a steak, head for *GJ's Stekhuset* on Föreningsgatan, where a lunchtime slab goes for 50kr; avoid the overpriced restaurant at *Hotell Jokkmokk*.

For traditional *Sami* dishes head for the restaurant at the Ájtte museum – the cloud-berry and ice cream is simply divine. Perfectly okay meals are also served up at the restaurant out at the campsite. Your first choice for drinking should be *Restaurang Opera* (beer costs 35kr); failing that try *Restaurang Milano,* and of an evening the *Bakfickan* bar inside *Hotell Jokkmokk* – if you've supped your way round Jokkmokk this far you won't mind the late-night drunken company here.

## Vuollerim and Porjus

Forty-five kilometres southeast of Jokkmokk on Route 97 to Boden and Luleå lies the tiny village of **VUOLLERIM**, site of a six-thousand-year-old **Stone Age winter settlement**. Archeological digs have uncovered well-preserved remains of houses, storage pits, tool and weapon shards, fires, rubbish dumps and drainage works. A small and excellent **museum** on the edge of the village (June–Aug Mon–Fri 9am–6pm; rest of the year Mon–Fri 9am–4pm; 50kr) covers the development of the various sites and finds, and a slide show takes you on a local journey through time depicting the probable life of the inhabitants. The whole thing really comes alive when a minibus carts you off to the digs themselves, with archeologists providing a guided tour in English – without them the whole thing would be nothing more than a mudbath to the untrained eye. To get here from Jokkmokk, you can take the Boden/Luleå bus and get off at the *Statoil* filling station, from where it's a 1km walk up the road towards the village; the bus to Murjek goes via Vuollerim and right to the museum. The site is on a narrow, wooded promontory that juts out into the lake – a great place for a picnic.

North of Jokkmokk, Route 45 and the *Inlandsbanan* pass through pretty **PORJUS**, blighted only by the ugly hydroelectric power station begun in 1910. The town was an obvious choice of site, *Swedish State Railways* requiring power for the electrification of the new line between Luleå and the Norwegian border, but logistically it was a disaster. The nearest train station was then 50km away at Gällivare, and there was no road to Porjus. For the first year until the inland rail stretch was complete, men carried up to seventy kilo loads on their backs along planked paths for the whole distance. The **heritage park** at **Porjus Kraftbyggarland** (mid-June to mid-Aug daily 9am–6pm), by the station, documents the power station's history.

# Gällivare

The last stop on the *Inlandsbanan*, **GÄLLIVARE** ("Yell-i-vaa-re") is one of the most important areas for iron ore in Europe and, if you have any interest in seeing a working mine, don't wait until Kiruna's tame "tourist tour" (see p.401); instead take a trip down the more evocative mines here. The town is also a good starting point for walking in the national parks, which fill most of the northwestern corner of the country (these are covered on pp.395–400).

## Arrival and information

The **train station** is on Lasarettsgatan, about five minutes' walk from the tourist office. It's also worth noting that *Skyways* flies from Gällivare to Stockholm several times daily and covers the 1200km in just two hours; the train takes around twenty. The very accommodating **tourist office** (June to mid-Aug daily 9am–8pm; rest of the year Mon–Fri 9am–4pm; ☎0970/166 60), Storgatan 16, has good free maps and hiking information; downstairs in the same building there's a **café**, and upstairs a simple **museum** dealing with *Sami* history and forestry. Gällivare is an easy place to walk around, with nearly everything you could want east of the train line, except the youth hostel, which is west of the tracks, and the one main sight, the mines (just outside town in Malmberget), which you are ferried to on a tourist office bus. **Bike rental** is available from the *Malm Hotell*; see below.

# Accommodation

The tourist office can fix you up with a **private room** for around 125kr per person, plus a booking fee of 20kr. The **youth hostel** (open all year but bookings required in Oct; ☎0970/143 80; 100kr or dorm beds for 70kr), which is behind the train station (cross the tracks by the metal bridge), offers accommodation in small cabins and a good sauna; because of the town's strategic transport position (see p.395) booking ahead in summer is advised. The hostel is a wonderful place to stay in winter when the Vassara träsk lake is frozen – snow scooters whizz up and down its length under the eerie Northern Lights, which are clearly visible in Gällivare. If it's full, try the small **private hostel**, *Lapphärberget* (☎0970/125 34; 100kr), near the Lappkyrkan, although be prepared for a less than warm welcome by the host. There are also other hostel-style places and several **hotels** to choose from (see below), but with your own transport the premier place to stay is in the reconstructed shantytown, **Kåkstan**, up at Malmberget (take bus #1). You can rent one of the simple four-berth wooden huts (toilet and shower across the unmade road) and pretend you're back in 1888, when iron ore was first loaded onto trains and marked the beginning of the great iron ore boom – ring ☎0970/183 96 or mobile ☎070/537 6977 or book through the tourist office. There's also a **campsite** (mid-May to mid-Sept; ☎0970/186 79) by the river and off the main Road 45 (Porjusvägen to Jokkmokk).

## Hotels and pensions

**Dundret**, Per Högströmsgatan 1 (☎0970/145 60). Actually a small pension, with just seven rooms and shower and toilet off the corridor. ②/①

**Gällivare Värdshus**, Klockljungsvägen 2 (☎0970/162 00). A central German-run cheapie with small youth-hostel style rooms, it looks dreadfully grotty on the outside but inside is perfectly okay. ③/②

**Lokstallarna**, at the Homstead Museum, Storgatan 16 (☎0970/153 75). More hostel-style en-suite accommodation. ①

**Malm**, Torget 18, in Malmberget (☎0970/244 50). Rooms here are basic, without bathrooms, but very cheap all year round (150kr per person in summer). The hotel rents out 21-gear **city bikes** for 100kr per day – if you book one day in advance, they'll bring them down to the tourist office for collection, otherwise take bus #1. ①

**Nex**, Lasarettsgatan 1 (☎0970/110 20, fax 154 75). The best of the bunch in town, with smart, tastefully decorated rooms and good restaurant (see p.395), and handy for the station – but closed on weekends. ④/②

**Nya Dundret** (☎0970/145 60, fax 148 27). The best hotel around, but it's at the top of the Dundret mountain, so you'll need your own transport to get here. ⑤/③

# The Sites

Gällivare is far more pleasant than the surrounding industry suggests. It's the biggest town since Östersund, and strolling around its open centre, heavily glazed and insulated against the biting cold of winter, is a great antidote to the small inland villages along the *Inlandsbanan*. There's a gritty ugliness to Gällivare that gives the place a certain charm: a steely grey mesh of modern streets that has all the hallmarks of a city, although everything is far too modest for the title to be applied with any justification. It occupies the site of a *Sami* village, and one theory has it that the town's name comes from the *Sami* language: a crack or gorge (*djelli*) in the mountain (*vare*). The *Sami* church, **Lappkyrkan** (mid-June to late Aug 10am–2pm), down by the river near the train station, is a mid-eighteenth-century construction and recalls the importance of the *Sami*. It's known as the *Ettöreskyrkan* ("one öre" church) after the subscription drive throughout Sweden

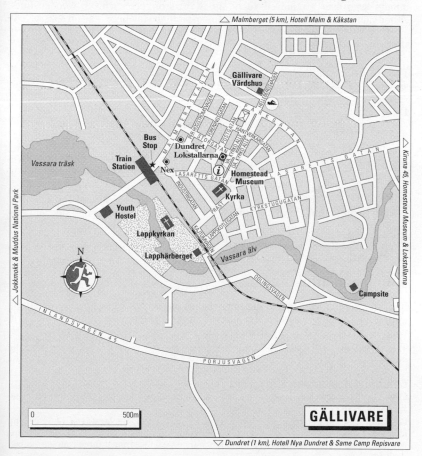

△ Malmberget (5 km), Hotell Malm & Kåkstan

Gällivare Värdshus

Bus Stop
Dundret Lokstallarna

Train Station
Nex

Vassara träsk

Homestead Museum

Kyrka

Youth Hostel

Lappkyrkan

Lapphärberget

Vassara älv

N

Campsite

◁ Jokkmokk & Muddus National Park

▷ Kiruna 45, Homestead Museum & Lokstallarna

INLANDSVÄGEN 45

PORJUSVÄGEN

ÖDLINGSVÄGEN

0          500m

**GÄLLIVARE**

▽ Dundret (1 km), Hotell Nya Dundret & Same Camp Repisvare

that paid for it. If you want to dip into *Sami* culture – meet the reindeer, see how the *Sami* make their handicrafts and throw lassoes – you can visit a **Sami camp** at **Repisvare**, 2.5km from the town centre, through *Vägvisaren-Samiska Upplevelser* (☎0970/555 60; mobile ☎010/694 9810; 40kr).

Tucked away at **MALMBERGET** on Dundret, one of the two hills that overlook the town, the modern mines and works are distant, dark blots down which the tourist office ferries relays of tourists in summer. There are two separate tours, both running from June to August: one of the underground **iron ore mine** (Mon–Fri 10am & 2pm; 160kr), the other to the opencast **copper mine** (Mon–Fri 2pm; 140kr), which is the biggest in Europe and also Sweden's biggest gold mine – gold is recovered from the slag produced during the extraction of the copper. The earsplitting noise produced from the mammoth-sized trucks in the iron ore mine (they're five times the height of a person) can be quite disconcerting in the confined darkness. The tour also takes in **Kåkstan**, the shantytown where the miners lived over a hundred years ago – rows of reconstructed wooden huts either side of an unmade street (it's also possible to stay here – see p.392).

## Walks around Gällivare

There's precious little else to see or do in Gällivare, but the town is well positioned as a base for walking. For a fairly gentle walk, you can head up to the *Björnfällan* **restaurant** (the name means "bear trap"), a 4km hike on a well-marked path up **Dundret** hill, from where the views are magnificent. To get right to the top, special buses are laid on for the Midnight Sun, making the journey from the train station to the end of the winding road (mid-June to mid-July daily 11pm, returning 1am; exact dates vary from year to year); tickets, available from the tourist office, cost 140kr return and include the ubiquitous Swedish waffle covered with cloudberries and cream.

Alternatively, explore the marshes and forests of one of the nearby national parks (see the following section). The nearest is **Muddus National Park**, which lies just to the south of town, hemmed in by the *Inlandsbanan* on one side and the train line from Boden to Gällivare on the other. The park is easy to reach with your own car, but public transport will only take you within 12km: take the bus to **Ligga** and then walk to **Skaite** and the beginning of the network of trails.

## Eating and drinking

If you're arriving from one of the tiny villages on the *Inlandsbanan*, the wealth of **eating** possibilities in town will make you dizzy; if you're coming from Luleå grit your teeth and bear it. As for **drinking**, the place to be seen is the rustic *Kai's Pub* at Storgatan 15, which has beer for 33kr between 3pm and 8pm – more after. The bar in the *Nex Hotell* is also a popular drinking hole.

### Cafés and Restaurants
**Café Forell**, Hantverkaregatan 7. For salad and good-quality lunches only – fish dishes a speciality.

**Gourmet Restaurangen**, in the out-of-town Ericssons Center, Upplagsvägen 17. Excellent food here, despite the plastic surroundings, but you need your own transport. The eat-until-you-drop pizza and pasta buffet is a good lunch-time deal; occasional three-course evening deals for 150kr.

**Nex Hotell**, Lasarettsgatan. The restaurant here does a range of good lunches and, although pretentious and expensive, it does serve excellent local delicacies such as Arctic char and reindeer.

**Pizzeria Dylan** in the Arkaden shopping centre. The best pizzeria in town, it also does takeaways – open daytime only.

**Restaurant Nya Dundret** inside the *Björnfällan* restaurant (see above). Good northern Swedish food but at a price – nothing under 150kr.

**Restaurang Peking**, Storgatan 21 B. A good place for lunch, with reasonable Chinese food and pizzas. Closed Mon.

**Åhults Bageri & Café**, Lasarettsgatan 19. Great for coffee and cakes.

## Moving on

Gällivare is what the Swedes call a *knutpunkt,* a travel interchange. From here **trains** run south in summer to Östersund and Mora on the *Inlandsbanan*, northwest to Kiruna and onto Narvik in Norway and southeast to Boden, Luleå and then all points south. **Buses** run west to the Stora Sjöfallet National Park (see p.397) and Ritsem, east to Pajala (see p.405) and northeast to Svappavaara, where connections can be made to Karesuando (see p.406); and from there via Finland to Treriksröset (see p.406) – the northernmost point in Sweden, where the country meets Norway and Finland. The year-round *Inlandsexpressen* buses run south via Jokkmokk and Arvidsjaur to Östersund, which are handy when the *Inlandsbanan* isn't running.

# Hiking in the national parks

It's not a good idea to go **hiking in the national parks** of northern Sweden on a whim. Even for experienced walkers, the going can be tough and uncomfortable in parts, downright treacherous in others. **Mosquitoes** are a real problem: it's difficult to describe the utter misery of being covered in a blanket of insects, your eyes, ears and nose full of the creatures (for more on practicalities and safety guidelines see "Hiking information" overleaf). Yet the beautiful landscape is one of the last wilderness areas left in Europe – it's little more than a vast expanse of forest and mountains, and roads and human habitation are the exception rather than the norm. **Reindeer** are a common sight, since the parks are breeding grounds and summer pasture, and **Sami** settlements are dotted throughout the region – notably at **Ritsem** and **Vaisaluokta**.

Although there are some good short trails, especially for beginners, that run within one of the five national parks, the grand master of them all is the northern section of the **Kungsleden**, which leads through several parks and is divided into five sections. A good map of the area is *Lantmäteriet Kartförlaget*'s "Norra Norrland" (scale 1:400 000), available in Gällivare.

## The national parks and shorter trails

There are five **national parks** in northern Sweden that range in difficulty from a gentle gander to a positive assault course. To the south of Gällivare is the easygoing **Muddus National Park** (accessible from Gällivare), and beginning about 120km northwest of Gällivare, the tract of wilderness edging Norway contains four others. Here the low fells, large lakes and moors of **Padjelanta, Stora Sjöfallet** and **Abisko** parks act as the eyebrows to the sheer face of the moun-

## HIKING INFORMATION

The best time to go **hiking** in the Swedish mountains is from late June to September. During May and early June the ground is very wet and boggy as a result of the rapid snow melt. Once the snow has gone, wild flowers burst into bloom to make the most of the short summer months. The weather is very changeable – one moment it can be hot and sunny, the next it can be cold and rainy – and snow showers are not uncommon in summer.

If you're a novice, it's imperative to keep to the **marked trails**, which in summer are worn paths denoted here and there by stone cairns or coloured ribbons on trees and poles. A red "X" on a pole marks the spot where winter and summer trails meet. Many routes cross large streams – bridges or rowing boats are provided. **Rest shelters** are always open but aren't intended for overnight stays; head instead for **cabins** or **STF fell stations**, which appear at intervals of roughly 15–20km and are listed, along with the distances between them, in the text below. The fell stations can be booked in advance and offer bed and breakfast accommodation; *HI* members get a 50kr discount at all fell stations. Cabins can't be booked, and you'll need your own sheets or sleeping bags, but during the summer season there are hosts in attendance. There are telephones in cabins and some rest shelters. Posted at the entrances and on huts and cabins throughout the parks are some special regulations on how to reduce damage to the land and safety advice; these are worth reading and remembering.

A few tips:

- Get decent **maps**, boots and proper advice before setting out.
- Bring several bottles of **mosquito repellent**.
- Take a good **sleeping bag**, and for longer treks a **tent**, as parts of some trails don't have overnight cabins.
- **Other essentials** for a day-hike pack include rain gear, scarf, gloves, cap, matches, a compass and a knife.
- When **fording streams** never wade in water above your knees. Wade across where the stream is shallow and wide. Go one at a time and wear training shoes if possible. Unbuckle the hip belt and chest strap on your pack.
- Watch out for **snow bridges** across streams – take great care not to fall into the water, which is likely to be deep and cold.
- Never go on a **glacier** without a guide – concealed crevasses can be fatal.

For additional information contact **Fjällsäkerhetsrådet** (The Council of Mountain Safety) at Naturvårdsverket, S-171 85, Solna. Detailed information, advice and encouragement for all the routes and parks covered here is given out by **Svenska Turistföreningen** (*Swedish Touring Club*), which has offices at Drottninggatan 31–33 in Stockholm and at Drottningtorget 6 in Gothenburg; or speak to any of the tourist offices in Ammarnäs, Jokkmokk, Gällivare, Kiruna or Tärnaby.

tainous and inhospitable **Sarek**. Classed as "extremely difficult", Sarek has no tourist facilities, trails, cabins or bridges; the rivers are dangerous and the weather rotten – in short, you need good mountaineering experience to tackle this one. For up-to-the-minute information on walking in the parks contact *Fjällenheten* (Mountain Advice Centre) at Åsgatan 20, Jokkmokk (☎0971/123 30), or the fell stations at Saltoluokta (☎0973/410 10) and Kvikkjokk (☎0971/210 22).

## Muddus National Park

**Muddus National Park** is the place recommended for beginnners, a pine-forested and marshland park between Jokkmokk and Gällivare, home to bears, lynx, martens, weasels, hares, elk and in summer also reindeer; among birds, the whooper swan is one of the most common sights. The park's western edges are skirted by Road 45 and the easiest approach is to leave the highway at **Liggadammen** (also buses here from Gällivare) and then follow the small road to **Skaite**, where an easy hiking **trail** of 55km begins. There are cabins (April–Sept; rest of the year keys from Jokkmokk & Gällivare tourist offices) along the trail, with a campsite at Muddus Falls. Distances between the cabins are as follows: Liggadammen to Skaite 13km; Skaite to Muddus Falls 7km; Muddus Falls to Muddusluobbal 9km; Muddusluobbal to Manson 5km; Sarkavare to Muddus Falls 14km; Solaure to Manson 7km. There are no outlets for buying food or other provisions.

## Padjelanta National Park

**Padjelanta** is the largest national park in Sweden; the name comes from the *Sami* language and means "the higher country", an apt description for a high tableland almost exclusively above the tree line and home to thousands of reindeer. The **Padjelanta Trail** (150km) runs from **Vaisaluokta** south through **Stora Sjöfallet** to **Kvikkjokk** and is good for inexperienced walkers – allow at least a week. You can get to Vaisaluokta by **bus** from Gällivare, then take a boat across the lake to Ritsem; to get to Kvikkjokk hop on a bus in Jokkmokk (note this trail incorporates part of the Kungsleden). For times of buses contact *Länstrafiken Norrbotten* (☎020/91 00 19) or any tourist office in the area. There's also a **helicopter** service operated by *Norrlandsflyg* between Kvikkjokk, Saltoluokta and Ritsem (July–Aug; 1170kr per person, 650kr over part of route; ☎0970/140 65 or ☎0971/210 68). There are two *STF* fell stations along the trail and distances between accommodation points are as follows: Ristem to Vaisaluokta (boat) 16km; Vaisaluokta to Kutjaure 18km; Kutjaure to Låddejokk 19km; Låddejokk to Arasluokta 12km; Arasluokta to Saltoluokta 10km; **Saltoluokta fell station** (mid-March to early May & mid-June to mid-Sept; ☎0973/410 10; 190–415kr) to Tuottar 18km; Tuottar to Tarraluoppal 11km; Tarraluoppal to Såmmarlappa 15km; Såmmarlappa to Tarrekaise 13km; Tarrekaise to Njunjes 7km; Njunjes to **Kvikkjokk fell station** 17km (late March to early May & mid-June to mid-Sept, ☎0971/210 22; 195–220kr). Ask the wardens at the cabins or fell stations for the nearest food stores.

# Kungsleden: Abisko to Hemavan

**Kungsleden** (the King's Route) is the most famous and popular of the trails; a 500km route from **Abisko** in the north to **Hemavan**, near Tärnaby (see p.381), it takes in Sweden's highest mountain, **Kebnekaise** (2078m). A well-marked trail, passing through various sections of the national parks (see above), it is traditionally split into **five sections**. There are cabins along the entire trail, and from Abisko to Kvikkjokk, north of the Arctic Circle, and in the south between Ammarnäs and Hemavan, there are *STF* fell stations. The ground is easy to walk, and where there are streams to cross bridges have been built. Wooden planks have been laid down across marshy ground, and there are either boat services or rowing boats to cross several large lakes.

### TRANSPORT TO THE KUNGSLEDEN

If you are starting the trail in Abisko, you can get there pretty easily by **train**; it's just before the Norwegian border on the Kiruna–Narvik run; while the **Inlandsbanan** stops in Jokkmokk, from where you can get a bus to Kvikkjokk.

There are also several useful **bus** routes that you can take to link up with the trail, most of which are run by *Länstrafiken Norrbotten* (☎020/91 00 19), the last two by *Länstrafiken Västerbotten* (☎020/91 00 19):

#004 Kiruna to Nikkaluokta (19km from Kebnekaise fell station)

#103 Gällivare to Ritsem (passes through Vakkotavare)

#253 Murjek to Jokkmokk and Kvikkjokk

#303 Arjeplog to Adolfström

#306 Arjeplog to Sandviken (passes through Jäkkvik)

#341 Ammarnäs to Sorsele

#31 Hemavan to Umeå

A **helicopter** service also operates between Nikkaluokta and Kebnekaise; contact *Norrlandsflyg* (late June to early Sept; ☎0970/140 65 or 550 30; 380kr per person).

If you're looking for splendid isolation this is not the trail for you. It's the busiest in the country, although a handy tip is to go against the flow: the most popular section is from Abisko down to Kebnekaise and most people walk in this direction, so by walking the route in reverse it'll be easier going.

### Abisko to Kebnekaise – 7 days, 105km

The Kungsleden begins at **Abisko Turiststation** (not at Abisko Ö station, which is in the village of Abisko). At the start the vegetation is lush and dense: beech forest stretches across the valley bottom. At the Alesjaure cabins, perched on a mountain ridge, you get a fantastic view over the open countryside below; there's a sauna here, too. The highest point is Tjäktja pass (1105m), from where there are also wonderful views. Accommodation distances are: from the **fell station** at Abisko Turiststation (late March to early May & June to late Sept; ☎0980/402 00; 160–395kr) to Abiskojaure 15km; Abiskojaure to Alesjaure 20km; Alesjaure to Tjäktja 13km; Tjäktja to Sälka 12km; Sälka to Singi 12km; Singi to Kebnekaise fell station 14km; **Kebnekaise fell station** (mid-March to early May & mid-June to mid-Sept; ☎0980/550 00; 220–330kr) to Nikkaluokta 19km (if you carry on to Nikkaluokta you have to double back to start the second section). **Provisions** are available at Abisko, Alesjaure, Sälka and Kebnekaise.

### Kebnekaise to Saltoluokta – 4 days, 51km

One of the **quietest** sections of the trail, this covers beech forest, open fells and deep valleys. First of all you backtrack to **Singi**, before heading south again with an unobstructed view of the hills and glaciers of Sarek National Park. You then paddle across the river at **Teusajaure** and climb over a plateau, from where you drop steeply through more beech forest to **Vakkotavare**. Here a bus runs to the quay at Kebnats, and then a short boat trip brings you to Saltoluokta fell station and the start of the next section (see below for details). From **Kebnekaise fell station** (see above for details) it's 14km to Singi; from Singi to Kaitumjaure 13km; Kaitumjaure to Teusajaure 9km; and Teusajaure to Vakkotavare 15km. **Provisions** are available at Kebnekaise, Kaitum and Saltoluokta.

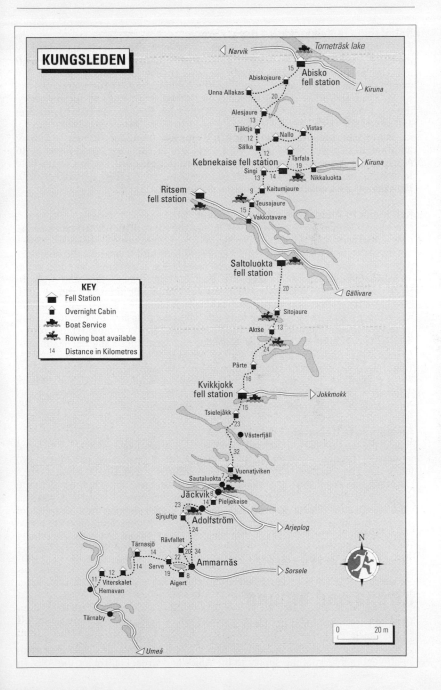

**KUNGSLEDEN**

◁ *Narvik*  ⟩ *Torneträsk lake*

15

Abiskojaure  **Abisko**
**fell station**  ⟩ *Kiruna*

Unna Allakas

20

Alesjaure
13
Tjäktja  Vistas
12  Nallo
Sälka
12  Tarfala
**Kebnekaise fell station**  19  ⟩ *Kiruna*
Singi
13  14  Nikkaluokta

Kaitumjaure
**Ritsem**  9
**fell station**  Teusajaure
15
Vakkotavare

**Saltoluokta**
**fell station**

20  ◁ *Gällivare*

Sitojaure
Aktse  13

24

Pårte
16

**Kvikkjokk**
**fell station**  ⟩ *Jokkmokk*

Tsielejåkk  15

23
Västerfjäll

32

Vuonatjviken
7
Sautaluokta
**Jäckvik** 8
23  14  Pieljekaise
Sjnjultje
**Adolfström**  ⟩ *Arjeplog*
24
Rävfallet
Tärnasjö  26  34
14  22
14  Serve  **Ammarnäs**  ⟩ *Sorsele*
12  19  8
11  Viterskalet  Aigert
Hemavan

Tärnaby

◁ *Umeå*

**KEY**
Fell Station
Overnight Cabin
Boat Service
Rowing boat available
14  Distance in Kilometres

N

0        20 m

## Saltoluokta to Kvikkjokk – 4 days, 73km

This involves crossing two lakes and passes through a bare landscape edged by pine and beech forests. A long uphill climb leads first to **Sitojaure** on a bare high fell. The lake here, which you have to cross, is shallow and choppy in the strong wind; take the boat service operated by the cabin caretaker. You then cross the wetlands on the other side of the lake on the wooden planks to **Aktse**, where there's a vast field of yellow buttercups in summer. Row across **Lake Laitaure**, and as you approach Kvikkjokk there's pine forest. The distances between accommodation are as follows: **Saltoluokta fell station** (mid-March to early May & mid-June to mid-Sept; ☎0973/410 10; 190–415kr) to Sitojaure 20km; Sitojaure to Aktse 13km; Aktse to Pårte 24km; Pårte to **Kvikkjokk fell station** 16km (late March to early May & mid-June to mid-Sept, ☎0971/210 22; 195–220kr). **Provisions** are available at Saltoluokta, Aktse and Kvikkjokk.

## Kvikkjokk to Ammarnäs – 8 days, 166km

Not recommended for novices, this is one of the most **difficult** stretches of the trail – distances between cabins can be long and there are four lakes to cross – but it's also one of the quietest stretches. From **Kvikkjokk** you take the boat over Saggat lake and walk to the first cabin at **Tsielejåkk**. It's 55km to the next cabin at **Vuonatjviken**. You then take the boat across Riebnesjaure and walk to Hornavan for another boat across to the village of **Jäckvik**; there are rooms available here. It's a short hike to the next cabin, then onto the village of **Adolfström**, where once again there is accommodation. Then another boat over Iraft lake and on to the cabins at **Sjnjultje**. From here there's a choice of routes: 34km direct to Ammarnäs or 24km to a cabin at Rävfallet and from there another 20km into Ammarnäs. From **Kvikkjokk fell station** (see above for details) to Tsielejåkk it's 15km; from Tsielejåkk to Vuonatjviken 55km; Vuonatjviken to Jäkkvik (village) 7km; Jäkkvik to Pieljekaise 8km; Pieljekaise to Adolfström (village) 14km; Adolfström to Sjnjultje 23km; Sjnjultje to Rävfallet 24km; and Rävfallet to Ammarnäs 20km. **Provisions** available in Jäkkvik and Adolfström.

## Ammarnäs to Hemavan – 6 days, 78km

This is the **easiest** part of the trail: you'll pass over low fells and heather-covered moors and through beech forests and wetlands, the horizon lined with impressive fell peaks. The only steep climb is between **Ammarnäs** and **Aigert**, where there's a powerful waterfall and a traditional steam sauna in the cabin. On the way to the **Syter** cabin, you'll pass a network of bridges, which cross the various lakes in what is called the **Tärnasjö archipelago**. With no fell stations on this stretch of the trail, distances between cabins are: Ammarnäs to Aigert 8km; Aigert to Serve 19km; Serve to Tärnasjö 14km; Tärnasjö to Syter 14km; Syter to Viterskalet 12km; Viterskalet to Hemavan 11km. **Provisions** are available in Aigert, Serve, Tärnasjö, Syter and Viterskalet.

# Kiruna and around

**KIRUNA** was the hub of the battle for the control of the iron ore supply during World War II. From here ore was transported north by train to the great harbour at Narvik over the border in Norway. Much German firepower was expended in an attempt to interrupt the supply to the Allies and wrest control for the Axis. In

the process, Narvik suffered grievously, whilst Kiruna – benefitting from supposed Swedish neutrality – made a packet selling to both sides.

The train ride to Kiruna today rattles through sidings, slag heaps and ore
works, a bitter contrast to the surrounding wilderness. The **mines** still dominate
the town and do so much more depressingly than in Gällivare (see p.394). They
are ugly brooding reminders of Kiruna's prosperity, and despite the new central
buildings and open parks, the town retains a grubby industrial feel. The tourist
office arranges **guided tours** around the mines during the summer (July & Aug
4 daily; out of season for groups only; 90kr; minimum age 10). A bus takes visitors
through the underground road network and then stops off at a "tourist mine", a
closed-off section of a leviathan structure containing service stations, restaurants,
computer centres, trains and crushing mills. During the dark winter months, it's
possible to visit the mines on a Japanese mushroom tour – in search of shiitakes
(Mon–Fri 4pm returning 10pm, Sat & Sun 8am returning 8pm; 125kr per person,
mushrooms 25kr per 100g); book through the tourist office or direct on
☎0980/124 16.

All the other sights in town are firmly wedded to the all-important metal in one
way or another. The tower of the **Rådhus** (June–Aug daily 9am–6pm; rest of the
year Mon–Fri 9am–5pm) is obvious even from the train station: a strident metal

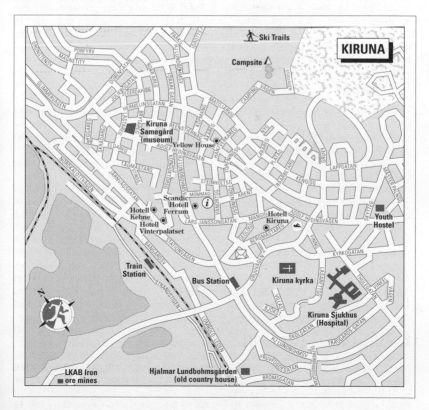

pillar harbouring an intricate latticework, clock face and sundry bells that chime raucously at noon. It was designed by Bror Marklun, and the whole hall unbelievably won the 1964 award for the most beautiful Swedish public building– but then it was 1964. Inside there's a tolerable art collection and *Sami* handicraft displays in summer.

Only a few minutes up the road, **Kiruna kyrka** (daily 11am–5pm; July till 10pm) causes a few raised eyebrows. Built in the style of a *Sami* hut, it's a massive origami creation of oak beams and rafters the size of a small aircraft hangar. *LKAB*, the iron ore company which to all intents and purposes *is* Kiruna and which paid for its construction, was also responsible for the nearby **Hjalmar Lundbohmsgården** (June–Aug daily 10am–8pm; rest of the year Mon–Fri 10am–4pm; free), a country house once used by the managing director of the company and the town's "founder". Displays inside mostly consist of turn-of-the-century photographs featuring the man himself and assorted *Sami* in their winter gear. Try to visit the house before going down the mine and everything will take on an added perspective: without the mine, Kiruna would be a one-reindeer town instead of the thriving place it is today, which is quite a feat when you consider its location on the map – don't be surprised to see snow on the slag heaps in the middle of June.

The **Kiruna Samegård** (mid-June to Sept daily 8am–6pm; rest of the year Mon–Fri 8am–4pm; 20kr), at Brytaregatan 14, is the most rewarding exhibition of *Sami* culture in town. The handicrafts may be familiar but what won't be is the small but impressive display of *Sami* art. There's also a café and a souvenir shop, where you can buy a piece of antler bone or reindeer skin.

## Practicalities

**Arriving by train** (there are also regular daily **buses** from Gällivare), it's a brisk ten-minute walk from the station up the steep hill to the **tourist office** (mid-June to end Aug Mon–Fri 9am–8pm, Sat & Sun 9am–6pm; rest of the year Mon–Fri 9am–4pm; ☎0980/188 80) in Folkets Hus in the central square off Mommagatan. If you're passing through you can leave your bags in the coin-operated lockers at the station (15kr, 20kr & 25kr). The **youth hostel** (mid-June to mid-Aug; ☎0980/171 95; 100kr) is 2km from the train station at Skyttegatan 16 A & B; as you come out from the station turn right and follow the signs. It fills quickly in summer as does the **campsite** (☎0980/131 00), a twenty-minute walk north of the centre on Campingvägen in the Högalid part of town, with cabins available, too.

Kiruna also has a number of central **hotels**. Try *Hotell Vinterpalatset*, Järnvägsgatan 18 (☎0980/831 70, fax 130 50; ⑤/③), with its wooden floors, large double beds, and superb sauna and jacuzzi suite on the top floor; there are cheaper, more basic rooms in the annexe (③/①). Round the corner at Konduktörsgatan 7, *Hotell Kebne* (☎0980/123 80; ⑤/③) is also handy for the train station and has good-quality rooms, wooden floors and marble bits here and there. The characterless *Scandic Hotell Ferrum*, Lars Jansongatan 17 (☎0980/186 00, fax 145 05; ⑤/③), is best avoided – the usual big chain indifference from staff and tedious rooms. Low-price hotel options include: *Yellow House*, Hantverkaregatan 25, which has youth hostel-style accommodation for 100kr per person; and *Hotell Kiruna*, Bergmästaregatan 7, which again has basic rooms but offers a little more comfort (②/①) – the rooms at both hotels, none of which are en suite, can be booked on ☎0980/137 50.

Kiruna's hardly a centre of haute cuisine, but **eating** at the inordinately popular *Mats & Mums*, Bergmästaregatan 10, is the best option – although the window through to the adjacent swimming pool makes for an unusual setting. Burgers, meat, fish dishes and Arctic specialities are the order of the day, with some of the more fancy dishes getting expensive – there's free coffee after dinner, though. Good food is also served at *Restaurang Lapplandia* in the same building as *Hotell Kiruna* at Bergmästaregatan 7; lunch and evening meals go for reasonable prices. Coffee and cakes are served up at *Brända Tomten* on Meschplan. The most popular **bar** is *Mommas* in the main square at the side of the tourist office – an American-style place. The grotty **drinking** den that is *Restaurang Arran* across the square at Föreningsgatan 9 has beer for a staggeringly cheap 19kr until 11pm some days (otherwise it's 35–40kr) and attracts a corresponding clientele – go in with a friend.

## Around Kiruna: the ice hotel at Jukkasjärvi

The tiny village of **JUKKASJÄRVI** (from Kiruna bus #006 Mon–Fri 1 daily) is an obvious destination for any tourist travelling in Lapland in winter: the **ice hotel** (550kr per person in a four-bed room; a private suite is 680kr per person), built here late every October, is also the world's biggest igloo and stands proudly by the side of the Torneälven river, until it melts in May. One thousand tons of ice and two thousand tons of snow are used to make the igloo, whose exact shape and design changes from year to year. However, there is usually a bar in the entrance hall (don't leave your beer on the bar for too long, or it'll freeze), several bedrooms with beds made out of blocks of compact snow covered with reindeer hides, an exhibition hall, a cinema, and a chapel where local couples can marry. The temperature here in winter is generally around -20°C to -30°C, which makes for a temperature inside the igloo of around -5°C. Guests who choose to stay are provided with specially made sleeping bags. Tried and tested by the Swedish army, who use the hotel for Arctic survival training, the bags are appproved for temperatures down to -35°C. In the morning, you can refresh yourself with a sauna and then eat a hearty breakfast. There are also **cabins** for rent on the site – if you chicken out – which along with the hotel can be booked through *Jukkas AB*, Marknadsvägen 63 (☎0980/211 90, fax 214 06); four-berth cabins cost 800kr. Activities here include: a half-day's dog sledging for a hefty 3000kr for four people, or you can rent a snow scooter for 885kr per day per person; skis cost 40kr per day. In summer there is river rafting, canoe paddling and hiking – details from *Jukkas AB*. You can **eat** across the road at *Jukkasjärvi Wärdshus* (11am–10pm).

The village itself is very small but at the end of Marknadsvägen, a dead-end road, there's an old wooden *Sami* church dating from 1608. Check out the richly decorated altarpiece by Bror Hjort. Under the floor are the remarkably well-preserved mummified remains of villagers who died here in the 1700s – although not on public display.

## On from Kiruna to the Norwegian border

From Kiruna, the most obvious route is northwest into Norway and to Narvik. Since 1984, there have been two choices: by **train** on the last leg of the long run from Stockholm or Luleå, and also by road (see overleaf). The train route from Luleå to Narvik, known as the **Malmbanan** (it meets up with the *Inlandsbanan* at Gällivare), is Europe's northernmost line, and would never have been built had it not been for the rich deposits of iron ore around Gällivare and Malmberget. The idea of building the line, which connects the Bothnian coast with the Atlantic coast (170km) and passes through some of the remotest and most inhospitable parts of Europe, was mooted on and off throughout the nineteenth century, when the only means of transporting the ore was by reindeer and sleigh. Finally in 1884, an English company was awarded the contract; by 1888, the line had reached Gällivare, and the company were bankrupt. Ten years passed before the State took over, and finally, the navvies, who'd been subject to temperatures of below -30°C and great isolation, shovelled their way through deep snow at Riksgränsen to meet the Norwegian border in July 1902. A year later, the route was officially opened by King Oscar II.

The much newer **road**, the **Nordkalottvägen** (North Calotte Highway), runs parallel to the rail line on the Swedish side of the border, threading its way across barren plateaux (the lakes up here are still frozen in mid-June), before slicing through the mighty Norwegian mountains. By train or by car, it's an exhilarating run that passes the start of the Kungsleden trail at Abisko (see p.398), continuing onto **RIKSGRÄNSEN**, the last settlement in Sweden, where it's possible to ski until late June. There's a **hotel** here, *Hotell Riksgränsen* (☎0980/400 80, fax 431 25 ④/③) opposite the train station – but nothing more.

# The Torne Valley

The gently sloping sides of the lush **Torne Valley** (Tornedalen) are one of the most welcoming sights in northern Sweden. Stretching over 500km from the mouth of the Gulf of Bothnia to Sweden's remote northern tip, the three rivers, Torne, Muonio and Könkämä, mark out the long border between Sweden and Finland. The valley is home to Swedes, Finns and *Sami*, who all speak an archaic **dialect** known, in Swedish at least, as *tornedalsfinska* – **Torne Valley Finnish**. The area is refreshingly different from the coast and from the heavily wooded inland regions of the country; the villages here are small, often no more than a couple of wooden cottages surrounded by open flower meadows running down to the river's edge – the open plains providing much-needed grazing land for the farmers' livestock.

To get to the Torne Valley, the main **bus** route (there are no trains through the valley) is #052 (Mon–Fri 3 daily, Sat & Sun 1 daily; 3hr) from Haparanda to Pajala. It is also possible to come into the valley at the halfway point at Pajala from Gällivare (bus #051 Mon–Fri 3 daily, Sat & Sun 1 daily; 2hr 30min), or from Kiruna (bus #003 Mon–Fri 3 daily, Sat & Sun 1 daily; 3hr 30min). From the north bus #002 runs from Karesuando to Vittangi (1 daily), where you change for the #003 for Pajala.

## Övertorneå

Buses run daily from Haparanda (see p.348) up the valley as far as **ÖVERTORNEÅ**, which is the first place of note. The only sight as such is the large wooden **Övertorneå kyrka**, with its medieval wood carvings. Dating from 1615, the structure was enlarged to its present crucifix shape in 1735. However, it is much better to break your journey before reaching the village and take in one of the many local lakes swirling in mist, dangle your toes in the water and listen to the mooing of the cows and the whisper of the birch trees – this is what the Torne Valley is really all about.

The **tourist office**, Matarengvägen 27 (mid June to mid-Aug daily 9am–7pm; rest of the year Mon–Fri 9am–4pm; ☎0927/105 35), can arrange **cabin** accommodation. There's a pleasant enough modern **hotel**, *Hotell Tornedalia* (☎0927/775 50, fax 103 50; ④/②). Alternatively, fifteen minutes before the bus arrives in Övertorneå, there's a **youth hostel** (June–Aug; ☎0927/303 50; 100kr) in the village of **HEDENÄSET**, beautifully situated by a lake with views across to Finland.

# Pajala

The valley's main village is pretty **PAJALA** (pronounced "Pie-allah") – a place that has earned itself a reputation and a half throughout Sweden. To celebrate the village's recent four-hundredth anniversary, the local council placed ads in the national papers inviting women from the south of the country up to Lapland to take part in the birthday festivities: the predominance of heavy labouring jobs in the north of Sweden has produced a population imbalance – around three men to every woman. It also explains the ridiculously macho behaviour that prevails in these parts. Journalists outside Sweden soon heard of the ads, and articles about the unusual invitation began to appear in newspapers across Europe. Before long busloads of women from all over the continent were heading north. It was a drunken, debauched bash that tiny Pajala won't forget in a long time, but it did help to redress the problem: dozens of east European women lost their hearts to gruff Swedish lumberjacks and began new lives north of the Arctic Circle. However, the effects of several winters spent in darkness, coupled with temperatures of -25°C, may still tip the balance back.

Taking place in the third week in September, the **Römpäviiko** – the "romp week", as this ongoing cultural festival is called – is undoubtedly the liveliest time to be in the village. At any other time Pajala is a great place to rest up in for a day or so – take a walk along the riverside or head off in search of the great grey owl (strix nebulosa) that sweeps through the nearby forests. The huge wooden model in the bus station will give you an idea of what the owl looks like: lichen grey with long slender tail feathers and a white crescent between its black and yellow eyes.

## Practicalities

**Buses** from Övertorneå stop at the central bus station. The **tourist office** is inside the station (mid-June to Sept Mon–Fri 9am–6pm, Sat & Sun 9am–1pm; rest of the year Mon–Fri 9am–5pm; ☎0978/714 41). Close by at Soukolovägen 2, *Pajala Wärdshus* (☎0978/101 00 or 712 00, fax 714 64; ④/②) has cosy little **rooms**, where all meals are included in the price. *Hotell Smedjan*, Fridhemsvägen 1 (☎0978/108 15, fax 717 75; ④/②), has similar en-suite rooms for much the same price. But the best place to stay is right at the other end of the village at *Pajala Camping* (May–Sept only; ☎0978/718 80 or 719 32), with its stunning views over the lazy Torne river; there are also simple **cabins** here with cold water only (numbers 1–16 have good river views; 250kr per person). For **eating** and **drinking**, the *Pajala Wärdshus* has *Dagens Rätt* for 52kr; while for traditional northern Swedish delicacies count on at least double that. At the weekends, there's also a popular disco in the basement and beer goes down 25kr. *Bykrogen* just round the corner is a cheap and cheerful pizzeria.

# Heading north: Karesuando and Treriksröset

A bus leaves Pajala once daily for Sweden's northernmost village, **KARESUAN-DO** (change in Vittangi). A singularly ugly place, 250km north of the Arctic Circle, the land here is in the grip of permafrost all year round and life is pretty tough. This is *Sami* heartland and national borders carry little significance; people cross them without as much as a bat of an eyelid, as they go about their everyday business.

If you're heading north for **Treriksröset** – a cairn where Sweden, Norway and Finland meet – you'll be forced to stay the night in Karesuando because the bus doesn't connect with services on the other side of the border in Finland (see below). To kill time you can stock up on tourist brochures from the **tourist office** (mid-June to mid-Aug daily 9am–6pm; ☎0981/202 05). Your two choices of **accommodation** are the basic *Hotell Grape* (☎0981/200 22, fax 202 65; ③/②) or *Karesuando Camping* (☎0981/201 39). Alternatively, there's a **youth hostel** across the river in Finnish **KAARESUVANTO** (from Sweden ☎009 358/696 777 71).

To continue to Treriksröset, take the bridge across the river Könkämä to Kaaresuvanto (remember Finland is one hour ahead of Sweden), from where buses leave in summer (June–Aug) for **Kilpisjärvi** (there's no road on the Swedish side of the border). From here there are two choices: a hike of 11km down a track to the cairn or a boat ride across the lake, which shortens the hike to just 3km. The boat (July to mid-Aug 10am, 1pm & 5pm Finnish time; 85kr return; 20min) requires at least four passengers if it's to sail; for boat information call the Swedish mobile number ☎010/666 8715.

## travel details

### Trains

Timetables change slightly from year to year, but the following is a rough idea of the **Inlandsbanan** services and times (latest information on ☎020/53 53 53). The *Inlandsbanan* runs from Mora to Gällivare via Östersund. **Northbound** trains leave Mora at 7am on Tues, Wed, Fri & Sun calling at Orsa and Sveg and many other wayside halts en route for Östersund. Northbound trains leave Östersund for Gällivare at 6.50am on Tues, Wed, Fri and Sun calling at Ulriksfors (for Strömsund), Dorotea, Vilhelmina, Storuman, Sorsele, Arvidsjaur, the Arctic Circle, Jokkmokk and Gällivare; there's an additional train from Östersund to Arvidsjaur on Mon, Thurs and Sat at 8.40am. Another northbound train leaves Arvidsjaur on Mon & Thurs at 8am for Gällivare. **Southbound** trains leave Gällivare at 7.15am on Mon, Wed, Thurs & Sat for stations to Östersund. An additional train leaves Gällivare on Tues & Fri at 10.05am for

Arvidsjaur. On Tues, Fri & Sun there's also a service from Arvidsjaur at 8.20am to Östersund. From Östersund southbound trains leave at 7am on Tues, Wed, Fri & Sun for Mora.

**From Borlänge** to Gävle (5 daily; 1hr 30min); Falun (8 daily; 15min); Malung (5 daily; 2hr); Mora (7 daily; 1hr 20min); Stockholm (10 daily; 2hr 40min); Uppsala (10 daily; 2hr); Örebro (4 daily; 2hr).

**From Falun** to Borlänge (8 daily; 15min); Gävle (5 daily; 1hr); Stockholm (8 daily; 3hr); Uppsala (8 daily; 2hr 45min); Örebro (4 daily; 1hr 45min).

**From Gällivare** to Boden (3 daily; 2hr); Gothenburg (1 daily; 19hr 30min); Gävle (2 daily; 14hr); Kiruna (3 daily; 1hr); Luleå (3 daily; 2hr 20min); Stockholm (2 daily; 16hr 30min); Umeå (1 daily; 7hr); Uppsala (2 daily; 15hr 30min).

**From Kiruna** to Abisko (3 daily; 1hr 20min); Boden (3 daily; 3hr); Gothenburg (1 daily; 20hr 30min); Luleå (3 daily; 3hr 20min); Narvik (3

daily; 3hr); Riksgränsen (3 daily; 2hr); Stockholm (2 daily; 17hr 30min); Uppsala (2 daily; 16hr 30min).

**From Kristinehamn** to Stockholm (10 daily; 2hr 45min); Oslo (2 daily; 4hr).

**From Mora** to Borlänge (7 daily; 1hr 20min); Leksand (7 daily; 45min); Rättvik (7 daily; 30min); Stockholm (7 daily; 4hr by X2000, 5hr by intercity); Tällberg (7 daily; 35min); Uppsala (7 daily; 3hr 15min by X2000, 4hr 15min by intercity).

**From Östersund** to Gothenburg (1 daily; 11hr); Stockholm (4 daily; 6hr); Storlien (4 daily; 3hr); Sundsvall (6 daily; 4hr 15min); Trondheim (3 daily; 5hr 30min); Uppsala (4 daily; 5hr 15min); Åre (4 daily; 1hr 45min).

## Buses

The **Inlandsexpressen** (#45) runs **north** from Mora to Gällivare via Orsa, Sveg, Åsarna, Östersund, Strömsund, Dorotea, Vilhelmina, Storuman, Sorsele, Arvidsjaur, Moskosel, Jokkmokk and Porjus. It operates daily all year round leaving Mora at 8am and 2pm for Östersund, from Östersund at 7am for Gällivare and at 1.40pm for Arvidsjaur. **Southbound** a bus leaves Gällivare at 9.30am for Östersund, and from Arvidsjaur at 8.50am for Östersund. From Östersund two buses operate to Mora at 7am and 12.30pm.

*Swebus Express* operates a **long-distance** service from Mora to Stockholm (#890) via Rättvik, Leksand, Falun, Borlänge and Uppsala. Another service (#801) runs from Sälen via Malung, Filipstad, Kristinehamn and Mariestad to Gothenburg. From Kristinehamn service #845 runs west to Oslo via Karlstad and east to Stockholm via Karlskoga and Öre-bro. For more information ☎020/64 06 40 or from abroad ☎08/655 00 90. Alternatively, *Svenska Buss* run from Falun and Borlänge to Stockholm and from Kristinehamn west to Gothenburg and east to Stockholm; more information on ☎020/67 67 67.

**From Ammarnäs** to Sorsele (3 daily; 1hr 20min).

**From Arjeplog** to Arvidsjaur (3 daily; 1hr 15min).

**From Arvidsjaur** to Arjeplog (3 daily; 1hr).

**From Gällivare** to Jokkmokk (4 daily; 1hr 30min); Kiruna (4 daily; 2hr 10min); Luleå (2 daily; 3hr 15min); Pajala (3 daily; 2hr 20min); Ritsem (1 daily; 3hr 30min).

**From Jokkmokk** to Gällivare (4 daily; 1hr 30min); Kvikkjokk (2 daily; 1hr 50min); Murjek (4 daily; 50min).

**From Kiruna** to Gällivare (4 daily; 2hr 10min); Jukkasjärvi (6 daily; 40min); Karesuando (1 daily; 3hr 30min); Luleå (2 daily; 4hr 45min); Pajala (3 daily; 3hr 30min); Nikkaluokta (2 daily; 1hr 10min).

**From Kvikkjokk** to Jokkmokk (2 daily; 1hr 50min).

**From Mora** to Grönklitt bear peak (1 daily; 1hr); Idre (2 daily; 3hr); Malung (2 daily; 2hr); Orsa (12 daily; 20min); Sälen (1 daily; 1hr 40min); Särna (4 daily; 1hr 50min).

**From Sorsele** to Ammarnäs (3 daily; 1hr 40min).

**From Storuman** to Tärnaby (5 daily; 2hr); Hemavan (4 daily; 2hr 20min).

**From Åsarna** to Klövsjö (4 daily; 15min); Östersund (7 daily; 1hr 20min).

**From Östersund** to Umeå (2 daily; 6hr).

PART THREE

# THE CONTEXTS

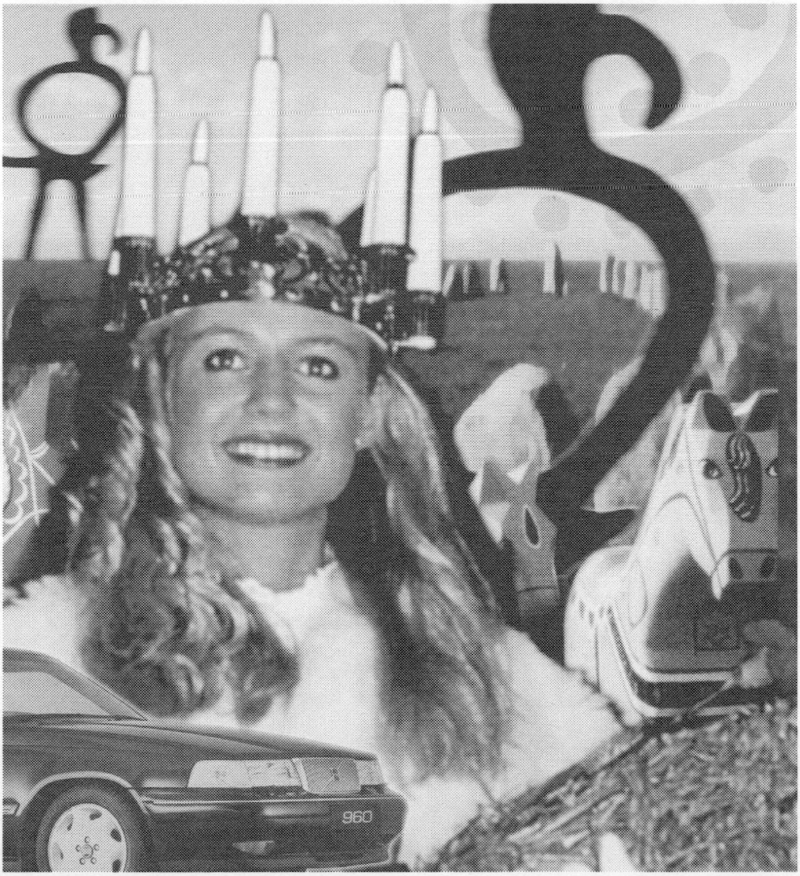

# A BRIEF HISTORY OF SWEDEN

Sweden has one of Europe's longest documented histories, but for all the upheavals of the Viking times and the warring of the Middle Ages, during modern times the country has seemed to delight in taking a historical back seat. For one brief period, when Prime Minister Olof Palme was shot dead in 1986, Sweden was thrust into the international limelight. Since then, however, it's regained its poise, even though the current situation is fraught. Political infighting and domestic disharmony are threatening the one thing that the Swedes have always been proud of and that other countries aspire to: the politics of consensus, the passing of which, arguably, is of far greater importance than even the assassination of their prime minister.

## EARLY CIVILISATIONS

It was not until around 6000 BC that the **first settlers** roamed north and east into Sweden, living as nomadic reindeer hunters and herders. By 3000 BC people had settled in the south of the country and were established as farmers; and dating from 2000 BC there are indications of a development in burial practices, with **dolmens** and **passage graves** found throughout the southern Swedish provinces. Traces also remain of the **Boat Axe People**, named after their char-

acteristic tool/weapon shaped like a boat. The earliest Scandinavian horse riders, they quickly held sway over the whole of southern Sweden.

During the **Bronze Age** (1500–500 BC) the Boat Axe People traded furs and amber for southern European copper and tin. Large finds of finished ornaments and weapons show a comparatively rich culture. This was emphasized by elaborate burial rites, the dead laid in single graves under mounds of earth and stone.

The deterioration of the Scandinavian climate in the last millennium before Christ coincided with the advance across Europe of the Celts, which halted the flourishing trade of the Swedish settlers. With the new millennium, Sweden made its first mark upon the Classical world. Pliny the Elder (23–79 AD) in the *Historia Naturalis* mentioned the "island of Scatinavia" far to the north. Tacitus was more specific: in 98 AD he referred to a powerful people, the *Suinoes*, who were strong in men, weapons and ships: a reference to the **Svear**, who were to form the nucleus of an emergent Swedish kingdom by the sixth century.

The Svear settled in the rich land around Lake Mälaren and became rulers of the whole country except the south. They gave Sweden its modern name: *Sverige* in Swedish or *Svear rike*, the kingdom of the Svear. More importantly, they gave their first dynastic leaders a taste for expansion, trading with Gotland and holding suzerainty over the Åland Islands.

## THE VIKING PERIOD

The Vikings – raiders and warriors who dominated the political and economic life of Europe and beyond from the ninth to the eleventh centuries – came from all parts of southern Scandinavia. But there is evidence that the **Swedish Vikings** were among the first to leave home, the impetus being a rapid population growth, domestic unrest and a desire for new lands. The raiders turned their attention largely eastwards, in line with Sweden's geographical position and knowing that the Svear had already reached the Baltic. By the ninth century the trade routes were well established, Swedes reaching the Black and Caspian seas and making valuable trading contact with the **Byzantine Empire**. Although more commercially inclined than their Danish and Norwegian counterparts, Swedish Vikings were quick to use force if profits were slow to materialize. From 860 onwards Greek and Muslim records relate a series of raids across the Black Sea against Byzantium, and across the Caspian into northeast Iran.

But the Vikings were settlers as well as traders and exploiters, and their long-term influence was marked. Embattled Slavs to the east gave them the name **Rus**, and their creeping colonization gave the area in which the Vikings settled its modern name, Russia. Russian names today – Oleg, Igor, Vladimir – can be derived from the Swedish – Helgi, Ingvar, Valdemar.

Domestically, **paganism** was at its height. Freyr was "God of the World", a physically potent God of Fertility through whom dynastic leaders would trace their descent. It was a bloody time. Nine **human sacrifices** were offered at the celebrations held every nine years at Uppsala. Adam of Bremen recorded that the great shrine there was adjoined by a sacred grove where "every tree is believed divine because of the death and putrefaction of the victims hanging there".

Viking **law** was based on the *Thing*, an assembly of free men to which the king's power was subject. Each largely autonomous province had its own assembly and its own leaders: where several provinces united, the approval of each *Thing* was needed for any choice of leader. For centuries in Sweden the new king had to make a formal tour to receive the homage of each province.

## THE ARRIVAL OF CHRISTIANITY AND THE EARLY MIDDLE AGES

Christianity was slow to take root in Sweden. Whereas Denmark and Norway had accepted the faith by the turn of the eleventh century, Swedish contact was still in the east and the people remained largely heathen. Missionaries met with limited success and no Swedish king was converted until 1008, when **Olof Skötonung** was baptized. He was the first known king of both Swedes and Goths (that is, ruler of the two major provinces of Västergötland and Östergötland), and his successors were all Christians. Nevertheless, paganism retained a grip on Swedish affairs, and as late as the 1080s the Svear banished their Christian king, Inge, when he refused to take part in the pagan celebrations at Uppsala. By the end of the eleventh century, though, the temple at Uppsala had gone and a Christian

church was built on its site. In the 1130s Uppsala replaced Sigtuna – original centre of the Swedish Christian faith – as the main episcopal seat and, in 1164, Stephen (an English monk) was made the first archbishop.

The whole of the early Middle Ages in Sweden was characterized by a succession of struggles for control of a growing central power. Principally two families, the Sverkers and the Eriks, waged battle throughout the twelfth century. **King Erik** was the first Sverker king to make his mark: in 1157 he led a crusade to heathen Finland, but was killed in 1160 at Uppsala by a Danish pretender to his throne. Within 100 years he was to be recognized as patron saint of Sweden, and his remains interred in the new Uppsala Cathedral.

Erik was succeeded by his son **Knut**, whose stable reign lasted until 1196 and was marked by commercial treaties and strengthened defences. Following his death, virtual civil war weakened the royal power with the result that the king's chief ministers, or **Jarls**, assumed much of the executive responsibility for running the country; so much so that when Erik Eriksson (last of the Eriks) was deposed in 1229, his administrator **Birger Jarl** assumed power. With papal support for his crusading policies he confirmed the Swedish grip on the southwest of Finland. His son, Valdemar, succeeded him but proved a weak ruler and didn't survive the family feuding after Birger Jarl's death. Valdemar's brother Magnus assumed power in 1275.

**Magnus Ladulås** represented a peak of Swedish royal power not to be repeated for 300 years. His enemies dissipated, he forbade the nobility to meet without his consent and began to issue his own authoritative decrees. Preventing the nobility from claiming maintenance at the expense of the peasantry as they travelled from estate to estate earned him his nickname Ladulås or "Barn-lock". He also began to reap the benefits of conversion: the clergy became an educated class upon whom the monarch could rely for diplomatic and administrative duties. By the thirteenth century, there were ambitious Swedish clerics in Paris and Bologna, and the first stone churches were appearing in Sweden. The most monumental is the early Gothic **cathedral** built at Uppsala.

Meanwhile the nobility had come to form a military class, exempted from taxation on the understanding that they would defend the crown. In the country the standard of living was still low, although an increasing population stimulated new cultivation. The forests of Norrland were pushed back, more southern heathland turned into pasture, and crop rotation introduced. Noticeable, too, was the increasing **German influence** within Sweden as the Hansa traders spread. Their first merchants settled in Visby and, by the mid-thirteenth century, in Stockholm.

## THE FOURTEENTH CENTURY – TOWARDS UNITY

Magnus died in 1290, power shifting to a cabal of magnates led by **Torgil Knutsson**. As Marshal of Sweden, he pursued an energetic foreign policy, conquering western Karelia to gain control of the Gulf of Finland; and building the fortress at Viborg, lost only with the collapse of the Swedish Empire in the eighteenth century.

Magnus's son Birger came of age in 1302 but soon quarrelled with his brothers Erik and Valdemar. They had Torgil Knutsson executed, then rounded on Birger, who was forced to divide up Sweden among the three of them. An unhappy arrangement, it lasted until 1317 when Birger had his brothers arrested and starved to death in prison – an act that prompted a shocked nobility to rise against Birger and force his exile to Denmark. The Swedish nobles restored the principle of elective monarchy by calling on the three-year-old **Magnus** (son of a Swedish duke and already declared Norwegian king) to take the Swedish crown. During his minority a treaty was concluded with Novgorod (1323) to fix the frontiers in eastern and northern Finland. This left virtually the whole of the Scandinavian peninsula (except the Danish provinces in the south) under one ruler.

Yet Sweden was still anything but prosperous. The **Black Death** reached the country in 1350, wiping out whole parishes and killing perhaps a third of the population. Subsequent labour shortages and troubled estates meant that the nobility found it difficult to maintain their positions. German merchants had driven the Swedes from their most lucrative trade routes: even the copper and iron ore **mining** that began around this time in Bergslagen and Dalarna relied on German capital.

Magnus soon ran into trouble, threatened further by the accession of Valdemar Atterdag to the Danish throne in 1340. Squabbles over sovereignty of the Danish provinces of Skåne and Blekinge led to Danish incursions into Sweden and, in 1361, Valdemar landed on Gotland and sacked **Visby**. The Gotlanders were massacred outside the city walls, refused refuge by the Hansa merchants.

Magnus was forced to negotiate and his son **Håkon** – now king of Norway – was married to Valdemar's daughter Margaret. With Magnus later deposed, power fell into the hands of the magnates who shared out the country. Chief of the ruling nobles was the Steward **Bo Jonsson Grip**, who controlled virtually all Finland and central and southeast Sweden. Yet on his death, the nobility turned to Håkon's wife **Margaret**, already regent in Norway (for her son Olof) and in Denmark since the death of her father, Valdemar. In 1388 she was proclaimed "First Lady" of Sweden and, in return, confirmed all the privileges of the Swedish nobility. They were anxious for union, to safeguard those who owned frontier estates and strengthen the crown against any further German influence. Called upon to choose a male king, Margaret nominated her nephew, **Erik of Pomerania**, who was duly elected king of Sweden in 1396. As he had already been elected to the Danish and Norwegian thrones, Scandinavian unity seemed assured.

## THE KALMAR UNION

Erik was crowned king of Denmark, Norway and Sweden in 1397 at a ceremony in **Kalmar**. Nominally, the three kingdoms were now in union but, despite Erik, real power remained in the hands of Margaret until her death in 1412.

Erik was at war throughout his reign with the Hanseatic League. He was vilified in popular Swedish history as an evil and grasping ruler, and the taxes he raised went on a war that was never fought on Swedish soil. He spent his time instead in Denmark, directing operations, leaving his queen Philippa (sister to Henry V of England) behind. Erik was deposed in 1439 and the nobility turned to **Christopher of Bavaria**, whose early death in 1448 led to the first major breach in the union.

No one candidate could fill the three kingships satisfactorily, and separate elections in Denmark and Sweden signalled a renewal of the infighting that had plagued the previous century. Within Sweden, unionists and nationalists skirmished, the powerful unionist **Oxenstierna** family opposing the claims of the nationalist **Sture** family, until 1470 when **Sten Sture** (the Elder) became "Guardian of the Realm". His victory over the unionists at the **Battle of Brunkeberg** (1471) – in the middle of modern Stockholm – was complete, gaining symbolic artistic expression in the **statue of St George and the Dragon** that still adorns the Great Church in Stockholm.

Sten Sture's primacy fostered a new cultural atmosphere. The first **university** in Scandinavia was founded in Uppsala in 1477, the first printing press appearing in Sweden six years later. Artistically, German and Dutch influences were great, traits seen in the decorative art of the great Swedish medieval churches. Only remote **Dalarna** kept alive a native folk art tradition.

Belief in the union still existed though, particularly outside Sweden, and successive kings had to fend off almost constant attacks and blockades emanating from Denmark. With the accession of **Christian II** to the Danish throne in 1513, the unionist movement found a leader capable of turning the tide. Under the guise of a crusade to free Sweden's imprisoned archbishop Gustav Trolle, Christian attacked Sweden and killed Sture. After Christian's coronation, Trolle urged the prosecution of his Swedish adversaries (gathered together under an amnesty) and they were found guilty of heresy. Eighty-two nobles and burghers of Stockholm were executed and their bodies burned in what became known as the **Stockholm Blood Bath**. A vicious persecution of Sture's followers throughout Sweden ensued, a move that led to widespread reaction and, ultimately, the downfall of the union.

## GUSTAV VASA AND HIS SONS

Opposition to Christian II was vague and unorganiszed until the appearance of the young **Gustav Vasa**. Initially unable to stir the locals of the Dalecarlia region into open revolt, he left for exile in Norway, but was chased on skis and recalled after the people had had a change of heart. The chase is celebrated still in the **Vasalopet** race, run each year by thousands of Swedish skiers.

Gustav Vasa's army grew rapidly and in 1521 he was elected regent, and subsequently, with the capture of Stockholm in 1523, king.

Christian had been deposed in Denmark and the new Danish king, Frederick I, recognized Sweden's *de facto* withdrawal from the union. Short of cash, Gustav found it prudent to support the movement towards religious reform propagated by Swedish Lutherans. More of a political than a religious **Reformation**, the result was a handover of church lands to the crown and the subordination of church to state. It's a relationship that is still largely in force today, the clergy being civil servants paid by the state.

In 1541 the first edition of the Bible in the vernacular appeared. Suppressing revolt at home, Gustav Vasa strengthened his hand with a centralization of trade and government. On his death in 1560 Sweden was united, prosperous and independent.

Gustav Vasa's heir, his eldest son **Erik**, faced a difficult time, not least because the Vasa lands and wealth had been divided among him and his brothers Johan, Magnus and Karl (an atypically imprudent action of Gustav's before his death). The Danes, too, pressed hard, reasserting their claim to the Swedish throne in the inconclusive **Northern Seven Years' War**, which began in 1563. Erik was deposed in 1569 by his brother who became **Johan III**, his first act being to end the war at the **Peace of Stettin**. At home Johan ruled more or less with the goodwill of the nobility, but upset matters with his Catholic sympathies. He introduced the liturgy and Catholic-influenced *Red Book*, and his son and heir Sigismund was the Catholic king of Poland. On Johan's death in 1592, Sigismund agreed to rule Sweden in accordance with Lutheran practice but failed to do so. When Sigismund returned to Poland the way was clear for Duke Karl (Johan's brother) to assume the regency, a role he filled until declared king **Karl IX** in 1603.

Karl had ambitions eastwards but, routed by the Poles and staved off by the Russians, he suffered a stroke in 1610 and died the year after. He was the last of Vasa's sons, and his heir was the seventeen-year-old Gustav II, better known as Gustavus Adolfus.

The rule of Vasa and his sons made Sweden a nation, culturally as well as politically. The courts were filled and influenced by men of learning; art and sculpture flourished. The **Renaissance** style appeared for the first time in Sweden, with royal castles remodelled – Kalmar being a fine example. Economically, Sweden remained mostly self-sufficient, its few imports luxuries like cloth, wine and spices. With around 8000 inhabitants, Stockholm was its most important city, although **Gothenburg** was founded in 1607 to promote trade to the west.

## THE RISE AND FALL OF THE SWEDISH EMPIRE

During the reign of **Gustavus II Adolfus** Sweden became a European power. Though still in his youth he was considered able enough to rule, and proved so by concluding peace treaties with Denmark (1613) and Russia (1617), the latter isolating Russia from the Baltic and allowing the Swedes control of the eastern trade routes into Europe.

In 1618 the **Thirty Years' War** broke out in Germany. It was vital for Gustavus that Germany should not become Catholic, given the Polish king's continuing pretensions to the Swedish crown and the possible threat it could pose to Sweden's growing influence in the Baltic. The Altmark treaty with a defeated Poland in 1629 gave Gustavus control of Livonia and four Prussian sea ports, and the income this generated financed his entry into the war in 1630 on the Protestant side. After several convincing victories Gustavus pushed through Germany, delaying an assault upon undefended Vienna. It cost him his life. At the **Battle of Lützen** in 1632 Gustavus was killed, his body stripped and battered by the enemy's soldiers. The war dragged on until the **Peace of Westphalia** in 1648.

With Gustavus away at war for much of his reign, Sweden ran smoothly under the guidance of his friend and chancellor, **Axel Oxenstierna**. Together they founded a new Supreme Court in Stockholm (and the same, too, in Finland and the conquered Baltic provinces); reorganized the national assembly into four Estates of nobility, clergy, burghers and peasantry (1626); extended the university at Uppsala (and founded one at Åbo – modern Turku); and fostered the mining and other industries that provided much of the country's wealth. Gustavus had many other accomplishments, too: he spoke five languages and designed a new light cannon, which assisted in his routs of the enemy.

## THE CAROLEANS

The Swedish empire reached its territorial peak under the **Caroleans**. Yet the reign of the last of them was to see Sweden crumble.

Following Gustavus Adolfus's death and the later abdication of his daughter Christina, **Karl X** succeeded to the throne. War against Poland (1655) led to some early successes and, with Denmark espousing the Polish cause, gave Karl the opportunity to march into Jutland (1657). From there his armies marched across the frozen sea to threaten Copenhagen; the subsequent **Treaty of Roskilde** (1658) broke Denmark and gave the Swedish empire its widest territorial extent.

However, the long regency of his son and heir, **Karl XI**, did little to enhance Sweden's vulnerable position, so extensive were its borders. On his assumption of power in 1672 Karl was almost immediately dragged into war: beaten by a smaller Prussian army at Brandenberg in 1675, Sweden was suddenly faced with war against both the Danes and Dutch. Karl rallied, though, to drive out the Danish invaders, and the war ended in 1679 with the reconquest of Skåne and the restoration of most of Sweden's German provinces.

In 1682 Karl XI became **absolute monarch** and was given full control over legislation and *reduktion* – the resumption of estates previously alienated by the crown to the nobility. The armed forces were reorganized too and by 1700 the Swedish army had 25,000 soldiers and twelve regiments of cavalry; the naval fleet was expanded to 38 ships and a new base built at **Karlskrona** (nearer than Stockholm to the likely trouble spots).

Culturally, Sweden began to benefit from the innovations of Gustavus Adolfus. *Gymnasia* (grammar schools) continued to expand and a second university was established at **Lund** in 1668. A national literature emerged, helped by the efforts of **George Stiernhielm**, "father" of modern Swedish poetry. **Olof Rudbeck** (1630–1702) was a Nordic polymath whose scientific reputation lasted longer than his attempt to identify the ancient Goth settlement at Uppsala as Atlantis. Architecturally, this was the age of **Tessin**, both father and son. Tessin the Elder was responsible for the glorious palace at **Drottningholm**, work on which began in 1662, as well as the cathedral at **Kalmar**. His son, Tessin the Younger, succeeded him as royal architect and was to create the new royal palace at Stockholm.

In 1697 the fifteen-year-old **Karl XII** succeeded to the throne and under him the empire collapsed. Faced with a defensive alliance of Saxony, Denmark and Russia, there was little the king could have done to avoid eventual defeat. However, he remains a revered figure for his valiant (often suicidal) efforts to prove Europe wrong. Initial victories against Peter the Great and Saxony led him to march on Russia, where he was defeated and the bulk of his army destroyed. Escaping to Turkey, where he remained as guest and then prisoner for four years, Karl watched the empire disintegrate. With Poland reconquered by Augustus of Saxony, and Finland by Peter the Great, he returned to Sweden only to have England declare war on him.

Eventually, splits in the enemy's alliance led Swedish diplomats to attempt peace talks with Russia. Karl, though, was keen to exploit these differences in a more direct fashion. In order to strike at Denmark, but lacking a fleet, he besieged Fredrikshald in Norway in 1718 and was killed by a sniper's bullet. In the power vacuum thus created, Russia became the leading Baltic force, receiving Livonia, Estonia, Ingria and most of Karelia from Sweden.

## THE AGE OF FREEDOM

The eighteenth century saw absolutism discredited in Sweden. A new constitution vested power in the Estates, who reduced the new king **Frederick I**'s role to that of nominal head of state. The chancellor wielded the real power and under **Arvid Horn** the country found a period of stability. His party, nicknamed the "Caps", was opposed by the hawkish "Hats", who forced war with Russia in 1741, a disaster in which Sweden lost all of Finland and had its whole east coast burned and bombed. Most of Finland was returned with the agreement to elect **Adolphus Frederick** (a relation of the crown prince of Russia) to the Swedish throne on Frederick I's death, which duly occurred in 1751.

During his reign Adolphus repeatedly tried to reassert royal power, but found that the constitution was only strengthened against him. The Estates' power was such that they issued a stamp with his name when Adolphus refused to sign any bills. The resurrected "Hats" forced entry into the **Seven Years' War** in 1757 on the French side, another disastrous venture as the Prussians repelled every Swedish attack.

The aristocratic parties were in a state of constant flux. Although elections of sorts were held to provide delegates for the *Riksdag* (parliament), foreign sympathies, bribery and bickering were hardly conducive to a democratic administration. Cabals continued to rule Sweden, the economy was stagnant, and reform delayed. It was, however, an age of intellectual and scientific advance, surprising in a country that had lost much of its cultural impetus. **Carl von Linné**, the botanist whose classification of plants is still used, was professor at Uppsala from 1741 to 1778. **Anders Celsius** initiated the use of the centigrade temperature scale; **Carl Scheele** discovered chlorine. A royal decree of 1748 organized Europe's first full-scale census, a five-yearly event by 1775. Other fields flourished, too. The mystical works of **Emmanuel Swedenborg**, the philosopher who died in 1772, encouraged new theological sects; and the period encapsulated the life of **Carl Michael Bellman** (1740–95), the celebrated Swedish poet whose work did much to identify and foster a popular nationalism.

With the accession of **Gustav III** in 1771, the crown began to regain the ascendancy. A new constitution was forced upon a divided *Riksdag* and proved a balance between earlier absolutism and the later aristocratic squabbles. A popular king, Gustav founded hospitals, granted freedom of worship and removed many of the state controls over the economy. His determination to conduct a successful foreign policy led to further conflict with Russia (1788–90) in which, to everyone's surprise, he managed to more than hold his own. But with the French Revolution polarizing opposition throughout Europe, the Swedish nobility began to entertain thoughts of conspiracy against a king whose growing powers they now saw as those of a tyrant. In 1792, at a masked ball in Stockholm Opera House, the king was shot by an assassin hired by the disaffected aristocracy. Gustav died two weeks later and was succeeded by his son **Gustav IV**, with the country being led by a regency for the years of his minority.

The wars waged by revolutionary France were at first studiously avoided in Sweden but, pulled into the conflict by the British, Gustav IV entered the **Napoleonic Wars** in 1805. However, Napoleon's victory at Austerlitz two years later broke the coalition and Sweden found itself isolated. Attacked by Russia the following year, Gustav was later arrested and deposed, and his uncle was elected king.

A constitution of 1809 established a liberal monarchy in Sweden, responsible to the elected *Riksdag*. Under this constitution **Karl XIII** was a mere caretaker, his heir a Danish prince who would bring Norway back to Sweden – some compensation for finally losing Finland and the Åland Islands to Russia (1809) after 500 years of Swedish rule. On the prince's sudden death, however, Marshal Bernadotte (one of Napoleon's generals) was invited to become heir. Taking the name of **Karl Johan**, he took his chance in 1812 and joined Britain and Russia to fight Napoleon. Following Napoleon's first defeat at the Battle of Leipzig in 1813, Sweden compelled Denmark (France's ally) to exchange Norway for Swedish Pomerania.

By 1814 Sweden and Norway had formed an uneasy union. Norway retained its own government and certain autonomous measures. Sweden decided foreign policy, appointed a viceroy and retained a suspensive (but not absolute) veto over the Norwegian parliament's legislation.

## THE NINETEENTH CENTURY

Union under Karl Johan, or **Karl XIV** as he became in 1818, could have been disastrous. He spoke no Swedish and just a few years previously had never visited either kingdom. However, under Karl and his successor **Oscar I**, prosperity ensued. The **Göta Canal** (1832) helped commercially, and liberal measures by both monarchs helped politically. In 1845 daughters were given an equal right of inheritance. A Poor Law was introduced in 1847, restrictive craft guilds reformed, and an Education Act passed.

The 1848 revolution throughout Europe cooled Oscar's reforming ardour, and his attention turned to reviving **Scandinavianism**. It was still a hope, in certain quarters, that closer cooperation between Denmark and Sweden–Norway could lead to some sort of revived Kalmar Union. Expectations were raised with the **Crimean War** of 1854: Russia could be neutralized as a future threat. But peace was declared too quickly (at least for Sweden) and there was still no real guarantee that Sweden would be sufficiently protected from Russia in

the future. With Oscar's death, talk of political union faded.

His son **Karl XV** presided over a reform of the *Riksdag* that put an end to the Swedish system of personal monarchy. The Four Estates were replaced by a representative two-house parliament along European lines. This, together with the end of political Scandinavianism (following the Prussian attack on Denmark in 1864 in which Sweden stood by), marked Sweden's entry into modern Europe.

**Industrialization** was slow to take root in Sweden. No real industrial revolution occurred and developments – mechanization, introduction of railways, etc – were piecemeal. One result was widespread **emigration** amongst the rural poor, who had been hard hit by famine in 1867 and 1868. Between 1860 and 1910 over one million people left for America (in 1860 the Swedish population was only four million). Given huge farms to settle, the emigrants headed for land similar to that they had left behind – to the Midwest, Kansas and Nebraska.

At home, Swedish **trade unionism** emerged to campaign for better conditions. Dealt with severely, the unions formed a confederation (1898) but largely failed to make headway. Even peaceful picketing carried a two-year prison sentence. Hand in hand with the fight for workers' rights went the **temperance movement**. The level of spirit consumption was alarming and various abstinence programmes attempted to educate the drinkers and, if necessary, eradicate the stills. Some towns made the selling of spirits a municipal monopoly – not a long step from the state monopoly that exists today.

With the accession of **Oscar II** in 1872, Sweden continued on an even, if uneventful, keel. Keeping out of further European conflict (the Austro-Prussian War, Franco-Prussian War and various Balkan crises), the country's only worry was a growing dissatisfaction in Norway with the union. Demanding a separate consular service, and objecting to the Swedish king's veto on constitutional matters, the Norwegians brought things to a head, and in 1905 declared the union invalid. The Karlstad Convention confirmed the break and Norway became independent for the first time since 1380.

The late nineteenth century was a happier time for Swedish culture. **August Strindberg** enjoyed great critical success and artists like **Anders Zorn** and **Prince Eugene** made their mark abroad. The historian **Artur Hazelius** founded the Nordic and Skansen museums in Stockholm; and the chemist, industrialist and dynamite inventor **Alfred Nobel** left his fortune to finance the Nobel Prizes. It's an instructive tale; Nobel hoped that the knowledge of his invention would help eradicate war – optimistically believing that humankind would never dare unleash the destructive forces of dynamite.

## FROM WORLD WAR I TO WORLD WAR II

Sweden declared a strict neutrality on the outbreak of **World War I**, tempered by much sympathy within the country for Germany, sponsored by the longstanding language, trade and cultural links. It was a policy agreed with the other Scandinavian monarchs, but a difficult one to pursue. Faced with British demands to enforce a blockade of Germany and the blacklisting and eventual seizure of Swedish goods at sea, the economy suffered grievously; rationing and inflation mushroomed. The **Russian Revolution** in 1917 brought further problems to Sweden. The Finns immediately declared independence, waging civil war against the Bolsheviks, and Swedish volunteers enlisted in the White army. But a conflict of interest arose when the Swedish-speaking Åland Islands wanted a return to Swedish rule rather than stay with the victorious Finns. The League of Nations overturned this claim, granting the islands to Finland.

After the war, a Liberal–Socialist coalition remained in power until 1920, when **Branting** became the first socialist prime minister. By the time of his death in 1924, the franchise had been extended to all men and women over 23 and the state-controlled alcohol system (*Systembolaget*) set up. Following the Depression of the late 1920s and early 1930s, conditions began to improve after a Social Democratic government took office for the fourth time in 1932. A **Welfare State** was rapidly established, meaning unemployment benefit, higher old-age pensions, family allowances and paid holidays. The **Saltsjöbaden Agreement** of 1938 drew up a contract between trade unions and employers to help eliminate strikes and lockouts. With war again looming, all parties agreed that Sweden should remain neutral in any struggle and rearmament was negligible, despite Hitler's apparent intentions.

**World War II** was slow to affect Sweden. Unlike in 1914, there was little sympathy for Germany, but neutrality was again declared. The Russian invasion of Finland in 1939 brought Sweden into the picture, providing weapons, volunteers and refuge for the Finns. Regular Swedish troops were refused though, fearing intervention from either the Germans (then Russia's ally) or the Allies. Economically, the country remained sound – less dependent on imports than in World War I and with no serious shortages. The position became stickier in 1940 when the Nazis marched into Denmark and Norway, isolating Sweden. Concessions were made – German troop transit allowed, iron ore exports continued – until 1943–44 when Allied threats were more convincing than the failing German war machine. Sweden became the recipient of countless refugees from the rest of Scandinavia and the Baltic. Instrumental, too, by rescuing Hungarian Jews from the SS, was **Raoul Wallenberg**, who persuaded the Swedish government to give him diplomatic status in 1944. Unknown thousands (anything up to 35,000) of Jews in Hungary were sheltered in "neutral houses" (flying the Swedish flag), fed and clothed by Wallenberg. But when Soviet troops liberated Budapest in 1945, Wallenberg was arrested as a suspected spy and disappeared – later reported to have died in prison in Moscow in 1947. However, unconfirmed accounts had him alive in a Soviet prison as late as 1975, and in 1989 some of his surviving relatives flew to Moscow in an attempt to discover the truth about his fate.

The end of the war was to provide the country with a serious crisis of conscience. Physically unscathed, Sweden was now vulnerable to Cold War politics. Proximity to Finland and, ultimately, to the Soviet Union, meant that Sweden refused to follow the other Scandinavian countries into **NATO** in 1949. The country did, however, much to Conservative disquiet, return most of the Baltic and German refugees who had fought against Russia during the war into Stalin's hands – their fate not difficult to guess.

## POSTWAR POLITICS

The wartime coalition quickly gave way to a purely **Social Democratic** government committed to welfare provision and increased defence expenditure – non-participation in military alliances didn't mean a throwing down of weapons.

Tax increases and a trade slump lost the Social Democrats seats in the 1948 general election and by 1951 they needed to enter a coalition with the Agrarian (later the Centre) Party to survive. This coalition lasted until 1957, when disputes over the form of a proposed extension to the pension system brought it down. An inconclusive referendum and the withdrawal of the Centre Party from government forced an election which saw no change. Although the Centre gained seats and the Conservatives replaced the Liberals as the main opposition party, the Social Democrats still had a (thin) majority.

Sweden regained much of its international moral respect (lost directly after World War II) through the election of **Dag Hammarskjöld** as Secretary-General of the United Nations in 1953. His strong leadership greatly enhanced the prestige (and effectiveness) of the organization, which under his guidance participated in the solution of the Suez crisis (1956) and the 1958 Lebanon–Jordan affair. He was killed in an air crash in 1961, towards the end of his second five-year term.

Throughout the 1950s and 1960s, domestic reform continued unabated. It was in these years that the country laid the foundations of its much-vaunted social security system, although at the time it didn't always bear close scrutiny. A **National Health Service** gave free hospital treatment, but only allowed for a small refund of doctor's fees, medicines and dental treatment – hardly as far-reaching as the British system introduced immediately after the war.

The Social Democrats stayed in power until 1976, when a **non-Socialist coalition** (Centre–Liberal–Moderate) finally unseated them. In the 44 years since 1932, the Socialists had been an integral part of government in Sweden, tempered only by periods of war and coalition. It was a remarkable record, made more so by the fact that modern politics in Sweden has never been about ideology so much as detail. Socialists and non-Socialists alike share a broad consensus on foreign policy and defence matters, even on the need for the social welfare system. The argument instead has been economic, and a manifestation of this is the **nuclear issue**. A second non-Socialist coalition formed in 1979 presided over a referendum on nuclear power (1980); the pro-nuclear lobby

secured victory, with the result an immediate expansion of the nuclear programme.

## OLOF PALME

The Social Democrats regained power in 1982, subsequently devaluing the krona, introducing a price freeze and cutting back on public expenditure. They lost their majority in 1985, having to rely on Communist support to get their bills through. Presiding over the party since 1969, and prime minister for nearly as long, was **Olof Palme**. He was assassinated in February 1986, and his death threw Sweden into modern European politics like no other event. Proud of their open society (Palme was returning home unguarded from the cinema), the Swedes were shocked by the gunning down of a respected politician, diplomat and pacifist. The country's social system was placed in the limelight, and shock turned to anger and then ridicule as the months passed without his killer being caught. Police bungling was criticized and despite the theories – Kurdish extremists, right-wing terror groups – no one was charged with the murder.

Then the police came up with **Christer Pettersson**, who – despite having no apparent motive – was identified by Palme's wife as the man who had fired the shot that night. Despite pleading his innocence, claiming he was elsewhere at the time of the murder, Pettersson was convicted of Palme's murder and jailed. There was great disquiet about the verdict, however, both at home and abroad: the three legal representatives in the original jury had voted for acquittal at the time; it was believed that Palme's wife couldn't possibly be sure that the man who fired the shot was Pettersson, since she had only seen him once, on the dark night in question and then only very briefly. On appeal, Pettersson was acquitted and released in 1989. The police appear to believe they had the right man all along, but in recent years some convincing evidence of the involvement of the South African secret services has come to light.

## CARLSSON AND BILDT

**Ingvar Carlsson** was elected the new prime minister after Palme's murder, a position confirmed by the **1988 General Election** when the Social Democrats – for the first time in years – scored more seats than the three non-socialist parties combined. However, Carlsson's was a minority government, the Social Democrats requiring the support of the Communists to command an overall majority – support that was usually forthcoming but that, with the arrival of the **Green Party** into parliament in 1988, could no longer be taken for granted. The Greens and Communists jockeyed for position as protectors of the Swedish environment, and any Social Democrat measure seen to be anti-environment cost them Communist support. Perhaps more worryingly for the government, a series of **scandals** swept the country, leading to open speculation about a marked decline in public morality. The Bofors arms company was discovered to be involved in illegal sales to the Middle East, and early in 1990 the Indian police charged the company with paying kickbacks to politicians to secure arms contracts. In addition, there was insider dealing at the stock exchange, and the country's Ombudsman resigned over charges of personal corruption.

The real problem for the Social Democrats, though, was the **state of the economy**. With a background of rising inflation and slow econom-ic growth, the government announced an aus-terity package in January 1990, which included a two-year ban on strike action, and a wage, price and rent freeze – strong measures which astounded most Swedes, used to living in a lib-eral, consensus-style society. The Greens and Communists would have none of it and the Social Democrat government resigned a month later. Although the Social Democrats were soon back in charge of a minority government, having agreed to drop the most draconian measures of their programme, the problems didn't go away.

The **General Election of 1991** merely con-firmed that the model consensus had finally bro-ken down. A four-party centre-right coalition came to power, led by **Carl Bildt**, which promised tax cuts and economic regeneration, but the recession sweeping western Europe didn't pass Sweden by. Unemployment hit a post-war record and in autumn 1992 – as the British pound and Italian lira collapsed on the interna-tional money markets – the krona came under severe pressure. Savage austerity measures did little to help: VAT on food was increased, statu-tory holiday allowances cut, welfare budgets slashed, and – after a period of intense currency speculation – short-term marginal interest rates raised to a staggering 500 percent. In a final attempt to steady nerves, Prime Minister Bildt and Carlsson, leader of the Social Democratic

opposition, made the astonishing announcement that they would ignore party lines and work together for the good of Sweden – and then pro-ceeded with drastic public expenditure cuts.

The fat was trimmed off the welfare state – benefits were cut, health care was opened up to private competition and education was given a painful shake-up. But it was too little too late. Sweden was gripped by its worst recession since the 1930s and unemployment had reached record levels of fourteen percent – the days of a jobless rate of one or two percent were well and truly gone. Poor economic growth coupled with generous welfare benefits, runaway spec-ulation by Swedish firms on foreign real estate and the world recession all contributed to Sweden's economic woes. With the budget deficit growing faster than that of any other western industrialized country, Sweden also decided it was time to tighten up its asylum laws – in a controversial step it introduced visas for Bosnians, to try to prevent the flood of refugees escaping the Bosnian War.

## THE RETURN OF THE SOCIAL DEMOCRATS

A feeling of nostalgia for the good old days of Social Democracy swept through the country in September of 1994, and Carl Bildt's minority conservative government was booted out. Swedes voted in massive numbers to return the country's biggest party to power, headed by **Ingvar Carlsson**. He chose a government con-taining fifty percent women ministers. Social Democracy was back with all its quirks and foibles – two ministers even decided they no longer wanted to work in Stockholm. The Minister for Culture upped sticks and moved her office out to Lake Vänern to be with her family, while the Minister for Employment thought he could be closer to the people by working from home in Piteå, up in the far north.

During 1994 negotiations on Sweden's planned **membership of the European Union** were completed and the issue was put to a referendum which succeeded in splitting Swedish public opin-ion right down the middle. The *Ja till EU* lobby argued that little Sweden would have a bigger voice in Europe and would be able to influence pan-European decisions if it joined, whereas *Nej till EU* warned that Sweden would be forced to lower its standards to those of other EU countries, unemployment would rise, drug trafficking would increase and democracy would be watered down – they also argued that the additive-free Swedish food market would be swamped with cheap additive-packed Eurosausages. But in November the Swedes followed the Austrians and the Finns in voting for membership from 1 January 1995 – but by the narrowest of margins, just five percent – a sign of unease to come.

More Social Democracy in action came in 1995 when Sweden allowed gay couples to marry, adopting a law on registered partnerships similar to that already in force in neighbouring Denmark and Norway. Same-sex couples won virtually the same rights as straight couples, the exceptions being that gay couples can't adopt children together, lesbians can't apply for insemination and the partnership ceremony can't be carried out in a church.

The Swedish authorities also faced the seemingly impossible task of stopping the smuggling of refugees into the country by organized gangs based in Iraq, Afghanistan and Pakistan. But the influx of illegal refugees was overshadowed by the problem of how to get the massive **state debt** under control. The krona fell to new lows as market fears grew that the minority government wouldn't be able to persuade parliament to approve cuts in state spending. However, the cuts came in the budget – the welfare state was trimmed back further and new taxes were announced to try to rein in the spiralling debt. Unemployment benefit was cut to 75 percent of previous earnings, benefits for sick leave were reduced and lower state pension payments also came into force. A new tax was also slapped on newspapers but to try to keep public support on his side, Finance Minister **Göran Persson** reduced the tax on food from a staggering twenty-one percent to just twelve percent.

Just when everything appeared under control, Carlsson announced his resignation – he was retiring to spend more time with his family, a very Swedish way of bowing out. He was replaced by the bossy Persson, known to friends and enemies alike as *HSB* – the Swedish initials for *han som besta//mmer*, he who decides.

Just as the year was nearing its close, a scandal rocked the ruling Social Democrats which led to the resignation of the deputy prime minister, Mona Sahlin. The tabloid *Expressen* revealed that she had been using her government credit card for private purchases which ranged from nappies to a family holiday – and all this from a woman who claimed to be a politician from the people, for the people. Mona Sahlin claimed she'd paid back every krona but it was too late – her party was losing credibility and she tendered her resignation.

Sweden's economy has recently improved to the point that the country will probably qualify to join the Single European Currency in 1999, but at the same time opposition to EU membership has grown so far that polls show a majority of Swedes would now like to leave the European Union. The government has acknowledged this fact by declaring that Sweden won't join the single currency – a curious statement given that the country hasn't negotiated an opt-out clause, unlike Britain.

Another current preoccupation is race relations, as many Swedes mistakenly blame their troubles on the rise in the immigrant population (Sweden has one million immigrants out of a total population of nearly nine million). Tension began to surface in the early 1990s when refugee housing centres were set on fire and immigrants in Stockholm lived in fear of the "laser man", who shot dead several dark-skinned foreigners with a laser-sighting gun. The government has done little to stamp out the violence, and neo-Nazi groups are on the rise – attacks and even murders have become all too frequent, and it's no longer unusual to hear of foreigners being forced from their homes by racial abuse and violence.

As the cradle-to-grave pattern of welfare is abandoned and the gap between rich and poor widens, racial tension will continue to pose a major threat to social order. Only renewed economic prosperity will bring about a change in public opinion. As the millennium approaches, debate is also likely to intensify over the pros and cons of Sweden's continued membership of the European Union. Equally, the planned decommissioning of the country's nuclear power stations, which produce fifty percent of all Sweden's energy, will become a focus for debate. The Swedish people voted in a referendum to close all nuclear stations by 2010 but already the government is trying to wriggle out of its commitment in view of the vast cost of making up the energy shortfall.

# SWEDISH ARCHITECTURE

## PREHISTORIC BUILDINGS

Discussion of **Prehistoric** building in Sweden is mostly a matter of conjecture, for the only structures to have survived from before 1100 are ruined or fragmentary. The most impressive structures of **Bronze Age** Sweden are the numerous grassy burial barrows and the coastal burial sites (particularly apparent on the island of Gotland) that feature huge boulders cut into the shapes of a prow and stern. One of the best known of the latter type is at **Ales Stennar** on the South Skåne coast – a Swedish Stonehenge set above windy cliffs.

More substantial are the **Iron Age** dwellings from the **Celtic** period (c. 500 BC to 800 AD). The best example of a fortification from this era is at **Ismantorp** on the Baltic island of Öland. Dating from the fifth century AD, this remarkable site has limestone walls up to fifteen feet high and some eighty foundations arranged into quarters, with streets radiating like spokes of a wheel.

From the remnants of pre-Christian era houses a number of dwelling types can be identified. The open-hearth hall, for example, was a square house with an opening in the roof ridge by which light entered and smoke exited. The two-storey gallery house had an open upper loft reached via an exterior stair, while the post larder was a house on stilts allowing for ventilation and protection from vermin.

## ROMANESQUE TO GOTHIC

The Christianization of Sweden is dated from 1008, the year Saint Sigfrid is said to have baptized King Olof. In the eleventh and twelfth centuries the Church and the monastic orders were the driving force behind the most significant building projects, with the most splendid example of Romanesque architecture being **Lund Cathedral**. Consecrated in 1145, when Lund was the largest town in Scandinavia and the archiepiscopal see, this monumental building was designed as a basilica with twin western towers, and boasts some tremendously rich carvings in the apsidal choir and vast crypt. The chief centre of Romanesque church building, however, was the royal town of **Sigtuna** to the northwest of Stockholm. Apart from boasting Sweden's oldest street, Sigtuna has the ruins of three eleventh-century churches – one of which, St Peter's, features the country's oldest groin vault.

Round arches, a distinctive feature of Romanesque architecture, flourished wherever limestone and sandstone were found – principally in regions of southern and central Sweden, such as Västergötland, Östergötland and Närke as well as Skåne. An easy supply of both types of stone was to be found on the Baltic island of Gotland, from where numerous baptismal fonts and richly carved sandstone decorations were exported to the mainland both to the west (Sweden proper) and the east (Swedish-controlled Finland).

Of the great monastic ruins of this period, the finest is **Alvastra Monastery** (1143), just south of Vadstena near the eastern shores of Lake Vättern. A portion of the huge barrel-vaults can still be seen, though much of the graceful structure was carted off by Vasa to build his castle at Vadstena.

**Gothic** architecture emerged in the thirteenth century, one of the finest early examples being the **Maria Church** in Sigtuna (1237), which with its red-brick step gables is markedly unlike the austere grey stone churches of a century earlier. The cathedral at **Strängnäs**, due east of Stockholm, is another superb piece of Gothic brick architecture, while in Sweden's third city of Malmö, the German-inspired **St Peter's Church** survives as a fine example of brick Gothic, a style often known as the Hanseatic Style. The cathedral at Uppsala (the largest in Scandinavia) is another intriguing specimen, designed by Parisian builders as a limestone structure to a French High Gothic plan, but eventually built in brick in a simpler, **Baltic Gothic** form. A good example of late Gothic is **Vadstena Convent Church**; begun in 1384, this austere limestone and brick hall was built exactly as decreed by Saint Birgitta, the founder of the church, and is flanked by her monastery and nunnery. However, the most rewarding place to explore Sweden's Gothic architecture is **Gotland** – the countryside is peppered with almost one hundred richly sculpted medieval churches, while the island's capital, the magnificently preserved Hanseatic seat of **Visby**, is replete with excellent domestic as well as ecclesiastical Gothic.

Few examples of the castles and fortifications of this period exist today. One of the best examples, **Varberg's Fortress** in Halland, just south of Gothenburg, was built by the Danes, while the best Swedish-built medieval fortifications are in Finland, a Swedish province until the early nineteenth century. One stark and beautifully unmolested example of a fortification in Danish-controlled Skåne is the castle of Glimmingehus; dating from around 1500, it was built by Adam van Duren, who also supervised the completion of the cathedral of Lund.

## RENAISSANCE AND BAROQUE ARCHITECTURE

**Gustav Vasa** (1523–60) could not have had more pronounced an effect on Swedish architecture. In 1527, with his reformation of the Church, Catholic properties were confiscated, and in many instances the fabric of monasteries and churches was used to build and convert castles into resplendent palaces. Wonderful examples of such Renaissance palaces are **Kalmar Castle**, in the south of Småland, and **Vadstena's Castle** – though unlike Kalmar, the latter's interior has been stripped of its original furnishings. Another magnificent Vasa palace, a glorious ruin since a nineteenth-century fire, is **Borgholm Castle** on the Baltic island of Öland.

While few churches built in this period enjoyed much prominence, one of outstanding elegance is the **Trefaldighetskyrkan** (Trinity Church) in Kristianstad, Danish king Christian IV's model Renaissance city in Skåne. With its tall windows, slender granite pillars and square bays, it is the epitome of sophistication and simplicity.

By the time Gustav II Adolf (Gustavus Adolphus) ascended the throne in 1611 a greater opulence was becoming prevalent in domestic architecture, a tendency that became even more marked in the **Baroque** area, which in Sweden commenced with the reign of Queen Kristina, art-loving and extravagant daughter of Gustav II Adolf. The first wave of Baroque, so-called Roman Baroque, was largely introduced by the German Nicodemus Tessin the Elder, who had spent much time in Italy.

The most glorious of palatial buildings from this era is **Drottningholm** outside Stockholm, a Baroque masterpiece created by Tessin for the Dowager Queen Hedvig Eleonora. Tessin's other masterpiece was **Kalmar Cathedral**, the finest church of the era and a truly beautiful vision of Italian Baroque. Nicodemus Tessin the Younger followed his father as court architect. He designed in Baroque style the new **Royal Palace at Stockholm** following the city's great fire of 1697 and the two contrasting **Karlskrona** churches: the domed rotunda of the Trefaldighetskyrkan (Trinity Church) and the barrel-vaulted basilica of the Fredrikskyrkan (Fredrik's Church). Karlskrona, like **Gothenburg**, is a fine example of regulated town planning, a discipline that came into being with the Baroque era.

## THE EIGHTEENTH CENTURY

In the eighteenth century **Rococo** emerged as the style favoured by the increasingly affluent Swedish middle class, who looked to France for their models. This lightening of architectural style paved the way for the Neoclassical elegance which would follow with the reign of Gustav III, who was greatly impressed by the architecture of classical antiquity. Good examples of this clear Neoclassical mode are the **Inventariekammaren** (Inventory Chambers) at Karlskrona, and the **King's Pavilion at Haga**, designed for Gustav III by Olof Temelman, complete with Pompeiian interiors by the painter Louis Masreliez.

Another, and quite distinct aspect of late eighteenth-century taste, was the fascination with **chinoiserie**, due in large measure to the power and influence of the Gothenburg-based Swedish East India Company, which was founded in 1731. The culmination of this trend was the **Kina Slott** (Chinese Pavilion) at Drottningholm, a tiny

Palladian villa built in 1763 and now beautifully restored.

## THE NINETEENTH CENTURY

Two vast projects dominated the Swedish architectural scene at the beginning of the nineteenth century: the remarkable **Göta Canal,** a 190-kilometre waterway linking the great lakes of Vänern and Vättern, Gothenburg and the Baltic; and the **Karlsborg Fortress** on the western shores of Vättern, designed to be an inland retreat for the royal family and the gold stocks, but eventually abandoned ninety years later in 1909.

By the mid-nineteenth century, a new style was emerging, based on Neoclassicism but flavoured by the French-born king's taste. This **Empire Style** (sometimes referred to as the Karl Johan Style) is most closely associated with the architect **Fredrik Blom** of Karlskrona, whose most famous building is the elegant pleasure palace **Rosendal** on Djurgården, Stockholm.

During the reign of Oskar I (1844–59), while the buildings of Britain's manufacturing centres provided models for Sweden's industrial towns, the styles of the past couple of centuries began to reappear, particularly Renaissance and Gothic. One of the most glamorous examples of late nineteenth-century neo-Gothic splendour is **Helsingborg Town Hall**, built around 1890 as a riot of fairy-tale red-brick detail. The names which crop up most often in this era include Fredrik Scholander, who designed the elaborate **Stockholm Synagogue** in 1861, and Helgo Zetterwall, whose churches of the 1870s and 1880s bear a resemblance to neo-Gothic buildings in Britain and Germany.

## THE TWENTIETH CENTURY

Some of the most gorgeous buildings in Sweden's cities are the result of a movement germinated in the final, resurgent years of the nineteenth century – **National Romanticism**, a movement that set out to simplify architecture and use local materials to create a distinctive Swedish style. The finest example of this new style, which was much influenced by the Arts and Crafts movement in Britain, is **Stockholm City Hall**, built in 1923 from plain brick, dressed stone and rustic timber, a combination that created a feeling of natural power. Another luscious example is Lars Israel Wahlmann's **Tjolöholm Castle**, just south of Gothenburg – a city in which some of the finest apartment buildings are those produced in the associated **Art Nouveau** style. One beautifully renovated building in full-blown Art Nouveau form is the theatre in Tivoli Park in **Kristianstad,** a town otherwise known for its Renaissance buildings.

In the second quarter of the century a new movement – **Functionalism** – burst onto the scene, making great use of "industrial" materials such as stainless steel and concrete. The leading architect of his generation was **Gunnar Asplund**, famed for Stockholm City Library (mid-1920s) and his contribution to many other buildings – his interior of the law courts in **Gothenburg's Rådhus** is a mecca for architecture students and enthusiasts today, with its flowing laminates and curving glass and steel elevators. Asplund was also responsible for the famed **Woodland Cemetery** in Stockholm, a magnificent project that also involved another designer, **Sigmund Lewerentz**.

The creation of the Welfare State went hand in hand with the ascendancy of a functionalist approach to architecture which rejected many of the individualistic features of traditional Swedish design. By the 1960s, the faceless International Style had gained dominance in Sweden, as town planning gave way to insensitive clearance of old houses and their replacement with bland high-rises. Since the late 1980s, however, restoration has become the order of the day (despite one-offs like Ralph Erskine's playful Ukkiken office block in Gothenburg), and areas that had been left to decay – such as the old working-class area of **Haga** in Gothenburg – have been gentrified and preserved. For now, this forward-looking country is concentrating on its rear-view mirror.

# SWEDISH LANDSCAPE AND WILDLIFE

## THE REGIONS OF SWEDEN

The look of the Swedish terrain owes most to the last **Ice Age**, which chafed the landscape for 80,000 years before finally melting away 9000 years ago. Grinding ice masses polished the mountains to their present form, a process particularly evident in scooped-out U-shaped mountain valleys such as **Lapporten** (The Lapp Gateway) near Abisko, in the extreme north. Subsequent to the thaw the land-mass rose, so that former coastlines are now to be seen many kilometres inland, in the form of huge fields of rubblestone, while the plains of Sweden were created by the deposition of vast quantities of silt by the meltwater.

## THE NORTH

The mountains of Sweden's north are part of the **Caledonian range**, the remains of which are also to be found further south in Europe, notably in Scotland and Ireland. Formed around 400 million years ago, the range reaches its highest points – with peaks higher than 2000m – in **Kebnekaise** and **Sarek**, in the extreme northwest. Ancient spruce, pine and birch forest extends continuously along most of the 1000-kilometre range, providing an unspoilt habitat for birds such as the golden eagle, which nests in trees that are on average 350 years old. The treeline lies at around 800m above sea level, giving way to great expanses of bare rockface and heathland, the latter often covered in wild orchids. In addition to eagles, the bird life in these raw mountain areas includes snow bunting, golden plovers and snowy owls, while the woodlands support willow grouse and bluethroat, among other species.

## CENTRAL SWEDEN

The most extensive of Sweden's plains is in the **central Swedish lowlands**, a broad belt spanning from Bohuslän on the west coast to Uppland and Södermanland on the east. Divided by steep ridges of rock, this former seabed was transformed by volcanic eruptions that created rocky plateaux such as Ålleberg and **Kinekulle**

---

### ALLEMANS RATT

The relationship between the Swedish people and their environment is characterized by an intense reverence – as one might expect from the country that produced Carl von Linne, who devised the universally accepted system of botanical categories. Many Swedes regard a regular communion with the lakes and forests as an absolute necessity, and their respect for the natural world is encapsulated by the **Allemans Ratt** or **Right of Common Access**. An unwritten right, it permits anyone to walk anywhere and spend a night anywhere as long as this does not infringe the privacy of home-owners or impinge on land where crops are grown. The only other exceptions are nature reserves and other protected zones at sensitive times of the year, such as bird sanctuaries, which are entirely closed to visitors during breeding season.

The general rules of the Allemans Ratt, which appear in English-language leaflets all over the country, forbid such things as tree felling and the removal of twigs or bark from living trees, the lighting of fires in dry terrain or on bare rock, and off-road driving, unless snow is on the ground. Fishing is allowed along the coasts of the country's five largest lakes. In all other instances, permits are required.

(Flowering Mountain) to the west of Lidköping. The latter is Sweden's most varied natural site, comprising deciduous woodland, evergreens, meadows and pastures, and treeless limestone flats. Flora abounds here, particularly cowslips, lady's-slipper, wild cherry and, in early summer, the unusual and intensely fragrant bear-garlic.

One of the region's most splendid areas of virgin forest is **Tiveden National Park**, around 50km northeast of Karlsborg and just to the northwest of **Lake Vättern**, one of the two enormous lakes in this part of Sweden. So huge is the other, **Lake Vänern**, that seabirds such as the turnstone, water pipit and Caspian tern all nest here. Fishing is big sport in Sweden, and Vänern and Vättern attract thousands to try their luck each year. Around 1300 tonnes of fish are taken from Vänern alone each year, with commercial fishery accounting for around eighty percent of the catch. Vänern was once the most productive salmon waters in Sweden, but the construction of hydroelectric dams ruined the spawning grounds, and by the 1970s salmon was almost extinct here. In an effort to complement natural reproduction, salmon and brown trout have been raised in hatcheries and released into the lake with considerable success, though stocks are still low.

The plains are dotted with lakes, and many wetland and migratory birds shelter here. **Kvismaren**, near Örebro, is an area of reed marsh and open waters where geese and ducks live in their thousands. Just to the west of Örebro, **Lake Tysslingen** is also well worth heading for, especially during March and April, when as many as 2500 whooper swans assemble. Just east of Vättern, **Lake Tåkern** is one of northern Europe's finest bird habitats. Like Kvismaren, it was largely drained in the nineteenth century and has an average depth of just a metre.

Some 250 bird species spend time here, particularly huge flocks of geese in autumn time. Sweden's most famous lowland lake, though, is **Hornborgasjön**, which boasts 120 species of wetland birds, while thousands of cranes briefly settle in the potato fields just to the south of the lake on their migration to the northern marshes every April.

## THE SOUTH

The southernmost third of Sweden, the most highly populated and industrialized region, is a mixture of highlands (in the north of the region), forests, lakes and cultivated plains. In southeastern Sweden, the high-yielding forests of **Småland** have kept the furnaces of glass factories alight since the seventeenth century. To the south, where the highlands give way to a gently undulating landscape, the mix of poppy fields, rape fields and pastures makes for some glorious summer-time scenery in **Skåne**. This province has a reputation for being monotonous and agricultural, but while this is true of much of the southwest of Skåne, it also boasts tracts of conifers, a dramatic coastline and lush forests of beech, best seen in the first weeks of May. The most dramatic natural rock formations in Skåne are at **Hovs Hallar**, a stunning castellation of red rock sea-stacks on the northern coast of the Bjäre peninsula.

To the east of Skåne, the **Stenshuvud National Park** has rocky coastal hills surrounded by woods of hornbeam, alder and moorlands full of juniper. Animals unusual for Sweden live here, such as tree frogs, sand lizards and dormice.

## THE ISLANDS

Sweden's two largest islands, **Gotland** and **Öland**, lying in the Baltic Sea to the east of the mainland, have excited botanists and geologists for centuries. When Carl von Linne first arrived in Öland in the mid-eighteenth century, he noted that the terrain was "of an entirely different countenance" from the rest of Sweden, and indeed the islands' limestone plateaux – known as alvar – are unique in Sweden.

**Stora Alvaret** (Great Limestone Plain) in southern Öland is a thin-soiled heathland with vividly coloured flora in spring and summer – Öland rockrose, red kidney vetch and blue globe daisy are among the unusual flowers which grow here. Birdlife is also rich and varied on Öland. The Öland goose, one of the oldest domesticated breeds in the country, originated here from interbreeding with wild geese. **Ottenby**, on the southern point, is the island's largest nature reserve, supporting golden oriole as well as fallow deer which have lived here since the whole island was a royal hunting ground.

**Gotland** is the more dramatic of the two great islands, thanks to its high sea-stacks, the remains of old coral reefs which loom like craggy ghosts along the island's shoreline. Like

Öland, Gotland sustains rich floral life, including at least 35 species of orchid, and it's also the home of the Gotland sheep, an ancient (and now rare) breed characterized by its dark, shaggy coat and powerful, bow-shaped horns. While on Gotland, it's also well worth crossing by ferry to Stora Karlsö island, a breeding ground for guillemot and razorbill.

## SWEDEN'S MAMMALS

The animal with the highest profile in Sweden is the **reindeer**, and warning signs about "reindeer crossing" are common all over Sweden, as is serious damage to vehicles involved in collisions with them. Throughout the year, reindeer are to be seen not just on mountainsides but also in the wooded valleys and lowlands.

One of the best places to see **red deer, roe deer** and particularly **elk** is the plateau of Halleberg, just south of Vanersborg in Västergötland. Used as a royal hunting ground for elk since the 1870s, Hallcbcrg has around 140 elk during the winter and 200 in the summer. The best times to see the elk and the deer (there are around 70 red deer and 1000 roe deer) are dawn and dusk, when they emerge to seek food in clear-felled areas. Other animals seen in this area are Swedish **woodland hare** and **badgers** – even **lynx** is the only member of the cat family living in the wild in Sweden.

Sweden's **wolves** have been hunted almost to extinction. A rare few still live in the north, where **Arctic foxes** have adapted to conditions of extreme cold, surviving at temperatures as low as -70°C. Although the animals were common in Sweden at the beginning of the twentieth century, excessive hunting for their costly fur has reduced numbers dramatically. **Wolverines** are far closer to extinction – they were placed under protection in 1969, and there are now just 150 individuals left, mostly in the north. **Bears**, though rarely seen, still live in the northernmost reaches of Sweden; it is estimated that there are around 700 of them in the wild.

If you're interested in seeing endangered species from Sweden and around the world in a close-to-wild environment, it's well worth visiting **Nordens Ark**, near Lysekil on the Bohuslän coast. A non-profitmaking breeding park, it is home not only to wolves, wolverines and lynxes, but also to lesser pandas, Przewalski's horses and snow leopards from the Himalayas.

# BOOKS

Books on Sweden in English are remarkably scant. The books listed below are the pick of a meagre crop; those that are currently out of print (o/p) shouldn't be too difficult to track down. The UK publisher is given first in each listing, followed by the publisher in the US, unless the title is available in one country only, in which case we've specified which country. Where only one publisher is given, with no country indicated, it means the same publisher produces the title in both the US and the UK.

## TRAVEL AND GENERAL

**James William Barnes Steveni**, *Unknown Sweden* (Hurst & Blackett, o/p). Fascinating account of journeys through Sweden in the early years of the twentieth century. With its excellent illustrations, this book is a superb social record.

**Mary Wollstonecraft**, *A Short Residence in Sweden, Norway and Denmark* (Penguin). A searching account of Wollstonecraft's three-month solo journey through southern Scandinavia in 1795.

## HISTORY AND MYTHOLOGY

**H.R. Ellis Davidson**, *The Gods and Myths of Northern Europe* (Penguin). A Who's Who of Norse mythology, including some useful reviews of the more obscure gods. Displaces the classical deities and their world as the most relevant mythological framework for northern and western European culture.

**Eric Elstob**, *Sweden: A Traveller's History* (Boydell/Rowman & Littlefield, o/p). An introduction to Swedish history from the year dot to the twentieth century, with useful chapters on art, architecture and cultural life.

**Alan Palmer**, *Bernadotte* (John Murray, o/p). First English biography for over fifty years of Napoleon's marshal, later Sweden's King Karl Johan XIV. Lively and comprehensive.

**Michael Roberts**, *The Early Vasas; A History of Sweden 1523–1611* (Cambridge University Press, o/p). A clear account of the period, complemented by the same author's *Gustavus Adolphus and the Rise of Sweden* (English University Press/Lawrence Verry, both o/p) which, more briefly and enthusiastically, covers the period from 1612 to Gustavus's death in 1632.

## ART AND ARCHITECTURE

**Henrik O. Andersson and Fredric Bedoire**, *Swedish Architecture 1640–1970* (Swedish Museum of Architecture). Definitive survey of the subject, in English/Swedish parallel text, with superb colour plates.

**Görel Cavalli-Björkman and Bo Lindwall**, *The World of Carl Larsson* (Simon & Schuster, US). A charming and brilliantly illustrated volume, charting the life and work of one of Sweden's most admired painters.

**Barbro Klein and Mats Widbom**, *Swedish Folk Art* (Abrams). A lavishly illustrated and richly documented history of the subject, relating ancient crafts to modern-day design ideas.

**Mereth Lindgren, Louise Lyberg, Birgitta Sandström and Anna Greta Wahlberg**, *A History of Swedish Art* (Coronet, US). A fine overview of Swedish painting, sculpture and, to a lesser extent, architecture from the Stone Age to the present. Clear text and good, mostly monochrome, illustrations.

## LITERATURE

**Stig Dagerman**, *A Burnt Child* (Quartet, UK). Intense short narrative concerning the reactions of a Stockholm family to the death of the mother. A prolific young writer, Dagerman wrote four novels, four plays, short stories and travel sketches by the time he was 26, then committed suicide in 1954 at the age of 31. This is one of his best works.

**Kerstin Ekman**, *Blackwater* (Vintage/St Martin's Press). Set in the forests of northern Sweden, this tightly plotted thriller marks the debut in translation of one of Sweden's most highly rated novelists.

**Robert Fulton** (trans.), *Preparations for Flight* (Forest Books, UK). Eight Swedish short stories from the last 25 years, including two rare prose outings from the poet Niklas Rådström.

**Lars Gustafsson**, *The Death of a Beekeeper* (Harvill/New Directions). Keenly perceived novel structured around the journal of a dying schoolteacher-turned-beekeeper.

**P.C. Jersild**, *A Living Soul* (Norvik Press/Dufour). The work of one of Sweden's best novelists, this is a social satire based around the "experiences" of an artificially produced, bodiless human brain floating in liquid. Entertaining, provocative reading.

**Selma Lagerlöv**, *The Wonderful Adventures of Nils* (Dover/Skandisk). Lagerlöv is Sweden's best-loved children's writer, and it's an indication of her standing in her native land that she's featured on the 20kr banknote. The tales of Nils Holgren, a little boy who flies all over the country on the back of a magic goose, are continued in *The Further Adventures of Nils*.

**Sara Lidman**, *Naboth's Stone* (Norvik Press/Dufour). A novel set in 1880s' Västerbotten, in Sweden's far north, charting the lives of settlers and farmers as the industrial age – and the railway – approaches.

**Torgney Lindgren**, *Merab's Beauty* (HarperCollins). Short stories capturing the distinctive flavour of family life in northern Sweden.

**Vilhelm Moberg**, *Emigrant* series (Penguin, o/p /Minnesota Historical Society). A sequence of highly poignant novels dealing with the emigration of some one million Swedes to the US in the second half of the nineteenth century. Moberg himself stayed behind, and is regarded as the finest chronicler of his times.

**Leo Perutz**, *The Swedish Cavalier* (Harvill/Arcade). Two men meet in a farmer's barn in 1701 – one is a thief, the other an army officer on the run. An adventure story with a moral purpose.

**Agneta Pleijel**, *The Dog Star* (Peter Owen, UK). By one of Sweden's leading writers, *The Dog Star* is the powerful tale of a young girl's approach to puberty. Pleijel's finest novel yet, full of fantasy and emotion.

**Clive Sinclair**, *Augustus Rex* (Andre Deutsch, UK). August Strindberg dies in 1912 – and is then brought back to life by the Devil in 1960's Stockholm. Bawdy, imaginative and very funny treatment of Strindberg's well-documented neuroses.

**Bent Söderberg**, *The Mysterious Barricades* (Peter Owen/Dufour). Leading Swedish novelist writes of the Mediterranean during the wars – a part of the world he's lived in for many years.

**Hjalmar Söderberg**, *Short Stories* (Norvik Press/Dufour). Twenty-six short stories from the stylish pen of Söderberg (1869–1941). Brief, ironic and eminently ripe for dipping into.

**August Strindberg**, *Plays: One* (including *The Father*, *Miss Julie* and *The Ghost Sonata*); *Plays: Two* (*The Dance of Death*, *A Dream Play* and *The Stronger*) (both Methuen). The major plays by the country's most provocative and influential playwright, examining with deep psychological analysis the roles of the sexes both in and out of marriage. A fantastically prolific writer, only a fraction of his sixty plays, twelve historical dramas, five novels, numerous short stories, autobiographical volumes and poetry has ever been translated into English.

## BIOGRAPHY

**Peter Cowie**, *Ingmar Bergman* (Andre Deutsch/Scribner, both o/p). A fine critical biography of the great director; a well-written, sympathetic account of Bergman's life and career. Bergman's major screenplays are published by Marion Boyars.

**Michael Meyer**, *Strindberg* (Oxford University Press). The best and most approachable biography of the tormented genius of Swedish literature.

**Andrew Oldham, Tony Calder and Colin Irwin**, *Abba* (Pan/Music Book Services). The last word on the band here described as the "greatest composers of the twentieth century".

# A BRIEF GUIDE TO SWEDISH

Swedish is a North Germanic language, with a grammar and vocabulary that resemble German, albeit in simpler form. Few foreigners speak Swedish and a knowledge of even the most basic words and phrases is sure to impress. However, 95 percent of the population speaks English to some degree, and Swedes are always keen to practise their English, so perseverance is the name of the game if you're intent on learning Swedish. Of the phrasebooks, most useful is *Swedish for Travellers* (Berlitz) or use the Swedish section in the *Scandinavian Europe Phrasebook* (Lonely Planet). If you're more serious about learning, the excellent *Colloquial Swedish* by Philip Holmes and Gunilla Serin (Routledge) is the best starting point.

## A FEW BASICS

Verb endings are constant in Swedish (*jag är* = I am, *du är* = you are, *han är* = he is), and all verbs take the auxiliary *att ha* (to have) in the past tenses (eg *jag har gått* = I have gone, *jag har gjort* = I have done). Swedish has only two genders (neuter and common gender), and three-quarters of all words are *en*-words (ie the latter) – eg *en hund* = a dog, *en katt* = a cat. One peculiar feature of Swedish is that the definite article is suffixed to the end of the noun – eg *hunden* = the dog, *katten* = the cat. Forming plurals is a complicated business but once again the definite article is suffixed, eg *hundarna* = the dogs.

## BASIC PHRASES

| | | | |
|---|---|---|---|
| yes; no | *jånej* | open; closed | *öppet; stängt* |
| hello | *hej/tjänare* | women; men | *kvinnor; män* |
| good morning | *god morgon* | toilet | *toalett* |
| good afternoon | *god middag* | bank; change | *bank; växel* |
| good night | *god natt* | post office | *posten* |
| today/tomorrow | *idag/imorgon* | stamp(s) | *frimärke(n)* |
| please | *tack/var så god* | where are you from? | *varifrån kommer du?* |
| here you are/ | | I'm English | *jag är engelsmann/* |
| you're welcome | *var så god* | | *engelska* |
| thank you (very much) | *tack (så mycket)* | Scottish | *skotte* |
| where?; when? | *var; när/ hur dags* | Welsh | *walesare* |
| what?; why? | *vad; varför* | Irish | *irländare* |
| how (much)? | *hur (mycket)* | American | *amerikan* |
| I don't know | *jag vet inte* | Canadian | *kanadensare* |
| do you know? (a fact) | *vet du...?* | Australian | *australier* |
| could you...? | *skulle du kunna...?* | a New Zealander | *nyzeeländare* |
| sorry; excuse me | *förlåt; ursäkta* | what's your name? | *vad heter du?* |
| here; there | *här; där* | what's this called in | *vad heter det här på* |
| near; far | *nära; avlägsen* | Swedish? | *svenska?* |
| this; that | *det här; det där* | do you speak English? | *talar du engelska?* |
| now; later | *nu; senare* | I don't understand | *jag föstår inte* |
| more; less | *mera; mindre* | you're speaking too fast | *du talar för snabbt* |
| big; little | *stor; liten* | how much is it? | *hur mycket kostar det?* |

## PRONUNCIATION

Rest assured – you're never going to sound Swedish, for not only is **pronunciation** difficult but the sing-song **melody** of the language is beyond the reach of most outsiders.

**Vowels** can be either long (when followed by one consonant or in word-final position) or short (when followed by two consonants). Unfamiliar vowels are as follows:

**ej** as in m**a**te

**y** as in **ew**e

**å** when short, as in h**o**t; when long, sort of as in r**aw**

**ä** as in g**e**t

**ö** as in f**u**r

**Consonants** are pronounced approximately as in English except:

**g** before e, i, y, ä or ö as in **y**et; before a, o, u, å as in **g**ate; sometimes silent

**j, dj, gj, lj** as in **y**et

**k** before e, i, y, ä or ö approximately as in **sh**ut, otherwise hard

**qu** as in **kv**

**rs** as in **sh**ut

**s** as in **s**o (never as English z)

**sj, skj, stj** approximately as in **sh**ut (different from soft k sound and more like an sh-sound made through the teeth but with rounded lips – this sound varies widely throughout Sweden and takes practice)

**tj** approximately as in **sh**ut and with same value as a soft **k**

**z** as in **s**o (never as in **z**oo)

### GETTING AROUND

| | | | |
|---|---|---|---|
| how do I get to...? | *hur kommer jag till...?* | what time does it leave? | *hur dags går det?* |
| left; right | *till vänster/ till höger* | what time does it arrive in...? | *hur dags är det framme i...?* |
| straight ahead | *rakt fram* | | |
| where is the bus station? | *var ligger busstationen?* | which is the road to...? | *vilken är vägen till...?* |
| the bus stop for... | *busshållplatsen till...* | where are you going? | *vart går du?* |
| railway station | *järnvägsstationen* | I'm going to... | *jag går till...* |
| where does the bus to .... leave from? | *varifrån går bussen till...?* | that's great, thanks a lot | *jättebra, tack så mycket* |
| is this the train for Gothenburg? | *åker detta tåg till Göteborg?* | stop here please | *stanna här, tack* |
| | | ticket to | *biljett till* |
| | | return ticket | *tur och retur* |

### ACCOMMODATION

| | | | |
|---|---|---|---|
| where's the youth hostel? | *var ligger vandrarhemmet?* | it's too expensive, I don't want it now | *det är för mycket, jag tar det inte* |
| is there a hotel round here? | *finns det något hotell i närheten?* | can I/we leave the bags here until...? | *kan jag/vi få lämna väskorna här till...?* |
| I'd like a single/ double room | *jag skulle vilja ha ett enkelrum/dubbelrum* | have you got anything cheaper? | *har du något billigare?* |
| can I see it? | *får jag se det?* | with a shower | *med dusch* |
| I'll take it | *jag tar det* | can I/we camp here? | *får jag/vi tälta här?* |
| how much is it a night? | *hur mycket kostar det per natt?* | | |

### DAYS AND MONTHS

| | | | | | |
|---|---|---|---|---|---|
| Sunday | *söndag* | January | *januari* | August | *augusti* |
| Monday | *måndag* | February | *februari* | September | *september* |
| Tuesday | *tisdag* | March | *mars* | October | *oktober* |
| Wednesday | *onsdag* | April | *april* | November | *november* |
| Thursday | *torsdag* | May | *maj* | December | *december* |
| Friday | *fredag* | June | *juni* | | |
| Saturday | *lördag* | July | *juli* | *Days and months are never capitalized.* | |

## THE TIME

| | | | |
|---|---|---|---|
| what time is it? | *vad är klockan?* | one forty | *tjugo i två* |
| it's.... | *den/hon är...* | one forty-five | *kvart i två* |
| at what time...? | *hur dags...?* | one fifty-five | *fem i två* |
| at... | *klockan...* | two o'clock | *klockan två* |
| midnight | *midnatt* | noon | *klockan tolv* |
| one in the morning | *klockan ett på natten* | in the morning | *på morgonen* |
| ten past one | *tio över ett* | in the afternoon | *på eftermiddagen* |
| one fifteen | *kvart över ett* | in the evening | *på kvällen* |
| one twenty-five | *fem i halv två* | in ten minutes | *om tio minuter* |
| one thirty | *halv två* | ten minutes ago | *för tio minuter sedan* |
| one thirty-five | *fem över halv två* | | |

## NUMBERS

| | | | | | | | |
|---|---|---|---|---|---|---|---|
| 1 | *ett* | 10 | *tio* | 19 | *nitton* | 80 | *åttio* |
| 2 | *två* | 11 | *elva* | 20 | *tjugo* | 90 | *nittio* |
| 3 | *tre* | 12 | *tolv* | 21 | *tjugoett* | 100 | *hundra* |
| 4 | *fyra* | 13 | *tretton* | 22 | *tjugotvå* | 101 | *hundraett* |
| 5 | *fem* | 14 | *fjorton* | 30 | *trettio* | 200 | *två hundra* |
| 6 | *sex* | 15 | *femton* | 40 | *fyrtio* | 500 | *fem hundra* |
| 7 | *sjö* | 16 | *sexton* | 50 | *femtio* | 1000 | *tusen* |
| 8 | *åtta* | 17 | *sjutton* | 60 | *sextio* | 10,000 | *tio tusen* |
| 9 | *nio* | 18 | *arton* | 70 | *sjuttio* | | |

## GLOSSARY OF SWEDISH WORDS AND PHRASES

| | | | |
|---|---|---|---|
| *berg* | mountain | *rabatt* | discount |
| *bio* | cinema | *rea* | sale |
| *bokhandel* | bookshop | *restaurangsvagn* | train buffet |
| *bro* | bridge | *riksdagshus* | parliament building |
| *brygga* | jetty/pier | *rådhuset* | town hall |
| *båt* | boat/ferry | *simhallen* | swimming baths |
| *cyckelstig* | cycle path | *sjö* | lake |
| *dal* | valley | *skog* | forest |
| *domkyrka* | cathedral | *slott* | palace/castle |
| *drottning* | queen | *sovvagn* | sleeping car |
| *extrapris* | special offer | *spår* | track |
| *färja* | ferry | *stadshus* | city hall |
| *färjeläge* | ferry terminal/berth | *stängt* | closed |
| *gamla* | old | *stora* | big |
| *gamla stan* | old town | *strand* | beach |
| *gata (g.)* | street | *stuga* | cottage |
| *gränd* | alley | *torg* | square/market place |
| *hamn* | harbour | *tunnelbana* | underground |
| *järnvägsstation* | railway station | *tåg* | train |
| *kapell* | chapel | *universitet* | university |
| *klockan (kl.)* | o'clock | *väg (v.)* | road |
| *kyrka* | church | *vrakpris* | bargain |
| *liggvagn* | couchette car | *ångbåt* | steamboat |
| *lilla* | little | *öppet* | open |
| *museet* | museum | *öppettider* | opening hours |
| *pressbyrå* | newsagent | | |

# INDEX

| | | | | |
|---|---|---|---|---|
| Amsterdam | 1-85828-086-9 | £7.99 | US$13.95 | CAN$16.99 |
| Andalucia | 1-85828-094-X | 8.99 | 14.95 | 18.99 |
| Australia | 1-85828-141-5 | 12.99 | 19.95 | 25.99 |
| Bali | 1-85828-134-2 | 8.99 | 14.95 | 19.99 |
| Barcelona | 1-85828-221-7 | 8.99 | 14.95 | 19.99 |
| Berlin | 1-85828-129-6 | 8.99 | 14.95 | 19.99 |
| Brazil | 1-85828-102-4 | 9.99 | 15.95 | 19.99 |
| Britain | 1-85828-208-X | 12.99 | 19.95 | 25.99 |
| Brittany & Normandy | 1-85828-224-1 | 9.99 | 16.95 | 22.99 |
| Bulgaria | 1-85828-183-0 | 9.99 | 16.95 | 22.99 |
| California | 1-85828-181-4 | 10.99 | 16.95 | 22.99 |
| Canada | 1-85828-130-X | 10.99 | 14.95 | 19.99 |
| China | 1-85828-225-X | 15.99 | 24.95 | 32.95 |
| Corsica | 1-85828-089-3 | 8.99 | 14.95 | 18.99 |
| Costa Rica | 1-85828-136-9 | 9.99 | 15.95 | 21.99 |
| Crete | 1-85828-132-6 | 8.99 | 14.95 | 18.99 |
| Cyprus | 1-85828-182-2 | 9.99 | 16.95 | 22.99 |
| Czech & Slovak Republics | 1-85828-121-0 | 9.99 | 16.95 | 22.99 |
| Egypt | 1-85828-188-1 | 10.99 | 17.95 | 23.99 |
| Europe | 1-85828-159-8 | 14.99 | 19.95 | 25.99 |
| England | 1-85828-160-1 | 10.99 | 17.95 | 23.99 |
| First Time Europe | 1-85828-270-5 | 7.99 | 9.95 | 12.99 |
| Florida | 1-85828-184-4 | 10.99 | 16.95 | 22.99 |
| France | 1-85828-124-5 | 10.99 | 16.95 | 21.99 |
| Germany | 1-85828-128-8 | 11.99 | 17.95 | 23.99 |
| Goa | 1-85828-156-3 | 8.99 | 14.95 | 19.99 |
| Greece | 1-85828-131-8 | 9.99 | 16.95 | 20.99 |
| Greek Islands | 1-85828-163-6 | 8.99 | 14.95 | 19.99 |
| Guatemala | 1-85828-189-X | 10.99 | 16.95 | 22.99 |
| Hawaii: Big Island | 1-85828-158-X | 8.99 | 12.95 | 16.99 |
| Hawaii | 1-85828-206-3 | 10.99 | 16.95 | 22.99 |
| Holland, Belgium & Luxembourg | 1-85828-087-7 | 9.99 | 15.95 | 20.99 |
| Hong Kong | 1-85828-187-3 | 8.99 | 14.95 | 19.99 |
| Hungary | 1-85828-123-7 | 8.99 | 14.95 | 19.99 |
| India | 1-85828-200-4 | 14.99 | 23.95 | 31.99 |
| Ireland | 1-85828-179-2 | 10.99 | 17.95 | 23.99 |
| Italy | 1-85828-167-9 | 12.99 | 19.95 | 25.99 |
| Kenya | 1-85828-192-X | 11.99 | 18.95 | 24.99 |
| London | 1-85828-231-4 | 9.99 | 15.95 | 21.99 |
| Mallorca & Menorca | 1-85828-165-2 | 8.99 | 14.95 | 19.99 |
| Malaysia, Singapore & Brunei | 1-85828-103-2 | 9.99 | 16.95 | 20.99 |
| Mexico | 1-85828-044-3 | 10.99 | 16.95 | 22.99 |
| Morocco | 1-85828-040-0 | 9.99 | 16.95 | 21.99 |
| Moscow | 1-85828-118-0 | 8.99 | 14.95 | 19.99 |
| Nepal | 1-85828-190-3 | 10.99 | 17.95 | 23.99 |
| New York | 1-85828-171-7 | 9.99 | 15.95 | 21.99 |
| Pacific Northwest | 1-85828-092-3 | 9.99 | 14.95 | 19.99 |

In the UK, Rough Guides are available from all good bookstores, but can be obtained from Penguin by contacting: Penguin Direct, Penguin Books Ltd, Bath Road, Harmondsworth, West Drayton, Middlesex UB7 0DA; or telephone the credit line on 0181-899 4036 (9am–5pm) and ask for Penguin Direct. Visa, Access and Amex accepted. Delivery will normally be within 14 working days. Penguin Direct ordering facilities are only available in the UK and the USA. The availability and published prices quoted are correct at the time of going to press but are subject to alteration without prior notice.

# around the world

| | | | | |
|---|---|---|---|---|
| Paris | 1-85828-235-7 | 8.99 | 14.95 | 19.99 |
| Poland | 1-85828-168-7 | 10.99 | 17.95 | 23.99 |
| Portugal | 1-85828-180-6 | 9.99 | 16.95 | 22.99 |
| Prague | 1-85828-122-9 | 8.99 | 14.95 | 19.99 |
| Provence | 1-85828-127-X | 9.99 | 16.95 | 22.99 |
| Pyrenees | 1-85828-093-1 | 8.99 | 15.95 | 19.99 |
| Rhodes & the Dodecanese | 1-85828-120-2 | 8.99 | 14.95 | 19.99 |
| Romania | 1-85828-097-4 | 9.99 | 15.95 | 21.99 |
| San Francisco | 1-85828-185-7 | 8.99 | 14.95 | 19.99 |
| Scandinavia | 1-85828-039-7 | 10.99 | 16.99 | 21.99 |
| Scotland | 1-85828-166-0 | 9.99 | 16.95 | 22.99 |
| Sicily | 1-85828-178-4 | 9.99 | 16.95 | 22.99 |
| Singapore | 1-85828-135-0 | 8.99 | 14.95 | 19.99 |
| Spain | 1-85828-240-3 | 11.99 | 18.95 | 24.99 |
| St Petersburg | 1-85828-133-4 | 8.99 | 14.95 | 19.99 |
| Thailand | 1-85828-140-7 | 10.99 | 17.95 | 24.99 |
| Tunisia | 1-85828-139-3 | 10.99 | 17.95 | 24.99 |
| Turkey | 1-85828-242-X | 12.99 | 19.95 | 25.99 |
| Tuscany & Umbria | 1-85828-243-8 | 10.99 | 17.95 | 23.99 |
| USA | 1-85828-161-X | 14.99 | 19.95 | 25.99 |
| Venice | 1-85828-170-9 | 8.99 | 14.95 | 19.99 |
| Vietnam | 1-85828-191-1 | 9.99 | 15.95 | 21.99 |
| Wales | 1-85828-245-4 | 10.99 | 17.95 | 23.99 |
| Washington DC | 1-85828-246-2 | 8.99 | 14.95 | 19.99 |
| West Africa | 1-85828-101-6 | 15.99 | 24.95 | 34.99 |
| More Women Travel | 1-85828-098-2 | 9.99 | 14.95 | 19.99 |
| Zimbabwe & Botswana | 1-85828-186-5 | 11.99 | 18.95 | 24.99 |
| *Phrasebooks* | | | | |
| Czech | 1-85828-148-2 | 3.50 | 5.00 | 7.00 |
| French | 1-85828-144-X | 3.50 | 5.00 | 7.00 |
| German | 1-85828-146-6 | 3.50 | 5.00 | 7.00 |
| Greek | 1-85828-145-8 | 3.50 | 5.00 | 7.00 |
| Italian | 1-85828-143-1 | 3.50 | 5.00 | 7.00 |
| Mexican | 1-85828-176-8 | 3.50 | 5.00 | 7.00 |
| Portuguese | 1-85828-175-X | 3.50 | 5.00 | 7.00 |
| Polish | 1-85828-174-1 | 3.50 | 5.00 | 7.00 |
| Spanish | 1-85828-147-4 | 3.50 | 5.00 | 7.00 |
| Thai | 1-85828-177-6 | 3.50 | 5.00 | 7.00 |
| Turkish | 1-85828-173-3 | 3.50 | 5.00 | 7.00 |
| Vietnamese | 1-85828-172-5 | 3.50 | 5.00 | 7.00 |
| *Reference* | | | | |
| Classical Music | 1-85828-113-X | 12.99 | 19.95 | 25.99 |
| Internet | 1-85828-198-9 | 5.00 | 8.00 | 10.00 |
| Jazz | 1-85828-137-7 | 16.99 | 24.95 | 34.99 |
| Opera | 1-85828-138-5 | £16.99 | 24.95 | 34.99 |
| Rock | 1-85828-201-2 | 17.99 | 26.95 | 35.00 |
| World Music | 1-85828-017-6 | 16.99 | 22.95 | 29.99 |

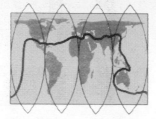